SolidWorks® 2007 Bible

SolidWorks®

SolidWorks® 2007 Bible

Published by
Wiley Publishing, Inc.
10475 Crosspoint Boulevard
Indianapolis, IN 46256
www.wiley.com

Copyright © 2007 by Wiley Publishing, Inc., Indianapolis, Indiana

Published simultaneously in Canada

ISBN: 978-0-470-08013-9

Manufactured in the United States of America

10 9 8 7 6 5 4 3 2 1

For general information on our other products and services or to obtain technical support, please contact our Customer Care Department within the U.S. at (800) 762-2974, outside the U.S. at (317) 572-3993 or fax (317) 572-4002.

Library of Congress Control Number: 2007924101

About the Author

Matt Lombard holds a mechanical engineering degree from Rochester Institute of Technology in Rochester, New York. Matt has worked as a design and manufacturing engineer in the medical and microelectronics industries. Currently, through his company Dezignstuff, he works mainly as a consumer product modeling consultant and technical writer.

Before becoming an engineer, Matt went to music school for two years and performed with the Navy band for four years. He still plays in local community groups for fun. Having grown up in the Adirondack Mountains of northeastern New York, he now calls the Shenandoah Valley of Virginia home.

This work is dedicated to my grandparents, Earl "Boots" Woods and Mildred "Mid" Woods, who taught me that the value of hard work goes beyond the numbers on a paycheck.

Credits

Acquisitions Editor
Jenny Watson

Project Editor
Martin V. Minner

Technical Editor
Richard Doyle

Copy Editor
Marylouise Wiack

Editorial Manager
Robyn Siesky

Business Manager
Amy Knies

Vice President and Executive Group Publisher
Richard Swadley

Vice President and Publisher
Barry Pruett

Project Coordinator
Lynsey Osborn

Graphics and Production Specialists
Stacie Brooks
Denny Hager
Jennifer Mayberry
Barbara Moore
Heather Pope

Quality Control Technicians
Laura Albert
Brian Walls

Proofreading
Aptara

Indexing
Aptara

Cover Design
Michael Trent

Cover Illustration
Joyce Haughey

Contents

Contents

Part II: Building Intelligence into Your Parts   181

Chapter 6: Getting More from Your Sketches 183

Chapter 7: Choosing a Feature Type 205

Contents

Contents

Part III: Working with Assemblies   389

Chapter 12: Organizing Assemblies 391

Contents

Contents

Contents

Preface

Welcome to the *SolidWorks 2007 Bible*. This book has been written as a desk reference for beginning and intermediate SolidWorks users. SolidWorks is such an immense software program that trying to cover all of its functions is an extremely ambitious undertaking, and I know that a few have been left out. Because of the scope of the topic, I have limited the book to covering the basic SolidWorks package, without the Office, Office Professional, or Office Premium add-ins, although I have devoted half of a chapter to Toolbox.

You will find enough information here that the book can grow with your SolidWorks needs. I have written tutorials for most of the chapters with newer users in mind, because for them it is most helpful to see how things are done in SolidWorks step by step. The longer narrative examples give more in-depth information about features and functions, as well as the results of various settings and options.

I have included an extensive appendix covering the Tools, Options settings. This offers an in-depth explanation of each option, including both System Options and Document Properties. This appendix uses special symbols to identity items that are new for SolidWorks 2007 or that affect file size or speed.

Icons

This book uses a set of icons to point out certain details in the text. While they are relatively self-explanatory, here is what each of these icons indicates:

NOTE Notes highlight useful information that you should take into consideration, or an important point that requires special attention.

TIP Tips provide you with additional advice that makes the software quicker or easier to use.

CAUTION Caution icons warn you of potential problems before you make a mistake.

NEW FEATURE The New Feature icon highlights features and functions that are new to SolidWorks 2007.

CROSS-REF Cross-Ref icons point out where you can find additional information about a topic elsewhere in the book.

ON the CD-ROM This icon points you toward related material on the book's CD.

The *SolidWorks 2007 Bible* is unique in its use of these two icons:

BEST PRACTICE Best practice icons point out recommended settings or techniques that are safe in most situations.

PERFORMANCE Performance icons elaborate on how certain settings, features, or techniques affect rebuild speed or file size.

These icons point out and describe techniques and settings that are either recommended or not recommended for specific reasons. Best Practice is usually considered to be very conservative usage, where the stability of the parametrics and performance (a euphemism for *rebuild speed*) are the ultimate goals. These two aspects of SolidWorks models are usually weighed against modeling speed (how long it takes you to create the model).

Best Practice and Performance recommendations need to be taken seriously, but you should treat them as guidelines rather than as rules. When it comes right down to it, the only hard and fast rule about SolidWorks is that there are no hard and fast rules. In fact, I believe that the only reason to have rules in the first place is so that you know when you can break them. Parametric stability and modeling speed are not always the ultimate goals, and are often overridden when workaround techniques are used simply to accomplish a geometric goal.

Because not everyone models with the same goals in mind, a single set of rules can never apply for everyone. You must take the best practice suggestions and apply them to your situation using your own judgment.

My point of view while writing this book has been that of someone who is actually using the software, not of someone trying to sell ideas, nor of someone trying to make the software look good. I try to approach the software objectively as a tool, recognizing that complex tools are good at some things and not so good at others. Both kinds of information (good and not-so-good) are useful to the reader. Pointing out negatives in this context should not be construed as criticizing the SolidWorks software, but rather as preparing the reader for real-world use of the software. Any tool this complex is going to have imperfections. Hopefully some of my enthusiasm for the software also shows through and is to some extent contagious.

Terminology

An important concept referred to frequently in SolidWorks is *design intent*. As a practical matter, I use the phrase *design for change* to further distinguish design intent from other design goals.

The reader needs to be familiar with some special terminology before continuing. In many cases, a SolidWorks vernacular or slang is used when the official terminology is either not descriptive enough or, as is sometimes the case, has multiple meanings. For example, the word *shortcut* has multiple meanings in the SolidWorks interface. It is used to describe right mouse button menus as well as hotkeys. As a result, I have chosen not to use the word shortcut and instead substitute the words *RMB* and *hotkey*.

I frequently use RMB to refer to Right Mouse Button menus, or other data that you access by clicking the right mouse button on an item. The word *tree* refers to the list of features in the FeatureManager. Also, command and option names are referred to using all initial capitals, even when SolidWorks does not use the same capitalization. For example, the setting Single Command Per Pick is listed in Tools ⇨ Options as Single command per pick.

Differences are frequently found between the names of features on toolbars and the names in the menus or PropertyManager titles. In these cases, the differences are usually minor, and either name may be used.

Most functions in SolidWorks can work with either the object-action or the action-object scenarios. These are also called *pre-select* and *select*, respectively. For example, the Hole Wizard is one tool for which pre-selection is definitely recommended because a difference in functionality is seen between pre-selection and selection. The Fillet feature shows no difference between using pre-selection and selection. Most features allow pre-selection, and some functions, such as inserting a design table, require pre-selection. Although you cannot identify a single rule that covers all situations, *most* functions accept both.

Frequently in this book, I have suggested enhancement requests that the reader may want to make. This is because SolidWorks development is driven to a large extent by customer requests, and if a large number of users converge on a few issues, then those issues are more likely to be fixed or changed. Again, the enhancement request suggestions are not made to criticize the software, but to make it better. I hope that several of you will join me in submitting enhancement requests.

SolidWorks is an extremely powerful modeling tool, very likely with the best combination of power and accessibility on the MCAD market today. This book is meant to help you take advantage of its power in your work and even hobbyist applications. If I could impart only a single thought to all readers of this book, it would be that with a little curiosity and some imagination, you can begin to access the power of SolidWorks for geometry creation and virtual product prototyping. You should start with the assumption that there is a way to do what you are imagining, and that you should be open to using different techniques.

For AutoCAD users making the transition to SolidWorks, you should simply forget everything you know about AutoCAD, because most of it, except for the most general geometric concepts, will not apply to SolidWorks, and will often simply confuse you.

Whoever you are, I hope that you find insight deeper than simply "what does this button do?" in this book. I hope that you will find an intuition for thinking like the software. Jeff Ray of the SolidWorks Corporation has said that the goal is to make the software as "intuitive as a light switch." While most people will agree that they have some work left to achieve that particular goal, I believe that approaching the interface intuitively, rather than attempting to remember it all by rote, is the best method. Good luck to you all.

Acknowledgments

The ideas that go into a book of this size do not all originate with a single individual. Research for many of the topics was done at user group meetings, the newsgroup `comp.cad.solidworks`, SolidWorks Corporation's discussion forums, and SolidWorks Customer Portal, as well as the Web sites of many individuals. I would like to thank all of the individuals who have posted to the public forums or created personal Web sites. Many of these people have knowingly or unknowingly contributed to my SolidWorks education, as well as that of many other SolidWorks users around the world.

I would especially like to thank Richard Doyle, the technical editor for this book, for keeping me on the straight and narrow when possible. This would not have been possible without Marty Minner and Courtney Allen, Wiley editors who with great patience have provided guidance and advice as necessary. Thanks also to those who have encouraged me along the way, including Kim Hardy, Chris Cole, Stan Kujawski, and the guys from Spark Engineering.

Part I

SolidWorks Basics

Chapter 1

Getting Familiar with SolidWorks

Let's face it; people develop brand loyalty to CAD software programs. It sounds silly, but you know it's true. If you are coming to SolidWorks from another CAD program, you are probably feeling a level of unease that is proportional to the amount of time you spent using the other program. You will get past that, and everything will be fine, I promise. As you will see, SolidWorks does everything as well as, or better than, your old software, and you will never crave your old software after you drink this Kool-Aid.

The biggest hurdle that many users face in learning a new CAD program is letting go of the old one. In some cases, the old software helps you to understand the new one, but in others, the thinking is just too different, and you may need to forget everything you thought you knew about CAD.

Switching to SolidWorks can involve a little of both. For example, if you are coming from Inventor, Solid Edge, or another program in that class, you will find SolidWorks to be very familiar territory, with a similar if not identical design philosophy. SolidWorks also shares a lot of underlying structure with Pro/ENGINEER, and if you are coming from that product, there will be some relearning, but much of your training will be transferable.

If you are coming from 2D AutoCAD, SolidWorks may at first cause a bit of culture shock for you. However, after you accept the concept that getting the model correct is dependent on the process, things will go more easily. As you will see, SolidWorks, and in fact most solid modeling in general, is very process-based.

SolidWorks is also a very Windows-based software, and so if you are familiar with Windows conventions, then you already know a lot about the SolidWorks interface and shortcuts. The regular and context-sensitive menus, toolbars, and keyboard shortcuts, as well as many other interface elements, all work the same as they do in Word, Excel, or PowerPoint. OS X and Linux users should not hold their breath for SolidWorks to be ported to those operating systems, although there have been third-party developments that allow Windows software to run on other operating systems and hardware.

In any case, regardless of how you arrived here with this SolidWorks Bible in your hand, here you are. Together we will progress from basic concepts to advanced techniques, everyday settings, and subtle nuances. This book will serve as your friend, tutor, and desk reference for learning about SolidWorks software.

Understanding Feature-Based Modeling

There is some terminology that you need to come to grips with before we dive into building models with SolidWorks. Notice that I talk about "modeling" rather than "drawing." This is because SolidWorks is really virtual prototyping software. Whether you are building an assembly line for automotive parts or designing decorative perfume bottles, SolidWorks can help you visualize your product in the most realistic way possible without actually having it in your hand. This is more akin to making a physical model in the shop than drawing on paper.

"Feature-based" modeling means that you build the model by incrementally identifying functional shapes, and applying processes to create the shapes. For example, you can create a simple box by using the Extrude process, and you can create a sphere by using the Revolve process. However, you can make a cylinder by using either process, by revolving a rectangle or extruding a circle. You start by visualizing the 3D shape, and then apply a process to a 2D sketch to create that shape. This concept on its own is half of what you need to know to create models with SolidWorks.

Figure 1.1 shows images of simple feature types with the 2D sketches from which they were created.

Many different feature types in SolidWorks enable you to create everything from the simplest geometry shown above to free-form shapes. In general, when I talk about modeling, I am talking about *solid* modeling, although SolidWorks also has a complete complement of surfacing tools. I will discuss the distinction between solid and surface modeling in a later chapter.

Table 1.1 lists some of the most common features that are found in SolidWorks, and classifies them according to whether they always require a sketch, a sketch is optional, or they never require a sketch.

TABLE 1.1

Feature Types

Sketch Required	Sketch Optional	No Sketch (Applied Features)
Extrude	Loft	Fillet
Revolve	Sweep	Chamfer
Rib	Dome	Draft
Hole Wizard	Shape	Shell
Wrap	Deform	Flex

FIGURE 1.1

Simple extruded and revolved features

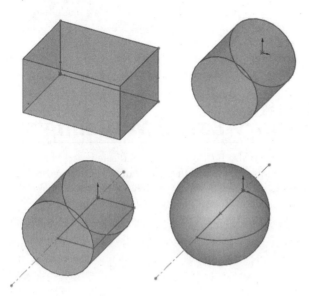

While the bulk of this book focuses on the use of solid features, I believe that no set of modeling tools is complete without surface-modeling functions. Hybrid features combine the use of solids and surfaces in some way, and are discussed in more detail in Chapter 27. The surfacing and hybrid features available in SolidWorks are:

- Lofted surface
- Swept surface
- Fill surface
- Boundary surface
- Freeform surface
- Offset surface
- Knit surface
- Radiate surface
- Ruled surface
- Replace Face
- Trim surface

- Untrim surface
- Cut with surface
- Thicken surface
- Cut Thicken surface

In addition to these features, there are many other types that create reference geometry (such as curves, planes, and axes), or perform some operation on existing geometry.

Understanding History-Based Modeling

In addition to being feature-based, SolidWorks is also history-based. To indicate process history, there is a panel to the left side of the SolidWorks window called the *FeatureManager design tree*. The FeatureManager keeps a list of the features in the order in which you have added them. It also enables you to reorder items in the tree (in effect, to change history). As a result, the order in which you perform operations is important. For example, consider Figure 1.2. This model was created by the following process:

1. Create a sketch.
2. Extrude the sketch.
3. Create a second sketch.
4. Extrude the second sketch.
5. Create a third sketch.
6. Extrude Cut the third sketch.
7. Apply fillets.
8. Shell the model.

If the order of operations used in the above part were slightly reordered, the resulting part would also look slightly different, as shown in Figure 1.3.

Figure 1.4 shows a comparison of the FeatureManager design trees for the two different feature orders. You can reorder features by dragging them up or down the tree. Relationships between features can prevent reordering; for example, the fillets are dependent on the second extruded feature, and cannot be reordered before it. This is referred to as a Parent/Child relationship.

CROSS-REF Reordering and Parent/Child relationships are discussed in more detail in Chapter 11.

FIGURE 1.2

Features that are used to create a simple part

FIGURE 1.3

Using a different order of features for the same part

FIGURE 1.4

Compare the FeatureManager design trees for the parts from Figure 1.2 and Figure 1.3.

ON the CD-ROM The part used for this example is available in the material from the CD-ROM, named Chapter 1 – Features.SLDPRT.

The order of operations, or *history*, is important to the final state of the part. For example, if you change the order so that the shell comes before the extruded cut, the geometry of the model changes, creating a sleeve inside instead of just a hole on top. You can try this for yourself by opening the part indicated above, dragging the Shell1 feature in the FeatureManager, and dropping it just above the Cut-Extrude1 feature.

In some cases, reordering the features in the FeatureManager may result in geometry that might not make any sense; for example, if the fillets are applied after the shell, they might break through to the inside of the part. In these cases, SolidWorks gives an error that helps you to fix the problem.

In 2D CAD programs where you are just drawing lines, the order in which you draw the lines does not matter, because the results are the same. This is one of the fundamental differences between history-based modeling and non-history-based drawing.

Features are really just like steps in building a part; the steps can either add material or remove it. However, when you make a part on a mill or lathe, you are only removing material. The FeatureManager is like an instruction sheet to build the part. When you reorder and revise history, you change the final result.

Sketching with Parametrics

You have already seen that sketching is the foundation that underlies the most common feature types. We will now find that sketching in parametric software is vastly different from drawing lines in 2D CAD.

Dictionary.com defines the word *parameter* as "one of a set of measurable factors . . . that define a system and determine its behavior and [that] are varied in an experiment." What this means to us as SolidWorks users in a practical sense is that we can create sketches that change according to certain rules, and maintain relationships through those changes. This is the basis of parametric design. It extends beyond sketching to curve elements, surface features, and solid features.

SolidWorks makes 2D and 3D sketching possible. Of the two methods, 2D sketches are by far the more widely used. You create 2D sketches on a selected plane, planar solid or surface face, and use them to establish shapes for features such as Extrude, Revolve, and others. Relations in 2D sketches are often created between sketch entities and other entities that may or may not be in the sketch plane. In situations where other entities are not in the sketch plane, the out-of-plane entity is projected into the sketch plane in a direction that is normal to the sketch plane. This does not happen for 3D sketches.

You use 3D sketches for the Hole Wizard, piping, wiring, and weldments, among other applications such as complex shape creation.

Both 2D and 3D sketches share some relation types, although some of these relations work differently in the two types of sketches. Some relations that are unique to each type of sketch. The available sketch relations are:

- **Along X, Along Y, Along Z:** 3D sketch only. Along X means that the Y and Z coordinates do not change — only the X coordinates. This is similar for the other relations.

- **Intersection:** 2D and 3D sketches. This relation is created by the Intersection Curve sketch tool. You cannot apply it manually.

- **Coincident:** 2D and 3D sketches. In a 2D sketch, a point can be coincident with an entity that is not on the sketch plane because SolidWorks considers the external entity to be projected into the sketch plane. In a 3D sketch, the coincident relation is explicit rather than projected.

- **Concentric:** 2D and 3D sketches. Available between arcs, circles, and ellipses, as well as items that project into a 2D sketch plane as arcs, circles, or ellipses.

- **Coradial:** 2D and 3D sketches. This applies to arcs or circles that have the same center and radius.

- **Collinear:** 2D and 3D sketches. Only available between a linear sketch entity and another linear sketch, edge, or curve entity.

- **Equal:** 2D and 3D sketches. This is used to make lines of equal length or arcs and circles of equal radius.

- **Equal Curvature:** 2D and 3D sketches. This relation only applies to splines, although you can apply it between a spline and other sketch entities, edges, or curves. This is similar to Tangent, except that in addition to being tangent, the spline also matches the curvature of the other item at the end of the spline. The curvature value cannot be set explicitly for any sketch entity except in the form of an arc or circle radius. Curvature = 1/radius.

- **Fix:** 2D and 3D sketches. This clamps a sketch entity wherever it is when you apply the relation. It is not considered best practice to make extensive use of the Fix relation. When it is used, it is a frequent cause of overdefined sketches and troubleshooting difficulties.

- **Horizontal:** 2D and 3D sketches. Horizontal and vertical relations are relative to the local sketch origin, not the global part origin. When used in a 2D sketch, Horizontal is indicated by the short leg of the red sketch origin. When used in a 3D sketch, Horizontal can be applied only when sketching on a plane within the 3D sketch, and it has no relation to geometry outside the plane.

- **Midpoint:** 2D and 3D sketches. An endpoint, sketch point, or centerpoint may be placed at the midpoint of a line or arc. In 3D sketches, only a line can receive a midpoint relation.

- **On Edge:** 2D and 3D sketches. This relation is created by the Convert Entities sketch tool. You cannot apply it manually.

- **Parallel:** 2D and 3D sketches. This may be used between sketch lines and linear edges, as well as curves or other sketch lines. When applied in a 2D sketch between a sketch line and an out-of-plane entity, the out-of-plane entity must project into the sketch plane as a straight line, and the parallel will apply to the projection.

- **Pierce:** 2D sketch only. A sketch point, centerpoint, or endpoint can be pierced by an edge, curve, or sketch that is external to the sketch and out-of-plane. The point where the out-of-plane curve goes through the sketch plane is the pierce point. The out-of-plane entity is not projected into the sketch plane. It is the only 2D sketch relation that does not use projected out-of-plane entities. If the curve entity does not cross the sketch plane, the relation fails. If the curve crosses the sketch plane at more than one location, the pierce point becomes the closest crossing to the selected sketch point.

- **Symmetric:** 2D sketch only. Symmetric relations are created by mirroring items around a sketch centerline, and you can also apply them manually to pre-existing sketch entities, by using a centerline for reference.

- **Tangent:** 2D and 3D sketches.

- **Vertical:** 2D and 3D sketches. Horizontal and vertical relations are relative to the local sketch origin, not the global part origin. When used in a 2D sketch, Vertical is indicated by the long leg of the red sketch origin. For planes in 3D sketches, horizontal and vertical relate only to the local plane, not to the 3D sketch origin. As a result, if a line is constrained to a plane in a 3D sketch, the plane is still allowed to rotate unless there is sketch geometry constrained to geometry outside of the sketch.

- **On Surface:** 3D sketch only. Planar sketch entities such as lines and arcs in a 3D sketch can be given the On Surface relation to planes or planar faces. Sketch points can be given the relation to any surface type. The On Surface constraint is created automatically by the Spline On Surface sketch tool.

- **At Intersection Of Two Faces:** 2D and 3D sketches. This sketch relation is only created by the Intersection Curve sketch tool, which draws sketch entities where surfaces, solid faces, or planes intersect. This relation cannot be created manually.

For a simple example of working with sketch relations in a 2D sketch, consider the sketch that is shown in Figure 1.5. The only relationships between the four lines are that they form a closed loop that is touching end to end, and one of the corners is coincident to the part origin. The small square icon near the origin is the symbol for a *coincident* sketch relation. The setting to enable or disable these sketch relation symbols is found at View ➪ Sketch Relations.

FIGURE 1.5

A sketch of four lines

If you drag any of the unconstrained corners (except for the corner that is coincident to the origin), the two neighboring lines will follow the dragged endpoint, as shown in Figure 1.6. Notice the ghosted image left by the original position of the sketch. This is helpful when experimenting with changes to the sketch because you can see both the new and the old states of the sketch. The setting to enable or disable this ghosted position is found at Tools ➪ Options ➪ Sketch ➪ Ghost Image On Drag.

FIGURE 1.6

Dragging an endpoint

If you add a parallel relation between opposing lines, they now act differently, as shown in Figure 1.7.

FIGURE 1.7

Dragging an endpoint where lines have relations

Next, a second parallel and a horizontal relation are added, as shown in Figure 1.8. If you are following along by recreating the sketch on your computer, you will notice that one line has turned from blue to black.

FIGURE 1.8

Horizontal and parallel relations are added.

The colors represent sketch states. Sketch states include Underdefined, Overdefined, Fully Defined, Unsolvable, Zero Length, and Dangling. There can be entities with different states within a single sketch. Also, endpoints of lines can have a different state than the rest of the sketched entity. For example, a line that is sketched horizontally from the origin has a *coincident* at one endpoint to the origin, and the line itself is *horizontal*. As a result, the line and first endpoint are black, but the other endpoint is underdefined because the length of the line is not defined. Sketch states are indicated in the lower-right corner of the graphics window and also in the status bar.

- **Blue:** Underdefined. The sketch entity is not completely defined. You can drag it to change size, position, or orientation.
- **Black:** Fully Defined. The sketch entity is fully defined by a combination of sketch relations and dimensions. A sketch cannot be fully defined without being connected in some way to something external to the sketch, such as the part origin or an edge. Multiple external entities may be used, as appropriate. (The exception to this rule is the use of the Fix constraint, which, although effective, is not a recommended practice.)

- **Red:** Overdefined. This can mean a number of things, but it is usually caused by conflicting relations or dimensions. For example, if a line has both horizontal and vertical relations, it becomes overdefined because one of the relations is satisfied, while the other is not.

- **Pink:** Unsolvable. The difference between pink and red is that red is in one of several possible correct locations, whereas pink is not able to move to a correct location, generally because of another red entity.

- **Yellow:** Zero Length. Solving the sketch relations would result in a zero-length entity; for example, this can occur where an arc is tangent to a line, and the centerpoint of the arc is also coincident to the line.

- **Brown:** Dangling. The relation has lost track of the entity to which it was connected.

Now you can see that dragging one corner only allows the lines to move in certain ways, as shown in Figure 1.9.

FIGURE 1.9

Sketch motion is becoming more constrained.

Dimensions are also part of the parametric scheme. If you apply an angle dimension about the origin and try dragging again, as shown in Figure 1.10, you see that the only aspect that is not locked down is the length of the sides. Notice also that when the angle dimension is added, another line turns black.

FIGURE 1.10

Open degrees of freedom can be dragged.

Finally, adding length dimensions for the unequal sides completes the definition of the sketch, as shown in Figure 1.11. At this point, all lines have turned black. This is the state that we call "fully defined." Between the dimensions and sketch relations, there is enough information to recreate this sketch exactly.

It is considered best practice to fully define all sketches. However, there are times when this is not practical. When you create freeform shapes, generally through the use of splines, these shapes cannot easily be fully defined, and even if they are fully defined, the extra dimensions are usually meaningless, because it is impractical to dimension splines on manufacturing drawings.

FIGURE 1.11

The fully defined sketch cannot be dragged, and there are no degrees of freedom.

It is the idea of reacting to change that most concerns us regarding parametric design. There are other factors that can also drive the sketch, such as equations, other model geometry that is external to the sketch, and even geometry from another part in an assembly, as you shall see later.

Understanding Design Intent

"Design Intent" is a phrase that you will hear SolidWorks users say a lot. I like to think of it as "design for change." Design Intent means that when you put the parametric sketch relations together with the feature intelligence, you can build models that react to change in predictable ways.

An example of Design Intent could be a statement in words that describes general aspects that help define the design of a part, such as "This part is symmetrical, with holes that line up with Part A, and thick enough to be flush with Part B." From this description, and the surrounding parts, it is possible to recreate the part in such a way that if Part A or Part B changes, the part being described updates to match.

There are some types of changes that cause features to fail or sketch relations to conflict. In most situations, SolidWorks has ample tools for troubleshooting and editing that allow you to either repair or change the model. In these situations, it is often the Design Intent itself that is changing.

When editing or repairing relations, it is considered best practice to edit rather than delete. Deleting often causes additional problems further down the tree. Many users find it tempting to simply delete anything that has an error on it, but the cause of the error may be something other than what is identified.

Editing Design Intent

Design Intent is generally thought of as a static concept that controls changing geometry. However, this is not always the way things are. Design Intent often changes, thus requiring the way in which the model reacts to geometric changes to also change. Fortunately, SolidWorks has many tools to help you deal with situations like this.

View, Sketch Relations

One of the most obvious tools necessary for visualizing existing Design Intent is to be able to see the sketch relations. You can show or hide icons that represent the relations using the menu selection View, Sketch Relations.

 View, Sketch Relations is an excellent candidate for use with a hotkey, thus allowing you to easily toggle the display on and off.

 For more information on creating and managing hotkeys, see Chapter 2.

You can use the sketch relation icons that are visible on the screen to delete relations by selecting the icon and pressing Delete on the keyboard. You can also use them to quickly tell the status of sketch relations, applying referring to the colors defined earlier.

Display/Delete Relations

You can find the Display/Delete Relations tool on the Sketch toolbar or by selecting a sketch entity in an open sketch. The sketch status colors that were defined earlier also apply here, with the relations being shown in the appropriate color. (Relations are not shown in blue or black, only the colors that cause errors, such as red, yellow, pink, and brown.) This tool also allows you to group relations by several categories:

- All in This Sketch
- Dangling
- Overdefining/Not Solved
- External
- Defined in Context
- Locked
- Broken
- Selected Entities

In the lower Entities panel, you can also replace one entity with another, or repair dangling relations.

Suppressed Sketch Relations

Suppressing a sketch relation means that the relation is turned off and not used to compute the position of sketch entities. Suppressed relations are generally used in conjunction with configurations.

 Configurations are dealt with in detail in Chapter 10.

Working with Associativity

Associativity in SolidWorks refers to links between documents, such as a part that has an associative link to a drawing. If the part changes, the drawing updates as well. Bi-directional associativity means that the part can actually be changed from the drawing. One of the implications of this is that you do not edit a SolidWorks drawing by simply moving lines on the drawing; you must change the model, which causes all views of the part or assembly to update correctly.

Other associative links include using base parts, where one part is inserted as the first feature in another part. This might be the case when you build a casting. If the part is designed in its "as cast" state, it is then inserted into another part where machining operations are performed by cut features and the part is transformed into its "as machined" state. This technique is also used for plastic parts where a single shape spans multiple plastic pieces. A "master part" is created and split into multiple parts that could, for example, become a mouse cover and buttons.

One of the most important aspects of associativity is file management. Associated files are kept connected by filenames. If a document name is changed, and one of the associated files does not know about the change, then the association between the files can become broken. For this reason, you should use SolidWorks Explorer to change names of associated files. There are other techniques that work, as well as some techniques that you should avoid.

BEST PRACTICE It is considered poor practice to change filenames of documents that are referenced by other documents with Windows Explorer. Links between parts, assemblies, and drawings can be broken in this way. Using SolidWorks Explorer or a Product Data Management, or PDM, application is the preferred method for changing filenames.

Summary

Product development is about design, but it is even more about change. You actually design something once, but you may modify it endlessly (or it may seem that way sometimes). Similarly, SolidWorks is about design, but it really enables change. Think of SolidWorks as virtual prototyping software that allows you to change your prototype rather than having to make a new one. Virtual prototypes will never completely replace physical models, but they may reduce your dependence on them to some extent.

SolidWorks is also about reusing data. Associativity allows you to model a part once and use it for Finite Element Analysis, or FEA, creating 2D drawings, building assemblies, creating photorealistic renderings, and so on. When you make changes to the model, your drawing is already updated, and you don't have to reapply FEA materials and conditions or redo the rendering setup. Associativity saves you time by reusing your data. Associativity and change driven by feature-based and history-based modeling can take some getting used to if you have had limited exposure to it, but with some practice it becomes intuitive and you will see the many benefits for enabling change. Parametric sketching and feature creation help you to maintain Design Intent and also adjust it as necessary.

Chapter 2

Navigating the SolidWorks Interface

The good news is that the SolidWorks interface is very flexible, and if you're a Windows veteran, most of it is perfectly intuitive. The bad news is that there's a lot of it to know. This chapter serves as a reference, and to help you decide how you want to use different portions of the interface. In this chapter, you learn how to effectively navigate and manipulate the interface, and you learn how to customize it both to suit your personal style and to help you work faster. This customization includes adding and removing toolbar buttons, displaying descriptions on toolbars, accessing dynamic help options, using standard and custom hotkeys, and making your interface customization portable to other computers.

Many aspects of the SolidWorks interface are controlled by settings, which are covered in detail in Appendix B. Each interface element that is identified in Figure 2.1 is explained in greater detail in its own section of this chapter.

Once you have mastered the various interface elements and customized your SolidWorks installation, working with the software becomes much more efficient and satisfying.

IN THIS CHAPTER

Identifying elements of the SolidWorks interface

Making the interface work for you

Tutorial: Getting to know the interface

FIGURE 2.1

Elements of the SolidWorks interface

FeatureManager

PropertyManager

ConfigurationManager

Display Pane expander arrows   Graphics window   SolidWorks Search

CommandManager   SolidWorks toolbars

SolidWorks
Resources
Design
Library
File
Explorer
Search
Results
View
Palette

Task pane

Display triad   Status bar   Part origin   Task pane
                                                    expander arrows

View orientation   Standard planes

Identifying Elements of the SolidWorks Interface

When communicating with other users and tech support, it is important to use names for the various interface components that other people understand. This chapter is about learning the terminology and finding the tools that you need.

Toolbars

The SolidWorks GUI (Graphical User Interface) is highly dependent on toolbar icons. While some icons are self-explanatory, others require some explanation. In this chapter, we discuss the Standard toolbar, button by button, in order to identify each of the available tools. Other toolbars have more specific functions and are explained in detail in their respective chapters.

Standard toolbar

The Standard toolbar has many of the basic tools that are familiar to most Windows users. It is used for basic functions such as creating and saving documents, changing colors, and undoing and redoing actions. Although there may be some commands that new users are not familiar with, this section serves as a reference for all user levels; the more advanced commands are covered in their respective sections.

The commands are shown in the order in which they appear on the Tools ⇨ Customize ⇨ Commands list for the Standard toolbar.

New

 The New command enables you to create new SolidWorks documents from existing templates. By default, SolidWorks uses the Novice interface for the New dialog box, which only allows you to select from default SolidWorks document templates, as shown in Figure 2.2.

FIGURE 2.2

The New SolidWorks Document dialog box, using the Novice interface

You can click the Advanced button in the lower-left corner of the dialog box to switch to the Advanced interface. The difference between the Novice and Advanced interfaces is that the Advanced interface allows you to use additional tabs and custom templates. You can create additional tabs by using Windows Explorer to add folders to the folder that is indicated in Tools ⇨ Options ⇨ File Locations ⇨ Document Templates. You can create custom templates by saving blank files with the desired settings as Template files, using the Files of type drop-down list in the Save As dialog box.

CROSS-REF   Templates are discussed in more detail in Chapter 3.

Figure 2.3 shows the Advanced interface of the New SolidWorks Document dialog box.

FIGURE 2.3

The New SolidWorks Document dialog box, using the Advanced interface

Open

The Open command is used to open SolidWorks documents and to import other types of data. Although many new users look for an Import command in SolidWorks, you must actually import all data through the Open dialog box. You can also use the Open dialog box in many respects like a standard Windows Explorer window, because it enables you to copy, move, delete, and rename files.

Figure 2.4 shows the Open dialog box.

FIGURE 2.4

The Open dialog box

The Preview option enables you to view document thumbnails in the Preview box that is located in the upper-right area of the Open dialog box.

When you use the Advanced option with an assembly document, it brings up the Configure Document dialog box, shown in Figure 2.5, which enables you to:

- Open the currently selected configuration.
- Create a new assembly configuration with a specified name that shows all referenced models.
- Create a new assembly configuration with a specified name that suppresses all parts in order to display only the assembly structure. (Suppressing all of the parts makes the assembly load instantly.).
- Load the assembly using a specified part configuration name. For example, if you specify "Simplified," the assembly opens all parts in their "Simplified" configuration, if it exists.

FIGURE 2.5

The Configure Document dialog box, which appears when you use the Advanced option in the Open dialog box

You can open the following types of documents from the Open dialog box:

NOTE The file types in the list are not alphabetized in the SolidWorks window, which makes it difficult to browse for file types. They are alphabetized here for ease of reference.

- **ACIS (*.sat):** ACIS files typically come from AutoCAD or CADKEY 3D models.

- **Add-Ins (*.dll):** If you have applications that run through a dynamic link library, or DLL, then you can start the DLL from the Open command.

- **Adobe Illustrator (*.ai):** You can open Adobe Illustrator files in SolidWorks as either sketch entities or sketch text.

- **CADKEY (*.prt, *.ckd):** CADKEY files.

- **Catia Graphics (*.cgr):** These are simply graphics files, not fully translated geometry files.

- **DWG (*.dwg):** DWG files can be either 2D or 3D. It is best to use the DWG format to transfer only 2D files. Use the ACIS format to transfer AutoCAD 3D files.

- **DXF (*.dxf):** DXF files can be either 2D or 3D. It is best to use the DXF format to transfer only 2D files. Use the ACIS format to transfer AutoCAD 3D files.

- **IDF (*.emn, *.brd, *.bdf, *.idb):** These file types are used to transfer circuit-board data into SolidWorks.

- **IGES (*.igs, *.iges):** IGES files can contain many types of information, but not all companies interpret it in the same way. SolidWorks works best with trimmed-surface IGES data. IGS data is sometimes used to transmit 2D data. SolidWorks does not typically do a good job of reading data in this format. You typically import 2D drawing data into SolidWorks as sketch entities. It is best to transfer 2D drawings as DWG or DXF files. Because of the variability of this data, it is not one of the preferred translation formats.

- **Inventor Part (*.ipt):** SolidWorks can open Inventor files up to and including version 9.0; however, it interprets just the geometry, not a complete feature tree.

- **Library Features (*.lfp, *.sldlfp):** Library features can include solid-feature geometry and sketches, and can also use configurations. These file formats are used for combinations of features that you use frequently, in order to save modeling time and to improve standardization.

- **Mesh (*.nxm, *.scn, *.3ds, *.obj, *.stl, *.wrl, *.ply, *.ply2):** These are mesh formats that include STL and 3D Studio Max files, which can be used in ScanTo3D to create a surfaced-solid model.

- **Parasolid (*.x_t, *.x_b, *.xmx_txt, *.xmt_bin):** There are two types of Parasolid files: binary and text. The binary files are typically about half the size of the text files, but you can read the text files with a text editor and extract certain information from the file header. SolidWorks is based on the Parasolid kernel, and so Parasolid is the preferred translation standard.

- **Point Cloud (*.xyz, *.txt, *.asc, *.vda, *.igs):** Point cloud files are typically brought in either for reference or to use ScanTo3D in order to create surfaced-solid models.

- **Pro/Engineer Part (*.prt, *.xpr):** SolidWorks can read versions 17 to 2001 of Pro/Engineer parts, as well as Wildfire versions 1 and 2.

- **Pro/Engineer Assembly (*.asm, *.xas):** SolidWorks can read versions 17 to 2001 of Pro/Engineer assemblies, as well as Wildfire versions 1 and 2.

- **Solid Edge Part (*.par):** SolidWorks reads the Parasolid data from Solid Edge files. To transfer Solid Edge drawings, DWG or DXF formats are preferred.

- **Solid Edge Assembly (*.asm):** SolidWorks reads the Parasolid data from Solid Edge files. To transfer Solid Edge drawings, DWG or DXF formats are preferred.

- **SolidWorks Parts, Assemblies, and Drawings (*.sldprt, *.sldasm, *.slddrw):** These are native SolidWorks-created documents or imported data saved as SolidWorks file type.

- **STEP AP 203/214 (*.step, *.stp):** STEP stands for "STandard for the Exchange of Product" model data. AP stands for "application protocol," which signifies different types of STEP data. The number 203 indicates Configuration Controlled Design, and 214 indicates Core Data for Automotive Mechanical Design Processes. STEP is a reliable translation standard, although Parasolid is preferred.

- **STL (*.stl):** STL is a tessellated or facetted format that is intended for the stereolithography process. You can import this format as a graphics body (with no selectable solid geometry), as a solid, or a surface. Keep in mind that because the data is tessellated, it cannot create smooth surfaces. Solid and surface imports severely degrade performance on any assembly into which they are placed. This is not a recommended format for import.

- **UGII (*.prt):** Unigraphics 10 and higher, including NX parts, can be opened in SolidWorks. However, you should keep in mind that UG drawings and assemblies have the same extension, and do not open if there is no Parasolid data in the file.

- **VDAFS (*.vda):** VDAFS is a German translation standard, which in my experience is at least as reliable as IGES.

- **VRML (*.wrl):** VRML stands for "Virtual Reality Markup Language." Its usage for CAD applications is limited, having been primarily a game geometry format. Large file sizes and tessellated geometry typically prevent its extensive use for transferring CAD data, but the format has special graduated color options that enable you to create 3D colored plots for analysis applications. This is not a recommended format for import.

Save

The first time you save a document, the Save command acts like the Save As command, giving you the option to assign a path, filename, file type, and description. Figure 2.6 shows the Save As dialog box. After the first save, the command doesn't display a dialog box, but just saves the data. You can specify whether or not to create backup copies by using the settings at Tools ⇨ Options ⇨ Backup/Recover.

FIGURE 2.6

The Save As dialog box

In addition to its native formats, SolidWorks can also save the following types of documents:

- **3D XML (*.3dxml):** This is a new XML-based 3D display format that was created in 2005 by Microsoft and Dassault Systems for the integration of 3D images into documentation, Web sites, manuals, and other materials.

- **ACIS (*.sat):** See the file-type description under the Open command list.

- **Adobe PDF (*.pdf):** Prints the current document to a PDF file.

- **Catia Graphics (*.cgr):** See the file-type description under the Open command list.

- **DWG (*.dwg):** See the file-type description under the Open command list.

- **DXF (*.dxf):** See the file-type description under the Open command list.

- **eDrawing (*.eprt, *.easm, *.edrw):** eDrawing is a display-only format that you can publish either as a standalone file that requires a separate viewer, or with a viewer built into the actual file. It features a small file size (relative to full CAD documents) and allows the viewer to view in 3D, mark up, section, and move parts.

- **Form Tool (*.sldftp):** This file type is specific to tools that form sheet metal. See Chapter 29 for more information.

- **IGES (*.igs):** See the file-type description under the Open command list.

- **HCG (*.hcg):** Catia Highly Compressed Graphics files. These files are display-only.

- **HOOPS HSF (*.hsf):** HOOPS is a 3D graphics display format that is used by several 3D viewers.

- **JPEG (*.jpg):** SolidWorks saves out the display as a JPEG image.

- **Library Feature Part (*.sldlfp):** See the file-type description under the Open command list.

- **Microsoft XAML (*.xaml):** Extensible Application Markup Language is a language for creating graphical interfaces for Windows Presentation Foundation, or WPF.

- **Parasolid (*.x_t):** See the file-type description under the Open command list.

- **Parasolid Binary (*.x_b):** See the file-type description under the Open command list.

- **Part (*.sldprt):** SolidWorks part format.

- **Part Template (*.prtdot):** SolidWorks part-template format. See Chapter 3 for more information on templates.

- **Pro/Engineer (*.prt, *.asm):** This file format does not save a feature-based part, but only a "dumb" solid.

- **ScanTo3D (*.xyz, *.wrl, *.stl, *.3ds):** See the file-type description under the Open command list, listed under the Mesh and Point Cloud headings.

- **Tiff (*.tif):** SolidWorks can save out the print image as a TIFF file. This is particularly useful for exporting high-resolution drawings.

- **Universal 3D (*.u3d):** This is a 3D display format that is used by Adobe.

- **VDAFS (*.vda):** See the file-type description under the Open command list.

- **VRML (*.wrl):** See the file-type description under the Open command list.

Save All

The Save All command saves all open documents. When saving a large number of files, settings can be important to avoid workflow interruption. One such setting, "Warn before saving documents with update errors," is found at Tools ➪ Options ➪ General. Another such setting, "Warn about saving referenced documents," is found at Tools ➪ Options ➪ External References.

Close

This command closes the active document. You might also consider using Close All, which is found in the Window menu.

Reload

One of the functions of the Reload command is the equivalent of closing the part without saving and reopening the same part. You can also use this command to change the read/write status of the file. The dialog box that displays also warns you when reloading causes you to discard changes, as shown in Figure 2.7.

FIGURE 2.7

The Reload options

Check Read-Only Files

This command becomes active only if the multi-user environment has been activated, and the option to check the status of read-only files has been activated in Tools ➪ Options ➪ Collaboration.

If these conditions are met and you click this button, you either receive a message that says that none of the read-only files in memory have been changed, or if they have been changed, the Reload dialog box displays with the changed parts in the dialog box, prompting you to reload the parts with write access.

Make Drawing from Part/Assembly

This command takes the current part or assembly and starts a new drawing, based on this part or assembly. How it behaves again depends on your settings. If you set the New dialog box to Novice, the Make Drawing command creates a new drawing of the active part or assembly from the default drawing template. If you set the New dialog box to Advanced, you are prompted to select a template.

Again, depending on your setup, the automatically created drawing may behave differently. If you use a template that contains pre-defined views, the views are automatically populated. Whether the View Palette appears depends on the setting at Tools ➪ Options ➪ Drawings ➪ Show View Palette.

Make Assembly from Part/Assembly

This tool works similarly to the Make Drawing tool in that if the New dialog box uses the Novice interface, it creates the new assembly from the default assembly template.

Another option that normally affects the function of this command is shown in Figure 2.8. The Make Assembly from Part/Assembly command opens a new assembly with the Insert Component PropertyManager dialog box open. The Start Command When Creating New Assembly option has no effect when you invoke a new assembly from the Make Assembly from Part/Assembly command. However, if you create a new assembly manually, this option controls whether or not the PropertyManager that selects models and places them in the assembly displays automatically.

FIGURE 2.8

The Insert Component dialog box opens when you apply the Make Assembly from Part/Assembly command.

Print

The Print command in the Standard toolbar is different from the Print command in the File menu. The hotkey Ctrl+P accesses the Print command from the menu. The difference is that from the toolbar, the Print command automatically prints using the current document settings to the current document printer. Using the Print command from the Menu displays the Print dialog box and enables you to select the printer and settings.

Print Preview

Print Preview displays a preview of what is to be printed. It allows you to zoom, but only with three limited zoom-scale options. These zoom options do not apply to printing, only to previewing. The Print button within the preview window takes you to the Print dialog box, where you can select settings and printers.

NOTE The Print Selection option is available only for drawings, and must be selected from the Print dialog box. It is assumed that when a model is printed, the selection is in the graphics window, which is printed for model documents.

Print3D

Print3D takes you to a Web site that allows you to choose from one of several services to create a rapid prototype of the active part.

This is different from 3D Printing, which is an option in the File menu that interfaces with 3D printer hardware that is connected to your computer.

Cut

This command cuts the selected item and places it on the Clipboard. Consider using Delete if you do not intend to paste the cut item. You can also apply the Cut command by using the Ctrl+X hotkey. This is standard Windows functionality.

Copy

This command copies the current selection to the Clipboard. The Copy command is also available by using the Ctrl+C hotkey. This is standard Windows functionality.

Paste

This command pastes whatever is on the Clipboard to the currently selected location. Not all items can be placed this way. You can also apply the Paste command by using the Ctrl+V hotkey. This is standard Windows functionality.

Delete

This command deletes the current selection. The Confirm Delete dialog box has some options that are shown in Figure 2.9. For example, the Also Delete Absorbed Features option deletes a feature and absorbed sketches. The Also Delete All Child Features option is not always available, but when it is, it automatically deletes dependent features. Turning this setting off causes dependent features to lose references, and to encounter dangling errors, but otherwise remain intact.

The Delete command is also available in the right mouse button (RMB) menu and by using the Delete key on the keyboard.

FIGURE 2.9

The Confirm Delete dialog box

There are two special uses of the Delete command. The first is when the selection is a surface or solid body. In this case, the Delete command results in a Delete Bodies feature being added to the FeatureManager, and the bodies being removed from the part. This is a history-based deletion, which means that if you roll back to before you used the Delete Bodies feature, the bodies are there again.

The second special use is when the selection is a closed-loop open edge of a surface body (such as a circular hole that is trimmed in the middle of a surface, and not at the edge); SolidWorks asks if you are trying to delete the feature or to delete the hole. This is similar to the Untrim feature.

Undo

The Undo command for SolidWorks 2007 allows you to undo more functions than in previous versions, but you may still encounter certain functions that it cannot undo. The drop-down arrow to the right of the icon enables you to see a list of how many functions it can undo. You can also access this function using the Ctrl+Z hotkey. This is standard Windows functionality.

Redo

The Redo command enables you to redo actions that were undone with the Undo command. This command also has a drop-down list that shows all of the functions that you can redo. This is standard Windows functionality.

Rebuild

The Rebuild command recalculates any features in the FeatureManager of the current part or assembly that SolidWorks has marked for rebuilding. When SolidWorks detects that a feature needs to be rebuilt, it displays a rebuild symbol next to the name of the feature in the FeatureManager.

NOTE At times, a rebuild symbol may not disappear from a feature, forcing it to be rebuilt every time you make a change. In a component with a lot of features, this can create a serious performance problem.

Other times, the rebuild symbol may not be present, even when features need to be rebuilt. Whenever it looks like something is wrong with a feature, it is a good idea to use the Forced Rebuild command, which rebuilds everything whether or not the software thinks that it is necessary. There is no icon or menu selection for Forced Rebuild; it is only available through the Ctrl+Q hotkey.

Options

The Options icon displays the Tools ➪ Options settings dialog box, where most of the SolidWorks settings are located.

 The Tools ➪ Options settings are explained in detail in Appendix B.

Properties

The Properties button displays the PropertyManager. This is usually unnecessary if the Tools ➪ Options ➪ General ➪ Auto-show PropertyManager option is turned on.

Color

The Color button displays the Color PropertyManager window. This enables you to assign colors, transparency, and other visual properties to parts, bodies, features, and faces.

When you are not sure at what level the color was applied (for example, face, feature, part, or component), you can use the Display pane and Display Callouts to identify colored entities.

Materials

You can apply materials to SolidWorks parts. These materials define characteristics for display, section hatching, density, and other material properties that are associated with Finite Element Analysis, or FEA. Materials with RealView graphics capabilities can look more realistic without rendering. Display properties are covered in more detail in Chapter 3.

Screen Capture

The Screen Capture command copies the contents of the graphics window to the Clipboard.

Textures

You can apply texture images to parts to improve the realism of the display without rendering.

Select Color Scheme

The Select Color Scheme command enables you to toggle through all of the available color schemes one-by-one by clicking the button. You can also click the drop-down arrow, and select from a list of color schemes. If you want, you can also customize color schemes.

Select

You can use the Select command to clear any other active tool, although you can also press the Esc button for the same purpose. Select activates the normal arrow cursor, which allows you to select items.

Selection Filter

The Selection Filter command is a powerful tool that limits the selection to only certain types of entities. The F5 key toggles the display of the entire filter toolbar.

Web Toolbar

The Web Toolbar button displays the Web toolbar, which enables you to open Web sites from within SolidWorks.

Full Screen

The Full Screen command removes toolbars, menus, and the FeatureManager, displaying only the graphics window. You can also toggle this option using the F11 key. The F9 key toggles the display of the FeatureManager, and the F10 key toggles the toolbars.

New Window

The New Window command opens an additional window of the active document. This feature is different from using multiple viewports because the FeatureManager displays twice. This can be useful when there is a large list of features in the FeatureManager, and you want to see items at the top of the list as well as at the bottom.

Tile Horizontally

The Tile Horizontally command tiles all open windows so that they are stacked one on top of another.

Tile Vertically

The Tile Vertically command tiles all open windows so that they sit side-by-side.

Help

The Help command accesses the SolidWorks Help file.

Figures 2.10 to 2.25 show the most commonly used toolbars displaying their default icons. The SolidWorks interface uses over 500 icons.

The Annotation toolbar, shown in Figure 2.10, contains tools for notes, balloons, surface finish and weld symbols, Geometric Dimensioning and Tolerancing (GD&T), datums, hole callouts, cosmetic threads, center marks and centerlines, cross hatch, and dimensioning. By default, this toolbar appears on the drawings Command Manager, but it may also be added to parts or assemblies as needed. These tools are covered in detail in Chapter 21.

FIGURE 2.10

The Annotation toolbar

The Assembly toolbar, shown in Figure 2.11, contains tools that are used in assemblies only. These include visibility tools, mating and moving tools, exploded-view tools, and various analysis tools, among others. These tools are covered in depth in Chapters 12 to 16.

FIGURE 2.11

The Assembly toolbar

The Dimensions/Relations toolbar, shown in Figure 2.12, contains tools for creating all of the dimension types in SolidWorks, including ordinate dimensions. In addition to the Sketch toolbar, you can also find tools for working with sketch relations.

FIGURE 2.12

The Dimensions/Relations toolbar

The Drawing toolbar, shown in Figure 2.13, contains tools for drawing view creation. You can also add buttons that do not display by default on the toolbar, including Empty View, Predefined View, and Update View. Update View is not a view type, but a command that updates all drawing views to the current state of the model. The tools on this toolbar are discussed thoroughly in Chapter 21.

FIGURE 2.13

The Drawing toolbar

By default, the Features toolbar, shown in Figure 2.14, contains the most commonly used solid features. Because there are a total of 47 feature commands, displaying them all on the toolbar is not practical. Everyone uses these features differently, and so you should customize your interface to match how you use the software. Surface features appear on a separate toolbar.

FIGURE 2.14

The Features toolbar

The Reference Geometry toolbar, shown in Figure 2.15, contains all of the available reference geometry tools. These include Plane, Axis, Coordinate System, Point, and Mate Reference.

FIGURE 2.15

The Reference Geometry toolbar

The Selection Filter toolbar, shown in Figure 2.16, enables you to limit the selection to particular entity types. The filter works in conjunction with both manual selection and window selection.

FIGURE 2.16

The Selection Filter toolbar

The Sheet Metal toolbar, shown in Figure 2.17, contains all of the tools that are specific to sheet metal. Sheet Metal functionality is covered in detail in Chapters 29 and 30.

FIGURE 2.17

The Sheet Metal toolbar

The Sketch toolbar is the most frequently used toolbar in SolidWorks. Figure 2.18 shows the default sketch entities on the Sketch toolbar, but there are many other entities that do not appear on it and that you may want to use. These entities include Ellipse, Centerpoint Ellipse, Spline on Surface, Split Entities, and many more.

FIGURE 2.18

The Sketch toolbar

The SolidWorks Office toolbar, shown in Figure 2.19, displays buttons for each of the add-ins in SolidWorks Office. However, not all of the available add-ins appear by default on the toolbar. The add-ins are:

- **Photoworks:** Photo-rendering software
- **Animator:** Animation software that can work in conjunction with Photoworks
- **eDrawings:** Collaboration software
- **3D Instant Website:** Enables you to post a 3D rotatable model to a Web site using a SolidWorks server
- **Toolbox:** A library of hardware
- **Utilities:** A suite of tools including: Compare Documents, Compare Features, Compare Geometry, Feature Paint, Find and Replace Annotations, Find/Modify/Suppress/Simplify, Format Painter, Geometry Analysis, Power Select, Report Manager, and Thickness Analysis
- **FeatureWorks:** An add-in that helps you to parametrically rebuild imported parts
- **Design Checker:** An add-in that checks aspects of a document against a standard Checks document
- **COSMOSWorks Designer:** FEA application
- **COSMOSMotion:** Motion analysis application
- **SolidWorks Routing:** An add-in for piping, wiring, and tubing design
- **ScanTo3D:** An add-in that enables you to take point cloud data and create parametric surface/solid models from it

FIGURE 2.19

The SolidWorks Office toolbar

The Standard toolbar, shown in Figure 2.20, is discussed in depth earlier in this chapter.

FIGURE 2.20

The Standard toolbar

The Standard Views toolbar contains all of the orthogonal named views, as well as Isometric, Dimetric, and Trimetric. Standard Views also contains a button for Normal To, 2, and 4 viewports as well as the Link Views option. Figure 2.21 shows the Standard Views toolbar with the additional View Orientation button, which is part of the View toolbar.

You can also access standard view icons through the View Orientation dialog box, which you can access using the View Orientation button or by pressing the Spacebar.

FIGURE 2.21

The Standard Views toolbar

The Surfaces toolbar, shown in Figure 2.22, contains mainly surface features. However, several non-surface features are also included in this toolbar by default. These features include Freeform and Fillet, which belong to the Features toolbar, and the Reference Geometry and Curves flyouts.

FIGURE 2.22

The Surfaces toolbar

The Tools toolbar, shown in Figure 2.23, contains tools such as Spell Check, Measure, Mass Properties, Section Properties, Check, Import Diagnostics, Feature Statistics, Equations, Deviation Analysis, Design Table, and COSMOSXpress.

FIGURE 2.23

The Tools toolbar

The View toolbar, shown in Figure 2.24, is one that you may use very frequently. In this toolbar, you can change the view from shaded to wireframe, rotate the view, or turn off plane display. You can do many things with the tools on this toolbar, and they are examined in detail in Chapter 3.

FIGURE 2.24

The View toolbar

SolidWorks Weldments are for creating welded frames, as well as tubular or structural components that are welded together. The Weldments toolbar has tools that are specifically intended for those functions. Figure 2.25 shows this toolbar.

FIGURE 2.25

The Weldments toolbar

Tooltips

One way to learn about the individual icons is to use the Tooltips that appear after you hover your cursor over an icon for a few seconds. Tooltips come in two varieties, large and small. Large Tooltips show the name of the tool, along with a brief description of what it does. Small Tooltips show the tool's name but not the description. To change the Tooltip display from large to small, or to turn off the Tooltip display altogether, you can use the Tools ⇨ Customize menu option. In addition to the Tooltip balloons, tips also display in the status bar at the bottom of the screen when the cursor is over an icon. Figure 2.26 shows a comparison between large and small Tooltips.

FIGURE 2.26

SolidWorks uses large Tooltips by default, although it can also show small Tooltips.

To change the size of the Tooltips or to turn off Tooltips altogether, go to Tools, Customize, Toolbars.

NOTE   The Tools ⇨ Customize menu option is inactive unless a SolidWorks document is open. To access Tools, Customize, first open a SolidWorks part, assembly, or drawing. Tools, Customize is different from the Customize Menu option that is found in all SolidWorks menus. The Customize Menu option is discussed later in this chapter.

Toolbar Icon Size

You can set SolidWorks icons to be small or large by accessing the setting on the Tools ⇨ Customize ⇨ Toolbars ⇨ Options menu. Figure 2.27 shows the difference between large and small icons.

FIGURE 2.27

A comparison of large and small icon size

Managing toolbars

In SolidWorks 2007, it is easy to move, turn on and off, and add icons to toolbars. It is important to remember that different document types retain different toolbar settings; for example, the toolbars that you see with a part open are different from the toolbars that you see for drawings.

When you are working on parts, it is important to have both the Sketch and the Features toolbars active. When you are working on a drawing, you will never use the Features toolbar, but you will frequently use the Sketch toolbar. Likewise for assemblies, you may want to display some additional toolbars and eliminate others. For this reason, when you change from a part document to a drawing document, you may see your display adjust because the changing toolbars increase or decrease the amount of space that is required.

BEST PRACTICE It is best practice to set up the toolbars for each document type so that they take up the same amount of space — for example, two rows on top and one column to the right. This way, changing between document types is not so jarring, with the graphics area resizing for each change.

Moving Toolbars

To move a toolbar, you can click with the cursor at the double bar on the left end of the toolbar, as shown in Figure 2.28. The cursor changes to a four-way arrow, and you can then drag the toolbar where you want it. Toolbars dock either vertically or horizontally. You can resize undocked toolbars so that they have rows and columns. This arrangement is typically used with the Selection Filter toolbar, which is often left undocked and compressed into a block that is three or four columns wide.

FIGURE 2.28

Double bars enable you to move toolbars.

If the SolidWorks window is not wide enough for the toolbar to fit entirely in the screen, double arrows like those shown in Figure 2.29 display at the end of the truncated toolbar. When you click the double arrows, a flyout toolbar appears with the missing icons, as shown in Figure 2.30.

FIGURE 2.29

A truncated toolbar showing double arrows

FIGURE 2.30

You can display a flyout toolbar by clicking the double arrows.

Adding or Removing Toolbars and Icons

You can add or remove toolbars in several ways:

- Right-click any toolbar, and then activate or deactivate the toolbar.
- Click Tools ⇨ Customize, and then activate or deactivate the toolbar from the Toolbars tab.
- Right-click any toolbar, select Customize, and again select the toolbar from the Toolbars tab.
- Click View ⇨ Toolbars to activate or deactivate toolbars.

 NOTE There are two toolbar entries in the View menu: the topmost toolbars allow you to turn toolbars on or off, and the bottom toolbars toggle the display of all of the toolbars.

To add or remove icons from toolbars, you must open the Tools ⇨ Customize dialog box. You can access this dialog box in two ways. The first, most obvious method is to go through the menus to Tools ⇨ Customize. The second, less obvious way is to right-click any toolbar (other than the CommandManager), select Customize, and then click the Commands tab. You can then select the toolbar that you want to add from the list. With the Customize dialog box open, you can remove a toolbar icon by dragging the icon away from the toolbar into white space in the graphics window. You can also reorder or move toolbar icons between toolbars. Figures 2.31 and 2.32 show the Toolbars and Commands tabs in the Customize dialog box.

FIGURE 2.31

The Toolbars tab in the Customize dialog box allows you turn entire toolbars on and off.

Flyout Toolbars

You can use any toolbar as a flyout toolbar. Figure 2.32 shows the list of all flyout toolbars, which is exactly the same as the list of *all* toolbars. Flyout toolbars are a nice space-saving feature for tools that you use infrequently, but frequently enough to want to avoid going through the menus. To use a toolbar as a flyout, select it from the Flyout Toolbars list and drag it onto an existing toolbar. It displays with an arrow to the right. Clicking the arrow causes all of the tools to scroll out temporarily until you click either a toolbar icon or anything else.

To add icons to a flyout toolbar, temporarily show the regular toolbar that corresponds to the flyout toolbar, and add icons to the regular toolbar. When you are done adding or removing icons, turn off the regular toolbar; the changes are applied to the flyout.

> **TIP** If you want to create a separate toolbar, you can commandeer an existing one for your own purposes. For example, because I do not use the Tools toolbar, I have removed all of the regular icons from it and replaced them with relevant flyout toolbars, which I do use extensively. This allows me to consolidate space, and not have unused icons on my toolbars.

FIGURE 2.32

The Commands tab in the Customize dialog box

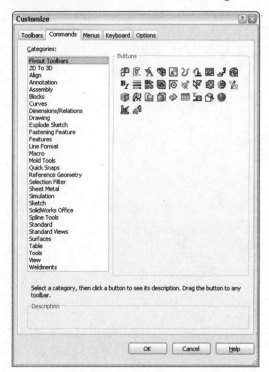

Full Screen Mode

Full Screen mode enables you to quickly toggle the display so that only the graphics window and the Task pane display; the FeatureManager, menus, toolbars, and status bar are all hidden. Alternatively, you can hide just the FeatureManager or the toolbars.

In Full Screen mode, you can still access the menus by clicking the cursor along the top border of the window.

- To toggle to Full Screen mode, press the F11 key.
- To toggle the toolbar display, press the F10 key (see Figure 2.33).
- To toggle the FeatureManager display, press the F9 key.

NEW FEATURE   Both Full Screen mode and the ability to hide the toolbars and the FeatureManager using hotkeys are new features in SolidWorks 2007.

FIGURE 2.33

The SolidWorks window with all toolbars hidden using the F10 key

Workflow customization

When you first install and run the SolidWorks software, you have the option to customize the interface using one of three pre-set option packages. Special menu and toolbar settings are made for Consumer Product Design, Machine Design, or Mold Design.

The three workflow customizations affect the interface as follows:

- Consumer Product Design adds the Surfaces toolbar to the CommandManager.
- Machine Design adds Sheet Metal and Weldments toolbars to the CommandManager.
- Mold Design adds Surfaces and Mold Tools toolbars to the CommandManager.

Similar changes are made to the menus to hide or show menu selections as appropriate. You can find more information about hiding and showing menu items later in this chapter.

If you want to select a different option after the initial setup, you can go to Tools ⇨ Customize ⇨ Options, where you can specify a different choice. Figure 2.34 shows the Options tab of the Customize dialog box.

FIGURE 2.34

The Options tab of the Customize dialog box, where you can select a different workflow customization

The CommandManager

The SolidWorks CommandManager works like a toolbar, but has much more flexibility. The CommandManager is divided into two areas, the Control Area and the Toolbar Area. The Control Area allows you to select which toolbar icons you want to display in the Toolbar Area. The default CommandManager is shown in Figure 2.35, and the Features and Sketch toolbars are listed in the Control Area. You can put any toolbar in the Control Area to save a lot of interface space.

At first, many users avoid using the CommandManager, but later come back to use it after seeing its flexibility and space-saving capabilities. I encourage you to give it a try. I was at first very skeptical of the benefits, until I used it for about a week, after which I was convinced.

The SolidWorks CommandManager

Control area　　　　　　　　　　Toolbar area

Minimizing the Size of the CommandManager

Many users are concerned about the amount of space that is taken up by the CommandManager when it uses the default settings. After all, it is supposed to save space, but it is so huge! You can make the icons the same size as normal icons and remove the descriptions. To do this, right-click the CommandManager and deselect the Use Large Buttons with Text option.

Adding Toolbars to the CommandManager

To add toolbars — such as Sheet Metal, Reference Geometry, or Tools — to the CommandManager, right-click the CommandManager, and select Customize CommandManager. This enables you to select additional toolbars. To reorder the toolbars in the Control Area, you must have Tools ⇨ Customize activated.

Using the CommandManager

You can use the CommandManager in two different ways. One way is to click the icon of the toolbar that you want to show in the Control Area, and then access the specific tools in the Toolbar Area. The other way is to use the Control Area icons as flyout toolbars, as shown in Figure 2.36.

Using CommandManager toolbar buttons as flyouts

Menus

Everyone has his or her own style of working. For example, some people like to use menus and others do not. An example of a tool that does not have a toolbar equivalent is View ⇨ Modify ⇨ Section View, which is used to change the active section view's settings.

The most frequently used menu items are in the View, Insert, and Tools menus. All of the menus shown in this section have all of the possible selections turned on. As a result, the View menu in Figure 2.37 may contain options that are not available on your computer. Customizing menus is covered later in this chapter.

The View menu is used primarily for turning on or off the visibility of entity types such as planes, sketches, or temporary axes. You can also do this by using hotkeys or by putting extra items on the View toolbar.

FIGURE 2.37

The View menu

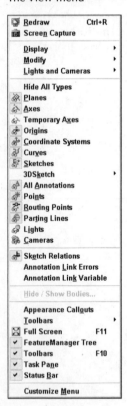

The Insert menu is used mostly for creating feature types for which you do not have a toolbar icon on the screen. For example, although the Move Face tool is only on the Mold Tools toolbar, it has many uses aside from mold design. You can find the Move Face tool on the Insert ⇨ Face menu, as shown in Figure 2.38.

FIGURE 2.38

The Insert menu

The Tools menu is used primarily for sketch entities or tools for which you have no icon on the screen. Several other commonly used tools, such as Measure, Equations, and Options, are also available in this menu. Figure 2.39 shows the complete Tools menu.

FIGURE 2.39

The Tools menu

You can customize menus by adding or omitting items. By using the Customize Menu option at the bottom of any menu — including shortcut (right mouse button) menus — you can limit the items in any menu, by removing tools that you do not use. To bring back the removed items, you can either go back to the Customize Menu or go to Tools, Customize, Options and click the Reset to Defaults buttons for menu and shortcut customization. Be careful not to confuse this Customize menu selection with the Customize Menu selection on the Tools menu. Figure 2.40 shows the Tools menu being customized. Notice that several items at the top have been turned off.

FIGURE 2.40

The Customize Menu option

The Tools ⇨ Customize ⇨ Options dialog box, shown in Figure 2.41, contains the Shortcut (right mouse button menu) and Menu customization options. These options enable you to show all of the menu items for both types of menus in a single stroke. By default, some items are hidden in various menus.

Keyboard customization is discussed later in this chapter.

NOTE SolidWorks terminology for Shortcut Menus and Shortcuts/Keyboard customization is slightly confusing because of these two overlapping, yet unrelated, terms. For this reason, we will refer to Shortcut Menus as RMB (right mouse button) menus from here on, because this is the standard terminology among SolidWorks users. Shortcuts are also generally referred to as *hotkeys* among users.

FIGURE 2.41

The Tools ⇨ Customize ⇨ Options dialog box

Cursors

SolidWorks cursors are context-sensitive, and change their appearance and function depending on the situation. Sketching cursors display a pencil and the type of sketch entity that you are presently sketching. Sketch cursors also display some dimensional information about the entity that you are sketching, such as its length or radius. Sketch cursor feedback is necessary for fast and accurate sketching.

CROSS-REF To learn more about sketch cursor feedback, see Chapter 4.

The Select cursor changes, depending the item over which you move it. Cursor symbols also help to remind you when selection filters are active.

The cursor is frequently available as an OK button. For example, after selecting edges for a Fillet feature, the RMB functions as an OK button.

FeatureManager and PropertyManager windows

The FeatureManager window is the panel to the left of the screen that shows an ordered record of features describing how the part was built. SolidWorks users spend a fair amount of time using the FeatureManager to edit or inspect models. Figure 2.42 shows the FeatureManager for a simple model.

FIGURE 2.42

The FeatureManager for a simple model

There is a splitter bar at the top of the FeatureManager that enables you to split the FeatureManager window into two windows, so that you can display the FeatureManager and another window, such as the PropertyManager. Small arrows in the middle of the right separator can collapse the FeatureManager to increase screen space. (The F9 key also collapses or opens the FeatureManager.) These elements are displayed in Figure 2.43.

You can open the Display-pane flyout from the FeatureManager by using the double arrows at the top-right corner, as shown in Figure 2.43. The Display pane helps you to visualize where colors, textures, transparency, or hidden bodies have been applied. Unfortunately, nothing can be changed from the Display pane, which would be the most intuitive. However, it is helpful when looking for colors that are applied to the model at some level other than the part level.

The Rollback bar at the bottom of the FeatureManager enables you to see the part in various states of history. All aspects of the FeatureManager are discussed in depth in Chapter 7.

FIGURE 2.43

Components of the FeatureManager

Splitter bar
Display pane arrows

Rollback bar   Collapse arrows

PropertyManager

ConfigurationManager

The PropertyManager is where most of the feature dialog boxes go, and where you can edit properties of selected items such as sketch elements. You can manually switch to the PropertyManager using the tabs on the top of the Display panel. The left-most icon is the FeatureManager tab, the middle one is the PropertyManager tab, and the one on the right is the ConfigurationManager tab. Other icons may appear in this area for drawings, or if you have add-ins such as PhotoWorks or Animator turned on.

One of the benefits of putting dialog boxes in the PropertyManager is that it saves a lot of space on the screen. On the other hand, you will often need to make a selection from the FeatureManager at the same time that the PropertyManager pops up and takes its place. This automatic pop-up behavior is controlled by a setting in the Tools ➪ Options ➪ System Options ➪ General ➪ Auto-show PropertyManager. When this window pops up, you may want to use either the splitter bars or the flyout FeatureManager. When creating or editing a feature, you can access the flyout FeatureManager by clicking the name of the feature at the top of the PropertyManager. The flyout FeatureManager is displayed just to the right of the regular FeatureManager, in the main graphics window, and is transparent to allow you to see the model through it. The flyout FeatureManager is shown in Figure 2.44, with a feature being edited in the PropertyManager.

FIGURE 2.44

The PropertyManager for a sketch entity

Task pane

By default, the Task pane sits to the right of the SolidWorks screen, although you can dock it on the left side or leave it undocked entirely. When the Task pane is expanded, you can collapse it by clicking outside of it. If you want to keep it open, click the pushpin in the upper-right corner of the pane. The Task pane is shown in Figure 2.45.

FIGURE 2.45

The Task pane

The Task pane is the home for several panels:

- **SolidWorks Resources:** These are useful links for templates, tutorials, tech support, news, GlobalSpec search, Tip-of-the-Day, and other resources.

- **Design Library:** This includes locally stored libraries, Toolbox, and 3D Content Central.

- **File Explorer:** This is a Windows Explorer–like interface that you can use to browse for files.

- **SolidWorks Search:** If you have installed the Windows Desktop Search with SolidWorks 2007 and indexed your files, you can perform searches that include filename and custom properties.

- **View Palette:** This palette allows you to visually select views and drag them onto a drawing sheet.

Status bar

The status bar is a non-intrusive way in which SolidWorks communicates information back to the user. It is located at the bottom of the screen, and you can enable it from the View menu. Figure 2.46 shows the status bar in action.

FIGURE 2.46

The status bar showing a Tooltip for the Sketch Circle tool

| Sketches a circle. Select the center of the circle, then drag to set its radius. | -1.99Sin | 0.364in | 0in | Under Defined | Editing Sketch2 |

The status bar can display the following information, indicators, and icons:

- Progress as parts, assemblies, or drawings load
- Tooltips for icons
- Measurements
- Sketch status for an active sketch
- In-context editing
- Suspend Automatic Rebuilds
- Icons that allow you to turn Quick Tips off or on
- Sheet scale for drawings
- Cursor position for drawings and sketches
- Whether you are editing the sheet, sheet format, or view of a drawing

2D Command Line Emulator

This is a tool specifically for people who are coming to SolidWorks from AutoCAD. As the name suggests, it adds a command line to the bottom of the SolidWorks window, that works like the AutoCAD command line in most respects. The available commands are somewhat limited compared to those that are available in AutoCAD. This tool only functions in the 2D sketch mode, on a drawing sheet, or in a drawing view; it does not work in a 3D sketch. The 2D Command Line Emulator is shown in Figure 2.47.

FIGURE 2.47
_____

The 2D Command Line Emulator in action

Available sketch tools in the 2D Command Line Emulator include: Align, Arc, Array, 'Cal, Chamfer, Chprop, Circle, 'Color, Copy, DDcolor, Dim, Dist, Ellipse, Erase, Exit, Extrude, Fillet, 'Grid, Line, List, Massprop, Mirror, Move, Offset, 'Ortho, 'Osnap, 'Pan, Plot, Point, Polygon, Qsave, Rectangle, 'Redraw, 'Redrawall, Revolve, Rotate, Save, Saveas, 'Snap, Spline, Trim, U (undo), 'Units, 'View, and 'Zoom. Commands that are preceded by an apostrophe (') can be used as transparent commands, without exiting an active command. Notice that even the cursor changes to crosshairs.

BEST PRACTICE The best way to learn a new software package is to embrace the new way, not to cling to the old way. Although you may find the 2D Command Line Emulator more comfortable to work with, you will not achieve the same results as you will with the SolidWorks default sketching mode. For example, the resulting sketch entities created using the 2D Command Line Emulator are not constrained in any way, and the endpoints do not even merge. You can turn off the 2D Command Line Emulator by going to Tools, Add-ins.

Making the Interface Work for You

As engineers and designers, we all like to tinker with things to optimize efficiency and to apply our personal stamp. When it is installed, the SolidWorks interface is functional, but not optimal. In the previous pages, we have discussed managing and customizing toolbars and menus. In the remainder of this chapter, we discuss more about customizing the interface, and suggest some strategies that you might use to help customize your work environment.

Customizing colors

You need to be aware of a few things before you change all of the standard colors in the SolidWorks interface to whatever strikes your fancy. The first is that SolidWorks does not automatically alter text color to contrast with your background. As a result, if you set the background to black, and the text is black, you won't be able to see the text. This may seem obvious to some people, but AutoCAD automatically changes text color to contrast with the viewport background, and so AutoCAD users may take this functionality for granted.

Some colors should be avoided for the background, or you should at least make some other changes if you choose these colors. Black is used with fully defined sketches, dimensions, FeatureManager text, and annotations. Blue backgrounds often mask the underdefined sketch color. Bright green backgrounds can cause problems with seeing selected items. Bright red, aside from being a terrible color to stare at all day, also does not contrast well with some of the red highlights and error colors.

You might say that whatever color background you select, it makes items or features difficult to see. For this reason, many users choose a gradient background, which allows you to pick colors where items are always visible on one half of the screen or the other. Staring at a white screen all day can be uncomfortable for your eyes, so pick colors that allow you to see everything with "reasonable" contrast, yet that are not glaringly bright. Very high contrast is hard on the eyes, and low contrast may make it difficult to distinguish items on the screen.

In addition to colors and gradients, you can use an image as the graphics window background. This gives you a wider range of customization capabilities, and several sample images are already available in the default settings.

Customization strategies

You can easily customize many aspects of the SolidWorks interface, including:

- Toolbars
- Menus
- Background colors or images
- PropertyManager skins

- Task pane location
- Hotkeys
- Macros
- Custom application programming

Whether or not you should customize each of the above items depends partially on how much time and energy you have to spend, as well as how much money you are ready to dedicate in the case of custom programming.

Hotkey approaches

Some of us old-timers prefer to use the keyboard over the mouse. If your hand-eye coordination is as bad as mine, you may also choose this approach. I can type without looking at the keyboard, but when I use the mouse, it takes me a few seconds to aim at an icon and hit it accurately. This means that I customize SolidWorks to use as many hotkeys as possible, and remove icons from the interface if I have them on a shortcut. Unfortunately, my memory is as bad as my eyesight, and so remembering 75 hotkey commands is a bit of a problem. I admit to having a printed list of hotkeys taped to the side of my monitor. While I know that needing to read the list to find a particular hotkey defeats most of the purpose of using them in the first place, I just accept it as a learning aid.

I generally do not advocate trying to standardize a hotkey scheme across multiple users, unless the users all agree to it. The underlying reason for writing a section entitled Hotkey Approaches is that everyone remembers things differently in the first place, and people have different tolerance levels for various irritations.

Any command that I use more than a few times an hour is worth assigning to a hotkey. I like to use alliteration when assigning keys to help with my faulty memory. Most-frequently used commands are assigned single-letter hotkeys, and less-frequently used commands are assigned combinations. Thus, Tools Options is linked to O, Measure to M, Select Vertex to Shift+V, and Curve Projected to Ctrl+J (Ctrl+P is the Windows standard for the Print command).

Other people like to group keys into easy-to-reach combinations, and so the Q, W, A, S, Z, and X keys are often assigned first for right-handed mouse users.

Organizing Hotkeys

Hotkeys are assigned and organized in the Tools ⇨ Customize ⇨ Keyboard dialog box, as shown in Figure 2.48. This interface enables you to see all of the hotkeys (called shortcuts in the list) easily. If you try to enter an existing hotkey, SolidWorks issues a prompt, telling you that the key is assigned to another command and what the command is, and asking you if you want to clear the other instance of the hotkey and make the new one active. You can also print out or copy to the Clipboard a list of only commands that use hotkeys.

Because the list of commands is so long, there is a Search function available, and a drop-down arrow that makes visible only the commands from a selected menu. The list of commands is organized by menu name, and the menus are listed as they occur in the interface. Fortunately, here on the Keyboard tab, SolidWorks allows you to sort using the column headers to list the menus, commands, or hotkeys in alphabetical order, simply by clicking the column header. This is a highly usable interface.

NEW FEATURE   This method for organizing and assigning hotkeys is new for SolidWorks 2007.

FIGURE 2.48

Tools ⇨ Customize ⇨ Keyboard — the hotkey interface

Using the keyboard

Moving between the mouse and the keyboard can be bothersome and time consuming. In addition to the hotkey approach, you can use another keyboard method to save time. Many users become adept at using the Alt-key combinations to invoke menu items. Most menu items in Windows applications contain a single underlined letter.

To access a top-level menu, you can hold down the Alt key and press the underlined letter for that menu, and then just press an underlined letter in the menu to access specific commands. This technique enables you to navigate most of the interface without using the mouse. For example, to exit SolidWorks, instead of using the mouse to click the red X in the upper-right corner, you could press Alt+F, X. In Figure 2.49, you can see that the F in File is underlined, as is the X in Exit.

FIGURE 2.49

Accelerator Keys in the File menu

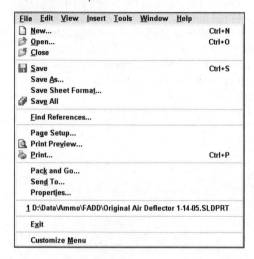

NOTE   The SolidWorks documentation terminology becomes further confused when talking about accelerator keys. It says that the general class of keys is called Shortcuts, which can be either accelerator keys or keyboard shortcuts. How these are distinguished from Shortcut Menus is not clear. Again, for our purposes in this book, we refer to the shortcut menus as *RMB* (right mouse button) menus, accelerator keys as *Alt-keys*, and keyboard shortcuts as *hotkeys*, which is more in line with standard usage than the documented terminology.

Fewest number of icons

In order to maximize valuable space on the monitor, many SolidWorks users strive to minimize the number of toolbar icons on the screen, or confine it to two rows of toolbars. You can do this by using the CommandManager, flyout toolbars, and hotkeys, and removing unused icons, as well as the other techniques discussed here.

Device approaches

If you have never used a Spaceball or equivalent view-manipulation device, you should consider it. They are wonderful devices and do far more than just spin the view. Most of the devices also have several programmable buttons that you can link to menu items. They can move drawing views, and parts within assemblies, and even manipulate selected objects in other Office applications and Web browsers. In addition, some game controllers, such as the Microsoft Sidewinder, are inexpensive and offer almost endless possibilities with button programming.

I have not yet come across a tablet that works well for SolidWorks command input. I believe that tablets have the same shortcomings as mice because they both require that you look at what your hands are doing.

Macros

Macros are short snippets of programming code that have a particular function. Most macros are small and intended for simple tasks that are repeated many times, such as drawing a rectangle centered on the origin of a selected plane, or changing selected dimensions to four decimal places. Macros may be recorded, written from scratch, or a combination where you record a particular action to be used as a starting point, and then embellish it manually from there. Recorded macros may not always record the parts of the action that you want to make into a macro, but you can edit them manually to include anything that you can program with VBA (Visual Basic for Applications), which is included with the base SolidWorks package at no extra cost.

CROSS-REF Macros are covered in more detail in Chapter32. Appendix C also contains sources for macros and macro-related help.

To access macros by using hotkeys, follow these steps:

1. Make a folder in your SolidWorks installation directory called "macros".

2. Copy macros into this folder.

3. Start (or restart) SolidWorks.

4. Go to Tools ➪ Customize ➪ Keyboard.

5. Scroll to the bottom of the list under the Macros category, and assign hotkeys as you would for standard SolidWorks commands.

Whether you are skilled at writing or recording macros, or you are just using macros collected from other people, they can be huge time savers and offer functionality that you would not otherwise be able to access.

Saving custom interface settings

Once you have set up your menus and toolbars, worked out all of the custom colors, figured out your hotkey usage, and connected your macros, you don't want to lose these settings when you reinstall the software or move to a different computer. Another user may want to share your settings, or you may want to transfer them to your home computer (for modeling the new deck or the doghouse, of course). Fortunately, these settings are very portable.

You can use the Copy Settings Wizard to save these settings out to a file. Access the wizard through Start, Programs, SolidWorks 2007, SolidWorks Tools, Copy Settings Wizard. This creates a file with an *.sldreg file extension. You can restore settings by double-clicking this file on a computer that has SolidWorks installed on it.

The SolidWorks settings are actually Windows registry settings. The file that is saved by the wizard is just a registry file that has a different extension to prevent it from being applied too easily. Saved-out registry files have a *.reg file extension, and are integrated into the registry by simply double-clicking them. If you are not familiar with the Windows registry, you should not make direct changes, because even small changes can cause serious problems with your operating system or even hardware. The settings that are saved out by the Copy Settings Wizard are safe to transfer between computers. In order for the Copy Settings Wizard to work, you need to have Administrator-level access to your computer. The Copy Settings Wizard is shown in Figure 2.50.

FIGURE 2.50

The Copy Settings Wizard

Working with multiple-document windows

In SolidWorks, as in other areas of life, things can become chaotic. You may sometimes have the luxury of working on a single part at a time, but more often, you will find yourself with several models open at once. This is a common situation for most users. Fortunately, SolidWorks has several methods for dealing with "information overload," to help you sort through it all.

Window management

Like most other Windows applications, SolidWorks can arrange the open document windows in one of several ways that are available through the Window menu, as shown in Figure 2.51:

- **Cascade:** Most useful for accessing documents that are to be edited one by one.
- **Tile Horizontally:** Most useful for wide and short parts.
- **Tile Vertically:** Most useful for tall, narrow parts, or documents where you want to compare items in the FeatureManager.
- **Arrange Icons:** When windows are minimized to icons, this menu selection arranges the icons neatly, starting in the lower-left corner of the window.

FIGURE 2.51

The Window menu

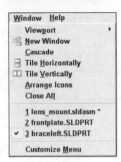

The images in Figure 2.52 show the window-management settings listed above.

FIGURE 2.52

Window Arrangements: Cascade, Tile Horizontally, and Tile Vertically

Also remember that you can use the F9 key to close the FeatureManager, and the F10 key to remove the toolbars to create extra interface space when arranging several windows in the graphics window.

Changing windows

You can use several techniques to change from one window to another. By clicking on the Window menu, you can view a list of open document windows, as shown in Figure 2.51. You can then select the desired window directly from this menu. If more than a few windows are open, a More Windows option appears at the end of the list, as shown in Figure 2.53. Clicking on this option brings up a separate window that enables you to select from the complete list.

FIGURE 2.53

You can select from a list of several windows.

When a smaller number of windows are open, a simpler way to change windows is to press Ctrl+Tab. This is a Windows standard technique that also works in other Office applications. Ctrl+Tab takes you in one direction in the list of open windows, and Ctrl+Shift+Tab takes you in the opposite direction through the list.

Tutorial: Getting to Know the Interface

By this point, you really have not learned much about making parts, assemblies, and drawings in SolidWorks, but you have learned quite a bit about using the interface. In this tutorial, you get some hands-on practice at making the changes that we have discussed in the rest of this chapter. The rest of the book also uses the settings that you create here.

Tutorial goals

This tutorial is intended to reinforce the following skills:

- Adding and removing toolbars
- Adding and removing toolbar buttons
- Adding and removing items from drop-down and RMB menus
- Setting up the CommandManager
- Setting up hotkeys
- Linking a hotkey to a macro
- Changing interface colors

Copy the existing settings

Regardless of what your initial settings are, you do not want to lose them. Before you start to make changes to your system, you should save out the existing settings to a file from which they can be recovered. You can do this using the Copy Settings Wizard, as shown in Figure 2.54.

FIGURE 2.54

The Copy Settings Wizard

To use the Copy Settings Wizard, follow these steps:

1. Close SolidWorks.
2. Click Start ➪ Programs ➪ SolidWorks 2007 ➪ SolidWorks 2007 Tools ➪ Copy Settings Wizard.
3. Select Save Settings, and click Next.

4. Enter a location and a name for the file.

5. Select the items that you would like to save. For the purposes of this tutorial, make sure that the following options are selected: Keyboard Shortcuts, Menu Customization, Toolbar Layout, and All Toolbars.

6. Click Finish.

Browse to the location where you saved the file and make sure that it is there.

Set all interface items to their default settings

You can set the interface back to the default settings using one of two methods. The first method, editing the Windows registry, may not be available to all users. It requires Administrator access to your computer and a good familiarity with Windows.

 Editing the Windows registry can be dangerous if you make a mistake. Do not attempt this method is you have any doubts about what you are doing.

To set SolidWorks back to its default settings, follow these steps:

1. Close SolidWorks.

2. Click Start ⇨ Run.

3. Type **regedit,** and click OK.

4. Browse to HKEY_CURRENT_USER\Software\SolidWorks\SolidWorks 2007 or the appropriate folder for the version that you are using.

5. To return all settings in SolidWorks back to default, delete the entire SolidWorks 2007 folder.

6. Close the Registry Editor.

7. The folder is recreated when SolidWorks starts up again, and is populated with default values.

The second method, which is less risky but less complete, is to go to the main locations and use the tools provided to return settings to their defaults. Restart SolidWorks and create a new blank document (you cannot display the Customize dialog box without a document open). To access the resets for the interface, do the following:

- Click Tools ⇨ Options ⇨ General ⇨ Reset, and go to the bottom-left area of the dialog box.
- Click Tools ⇨ Customize ⇨ Toolbars ⇨ Reset, and go to the bottom-left area of the dialog box.
- Click Tools ⇨ Customize ⇨ Menus ⇨ Reset All, and go to the right side of the dialog box.
- Click Tools ⇨ Customize ⇨ Keyboard ⇨ Reset to Defaults, and go to the upper-right area of the dialog box.
- Click Tools ⇨ Customize ⇨ Options; there are three Reset to Defaults buttons along the left side of the dialog box.

Customizing the CommandManager

Now that you have restored the default settings, you can begin customizing the interface with the CommandManager. To do this, RMB click anywhere on the CommandManager and deselect the Use Large Buttons with Text option, as shown in Figure 2.55. When you have done this, the check mark should no longer appear in front of the option.

FIGURE 2.55

Deselect the Use Large Buttons with Text option.

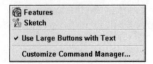

Next, add some toolbars to the Control Area of the CommandManager, as follows:

1. Again, RMB click the CommandManager, and select Customize CommandManager.

2. Select the Surfaces, Sheet Metal, and Annotations toolbars from this list, which is partially shown in Figure 2.56. Deselect the Sketch toolbar.

FIGURE 2.56

The Customize CommandManager

3. Click outside of the list; the list closes and applies the changes you made.

4. Click the Features toolbar button in the Control Area of the CommandManager, and make sure that the Features toolbar buttons appear in the Toolbar Area to the right.

5. RMB click any toolbar *other than* the CommandManager, and select Customize; this brings up the Tools ⇨ Customize dialog box, where you can add, remove, and reorder toolbar buttons.

6. Reorder the toolbars in the Control Area of the CommandManager so that the Annotations toolbar comes first. When you are done, The CommandManager should look like Figure 2.57. Leave the Customize dialog box open.

FIGURE 2.57

The CommandManager with your changes applied

7. Make sure that the Toolbars tab of the Customize dialog box is displayed.

8. Turn on the Sketch and Tools toolbars.

9. Place the Sketch toolbar to the right of the Task pane, and the Tools toolbar just above the Task pane.

10. Drag the Reference Geometry and Curves flyout toolbars from the end of the Features toolbar in the CommandManager over to the Tools toolbar, as shown in Figure 2.58. Use the Tooltips to identify the buttons.

FIGURE 2.58

Move these toolbar buttons from the Sketch toolbar to the Tools toolbar.

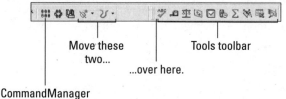

The display should now look like Figure 2.59. Close the Customize dialog box.

FIGURE 2.59

The customized SolidWorks interface

Customizing menus

If you always do the same types of work, or more importantly, *never* do certain types of work, then you might consider customizing some menus to remove items that you never use. Customization applies to both the main drop-down menus and the context-sensitive RMB menus. To customize a menu:

1. Click Insert ⇨ Customize Menu.

2. Turn off the menu items Sketch from Drawing, DXF/DWG, Object, Hyperlink, and Picture, as shown in Figure 2.60. Click anywhere outside of the list to close it.

3. Click the Insert menu to ensure that the deselected items have been removed.

4. RMB click the Right plane in the FeatureManager.

5. Select Customize Menu.

6. Turn off Section View. Click anywhere outside of the list to close it.

7. RMB click the Right plane to verify that Section View has been removed.

FIGURE 2.60

Customizing the Insert menu

Change interface colors

Edit the colors used in the interface:

1. Click the Select Color Scheme tool from the Standard toolbar. Each time you click this tool, the background color changes to a new scheme.

2. Click the drop-down arrow to the right of the button to see the entire list. Select another scheme from the list.

3. Click Tools ⇨ Options ⇨ Colors to display the dialog box shown in Figure 2.61.

4. Change the viewport background color to white (preview thumbnails use this background color).

5. Adjust the top gradient and bottom gradient colors to your personal taste, but choose colors that are both functional and attractive.

6. Set the Background Appearance toggle to Gradient.

7. Make sure that the Match Graphics Area and FeatureManager Backgrounds option is selected.

FIGURE 2.61

The Tools ➪ Options ➪ Colors dialog box

8. Deselect the Use Specified Color for Shaded With Edges Mode option. This makes the edges of models a similar hue to the part itself, rather than the cartoonish-looking black edges.

9. Click the Save As Scheme button, and save the scheme with your name or another file-name that is easily identifiable.

10. Click OK to close the Tools ➪ Options ➪ Colors dialog box.

11. Again, click the drop-down list next to the Select Color Scheme tool; your new custom color scheme should now have been added to the list.

Adding hotkeys

For many users, hotkeys are an integral part of the everyday experience of using SolidWorks. You can easily assign hotkeys and manage the assignments by following these steps:

1. Click Tools ➪ Customize ➪ Keyboard.

2. In the Search For text box, type **Options**.

3. Click in the Shortcut column, and type **O**.

4. Click again in the Search For text box, and type **Customize**.

5. Click in the text box next to the Tools ➪ Customize entry and press Ctrl+C. Answer no to the question of whether you want to reassign the hotkey. Press Ctrl+T instead.

6. Click OK to exit the Customize dialog box.

7. Press the O key to bring up Tools ⇨ Options. Click OK to exit.

8. Press Ctrl+T to bring up Tools ⇨ Customize. Click OK to exit.

9. Press Alt+F, and then press X to exit SolidWorks.

Combining macros with hotkeys

Macros are covered in Chapters 34 and 35, but the following steps show you how to link a macro to a hotkey:

 You can use the macro called rectangle.swp, located on the CD-ROM.

1. Find your SolidWorks installation directory. By default, this directory is C:\Program Files\SolidWorks.

2. Create a folder called Macros in the SolidWorks directory and put the rectangle.swp macro in it.

3. Start SolidWorks.

4. Create a new blank part document.

5. Press Ctrl+T to access the Customize dialog box.

6. Click the Keyboard tab.

7. In the Search For text box, type **rectangle**.

8. Click in the Shortcut column next to the listing with the Category of Macros, and press R.

9. Click OK to exit the Customize dialog box.

10. Press R. The rectangle macro runs and draws a sketch rectangle on the Front plane, centered on the origin.

11. Press Ctrl+S to access the Windows standard hotkey for the Save command. Name the part rectangle.sldprt and save it to a workspace directory.

12. Press Alt+F and then X to exit SolidWorks.

The use of Alt-keys and hotkeys is somewhat exaggerated in this tutorial, but it is intended to get you used to working with them.

Summary

The SolidWorks interface is quite busy, and you can access most items in multiple ways. This allows you to choose how you work, whether through toolbars, the CommandManager, or menus, among other choices. The fact that SolidWorks is so tightly integrated into Windows means that in most cases, you know what to expect from the interface, and much of your knowledge from using other applications is transferable.

The SolidWorks interface is also customizable through all of the standard Windows methods, such as rearranging toolbars, customizing menus and hotkeys, and changing background colors and skins. If you spend a significant amount of your workweek using this software, you want to take some time to configure it for efficiency and comfort. Because of the complexity of the interface and the myriad ways in which you can use it, each user is expected to create an interface that looks a little bit different from anyone else's.

Chapter 3

Getting Started with SolidWorks

SolidWorks uses several file types to accomplish tasks. The most frequently used types are parts, assemblies, and drawings. Beyond these, we have templates for each type and drawing format. The difference between drawing templates and drawing formats is cause for frequent confusion among many SolidWorks users, and so we will spend some extra time on this topic.

Other file types also exist, such as design tables, Bill of Materials, or BOM, templates, and table templates, sheet-metal gauge tables and bend tables, custom symbol and line type files, custom property files, color swatches, library features, and macros. This chapter contains a complete list of these file types. Some of them allow you to customize SolidWorks using simple but little-known techniques, such as the ability to add custom symbols that can be inserted into a string of text, or to create new line types, or to change how SolidWorks creates hole callouts.

If you are a CAD Administrator looking for advice on how to implement SolidWorks, this chapter includes some information, but you should also refer to Appendix A, "Implementing SolidWorks," for additional information and higher-level planning suggestions.

Tools for Beginners

SolidWorks has many tools for beginning users that are available when you install the software. A default installation presents you with several options when you launch the software for the first time. Following is a catalog of these options and how to benefit most from them.

If you plan to attend formal SolidWorks reseller-based training, it is a very good idea to first go through some of the tutorials in this section, so that you are prepared to ask educated questions and have an advantage over the rest of the class. You will also get more out of the training if you have seen the material once before.

SolidWorks license agreement

Although the license agreement does not have any bearing on learning how to use the software — other than the fact that it allows for a Home Use License — it is useful to be familiar with what it says. Many users find this part of the license agreement, shown in Figure 3.1, to be helpful. The primary user of the license at work is also allowed to use the license at home or on a portable computer. This is often a good option for learning, additional practice, or completing the design of a personal project such as a deck or soapbox derby car.

Once you finish reading the License Agreement page, you can select Accept to continue.

FIGURE 3.1

The SolidWorks license agreement

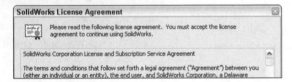

Welcome to SolidWorks

The Welcome to SolidWorks screen, shown in Figure 3.2, follows the License Agreement page. It helps you to establish what type of tools you would like to see in the interface, and offers some help options.

FIGURE 3.2

Welcome to SolidWorks screen

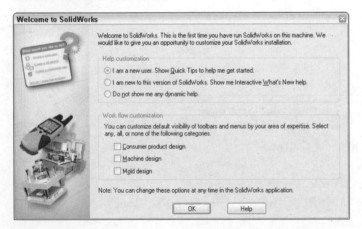

Quick Tips

The Quick Tips feature enables balloons with tips to help you get started with several tasks. For example, the first Quick Tip that you see may be the one shown in Figure 3.3. When you begin to create your first document in SolidWorks, a Quick Tip guides you through this process.

FIGURE 3.3

A New SolidWorks Document Quick Tip

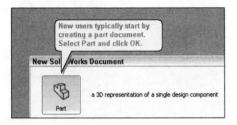

As you begin working, Quick Tips displays a dialog box at the lower-right corner of the graphics window that offers context-sensitive help messages, as shown in Figure 3.4. As you work with the software, these messages will change to reflect what you are doing.

FIGURE 3.4

The main Quick Tip window

You can turn Quick Tips on or off using the small icon on the taskbar in the lower-right corner, as shown in Figure 3.5. You can also turn Quick Tips on or off using the Help menu, by selecting Quick Tips. The on/off setting is document-type sensitive, and so if you turned this feature off in part mode, then you must also turn it off for assemblies and drawings. Quick Tips are a great way to get started if you are a beginner, as well as to refresh your memory if it has been a while since you worked with the program, or if several versions have gone by since you last used the software.

FIGURE 3.5

Turning Quick Tips on or off

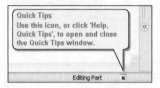

The first time that you create a document, you are prompted to select units for your default templates, as shown in Figure 3.6. This is an important step, although you can change this setting later if necessary. You can find more information on part and assembly templates later in this chapter, and drawing templates are described in detail in Chapter 20.

FIGURE 3.6

Selecting the default template units

The main significance of this default template unit option is not so much the units as the dimensioning standard that you are selecting. ISO and ANSI standards use different methods of projecting views. ISO is typically a European standard and uses First Angle Projection, while ANSI is an American standard and uses Third Angle Projection. Third Angle Projection is used throughout this book.

The difference between First and Third Angle Projections can cause parts to be manufactured incorrectly if those reading the prints do not notice the difference or see that there is some discrepancy. Figure 3.7 demonstrates the difference between these two methods. Make sure that you specify the correct option. If someone else, such a computer specialist who is not familiar with mechanical drafting standards, has initially set up SolidWorks on your computer, then you should verify that the default templates are correct.

FIGURE 3.7

Differences between First Angle Projection (left) and Third Angle Projection (right)

You can find another setting that affects projections by selecting Tools ➪ Options ➪ Display/Selection ➪ Projection Type For Four View Viewport. This does not follow the dimensioning standard that is selected for the default templates, or the country in which the software is installed.

CAUTION   The default setting for this option is First Angle Projection.

Online documentation

Several types of online documentation are available to help SolidWorks learners along their path. A great place to start is the SolidWorks Resources tab of the Task pane, on the right side of the screen. This is the first tab in the list, and displays the Home icon. The Getting Started section of the SolidWorks Resources tab is shown in Figure 3.8.

FIGURE 3.8

The Getting Started section of the SolidWorks Resources tab on the Task Manager

Making My First Part and Making My First Drawing

The Getting Started area contains two beginner-level tutorials that are aimed at helping you understand the basics of part and drawing creation, and also to get used to the interface. These tutorials are about 30 minutes long.

Online Tutorials

The Online Tutorials link takes you to a list of 35 basic tutorials on subjects from sheet metal to macros, in parts assemblies and drawings. These tutorials are certainly worth your time, and can build your skills and knowledge of basic functionality. This SolidWorks Bible distinguishes itself by going into far more detail and depth about each function, adding information such as best practice, performance considerations, and cautionary data, and acting as a thorough desk reference.

Moving from AutoCAD

The Help menu contains a selection called Moving from AutoCAD. This is intended to assist the transitioning user to acclimate to their new surroundings. Terminology is a big part of the challenge when making this switch, and prominently figures in the Moving from AutoCAD help file.

The most helpful tools in Moving from AutoCAD are probably the Approach to Modeling and Imported AutoCAD Data sections. They contain information that is useful whether you are coming to SolidWorks from AutoCAD or another CAD package.

Online User's Guide

The Online User's Guide is the traditional Help file. You can use either the Index or Search capabilities to find what you are looking for. The Online User's Guide contains screen captures and animations, sample files, and even a separate API (Application Programming Interface) help file.

What's New

With every release, SolidWorks publishes a What's New document to help you keep up to speed with the changes. This is typically a PDF file with accompanying example files. If you have missed a version or two, then you can read through the What's New files to get back on track.

Tip of the Day

The SolidWorks Tip of the Day displays at the bottom of the SolidWorks Resources tab on the Task pane. You can cycle through a few of these tips or use them to quiz coworkers to build useful skills.

Hardcopy documentation

Over time, software companies have reduced their hardcopy documentation. They often claim that keeping up with the changes in print is too much work and too inefficient, but most users prefer to have a physical book in their hands, to spread out on the desk next to them, to earmark, highlight, and mark with post-its. Hardcopy documentation still has an important role to play in the dissemination of information.

SolidWorks does publish some pamphlet-sized hardcopy documentation that ships in the box with new installation and upgrade CDs.

Quick Start

The Quick Start pamphlet acts as a rough outline for issues that range from installation to getting help.

Quick Reference Guide

The Quick Reference Guide is a foldout card that contains some of the symbols that display in the FeatureManager as well as other locations. This card also contains some of the default hotkeys and customization options.

Identifying SolidWorks Documents

Although SolidWorks uses three main types of data files, there are many more types of supporting files that you should know about if you are concerned with customization and creating implementation standards.

Document types

SolidWorks main design document file types:

Design Documents

- *.sldprt: SolidWorks Part file type
- *.sldasm: SolidWorks Assembly file type
- *.slddrw: SolidWorks Drawing file type

SolidWorks template document file types:

Templates and Formats

- *.prtdot: Part Template
- *.asmdot: Assembly Template
- *.drwdot: Drawing Template
- *.slddrt: Drawing Sheet Format
- *.sldtbt: General Table Template
- *.sldbombt: BOM Template (table-based)
- *.xls: BOM Template (Excel-based)
- *.sldholtbt: Hole Table Template
- *.sldrevtbt: Revision Table Template

- *.sldwldtbt: Weldment Cutlist Template
- journal.doc: Design Journal Template

SolidWorks library document file types:

Library Files

- *.sldlfp: Library Part File
- *.sldblk: Blocks

> **NOTE**   Forming Tools used to be created as *.sldlfp files, but are now simply *.sldprt.

Favorites

- *.sldweldfvt: Weld Favorite
- *.sldgtolfvt: Geometric Tolerance Favorite
- *.sldsffvt: Surface Finish Favorite
- *.sldnotefvt: Note Favorite
- *.sldsffvt: Surface Finish Symbol Favorite

Symbol Files

- gtol.sym: Symbol file that allows you to create custom symbols
- swlines.lin: Line Style definition file that allows you to create new line styles

Others

- *.sldreg: SolidWorks settings file
- *.sldmat: Material Database
- *.sldclr: Color Palette file
- *.txt: Custom Property file, Sheet Metal Bend Line Note File
- *.swp, *.swb: Macros, Macro Features
- *.btl: Sheet Metal Bend Table
- *.xls: Sheet Metal Gauge Table
- calloutformat.txt: Hole Callout Format file

Saving your setup

If you have taken time to set up a computer and then need to reinstall SolidWorks, move to another computer, or duplicate the setup for another user, then you need to copy out these files. Keep in mind that you need to copy only the files that you have used or customized. By default, all of these files are located in different folders within the SolidWorks installation directory. The previous chapter dealt with interface settings and creating a registry settings file to copy to other computers or use as a backup. However, you also need to copy the various file types that comprise a custom installation.

BEST PRACTICE When you create complex implementations that include templates for various types of tables or customized symbol files, it is important to have these files in a location other than the default installation folder. Otherwise, uninstalling SolidWorks or installing a new version will delete all of your hard work. You can use the Tools, Options, File Locations to locate these files in separate library folders, which may be on the local hard drive or on a network location.

Templates

When you create a new file, the New dialog box allows you to select one of several files to start from; these files are templates. Think of templates as "start parts" that contain all of the document-specific settings for a part (Tools ➪ Options ➪ Document Properties). The same concept applies to assemblies and drawings. Templates generally do not contain any geometry, although this is possible.

TIP The Novice interface for the File ➪ New SolidWorks Document dialog box only allows you to select default templates. The Advanced interface allows you to select any available templates.

As shown in Figure 3.9, several tabs can display on the Advanced interface. Each of these tabs is created when you create a folder in the template directory by selecting Tools ➪ Options.

Using Multiple Document Templates

Using multiple templates enables you to start working from multiple starting points. This offers you an advantage in many situations, such as:

- Standardization for a large number of users
- Working in various units
- Pre-set materials or colors
- Pre-set custom properties
- Parts with special requirements, such as sheet metal or weldments
- Drawings of various sizes with formats (borders) already applied
- Drawings with special notes already on the sheet

CROSS-REF Drawing templates and formats are complex enough that they are dealt with in their own separate chapter. Chapter 20 discusses in-depth the differences between templates and formats, as well as how to use them to your best advantage. This chapter only discusses part and assembly templates.

Depending on what you need, you may want to have metric and inch part and assembly templates, part templates for steel and aluminum, separate templates for sheet metal parts, and another one for weldments, if you design these types of parts. If your firm has customers with different requirements, you may consider using separate templates for these customers. Over time, you will discover the types of templates that you need, because you will find yourself making the same changes over and over again.

FIGURE 3.9

The Novice and Advanced interfaces for the New SolidWorks Document dialog box

To create a template, open the appropriate document type (part or assembly), and make the settings that you want the template to have. For example, units are one of the most common reasons to make a separate template. In fact, any of the Document Property settings is a good reason for creating a template, from the dimensioning standard that is used to image quality settings.

CROSS-REF Document Property settings are covered extensively in Appendix B.

Some document-specific settings are not contained in the Document Properties dialog box. However, these settings are saved with the template. Settings that fall into this category are the View menu entity-type visibility options and the Tools ⇨ Sketch Settings options.

Custom Properties are another piece of the template puzzle. If you use or plan to use BOMs, PDM, or linked notes on drawings, then you need to take advantage of the automation options that are available by using custom properties. Setting up custom properties is covered in detail in Chapter 20.

The names of the standard planes are also template-specific. For example, the standard planes may be named Front, Top, and Side; or XY, XZ, and ZY; Plane1, Plane2, and Plane3; or North Plan, East or Elevation Plan, and Side for different uses.

Locating Templates

You can establish the templates folder at Tools ➪ Options ➪ File Locations ➪ Document Templates. This location may be a local directory or a shared network location. You can specify multiple folders in the list box, each of which will correspond to a tab in the New Document Advanced interface.

Once you specify all of the document properties, custom properties, and other settings the way you want them and you are ready to save the file as a template, click File ➪ Save As and in Files of Type, select Part Templates. SolidWorks prompts you to save the template in the first folder that appears in the File Locations list.

You can also create additional tabs on the New dialog box by making sub-folders in the main folder that is specified in the File Locations area. For example, if your File Locations list for Document Templates looks like Figure 3.10, then your New dialog box will look like Figure 3.11.

FIGURE 3.10

The Tools ➪ Options ➪ File Locations list

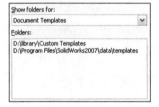

FIGURE 3.11

The New SolidWorks Document dialog box

When you add subfolders to either of the locations that are listed in File Locations, SolidWorks creates additional tabs in the New dialog box, as shown in Figures 3.12 and 3.13.

FIGURE 3.12

Additional subfolders added to a File Locations path

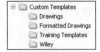

FIGURE 3.13

The resulting tabs in the New SolidWorks Document dialog box, based on the subfolders in Figure 3.12

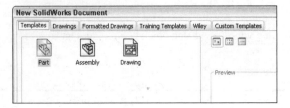

Default Templates

You can establish default templates at Tools ⇨ Options ⇨ Default Templates. The default templates must be in one of the paths that are specified in File Locations. Figure 3.14 shows the Default Templates settings.

FIGURE 3.14

The Tools ⇨ Options ⇨ Default Templates settings

These templates will be used for operations (such as File Import and Mirror Part) where SolidWorks does not prompt for a template.

Parts
D:\library\Custom Templates\part inch.prtdot   [...]

Assemblies
D:\library\Custom Templates\Assembly inch.asmdot   [...]

Drawings
D:\library\Custom Templates\Drawings\inch B.drwdot   [...]

○ Always use these default document templates
○ Prompt user to select document template

As shown in Figure 3.14, the Default Template settings contain two options: Always Use These Default Document Templates, and Prompt User to Select Document Template. These options apply to situations where a template is required by an automatic feature in the software, such as an imported part or a mirrored part. In these situations, depending on the option that you have selected, the system either automatically uses the default template or prompts the user to select a template.

PERFORMANCE If you allow the software to apply the default template automatically, this can greatly speed up program performance. This is especially true in the case of imported assemblies, which would require you to manually select templates for each imported part in the assembly if you selected the Prompt User to Select Document Template option.

Sharing templates

If you are administering an installation of a large number of users, or even if there are just a few users working on similar designs, then shared templates are a must. If every user is doing what they think is best, you may get an interesting agglomeration of ideas, but the overall consistency of the company's documentation may suffer. Standardized templates cannot make users model, assemble, and detail in exactly the same way, but they do create a baseline of consistency in user output.

To share templates among several users, you must create a folder for templates on a commonly accessible network location, preferably read-only for users and read-write for Administrators. Then direct each user's File Locations and Default templates to this location. Problems due to multiple users accessing the same files do not arise in this situation because templates are essentially copied to create a new document, and not used directly.

CAUTION One of the weaknesses of this arrangement is that if the network goes down, users no longer have access to their templates. This can be handled by also putting copies of the templates on the local computers; however, this tends to undermine the original goal of consistent documentation. Users may prefer to use and customize the local templates rather than use the standardized network copies.

CAD administration, and indeed organizing any group of people, always comes down to trusting employees to do the right thing. There is no way to completely secure any system against all ignorance and malice, and so you must rely on having hired people that you can train and trust.

Opening Existing Documents

There are many ways to open SolidWorks documents, and you should be familiar with a few of them before we go on. Many of these techniques also apply to other Microsoft-compliant software, and so you may already know them; you may also learn something that you can apply to other applications.

Opening a document

Notice that we have several ways of referring to SolidWorks data. *Files* is generic enough to cover all three data types, part, assembly, and drawing. You may have already noticed that the word *documents* is also frequently used. The word *documents* is often used to reinforce the idea that the data inside the file has some business value to your organization, as well as to separate these files from other more generic files such as settings or favorites. For good or ill, the words are often used interchangeably.

You can open SolidWorks documents in many ways, and the same procedures apply, regardless of the type of document. The Open dialog box can be used slightly differently; you can use it to filter for different file types. For example, if SolidWorks Part is listed in the Files of type drop-down menu, then you will only see parts. SolidWorks documents can be opened in the following ways:

- From the File ⇨ Open menu
- Browsing through Windows Explorer and double-clicking the file
- Browsing through Windows Explorer and dragging the file into the SolidWorks window
- Browsing through Windows Explorer, right-clicking the file, and selecting Open
- Using File Explorer in the Task pane to browse to the part
- If the document was open recently, selecting it from the Recent File list, either in the File menu or in the Task Pane File Explorer
- Selecting Open in SolidWorks from SolidWorks Explorer
- Selecting the document from the Start menu, Documents list

Looking inside a SolidWorks document

What kind of data is actually stored inside a SolidWorks document? Obviously the feature definitions must be stored, as the settings used to create each feature. The document properties mentioned earlier are also stored in the file. Configuration data and design tables are stored, as well as feature comments, and the Design Journal Word document. Other types of information include Parasolid data for the finished part. Parasolid data is also stored for rollback states and configurations. This is one of the reasons why parts can grow dramatically in size as you work on them. Display information is stored for the thumbnail previews, as well as information that can be read by eDrawings to rotate the parts in 3D. For this reason, the image-quality settings can also cause the file size to jump again, particularly for curvaceous models with a lot of small detail. Photoworks and COSMOS data may also be stored in the parts, depending on settings.

PERFORMANCE Increasing file size is not necessarily a bad thing, as long as there is a way to reduce the size again. In many situations, the increase in file size is a result of the file storing information for later use, rather than recalculating it again when it is needed. This is particularly true with rollback states and configurations. As a result, the larger file sizes are intended to improve performance.

The one situation in which performance is adversely affected by file size is when files must be transferred over limited-bandwidth connections. A Zipped-down 200MB file takes time on both ends, first to upload and then to download.

Assembly files store information such as the paths to all of the referenced parts, and the part configuration that is used. Assembly configuration data is also stored, with component colors, display states, exploded views, and mates. Assembly features must also be stored, along with in-context reference information. Any Smart Fasteners or component patterns are also defined in the assembly document. Lightweight assemblies actually store the part display data in the assembly file, and so for assemblies with a lot of parts, this can require a sizeable amount of information. Flexible subassemblies cause the subassembly mate to be solved in the upper-level assembly, and so the flexible subassembly mates must also be stored in the assembly.

Of course, because the Drawing document is the top of the food chain, these documents tend to become the biggest, particularly when several section, broken-out section, or detail views are added.

Microsoft Shadow Data

If you pay close attention to the size of your files after you save them, you may notice that SolidWorks files alternately double or halve in size. What is happening is that SolidWorks makes a copy of the data within the file, which effectively doubles the file size. When you perform a Save As function, the size may return to normal. However, this technique does not continue to cut the file size in half every time you do it. Under normal circumstances, files range between the normal file size and twice the normal file size. It should also be noted that the file size reduction is not permanent, and the file size is likely to double again the next time you save it.

NOTE   This is not the same as Microsoft Volume Shadowing, which is a server-based drive-copying technique.

CAUTION   Using the Save As command can seriously affect file management. Save As replaces referenced files if the referencing assembly or drawing document is open when you save a referenced part using Save As. This technique is often used by applying the Save As command and keeping the filename the same.

As you can see, a lot of information is stored in the SolidWorks files, but with good reason. However, there are also some ways to reduce the file size beyond the Save As technique.

Understanding file references

SolidWorks assemblies and drawings do not contain any geometry aside from sketches and assembly features; they only display geometry that is ultimately created in part documents. When you open an assembly, the assembly is in turn opening one, or several, or several thousand other part files. In the CAD industry, this is known as associativity. SolidWorks is said to be bi-directionally associative because if you change a part in the assembly window, the part updates, and if you change it in the part window, the assembly updates. This associativity also holds true for drawings.

CROSS-REF   In Chapters 16 and 21, we discuss making changes to part documents from assembly and drawing windows, respectively.

When an assembly opens file references — which may be parts or other assemblies (subassemblies) — you might think that there is some magic and infallible formula that never fails. Of course, you would be wrong if you thought this. To find referenced files, SolidWorks actually goes through a well-defined (if poorly understood) search routine.

Reducing File Sizes

SolidWorks files can become immense. By *immense,* I mean any single file that is over 100MB. This happens more often than you might think, especially in large parts that are highly detailed and with many small radius faces.

CAUTION I do not recommend becoming overly concerned about the size of files that are sitting on a local hard drive and being accessed regularly. It does not help you to try to control files that are going to grow in size anyway. Generally, reducing file size (except for the shadow data) means that the data is going to need to be recalculated at some point, and so it actually slows you down. However, if you are working across a network, or worse yet, across a VPN (virtual private network) or the Internet, you have a more valid concern. The cost of hard drive space is cheap compared to the cost of Internet bandwidth.

Given some of the information above, several techniques exist that can help you control file sizes:

- **Save As:** As noted earlier, a Save As can remove the shadow data, potentially reducing the file size by half.

- **Forced rebuild:** When things just simply look wrong with your file, one technique that often sets them right is the forced rebuild. You can apply this command only by pressing Ctrl+Q; there is no other way to access it. It goes through the SolidWorks document and recalculates everything, whether or not SolidWorks thinks it needs to. This is just a way to force everything to be updated, and it sometimes catches errors or eliminates extra data. Early versions of SolidWorks 2007 required a forced rebuild to get rid of extraneous data caused by rollback states.

- **Enclosing a part in a Box:** This solution probably sounds strange to you, but if you enclose a part in an extruded rectangle, then you are reducing two different sources of file size, the preview and the Parasolid body data. A rectangle is better than a circle, because graphics data is stored as triangles. Flat rectangular faces require only two triangles, but curved faces, especially at high display accuracy, can require hundreds or thousands of triangles. Curve faces also require more data to describe than flat faces.

- **Removing configuration data:** If you are following this book in a linear way, from the beginning to the end, then you may not yet have read about configurations or some of the other more advanced topics; however, they must be included in the discussion on file sizes. SolidWorks saves body data for each configuration, and so with a lot of configurations, you are going to have a very large file size. If you need to transfer a part across the Internet, it is best to remove any unnecessary configuration data from parts and assemblies. Another technique is to auto-create a Design Table, save the table externally, and then delete all of the configurations. The configurations can then be recreated from the Design Table when needed.

- **Changing the display to HLR mode:** HLR (hidden line removed) display mode is a wireframe display, which does not have the shaded display data.

> ■ **Minimize the window, push the part off the screen, and save:** This is another attempt to reduce the display data that is saved with the part or assembly. Starting with SolidWorks 2007, the software now has an internal routine for creating preview thumbnails. When you save with the part in any orientation or even off of the screen — or worse yet, when the part is last saved from an assembly document where no part-only preview is available — SolidWorks internally takes a snapshot of the part from an isometric view, zoomed to fit the thumbnail image, to use as the thumbnail preview.

Whenever I ask people where they think that an assembly first looks for referenced files, they usually respond that the assembly should look for the files in the same place it found them when the assembly was last saved, or something to that effect. Intuitively, this answer makes a lot of sense, but again, it is incorrect. This actually turns out to be number 8 (of 13) on the list of places that it looks.

The first place that it looks is to see if there are currently any other documents open with the same name. This means that you cannot have two different parts called Cover.sldprt open at the same time in a single session of SolidWorks. This is a basic file management concept that you need to understand early on: files need to have unique names. Whether it is a copy of the original or a completely different file with the same name, you need to be careful not to have duplicate filenames, especially as your assemblies become larger and make more use of subassemblies. This means that if you have a large machine with 4,000 unique parts, they all must have different names.

BEST PRACTICE From the start, you should use unique filenames. This usually means including some sort of a sequential number in the filename. Descriptive names are popular, but often cause conflicts due to naming issues; for example, how many *covers* do you have in a typical assembly?

The second place SolidWorks looks for referenced files is a location that you specify in Tools, Options, File Locations, Referenced Documents. As a result, if you *do* have multiple files with the same name, you can force SolidWorks to look in a particular location.

Using Visualization Tools

One of the most important skills in SolidWorks is manipulating the view. This is something users do more frequently than any other function in SolidWorks, and so learning to do it efficiently and effectively is very important.

Changing the view

Whether you look at it as rotating the model or rotating the point of view around the model, view manipulation is an important skill to master in SolidWorks. The easiest way to rotate the part is to hold down the middle mouse button (MMB) or the scroll wheel, and move the mouse. If your mouse does not have a middle button or a scroll wheel that can be used as a middle mouse button, then you can use the Rotate View icon on the View toolbar.

> **TIP**   Some mouse drivers change the middle button or scroll-wheel settings to do other things. Often, you can disable the special settings for a particular application if you want SolidWorks to work correctly and still use the other functionality. For example, the most common problem with mouse drivers is that when the model gets close to the sides of the graphics window and the scroll bars engage, the middle mouse button suddenly changes its function. If this happens to you, you should change the function of the middle mouse button to "Middle Mouse Button" from its present setting.

Arrow keys

The arrow keys rotate the view:

- **Arrow:** Rotate 15 degrees (you can customize this setting through Tools ➪ Options ➪ View Rotation)
- **Shift-arrow:** Rotate 90 degrees
- **Alt-arrow:** Rotate in a plane flat to the screen
- **Ctrl-arrow:** Pan

Middle mouse button

The middle mouse (MMB) button or scroll wheel has several uses in view manipulation:

- **MMB alone:** Rotate
- **Click on edge, face, or vertex with MMB, and then drag MMB:** Rotate around selected entity
- **Ctrl-MMB:** Pan
- **Shift-MMB:** Zoom
- **Alt-MMB:** Rotate in a plane flat to the screen

Using the View toolbar

The View toolbar, shown in Figure 3.15, contains the tools that you need to manipulate the view in SolidWorks. Not all of the available tools are on the toolbar, and so they are all described here. You can use these tools with models but not drawings.

FIGURE 3.15

The View toolbar

Zoom To Fit: Resizes the graphics window to include everything that is shown in the model. You can also access this command by pressing the F key.

Zoom To Area: When you drag the diagonal of a rectangle in the display area, the display resizes to fit it.

Zoom In/Out: Drag the mouse up or down to zoom in or out, respectively. You can also access this command by holding down the Shift key and dragging up or down with the MMB.

Zoom To Selection: Resizes the screen to fit the selection. You can also access this command from the right-mouse button, or RMB, on the FeatureManager. For example, if you select a sketch from the FeatureManager and click Zoom to Selection, the view positions the sketch in the middle of the screen and resizes the display to match it. The view does not rotate with Zoom to Selection.

> **TIP** There is a reciprocal function that enables you to find an item in the tree from graphics window geometry. If you right-click a face of the model, then you can select Go To Feature in Tree, which highlights the parent feature.

Rotate View: Enables you to orbit around the part or assembly using the left-mouse button. You can also access this command by using the MMB without the Toolbar icon.

Pan: Scrolls the view. You can also access this command by holding down the Ctrl key and dragging the MMB without using the Toolbar icon.

3D Drawing View: Enables you to rotate the model within a drawing view to make selections that would otherwise be difficult or impossible.

Standard Views flyout toolbar: The Standard Views toolbar will be discussed later in this chapter. The flyout enables you to access all of the Standard Views tools.

Wireframe: Displays the model edges without the shaded faces. No edges are hidden.

Hidden Lines Visible (HLV): Displays the model edges without the shaded faces. Edges that would be hidden are displayed in a font.

Hidden Lines Removed (HLR): Displays the model edges without the shaded faces. Edges that are hidden by the part are removed from the display.

Shaded with Edges: The model is displayed with shading, and edges are shown using HLR. Edges can either be all a single color that you set in Tools, Options, Colors (typically black), or they can match the shaded color of the part.

Shaded: The model is displayed with shading, and edges are not shown.

Shadows in Shaded Mode: When the model is displayed shaded, a shadow displays "under" the part. Regardless of how you rotate the model, when Shadows are initially turned on, the shadow always starts out parallel to the Standard plane that is closest to the bottom of the monitor. As you rotate the model, the shadow moves with it. If Shadows are turned off and then back on again, they again display parallel to the standard plane that is closest to the bottom of the monitor.

Section View: Sections the display of the model. Figure 3.16 shows the Section View command at work. You can use up to three section planes at once. Solid models and assemblies can be sectioned, but surface models cannot. You can use the spin boxes, enter numbers manually, or drag the arrows that are attached to the section planes to move the section through the model. Section planes can also be rotated by dragging the border of the plane.

The Section View tool

Clicking the check mark icon in the Section View PropertyManager enables you to continue working with the sectioned model, although you may not be able to reference edges or faces that are created by the section view. It is only a displayed section; the actual geometry is not cut.

NEW FEATURE   Starting with SolidWorks 2007, you can save the section view to an annotation view for later use in a drawing.

 RealView: Creates a more realistic reflective or textured display for advanced material selections. This feature does not work with all graphics hardware, so check the SolidWorks Web site to see if it supports your hardware.

The following toolbar buttons are not on the View toolbar by default, but you can add them if you want:

Camera View: Views the model through a Camera. You can use Cameras for:

- Viewing the model from a particular point of view.

- Creating renderings with perspective and depth-of-field (focus) blur; this feature is only available when PhotoWorks is added in.

- Animating the position and target of the point of view in an animation; this feature is only available when Animator is added in.

Cameras are created through the RMB menu on the Lights and Cameras folder in the FeatureManager, as shown in Figure 3.17.

FIGURE 3.17

Adding a new Camera

When you add a Camera, an interface displays in the PropertyManager, as shown in Figure 3.18.

In this interface, you can position the Camera object by dragging the triad, and you can resize the Field of View box by dragging the border. In the graphics window, you can use the left panel to target and position the Camera, while the right panel shows the view through the Camera.

The Depth of Field panel of the Camera PropertyManager is not shown because it requires that PhotoWorks be added in.

There are three methods to switch the graphics window to the Camera view:

- Through the View Orientation dialog box (accessed through the spacebar)

- Through the View Orientation pop-up (in the lower-left area of the graphics window)

- Through the RMB menu on the Camera in the Lights and Cameras folder in the FeatureManager

---

FIGURE 3.18

Camera Options and Interface

Triad

Field of View box

When you switch the view to the Camera view, the regular Rotate View command does not function. Rotating the view means moving the Camera. There are two ways to move the Camera:

- Edit the Camera properties and reposition the Camera by dragging the triad
- Use the Turn Camera tool to rotate the view while looking through the Camera

 Turn Camera: Allows you to rotate the view when looking through the Camera without editing the Camera properties.

 Draft Quality HLR/HLV: Toggles between low-quality (draft) and high-quality edge HLR or HLV display. This affects display speed for complex parts or large assemblies. When in draft-quality mode, edge display may be inaccurate.

 Perspective: Displays the model in perspective view without using a Camera. If you want to create a perspective view on a drawing, you must create a custom view in the View Orientation dialog box with the Perspective tool turned on. Perspective can be adjusted through View ➪ Modify ➪

Perspective by adjusting the relative distance from the model to the point of view. Relative distance is measured by the size of the bounding box of the model, and so if the model fits into a box roughly 12 inches on a side, and the perspective is set to 1.1, then the point of view is roughly 13 inches from the model. For more accurate perspective, you can use a Camera.

 Curvature: A geometrical analysis tool that applies a color gradient to the part, based on the local curvature. You can also apply curvature display to individual surfaces through the RMB menu. With some hardware, curvature display can take more time to generate for complex models.

PERFORMANCE Settings in Tools ➪ Options ➪ Performance can greatly affect rebuild speed if curvature display data is regenerated for each part rebuild. You should leave this setting at the default setting, which is Only On Demand.

 Zebra Stripes: Another geometrical analysis tool that helps you to visualize the quality of transitions between faces across edges. Zebra Stripes simulates putting a perfectly reflective part in a room that is either cubic or spherical and where the walls are painted with black-and-white stripes. In high-end shape design, surface quality is measured qualitatively by using light reflections from the surface. Reflecting stripes makes it easier to visualize when an edge is not smooth.

The three cases that Zebra Stripes can help you identify are as follows (see Figure 3.19):

- **Contact:** Surfaces intersect at an edge, but are not tangent across the edge. This condition exists when stripes do not line up on either side of the edge.

- **Tangency:** Surfaces are tangent across an edge, but have different radius of curvature on either side of the edge (non-curvature continuous). This condition exists when stripes line up across an edge but the stripe is not tangent across the edge.

- **Curvature Continuity:** Surfaces on either side of an edge are tangent and match in radius of curvature. Zebra Stripes are smooth and tangent across the edge.

FIGURE 3.19

Zebra Stripes

In Figure 3.19, the Zebra Stripes in example A do not match at all. This is clearly the non-tangent, contact-only case. Example B shows that the stripes match in position going across the indicated edge, but they change direction immediately. This is the tangent case. Example C shows the stripes flowing smoothly across the edge. This is the curvature continuous case.

You can use the remaining icons in the View toolbar to toggle the display of various types of entities from reference geometry to sketches. The following images identify the icons:

	View Planes
	View Axes
	View Temporary Axes
	View Origins
	View Coordinate Systems
	View Curves
	View Sketches
	View 3D Sketch Planes
	View 3D Sketch Dimensions
	View All Annotations
	View Points (refers to Reference Points)
	View Routing Points (refers to points for the Routing add-in)
	View Parting Lines (refers to Mold Tools parting lines)
	View Lights (refers to the light icons, not the illumination from the light)
	View Cameras
	View Sketch Relations (this is a good candidate for a hotkey)

View Orientation

Accesses the View Orientation dialog box, shown in Figure 3.20, which contains all of the standard named views, such as Front, Top, and so on. You can also activate View Orientation by pressing the spacebar.

The View Orientation dialog box

The View Orientation dialog box contains the following controls:

 Push Pin: Keeps the dialog box active.

 New View: Creates a new custom-named view (the Wiley view was created this way).

 Update Standard Views: Sets the current view to be the new Front view; all other views update relative to this change. This also updates any associated drawing views, but does not move any geometry or change plane orientation.

 Reset Standard Views: Resets the standard views so that the Front view looks normal to the Front plane (Plane1, XY plane).

View Orientation can also be manipulated from two other locations: the Standard Views toolbar, which is discussed later in this chapter, and the View Orientation pop-up, shown in Figure 3.21. This function allows you to select the orientation or the arrangement of viewports. The pop-up also displays any existing Cameras, which are described earlier in this section.

 Previous View (undo view change): You can access this tool using the default hotkey Shift+Ctrl+Z.

FIGURE 3.21

The View Orientation pop-up

View Orientation pop-up

The Standard Views toolbar

We have already mentioned the Standard Views flyout on the View toolbar, but here we will describe the tools that it contains in detail. Figure 3.22 shows the Standard Views toolbar in its default configuration.

FIGURE 3.22

The Standard Views toolbar

By default, the Standard Views toolbar contains the View Orientation button, a tool from the View toolbar. The View Orientation button is discussed in detail earlier in this section.

 Normal To has three modes of operation:

■ **First Selection:** Click a plane, planar face, or 2D sketch. When you click Normal To, the view reorients normal to the selected plane, face, or sketch, and zooms to fit the model in the view. This method is shown in Figure 3.23.

FIGURE 3.23

The result of using Normal To on the end rib angled face

Selected face

- **Second Selection:** Click Normal To a second time. The view rotates 180° to display the opposite direction.
- **Third Selection:** After making the first selection, Ctrl-select another planar entity. The second entity is rotated to the top. This method is shown in Figure 3.24.

FIGURE 3.24

Using Normal To with Second Selection to define the top

First selection

Second selection

Annotation views

Annotation views enable you to group annotations that were made in the 3D model into views that will be used on the drawing. They can be displayed under the Annotations folder in the FeatureManager for parts and assemblies. Annotation views can be created either automatically, when 3D annotations are added, or manually. An Unassigned Items annotation view acts as a catchall for annotations that are not assigned to any particular views. In the 3D model, you can use the views to reorient the model and display annotations. As mentioned earlier, annotation views can also capture a model section view to be shown in a drawing view. The Annotation views are shown for the Chapter3SampleCasting part in Figure 3.25.

FIGURE 3.25

Annotations views for Chapter3SampleCasting.sldprt

Using color and optical properties

Both color and transparency can be very effective tools to help you visualize design geometry. Color can be used in many ways, including coloring certain types of features that need special treatment, such as reamed holes or polished surfaces, or features created by secondary operations after molding or casting the base part.

The tool that you can use for controlling color is the Color button from the Standard toolbar, both of which are discussed in Chapter 2. Figure 3.26 shows the Color and Optics interface.

Color hierarchy

One of the things that confuse many users about applying color is that colors can be applied on many levels, and may override or be overridden by other colors. This means that in a part, a color may be applied to a face, a feature, a body, or the entire part. (If you are reading this book from beginning to end, then you will notice that several of these entity types have not yet been discussed.) There is a specific hierarchy to this coloring scheme, as follows:

- **Part:** When you apply color or optical properties at the level of the part (the name of the part shows in the Color and Optics PropertyManager), any other entity color will override it.

- **Body:** You can assign Solid or Surface bodies a color that overrides the part color.

- **Feature:** When a feature is selected from the FeatureManager, the applied color goes to the feature. The selection box has selection filter buttons to control the type of entity that is selected.

■ **Face:** If you click on a part in the graphics window, you select a face. The face may be part of a part, a feature, or a body. Face colors override all other part-level colors.

■ **Component:** When you use a part or subassembly in an upper-level assembly, it is considered a component. You can apply colors to a component that override all other applied colors.

■ **Automatic color changes:** Some color changes are automatic; for example, when editing parts in the context of an assembly, they can change colors or become transparent, which overrides everything else.

For complex surfaces, surface transition quality is often measured by reflections, and so setting up a reflective model can be key to finding shape imperfections. In lieu of reflective RealView materials, using lights with specularity can help you to evaluate curved surfaces, although it is generally not useful for flat faces.

Other entity colors

You can color other entities in addition to the 3D shaded model. Curve entities (such as a helix or projected curve) can be colored in addition to sketches. You can only view sketch colors when the sketch is closed and shown, because when the sketch is open, the entity colors have special significance for dealing with the sketch status.

FIGURE 3.26

The Color and Optics interface

The Display pane

The Display pane flies out from the right side of the FeatureManager and displays a quick list of which entities have colors, materials, or textures assigned. It also shows hidden parts or bodies for assemblies and multibody parts. The Display pane is shown in Figure 3.27. You may notice that it does not display colors for faces, and it does not enable you to change anything from the Display pane; it just keeps and displays the record of where the color or optical properties were assigned. We will revisit the Display pane again in Chapter 12 to see how it is used in assemblies.

Automatic colors

The settings found at Tools ➪ Options ➪ Document Properties ➪ Colors can be used to automatically color certain types of features with specific colors. For example, all Shell features can be colored red as they are created.

 I find this functionality particularly useful with surface features. I have surface features set to show up as yellow, which to me sets the surfaces apart from the solids.

 Certain types of surface features do not follow the automatic feature color settings. This is a bug that has been reported and exists as late as 2007 sp2.1.

FIGURE 3.27

The Display pane in action

Tutorial: Creating a Part Template

This simple tutorial guides you through the steps of making a few standard part templates for use with inch and millimeter parts. It also guides you through the creation of some templates for a couple of materials.

1. Select Tools ➪ Options ➪ System Options ➪ File Locations, and then select Document Templates from the Show Folder For drop-down list.

2. Click the Add button to add a new path to a location outside of the SolidWorks installation directory; for example, D:\Library\Templates.

3. Click OK to close the dialog box and accept the settings.

4. Select File ⇨ New.

5. Create a new Part document, selecting any template if you are using the Advanced interface.

6. Select Tools ⇨ Options ⇨ Document Properties ⇨ Detailing.

7. Ensure that the ANSI standard is selected.

8. Change to the Units page.

9. Change the unit system to IPS, inches, with 3 decimal places, using millimeters as the dual units, with 2 decimal places. Set angular units to Degrees with 1 decimal place.

10. Change to the Grid/Snap page.

11. Turn the Display grid setting to OFF.

12. Change to the Image Quality page.

13. Move the slider two-thirds of the way to the right, so that it is closer to the High setting. Ensure that the Save Tessellation With Part Document option is ON.

14. Click OK to save the settings and exit the Tools, Options dialog box.

15. RMB click the Materials entry in the FeatureManager, and select 1060 Alloy from the list.

16. Select File ⇨ Properties, and click the Custom tab.

17. Add a property called *material* of type *Text*. In the Value/Text Expression column, click the down arrow and select Material from the drop-down list. Notice that the Evaluated Value shows 1060 Alloy.

18. Add another property called *description* and give it a default value of *Description*. At this point, the window should look like Figure 3.28.

FIGURE 3.28

Setting up custom properties

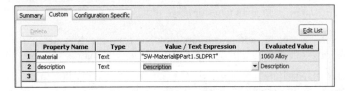

19. Click OK to close the Summary Information window.

20. Change the names of the standard planes by clicking them twice slowly or by clicking once and pressing the F2 key. (Selecting Properties from the RMB menu also enables you to edit the name of a sketch or feature.) Rename them to **Front**, **Top**, and **Side**, respectively.

21. Ctrl-select the three planes from the FeatureManager, RMB click, and select Show.

22. From the View menu, ensure that Planes is selected.

23. RMB click the Front plane and select Insert Sketch.

24. Select the Line tool, and click and drag anywhere to draw a line.

25. Select the Smart Dimension tool and click the line; then click in the graphics window to place the dimension. If you are prompted for a dimension value, press 1 and click the check mark icon, as shown in Figure 3.29.

FIGURE 3.29

Drawing a line and applying a dimension

26. Press Esc to exit the Dimension tool, RMB click the displayed dimension, and select Link Value.

27. Type **thickness** in the Name text box, and click OK.

28. Press Ctrl-B (rebuild) to exit the sketch, select the sketch from the FeatureManager, and press Delete.

NOTE This exercise of creating the sketch and deleting it was done only to enter the link value "thickness" into the template. Once this is done, every part made from this template, which uses an Extrude feature, will have a check box for Link to Thickness, which allows you to automatically establish a thickness variable for each part that you create. This is typically a sheet-metal part feature, but it can be used in all types of parts.

29. Click File ⇨ Save As, and select Part Template from the drop-down list. Ensure that it is going into your template folder, give it an appropriate name, and then click Save.

30. Edit the material that you applied to change it from 1060 Alloy to Plain Carbon Steel, and save it as another template with a different name.

31. Change the primary units to millimeters with 2 places, and save it as a third template file.

32. Exit the file.

Tutorial: Visualization Techniques

Visualization is a key factor in SolidWorks. Whether it is for a presentation of your design to customers or management or simply checking the design, it is important to be able to see the model in various ways. This tutorial guides you through using several tools and techniques.

1. If the part named Chapter3Sample.sldprt is not already opened, then open it from the CD-ROM. If it is open and changes have been made to it, then click File ➪ Reload ➪ OK.

2. Practice using some of the controls for rotating and zooming the part. In addition to the View toolbar buttons, you should also use Z and Shift-Z (Zoom Out and In, respectively), the arrow keys, and the Ctrl-, Shift-, and Alt-arrow combinations.

3. Use the MMB to select a straight edge on the part, and then drag with the MMB. This rotates the part about the selected entity. Also apply this technique when selecting a vertex and a flat face.

4. Select the name of the part at the top of the FeatureManager.

5. Click the Color button from the Standard toolbar.

6. Click the color you want in the Favorite panel. The model should change color. If you click and drag the cursor over the colors, the model changes color as you drag over each new color. Figure 3.30 identifies some of the buttons.

FIGURE 3.30

The Color and Optics interface elements

7. If the Color Properties panel is not expanded, click the double arrows to the right to expand it. Select the colors you want from the continuous color map. Again, click and drag the cursor to watch the part change color continuously.

8. Create a swatch. In the Favorite panel, select the Create New Swatch button and call the new swatch color file BibleColors.

9. Select a color from the Color Properties continuous map; the Add Selected Color button becomes active. Clicking the button adds the color to the swatch palette. You can add several colors to the palette to use as favorites later on.

 TIP You will be able to access these colors again later by selecting BibleColors from the drop-down list in the Favorite panel. You can transfer the colors to other computers or SolidWorks installations by copying the file BibleColors.slddclr from the <SolidWorks installation directory>\lang\english folder (or the equivalent file for your installed language).

10. In the Optical Properties panel, move the Transparency slider to the right, and watch the part become transparent.

11. To prevent the Color and Optics window from closing after every change, click the push-pin icon at the top of the window.

12. Click the green check mark icon to accept the changes; note that with the push-pin icon selected, the window remains available.

13. Expand the flyout FeatureManager in the upper-left corner of the graphics window, as shown in Figure 3.31, so that all of the features in the part are visible.

FIGURE 3.31

The Flyout FeatureManager

14. Select the features Extrude1, Fillet7, and Fillet6 from the FeatureManager so that they are displayed in the Selection list of the Color and Optics window. Select a color from the BibleColors swatch palette that you have just created.

15. Click the check mark icon to accept the changes and clear the Selection list.

16. Select the inside face of the large cylindrical hole through the part, and assign a separate color to the face.

17. Click the check mark icon to accept the changes, and click the red X icon to exit the command.

18. Expand the Display pane (upper-right area of the FeatureManager). You should see color and transparency symbols for the overall part, and color symbols for three features. There is no indication of the face color that is applied.

19. Remove the colors. Open the Color and Optics window again, re-select the three features (Extrude1, Fillet7, and Fillet6), and click the Remove Color button below the Selection list. Do the same with the colored face. Return the part transparency to fully opaque.

20. Click the check mark icon to accept the changes.

21. Change the edge display to Shaded (without edges). Then change to a Wireframe mode. Finally, change back to Shaded With Edges.

22. Now select View ➪ Display ➪ Tangent Edges as Phantom. Figure 3.32 shows the difference between Tangent Edges Visible, as Phantom, and Removed settings.

FIGURE 3.32

Tangent Edge display settings for a shaded model

TIP Using the Tangent Edges as Phantom setting is a quick and easy way to look at a model to determine whether or not face transitions are tangent. It does not help to distinguish between tangency and curvature continuity; you need to use Zebra Stripes for that.

23. Switch back to Shaded display.

24. If you do not have a RealView-capable computer, then skip this step. Ensure that the RealView button in the View toolbar is depressed. RMB click the Material folder in the FeatureManager. Select Edit Material, and then select Steel, AISI 304. Rotate the part. Notice that the finish is semi-reflective. Click the check mark icon to accept the change.

25. If the Texture button is not on your Standard toolbar, use Tools ⇨ Customize ⇨ Commands to add it to the toolbar.

26. Turn the part over, select the bottom face, and apply a texture of Steel, Cast, Cast Rough. The rest of the part should retain the semi-reflective surface, as shown in Figure 3.33. Click the check mark icon to accept the change.

FIGURE 3.33

Applying a material to a part

27. Click the Section View button on the View toolbar. Drag the arrows in the middle of the section plane back and forth with the cursor to move the section dynamically through the part, as shown in Figure 3.34.

28. Click the check box next to the Section 2 panel name, and create a second section that is perpendicular to the first.

29. Click the green check mark icon to accept the section. Notice that while in the Section View PropertyManager, the RealView material does not display, but once you close the dialog box, RealView returns.

FIGURE 3.34

A section view

Summary

Learning to manipulate the view is essential to being able to interpret the visual data on the screen. As a result, you need to be familiar with opening and viewing SolidWorks documents before we can discuss the modeling aspects of the software.

When you start using SolidWorks, several resources are available to help you learn the basic tasks. There are also some important options that you need to select up front, when using the software for the first time. Properly setting up templates can save you a lot of time and automate other tasks in the future, particularly drawings and PDM data entry. Customizing your SolidWorks installation and knowing which files are and are not important is also key to your role as Administrator.

Chapter 4

Working with Sketches

This is where the fun begins, or begins to begin. To me, training animals has always been fun, especially when the animal begins to respond to my instructions. Learning SolidWorks is like working with an animal that has already been trained. You know it is supposed to respond to you in certain ways, but there is always this little thrill of having communicated with something outside of yourself when it actually responds with a predicted behavior. This is not to say that it is surprising; it is just somehow a little thrilling. SolidWorks programmers have created an animal that responds to your input with intelligence and comprehension.

So far in this book, we have looked mainly at settings and setup, which is pretty mundane business. However, here we begin to build models, simple at first, but gaining in complexity and always demonstrating new techniques and features that build your modeling vocabulary. Beyond this, we move into putting the parts together into assemblies, which helps to make the "pretty pictures" look like something useful. Finally, we use the parts and assemblies to create drawings.

Several basic facts about sketches may be helpful before we start. While a part may have many sketches, only one sketch can be open at a time. This is due in part to the history-based nature of the software because every entry in the FeatureManager tree must be edited in the order in which it sits in the tree.

While you can create both 2D and 3D sketches, you will use 2D sketches most of the time. When referring to a generic *sketch*, a 2D sketch is always assumed. You will use 3D sketches in specific situations, and they will be explicitly called for when needed.

CROSS-REF We discuss 3D sketches in detail in Chapter 31.

When you open a sketch, several tools become unavailable. For example, you cannot apply a Fillet feature while a sketch is open. Conversely, there are several things that you cannot do *until* you open a sketch. When I used to teach SolidWorks classes for a reseller, I had only one rule: you were not allowed to throw the monitor out the window because of frustration until you checked to see if you were in or out of Sketch mode and if the selection filter was turned on. These features are two very common sources of frustration for new users.

There are several indicators that let you know when you are in Sketch mode:

- The top bar of the SolidWorks window displays the text, Sketch X of Part Y.
- The lower-right corner of the status bar displays the text, Editing Sketch X.
- The Confirmation Corner displays a sketch icon in the upper-right corner of the graphics window.
- The Sketch toolbar button now displays the text, Exit Sketch, and is pressed in.
- The red sketch Origin displays.
- If you are using the grid, it displays only in Sketch mode.

While most users find the sketch grid to be annoying and distracting, when teaching, I always used the grid to remind students when they were in Sketch mode. If you find that you forget or would like a visual cue, the sketch grid is a useful, if less than fashionable, option.

Opening a Sketch

There are several ways to open a new sketch in SolidWorks:

- Click a sketch entity toolbar button from the Sketch toolbar; SolidWorks prompts you to select a sketch plane. When you select the plane, the sketch opens.
- Preselect a plane or planar face and then click either a sketch entity button or the Sketch button.
- Right-mouse button (RMB) click a plane or planar face and select Insert Sketch.

You can open existing sketches in several ways:

- RMB click a sketch in the FeatureManager or graphics window, and select Edit Sketch.
- Select a sketch from the FeatureManager or graphics window, and click the Sketch button on the Sketch toolbar.
- Double-click a sketch with the Move/Size Features tool active.

Identifying Sketch Entities

The first step in creating most SolidWorks parts is a sketch. This will usually be a 2D sketch, although 3D sketches are also used and are discussed in Chapter 31. A 2D sketch is simply a collection of 2D lines, arcs, and other elements that lie together on a plane; it usually also contains relations and/or dimensions between the entities.

SolidWorks sketch entities include many types, some of which you will use all of the time, and some of which you may not use, even if you spend years working with the software. Here we will identify each entity type so that you see it at least once, and know that it is available if you need it at some point.

The Sketch toolbar

The default buttons on the Sketch toolbar are identified first, followed by the rest of the entities that you can access through Tools ➪ Customize ➪ Commands ➪ Sketch.

 Sketch opens and closes sketches. If you preselect a plane or planar face and then click the Sketch button, SolidWorks opens a new sketch on the plane or face. If you preselect a sketch before clicking the Sketch button, SolidWorks opens this sketch. If you do not use preselection, SolidWorks prompts you to select a plane on which you want to put a new sketch, or an existing sketch to edit.

 3D Sketch opens and closes 3D sketches.

 Smart Dimension can create several types of dimensions, such as horizontal, vertical, aligned, radial, diameter, angle, and arc length.

- **Horizontal, Vertical, and Aligned:** You can create dimensions in three ways, as shown in Figure 4.1:

  - By selecting a line and placing the dimension

  - By selecting the endpoints of the line and placing the dimension

  - By selecting lines at the ends of the line and placing the dimension

  Selecting the line is the easiest and fastest method. Selecting the lines on the ends is not recommended because if you delete either of the selected lines, the dimension is also deleted.

  You can use the first and second techniques for the angled line shown in Figure 4.1 to create any of the three dimensions shown. You can do this by dragging the cursor while placing the dimension until the witness lines snap to the orientation you want.

 To lock the orientation of a dimension while moving the cursor to place the actual dimension value, RMB click. To unlock it, just RMB click again.

FIGURE 4.1

Selection options for linear Smart Dimension

In this case, the third technique locks you into the horizontal orientation because of the orientation of the selected lines.

CAUTION   When you select end lines to establish a dimension instead of endpoints, both of the end lines will gain an implied relation that prevents them from moving as you might predict. In the case shown in Figure 4.1, neither of the end lines can be angled unless you remove the dimension.

Another issue that arises for adding dimensions to end lines is that if you delete either of the end lines, the dimension is also deleted. This is not true for the first and second techniques, where as long as the endpoints remain, the dimension also remains.

- **Radial:** You create the dimension by selecting an arc and placing the dimension. If you want a radial dimension of a complete circle, you must RMB click the dimension after you create it, select Properties, and deselect the Diameter Dimension option, as shown in Figure 4.2.

- **Diameter:** You can create the dimension by selecting a complete circle and placing the dimension. If you want a diameter dimension for an arc, use the Dimension Properties dialog box shown in Figure 4.2 and select the Diameter Dimension option.

- **Angle:** You can create the dimension in one of two ways. If the angle to be driven is between two straight lines, simply select the two straight lines and place the dimension. If you are creating an included angle dimension for an arc where there are not necessarily any straight lines drawn, then with the Smart Dimension tool active, first select the vertex of the angle, and then the two outlying points, as shown in Figure 4.3.

- **Arc Length:** You can create the dimension by selecting an arc and its endpoints with the Smart Dimension tool.

FIGURE 4.2

The Dimension Properties interface

FIGURE 4.3

Creating an included angle dimension

Line creates straight lines using one of two methods:

- **Click-Click:** Used for drawing multiple connected end-to-end lines. Click and release the left-mouse button to start the line; each click-and-release ends the previous line and starts a new one. Double-click, press Esc, or deselect the Line tool to end.

- **Click-Drag:** Used to draw individual or unconnected lines. Click, drag, and drop. The first click initiates the line, and the drop ends it.

Alternate methods for drawing lines include horizontal, vertical, angle, and infinite lines. The interface for these options displays in the PropertyManager, as shown in Figure 4.4.

- **Horizontal, Vertical:** These settings require you to select a starting point, and an ending vertical or horizontal position. There does not seem to be any compelling reason for you to use this instead of the regular line command.

- **Angle:** Enables you to specify an angle and drag a line at this angle. Again, I can find no compelling reason to use this tool.

- **Infinite Lines:** This is truly puzzling. SolidWorks parts have a working space limited to 1000 meters on a side, centered on the Origin. Infinite lines extend well beyond this, although you cannot draw or dimension a regular line outside of this box. I have not come across a compelling use for this feature, and I am quite sure that it was added only to appease unrepentant AutoCAD users.

FIGURE 4.4

The Insert Line PropertyManager interface

 Rectangle creates a rectangle by clicking one corner and dragging to the diagonal corner. This action creates four lines with Horizontal and Vertical sketch relations, as appropriate.

Circle creates a circle using one of two methods:

- **Center Creation:** Click the center of the circle and drag the radius. The Circle PropertyManager calls this function *center creation*.

- **Perimeter Creation:** This only creates tangent relations with other entities in the current sketch, and so if you are building a circle from model edges or entities in other sketches, you need to apply the relations manually. SolidWorks calls these functions *perimeter creation*. To create a circle using this technique, you must select the Perimeter Creation option from the Circle PropertyManager window after clicking the Circle tool. There is also a separate Perimeter Creation toolbar button, and a menu selection for Tools ➪ Sketch Entities ➪ Perimeter Circle.

  - **Tangent to Two Entities:** Start the circle with the cursor near one line in the sketch. A Tangent symbol appears by the cursor with a yellow background. Click and drag the diameter to the second tangent entity, where a similar cursor symbol should appear. Release the mouse button and RMB click the green check mark icon. This process is shown in Figure 4.5.

  - **Tangent to Three Entities:** Use the process for Tangent to two entities, but omit the RMB click of the green check mark icon. After dropping on the second tangent, drag again to the third tangent entity.

FIGURE 4.5

Creating a perimeter creation circle

R = 6.11

Centerpoint Arc creates an arc by clicking the center, dragging the radius, and then clicking and dragging the included angle of the arc. The first two steps are exactly like the Center-Radius circle.

 Tangent Arc creates an arc tangent to an existing sketch entity. Depending on how the cursor moves away from the end of the existing sketch entity, the arc can be tangent, reverse tangent, or perpendicular, as shown in Figure 4.6.

FIGURE 4.6

Using the Tangent Arc feature

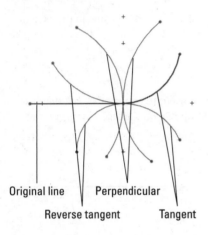

Original line   Perpendicular

Reverse tangent   Tangent

Another way to create a tangent arc is to start drawing a line from the end of another sketch entity, and while holding the left mouse button, to press the A key, or to return the cursor to the starting point and drag it out again. This method can be difficult to master, but it saves time when compared to any of the techniques for switching sketch tools.

 3 Point Arc creates an arc by first establishing endpoints, and then establishing the included arc, as shown in Figure 4.7. Again, this tool also works using the Click-Click or Click-Drag methods.

FIGURE 4.7

Creating a three point arc

Click-Drag   Click-Drag

Sketch Fillet creates a sketch fillet in one of two ways. You can either select the endpoint where the sketch entities intersect, or you can select the entities themselves, selecting the portion of the entity that you want to keep. Figure 4.8 illustrates both techniques.

FIGURE 4.8

Creating a sketch fillet

Select lines   Select   Result

 Centerline follows the same methods as regular lines, and is also called a *construction line* in some cases. Other construction entities such as construction circles are not available, but you can create them by selecting the For Construction option in the PropertyManager for any entity.

Sketch Fillets

While the Sketch Fillet tool is easy to use, applies immediately, and may align with your way of working in a 2D program, it is not considered best practice to use sketch fillets extensively. Some reasons for this include:

- Large changes in the size or shape of the rest of the sketch can make the fillets cause the feature built from the sketch to fail.

- SolidWorks (and other parametric programs as well) often has difficulty solving tangent arcs in some situations. You may see them flip tangency or go around 270° instead of just 90°. Using a lot of fillets in a sketch can often cause trouble.

- If you want to remove the fillets temporarily, there is no good way to do this if you have used sketch fillets.

- Sometimes feature order requires that other features, such as draft, come before the fillet.

- Sometimes a 2D fillet simply cannot create the required geometry.

Fillet features are the preferred method for creating rounds and fillets. The same can be said for chamfers.

Spline draws a freeform curve. Splines may form either a single closed loop or an open loop. You can draw a spline by clicking each location where you want to add a control point. Figure 4.9 identifies the elements of a spline. The detail image shows the structure of a spline handle.

FIGURE 4.9

The structure of a spline and a spline handle

Control polygon   Spline points   Minimum radius

Inflection point

Combination
(direction and magnitude)   Direction handle

Magnitude handle

Splines are used mainly for freeform complex shapes in 2D and 3D sketches, although you can also use them for anything that you would use other sketch elements for.

 Point creates a sketch point. Aside from limited cases of lofting to a point or using a point as a constraint sketch in a Fill feature, sketch points are usually used for reference or for the location of the centerpoint of Hole Wizard features.

You can also use the sketch point as a virtual sharp. If two sketch entities do not actually intersect because of a fillet or chamfer, selecting the two entities and clicking the Point tool creates a point at the location where they would intersect if they were extended. This is useful for dimensioning to the sharp. Virtual sharp display is controlled by a Document Property setting that is described in more detail in Appendix B.

 3D Sketch Plane creates a plane in a 3D Sketch. I discuss 3D Sketches in more detail in Chapter 31.

 Add Relation displays a PropertyManager window that allows you to apply sketch relations. This interface appears to be obsolete because it is easier to simply select sketch items and apply relations in the PropertyManager window that appears automatically when you select them; however, there are some subtle workflow-related reasons for using this tool.

When the Add Relation PropertyManager is active, you do not need to use the Ctrl key to select multiple entities. You also do not need to clear a selection before making a new selection for the next relation. These two reasons sound minor, but if you have a large number of sketch relations to apply, the workflow goes much more smoothly using this tool than the default method.

 Display/Delete Relations enables you to look through the relations in a sketch, and sort them according to several categories. From this window, you can delete or suppress relations and replace entities in relations.

 Quick Snaps flyout allows you to quickly filter types of entities that sketch elements will snap to when you move or create them. To access the tools, click the drop-down arrow to the right of the toolbar button.

 Mirror Entities mirrors selected sketch entities about a single selected centerline, and applies a Symmetric sketch relation. There is also a Dynamic Mirror function that is described later in this chapter.

 Convert Entities converts edges, curves, and sketch elements from other sketches into entities in the current sketch. When edges are not parallel to the sketch plane, the Convert Entities feature projects them into the sketch plane. Some elements may be impossible to convert, such as a helix, which would produce a projection that overlaps itself. Sketch entities that are created using Convert Entities get an On Edge sketch relation.

Offset Entities works like the Convert Entities feature, except that it offsets the sketch to one side or the other of the projection of the original edge, sketch, or curve. Figure 4.10 shows the interface for this command.

FIGURE 4.10

The Offset Entities interface

The options available in the Offset Entities interface are as follows:

- **Add Dimensions:** Constrains offset sketch entities. Instead of the On Edge relations, Offset Entities creates an Offset sketch relation that cannot be recreated manually.

- **Reverse:** Changes the direction of the offset.

- **Select Chain:** Selects continuous end-to-end sketch entities.

- **Bi-directional:** Offsets to both sides simultaneously.

- **Make Base Construction:** If you are offsetting sketch entities within the active sketch, this option converts the original sketch entities to construction sketch geometry.

- **Cap Ends:** Is available only when you have selected the Bi-directional option. Capping the ends with arcs is an easy way to create a slot from a sketch of the centerline. This function works with all sketch entities, and so it is not limited to straight slots. Figure 4.11 shows examples of the Cap Ends option.

 The Offset Entities command may fail if the offset distance is greater than the smallest radius of curvature, and you are attempting to offset to the inside of the arc.

FIGURE 4.11

The results of using offset entities cap ends

 Trim Entities is actually several functions rolled into one, and it is an extremely powerful tool for editing sketches. Trim Entities allows several methods for trimming, as well as extending and deleting sketch entities. Figure 4.12 shows the PropertyManager interface for this function.

FIGURE 4.12

The Trim Entities interface

- **Power Trim:** Trims by dragging a cursor trail over multiple entities. The entities that you drag the cursor over are trimmed back to the next intersecting sketch entity. Each time you trim an entity, a red box is left behind that remains until you trim the next entity. If you backtrack with the cursor and touch the red box, this trim is undone. This option is best used when you need to trim a large number of entities that are easy to hit with a moving cursor. Figure 4.13 shows the Power Trim feature in action.

You can also use power trim to extend sketch entities along their paths by dragging the endpoints. Regular dragging can also change the position or orientation of the rest of the entity, but by using the Power Trim feature, you affect only the length.

The Power Trim feature in action

■ **Corner:** Trims or extends two selected entities to their next intersection. When you use the Corner option to trim, the selected portion of the sketch entities is kept, and anything on the other side of the corner is discarded. Figure 4.14 shows two ways that the Corner option can work.

Using the Corner option

- **Trim Away Inside:** Trims away selected entities inside a selected boundary. The boundary may consist of a pair of sketch entities or a model face (edges of the face are used as the boundary). Only entities that cross both selected boundaries (or cross the closed loop of the face boundary twice) can be trimmed. This option does not trim a closed loop such as a circle, ellipse, or closed spline.

- **Trim Away Outside:** Functions exactly like the Trim Away Inside option, except that sketch entities outside of the boundary are discarded. The Trim Away Inside and Outside option are illustrated in Figure 4.15.

FIGURE 4.15

Using the Trim Away Inside and Outside options

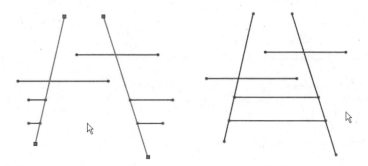

- **Trim to Closest:** This is the default setting. Clicking on a sketch entity will:

  - Trim it back to the next entity if there is only one crossing entity.

  - Trim between two crossing entities if there are more than one.

  - Delete the entity if there are no crossing entities.

  In all cases, the selected section of the entity is removed.

  The Trim to Closest option can also extend by dragging one entity to another; if an intersection is possible, the first entity is extended to the second entity. Figure 4.16 illustrates how the Trim to Closest option functions.

 Construction Geometry toggles between regular sketch entities and construction entities.

 Move Entities enables you to move entities within a sketch by dragging or by keying in XY points. Figure 4.16 shows the simple interface for the Move Entities command. Select the entities to move in the upper box, and the method to move them below.

FIGURE 4.16

The Move Entities interface

 Select is usually used to turn off the previous command.

 Grid/Snap is used to open the Grid/Snap section of Tools, Options, Document Properties.

 Parallelogram can be used in two different ways:

- To draw a rectangle at an angle, click one corner of the rectangle, and then drag a side connected to that corner. Then click and drag the length of the second direction.

- To draw a parallelogram (adjacent sides are not perpendicular, but opposite sides are parallel), draw the first side of the parallelogram in the same way as the first side of the rectangle, but hold down the Ctrl key when dragging the second side; you can set the angle as well as the length.

 Polygon creates a regular *n*-sided polygon in the same way as a circle. Click the center and drag the radius. You need to set the number of sides in the PropertyManager before clicking in the graphics window.

 Perimeter Circle. See Circle mentioned earlier.

 Ellipse is created by clicking the center, dragging one axis, and then dragging the other axis.

Partial Ellipse is created by clicking the center, dragging one axis, dragging the other axis, and then clicking and dragging the included angle of the partial ellipse. The Partial Ellipse feature works like the centerpoint arc.

 Parabola is created by clicking the location for the Focus, and then dragging the position of the Apex. You then click and drag the included angle of the parabola, as shown in Figure 4.17.

FIGURE 4.17

Drawing a parabola

 Spline on Surface is used in 3D sketches to draw a freeform spline on any 3D surface. The Spline on Surface feature is constrained to working only on a single face at a time; it cannot bridge between faces.

 Sketch Text creates editable text in sketches using TrueType fonts. Some fonts produce sketches that are unusable for solid features. Sketch Text may be dissolved into lines and arcs so that you can edit them manually. Figure 4.18 points out the key elements of the Sketch Text interface.

FIGURE 4.18

The Sketch Text interface

Curve for text to follow

Sketch text

Bold, italics, rotate

Justification

Spacing   Width

Direction and orientation

 Intersection Curve in 2D sketches, creates sketch entities where the sketch plane intersects selected faces. In 3D sketches, the Intersection Curve feature creates sketch entities where any types of selected surfaces intersect. This can be an extremely useful tool in many situations.

 Face Curves applies the underlying U-V isoparameter mesh to a selected face. It is most commonly used as an analysis tool for complex surfaces, but you can also use it to create curves to rebuild faces. Accepting the results by clicking OK creates a separate 3D sketch for each spline. Figure 4.19 shows the original surface and the results of using face curves on a complex lofted surface.

Extend extends a sketch entity up to its next intersection with another sketch entity.

Split Entities splits a sketch entity into two segments. You can also delete it later to rejoin the entity back into a single segment.

FIGURE 4.19

Using face curves on a complex surface

 Dynamic Mirror can be used when you preselect a centerline, and Dynamic Mirror is turned on. Any new sketch entity that you draw is automatically mirrored to the other side of the centerline.

 Rotate Entities rotates selected sketch entities.

 Scale Entities scales selected sketch entities about a specified point by a specified scale ratio. This function does not scale dimensioned entities, and may remove external sketch relations to complete the task.

 Copy Entities can copy multiple instances of selected sketch entities. This feature functions like the Move Entities feature. Unfortunately, a combination of the Copy and Rotate features does not seem to exist.

 Linear Sketch Pattern creates a one- or two-directional pattern of sketch entities. You can define spacing and angles. Figure 4.20 shows the interface and the results of this function.

 Circular Sketch Pattern creates a circular pattern of sketch entities.

BEST PRACTICE You should use sketch patterns as little as possible. For much the same reasons that fillet features are preferred over sketch fillets, pattern features are also preferred over sketch patterns. Sketch patterns are not as editable or as flexible as feature patterns. They solve slowly, especially when you pattern a lot of entities. Best practice is to avoid sketch patterns unless there is no alternative.

 Make Path is intended to help create machine-design motion in sketches, in particular, cam type motion. Although it is helpful, you do not need to make a block of the cam first. You can then RMB click the block and select Make Path. A tangent relation to a path enables a follower to roll around the entire perimeter.

FIGURE 4.20

The Linear Sketch Pattern interface

 Modify Sketch is one of my favorite sketch tools, but it has been falling out of favor in more recent versions of SolidWorks because of the improvement of tools such as Move Sketch. The Modify Sketch feature is flexible and powerful, and enables you to move, rotate, and scale the sketch, as well as mirror about a horizontal or vertical axis or about both axes simultaneously. Figure 4.21 shows the interface, which consists of a dialog box, a special Origin, and a context-sensitive cursor.

FIGURE 4.21

The Modify Sketch interface

Both the left- and right-mouse buttons have special functions, which change when the cursor is moved over the three knots on the special Origin. The RMB allows you to mirror or rotate the sketch, and the left-mouse button, or LMB, allows you to move the Origin or move the sketch.

This function has some limitations when you use it with sketches that have external relations. Certain functions may be disabled, or a warning message may appear, saying that you need to remove external relations to get a particular function to, well, function.

 No Solve Move enables the moving of sketch entities without solving any relations in the sketch. If you select this option and you move an entity with relations that would otherwise not allow it to move (such as a collinear relation), then you are prompted with a choice to either delete the existing relation and continue, or to copy the entity without the relation.

 Sketch Picture is a picture that is placed in the sketch, lies on the sketch plane, and is listed in the FeatureManager that is indented under the sketch. The sketch picture may be suppressed independently from the rest of the sketch, and when the sketch is hidden, the picture is not visible. You can easily move, resize, and rotate sketch pictures, as well as apply a transparent background to them. They are usually used for tracing over or as a planar decal without the need for PhotoWorks. Figure 4.22 shows the controls for manipulating the Sketch Picture feature.

FIGURE 4.22

The Sketch Picture interface

The Dimensions/Relations toolbar

The Dimensions/Relations toolbar has a few tools that we have already seen, but as the name suggests, it also contains tools that will either help you to create or investigate dimensions and sketch relations. Figure 4.23 shows the default toolbar, but in the following pages, we look at all of the available tools that are available through Tools ➪ Customize ➪ Commands ➪ Dimensions/Relations.

FIGURE 4.23

The Dimensions/Relations toolbar

 Smart Dimension is described in the Sketch toolbar section, and is shown in Figure 4.1.

 Horizontal Dimension applies a dimension to a sketch entity that drives the horizontal distance between the endpoints.

 Vertical Dimension works like a horizontal dimension, but vertically.

 Baseline Dimensions are different from most of the dimension tools that you find on the Dimensions/Relations toolbar in that they create only *reference* dimensions (they are driven, they only measure distances rather than drive them), and they are applicable only in *drawing* documents. Baseline Dimensions start from a single reference; then, as you select additional references, additional dimensions are stacked, as shown in Figure 4.24.

FIGURE 4.24

Baseline Dimensions on a drawing

Ordinate Dimensions are driving dimensions where a set of ordinate dimensions originate from a common zero point. To use these dimensions, simply click a zero location, place the zero dimension, and then click additional points. The dimensions are placed and are automatically aligned to the rest of the dimensions.

NOTE   If a line is *not* selected as the zero reference entity, the Ordinate Dimension feature defaults to a Horizontal Ordinate.

You can remove Ordinate Dimensions from the common alignment by RMB clicking the dimension and selecting Break Alignment.

Ordinate Dimensions will jog automatically if SolidWorks senses that the dimensions are getting too close to one another. You can also jog them manually.

After you create the Ordinate Dimension set, you can add to it by accessing the Add to Ordinate command through the RMB menu.

All of these options for Ordinate Dimensions are shown in Figure 4.25.

FIGURE 4.25

Options for Ordinate Dimensions

Not all of the listed options are available in the model sketch environment; some are available only in drawings.

 Horizontal Ordinate Dimensions are simply ordinate dimensions that are forced to drive dimensions in a horizontal direction.

 Horizontal and **Vertical Ordinate Dimensions** have the same function as the regular Ordinate, except that they only drive horizontal and vertical dimensions, respectively.

Chamfer Dimension is another type of dimension that is only driven and only applied in drawing documents. It works by first selecting the chamfered edge, and then selecting the angle reference edge. It produces dimensions like the one shown in Figure 4.26.

FIGURE 4.26

Applying a chamfer dimension

.273 X 45.00°

Select first

Select second

 Auto Dimension also functions only in a drawing. You need to select reference edges for X and Y directions and specify either all edges or only selected edges. SolidWorks then dimensions everything, based on the reference edges. Hole diameters are also dimensioned.

BEST PRACTICE While the Auto Dimension feature can clearly save you a lot of time dimensioning parts on a drawing, it does not necessarily use the best dimensioning practice for manufacturing drawings. This tool is best used in situations when baseline dimensions are appropriate.

 Add Relations is described in depth in the Sketch toolbar section.

Automatic Relations toggles to enable or disable the automatic creation of sketch relations while sketching. This toggle is also available through Tools ⇨ Sketch Settings ⇨ Automatic Relations. Automatic relations help you to create intelligent sketches with less manual intervention. Although using them takes a little practice, it is well worth the effort.

CAUTION As with any automatic function, there are times when automatic relations will do things that you do not expect or want. While you are sketching, it is recommended that you watch the cursor and the relations that it automatically applies.

While sketching, symbols appear on the cursor to show that a relation will automatically be created. These symbols have a yellow background, and will apply horizontal, vertical, coincident, tangent, parallel, and perpendicular relations. Figure 4.27 shows two situations where automatic relations are applied — a horizontal and a tangent relation.

FIGURE 4.27

Some automatic relations that appear on the cursor

Inferencing in Sketch

Although Inferencing and Automatic Relations are often confused, even by experienced
SolidWorks users, these functions are not the same. *Inferencing* refers to the blue dotted lines that
display in Sketch mode when the cursor aligns with endpoints, centerpoints, or the Origin.
Inferencing does not create sketch relations, with one exception. If the cursor is aligned to one side
of the endpoint of another line, and you draw a horizontal line, then an automatic Coincident relation is applied between the line and the endpoint. This also holds true if the cursor starts above or
below the point and you draw a vertical line.

When the cursor displays a small symbol with a yellow background, this means that an automatic
relation is going to be applied. If the relation symbol has a white background, the relation is infer-
enced, but not applied as an actual sketch relation. The symbols with the blue background are
relations that have been applied to existing sketch entities. The symbols look the same, regardless
of background color.

The following are the symbols for the various inferences, automatic relation cursors, and applied
sketch relations. The difference between the three types is simply the background colors, white,
yellow, and blue, respectively.

CROSS-REF These relations are defined in the Sketching with Parametrics section of Chapter 1.

- Along X
- Along Y
- Along Z
- **At Intersection of Two Faces**: This uses the same symbol as the Intersection relation.
- Coincident
- Collinear
- Concentric

Coradial

Equal

Equal Curvature

Fix

Horizontal

Intersection: This uses the same symbol as At Intersection of Two Faces.

Midpoint

Offset

On Edge

On Surface: This is the same as the Coincident symbol.

Parallel

Perpendicular

Pierce

Symmetric

Tangent

Vertical

Display/Delete Relations is described in detail in the Sketch toolbar section.

Fully Define Sketch interface uses sketch relations and dimensions to fully define the active sketch. It allows you to select what types of sketch relations and dimensions will be used to do this. Figure 4.28 shows the Fully Define Sketch interface.

Scan Equal scans a sketch for entities with either the same length or the same radius, and applies Equal relations.

FIGURE 4.28

FIGURE 4.28

The Fully Define Sketch interface

Exploring Sketch Settings

In addition to sketch tools, another important aspect of controlling sketches is sketch settings. Sketch settings are found in two different locations. The first location is at Tools ⇨ Options ⇨ Sketch. In this chapter, we cover the settings found at the second location, Tools ⇨ Sketch Settings. These settings mainly affect sketch relations.

 The sketch settings at Tools ⇨ Options ⇨ Sketch are discussed in detail in Appendix B. They mainly affect sketch display issues, and have some overlap with Tools, Sketch Settings.

Automatic Relations is covered in depth in the Dimensions/Relations toolbar section.

Automatic Solve is turned on by default. As you make changes to a sketch by adding relations or changing dimensions, SolidWorks automatically and immediately updates the sketch to reflect the changes. When the Automatic Solve setting is turned off, these changes are deferred until you exit the sketch or turn the Automatic Solve setting back on. The setting can be useful to prevent intermediate solutions (for example, when half of the changes are made) that may cause problems with the sketch, and when you are confident that the outcome will be correct.

If you import a large drawing from the DXF or DWG formats, these drawings import as sketch entities into either a SolidWorks sketch or a drawing. SolidWorks may automatically turn off the Automatic Solve setting for performance (speed) reasons on files of this type.

Enable Snapping is turned on by default. It enables the cursor to snap to the endpoints of existing sketch entities to help you make cleaner sketches. When you turn this setting off, Automatic Relations is also disabled (although the icon for the setting remains depressed, Automatic Relations are not created).

No Solve Move is discussed in the Sketch toolbar section.

Detach Segment on Drag is turned off by default. When you turn this setting on, the Detach Segment on Drag feature enables you to pull a single sketch element away from a chain of elements. For example, if you have a rectangle and you want to detach one of the lines from the rest of the rectangle, without using this setting, you would have to draw extra geometry and then trim and delete lines in order to release the endpoints.

BEST PRACTICE It is recommended that you leave this setting off. Turn it on only when you need it, and then immediately turn it off again. This setting can be hazardous for everyday use, since it enables you to simply drag sketch elements that may be otherwise fully defined.

Override Dims on Drag is off by default. When you turn this setting on, it enables you to drag fully defined sketch geometry, and the dimensions will update to match the dragged size. This is another setting that you should use sparingly. It can be useful for doing concept work, but you should leave it off when working with production data for obvious reasons.

Using Sketch Blocks

Sketch blocks are collections of sketch entities that can be treated as a single entity. You can use sketch blocks in parts, assemblies, and drawings. To create a sketch block, select a group of sketch entities and click the Make Block button on the Blocks toolbar, or select Tools ➪ Blocks ➪ Make.

Blocks may be internal to a particular document, or they may be saved as an external file. The externally saved block may be linked to each document where it is used, so that if the block is changed, it updates in the documents where it is used.

You can use blocks in conjunction with the Make Path function mentioned earlier in this chapter to create functional layouts for mechanisms.

The following is a description of the various tools that are available on the Blocks toolbar.

 Make Block creates a sketch block from selected sketch entities. You can position a manipulator to denote the insertion point for the block. Blocks may attach at any entity endpoint, but the insertion point follows the cursor.

 Edit Block enables you to edit an existing block as if it were a regular sketch.

 Insert Block allows you to select from a list of open blocks or browse to a location where blocks are stored. You can edit the insertion point by using the Edit Block function.

Add/Remove, while editing a block, allows you to add or remove sketch entities from the block without deleting them from the sketch.

 Rebuild Block allows changes to a block to be reflected in any external relations without exiting the block. For example, if you have a block in a sketch, and a sketch line is coincident to one of the endpoints in the block, you may edit the block such that the referenced endpoint moves. As a result, the line in the sketch will not move until you either exit the block or use the Rebuild Block function.

 Save Block saves a selected block to an external file (with the *.sldblk extension).

 Explode Block removes all of the sketch entities from a block and brings them into the current sketch.

 Belt/Chain enables you to make a belt or chain around a set of pulleys. Each pulley must be a block. After activating the command, you can select each pulley and use the arrow on the pulley to switch the side of the pulley to which the belt goes. You can also compensate for the thickness of the belt (this is important when both sides of the belt are in contact with pulleys), and drive the pulley arrangement using the length of the belt. Figure 4.29 shows the Belt/Chain dialog box.

FIGURE 4.29

The Belt/Chain dialog box

Tutorial: Learning to Use Sketch Relations

While it is useful to read through the definitions and functions of all of the sketch entities, tools, and relations, using your mouse to create is what this is all about. This tutorial makes sure that you get to know all of the major functions in SolidWorks sketches. Almost every part that you build will start with a sketch, so this is a skill worth mastering. Follow these steps to learn about sketch relations:

1. Open a new part using a template that you set up in the Template tutorial from Chapter 3. If you do not have this template, there is one provided for you on the CD-ROM named BibleInchTemplate.prtdot. Copy it to your templates folder and use it to create a new part. You may also use a SolidWorks default template.

2. Select the Front plane in the FeatureManager, and click the Sketch button on the Sketch toolbar. Click the Line tool from the Sketch toolbar.

3. Move the cursor near the Origin; the yellow Coincident symbol appears.

4. Draw a line horizontal from the Origin. Remember that there are two ways to sketch the line, Click-Click or Click-Drag. Make sure that the line snaps to the horizontal and that there is a yellow Horizontal relation symbol. The PropertyManager for the line should show that the line has a Horizontal relation. Also notice that the line is black, but the free endpoint is blue. This means that the line is fully defined except for its length. You can test this by dragging the blue endpoint.

5. Click the Smart Dimension tool on the Sketch toolbar, use it to click the line that you just drew, and place the dimension. If you are prompted for a dimension, type **1.000**. If not, then double-click the dimension; the Modify dialog box will appear, enabling you to change the dimension.

6. Draw two more lines to create a right triangle to look like Figure 4.30. If the sketch relations symbols do not show in the display, turn them on by clicking View ➪ Sketch Relations. You may want to set up a hotkey for this, because having sketch relations is useful, but often gets in the way.

FIGURE 4.30

Draw a right triangle.

7. Drag the blue endpoint of the triangle. Dragging endpoints is the most direct way to change the geometry. Dragging the line directly may also work, but this sometimes produces odd results, particularly in versions earlier than SolidWorks 2007. The sketch leaves a ghost when dragging so that you can see where you started.

8. Click the Smart Dimension tool, and then click the horizontal line and the angled line. This produces an angle dimension. Place the angle dimension inside the triangle, and give it a value of 30°.

9. Click the Sketch Fillet tool, set the radius value to 0.10 inches, and click each of the three endpoints. Where the 1.000-inch dimension connects to the sketch, SolidWorks has created *virtual sharps*. Figure 4.31 shows the sketch at this point. You may now want to turn off the Sketch Relations display because the screen is getting pretty busy. You can find this setting at View ⇨ Sketch Relations.

FIGURE 4.31

The resulting sketch after you perform step 9

10. Draw a line starting from the midpoint of the angled line. The midpoint should highlight when you move the cursor close to it. Draw the line perpendicular to the angled line. A dotted gray line appears, showing where the perpendicular lies. When you follow this line, the yellow perpendicular symbol appears on the cursor. Make this line approximately .75 inches long. Feedback on the cursor also shows the length of the line as you draw it.

11. Draw two more lines ending at the endpoint of the sketch fillet, as shown in Figure 4.32. Use the Inferencing lines to line up the second angled line with the end of the arc. The last line drawn is thin, and the second line drawn is blue. The thin line indicates that there is a potential problem with the sketch, but not an error in solving the relations. The problem is that an extrude requires a single closed loop, and this sketch is not a closed loop.

12. Click the Trim tool from the Sketch toolbar. Make sure that the Trim option is set to Closest. Click the angled line of the triangle between the thin line and the line at the midpoint. This trims out that section, and makes the sketch a closed loop, so that the thin line now has a regular thickness. A warning may appear because you have a Midpoint relation to the line being trimmed, and you no longer want this relation, but you want the lines to intersect at their endpoints. Select Yes at the prompt.

FIGURE 4.32

The resulting sketch after you perform step 11

13. Click the Smart Dimension tool. Use it to create aligned dimensions on the short line (.25 inches) and one of the long lines (.125 inches). You may now want to reorganize some of the dimensions if the display is becoming crowded.

14. At this point, two of the lines should be blue, but it may not be clear why they are not defined. Select one of the blue lines and drag it. Notice that what changes is the arc nearest the Origin. This changes in a way that is not useful for this part. To lock this line where it needs to be, select the blue line nearest the Origin and the centerpoint of the arc nearest the Origin, and give them a Coincident relation in the PropertyManager. The result is a fully defined sketch, as shown in Figure 4.33.

FIGURE 4.33

The resulting sketch after you perform step 14

15. Save the part with the name Sketch Relations Tutorial.sldprt. Close the part.

Tutorial: Using Blocks and Belts

Sometimes I am amazed at the things that can be done in SolidWorks, even with fairly simple tools. This is one of those times. If you design machines, then this tutorial will have some extra meaning for you. If you do not design machines, then these are still valuable tools to have in your toolbox ready to use in various situations. Follow these steps to learn about using Blocks and Belts.

1. Open a new part with inches as the units.

2. Draw a sketch on the Front plane as shown in Figure 4.34, with four lines connected to the Origin. Exit the sketch and rename it as Layout Sketch, either by clicking twice on the name of the feature in the FeatureManager or by selecting it and pressing F2.

FIGURE 4.34

The layout sketch

3. Open a second sketch on the Front plane, and draw a circle centered on the Origin with a 6-inch diameter.

4. Inside the circle, draw a rectangle around the Origin.

5. Select two adjacent sides of the rectangle and make an Equal sketch relation between them (this makes the rectangle into a square).

6. Draw a diagonal construction line (using the Centerline tool) across the square from corner to corner.

7. Press Esc to exit the Centerline command.

8. Select the centerline, Ctrl-select the Origin, and apply a Midpoint relation to them. This is a very common technique for centering a rectangle on a point.

The CD-ROM for Chapter 2 contains a macro that automatically draws a rectangle that is centered on the Origin.

9. Click the Smart Dimension tool, and apply a 1.000-inch dimension to one side of the square. Turn off the Smart Dimension tool by clicking it again on the toolbar or pressing Esc.

10. If the Blocks toolbar is not active, then activate it and select Make Block. You can also access this command through Tools ➪ Block ➪ Make.

11. Window select the circle and the square by clicking and dragging a box that includes all of the items in the sketch. The PropertyManager to the left displays a circle and five lines that are to be made into a block.

12. Expand the Insertion Point panel in the PropertyManager. This causes a blue manipulator Origin to appear in the graphics window. Click this Origin and drag it onto the center of the circle. Then click the green check mark icon to exit the Make Block dialog box. This is shown in Figure 4.35.

FIGURE 4.35

Creating a block

13. The items in the block now turn gray. Click anywhere on the block and drag it out of the way. Then drag the center of the circle and drop it on the part Origin.

14. Click the Insert Block tool on the Blocks toolbar. Place the block on the opposite sharp corner of the layout sketch.

15. Create another block that is identical to the first one, except that it has a diameter of three inches instead of six inches. You can do this by selecting the first block, clicking Edit Block from the toolbar, and copying (window select and Ctrl+C). Then exit the Edit Block and paste (Ctrl+V) in the regular sketch. Make sure to also change the insertion point for this second block to the center of the circle.

16. Insert a second instance of this second block, and make sure that both of them have the center of the circle at the two remaining intersection points of the four-sided shape of the layout sketch. At this point, your sketch should look like Figure 4.36.

FIGURE 4.36

Block placement

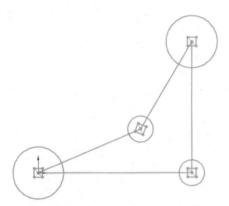

17. Click the Belt/Chain tool on the Blocks toolbar. Select the blocks in counter-clockwise order, starting at the Origin. On the last pulley, you will have to click the arrow to get the belt to go the correct way around the pulley.

18. Make sure that the Engage Belt option is selected. This allows you to make the pulleys move in the same way that they would in a real mechanism.

19. Click the Use Belt Thickness option, and assign .25 inches for the thickness. The belt should be offset from the pulleys.

20. Click the green check mark icon.

21. Click and drag one of the corners of the square in a pulley. All of the pulleys should turn as if this were a real mechanism. The ratios are also observed because the small pulleys rotate faster than the large ones.

22. Save this part as Blocks and Belts Tutorial.sldprt. Exit the part.

Summary

Sketching in SolidWorks is something that you will do almost every time you open the software. There are a lot of automated features available that you can allow to do the work for you. You also have a lot of control to make changes manually.

The options for creating intelligent relationships that establish your design intent, as well as SolidWorks' capabilities in laying out mechanisms, is only limited by your imagination. The more familiar you become with the tools in your toolbox, the more of a craftsman you can become with this software.

Chapter 5

Creating Simple Parts, Assemblies, and Drawings

IN THIS CHAPTER

Asking the right questions

Tutorial: Creating a simple part

Tutorial: Creating a simple assembly

Tutorial: Making a simple drawing

When you begin to build a model in SolidWorks, there are a few things to consider before you start. If you spend some time considering what you are doing first, then it will benefit you later in the process. Good modeling practice is based on robust design intent, which just means that you build a part that can adapt easily to changes. This section begins with questions that you need to ask.

Asking the Right Questions

Asking the right questions is the first step to getting the right answers. By asking questions about the part now, you can create a model that will be easier to edit, easier to properly place into an assembly, easier to detail in drawings, and easier for other SolidWorks users to understand when someone else has to work on your models. The questions focus on the physical manufactured part. Sometimes you will be able to find answers for the questions, and other times not. Whether you are doing the modeling for someone else, or doing the design and modeling yourself may make a difference in how you approach the modeling task.

The purpose of these questions is to help you establish design intent. The term *design intent* is difficult to define, but it is basically a statement of how the part functions and how the model reacts to modeling changes.

It may help to try to put the design intent into words to help you focus on what is important in the design. An example of a statement of design intent might be: "This part is symmetric about two planes, is used to support a 1.00" diameter shaft with a constant downward load of 150 pounds using a bronze bushing, and is bolted to a plate below it." This does not give you enough information to design the part, but it does give you information about two surfaces that are important (a hole for the bushing and the bottom that touches the mounting plate), as well as some general size and load requirements.

The following questions can help you to develop the design intent for your own projects.

Is the part symmetrical?

Symmetry is an important aspect of design intent. Taking advantage of symmetry can significantly reduce the time needed to model the part. Symmetry can exist on several levels:

- Sketch symmetry
- Individual feature symmetry
- Whole-part symmetry
- Axial symmetry (a revolved part)
- "Almost" symmetry (the whole part is symmetrical, except for a few features)
- Left and right symmetrical versions of the part

What are the primary or functional features?

This is probably the most important question. Primary or functional features include how the part mounts or connects to other parts, motion that it needs to accommodate, and additional structure to support loads.

Often it is a good idea to create a special sketch as the first feature in the part that lays out the functional features. This could be as simple as a straight line to denote the bottom and a circle to represent the position and size of a mating part, or as complex as full outlines of parts and features from all three standard planes. This technique is called a *layout sketch*, and it is an important technique in both simple and complex parts. You can use layout sketches for anything from simply drawing a size-reference bounding box to creating the one point of reference for all sketched features in the part. You can use multiple layout sketches if a single sketch on one plane is not sufficient.

In what ways is the part likely to change?

When the marketing department gets out of their meeting at 4:45 pm, what changes do you need to be prepared for so that you can still be out the door by 5:00 pm? No one expects you to be able to tell the future, but you do need to model in such a way that your model easily adapts to future changes. As you gain experience with the software, and you keep this idea in mind, then you will develop some instincts for the type of modeling that you do.

What is the manufacturing method?

Modeling for the casting process is very different from modeling for the machining process. The process should be evident in your modeling. There are times when you will not know which process will be used to create the part when you start to create a model. If you are simply making an initial concept model, then you may not need to be concerned about the process. In these cases, it may or may not be possible to reuse your initial data if you need to make a detailed cast part from your non-process-specific model. Decisions like this are usually based on available time, how many changes need to be made, and a determination of the risk of making the changes versus not making the changes, as well as which decision will cost you the most time in the long run.

BEST PRACTICE As engineers, we are typically perfectionists. However, there always needs to be a balance between perfection and economy. Achieving both simultaneously is truly a rare event. Still, you should be aware that problems left by the designer for other downstream applications to solve (such as machinists, mold makers, and assemblers) also have an impact on the time and cost of the project.

The best practice in this case is a judgment call. When faced with assembling a model sloppily or remodeling it perfectly, I usually choose to remodel because doing it the second time is always faster. Also, if additional changes are required, then you do not need to struggle with the sloppily assembled model. You can easily copy sketches from one part to another, while keeping the old part open as you build the new part. As a result, you may be surprised how quickly things go.

Will there be secondary operations?

When working with any manufacturing process, some secondary processes are generally required. For example, if you have a cast part, then you may need to machine the rough surface to create a flat face in some areas. You may also need to ream or tap holes. In plastic parts, you may need to press in threaded inserts.

There are some special tools in SolidWorks that you can use to document secondary operations:

- A technique called *Configurations* in SolidWorks allows you to create different versions of a part. For example, one configuration may have the features for the secondary operations suppressed (turned off), and showing just the part as cast, while the other configuration shows the part as machined.

CROSS-REF Chapter 10 discusses configurations and feature suppression in depth.

- A technique called *Insert Part* allows you to use one SolidWorks part as the starting point for a second part. For example, the as-cast part has all of the features to make the part, but it is inserted as the first feature in the as-machined part, which adds the cuts required by the machining process.

Will there be other versions?

Sometimes there are size-based versions of parts that have to be created, or versions based on additional features. If these are fairly simple, they can also be handled with configurations, but you need to plan this flexibility in advance.

Creating a Simple Part

In this section, we build the simple part shown in Figure 5.1. While the shape is simple, the techniques used and discussed here are applicable to a wide variety of real-world parts.

FIGURE 5.1

A simple machined part

Where to start?

When you start a new part from a template and are confronted with the blank screen with only the part Origin showing, this is the question that first comes to mind. Of course, it depends on the shape and function of your part, but for the time being, you can assume that you are working with the rectangular part shown in Figure 5.1.

The first feature that you create should somehow be positioned relative to the Origin. Whether there is a corner of a rectangle that is coincident to the Origin, the rectangle is centered on the Origin, or dimensions are used to stand the rectangle off from the Origin at some distance, you need to lock the first feature in two-dimensional space to the Origin.

When working with a simple part, the entire part can be described as rectangular or cylindrical. In these cases, it is easy to know where to start: you simply draw a rectangle or a circle, respectively. On complex parts, it may not be obvious where to start, and the overall part cannot be said to have any simple shape. In cases like this, it may be best to select *the* (or *a*) prominent feature, mounting location, functional shape, or focus of the mechanism. For example, if you were to design an automobile, what would you designate as the 0,0,0 Origin? The ground may be a reasonable location, or the plane of the centers of the wheels. Much of the automotive industry uses the center of the end of the crankshaft in the engine as the assembly Origin. That may seem arbitrary, but as long as everyone working on the vehicle agrees, it is as good a location as any.

With that in mind, it seems logical to start the part shown in Figure 5.1 by sketching a rectangle. Select the Top plane, and sketch a rectangle centered on the part Origin.

Symmetry

The next decision is about part symmetry. This part is not completely symmetrical, and so modeling a quarter of it and mirroring the entire model twice is not going to be the most effective technique. Instead, you should build the part symmetrically around the Origin, and mirror individual features as appropriate. To start with this type of symmetry, you need to sketch a rectangle centered around the Origin. The centered rectangle is something that you will create frequently enough to warrant using a macro.

> **ON the CD-ROM** A macro that creates a rectangle centered on the Origin is provided on the CD-ROM in the materials for Chapter 2.

Figure 5.2 shows two common techniques for centering a rectangle on the Origin. You can use the sketch relation symbols to identify the relations that have been applied to this sketch.

FIGURE 5.2

Centering a rectangle on the Origin

TIP To make a rectangle work like a square, use an Equal sketch relation on two adjacent sides. This only requires a single dimension to drive the size of the square.

Beginning with the rectangle that you sketched in the previous section, apply one horizontal dimension (4.00 inches) and one vertical dimension (6.00 inches). The sketch is fully defined at this point because both the size and position of the rectangle have been established.

BEST PRACTICE If you are dimensioning a horizontal line, the best way to do it is to simply select the line and place the dimension. Selecting the line endpoints can also work, but selecting the vertical lines on either side of the horizontal lines is not as robust. The problem is that if you use this third method, deleting either of the vertical lines causes the dimension to also be deleted. In the first two dimensioning methods, dimensions are not deleted unless you remove one of the endpoints, which requires deleting two lines, the horizontal line, and one of the vertical lines.

Make it solid

Next, click Extrude from the Features toolbar, or click Insert ➪ Features ➪ Extruded. In the Direction 1 panel, select Mid Plane as the end condition. SolidWorks takes the distance that you entered and extrudes it symmetrically about the sketch plane. Enter 1.00 inch as the distance.

By centering the sketch on the Origin and extruding by using a Mid Plane end condition, the initial block is built symmetrically about all three standard planes, with the part Origin at the center. In many parts, this is a desirable situation. It enables you to create mirrored features using the standard planes, and also helps you to assemble parts together in an assembly later, when parts must be centered and do not have a hard face-to-face connection with other parts. Figure 5.3 shows the initial feature with the standard planes.

FIGURE 5.3

An initial extruded feature centered on the standard planes

Extrude Feature Options

The Extrude feature is one of the staples of SolidWorks modeling. Depending on the type of modeling that you do, the Extrude feature may be one of your main tools.

The Extrude interface

From

The From panel establishes where the Extrude feature starts. By default, SolidWorks extrudes from the sketch plane. Other available options are:

■ **Surface/Face/Plane:** The extrude begins from a surface body, a face of a solid, or a reference plane.

Extruding from a surface

continued

153

continued

CROSS-REF   Surface features are discussed in detail in Chapter 27.

- **Vertex:** The distance from the sketch plane to the selected vertex is treated as an offset distance.

- **Offset:** You can enter an explicit offset distance, and you can also change the direction of the offset.

Direction 1 and Direction 2

Direction 1 and Direction 2 are always separated by 180 degrees. Direction 2 becomes inactive if you select Mid Plane for the end condition of Direction 1. The arrows that display in the graphics window show a single arrow for Direction 1 and a double arrow for Direction 2. For the Blind end condition, which is described below, dragging the arrows determines the distance of the extrude.

 Each of the end conditions is affected by the Reverse Direction toggle. This toggle simply changes the default direction by 180 degrees. You need to be careful when using this feature, particularly when using the Up to end conditions, because if the entity that you are extruding up to is not in the selected direction, then an error results.

Following is a brief description of each of the available end conditions for the Extrude feature:

- **Blind**: Blind in this case means an explicit distance. The term is usually used in conjunction with holes of a specific depth, although here it is associated with a boss rather than a hole.

- **Up to Vertex**: In effect, Up to Vertex works just like the Blind end condition, except that the distance is parametrically controlled by a model vertex or sketch point.

- **Up to Surface**: Up to Surface could probably be better named *Up to Face*, because the end does not necessarily have to be an actual surface feature. This end condition may display a warning if the projection of the sketch onto the selected face extends beyond the boundary of the face. In that case, it is advisable to knit several faces together into a surface body and to use the Up to Body end condition.

- **Offset from Surface**: By default, Offset from Surface extrudes until it reaches a specified distance from a selected surface. There are two methods for determining the type of offset and one to determine direction.

  - The default offset method behaves as if the selected surface were offset radially, so that a surface with a 4-inch radius and a 1-inch offset would give a curvature on the end of the extrude of a 3-inch radius.

  - The second method, called Translate Surface, behaves as if the surface were *moved* by the offset distance.

Offset from surface using the default and Translate Surface options

■ Reverse Offset refers to when the offset stops short of the selected face or when it goes past it. These options are illustrated in the following figure.

The Reverse Offset option

continued

continued

- **Up to Body**: The Up to Body end condition is very useful in many situations, especially when receiving the error message, "The end face cannot terminate the extrusion," from the Up to Face end condition.

- **Mid Plane**: The Mid Plane end condition eliminates the Direction 2 options and divides the extrude distance equally in both directions, so that if you specify a 1.00-inch Mid Plane, then SolidWorks extrudes .50 inches in one direction and .50 inches in the other direction.

- **Through All**: The Through All end condition is available only when there is already solid geometry existing in the part. When used for an extruded boss (which adds material), it extrudes to the distance of the farthest point of the solid model in a direction perpendicular to the sketch plane. When used for a cut, it simply cuts through everything.

- **Up to Next**: Up to Next extrudes the feature until it runs into a solid face that completely intercepts the entire sketch profile. If a portion of the sketch hangs over the edge of the face, the extrude feature will keep going until it runs into a condition that matches that description, which may be the outer face of the part in the direction of the extrusion.

The Up to Next end condition used with a Cut extrude

By default, the Direction of Extrusion is normal to the sketch plane, but you can also select a linear entity such as an edge or axis as the direction. All of the end-condition options are still available when you manually define the Direction of Extrusion as something other than the default.

You can also assign a Draft option to an extrusion as it is created, and you can control the draft separately for Direction 1 and Direction 2.

BEST PRACTICE When dealing with molded or cast parts, certain types of features, such as drafts, fillets, and shells, are often the targets of users trying to assign best practices. This is partially because using drafts, fillets, and shells is very much like playing Rock, Paper, Scissors; you can never really win this game except by luck. Arranging the features in the correct order so that the model is efficient and achieves the desired results is challenging and resistant to rules that apply in most situations. It is usually best to apply draft as a separate feature rather than using it in the definition of the Extrude feature. It is also best to apply draft after most of the modeling is done, but before you apply the cosmetic fillets, and before using the shell feature.

Thin Feature

The Thin Feature panel is activated by default when you try to extrude an open loop sketch (a sketch that does not fully enclose an area). The end-condition options remain the same, but what changes is that the feature applies a thickness to the sketch elements, in the manner of a sheet metal, thin-walled plastic part, or a rib. The Thin Feature panel of the Extrude PropertyManager, along with a representative thin feature extrusion, is shown in the following figure.

The Cap Ends option is available only when you specify a Thin Feature to be created from a closed loop sketch. This creates a hollow, solid body in a single step.

You can also use Thin Features with cuts, and they are very useful for creating slots or grooves.

The Thin Feature panel, and a thin feature extrusion

Contour Selection

SolidWorks works best when the sketches are neat and clean, when nothing overlaps, and there are no extra entities on closed loops. However, when you need to use a sketch that does not meet these parameters, you can use an alternative method called Contour Selection.

Contour Selection enables you to select enclosed areas to be used for features, regardless of how many normal sketch rules the rest of the sketch violates.

BEST PRACTICE It is my opinion that this feature was introduced into SolidWorks only to keep up with other CAD packages, not because it is a great feature. I do not recommend using Contour Selection on production parts. It is useful for creating quick models, but the selection is too unstable for any data that you may want to rely on in the future. The main problem is that if the sketch changes, the selected area may also change, or SolidWorks may lose track of it entirely.

Making the groove

The next modeling step is to create a groove on the back of the part. How is this feature going to be made? You can use several techniques to create this geometry. List as many techniques as you can think of, whether or not you know how to use them. Later, we will sort through which techniques work and which do not.

> **TIP**   One of the secrets to success with SolidWorks, or indeed any tool-based process, is to know several ways to accomplish any given task. By working through this exercise, you gain problem-solving skills as well as the ability to improvise when the textbook method fails.

FIGURE 5.4

Methods for creating the groove

In Figure 5.4, the first image shows a nested loop sketch, with one closed loop inside another. This technique cuts away the material between the loops. The second image shows a swept cut, with a path for the cut and a cross-section. The third image shows a Thin Feature cut, with only the centerline of the groove used as a sketch. Another option could include a large pocket being cut out, with a boss adding material back in the middle.

Relative size or direct dimensions?

Of these methods, the Thin Feature cut is the simplest and most direct because the sketch is easiest to create and control. The sketch for this feature is simply a rectangle. In this case, it makes sense to use sketch fillets to round the corners rather than fillet features. There are a few ways to create the rectangle, and the method that you choose depends on the design intent. For example, although the rectangle needs to remain centered and symmetrical, you also have to consider which is the more important aspect: the size of the groove or the overall size of the part? If the size of the part is more important than the size of the groove, then it might be best to create the groove as an offset of the outer shape of the block, rather than driving its dimensions independently. To summarize, the groove dimensions are driven by the overall shape of the block.

To create a groove, you can create a rectangle by offsetting the block shape, and use sketch fillets to round the corners.

Creating the offset

There is one more thing to consider before you create the sketch. What should you use to create the offset: the actual block edges or the original sketch? The answer to this is a Best Practice type issue.

BEST PRACTICE When creating relations that need to adapt to the biggest range of changes to the model, it is best to go as far back in the model history as you can to pick up those relations. In most cases, this means creating relations to sketches rather than to edges of the model. Model edges can be fickle, with the use of fillets, chamfers, and drafts.

This best practice tip will become more significant the first time you create a feature built from model edges, and then make changes that break relations.

To create the offset for your part, follow these steps:

1. Open a sketch on the face of the part. To create the offset, expand the Extrude feature by clicking the plus icon next to it in the FeatureManager so that you can see the sketch. Regardless of how it displays here, this sketch appears before the extrude in the part history. RMB click the sketch and select Show.

TIP You can view individual sketches and reference geometry entities such as planes from the RMB menu. However, the global settings for the visibility of these items are found in the View menu. You can access these items faster by using the View toolbar, or by linking the commands to hotkeys.

2. Next, RMB click the sketch in the graphics window and click Select Chain. This selects any non-construction, end-to-end sketch entities. Click Offset Entities on the Sketch toolbar. Offset to the inside by .400 inches. Apply .500-inch sketch fillets to each of the corners.

3. Click Extruded Cut on the Feature toolbar. By default, the extruded cut will cut away everything inside the closed profile of the sketch. Look down the FeatureManager window and click the check box on the top bar of the Thin Feature panel. Make the cut Blind, .100 inch. The Thin Feature type should be set to Mid Plane with a width of .400 inches. The PropertyManager and graphics window should look like Figure 5.5.

FIGURE 5.5

Using the Groove feature

Sketch techniques

Although the next two features could be more easily and efficiently created by using a cut, I will create them as two extrudes. The main point here is to show some useful sketch techniques, rather than optimum efficiency. Begin with the part from the previous section and follow these steps:

1. Open a new sketch on the large face opposite from the groove. Draw a rectangle picking up the automatic coincident relation to one corner and then dragging across the part and picking up another coincident to the edge on the opposite side. Figure 5.6 shows the rectangle before and after this edit.

TIP If you want to continue using the recommended best practice mentioned earlier of making relations to sketches rather than model edges, here are a few tips. In some situations (such as the current one) the sketch plane is offset from the sketch that you want to make relations to, and so the best bet is to use the Normal To view. The next obstacle is making sure that automatic relations pick up the sketch rather than the edge, and so you can use the Selection Filter to only select sketch entities.

2. Delete the Horizontal relation on the line that is not lined up with an edge. This enables you to drag it to an angle or apply the dimensions shown.

   You can delete the Horizontal relation by selecting the icon on the screen. As a reminder, you can show and hide the sketch relation icons from the View menu. You can check to ensure that the relations were created to the sketch rather than the model edges by clicking the Display/Delete Relations button on the Sketch toolbar, clicking the relation icon to check, and expanding the Entities panel in the PropertyManager. The Entities box shows where the relation is attached to, as shown in Figure 5.7. In this case, it is a point in Sketch1. Without custom programming, there is no way to identify items in a sketch by name, but you already know which point it is; you just needed to know whether it was in the sketch or on the model.

FIGURE 5.6

Edits to a rectangle

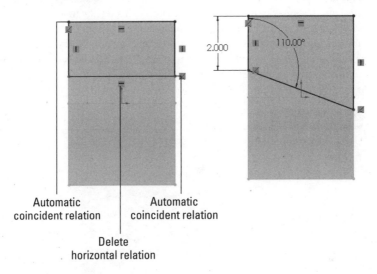

Automatic coincident relation

Automatic coincident relation

Delete horizontal relation

FIGURE 5.7

The Display/Delete Relations dialog box

3. The second sketch trick involves the use of a setting. Before you try this, go to Tools ⇨ Options ⇨ Sketch, and ensure that Prompt To Close Sketch is turned on; then click OK to close the dialog box.

4. Open another new sketch on the same face that was used by the last extrusion. Draw an angled line across the left and bottom sides of the box, with the dimensions shown in Figure 5.8. In this case, in order for this technique to work, the endpoints of the line have to be coincident with the model edges rather than the sketch entities.

This line by itself constitutes an open sketch profile, meaning that it does not enclose an area, and has unshared endpoints. Ordinarily, this results in a Thin Feature, as described earlier, but when the endpoints are coincident with model edges that form a closed loop, and the setting mentioned previously is turned on, SolidWorks automatically gives you the option of using the model edges to close the sketch. This saves several steps when compared to selecting, converting, and trimming manually.

FIGURE 5.8

Using the prompt to close a sketch setting

5. Click the Extrude tool on the Features toolbar. Answer Yes to the prompt, and double-click the face of the previous extrusion. SolidWorks automatically uses the face that you double-clicked for an Up to Surface end condition. This is a simple way of linking the depths of the two extrusions automatically. Again, this entire operation could have been handled more quickly and efficiently with a cut, but these demonstrate an alternative method which in some situations may be useful.

Hole Wizard

The next features that you will apply are a pair of counterbored holes. SolidWorks has a special tool that you can use to create common hole types, called the Hole Wizard. The Hole Wizard is a tool that helps you to create standard hole types using standard or custom sizes. You can place holes on any face of a 3D model or constrain them to a single 2D plane or face. A single feature created by the Hole Wizard may create a single or multiple holes, and a feature that is not constrained to a single plane can create individual holes originating from multiple faces, non-parallel, and even non-planar faces (holes may go in different directions). All holes in a single feature that you create by using the Hole Wizard must be the same type and size. If you want multiple sizes or types, then you must create multiple features.

Hole Wizard: Using 2D versus 3D Sketches

Hole Wizard holes use either a 2D or a 3D sketch for the placement of the hole centers. You can define the centers by simply placing and dimensioning sketch points. The 3D sketch type is used by default, with the 2D sketch type only being used when you select a planar face *prior* to clicking the Hole Wizard tool.

Because the 3D placement of holes seems so much more flexible, why would anyone want to use the 2D placement method? 3D sketches have several limitations with respect to dimensioning and sketch relations. Recent releases of SolidWorks have added relations such as Midpoint and Equal to 3D sketches, which are an improvement over previous versions, but still do not make the 3D sketch as usable as a 2D sketch in the end.

CROSS-REF Three-dimensional sketches are discussed in Chapters 17 and 31. Chapter 17 also gives a more detailed description of the Hole Wizard. Chapter 22 has additional information on the display of threads.

The following image shows a part with various types of holes created by the Hole Wizard, including counterbored, countersunk, drilled, tapped, and pipe-tapped holes. The part is shown in section view for clarity. The drilled hole is not shown in the figure.

Countersunk   Counterbored

Tapped   Pipe tap

Holes created by the Hole Wizard

To apply counterbored holes to your part, follow these steps:

1. Select the face that the groove feature was created on, and click the Hole Wizard tool on the Features toolbar. Then set the hole to Counterbored, set the type to Socket Head Cap Screw, the size to one-quarter, and the end condition to Through All, as shown in Figure 5.9.

FIGURE 5.9

The Hole Wizard Hole Specification interface

2. Next, click to select the Positions tab at the top of the PropertyManager. This is where you place the centerpoints of the holes using sketch points. It is often useful to create construction geometry to help line up and place the sketch points.

CAUTION   When you select a face to create a 2D Hole Wizard hole, SolidWorks always creates a sketch point at the location where you selected the planar face, and then activates the Point sketch tool. If you click anywhere in the graphics window with the Point tool active, you place additional points, which are used to create additional holes. If those points are off of the solid model, then they may cause errors. To exit the Point tool, just press Esc.

3. Draw two construction lines, horizontally across the part, with Coincident relations to each side. Select both lines and give them an Equal relation. The point of this step is to evenly space holes across the part without dimensions or equations.

> **TIP** Although several methods exist to make multiple selections, a box or window selection technique may be useful in this situation. If the box is dragged from left to right, then only the items completely within the box are selected. If the box is dragged from right to left, then any item that is at least partially in the box is selected.

> **TIP** SolidWorks displays an error if you try to place a sketch point where there is an existing sketch entity endpoint. If you build construction geometry in a sketch and want to place a sketch point at the end of a sketch entity, then you have to create the sketch point to the side where it does not pick up other incompatible automatic sketch relations, and then drag it onto the endpoint.

4. Place sketch points at the midpoint of each of the construction lines. If there is another sketch point other than the two that you want to make into actual holes, then delete the extra points. Dimension one of the lines down from the top of the part, as shown in Figure 5.10. All of the sketch relation icons display for reference. Click OK to accept the feature once you are happy with all of the settings, locations, relations, and dimensions.

FIGURE 5.10

Placing the centerpoints of holes

Cutting a slot

The Hole Wizard does not specifically allow you to cut slots, nor is there a Slot feature. However, you can use one of the following methods to cut a slot:

- **Explicitly drawing the slot**: Draw a line, press A to switch to the Tangent Arc tool, draw the tangent arc, press A to switch back to the Line tool, and so on. Although you can press the A key to toggle between the line and arc functions, you can also toggle between a line and a tangent arc by returning the cursor to the line/arc first point.

- **Rectangle and arcs**: Draw a rectangle, place a tangent arc on both ends, and then turn the ends of the rectangle into construction entities.

- **Thin Feature cut**: As you did earlier with the groove, you can also create a Thin Feature slot, although you need to follow additional steps to create rounded ends on it.

- **Offset in Sketch**: By drawing a line, and using the Offset with Bi-directional, Make Base Construction, and Cap Ends settings, it is easy to create a slot from any shape by drawing only the centerline of the slot.

- **Library feature**: A library feature can be stored and can contain either simple sketches or more complex sets of combined features. The library feature is a good option for the counterbored slot used in this example. Library features are discussed in depth in Chapter 19.

To cut slots in your part, follow these steps:

1. In this case, use the Offset in Sketch option. Draw a line that represents the centerline of the slot, and use the sketch offset to create the rest of the sketch. Draw the line such that it is symmetrical about the Origin, using a construction line that is coincident to the Origin on one end and that has a Midpoint relation to the line to be offset on the other end.

2. Use an offset distance of .219 inches — as shown in Figure 5.11 — which is half of the counterbore diameter that is used in the Hole Wizard holes. From this sketch, create an extruded cut that extrudes up to the surface of the counterbore in the holes.

3. The through hole for the counterbored slot is also a slot, and so you can use the same technique. Open a sketch on the bottom of the previous slot, and draw a line that picks up automatic relations to the centers of the two rounded ends for the slot.

   When you have drawn this line, use the Sketch Offset as before, and apply the Through All end condition to the cut.

TIP   Picking up these relations automatically may seem difficult at first, but with some practice, it becomes automatic. When trying to find the center of an arc, the centerpoint is usually displayed and is easy to select. However, when making a relation to an edge, the centerpoint does not display by default. To display it, hold the cursor over the arc edge for a few seconds; a marker that resembles a plus sign inside a circle will show you where the center is, thus allowing you to select it with a sketch tool and pick up the automatic relations.

FIGURE 5.11

Creating a slot

In Figure 5.12, the first centerpoint has already been referenced, and the cursor is trying to find the centerpoint of the other end of the slot.

FIGURE 5.12

Applying automatic relations to a circular edge

Fillets and chamfers

Several chapters could be written just about fillet types, techniques, and strategies in SolidWorks. Chapter 7 deals with more complex fillet types.

As mentioned earlier, it is considered a best practice to avoid sketch fillets when possible, using feature fillets instead. Another best practice guideline is to put fillets at the bottom of the design tree, or at least after all of the functional features. You should not dimension sketches to model edges created by fillets unless there are no better methods available. There are too many ways, and reasons, to change sketches to make other features, especially important features, dependent on them.

Do not dimension sketches to model edges that are created by fillets. While the previous best practice about relations to sketch entities instead of model edges was a mild warning, you must heed this one more carefully.

To add fillets and chamfers to your part, follow these steps:

1. Initiate a Fillet feature, and select the four short edges on the part. Set the radius value to .600 inches. Click OK to accept the Fillet feature.

TIP When selecting edges around a four-sided part, the first three edges are usually visible and the fourth edge is not. You can select invisible edges by expanding the Fillet Options panel of the Fillet PropertyManager, and selecting the Select Through Faces option. When you have a complex part with a lot of hidden edges, this setting can be bothersome, but in simple cases like this, it is useful. Figure 5.13 shows this option in action.

FIGURE 5.13

Selecting an edge through model faces

2. Apply chamfers to the edges of the angled slot through the part, as indicated in Figure 5.14. Make the chamfers .050 inches by 45 degrees.

Chamfers observe many of the same best practices as fillets.

TIP Feature order is important with features like chamfers and fillets because of how they both tend to propagate around tangent edges. Although you can turn this setting off for both types of feature, it is best to get the correct geometry by applying the features in order.

CROSS-REF   The Fillet Xpert, which helps you to manage large numbers of overlapping fillets by automatically sorting through feature order issues, is discussed in detail in Chapter 27.

3. Select the four edges that are indicated for fillets in Figure 5.14. Apply .050-inch-radius fillets.

4. Apply a last set of .050-inch chamfers to the back side of the counterbores and slot.

FIGURE 5.14

Edges for Fillet and Chamfer features

Chamfer edges   Fillet edges   Select to chamfer

The finished part is simple, but you have learned many useful techniques along the way. In the rest of this chapter, you will put the part together with other parts to form an assembly, and then create a quick 2D drawing of the part and the assembly to document the design.

Tutorial: Creating a Simple Assembly

Up to this point, you have been learning about how to create geometry, or parts. Assemblies involve organizing that geometrical data to represent real products or parts of products. Assemblies can be complex or simple. They can be structured in a single level or use many subassemblies. Assemblies can be static or allow Dynamic Assembly Motion. Relationships in the assembly can also drive part geometry.

This part of this chapter serves as an introduction to some of the basic functions and main features of assemblies. Because all of the geometry creation is done in the part document, most of what goes on in the assembly document has to do with organizing that geometry in space.

CROSS-REF Chapters 12 to 16 discuss various aspects of assemblies in greater detail.

The following pages describe common techniques that are used in assemblies. The part created earlier in this chapter is assembled with some additional parts that have already been created. The main point here is to give you a basic understanding of the assembly functions that exist and how they work, before exploring various aspects of the software in greater detail in Part II. To create a simple assembly, follow these steps:

ON the CD-ROM This tutorial uses parts called Chapter5Frame.sldprt and Chapter5Screw.sldprt from the CD-ROM, in the material for Chapter 5.

1. From the CD-ROM, open the part named Chapter5Frame.sldprt. With the part open, click the Make Assembly From Part button on the Standard toolbar. If you have not made a custom template for assemblies, use the default assembly template that installed with SolidWorks. Move the cursor to the assembly Origin, where the cursor changes to indicate that the part Origin will be lined up with the assembly Origin. If the Origin is not visible on the screen, use the View, Origins menu selection to turn it on.

   The first part that you insert into an assembly has a Fixed constraint applied to it. This constraint is indicated by the (f) in front of the name of the part in the FeatureManager. Figure 5.15 shows the placement preview and cursor from step 1, as well as the FeatureManager after the part has been added.

FIGURE 5.15

Placing a part in a new assembly

CROSS-REF The Frame part is a weldment. Weldments are discussed in detail in Chapters 31, 32, and 33. They are made of multiple bodies within a single part file. Multiple bodies are discussed in detail in Chapter 26.

2. Open the part that you created in the previous tutorial. If you do not have it, then you can open a pre-built copy from the CD-ROM materials for Chapter 5. Once you open the part, change to the assembly window.

You can press Ctrl+Tab to change between open documents, and Alt+Tab to change between open applications. These are Windows conventions that are not exclusive to SolidWorks.

3. From the assembly menus, click Insert ⇨ Component ⇨ Existing Part/Assembly. This displays the PropertyManager, as shown in Figure 5.16. Select the machined part from the selection box and click in an open space in the graphics window to place it.

Newly placed parts in the assembly (except for the very first part) are completely undefined in terms of position or location. Instead of the (f) symbol, for Fixed, the newly placed part displays a (-) symbol, which means Underdefined. You can change a Fixed part to underdefined by selecting Float in the RMB menu. Figure 5.16 also shows the FeatureManager with the new part in it. It is a little confusing that (f) stands for Fixed when the opposite condition, Float, also starts with an f.

FIGURE 5.16

The Insert Component interface

 Parts in an assembly are positioned relative to one another with mates. Mates are in many ways similar to sketch relations.

4. Click the Mate button from the Assembly toolbar. The mate options that are not grayed out are available with the current selection. For example, in Figure 5.17, the corresponding faces of the weldment and the machined part are selected, and these faces can be mated coincident, parallel, perpendicular, at a distance, or at an angle.

FIGURE 5.17

Mate options

 TIP You can move a part in an assembly by clicking the part and dragging it with the LMB (left mouse button). It follows whatever mates you have applied to it. To rotate a part that does not have any mates applied to it, drag the part with the RMB. The MMB still rotates the view.

5. Select the Coincident mate, and then the faces as shown in the figure. If the machined part is turned as it is in Figure 5.17 (so that it interferes with the welded frame if the selected surfaces touch), then click the Flip Mate Alignment button on the popup toolbar or toggle the Mate Alignment buttons in the PropertyManager. Close the popup toolbar by clicking the green check mark icon.

BEST PRACTICE In contrast to sketch relations, most assembly mates have alignment orientation. Flat faces can be coincident in one of two orientations separated by 180 degrees. The same is true of concentric relations, as well as others. SolidWorks orients a part to the closest orientation that works. This means that it is often best to pre-position a part so that it picks up the correct mate orientation. This usually involves some combination of rotating the view and rotating the part.

6. Select the top angled face of the angled frame member and the corresponding flat face of the machined part. Make these faces coincident. In this case, the parts are already in the correct orientation, and so there is no need to pre-position them. Click the green check mark icon to accept the mate.

7. One more mate is required to fully define the position of the machined part. Drag the part and verify that it slides up and down the angled weldment member. Find the two tapped holes in the weldment and slide the machined part so that the holes appear in the counterbored slot. Ideally the holes should be symmetrical with the part, but the slot was created to allow room for adjustment.

172

8. Expand the machined part in the FeatureManager and select its Front plane. From the View menu, turn on the display of temporary axes, and Ctrl-select the temporary axes in the centers of the threaded holes in the frame, as shown in Figure 5.18. Select the Symmetric mate on the Advanced Mates panel. Turn off the display of temporary axes when the mate is complete.

FIGURE 5.18

Creating a Symmetric mate

Front Plane

Temporary axes

9. Through the menus or Assembly toolbar, click Insert Component, and use the Browse button to find the existing Chapter5Screw.sldprt part on the CD-ROM, or on your hard drive if you have copied it there.

10. Notice that this part behaves differently in certain situations. For example, when the cursor is over empty space, it is attached to the centroid of the part, but when the cursor is over a flat or cylindrical face, the part snaps to that face. This is because the part uses a Mate Reference, enabling planar and cylindrical faces to automatically get Coincident and/or Concentric mates when the part is dropped on them.

11. Make sure that the Pushpin feature is activated in the Insert Component PropertyManager, and then drop the part at the bottom of each counterbored hole. The part will automatically get Concentric and Coincident mates. Figure 5.19 illustrates the location where you should drop the part. Click OK to accept the part placement.

FIGURE 5.19

Using a Mate Reference

12. You need to place two more screws in the assembly, but these ones cannot be automatically mated; you need to do this manually. Copy two instances of the screws. To copy a screw, Ctrl-drag the part either from the graphics window or from the FeatureManager and drop it into the graphics window.

13. Position the part and the view so that you can see the cylindrical body of the screw and the cylindrical face of the threaded hole in the C-channel. With the Mate function active, select both faces and click OK. Click the other pair of mating faces and click OK again.

14. Now click the underside of the screw head and the counterbored surface of the slot, make sure that they will be coincident, and click OK.

15. Save and close the assembly.

This is a quick overview of the basic assemblies' functionality, which is expanded on in later chapters.

Tutorial: Making a Simple Drawing

If you are coming to SolidWorks from a dedicated 2D software, you will be creating drawings very differently from what you may be used to. In 2D design software, you draw each view individually, and when a change occurs, you have to go back through the views and ensure that each view is updated appropriately. In 2D, views are sometimes created sparingly because they are difficult to create and to update. This includes view types such as Isometric views, complex sections, and views projected at non-orthogonal angles.

In SolidWorks, drawing views are almost free, being simply projected from the 3D model. Updates are made in the model, and all views update automatically from there. You can handle dimensions in a couple of ways, either using the dimensions that you used to create the model, or placing new dimensions on the drawing (best practice for modeling is not necessarily the same as best practice for manufacturing drawings). To make a simple drawing, follow these steps:

1. Press the New button from the Standard toolbar, or click File ➪ New. From the New SolidWorks Document window, select the Drawing template. The template contains all of the document-specific settings.

2. After selecting the drawing template, the Sheet Format/Size dialog box displays, as shown in Figure 5.20. Select the D-Landscape sheet size, as well as the format that automatically associates with that sheet size, and click OK. If the Model View PropertyManager appears, click the red X icon to exit.

FIGURE 5.20

The Sheet Format/Size dialog box

Paper size

Use this for custom size paper

Border and associated text

Turn this off if you want a blank drawing sheet

3. Before creating any views on the drawing, set up some fields in the format to be filled out automatically when you bring the part into the drawing. RMB click anywhere on the drawing sheet (on the paper), and select Edit Sheet Format.

4. Zoom in to the lower right-hand corner of the drawing. Notice that there are several variables with the format $PRPSHEET:{Description}. These are annotations that are linked to custom properties. Some of them have properties with values (such as the Scale note), and some of the properties do not have values (such as the Description).

Sheet versus Format

With new and even experienced users, there is some confusion around the Sheet versus Sheet Format issue. Part of the confusion is due to SolidWorks terminology. SolidWorks names the two items Sheet and Sheet Format. In this book, I simply use the terms *Sheet* and *Format*, to avoid linking the two items with a common first name. It would be better yet if *Format* were changed to *Border* or *Title Block* so that the name more closely matched the function. (The confusion goes deeper for long-time users because there was a time around SolidWorks 98 when Templates as we know them did not exist, and what is now called the Format was called the Template, which is why templates have the file extension *.slddrt [DRawing Template]).

In a SolidWorks drawing, you are either editing the sheet or the format. When editing the sheet, you can perform actions such as view, move, and create views, but you cannot select, move, or edit the lines and text of the drawing border. When editing the format, you can edit the lines and text that make up the drawing border, but the drawing views disappear.

Often, users save a template that already uses a format, and save themselves some time by selecting everything all at once when they first select the drawing template for a new drawing.

While you cannot change templates after you create a document, you can swap formats, and change sheet sizes.

5. Add an annotation in the Drawn row, in the Date column. You can add annotations by clicking Insert ➪ Annotations ➪ Note, or by activating the Annotations toolbar in the CommandManager and clicking the Note button. Type today's date as the text of the note.

CAUTION If you are using a SolidWorks default template and a circle appears around your note, then use the Text Format PropertyManager that appears when you are creating a note, expand the Border panel, and change the Circle option to None.

6. Add another note, this time to the Name column. Do not type anything in the note, but use the Link to Properties button in the Note PropertyManager to create a link to a custom property. In the Link to Property dialog box, click the Model in View Specified option in Sheet Properties. Type **user** in the drop-down text box below the option. This now accesses a custom property in a part or assembly that is put onto this drawing and called "user," and will put the value where the note is placed.

7. To return to Edit Sheet mode (out of Edit Format mode), select Edit Sheet from the RMB menu. A little text reminder message appears in the lower-right corner on the status bar, to indicate whether you are editing the Sheet or the Format.

8. From the Drawings toolbar, select the Standard 3 View button, or through the menus, click Insert ➪ Drawing View ➪ Standard 3 View. If the Chapter5SimpleMachinedPart document does not appear in the list box in the PropertyManager, then use the Browse button to select it. When you click the OK button, the three drawing views are created.

9. Drawing views can be sized individually or for each sheet. The Sheet Properties dialog box in Figure 5.21 shows the sheet scale. If this is changed, all of the views on the sheet that use the sheet scale are updated. If you select a view and activate the Drawing View PropertyManager, you can use the Scale panel to toggle from Use Sheet Scale to Use Custom Scale.

CAUTION In the United States, drawings are traditionally made and understood using the Third Angle Projection, which is the ANSI standard. In Europe, drawings typically use First Angle Projection, which is the ISO standard. If you are not careful about making and reading your drawings, then you could make a serious mistake. There are times when in the United States, the SolidWorks software will install with ISO standard templates, which will project views using First Angle Projection.

When using a template that you are unfamiliar with, it is a good idea to check the projection method. To do this, RMB click the drawing sheet and select Sheet Properties. The Type of Projection setting appears in the top middle of the dialog box, as shown in Figure 5.21. This dialog box looks similar to the Sheet Format/Size dialog box, but it has some additional options, including the projection type.

FIGURE 5.21

First-angle versus third-angle projections

10. To create an Isometric view, activate the Drawings toolbar in the CommandManager, and click the Projected View button. Then select one of the existing views, and move the cursor at a 45-degree angle. If you cannot place the view where you would like it to go, then press the Ctrl key to break the alignment, and place the view where you want it.

11. You can change the appearance of the drawing view in several ways.

   ■ **View ➪ Display ➪ Tangent Edges with Font** uses phantom line type for any edge between tangent faces.

   ■ **View ➪ Display ➪ Tangent Edges Removed** completely removes any tangent edges. This is not recommended, especially for parts with a lot of filleted edges, because it generally displays just the outline of the part.

   ■ **Shaded** or **Wireframe** modes can be used on drawings, accessed from the View toolbar.

   ■ **Perspective** views must be saved in the model as a named view and placed in the drawing using the view name.

   ■ **RealView** drawing views are not available on a drawing except by capturing a screen shot from the model and placing this screen shot in a drawing. The same applies to PhotoWorks renderings.

12. Look at the custom properties that you created in the title block. The date is there because you entered a specific value for it, but the Name field is not filled in. This is because there is no User property in the part. RMB click the part in one of the views and select Open Part. In the part window, click File ➪ Properties, and in the Property Name column, type the property name **user**, with a value of your initials, or however your company identifies people on drawings. The Properties dialog box, also called Summary Information, is shown in part in Figure 5.22.

FIGURE 5.22

The Custom Properties entry table

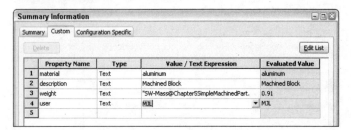

CROSS-REF When used in models and formats, Custom Properties are an extremely powerful combination, especially when you want to automatically fill in data in the format, in a BOM, or a PDM product. These topics are discussed in more detail in Chapters 20 and 24.

13. When you flip back to the drawing (using Ctrl+Tab), the Name column now contains the value of your initials.

14. Click the Section View button on the Drawings toolbar. This activates the Line command so that you can draw a section line in a view. When sketching, a line can go either on the Sheet or in a view. This is similar to the distinction between the Sheet and the Format. To make a section view, the section line sketch must be in the view. You will know that you are sketching in a view when a pink border appears around the view. You may also use Lock View Focus from the RMB menu to manually control the view.

15. Bring the cursor down to the circular edge of the slot to activate the center point of the arc. Once the center point is active, you can use the dotted inference lines to ensure that you are lined up with the center. Another option is to manually create sketch relations. Turning on temporary axes displays center marks in the centers of arcs and circles. Figure 5.23 shows the technique with the inference lines being used. Draw the section line through the slot, and then place the section view.

FIGURE 5.23

Creating a section view

SECTION B-B

16. As mentioned earlier, you can use two fundamentally different methods for dimensioning drawings:

   ▪ **Model Items** imports the dimensions used to build the SolidWorks model and uses them on the drawing. These dimensions are *bi-directionally associative*, meaning that changing them on the drawing updates the model, and changing them on the model updates them in the drawing. On the surface of things, this sounds too good to be true, and it is. The potential problems are that you might not model things the way you would dimension them for the shop. You have to answer several questions for yourself such as do the leader lines go to the right locations or can they be moved and the dimensions usually come in in such a way that they require quite a bit of moving them around.

■ **Reference (driven) Dimensions** can be applied to the drawing view directly. These are only associative in one direction, meaning that they measure what is there, but they do not drive the size or position of the geometry. All changes must be made from the model. Again, on the face of things, this appears to be redundant and a waste of time, but in my personal estimation, by the time you finish rearranging dimensions, checking to ensure that you have everything you need, and hiding the extraneous dimensions, you are usually far better off using reference dimensions.

BEST PRACTICE   Users have strong opinions on both sides of this issue. The best thing for you to do is to use both methods and decide for yourself.

17. If you choose to use the Model Items approach, you can do this by clicking Insert ➪ Model Items. Then specify whether the dimensions should come from the entire model or just a selected feature. You also need to ask whether the dimensions should come into all views or just the selected one, and whether you want just a certain type of dimension, annotation, or reference geometry.

18. Once the dimensions are brought in, you need to move some of them from one view to another, which you can do by Shift-dragging the dimension from the old location to the new location. Ctrl-dragging predictably copies the dimension. You can move views by dragging an edge in the view.

Summary

Part I, "SolidWorks Basics," has laid the foundation for the more detailed information that will follow. In the chapters in Part I, I have tried to give recommendations and answer questions that help you to develop an intuition for how SolidWorks software operates, which is the most crucial kind of knowledge when troubleshooting a modeling or editing problem.

This chapter has glossed over many of the important details in order to give you a quick overview of the basic functionality in SolidWorks for the three main data types: Parts, Assemblies, and Drawings. From here, Part II, "Building Intelligence into Your Parts," discusses in more detail how you can accomplish parametric design in SolidWorks.

Part II

Building Intelligence into Your Parts

Getting More from Your Sketches

Design work would be so much nicer if you could only start with a clean screen every time. Unfortunately, this is rarely the case. Design turns out to be mainly about change. For example, when it comes to sketches, you draw the sketch once, and then you change it several times. Rarely are you able to do something fresh. Because you will spend more time editing than drawing completely new sketches, it makes sense to focus on learning how to edit them.

In addition to editing sketches, this chapter covers sketch tools such as sketch pictures, which you can use for tracing; sketch text; and colors and line fonts, which you can use to make reference sketch entities distinguishable from other model elements.

Editing Sketch Relations

When I was teaching SolidWorks reseller classes, I frequently told my classes, "Delete is not an edit option." You will find that this is good advice. There are times to use the Delete command, but you should use it only when it is really necessary. In my own work, I sometimes go to extreme lengths to avoid deleting sketch entities, just to stay in practice.

The main reason for not deleting sketch entities is that when you are editing a sketch that has other features that are dependent on it, the dependent features may lose their references, or *go dangling*. Because of this, even when you can use the Delete command instead of editing, it is still a good practice to edit instead. Deleting relations is not as critical as deleting sketch entities, unless the relations are referenced by equations or design tables.

Display/Delete relations

 Display/Delete Relations is your primary tool when dealing with sketch relations. It is particularly useful to sort relations by the various categories that are shown in Figure 6.1.

Sketch relations in the Display/Delete Relations dialog box can be divided into the following categories:

■ **All in This Sketch:** Shows all of the relations in the active sketch.

■ **Dangling:** Shows only the dangling relations. Dangling relations appear in a brownish-green or olive color, and represent relations that have lost one of the entities that drives the relation. You can repair dangling relations by selecting the entity with the dangling relation, and then dragging the red dot onto the entity to which it should have the relation.

■ **Overdefining/Not Solved:** Overdefined relations are any set of conflicting or redundant instructions that are given to a sketch entity, and appear in red. For example, if a line is collinear with an edge and also vertical, but the edge itself is not vertical, then both the collinear and vertical relations appear in red.

FIGURE 6.1

The Display/Delete Relations PropertyManager

The Not Solved condition often accompanies Overdefined. Not Solved typically refers to a dimension or relation that cannot be applied because of the conflict. The lower-right corner of the screen and the status bar show flags warning that the sketch is overdefined, as shown in Figure 6.2.

FIGURE 6.2

An overdefined sketch

When an overdefined situation exists, all of the relations and dimensions in a sketch may often become overdefined. This can look like a daunting task to repair, when the entire problem is caused by a single relation. Do not automatically delete everything. Instead, try deleting or suppressing the last dimension or relation that was added. You can suppress a dimension by setting it to Driven in the RMB (right-mouse button) menu, and you can suppress relations in the Display/Delete Relations PropertyManager.

- **External:** External relations connect with an entity outside the active sketch. This includes the part Origin, or any model edges. The term *external relations* is also sometimes meant to signify any relations outside of the part.

- **Defined in Context:** Any relation between parts in an assembly is considered an in-context relation.

- **Locked:** External relations (outside the part) may be locked or broken to increase speed and to lock out changes.

- **Broken:** See Locked.

- **Selected Entities:** Sketch relations are shown only for the selected sketch entities.

CROSS-REF In-context design, also called *top-down*, as well as locked and broken relations, are covered in detail in Chapter 16.

CAUTION Some of the relations listed in the Display/Delete Relations dialog box may be colored to signify the state of the relation. Unfortunately, colored relations are typically placed at the top of the list to attract attention, but when you select them, they are always a dark blue, and so the advantage of color-coding is defeated. The only way around this is to select a relation other than the first one in the list. If there is only one relation in the list, you cannot see the state color.

A setting in Tools, Options controls the display of errors. You can select Tools ⇨ Options ⇨ FeatureManager to find an option called Display Warnings, where you can choose Always, Never, and All but Top Level. When a sketch contains sketch relations with errors, they display as warning signs on the sketch, and will propagate to the top level of a part or assembly if you have chosen the Always option.

SketchXpert

The SketchXpert, shown in Figure 6.3, can help you to diagnose and repair complex sketch relation problems. The Diagnose button at the top creates several possible solutions that you can toggle through using the forward and backward arrow buttons in the Results panel. The Manual Repair button displays all of the relations with errors in a window and allows you to delete them manually.

FIGURE 6.3

The SketchXpert dialog box

By selecting the option at the very bottom of the dialog box, you can make the SketchXpert display any time that a sketch error occurs. To display the SketchXpert manually instead of automatically, you can access it by RMB clicking in a sketch.

Copying and Moving Sketch Entities

SolidWorks offers several different tools to help you move sketch entities around in a sketch. In SolidWorks, it is usually recommended to keep the sketch as simple as you can, and to create patterns using feature patterns rather than sketch patterns. The following section discusses the main tools for moving and copying sketch entities.

Move entities

 Move entities enables you to move selected sketch entities by either selecting From and To points, or by typing in XY coordinates for the move. This entity detaches segments whose endpoints are merged, as shown in Figure 6.4. All of these tools have a pushpin icon in the interface, which allows you to use them many times when the pushpin icon is pushed in; they are deactivated after one use if the pushpin icon is not pushed in.

FIGURE 6.4

Using move entities

Rotate entities

 Rotate entities rotates selected entities in a sketch in the same way that Move entities works. You can drag the angle or type it in manually. The green check mark icon is on the RMB, as shown in the cursor display in Figure 6.5.

187

FIGURE 6.5

Using the Rotate entities feature

The Keep Relations option does not actually keep any relations — it deletes the Horizontal and Vertical relations in the sketch, as shown in Figure 6.5 — but it does keep the merged endpoints, as shown in the right-most image of Figure 6.5. This can be useful, especially considering how many sketch relations it would take to make a sketch move like this naturally.

Copy entities

 The Copy Entities tool works exactly like the Move Entities tool, except that it copies instead of moving.

Scale entities

 Scale entities is one of those functions that is probably best left alone. This is because the results appear erratic and unpredictable, particularly if there are dimensions on the sketch. This tool works on a selection of entities, particularly on an isolated selection that is not connected to other entities in the sketch. The PropertyManager for the Scale Entities tool is shown in Figure 6.6.

Modify sketch

 The Modify Sketch tool has been available in SolidWorks for a long time, but it has been super-seded by some of the newer tools mentioned above. However, it still has some unique functionality that is not covered by any other sketch tool. Modify sketch works on the entire sketch rather than on selections from the sketch, and it works best if there are no external relations. It can also work on a sketch without the sketch being active. While most features have been moved to the PropertyManager, Modify sketch still uses a dialog box that floats in the graphics window, as shown in Figure 6.7.

FIGURE 6.6

The Scale PropertyManager

FIGURE 6.7

The Modify Sketch dialog box

Scale About

The scaling function in the Modify Sketch tool enables you to scale about either the part Origin or the Moveable Origin. The Moveable Origin is the black origin symbol with knobs on the ends of the axes and at the intersection. The Moveable Origin can be moved and even snapped to entities that are internal or external to the sketch.

Translate

The Translate function of the Modify Sketch tool enables you to click and drag to move the entire sketch, or to select a point and move it to a specific set of coordinates that you type in. If the sketch is dragged onto an external entity and picks up an automatic relation, then a message may appear that you can now use Modify sketch only for rotating the sketch because there is an external relation.

Rotate

The Rotate function of the Modify Sketch tool enables you to position the Moveable Origin to act as the center of rotation, and to either type in a rotation angle or drag with the RMB to rotate, as indicated by the cursor.

Mirroring

When you place the cursor over the knobs on the Moveable Origin, the cursor symbols change to indicate the functionality of the RMB. These cursors are shown in action in Figure 6.8. The cursors enable mirroring about X, Y, or both simultaneously.

FIGURE 6.8

The Modify Sketch tool cursors

Copy and paste

Probably the simplest way to copy sketch entities in a sketch is to select the entities and use Ctrl+C and Ctrl+V or one of the many other methods available for this purpose (such as the RMB menu, the Edit menu, and Ctrl-dragging).

In addition to selected entities within an active sketch, you can also select a sketch from the FeatureManager and copy or paste it to a selected plane or planar face. This creates a new sketch feature in the FeatureManager that has no relation to the original, although it does maintain internal dimensions and relations. This is particularly useful when setting up certain types of lofts that use several profiles that can be created from a single copied profile. Copying and pasting is a fast and effective method of putting sketches on planes.

Simple drag

If a selected set of sketch entities has no external relations, then you can select it as a group and move it without distorting or resizing the sketch.

Derived sketch

A derived sketch is a parametrically linked copy. The sketches do not need to have any geometrical relation to one another, but when the parent sketch is changed, the dependent derived copy is updated to stay in sync.

To create a derived sketch, you can select a plane or planar face, Ctrl-select the sketch of which you want to make the parametric copy, and then click Insert ➪ Derived Sketch.

When you create a derived sketch, you cannot change its shape; it works like a block of a fixed shape. However, you can change the position and orientation of the derived sketch. Figure 6.9 shows a derived sketch and its parent.

FIGURE 6.9

A derived sketch and its parent

Original sketch   Derived sketch

Using Sketch Pictures

Sketch pictures are images that are placed in a sketch on a sketch plane. You can size and rotate the images, give them a transparent background, trace over them, and suppress them. They display as a child of the sketch. Image types that you can use as sketch pictures are BMP, GIF, JPEG, TIFF, and WMF.

To bring a picture into a sketch, the sketch must first be active. Click Sketch Picture on the Sketch toolbar (it is not there by default, and so you may need to drag it onto the Sketch toolbar from the Tools ➪ Customize ➪ Commands dialog box). You can also access this command through the menus at Tools ➪ Sketch Tools ➪ Sketch Picture. You cannot use sketch pictures in assembly sketches, but they can be shown in a part sketch in an assembly.

To change the size of a sketch picture, you can double-click it and drag one of the handles around the outside of the image. When the picture comes into the sketch, it is usually too big, having been sized at a ratio of 1 pixel to 1 mm. To size a picture accurately, you should include a ruler or an object of a known size in the image. If you cannot do this, the next best thing is to guess the size. Draw a line in your sketch and dimension it to approximately the size of something that is recognizable in the image, and then move the image by clicking and dragging it to lay the dimensioned sketch entity as close over the object in the image as possible.

Images are opaque, and you cannot see the model through them, but at the same time, you also cannot see the images through the model. They are like a flat piece of paper that is pasted to the model or hanging in space.

Sketch pictures cannot be shown on a drawing associatively. The only way to do this is to capture an image of the sketch picture that is being shown in the model, and putting this image in the drawing. PhotoWorks does not use sketch pictures, either, and PhotoWorks Decals are a separate item altogether.

> **TIP** Although the most common use for the sketch picture is as a tracing guide, you can use it for a wide variety of other purposes. For example, any sort of logo, decal, or display that is on a flat surface can be shown as a sketch picture.

> **BEST PRACTICE** Best practice for using sketch pictures is to put them into a separate sketch near or at the top of the FeatureManager. Even though you can have sketch entities in a Sketch Picture sketch, I prefer to keep them in separate sketches. This is because when you use the sketch entities for an extrude or a loft guide curve, this sketch will be consumed under that feature, which means that the image becomes buried somewhere in your model, rather than being easily accessible at the top of the FeatureManager.

Three views

When building a model from images, it is often helpful to have three or more images from orthogonal views, similar to recreating a part from a 2D drawing. If you have a left and a right view, it may be a good idea to put them on planes that are slightly separated so that the images are not exactly on top of one another, which makes them both hard to see. Putting them on slightly offset planes means that one will be clearly visible from one direction, and the other visible from the other direction.

Each sketch picture must be in a separate sketch. Figure 6.10 demonstrates the use of multiple sketch pictures to trace the outline of a vehicle, with the partially complete model shown with the images.

Perspective

Perspective in images can make it difficult to size items in the foreground or background. You should be aware of this, as well as that objects at different distances from the camera will appear at distorted sizes. If you are taking the pictures that will be used as sketch pictures, you can minimize the effects of perspective by standing farther away from the object and using zoom on the camera if possible.

Using multiple sketch pictures

Sharp edges

When you are drawing a sketch of an object, you are usually drawing theoretically sharp corners of the model. Real parts usually have rounded corners, and so you may have to use your imagination to project where the 3D surfaces would intersect at an edge.

When you are reverse-modeling a part from images, you are not using an exact science. It is better than not being able to put pictures into the sketch, but there is nothing about it that can be considered precise.

Using Sketch Text

Sketch text uses TrueType fonts to create text inside a SolidWorks sketch. This means that any TrueType font that you have can be converted to text in solid geometry; this includes Wingdings and symbol fonts. Keep in mind that some characters in certain fonts do not convert cleanly into SolidWorks sketches. Sketch text still has to follow the rules for sketching and creating features such as closed contours, as well as not mixing open and closed contours.

You can make sketch text follow a sketch curve; to space it evenly along the curve, you can control character width and spacing, as well as overall size by specifying points or actual dimensions. Sketch text can also be justified right, left, centered and evenly, as well as reversed, rotated, and flipped upside down. Figure 6.11 shows the Sketch Text PropertyManager and some of the possible uses of sketch text.

FIGURE 6.11

Examples of sketch text

Overlapping characters

The icons in the Sketch Text PropertyManager are fairly self-explanatory, other than the Rotated Text option, which rotates individual letters, and not the whole string of text.

You can use the Sketch Text tool multiple times in a single sketch to make pieces of text with different properties. Each string of text has a placement point located at the lower left of the text. This point can be given sketch relations or dimensions to locate the text.

If the text overlaps in places, as shown in Figure 6.10, you can correct this in a couple of ways. First, you can extrude it with the Merge option turned off so that each letter is created as a separate solid body. You can also explode sketch text so that it becomes simply lines and arcs in a sketch, which you can edit the same as any other sketch.

Using Colors and Line Styles with Sketches

Custom colors and line styles are usually associated with drawings, not sketches; in fact, they are most valuable when used for drawings. In sketches, this functionality is little known or used, but is still of value in certain situations.

Color Display mode

 In drawings, you can use the Color Display Mode button to switch sketch entities on the drawing between displaying the assigned line or layer color and displaying the sketch status color. It has exactly the same effect here in part and assembly sketches.

When you press the button, the sketch state colors are used. When the button is not pressed, any custom colors that you have applied to the sketch entities will display. If the button is not pressed and you have not applied colors to the entities, then the default sketch state colors are used.

You can use sketch colors for emphasis, to make selected sketch entities stand out, or to make sketches with various functions immediately distinguishable. Color Display mode only has an effect on an active sketch. Once a sketch is closed, it returns to the gray default color for inactive sketch entities.

Line color

 Line color enables you to assign color to entities in an active sketch. Whether the assigned color or the default sketch status colors are used is determined by the Color Display Mode tool.

Edit color

 You can use the Edit Color tool to assign color to an entire sketch. The color that you assign in this way displays only when the sketch is inactive, instead of the default gray color. The colors that are assigned to sketches in this way also follow the toggle state of the Color Display Mode button. For example, if the Color Display Mode button is depressed, then inactive sketches display as gray. When the Color Display Mode button is not pressed, then inactive sketches display in any color that you have assigned by using the Edit Color tool.

Line thickness and line style

 The Line Thickness and Line Style tools function independently from the Color Display Mode button, but they are still used only when the sketch is active. As soon as a sketch that contains entities with edited thickness and style is closed, the display goes back to the normal line weight and font.

195

To assign a thickness or a style, you can select the sketch entities to be changed, press the button, and select the thickness or style. Although a single sketch entity may have only a single thickness or style, you can use multiple thicknesses or styles within a single sketch. Figure 6.12 shows a sketch with the thickness and style edited.

FIGURE 6.12

A sketch with edited line thickness and line style

You can create custom line styles, but only in a drawing document; you cannot use custom line styles in the part environment.

CROSS-REF Line thickness and line styles are covered in more detail in the discussion of drawings in Chapter 20.

Tutorial: Editing and Copying

This tutorial guides you through some common sketch relation editing scenarios and using some of the Copy, Move, and Derive tools. Follow these steps to learn about editing and copying sketches:

1. Open the part named Chapter6 Tutorial1.sldprt from the CD-ROM. This part has several error flags on sketches. In cases where there are many errors, it is best to roll the part back and go through the errors one by one.

2. Drag the rollback bar from just after the last fillet feature to just after Extrude3. If Extrude3 is expanded so that you can see Sketch3 under it, then drop the rollback bar to after Sketch3. If a warning message appears, telling you that Sketch3 will be temporarily unabsorbed, then select Cancel and try the rollback again. Figure 6.13 shows before and after views for the rollback.

3. Edit Sketch3 and turn off the Sketch Relations display (View ⇨ Sketch Relations). Click Display/Delete Relations on the toolbar (the Eyeglasses tool), and set it to All in This Sketch. Notice that all of the relations conflict, but only one is unsolvable: the Equal Radius relation. This appears to be a mistake because the two arcs cannot be equal.

4. Delete the Equal Radius relation. The sketch is still not fixed.

5. Click the green check mark icon to close the Display/Delete Relations PropertyManager.

6. RMB click the graphics window and select SketchXpert. Click Diagnose.

FIGURE 6.13

Rolling the part back to Extrude3

Rollback bar   Rollback cursor

Model in rolled back state

7. Using the double arrows in the Results panel, toggle through the available solutions. All of the solutions except one remove sketch relations. Accept the one solution that removes the dimension, and click the green check mark icon to exit the SketchXpert. The sketch no longer shows errors.

8. Close the sketch. Notice that the error flag does not disappear until the sketch has been repaired and closed.

9. Use the rollback bar to roll forward to after Extrude2 and Sketch2. Figure 6.14 shows the tooltip message that appears if you place the cursor over the feature with the error. With time, you will begin to recognize the error messages by a single keyword or even by the shape of the message text. This message tells you that there is a *dangling* relation — a relation that has lost one of the entities.

FIGURE 6.14

The Error tooltip

10. Edit the sketch. Figure 6.15 points out the dangling errors. If you show the Sketch Relation icons again, the errors will be easier to identify. When you use Display/Delete Relations, the first two Coincident relations appear to be dangling. Clicking the relation in the Relations panel of the Display/Delete Relations PropertyManager shows that one point was connected to a line and the other point was connected to a point.

11. When you have fixed the errors, exit the sketch and confirm that the flag is no longer on Sketch2.

12. Drag the rollback bar to just before CutExtrude1. Edit 3DSketch1. This sketch is overdefined. If the Sketch Relations are not on at this point, then turn them on again.

TIP   Because this is a task that you will perform many times, this is a good opportunity to set up a hotkey for this function. As a reminder, to set up a hotkey, go to Tools ➪ Customize ➪ Keyboard, and in the Search box, type *relations*. In the Shortcut column for this command, select a hotkey to use.

13. Double-click one of the relation icons; the Display/Delete Relations PropertyManager appears. Notice that one of the sketch relations is a Fixed relation. Remove the Fixed relation, and exit the sketch.

14. RMB click anywhere in the FeatureManager and select Roll To End.

15. Click CutExtrude1 in the FeatureManager so that you can see it in the graphics window, and then click a blank space to deselect the feature.

16. Ctrl-drag any face of the cut feature, and drop it onto another flat face. The Ctrl-drag function copies the feature and the sketch, but the external dimensions and relations become detached.

FIGURE 6.15

Fixing dangling errors

Two points with dangling relations

1.18

Drag this point to this corner

Drag this point to this edge

17. In the prompt that appears, click Dangle in response to the prompt. This means that you will have to reattach some dangling dimensions rather than recreating them. Edit the newly created sketch, which now has an error on it.

18. Two of the dimensions that went to external edges now have the olive dangling color. Select one of the dimensions; a red handle displays. Drag the red handle and attach it to a model edge. Do this for both dimensions. The dimensions update to reflect their new locations. Exit the sketch and verify that the error flag has disappeared.

19. Expand CutExtrude1, and select Sketch5 under it. Ctrl-select a flat face on the model other than the one that Sketch5 is on. In the menu, select Insert ⇨ Derived Sketch. You are put into a sketch editing the derived sketch.

20. The sketch is blue, and so you should be able to resize it, right? You can test this by dragging the large circle; it only repositions the sketch as a unit.

21. Dimension the center of the large circle to the edges of the model.

22. Drag the smaller circle, and notice that it swivels around the larger circle. Create an angle dimension between the construction line between the circle centers and one of the model edges. Notice that the sketch is now fully defined.

23. Exit the sketch, and look at the name of the derived sketch in the FeatureManager. The term *derived* appears after the name, and the sketch appears as fully defined.

24. RMB click the sketch and select Underive Sketch. Notice that the sketch is now underdefined. The Underive command removes the associative link between the two sketches.

Tutorial: Controlling Pictures, Text, Colors, and Styles

This tutorial guides you through some of the miscellaneous functions in sketches, and shows you what they are used for and how they are used. Follow these steps to learn how to control these items:

1. Open a new part using a template with inches as units. Open a sketch on the Front plane, and draw a construction line 12 inches down (negative Y) from the Origin.

2. Insert a sketch picture in this sketch. Use Sketch Picture 1.tif from the CD-ROM for Chapter 6.

3. Resize the image so that the endpoints of the construction line are near the centers of the holes on the ends of the part. To move the image, just double-click it first, and then drag it. To resize it, drag the corners.

4. In the Transparency panel of the Sketch Picture PropertyManager, select the Eyedropper tool and click in the white background of the image. Make sure that the color field next to the Eyedropper tool changes to white.

5. Slide the Transparency and Matching Tolerance sliders all the way to the right, or type **1.00** in the number boxes.

6. Close the sketch, and rename it **Sketch Image Front View**.

7. Put the image Sketch Picture 2.tif, also from the CD-ROM, on the Right plane, and resize it to fit with the first image. Center it symmetrically about the Origin. Also set the transparency to the same setting as the first image.

8. Open a new sketch, also on the Front plane, and draw two circles to match the features on the ends. Extrude them using a Mid Plane extrusion to match the image in the other direction (about 2.5 inches), as shown in Figure 6.16.

9. Open another new sketch on the Front plane and draw the tangent lines to form the web in the middle of the part. Close the sketch to make a solid extrusion. Extrude this part .5 inches Mid Plane.

FIGURE 6.16

Using sketch pictures

10. Open a new sketch on the face of the large flat web that you created in the previous step, and offset the arc edge of the larger circular boss by 2.1 inches.

11. Change the arc to a construction arc and drag its endpoints to approximately the position shown in Figure 6.17. The endpoints of the arc are blue after you drag them. Give them a Horizontal relation, and then dimension them as shown in Figure 6.17.

FIGURE 6.17

Creating an offset arc

12. Click Tools ➪ Sketch Entities ➪ Text to initiate the creation of sketch text.

13. Select the construction arc to go into the Curves window.

14. In the Text window, type **SolidWorks**. Select the Full Justify option.

15. Deselect the Use Document Font option, click the Font button, and then set the Units to .50 inches. Click the Bold button to make the text thicker. Click OK to exit the dialog box. Click the green check mark icon to exit the sketch text, and then exit the sketch.

16. Extrude the text to a depth of .050 inches with 3 degrees of draft. The part at this point resembles Figure 6.18.

FIGURE 6.18

Creating extruded text

PERFORMANCE Sketch Text is a real performance killer. The more text that you use, the longer it takes to extrude. Draft on the extrusion adds to the time required.

17. Select the flat face on the other side of the part from where you just extruded the text, and open a sketch.

18. Select the face and click the Offset button to make a set of sketch entities offset to the inside of the face by .50 inches.

19. Turn on the Line Format toolbar (RMB click any toolbar other than the CommandManager and select Line Format).

20. Select all of the sketch lines, and change their color using the Line Color tool. Change the line thickness and the line style using the appropriate tools. The sketch now looks something like Figure 6.19.

21. When you click the Color Display Mode tool, the colors return to regular sketch colors. When you exit the sketch, the line weight and style also return to normal.

FIGURE 6.19

Using line thickness and line style

Summary

Many tools that are available in sketches are not commonly shown in the most popular sources of information, including official training manuals. The difference between a good CAD tool and a great communication tool can be some of these minor functions that just make life a little easier, or the presentation or editing of data a little better. When you explore the capabilities of SolidWorks, it usually rewards you with functionality that others might not find.

Chapter 7

Choosing a Feature Type

Whenever I do a woodworking project, the most frustrating part of the job is to envision a result, but not be able to accomplish it because I do not have the tools to get it done; worse yet is to actually have the tools but either not understand how to use them or not even realize that I have them. Getting the job done is so much more satisfying when you use the right tools and get the job done right — not just so that it *looks* right, but so that it really *is* right.

I see users run into the same issues with SolidWorks. SolidWorks offers so many "tools in the toolbox" that it is sometimes difficult to select the best one, especially if it is for a function that you do not use frequently.

This chapter helps you to understand how each feature functions, and offers situations when they are best applied or avoided.

Identifying When to Use Which Tool

I am always trying to think of alternate ways of doing things. Especially when working with complex features, it is important to have a backup plan, or sometimes multiple backup plans. Even when the part is not that complicated, every situation is different. You probably will not get away with just doing blind extrudes and cuts with simple chamfers and fillets for the rest of your career. And even if you could, who would want to?

As an exercise, I often try to see how many different ways a particular shape might be modeled, and how each modeling method relates to manufacturing methods, costs, editability, efficiency, and so on. You may also want to try this approach.

Extrude

 Extruded features can be grouped into several categories, with extruded Boss and Cut features at the highest level. Boss and Cut are two separate feature types and cannot be interchanged. Sketches may be shared between features or reused after a feature has been deleted.

The "Base" part of the Extruded Boss/Base is a holdover from when SolidWorks did not allow multibody parts, and the first feature in a part had special significance that it no longer has. This is also seen in the menus at Insert ➯ Boss/Base. The Base feature was the first solid feature in the FeatureManager, and you could not change it without deleting the rest of the features. The introduction of multibody support in SolidWorks has removed this limitation.

 CROSS-REF Multibody parts are covered in detail in Chapter 26.

Solid Feature

In this case, we use the term *solid feature* as opposed to *thin feature*. This is the simple type of feature that you create by default when you extrude a closed loop sketch. A closed loop sketch fully encloses an area without gaps or overlaps at the sketch entity endpoints. Figure 7.1 shows a closed loop sketch creating an extruded solid feature.

Thin Feature

The Thin Feature option is available to several types of features, but is most commonly used with Extruded Boss features. Thin features are created by default when you use an open loop sketch, but you can also select this option for closed loop sketches. Thin features are commonly used for ribs, thin walls, hollow circular bosses, and many other types of features that are common to plastic parts or castings.

Even experienced users tend to forget that thin features are not just for bosses, but can also be used for cuts. For example, you can easily create grooves and slots with thin feature cuts.

Figure 7.2 shows the Thin Feature panel in the Extruded Boss PropertyManager. In addition to the default options that are available for the Extrude feature, the Thin feature adds a *thickness* dimension, as well as three options to direct the thickness relative to the sketch: One-Direction, Mid-Plane, and Two-Direction. The Two-Direction option requires two dimensions, as shown in Figure 7.2.

FIGURE 7.1

A closed loop sketch and an extruded solid feature

FIGURE 7.2

The Thin Feature interface

Thin feature sketches are simpler, which always means that they are more robust through changes. You can create the simplest cube from a single sketch line and a thin feature extrude. However, in some respects, they are not as flexible when the design intent changes. For example, if a part is going to change from a constant width to a tapered or stepped shape, thin features do not handle this kind of change well. Figure 7.3 shows different types of geometry that are created from thin features.

FIGURE 7.3

Different types of geometry created from thin features

Sketch types

I have already mentioned several sketch types, including closed loop and open loop. Closed loop sketches make solid features by default, but you can also use them to make thin features. Open loop sketches make thin features by default, and you cannot use them to make solid features.

Sketch contours

 Sketch Contour is a feature that is used in other competing CAD packages and that SolidWorks has adopted, probably more to match features in the competing software than to create a better way of doing things. Using sketch contours seems to promote sloppy work, although in some cases, they act as valid time savers.

In general, sketch contours enable you to select enclosed areas where the sketch entities themselves actually cross or otherwise violate the usual sketch rules. One of these conditions is the self-intersecting contour.

SolidWorks works best with well-disciplined sketches that follow the rules. As a result, if you plan to use sketch contours, then you should make sure that it is not simply because you are unwilling to clean up a messy sketch.

When you define features by selecting sketch contours, they are more likely to fail if the selection changes when the selected contour's bounded area changes in some way. It is best practice to use the normal closed loop sketch when you are defining features. Contour selection is best suited to "fast and dirty" conceptual models, which are used in very limited situations for production models.

As shown in Figure 7.4, there are several types of contour selection.

3D sketch

You can make extrusions from 3D sketches, even 3D sketches that are not planar. While not necessarily the best way to do extrudes, this is a method that you can use when needed. You can establish direction for an extrusion by selecting a plane (normal direction), axis, sketch line, or model edge.

FIGURE 7.4

Types of contour selection

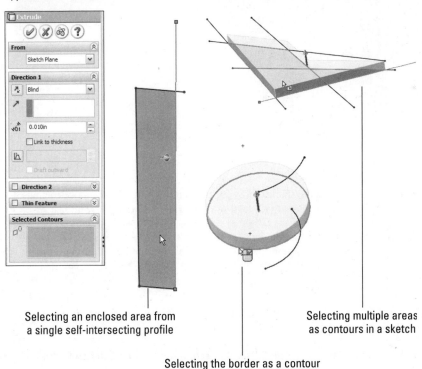

Selecting an enclosed area from a single self-intersecting profile

Selecting the border as a contour

Selecting multiple areas as contours in a sketch

When you make an extrusion from a 3D sketch, the direction of extrusion cannot be assumed or inferred from anything — it must be explicitly identified. Extrusion direction from a 2D sketch is always perpendicular to the sketch plane unless otherwise specified.

Non-planar sketches become somewhat problematic when you are creating the final extruded feature. The biggest problem is how you cap the ends. Figure 7.5 shows a non-planar 3D sketch that is being extruded. Notice that the end faces are, by necessity, not planar, and are capped by an unpredictable method. This is a problem only if your part is going to use these faces in the end; if it does not, then there may be no issue with using this technique. If you would like to examine this part, it is included on the CD-ROM as Chapter 7 Extrude 3D Sketch.sldprt.

FIGURE 7.5

Extruding a non-planar 3D sketch

If you need to have ends with a specific shape, and you still want to extrude from a non-planar 3D sketch, then you should use an extruded surface feature rather than an extruded solid feature.

 Surfacing features are covered in detail in Chapter 27. Chapter 5 contains additional details on extrude end conditions, thin features, directions, and the From options.

Revolve

 Like all other features, revolve features have some rules that you must observe when choosing sketches that can be used to create a revolve:

- Draw only half of the revolve profile (draw the section to one side of the centerline).
- The profile must not cross the centerline.

- The profile must not touch the centerline at a single point. It can touch along a line, but not at a point. Revolving a sketch that touched the centerline at a single point would create a point of zero thickness in the part.

You can use any type of line or model edge for the centerline, not just the centerline/construction line type.

End conditions

There are three Revolve end conditions:

- **One-Direction:** The revolve angle is driven in a single direction.
- **Two-Direction:** The revolve angle can be driven in two independent directions.
- **Mid-Plane:** The revolve angle is divided equally in opposite directions.

There is no equivalent for Up to Vertex, Up to Next, Up to Surface, or Up to Body with the Revolve feature.

Contour selection

Like extrude features, revolve features can also use contour selection; as with the extrude features, I recommend that you avoid using contours.

Loft

Many users struggle when faced with the option to create a loft or a sweep. Some overlap exists between the two features, but as you gain some experience, it becomes easier to choose between them. Generally, if you can create the cross-section of the feature by manipulating a single sketch, then a sweep might be the best feature. If the cross-section changes character or severely changes shape, then a loft may be best. If you need a very definite shape at both ends and/or in the middle, then a loft is a better choice because it allows you to explicitly define the cross-section at a point. However, if the outline is more important than the cross-section, then you should choose a sweep. If the path between ends is important, choose a sweep. If the ends themselves are more important and you just want to blend from one end to the other, then the loft is the better choice.

Both types of features are extremely powerful, but the sweep has a tendency to be fussier about details, setup, and rules, while the loft can be surprisingly flexible. I am not trying to dissuade you from using sweeps, because they are useful in many situations. However, in my own personal modeling, I probably use about ten lofts for every sweep. For example, while you would use a loft or combination of loft features to create a complex laundry detergent bottle, you would use the sweep to create a raised border around the label area.

Lofts are an example of *interpolated* geometry. That is to say that the loft is outlined by creating several loft sections and guide curves, and then the software interpolates the face geometry in between the sections. A good example of this is to put a circle on one plane and a rectangle on an offset plane and then loft them together. This arrangement is shown in Figure 7.6. The transition between shapes is the defining characteristic of a loft, and is also the reason for choosing a loft instead of another feature type. Lofts can create both Boss features and Cut features.

FIGURE 7.6

A simple loft

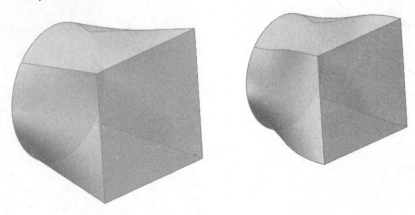

The two-profile loft with default end conditions always creates a straight transition, which is shown in the image to the left. A two-point spline with no end tangency creates a straight line in exactly the same way. By applying end conditions to either or both of the loft profiles, the loft's shape is made more interesting, as seen in the image to the right in Figure 7.6. Again, the same thing happens when applying end tangency conditions to a two-point spline: it goes from being a straight line to being more curvaceous, with continuously variable curvature. The Loft PropertyManager interface is shown in Figure 7.7.

Entities that you can use in a loft

For solid lofts, you can select faces, closed loop 2D or 3D sketches, and surface bodies. You can use sketch points as a profile on the end of a loft that comes to a point or rounded end. For surface lofts, you can use open sketches and edges in addition to the entities that are used by solid lofts.

Some special functionality becomes available to you if you put all of the profiles and guide curves together in a single 3D sketch. In order to select profiles made in this way, you must use the SelectionManager, which is discussed later in this chapter.

The Sketch Tools panel of the Loft PropertyManager enables you to drag sketch entities of any profile made in this way while you are editing or creating the Loft feature, without needing to exit and edit a sketch.

FIGURE 7.7

The Loft PropertyManager

CAUTION While this sort of functionality may be attractive for a lot of reasons, you should not choose this way. Unless you are dealing with the simplest of geometry and sketch relations, 3D sketches — and more specifically 3D sketch planes — are simply not up to the task. It is definitely true that 3D sketches in SolidWorks work far better than they used to, but I would still not put even a 3D sketch of medium complexity in a part that I had to depend on for production data. The specific problem is sketch relations. I discuss 3D sketches in more detail in Chapter 31.

The similarities between lofts and splines

The words "loft" and "spline" come to us from the shipbuilding trade. The word "spline" is actually defined as the slats of wood that cover the ship, and the spars of the hull very much resemble loft sections. With the splines or slats bending at each spar, it is easy to see how the modern CAD analogy came to be.

Lofts and splines are also governed by similar mathematics. You have seen how the two-point spline and two-profile loft both create a straight-line transition. Next, a third profile is added to the loft and a third point to the spline, which demonstrates how the math that governs splines and lofts is also related to bending in elastic materials. Figure 7.8 shows how lofts and splines react geometrically in the same way that bending a flexible steel rod would react (except that the spline and the loft do not have a fixed length).

FIGURE 7.8

Splines, lofts, and bending

Three-point spline, no end conditions

End tangency changed

Reacts like a pinned joint

Notice slight bulge, just like a real rod in bending

Profile(Sketch2)

With this bit of background, it is time to move forward and talk about a few of the major aspects of Loft features in SolidWorks. It is probably possible to write a separate book that only discusses modeling lofts and other complex shapes. In this single chapter, I do not have the space to cover the topic exhaustively, but coverage of the major concepts will be enough to point you in the right direction.

The need for surfaces

In this chapter, I deal exclusively with solid modeling techniques because they are the baseline that SolidWorks users use most frequently. Surfaces make it easier to discuss complex shape concepts because surfaces are generally created one face at a time, rather than by using the method with solid modeling that creates as many faces as necessary to enclose a volume.

From the very beginning, the SolidWorks modeling culture has made things easier for users by taking care of many of the details in the background. This is because solids are built through automated surface techniques. Surface modeling in itself can be tedious work because of all of the manual detail that you must add. Solid modeling as we know it is simply an evolutionary step that adds automation to surface modeling. The automation maintains a closed solid boundary around the volume.

Because surfaces are the underlying building blocks from which solids are made, it would make sense to teach surfaces first, and then solids. However, the majority of SolidWorks users never use surfacing, and do not see a need for it, and so surface functions are generally given a lower priority.

CROSS-REF You can refer to Chapter 27 for surfacing information.

Loft end constraints

Loft end conditions control the tangency direction and weighting at the ends of the loft. Some of the end constraints depend upon the loft starting or ending from other geometry. The optional constraints include the following:

None

The direction of the loft is not set by the None end constraint, but the curvature of the lofted faces at the ends is zero. This is the default end constraint for two-section lofts.

Default

The Default end constraint is not available for two-section lofts, only for lofts with three or more sections. This end constraint applies curvature to the end of the loft so that it approximates a parabola being formed through the first and last loft profiles.

The SolidWorks help file makes a special point to explain the difference between the None and Default end constraints, but the Default help makes it look as if it works with only two profiles, when in fact it does not.

Tangent to Face

The Tangent to Face end constraint is self-explanatory. This end constraint may fail or cause unwanted ripples or puckers in the part if profiles that are adjacent to one another or touch at an edge are lofted together. The Tangency to Face option includes a setting for tangent length. This is not a literal length dimension, but a relative weighting, on a scale from 0.1 to 10. The small arrow to the left of the setting identifies the direction of the tangency. Usually, the default setting is correct, but there are times when SolidWorks misidentifies the intended tangency direction, and you may need to correct it manually.

The Next Face option is available only when lofting from an end face where the tangency could go in one of two perpendicular directions. This is shown in Figure 7.9.

Apply to All refers to applying the Tangent Length value to all of the tangency-weighting arrows for the selected profile. When you select Apply to All, only one arrow displays. When you deselect it, one arrow should display for each vertex in the profile, and you can adjust each arrow individually.

FIGURE 7.9

Examples of end constraints

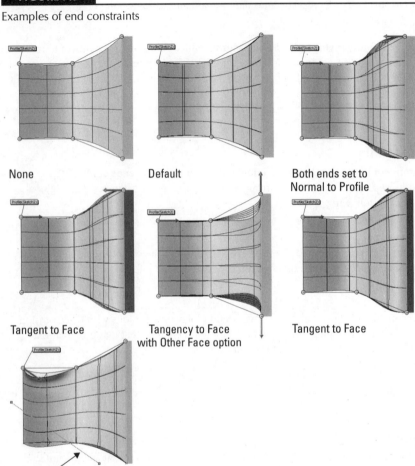

None

Default

Both ends set to
Normal to Profile

Tangent to Face

Tangency to Face
with Other Face option

Tangent to Face

Direction vector

Curvature to Face

The difference between tangency and curvature is that tangency is only concerned with the direction of curvature immediately at the edge between the two surfaces. Curvature must be tangent and in addition match the radius of curvature on either side of the edge between surfaces. This is often given many names, including curvature continuity, c2, and others. Lofted surfaces do not usually have a constant radius; because they are like splines, they are constantly changing in local radius.

Direction Vector

The Direction Vector end constraint forces the loft to be tangent to a direction that you define by selecting an axis, edge, or sketch entity. The angle setting makes the loft deviate from the direction vector, as shown in Figure 7.9. The curved arrows to the left identify the direction in which the angle deviation is going.

Isoparameter U-V lines

The mesh or grid shown in the previous images appears automatically for certain types of features, including lofts. The grid represents *isoparameter* lines, also known as NURBS mesh or U-V lines. This mesh shows the underlying structure of the faces being created by the feature. If the mesh is highly distorted and appears to overlap in places, then it is likely that the feature will fail.

You can show or hide the mesh through the RMB menu when editing or creating a Loft feature, unless the SelectionManager is active. In this case, you can see only SelectionManager commands in the RMB menu. In addition, planar faces do not mesh, only faces with some curvature.

Guide curves

Guide curves help to constrain the outline of a loft between loft profiles. Although it is best to try to achieve the shape you want by using appropriately shaped and placed loft profiles, I recognize that this is not always possible. The most appropriate use of guide curves for solid lofts is at places where the loft is going to create a hard edge, which is usually at the corners of loft profile sketches. Guide curves often (but not always) break up what would otherwise be a smooth surface, and you should avoid them in these situations, if possible.

BEST PRACTICE Do not try to push the shape of the loft too extremely with guide curves. Guide curves should be used mainly for tweaking and fine-tuning rather than coarse adjustment. Use loft sections and end constraints to get most of the overall shape correct. Pushing too hard with a guide curve can cause the shape to kink unnaturally.

Although guide curves may be longer than the loft, they may not be shorter. The guide curve applies to the entire loft. If you need to apply the guide curve only to a portion of the loft, then split the loft into two lofts, one that uses the guide curve, and the other that does not. The guide curve must intersect all profiles in a loft.

If you have more than one guide curve, the order in which they are listed in the box is important. The first guide curve helps to position the intermediate profiles of the loft. It may be difficult or impossible to visualize the effects of guide-curve order before it happens, but remember that it does make a difference, and depending on the difference between the curves, the difference may or may not be subtle.

Guide curves are also used in sweeps, which are dealt with later in this chapter. Figure 7.10 shows a model that is lofted using guide curves. The image to the left shows the sketches that are used to make the part. There are two sketches with points; you can use points as loft profiles. The image in the middle shows the Loft feature without guide curves, and to the right is the part with guide curves. If you would like to examine how this part is built, you can find it on the CD-ROM with the filename Chapter 7 Guide Curves.sldprt.

FIGURE 7.10

A loft with and without guide curves

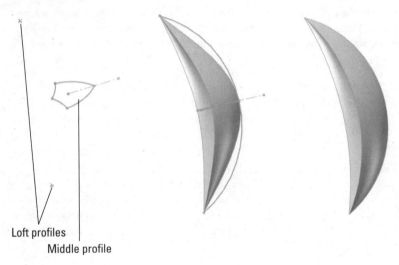

Loft profiles
     Middle profile

Centerline lofts

The Centerline panel of the Loft PropertyManager is used to set up a Centerline loft. You can use the Centerline of a loft in roughly the same way that you use a sweep path. In fact, the Centerline loft resembles a sweep feature where you can specify the shape of some of the intermediate profiles. Centerline lofts can also create intermediate profiles. You may prefer to use a centerline loft instead of either a sweep or a regular loft because the profile may change in ways that the Sweep feature cannot handle, and the loft may need some guidance regarding the order of the profiles or how to smooth the shape between the profiles.

Sweep features are covered later in this chapter. If you are creating a centerline loft, then you may want to examine the sweep functionality as well.

You can use centerlines simultaneously with guide curves. While guide curves must touch the profile, there is no such requirement for a centerline; in fact, the centerline works best if it does not touch any of the profiles.

The slider in the Centerline Parameters panel enables you to specify how many intermediate sections to create between sketched profiles.

SelectionManager

The SelectionManager simplifies the selection of entities from complex sketches that are not necessarily the clean, closed loop sketches that SolidWorks works with most effectively.

 The SelectionManager is new in SolidWorks 2007, and is used only for loft, sweep, and boundary surface features. It replaces Smart Selection and Contour Selection for these features.

The SelectionManager has been implemented in a limited number of features, and has limited functionality compared with the other selection options that are available in SolidWorks. Selection options in the SelectionManager include the following:

- **OK:** Accepts the selection. This feature is also available on the RMB.

- **Cancel:** Quits the SelectionManager

- **Clear:** Clears the current selection set

- **Pushpin:** Keeps the SmartSelection window available, even when it is not required for sketch entity selections

- **Select Closed Loop:** You can select two different types of loops with this tool:
  - A parametric closed loop in a 2D or 3D sketch
  - A parametric loop of edges around a surface

- **Select Open Loop:** Selects a chain (end-to-end sketch entities)

- **Select Group:** Selects entities individually. If you click the Propagate symbol, all tangent edges are selected.

- **Select Region:** Works like the Contour Selection described earlier in this chapter.

- **Standard Selection:** Disables special functions of the SelectionManager. This feature works like a regular selection tool.

- **Auto OK Selections:** Enabled when you use the Pushpin feature. This feature works for closed and open loop selection.

Loft options

You can choose from the following Loft options, as shown in Figure 7.11:

- **Merge Tangent Faces:** Model faces that are tangent are merged into a single face. This is done behind the scenes by converting profiles into splines, which make approximations but are smoother than sketches with individual tangent line and arc entities.

FIGURE 7.11

Loft options

- **Close Loft:** A closed loop is made of the loft. At least three loft profiles must exist in order to use this option. Figure 7.12 shows a loft where the Close Loft option is used, and the loft sections are shown. This model is on the CD-ROM with the filename Chapter 7 — Closed Loft.sldprt.

FIGURE 7.12

A closed loft

- **Show Preview:** This turns the preview of the Loft feature on or off, if the feature is not going to fail. All of the following loft preview options are system options, and remain on until you turn them off.

  - **Transparent Preview** is available from the RMB menu when you edit a loft, if the SelectionManager is not active.

  - **Mesh Preview** is also available on the same RMB menu.

  - **Zebra Stripe Preview** is also available on the same RMB menu, and is covered in more depth in Chapter 11.

- **Merge Result:** Merges the resulting solid body with any other solid bodies that it may contact.

Sweep

 The Sweep feature uses more than one sketch. A sweep is made from a profile (cross-section) and a path, and can create a boss or a cut feature. If you want, you can also use guide curves. Sweeps can run the gamut from simple to complex. Typical simple sweeps are used to create wire, tubing, or hose. More complex sweeps are used for creating objects such as bottles, involutes, and corkscrews.

The main criteria for selecting a sweep to create a feature are that you must be able to identify a cross-section and a path. The profile (cross-section) can change along the path, but the overall shape must remain basically the same. The profile is typically perpendicular to the path, although this is not a requirement.

Simple sweep

An example of a simple sweep is shown in Figure 7.13. The paper clip uses a circle as the profile, and the coiled lines and arcs as the path.

FIGURE 7.13

A simple sweep feature

Profile or cross-section

Sweep path

Simple sweeps such as that shown in Figure 7.13 essentially set up SolidWorks to create geometry from simpler features such as Extrude and Revolve. If you look at the faces, you can see that they are created from straight lines and arcs, which lend themselves well to extrudes and revolves.

Sweep with guide curves

More complex sweeps begin to control the size, orientation, and position of the cross-section as it travels through the sweep. When you use a guide curve, several analogies can be used to visualize how the sweep works. The cross-section/profile is solved at several intermediate positions along the path. If the guide curve does not follow the path, the difference between the two is made up by adjusting the profile. Consider the following example. In this case, the profile is an ellipse, the path is a straight line, and there are guide curves that give the feature its outer shape. Figure 7.14 shows all of these elements and the finished feature.

FIGURE 7.14

A sweep with two guide curves

ON the CD-ROM   The part shown in Figure 7.14 is on the CD-ROM with the filename Chapter7 Bottle.sldprt.

The sweep with guide curves does not create extrudes and revolves, although you can use simple lines and arcs with this feature. The changes in the cross-section are created from a more complex feature type, namely a loft. The PropertyManager for the Sweep function includes an option for Show Sections, which in this case creates almost 200 intermediate cross-sections. These sections are used to create a loft. You can think of complex sweeps as an automated setup for an even more complex loft. It is helpful to envision features such as this when you are troubleshooting or setting up more complex sweeps. If you open the part mentioned previously from the CD-ROM, you can edit the Sweep feature to examine the sections for yourself.

In most other published SolidWorks materials that cover these topics, sweeps are covered before lofts because many people consider lofts to be the more advanced topic. However, I have put lofts first because understanding lofts is necessary before you can understand complex sweeps, as complex sweeps really are just lofts.

Pierce relation

The Pierce sketch relation is the only sketch relation that applies to a 3D out-of-plane edge or curve without projecting the edge or curve into the sketch plane. It acts as if the 3D curve is a length of thread and the sketch point is the eye of a needle, where the thread pierces the needle eye. The Pierce relation is most important in the Sweep feature when it is applied in the profile sketch between endpoints, center points, or sketch points and the guide curves. This is because the Pierce relation determines how the profile sketch will be solved when it is moved down the sweep path to create a new intermediate profile.

Figure 7.15 illustrates the function of the Pierce relation in a sweep with guide curves. The dark section on the left is the sweep section that is sketched. The lighter sketches to the right represent the intermediate profiles that are automatically created behind the scenes.

FIGURE 7.15

The effects of the Pierce relation

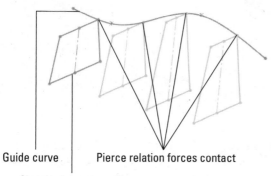

Guide curve   Pierce relation forces contact

Sketched sweep profile

Figure 7.16 shows a more complicated 3D sweep, where both the path and the guide curve are 3D curves. I cover 3D curves toward the end of this chapter, and so you can refer ahead to these features to understand how this part is made.

ON the CD-ROM The part shown in Figure 7.16 is on the CD-ROM with the filename Chapter 7 3D Sweep.sldprt.

This part is created by making a pair of tapered helices, with the profile sketch plane perpendicular to the end of one of the curves. The taper on the outer helix is greater than on the inner one, which causes the twist to become larger in diameter as it goes up.

To make the circle follow both helices, you must create two pierce relations, one between the center of the circle and a helix, and the other between a sketch point that is placed on the circumference of the circle and the other helix. This means that the difference in taper angles between the two helices is what drives the change in diameter of the sweep.

FIGURE 7.16

A 3D sweep

Creating Curve Features

Curves in SolidWorks are often used to help define sweeps and lofts, as well as other features. Curves differ from sketches in that curves are defined using sketches or a dialog box, and you cannot manipulate them directly or dimension them in the same way that you can sketches. Functions that you are accustomed to using with sketches often do not work on curves.

TIP   When you come across a function that does not work using a curve entity, but that works on a sketch (for example, making a tangent spline), then it may help to use the Convert Entities feature. Converting entities on a helix into a 3D sketch creates a spline that lies directly on top of the helix, and allows you to make another spline that is tangent to the new spline.

The following types of curves can be defined in SolidWorks:

- Helix/tapered helix/variable helix/spiral
- Projected curve
- Curve through XYZ points
- Curve through reference points
- Composite curve

You can find all of the curve functions on the Curves toolbar or through the menus at Insert ➪ Curve.

Helix

The Helix curve types are all based on a circle in a sketch. The circle represents the starting location and diameter of the helix. Figure 7.17 shows the PropertyManagers of the Constant Pitch and Variable Pitchhelix types.

FIGURE 7.17

The Helix PropertyManager

You can create all of the helical curve types by specifying any combination of total height, pitch, and the number of revolutions. The start angle is best thought of as a relative number. It is difficult to predict where zero degrees starts, and this depends on the relation of the sketch plane to the Origin. The start angle cannot be controlled outside of the PropertyManager, and cannot be driven by sketch geometry. The term *pitch* refers to the straight-line distance along the axis between the rings of the helix. Pitch for the spiral is different, and is described later.

Tapered Helix

The Tapered Helix panel in the Helix PropertyManager enables you to specify a taper angle for the helix. The taper angle does not affect the pitch. If you need to affect both the taper and the pitch, then you can use a variable pitch helix. Figure 7.18 shows how the taper angle relates to the resulting geometry.

FIGURE 7.18

The tapered helix

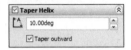

Variable Pitch Helix

You can specify the variable pitch helix either in the chart or in the callouts that are shown in Figure 7.19. Both the pitch and the diameter are variable. The diameter number in the first row cannot be changed, but is driven by the sketch. In the chart shown, the transition between 4 and 4.5 revolutions is where the pitch and diameter both change.

FIGURE 7.19

The variable pitch helix

Spiral

A spiral is a flattened (planar) tapered helix. The pitch value on a spiral is the radial distance between revolutions of the curve.

Projected curve

Many users have difficulty envisioning the concept of the projected curve. The two options available for projected curves are:

- Sketch onto Face
- Sketch onto Sketch

These names can be misleading if you do not already know what they mean. In both cases, the word *sketch* is used as a noun, not a verb, and so you are not actively sketching on a surface; instead, you are creating a curve by projecting a sketch onto a face.

Sketch Onto Face

The Sketch Onto Face option is the easiest to explain, and so I will describe this one first. With this option set, the projected curve is created by projecting a 2D sketch onto a face. The sketch is projected normal (perpendicular) to the sketch plane. This is like extruding the sketch and using the Up To Surface end condition. The sketch can be an open or closed loop, but it may not be multiple open or closed loops, nor can it be self-intersecting. Figure 7.20 shows an example of projecting a sketch onto a face to create a projected curve.

FIGURE 7.20

A projected curve using the Sketch Onto Face option

Sketch Onto Sketch

This is the concept that most frequently causes difficulty for users. The Sketch Onto Sketch Projected Curve option can be visualized in a few different ways.

Reverse 2D drawing visualization method

One way is to think of it as being the reverse of a 2D drawing. In a 2D drawing, 3D edges (you can think of the edges as curves) are projected onto orthogonal planes to represent the edge from the Front or Top planes. The Sketch Onto Sketch projection takes the two orthogonal views, placed on perpendicular planes, and projects them back to make the 3D edge or curve. This is part of the attraction of the projected curve, because making 3D curves accurately is difficult if you do it directly by using a tool such as a 3D sketch spline; however, if you know what the curve looks like from two different directions, then it becomes easy. Figure 7.21 illustrates this visualization method.

When you think of describing a complex 3D curve in space, one of the first methods that usually comes to mind is describing it as a 2D curve from perpendicular directions, exactly in the same way as you would if you created projected drawing views from it. From this, it makes sense to see the creation of the curve as the reverse process, drawing the 2D views first, from which you can then create the 3D curve.

FIGURE 7.21

The reverse 2D drawing visualization method for projected curves

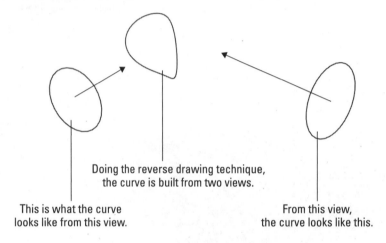

Doing the reverse drawing technique,
the curve is built from two views.

This is what the curve
looks like from this view.

From this view,
the curve looks like this.

Intersecting surfaces visualization method

A second method used for visualizing Sketch On Sketch projected curves is the intersecting surfaces method. In this method, you can see the curve being created at the intersection of two surfaces that are created by extruding each of the sketches. This method is shown in Figure 7.22.

Curve Through XYZ Points

The Curve Through XYZ Points feature enables you to either type in or import a text file with coordinates for points on a curve. The text file can be generated by any program that makes lists of numbers, including Excel. The curve reacts like a spline, and so the teeter-tottering effect may be noticeable, especially because you cannot set end conditions or tangency. To avoid this effect, it may be a good idea to overbuild the curve by a few points on each end.

If you import a text file, the file can have an extension of either *.txt or *.sldcrv. The data that it contains must be formatted as three columns of X-, Y-, and Z-coordinates using the document units (inch, mm, and so on), and the coordinates must be separated by comma, space, or tab.

Figure 7.23 shows both the Curve File dialog box displaying a table of the curve through X, Y, and Z points, and the *.sldcrv Notepad file. The file can be read from the Curve File dialog box by using the Browse button, but if you manually type the points, then you can also save the data out directly from the dialog box. Just like any type of sketch, this type of curve cannot intersect itself.

FIGURE 7.22

Using intersecting surfaces to visualize a Sketch on Sketch projected curve

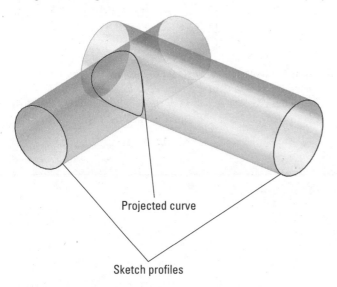

Projected curve

Sketch profiles

FIGURE 7.23

The Curve File dialog box showing a table of the curve through X, Y, and Z points, and a Notepad text file with the same information

Curve Through Reference Points

The Curve Through Reference Points feature creates a curve entity from selected sketch points or vertices. The curve can be an open or closed loop, but a closed loop requires that you select at least three points. You cannot set end conditions of the curve, and so this feature works like a spline in the same way as the XYZ curve.

The most common application of this feature is to create a simple two-point curve across the opening of a surface feature to close the opening by using a surface feature such as Fill, Boundary, or Loft.

Composite curve

The composite curve joins together multiple curves, edges, or sketches into a single curve entity. The part shown in Figure 7.24 was created by using a composite curve to join together a 3D sketch, variable pitch helix, and a projected curve. You can also use model edges with the composite curve. The curve is shown on half of the part; the rest of the part is mirrored.

FIGURE 7.24

A part created from a composite curve

Split lines

Split lines are not exactly curves; they are really just edges that split faces into multiple faces. Split lines are used for several purposes, but are primarily intended to split faces so that draft can be added. They are also used for creating a broken-out face for a color break, or to create an edge for a hold line fillet, which is discussed later in this chapter.

There are some limitations to using split lines. First, they must split a face into at least two fully enclosed areas. You cannot have a split line with an open loop sketch where the ends of the loop are on the face that is to be split; they must either hang off the face to be split or be coincident with the edges. Second, nested loops or multiple closed loops are not allowed, nor are self-intersecting sketches. If you need to do something with a sketch of one of these types, then you may be able to accomplish the same thing using multiple split-line features. If you want to create multiple stripes across a face, the best option may be to create an open loop sketch with many S-shaped zigzags.

One result of all of these limitations is that it becomes difficult to make split lines using sketch text or other complex sketches. There are several ways of bypassing these limitations, such as copying the surfaces with Knit or Offset at zero distance and then trimming the surface with the sketch, or creating a very shallow solid extrude (although this can be very detrimental to rebuild and graphics speed).

CAUTION   A word of caution is needed when using split lines, especially if you plan to add or remove split lines from an existing model. The split lines should go as far down the tree as possible. Split lines change the face IDs of the faces that they split, and often the edges as well. If you roll back and apply a split line before existing features, you may have a significant amount of cleanup to do. Similarly, if you remove a split line that already has several dependent features, then many other features may also be deleted or simply lose their references.

Filleting

SolidWorks offers very powerful filleting functions. Many filleting options are available, but most of them are relatively little used or even known. In fact, most users confine themselves to the Constant Radius or Variable Radius fillets. The following section describes all of the available fillet types and options:

- Constant Radius Fillet
    - Multiple Radius Fillet
    - Round Corners
    - Keep Edge/Keep Surface
    - Keep Feature
- Variable Radius Fillet
- Face Fillet
    - Curvature Continuous Fillet
    - Face Fillet with Help Point
    - Single Hold Line Fillet
    - Double Hold Line Fillet
    - Constant Width Fillet
- Full Round Fillet
- Setback Fillet
    - Setback Fillet with Variable Radius

Figure 7.25 shows the Fillet PropertyManager. There are other options that affect preview and selection of items, and these options are discussed in this section.

The Fillet feature comprises various types of functionality. Simple fillets on straight and round edges are handled differently from variable-radius fillets, which are handled differently from the single or double hold line fillet or setback fillets. Once you click the OK button to create a fillet as a certain type, you cannot switch it to another type. You can switch types before the OK button is clicked.

FIGURE 7.25

The Fillet PropertyManager

Creating a constant radius fillet

Constant radius fillets are the default type that are created if you select only edges, features, or faces without changing any settings. When applying fillets in large numbers, you should consider several best-practice guidelines and other recommendations that come later in this chapter.

There are still some long-time users who distinguish between fillets and rounds (where fillets add material and rounds remove it). SolidWorks does not distinguish between the two, and even two edges that are selected for use with the same fillet feature can have opposite functions, for example, both adding and removing material in a single feature.

Selecting entities to fillet

You can create fillets from several selections, including edges, faces, features, and loops. Edges offer the most direct method, and are the easiest to control. Figure 7.26 shows how you can use each of these selections to more intelligently create fillets on parts.

TIP To select features for filleting, you must select them from the FeatureManager. The Selection Filter only filters edges and faces for fillet selection. You can select loops in two ways, through the RMB Select Loop option, or by selecting a face and Ctrl-selecting an edge on the face.

Another option for selecting edges in the Fillet command is the Select Through Faces option, which appears on the Fillet Options panel. This option enables you to select edges that are hidden by the model. This can be a useful option on a part with few hidden edges, or a detrimental option on a part where there are many edges due to patterns, ribs, vents, or existing fillets. You can control a similar option globally for features other than fillets at Tools ⇨ Options ⇨ Display/Selection, Allow Selection In HLR and Shaded Modes.

Faces and Features selections are useful when you are creating fillets where you want the selections to update. In Figure 7.26, the ribs that are intersecting the circular boss are also being filleted. If the rib did not exist when the fillet was applied, but was added later and reordered so that it came before the Fillet feature, then the fillet selection automatically takes the rib into account. If the fillet used edge selection, then this automatic selection updating would not have taken place.

Tangent propagation

By default, fillets have the Tangent Propagation option turned on. This is almost always a good choice, although there may be times when you want to experiment with turning it off. Tangent propagation simply means that if you select an edge to fillet, and this edge is tangent to other edges, then the fillet will keep going along tangent edges until it forms a closed loop, the tangent edges stop, or the fillet fails.

If you turn off Tangent Propagation, but there are still tangent edges, then you may see different results. One possible result is that it could fail. One of the tricks with fillet features is to try to envision what you are asking the software to do. For example, if one edge is filleted and the next edge is not, then how is the fillet going to end? Figure 7.27 shows two of the potential results when fillets are asked not to propagate, whether or not to tangent edges. The fillet face may continue along its path until it runs off of the part, or until the feature fails.

FIGURE 7.26

Selection options for fillets

Radius: 0.2in

Radius: 0.1in

Radius: 0.1in

Select individual edges

Selecting a loop is just a
shortcut to selecting several edges

Selecting a feature fillets
all the edges
that touch the feature

Selecting a face fillets all
edges around the face

FIGURE 7.27

Turning off the Tangent Propagation option

TIP This may sound counter-intuitive, but sometimes when fillet features fail, it may be useful to turn off propagation and make the fillet in multiple features. There are times when creating two fillets like the one shown in Figure 7.27 will work when making the same geometry as a single feature will not. This may be due to geometry problems where the sharp edges come together and are eliminated by the fillet.

BEST PRACTICE In general, fillets should be the last features that are applied to a model, particularly the small cosmetic or edge break fillets. Larger fillets that contribute to the structure or overall shape of the part may be applied earlier.

Be careful of the rock-paper-scissors game that you inevitably get caught up in when modeling plastic parts and deciding on the feature order of fillets, draft, and shell. Most fillets should come after draft, and large fillets should come before the shell. Draft may come either before or after the shell, depending on the needs of the area that you are dealing with on the part. In short, there is no single set of rules that you can consistently apply and that works best in all situations.

Dealing with a large number of fillets

Figure 7.28 shows a model with a bit of a filleting nightmare. This is a large plastic tray that requires many ribs underneath for strength. Because the ribs may be touched by the user, the sharp edges need to be rounded. Literally hundreds of edges would need to be selected to create the fillets if you do not use an advanced technique.

FIGURE 7.28

A plastic tray with a large number of fillets

Selecting Entities

Some of the techniques outlined previously, such as face and feature selection, can be useful for quickly filleting a large number of edges. Another method that still selects a large number of edges, but is not as intuitive as the others, is window selection of the edges. To use this option effectively, you may want to first position the model into a view where only the correct edges will be selected, turn off the Select Through Faces option, and use the Edges Selection filter.

Using Preview

I like to use the fillet preview. It helps to see what the fillet will look like, and perhaps more important, the presence of a preview usually means that the fillet will work.

Unfortunately, when you have a large number of fillets to create, the preview can cause a significant slowdown. Turning it off or using the Partial Preview are both possible options. Partial Preview shows the fillet on only one edge in the selection, and is much faster when you are creating a large number of fillets.

PERFORMANCE For rebuild speed efficiency, you should make fillets in a minimum number of features. For example, if you have 100 edges to fillet, it is better for performance to do it with a single fillet feature that has 100 edges selected rather than 100 fillet features that have one edge selected. This is the one case where creating the feature and rebuilding the feature are both faster by choosing a particular technique (usually if it is faster to create, it rebuilds more slowly).

BEST PRACTICE Although creation and rebuild speed are in sync when you use the minimum number of features to create the maximum number of fillets, this is not usually the case. (There had to be a downside.) When a single feature has a large selection, any one of these edges that fail to fillet will cause the entire feature to fail. As a result, a feature with 100 edges selected is 100 times more likely to fail than a feature with a single edge. Large selection sets are also far more difficult to troubleshoot when they fail than small selection sets that fail.

Using folders

When you have a large number of fillet features, it can be tedious to navigate the FeatureManager. It is therefore useful to place groups of fillets into folders. This makes it easy to suppress or unsuppress all of the fillets in the folder at once. Separate folders can be particularly useful if the fillets have different uses, such as fillets that are used for PhotoWorks models, and fillets that are removed for FEA or drawings.

Multiple Radius Fillet

The Multiple Radius Fillet option in the Fillet PropertyManager enables you to make multiple fillet sizes within a single fillet feature. Figure 7.29 shows how the multiple radius Fillet feature looks when you are working with it. You can change values from the callout flags or in the PropertyManager.

FIGURE 7.29

Using the Multiple Radius Fillet option

This may seem like an attractive way to group several fillets into as small a space on the FeatureManager as possible, but I cannot think of a single reason that would drive me to use this option. While there may be a small performance benefit to condensing several features into one, there are many more downsides that adversely affect performance:

- Loss of control of feature order
- A single failed fillet causes the whole feature, and thus all of the fillets, to fail

- Troubleshooting is far more difficult
- Smaller groups of fillets cannot be suppressed without suppressing everything
- You cannot change the size of a group of fillets together

BEST PRACTICE   While this may be more personal opinion than best practice, I believe that there are good reasons to consider using techniques other than single features that contain a lot of fillets, or single features that drive fillets of various sizes. Best practice would lean more toward grouping fillets that have a similar use and the same size. For example, you may want to separate fillets that break corners on ribs from fillets that round the outer shape of a large plastic part.

Another consideration is feature order when it comes to the fillet's relationship to draft and shell features. If the fillets are all grouped into a single feature, then controlling this relationship becomes impossible.

Round Corners

The Round Corners option refers to how SolidWorks handles fillets that go around sharp corners. By default, this setting is off, which leaves fillets around sharp corners looking like mitered picture frames. If you turn this setting on, the corner looks like a marble has rolled around it. Figure 7.30 shows the resulting geometry from both settings.

FIGURE 7.30

The Round Corners option, both on and off

Round corners off   Round corners on

Keep Edge/Keep Surface

The Keep Edge/Keep Surface toggle determines what SolidWorks should do if a fillet is too big to fit in an area. The Keep Edge option keeps the edge where it is and tweaks the position (not the radius) of the fillet to make it meet the edge. The Keep Surface option keeps the surfaces of the fillet and the end face clean; however, to do this, it has to tweak the edge. There is often a tradeoff when you try to place fillets into a space that is too small. Sometimes it is useful to try to visualize what you think the result should look like. Figure 7.31 shows how the fillet would look in a perfect world, followed by how the fillet looks when cramped with the Keep Edge option, and how it looks when cramped with the Keep Surface option.

The Default option chooses the best option for a particular situation. As a result, it seems to use the Keep Edge option unless it does not work, in which case it changes to the Keep Surface option.

Keep Feature

The Keep Feature option appears on the Options panel of the Fillet PropertyManager. By default, this option is turned on. If a fillet completely surrounds a feature such as a hole (as long as it is not a through hole) or a boss, then turning off the Keep Feature option removes the hole or boss. When Keep Feature is on, the faces of the feature trim or extend to match the fillet, as shown in Figure 7.32.

FIGURE 7.31

The Keep Edge option and the Keep Surface option

FIGURE 7.32

The Keep Feature option, both on and off

Part before fillet

Keep feature off

Keep feature on

Creating variable radius fillets

Variable radius fillets are another powerful weapon in the fight against boring designs; they also double as a useful tool to solve certain problems that arise. Although it is difficult to define exactly when to use the variable radius fillet, you can use it when you need a fillet to round an edge, and it has to change in size to fit the available geometry.

BEST PRACTICE It may be easier to identify when *not* to use a variable radius fillet. Fillets are generally used to round or break edges, not to sculpt a part. If you are using fillets to sculpt blocky parts, unless you are actively trying to make blocky parts with big fillets, then you may consider another approach using complex modeling, which will give the part a better shape and make it more controllable. Other options exist that give you a different type of control, such as the double hold line fillet.

In some ways, variable radius fillets function like other fillets. For example, they offer propagation to tangent edges and preview options.

Applying the values

When you first select an edge for the variable radius fillet, the endpoints are identified by callout flags with the value *unassigned*. A preview does not display until at least one of the points has a radius value in the box. You can also apply radius values in the PropertyManager, but they are easier to keep track of using the callouts. Figure 7.33 shows a variable radius fillet after the edge selection, after one value has been applied, and after three values have been applied. To apply a radius value that is not at the endpoint of an edge, you can select one of the three colored dots along the selected edge. The preview should show you how the fillet will look in wireframe display.

By default, the variable radius fillet puts five points on an edge, one at each endpoint, one at the midpoint, and one each halfway between the ends and middle. If you want to create an additional control point, there are three ways to do this:

- Ctrl-drag an existing point.
- Select the callout of an existing point and change the P (percentage) value.
- Change the Number of Instances value in the Variable Radius Parameters panel of the PropertyManager.

FIGURE 7.33

Assigning values to a variable radius fillet

If you have selected several edges, and several unassigned values are on the screen, then you can use the Set Unassigned option in the PropertyManager to set them all to the same value. The Set All option sets all radius values to the same number, including any values that you may have changed to be different than the rest. Figure 7.34 shows the Variable Radius Parameters panel.

FIGURE 7.34

The Variable Radius Parameters panel of the Fillet PropertyManager

Another available option with the variable radius fillet is that you can set a value of zero at an end of the fillet. You need to be careful about using a zero radius, because it is likely to cause downstream problems with other fillets, shells, offsets, and even machining operations. You cannot assign a zero radius in the middle of an edge, only at the end. If you need to end a fillet at a particular location, you can use a split line to split the edge and apply a zero radius at that point. Figure 7.35 shows a part with two zero-radius values.

FIGURE 7.35

Zero radius values in the variable radius fillet

Straight versus smooth transitions

Variable radius fillets have an option for either a straight transition or a smooth transition. This works like the two-profile lofts that were mentioned earlier in this chapter. The names may be somewhat misleading because both transitions are smooth. The straight transition goes in a straight line, from one size to the next, and the smooth transition takes a swooping S-shaped path between the sizes. The difference between these two transitions is demonstrated in Figure 7.36.

FIGURE 7.36

Straight versus smooth transitions of a variable radius fillet

Straight transition

Smooth transition

Other reasons to use the variable radius fillet

Variable radius fillets use a different method to create the fillet geometry than the default constant radius fillet. Sometimes using a variable radius fillet can make a difference where a constant radius fillet does not work. This is sometimes true even when the variable radius fillet uses constant radius values. It is just another tool in the toolbox.

Face fillet

Face fillets may be the most flexible type of fillet because of the range of what they can do. Face fillets start as simply an alternate selection technique for a constant radius fillet and extend to the extremely flexible double hold line face fillet, which is more of a blend than a fillet.

Under normal circumstances, the default fillet type uses the selection of an edge to create the fillet. An edge is used because it represents the intersection between two faces. However, there can sometimes be a problem with the edge not being clean, or being broken up into smaller pieces, or any number of other reasons causing a constant radius fillet using an edge selection to fail. In cases like this, SolidWorks displays the error message, "Failed to create fillet. Please check the input geometry and radius values or try using the 'Face Fillet' option."

Users almost universally ignore these messages. In the situation shown in Figure 7.37, the Face Fillet option suggested in the error message is exactly the one that you should use. Here the face fillet covers over all of the junk on the edge that prevents the fillet from executing.

FIGURE 7.37

A face fillet covering a bad corner

Face fillets are sometimes amazing at covering over a mess of geometry that you might think you could never fillet. The main limitation on fillets of this type is that the fillet must be *big* enough to bridge the gap. That's right, I said *big* enough. Face fillets can fail if they are either too small or too large. Figure 7.38 shows a complex fillet situation that is completely covered by a face fillet.

FIGURE 7.38

A face fillet covering complex geometry

The model used for this image can be found on the CD-ROM, with the filename Chapter 7 Plastic Cover Fillets.sldprt.

Continuous curvature face fillets

Curvature continuity refers to the quality of a transition between two curves or faces, where the curvature is the same or continuous at and around the transition. The best way to convey this concept is with simple 2D sketch elements. When a line transitions to an arc, you have non-continuous curvature. The line has no curvature, and there is an abrupt change because the arc has a specific radius.

NOTE Radius is the inverse of curvature, and so $r = 1/c$. For a straight line, $r = \infty$, in which case $c = 0$.

In order to make the transition from $r = \infty$ to $r = 2$ smoothly, you would need to use a variable radius arc if such a thing existed. There are several types of sketch geometry that have variable curvature, such as ellipses, parabolas, and splines. Ellipses and parabolas follow specific mathematical formulas to create the shape, but the spline is a general curve that can take on any shape that you want, and its curvature can be controlled to change smoothly or continuously. Splines, by their very definition, have continuous curvature within the spline, although you cannot control the specific curvature or radius values directly.

All of this means that continuous curvature face fillets use a spline-based variable-radius section for the fillet, rather than an arc-based constant radius. Figure 7.39 illustrates the difference between continuous curvature and constant curvature. The spikes on top of the curves represent the curvature (1/r, and so the smaller the radius, the taller the spike). These spikes are called a *curvature comb*.

FIGURE 7.39

Using curvature combs to evaluate transitions

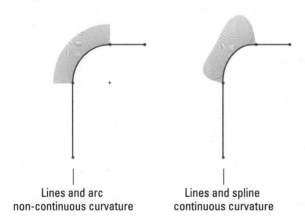

Lines and arc
non-continuous curvature

Lines and spline
continuous curvature

NOTE This screen shot was taken in SolidWorks 2007 sp1. The display of the curvature comb in SolidWorks 2006 will have a top curve on the curvature comb. This curve has been removed in the early versions of 2007, but it may be restored in a later service pack.

Notice how in Figure 7.39, the curvature comb immediately jumps from no curvature to the constant arc radius, but the spline image ramps up to a curvature that varies.

Face fillets with Help point

The Help point in the Face Fillet PropertyManager is a fairly obscure option. However, it is useful in cases where the selection of two faces does not uniquely identify an edge to fillet. For example, Figure 7.40 shows a situation where the selection of two faces could result in either one edge or the other being filleted (normally, I would hope that both edges would be filleted). The fillet will default to one edge or the other, but you can force it to a definite edge using the Help point.

FIGURE 7.40

Using a Help point with a face fillet

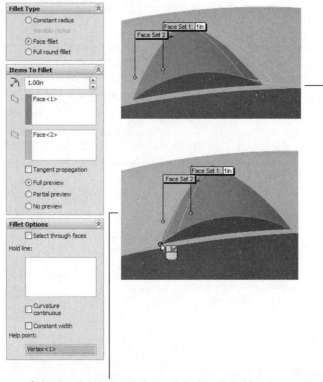

Selecting the Help point forces it to the other side

Face fillet defaults to the right side

In some cases, the Help point is ignored altogether. For example, if you have a simple box, and select both ends of the box as selection set 1, and the top of the box as selection set 2, then the fillet could go to either end. Consequently, assigning a Help point will not do anything in this case, because multiple faces have been selected. The determining factor is which of the multiple faces is selected first. If this were a more commonly used feature, the interface for it might be made a little less cryptic, but because this feature is rarely, if ever, used, it just becomes a quirky piece of trivia.

Single hold line fillet

A single hold line fillet is a form of variable radius fillet, but instead of it being defined using the variable radius fillet type, it is created using the face fillet. Rather than the radius being driven by specific numerical values, it is driven by a hold line, or edge, on the model. The hold line can be an existing edge, forcing the fillet right up to the edge of the part, or it can be created by a split line, which enables you to drive the fillet however you like. Figure 7.41 shows these two options, before and after the fillets. Notice that these fillets are still arc-based fillets; if you were to take a cross-section perpendicular to the edge between filleted faces, it would be an arc cross-section with a distinct radius. However, in the other direction, hold line fillets do not necessarily have a constant radius, although they may if the hold line is parallel with the edge between faces.

FIGURE 7.41

Single hold line fillets

Hold line (edge)   Hold line (split line)

You can select the Hold line in the Fillet Options panel of the Face Fillet PropertyManager, as shown in Figure 7.42. The top panel, Fillet Type, is available only when the feature is first created. When you edit it after it has been created, the Fillet Type panel does not appear. As a result, you cannot change from one type of fillet to another after it has been initially created.

FIGURE 7.42

The PropertyManager interface for the hold line face fillet

Double hold line fillet

There are times when a single hold line does not meet your needs. The single hold line controls only one side of the fillet, and in order to control both sides of the fillet, you must use a double hold line fillet. SolidWorks software does not specifically differentiate between the single and double hold line fillets, but they are radically different in how they create the geometry. When both sides of the fillet are controlled, it is not possible to span between the hold lines with an arc that is tangent to both sides unless you were careful about setting up the hold lines so that they are equidistant from the edge where the faces intersect. This means that the double hold line fillet must use a spline to span between hold lines, as shown in Figure 7.43.

To get this feature to work, you need to use the Curvature Continuous option in the Fillet Options panel. Remember that this option creates a spline-based fillet rather than an arc-based fillet, which is exactly what you need for a double hold line fillet. This makes the double hold line fillet more of a blend than a true fillet. Figure 7.44 shows examples of the double hold line fillet.

FIGURE 7.43

A double hold line uses a spline, not an arc.

Arc tangent on both ends
does not fit both edges

Spline tangent
on both ends fits

FIGURE 7.44

Examples of the double hold line fillet

Constant width fillet

The Constant Width option of the Face Fillet PropertyManager drives a fillet by its width rather than by its radius. This is most helpful on parts where the angle of the faces between which you are filleting is changing dramatically. Figure 7.45 illustrates two situations where this is particularly useful. The setting for constant width is found in the Options panel of the Face Fillet PropertyManager. The part shown in the images is on the CD-ROM, using the filename Chapter 7 Constant Width.SLDPRT.

The constant width fillet

No fillet   Default face fillet   Face fillet with Constant Width option

Full round fillet

The full round fillet is very useful in many situations. In fact, it may actually work in situations where you would not expect it to. It does require quite a bit of effort to accomplish the selection, but it compensates by allowing you to avoid alternate fillet techniques.

To create a full round fillet, you have to select three sets of faces. Usually one face in each set is sufficient. The fillet is tangent to all three sets of faces, but the middle set is on the end, and the face is completely eliminated. Figure 7.46 shows several applications of the full round fillet. Notice that it is not limited to faces of a square block, but also propagates around tangent entities and can create a variable radius fillet over irregular lofted geometry.

FIGURE 7.46

A full round fillet

Setback fillet

The setback fillet is the most complex of the fillet options. You can use the Setback option in conjunction with constant radius, multiple radius, and variable radius fillet types. A setback fillet blends several fillets together at a single vertex, starting the blend at some "setback" distance along each filleted edge from the vertex. At least three, and often more, edges come together at the setback vertex. Figure 7.47 shows the PropertyManager interface and what a finished setback fillet looks like. The following steps demonstrate how to use the setback fillet.

Setting up a setback fillet can take some time, especially if you are just learning about this feature. You must specify values for fillet radiuses, select edges and vertices, and specify six setback distances. If you are using multiple radius fillets or variable radius fillets, then this becomes an even larger task. The steps are as follows:

1. Determine the type of fillet to be used:

   ▪ Constant radius fillet

   ▪ Multiple radius fillet

   ▪ Variable radius fillet

FIGURE 7.47

The Setback Fillet Interface and a finished fillet

Setback vertices: all edges coming
to these vertices will be filleted

2. Select the edges to be filleted. Selected edges must all touch one of the setback vertices that will be selected in a later step.

3. Assign radius values for the filleted items. Figure 7.48 shows a sample part that illustrates this step.

FIGURE 7.48

The setback fillet setup for steps 1 through 3

4. Select the setback vertices. In the Setback Parameters panel of the PropertyManager, with the second box down highlighted, select the vertices. Although this box looks like it is only big enough for a single selection, it can accept multiple selections.

5. Enter setback values. As shown in Figure 7.49, the setback callout flags have leaders that point from a specific value to a specific edge. The dimensions refer to distances, as shown in the image to the right in Figure 7.49. The setback distance is the distance over which the fillet will blend from the corner to the fillet.

Entering setback values

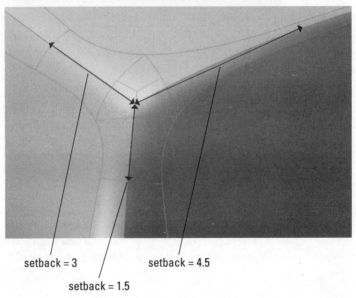

> **CAUTION** When you select multiple vertices, the preview arrows that indicate which edge you are currently setting the setback value for may be incorrect. The arrows can only be shown on one vertex, and so you may want to rely on the leaders from the callouts to determine which setback distance you are currently setting.

6. Repeat the process for all selected setback vertices. If you are using a preview, then you may notice that the preview goes away when starting a second set of setback values. Don't worry. This is probably not because the feature is going to fail. Once you finish typing the values, the preview will return. When you have spent as much time setting up a feature as you will spend on this, seeing the preview disappear can be frustrating; however, persevere, and it will return.

Selecting a Specialty Feature

SolidWorks contains several specialty features that perform tasks that you will use less often. Although you will not use these features as frequently as others, you should still at least be aware of them and what they do, because you never know when you will need them.

Dome and Shape

The Dome and Shape features are similar in many ways. For example, they both bulge or indent a single selected face. Neither of these features really offers you much control over the actual shape; instead, the shape is controlled by the following:

- The shape of the selected face
- An internal algorithm
- Various settings
- A constraint sketch

While each of these elements influences the shape of the feature, this influence is not predictable or controllable — it is more of a random or approximate affect. When SolidWorks first released the Shape feature, they advertised it as a complex shape-creation tool. In fairness, it does create complex shapes, but they are not truly intentional, predictable, or controllable, and are certainly not anything that you would use on a consumer product. Dome and Shape are quick approximations, and rarely achieve professional-looking results.

> **BEST PRACTICE** Dome and Shape features are best used when you are looking for a generic bulge or indentation, and are not too concerned about controlling the specific shape. Occasionally, one of these features may be exactly what you need, but when you need more precise, predictable control, then you should use the Loft feature. Of these two features, Dome is the most useful.

Because there are more similarities than differences between the Dome and Shape features, the differences are listed first to distinguish them:

- The Dome feature can create multiple domes on multiple selected faces in a single feature, although it creates only a single dome for each face. Shape can shape only a single face for each command.

- Using the Elliptical Dome setting, Dome can create a feature that is tangent to the vertical. Shape is always tangent to the face that you have selected to create it.

- Shape has controls named Pressure, Bend, and Stretch, implying that you should visualize its function as an elastic membrane with positive or negative fluid pressure that causes it to bulge or collapse inward.

The similarities between the features include the following:

- Both features can use constraint sketches to limit their shape.

- Both features work on non-planar faces.

- Neither feature can establish a tangent relationship to faces bordering the selected face.

- Neither feature can span multiple faces.

- Both features display a temporary untrimmed four-sided patch that extends beyond the selected face when you use them on a non-four-sided face.

- Both features function on solids.

- Neither feature functions on surfaces.

The Dome and Shape interfaces are shown in Figure 7.50. Notice that the Shape feature is not integrated into the PropertyManager. This is always a sign of a feature that is not used often. As is the case with a rarely used feature that is not very useful, the feature may disappear rather than be updated.

The Dome feature has two notable settings, the elliptical dome and continuous dome.

The elliptical dome is available only on flat faces where the boundary is either a complete circle or an ellipse. The cross-section of the dome is elliptical, and does not account for draft, which means that it is always tangent to the perpendicular from the selected flat face.

The continuous dome is a setting for any non-circular or elliptical face, including polygons and closed-loop splines. The setting results in a single unbroken face. If you turn the continuous dome setting off, it functions like the elliptical dome setting. Figure 7.51 shows the most useful settings for the Dome feature.

FIGURE 7.50

Dome and Shape interfaces

FIGURE 7.51

Settings for the Dome feature

Non-continuous dome

Elliptical dome   Non-elliptical dome

Continuous dome

Wrap feature

The Wrap feature enables you to wrap 2D sketches around cylindrical and conical faces. However, trying to wrap around 360 degrees can cause some difficulties. Although all of the available information on the Wrap feature says that you can wrap onto a conical surface, it fails to mention that the point of the cone must be cut off in order for it to work.

The Wrap feature works by flattening the face, relating the sketch to the flat pattern of the face, and then mapping the face boundaries and sketch back onto the 3D face. The reason why it is limited to cylindrical and conical faces is that these types of geometry are *developable*. This means that the faces can be mapped to the flat pattern through some relatively simple techniques that happen behind the scenes. Developable geometry can be flattened without stretching. You will see in a later chapter that sheet metal functions are limited in the same way and for the same reasons.

SolidWorks does not wrap onto other types of surfaces, such as spherical, toroidal, or general NURBS surfaces, because you cannot flatten these shapes without distorting or stretching the material. There is software that can flatten these shapes, but it is typically done for sheet-metal deep drawing applications, which highly deform the metal.

The Wrap feature has three main options:

- Emboss
- Deboss
- Scribe

Figure 7.52 shows the Wrap PropertyManager interface.

FIGURE 7.52

The Wrap PropertyManager interface

Scribe

Scribe is the simplest of the options to explain, and understanding it can help you understand the other options. Scribe creates a split line-like edge on the face.

Several requirements must be met in order to make a wrap feature work:

- A cylindrical or conical face.
- A closed loop or nested closed loop 2D sketch.
- The sketch must be on a plane that is either tangent to or parallel to another plane that is tangent to the face.
- The wrap should not be self-intersecting when it wraps around the part (self-intersection will not cause the feature to fail, but on the other types, Emboss and Deboss, it may produce unexpected results).

Scribes can be created on solid or surface faces. Scribed surfaces are frequently thickened to create a boss or a cut.

Emboss

The Wrap Emboss option works much like the scribe, but it adds material inside the closed loop sketch, at the thickness that you specify in the Emboss PropertyManager. Embossing can only be done on solid geometry. If the feature self-intersects, then the intersecting area is simply not embossed, and is left at the level of the original face. One result is that creating a full wrap-around feature, such as the geometry for a barrel cam, requires a secondary feature. This is because the Wrap feature always leaves a gap, regardless of whether the sketch to be wrapped is under or over the diameter-multiplied-by-pi length.

 To work around this problem, you can use a loft, extrude, or revolve feature to span the gap.

When you use the Emboss option, you can set up the direction of pull and assign draft so that the feature can be injection molded. This limits the size of the emboss so that it must not wrap more than 180 degrees around the part.

Deboss

Deboss is just like emboss, except that it removes material instead of adding it.

Figure 7.53 demonstrates all of these options. The part shown in the images is available on the CD-ROM with the filename Chapter 7 Wrap.sldprt. For each of the demonstrated cases, the original flat sketch is shown to give you some idea of how the sketch relates to the finished geometry.

FIGURE 7.53

The Wrap Feature options

Sketch

Scribed edge

Embossed barrel cam

Closed loop cam profile sketch

Scribed surface feature
thickened into a solid and patterned

Keep in mind that this feature is not like the projected sketch. A projected sketch is not foreshortened on the curved surface, but is projected normal from the sketch plane. A sketch that is one inch long will measure one inch along the curvature of the surface, and will measure less than one inch linearly from end to end.

The scribed part in the figure above was created on a conical surface body. The surface was then thickened as a separate body and patterned.

CROSS-REF   Chapter 26 covers working with multiple bodies, and Chapter 27 covers surfaces.

The embossed cam employed a workaround with a revolve feature to close the gap that is always created when wrapping all the way around a part.

The example with the debossed text employs a direction of pull and draft so that the geometry can be molded.

Flex

The Flex feature is different from most other features in SolidWorks. Most other features create new geometry, but Flex (and Deform, which follows) takes existing geometry and changes its shape. Flex can affect the entire part, or just a portion of it. Flex works on both solid and surface bodies, as well as imported and native geometry.

Figure 7.54 shows the Flex PropertyManager interface. Flex has four main options, and many settings. The four main options are as follows:

- **Bending**: Establish two trim planes to denote the ends of the bent area, and specify an angle or radius for the bend.

- **Twisting**: Establish two trim planes to limit the area of the twist, and enter the number of degrees through which to twist.

- **Tapering**: Establish two trim planes to limit the area of the taper. The body will be larger toward one end and smaller toward the other end.

- **Stretching**: Establish two trim planes to limit the area to be stretched. You can stretch the entire body by moving the trim planes outside of the body.

BEST PRACTICE   Flex is not the kind of feature that you should use to actually *design* parts, but it can be extremely valuable when you need to show a part in an "in use" state. A simple example would be a rubber strap that stretches over something when it is used, but that is designed and manufactured in its free state. The geometry that you can create by using the flex functions is not generally production-model quality, but it is usually adequate for a looks-like model.

Figure 7.55 shows examples of each flex option using a model of a rubber grommet. The part shown in the figure can be found on the CD-ROM with the filename Chapter 7 Flex.sldprt.

In some cases, the triad and trim planes are slightly disoriented. The best thing to do in situations like this is to simply reorient the triad using the angle numbers in the Triad panel of the PropertyManager. This is also a solution if the planes are turned in such a way that the axis of bending is not oriented to the bend that the part requires.

FIGURE 7.54

The Flex PropertyManager interface

The Flex feature is very conscious of separate bodies. In some cases this can be helpful, but in default situations when there is only one body in the part, it can be annoying. Remember to select the body to be affected in the very first selection box at the top of the PropertyManager.

TIP   If you want to bend only one of the tabs on the grommet, then the best solution is to split the single body into two bodies, and flex only one of the bodies. The examples shown for twisting and stretching use this technique.

CROSS-REF   Splitting a single body into multiple bodies is covered in Chapter 26.

FIGURE 7.55

A rubber grommet in various flex states

Twisting

Bending

Natural position

Stretching

Notice bodies have been split

You can place the trim planes by selecting a model vertex, by dragging the arrow on the plane, or by typing in a number. Be careful when dragging the plane arrows because dragging the border of the plane drags the flex value for the feature. (Dragging the plane in a bending operation is like changing the angle or radius for the bend.)

Using the triad can be very tricky. Moving the triad in the bending option moves the axis of the bend, and so it determines whether the bend will compress or stretch the material. The position of the triad also determines which side of the bent body will move or stay stationary, or if both sides will move. Placing the triad directly on a trim plane causes the material outside the bend on that side of the trim plane to remain stationary.

I highly recommend taking a look at the models that are provided with this chapter to examine the various functions of the Flex feature more carefully. The model uses configurations, which are covered in Chapter 10.

Deform

Like the Flex feature, Deform changes the shape of the entire model without regard to parametrics, features, history, or dimensions. Some software packages call this technique *global shape modeling*. Also like Flex, Deform works on surface bodies as well as solids. Deform can also handle imported geometry as well as SolidWorks native parts. Model complexity is not an issue unless the part runs into itself during deformation.

The Deform feature is also another feature type that you may not use to actually design anything, but that you may use to show a model in a deformed state.

BEST PRACTICE Typically, if you want a model to have a certain shape, then you need to intentionally and precisely model it with that shape. The problem with using deform and flex geometry for actual design data is that they both create fairly approximate geometry, and this process yields a result that is not completely intentional. The shape that you finally achieve is the result of arbitrary uncontrolled function of the feature, not necessarily creating a shape that you had clearly envisioned beforehand.

Deform has three types:

- **Point**: Deforms a portion of the model by pushing a point and the geometry around it.
- **Curve to Curve**: The most precise and useful deform type. Select an existing edge and force the edge to match a curve.
- **Surface Push**: This type of deform, while conceptually a very interesting function, is nearly unusable in practice. The part is deformed into a shape vaguely resembling an intermediate shape between the existing state of the part and a "tool" body.

Figure 7.56 shows the PropertyManager interface for the Deform feature. The interface is different for each of the three main types, and also changes, depending on selections within the individual types. The interface shown is for the curve to curve type because I believe this to be the most useful type.

FIGURE 7.56

The PropertyManager interface for the curve to curve deform

Point Deform

The Point Deform option enables you to push a point on the model, and the model deforms as if it were rubber. Figure 7.57 shows the PropertyManager, as well as a before-and-after example of the Point Deform function. The key to using this feature is to ensure that the Deform Region option is turned off. Aside from that, you just have to use trial and error when applying the Deform option. The depth, diameter, and shape of the deformation are not very precise. Also, you cannot specify the precise location for the point to be deformed. Again, this is best used for "looks-like" models, and not production data.

The Deform Point PropertyManager, and a before-and-after example

In the model from Figure 7.57, two Point Deform features are used, one to apply some shape to the back and one to apply some shape to the seat.

Curve to Curve Deform

Because this option uses curve (or sketch or edge) data, it is a more precise method than the other deform types. The main concept here is to transform a curve on the original model to a new curve, thus deforming the body to achieve the new geometry.

The model shown in Figure 7.58 has been created using the curve to curve deform. The part starts as a simple sweep (sweep an arc along an arc), and then a split line is created to limit the deform to a specific area of the model. The model is on the CD-ROM with the filename Chapter 7 Deform Curve to Curve.sldprt.

Surface Push Deform

I do not go into much detail on the Surface Push Deform type because it is not one of the more useful functions in SolidWorks. In order to use it, you must have the body of the part that you are modeling, and a tool body that will be used to shape the part that you are modeling. The finished shape does not fit the tool body directly, but looks about half-way between the model and the tool body, blended together in an abstract sort of way. It looks like the dent that would result from an object being thrown very hard at a car fender, in that neither the thrown part nor the fender are immediately recognizable from the result.

FIGURE 7.58

Using the curve to curve deform option

Indent

 The Indent feature is what the Surface Push Deform is trying to be, or should try to be. Indent uses the same ingredients as the Surface Push, but it produces a result that is both intelligible and useful. For example, if you are building a plastic housing around a small electric motor, then the Indent feature shapes the housing and creates a gap between the housing and the motor. Figure 7.59 shows the PropertyManager interface for the Indent feature, as well as a before-and-after shot of the indent.

FIGURE 7.59

Using the Indent feature

In this case, the small motor is placed where it needs to be, but there is a wall in the way. Indent is used to create an indentation in the wall using the same wall thickness, and placing a gap of .010 inches around the motor. The motor is brought into the wall part using the Insert ➪ Part command. This is a multibody technique. Multibodies are examined in detail in Chapter 26.

Tutorial: Bracket Casting

When you follow this tutorial, you are encouraged to follow the directions the first time to make sure that you understand the concepts involved, and then to go through it again, this time deviating from the instructions to see if you can expand your understanding by experimentation. To try bracket casting, follow these steps:

1. Open a new part using an inch-based template.

2. On the Right plane, draw a circle centered at the origin with a diameter of .150 inches, and a second circle placed 4.000 inches vertically from the first, with a diameter of 2.250 inches.

3. Extrude the sketch 1.000 inch using a From condition of Offset by 1.000 inch, such that the offset and the extrude depth are in the same direction. Rename this feature Bosses in the FeatureManager. Figure 7.60 shows the results of these steps.

FIGURE 7.60

The results of steps 1 to 3

NOTE These steps produce multiple bodies that will be merged in a later step. Multiple-body parts are covered in more detail in Chapter 26. You can tell that there are multiple bodies by looking at the Solid Bodies folder near the top of the tree, and expanding the folder. The bodies are listed in the folder.

4. On the Top plane, open a new sketch and draw a horizontal construction line across the cylinder, from the midpoint of one side to the midpoint of the other side. To pick up the automatic relations for the midpoints more easily, it is recommended that you orient the view, normal to the sketch, or use the Top view. It does not matter if you make the relations to the top or bottom cylinder, because the midpoints of the sides are in the same place when they are projected into the sketch plane.

5. Next, draw an ellipse (Tools ➪ Sketch Tools ➪ Ellipse) centered at the midpoint of the construction line and that measures .700 inches horizontally and 1.375 inches vertically. Exit the sketch.

6. Show the sketch for the Bosses feature (click the plus icon next to the Bosses extrude to show the sketch, and then RMB click the sketch and select Show).

7. Create a plane parallel to the Top plane at the center of the larger circle. You can access the Plane creation interface at Insert ➪ Reference Geometry ➪ Plane. If you select the Top plane from the flyout FeatureManager and the center of the larger sketch circle from the graphics window, then the interface will automatically select the Parallel Plane At Point option. Click OK to create the plane. Rename this plane Top Boss Plane.

8. Draw a second ellipse on the Top Boss Plane. Do not draw a construction line as you did for the first ellipse; instead, you can just make the center point of the second ellipse directly on top of the first ellipse's center point. The dimensions should be 1.000 inch horizontal by 1.750 inches vertical. Figure 7.61 shows the results up to this point.

FIGURE 7.61

The results up to step 8

TIP When you are sketching on parallel planes that are separated by some distance and try-ing to pick up automatic relations, it is often very helpful to be looking "normal to" the sketch, so that you can see how other entities are projected into the sketch plane.

9. Use the Loft feature to loft between the two ellipses. Be sure to select the ellipses in approximately the same location so that they do not twist. If the loft preview accidentally twists, then use the connectors (light-blue square dots on the sketches that are connected by a straight line) to straighten out the loft.

NOTE Notice that this feature joined together the other two disjoint bodies with the body that was created by the loft into a single body. This is a result of selecting the Merge Result option in the Options panel.

TIP If you want to experiment, expand the Start/End Constraints panel and apply end condi-tions for the loft. This causes the loft to change from a straight loft to a curved loft.

10. RMB click all sketches that are showing, and select Hide. Do the same for the Top Boss Plane. This cleans up the display to prevent it from becoming confusing. However, if you prefer to see the sketches, then you can leave them displayed.

TIP You can either hide or show different types of entities in groups by using the View menu. Hide All Types hides everything, and disables the options for individual entity types to be used.

11. Open a sketch on the Right plane. Sketch an ellipse such that the center is oriented 1.750 inches vertically from the Origin, and the ellipse measures .750 inches horizontally and 1.500 inches vertically.

12. Extrude this ellipse using the Up To Next end condition. If Up To Next does not appear in the list, then change the direction of the extrude and try it again.

13. Show the sketch of the Bosses feature and open a sketch on the Right plane. Sketch two circles that are concentric with the original circles, with the dimensions of .875 inches and 1.250 inches.

14. Create an extruded cut that goes Through All using the End Conditions options. If you get an error, then try reversing the direction of the extrude. Figure 7.62 shows the state of the model up to this step.

FIGURE 7.62

The results up to step 14

15. Start a fillet feature, and select the face of the Loft feature. Assign a radius of .200 inches.

NOTE   Although this fillet is created by selecting a face, it is not a face fillet. Selecting a face for a regular constant radius fillet simply fillets any edge that is on the face.

16. Create a mirror feature, using the Right plane as the mirror plane. In the Mirror PropertyManager, expand the Bodies To Mirror panel, and select anywhere on the part. Make sure that the Merge Solids option is selected. Click OK to accept the mirror.

17. Orient the view to the Front view, and then turn the view on its side (hold down Alt and press the left- or right-arrow key six times).

18. Open a new sketch on the Front plane. From the View menu, make sure that Hide All Types is not on, and show Temporary Axes. Draw and dimension a horizontal construction line, as shown in Figure 7.63.

19. With the construction line selected, start the Sketch Text command (Tools ⇨ Sketch Entities ⇨ Text). Make sure that the line appears in the Curves selection box.

20. Click in the text box, and type **Made in USA** (or your name or company name). Select the text and click the Bold button. Deselect the Use Document Font option, change the font to use units, and set the height to .175 inches.

21. Click OK to exit the Sketch Text PropertyManager, and click OK again to exit the sketch. You can turn off the Temporary Axis display.

FIGURE 7.63

The results up to step 18

1.750

.800

.600

22. Click Insert ➪ Features ➪ Wrap. You should be prompted to select a plane or a sketch. Use the Flyout FeatureManager to select the sketch that you just created with the sketch text in it. Next, select the cylindrical face of the boss to see a preview of the text wrapped onto the face. If the text appears backwards, then click the Reverse Direction option in the Wrap PropertyManager.

23. Select the Emboss option, and assign a thickness of .025 inches. Click in the Pull Direction selection box and select the Front plane. Click OK to accept the feature.

24. Save the part and close it. If you would like to examine a reference part, you can find it on the CD-ROM with the filename Chapter 7 Tutorial Bracket Casting.sldprt. The finished part is shown in Figure 7.64.

FIGURE 7.64

The finished part

Tutorial: Creating a Wire-Formed Part

Follow these steps to create a wire-formed part:

1. Open a new part using an inch-based template.

2. Open a sketch on the Right plane and sketch a circle that is centered on the Origin with a diameter of 1.500 inches.

3. Create a Helix, Constant Pitch, Pitch, and Revolution, where the Pitch = .250 inches, Revolutions = 5.15, and Start Angle = 0. The Helix command is found at Insert ➪ Curve ➪ Helix/Spiral.

4. Create a sketch on the Front plane, as shown in Figure 7.65. Pay careful attention when adding the construction line, as shown. This line is used in the next step to reference the end of the arc.

The results up to step 4

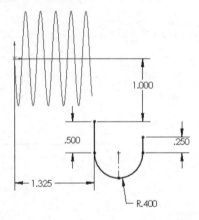

5. Open a sketch on the Right plane and use Figure 7.66 to add the correct relations and dimensions. Be aware that the two sketches shown are on different sketch planes, which makes it difficult to depict in 2D. You can also open the part from the CD-ROM for reference.

6. Exit the sketch and create a projected curve. The Projected Curve function is found at Insert ➪ Curve ➪ Projected Curve. Use the Sketch on Sketch option.

7. Open a 3D sketch. You can access a 3D sketch from the Insert menu. Select the helix and click Convert Entities on the Sketch toolbar. Then select the projected curve and click Convert Entities again. You now have two sections of a 3D sketch that are unconnected in space.

FIGURE 7.66

The sketch for step 5

Coincident

Dimension references
end of construction line

Vertical relation

8. Draw a two-point spline to join the ends of the 3D sketch entities that are closest to one another. Assign tangent relations to the ends to make the transition smooth. Figure 7.67 illustrates what the model should look like at this point.

FIGURE 7.67

The results up to step 8

Connecting spline

Adjust the length of this handle

You may have to adjust the length of one of the spline tangency length arrows to keep the spline from remaining inside the cylinder of the helix.

9. Open a sketch on the Right plane, and draw an arc that is centered on the Origin and coincident with the end of the 3D sketch helix. The 185-degree angle is created by activating the dimension tool and clicking first the center of the arc, and then the two endpoints of the arc. Now place the dimension. This type of dimensioning allows you to get an angle dimension without dimensioning to angled lines. Exit the sketch.

10. Create a Composite Curve (Insert ➪ Curve ➪ Composite) consisting of the 3D sketch and the new 2D sketch.

11. Create a new plane using the Normal to Curve option, selecting one end of the composite curve.

12. On the new plane, draw a circle that is centered on the end of the curve with a diameter of .120 inches. You need to create a Pierce relation between the center of the circle and the composite curve.

13. Create a sweep feature using the circle as the profile and the composite curve as the path. To create the sweep, you must first exit the sketch.

14. Hide any curves that still display.

15. Click Insert ➪ Cut ➪ With Surface. From the Flyout FeatureManager, select the Right plane. Make sure that the arrow is pointing to the side of the plane with the least amount of material. Click OK to accept the cut. The finished part is shown in Figure 7.68.

FIGURE 7.68

The finished part

Summary

SolidWorks has a wide range of feature types to choose from, ranging from simple extrudes and revolves to more complex lofts and sweeps. It also offers a range of specialty features that may not be useful on a day-to-day basis, but that have their place in the modeling techniques that you need to know to get the job done.

Some features, such as extrude, fillet, and flex, have so many options that it may be difficult to take them all in at once. You should browse through the models on the CD-ROM for this chapter and use the Rollback bar (described in detail in Chapter 11) to examine how the parts were built. You can then try to create a few on your own.

Chapter 8

Patterning and Mirroring

Patterning and mirroring in SolidWorks are great tools to help you improve your efficiency. The software provides many pattern types that also help you accomplish design tasks easily. In addition to the different types of patterns, there are many more detailed options that enable functionality that you may not have considered. A solid understanding of patterning and mirroring tools is necessary to be able to build the maximum amount of parametric intelligence into your models.

Patterning in a Sketch

You can use both pattern and mirror functions in Sketch mode, although sketch patterns are not a preferred choice. The distinction between patterning and mirroring in Sketch mode is important when it comes to sketch performance.

PERFORMANCE | Although there are many metrics for how software performs, in SolidWorks, the word *performance* means the same thing as *speed*. Sketch patterns have a very adverse effect on speed.

A little test

You can hear a lot of conflicting information about which features are better to use in different situations. Users coming from a 2D background often prefer to use functions such as sketch patterning because it looks familiar, without questioning whether there is a better way. When in doubt, you can perform a test to determine for yourself which is better.

In this test, I made a series of 20-by-20 patterns using circles, squares, and hexagons. The patterns were both sketch patterns and feature patterns, and were created with both Verification On Rebuild and Geometry Pattern turned on and off. Verification On Rebuild is a setting that you can access through Tools ⇨ Options ⇨ Performance ⇨ and Geometry Pattern is a setting that is applicable only to feature patterns.

Table 8.1 shows the rebuild times (in seconds) of certain types of patterns as measured by Feature Statistics (found at Tools ⇨ Feature Statistics). Sketch patterns are far slower than feature patterns, by a factor of about ten. The biggest speed reduction occurs when you use sketch patterns in conjunction with the Verification on Rebuild setting, especially as the number of sketch entities being patterned increases.

Generally, the number of faces being patterned has a significant effect on the speed of the pattern. The sketch pattern times are taken for the entire finished model, including the sketch pattern and a single extrude feature, using the sketch with the pattern to do an extruded cut. The sample parts are on the CD-ROM for reference. Look for the filenames beginning "Reference1" through "Reference7."

TABLE 8.1

Pattern Rebuild Times

Pattern Type	Default	Geometry Pattern	Verification on Rebuild
20x20 sketch circle	1.75	n/a	10.5
20x20 sketch square	10.8	n/a	143
20x20 sketch hex	19.4	n/a	294
20x20 feature circle	.19	.28	.19
20x20 feature square	.34	.55	.33
20x20 feature hex	.48	.70	.48

Figure 8.1 shows one of the parts used for this simple test.

Patterning a sketch

It is best to pre-select the sketch entities that you want to pattern before using the Sketch Pattern tool. If you do not pre-select, then after the PropertyManager is open, you can only select entities to pattern one by one because the window select is not available for this function.

 TIP   When creating a linear sketch pattern, be sure to select the Add Dimension check boxes. If these dimensions are not added, then editing the pattern becomes more difficult.

FIGURE 8.1

A pattern part used for the test

Linear Sketch Pattern

 The Linear Pattern PropertyManager is shown in Figure 8.2.

FIGURE 8.2

The Linear Pattern PropertyManager

The Direction 1 panel works predictably by establishing the direction and spacing, and then the number. The Angle setting enables you to specify a direction that does not rely on anything outside of the sketch.

Direction 2 works a little differently. You must first specify how many instances you want, and then the other information becomes available.

Circular Sketch Pattern

The Circular Sketch Pattern defaults to the sketch Origin as the center of the pattern. You can move and position this point using the numbers in the PropertyManager, but you cannot dimension it until after the pattern is created. Again, this is another feature where you need to pre-select because window selection is not available (patterned sketch entities must be selected one by one to go into the Entities to Pattern panel). Figure 8.3 shows the Circular Pattern PropertyManager.

FIGURE 8.3

The Circular Pattern PropertyManager

Mirroring in a Sketch

Mirroring in a sketch is a completely different matter from patterning in a sketch. It offers superior performance, and the interface is better developed. Mirrored entities in a sketch are an instrumental part of establishing design intent.

Two methods of mirroring items in a sketch are discussed here, along with a method to make entities work as if they have been mirrored when in fact they were manually drawn.

Mirror Entities

 Mirror Entities works by simply selecting the entities that you want to mirror along with a single centerline, and pressing the Mirror Entities button on the Sketch toolbar. It is a simple and effective tool that you can use on existing geometry.

One feature of Mirror Entities may sometimes cause unexpected results. For example, in some situations, Mirror Entities will mirror a line or an arc and merge the new element with the old one across the centerline. This happens in situations when the mirror and the original would form a single line or a single arc. SolidWorks may delete certain relations and dimensions in these situations.

Dynamic Mirror

 As the name suggests, Dynamic Mirror mirrors sketch entities as they are created. You can activate it by selecting a centerline and clicking the button on the Sketch toolbar. Dynamic Mirror is not on the toolbar by default; you need to select Tools, Customize, Commands to add it to the toolbar. You can also access Dynamic Mirror through the menus at Tools, Sketch Tools, Dynamic Mirror.

When you activate this function, the centerline displays with hatch marks on the ends, and remains active until you turn it off or exit the sketch. Figure 8.4 shows the centerline with hatch marks.

FIGURE 8.4

The Dynamic Mirror centerline with hatch marks

Symmetry sketch relation

The Symmetry sketch relation has been covered in previous chapters on sketching, but it is mentioned here because it offers you a manual way to mirror sketch entities. There are editing situations when you may not want to create new geometry, but instead use existing entities with new relations driving them.

To create the Symmetry sketch relation, you must have two similar items (such as lines or endpoints) and a centerline selected.

Geometry Pattern

The SolidWorks Help file says that the Geometry Pattern option in feature patterns results in a faster pattern because it does not pattern the parametric relations. This claim is valid only when there is an end condition on the patterned feature such that the feature will actually pattern the end condition's parametric behavior. The part shown in Figure 8.5 falls into this category. The improved rebuild time goes from .30 to .11 seconds. Although a 60-percent reduction is significant, the most compelling argument for the use of the Geometry pattern is to avoid the effect of patterning the end-condition parametrics.

FIGURE 8.5

A geometry pattern test

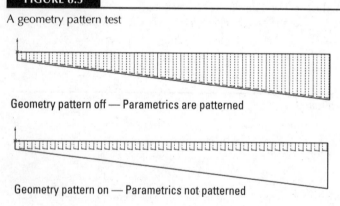

Geometry pattern off — Parametrics are patterned

Geometry pattern on — Parametrics not patterned

Under some conditions, Geometry Pattern will not work. One example is any time a patterned face would merge with an unpatterned face. These situations can be difficult to identify. Figure 8.6 shows a pattern that cannot be created using the Geometry Pattern option. The boss merges with the side face of the block, which generates the error message shown in the figure. The circular part shown in the image is an exception where the partial cylindrical bosses merge with the side of the cylinder, but Geometry Pattern works.

FIGURE 8.6

Merged faces

Patterning Bodies

The topic of multiple bodies is covered in depth in Chapter 26, but it must be dealt with briefly here. Any discussion of patterning is not complete without a discussion of bodies because using bodies is an available option with all of the pattern and mirror types.

SolidWorks parts can contain multiple solid bodies. A body is a solid that comprises a single contiguous volume. Surface bodies are defined differently, but they can also be patterned and mirrored as bodies.

There are both advantages and disadvantages to mirroring and patterning bodies instead of features. The advantages can include the simplicity of selecting a single body for mirroring or patterning. In cases where the geometry to be patterned is complex or there is a large number of features, patterning bodies also can be much faster. However, in the example used earlier with patterning features in a 20-by-20 grid of holes, when done by patterning a single body of 1" × 1" × .5" with a .5" diameter hole, patterning bodies gives a rebuild time of about 130 seconds with or without Verification On Rebuild. It is the function that combines the resulting bodies into a single body that takes most of the time. This says that for large patterns of simple features, patterning bodies is *not* an efficient technique. Although I do not have an experiment in this chapter to prove it, I believe that creating a pattern of a smaller number of complex bodies using a large number of features in the patterned body would show a performance improvement over patterning the features.

Another disadvantage of patterning or mirroring bodies is that it does not allow you to be selective. You cannot mirror the body minus a couple of features; without doing some shuffling of feature order in the FeatureManager. Another disadvantage is that if the base of the part has already been mirrored by a symmetrical sketch technique, then body mirroring is not going to help you mirror the subsequent features. Also, the Merge Bodies option does not work as you would want it to. It merges only those bodies that are part of the mirror to bodies that are part of the mirror. Pattern Bodies does not even have an option to merge bodies. Both of these functions are often going to require an additional combine (for solid bodies) or knit (for surface bodies) to put the final results together.

CROSS-REF   Bodies are discussed in more detail in Chapter 26. Surface modeling is covered in Chapter 27.

Patterning Faces

Most of the pattern types have an option for Pattern Faces. This option has a few restrictions, the main limitation being that all instances of the pattern must be created within the boundaries of the same face as the original. Figure 8.7 shows an example of the Pattern Faces option working with a Circular Pattern feature.

FIGURE 8.7

A circular pattern using the Pattern Faces option

To get around this limitation, you can knit and pattern the surface body, as shown in Figure 8.8.

FIGURE 8.8

Patterning a surface body

Split in face means faces
from feature on side cannot be
patterned all the way around

CROSS-REF   Working with surface bodies is covered in Chapter 27.

Patterning Fillets

You may hear people argue that you cannot pattern fillets. This is partially true and partially untrue. It is true that fillets as individual features cannot be patterned. For example, if you have a symmetrical box and a fillet on one edge and want to pattern only the fillet to other edges, this cannot be done. However, when fillets are patterned with their parent geometry, they are a perfectly acceptable candidate for patterning. This is also true for the more complex fillet types, such as variable radius and full radius fillets. You may need to use the Geometry Pattern option, and you may need to select all of the fillets affecting a feature, but it certainly does work.

Understanding Pattern Types

Up to now, I have discussed patterns in general, differentiated sketch patterns from feature patterns and body patterns, and looked at some other factors that affect patterning and mirroring. I will now discuss each individual type of pattern to give you an idea of what options are available.

Linear Pattern

The Linear Pattern feature has several available options:

- **Single direction or two directions:** Directions can be established by edge, sketch entity, axis, or linear dimension. If two directions are used, the directions do not need to be perpendicular to one another.

- **Spacing:** The spacing represents the center-to-center distance between pattern instances, and can be driven by an equation.

- **Number of Instances:** This number represents the total number of features in a pattern, which includes the original seed feature. It can also be driven by an equation. Equations are covered in detail in Chapter 9.

- **Direction 2:** The second direction works just like the first, with the one exception of the Pattern Seed Only option. Figure 8.9 shows the difference between a default two-direction pattern and one using the Pattern Seed Only option.

FIGURE 8.9

Using the default two-direction pattern and the Pattern Seed Only Option

Original feature   Pattern seed only

- **Instances to Skip:** This option enables you to select instances that you would like to leave out of the final pattern. Pink dots are the instances that remain, and the red dots are the ones that have been removed. Figure 8.10 shows the interface for skipping instances. You may have difficulty distinguishing the red and pink colors on the screen.

FIGURE 8.10

Using the Instances to Skip option

- **Propagate Visual Properties:** This option patterns the color, texture, or cosmetic thread display, along with the feature to which it is attached.

- **Vary Sketch:** This option in patterns is often overlooked and not widely used or understood. While it may have a niche application, it is a powerful option that can save you a lot of time if you ever need to use it.

  Vary Sketch allows the sketch of the patterned feature to maintain its parametric relations in each instance of the pattern. It is analogous to the Geometry Pattern. Where Geometry Pattern disables the parametric end condition for a feature, Vary Sketch enables the parametric sketch relations for a pattern.

  To activate the Vary Sketch option, the Linear Pattern must use a linear dimension for its Pattern Direction. The dimension must measure in the direction of the pattern, and adding the spacing for the pattern to the direction dimension must result in a valid feature.

  The sketch relations must hold for the entire length of the pattern. Figure 8.11 shows the sketch relations and the resulting pattern. The preview function for this feature does not work.

To adequately understand how this feature works, open the sample file from the CD-ROM called Chapter 8 Vary Sketch.sldprt, and edit Sketch2.

Edit the .40-inch dimension. Double-click it and use the scroll arrow to increase the dimension; watch the effect on the sketch. If a sketch does not do this, then it cannot be used with the Vary Sketch option. In this case, the .40-inch dimension was used as the direction. The direction dimension has to be able to drive the sketch in the same way that this one does. These dimensions cannot pass through the Zero value and cannot flip directions or move into negative values.

FIGURE 8.11

Using the Vary Sketch option

To make the sketch react this way to changes in the dimension, the slot was created using the bi-directional offset that was demonstrated in an earlier chapter, which means that the whole operation is being driven by the construction lines and arcs at the centerline of the slot. Sketch points along the model edges are kept at a certain distance from the ends of the slots using the .50-inch dimensions. The arcs are controlled by an Equal Radius relation and a single .58-inch radius dimension. The straight lines at the ends of the slots are controlled by an Equal Length relation.

This type of dimensioning and relation creation is really what parametric design is all about. The Vary Sketch option takes what is otherwise a static linear pattern and makes it react parametrically. If you model everything with the level of care that you need to put into a Vary Sketch pattern feature sketch, then your models will react very well to change.

Circular Pattern

The Circular Pattern feature requires a straight edge, an axis, or a temporary axis to act as the center of the pattern. All of the other options are the same as the Linear Pattern — except that the Circular Pattern does not have a Direction 2 option, and the Equal Spacing option works differently.

Equal Spacing takes the total angle and evenly divides the number of instances into that angle. The name *equal spacing* is a bit misleading because all Circular Patterns create equal spacing between the instances, but somehow everyone knows what they mean.

Without using the Equal Spacing option, the Angle setting represents the angular spacing between instances.

The Vary Sketch option is available in Circular Pattern as well. The principles for setup are the same, but you must select an angular dimension for the direction. The part shown in Figure 8.12 was created using this technique.

FIGURE 8.12

A Circular Pattern vary sketch

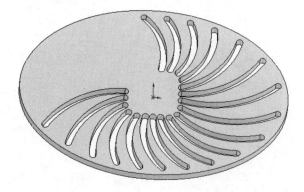

Curve Driven Pattern

A Curve Driven Pattern does just what it sounds like: it drives a pattern along a curve. The curve could be a line, an arc, or a spline. An interesting thing about the Curve Driven Pattern is that it can have a Direction 2, and Direction 2 can also be a curve. This pattern type is one of the most interesting, with many options available.

For an entire sketch to be used as a curve, the sketch must not have any sharp corners—all of the entities must be tangent. This could mean using sketch fillets or a fit spline. The example shown in Figure 8.13 is created using sketch fillets. This pattern uses the Equal Spacing option, which spaces the number of instances evenly around the curve. It also uses the Offset Curve option, which maintains the patterned feature's relationship to the curve throughout the pattern, as if an offset of the curve goes through the centroids of each patterned instance. The Align to Seed option is also used, which keeps all of the pattern instances aligned in the same direction.

FIGURE 8.13

The Curve Driven Pattern using sketch fillets

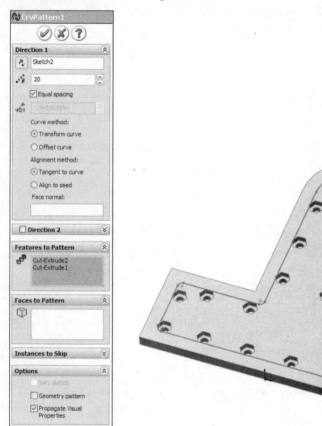

Figure 8.14 shows the same part using the Transform Curve positioning option and Tangent to Curve alignment option.

Instead of an offset of the curve going through the centroids of each patterned feature instance, in the Transform Curve, the curve is moved rather than offset. On this particular part, this causes a messy pattern. The Tangent to Curve option gives every patterned instance the same orientation relative to the curve as the original.

The Face Normal option is used for a 3D pattern, as shown in Figure 8.15. Although this functionality seems a little obscure, it is useful if you need a 3D curve-driven pattern on a complex surface. If you are curious about this example, it is on the CD-ROM with the filename Reference 3d Curve Driven.sldprt.

FIGURE 8.14

Using the Transform Curve and Tangent to Curve options

FIGURE 8.15

Using a 3D curve-driven pattern

Using a Direction 2 for a curve-driven pattern will create a result similar to that in Figure 8.16. This is another situation that, although rare, is good to know about.

Using Direction 2 with a curve-driven pattern

The rest of the Curve Driven Pattern works like the other pattern features that have already been demonstrated.

Sketch Driven Pattern

Sketch-driven patterns use a set of sketch points to drive the locations of features. The Hole Wizard drives the locations of multiple holes using sketch points in a similar way. However, the Sketch Driven Pattern does not create a 3D pattern in the same way that the Hole Wizard does. Figure 8.17 shows a pattern of several features that has been patterned using a sketch-driven pattern. A reference point is not necessary for the first feature.

The Centroid option in the Reference Point section is fine for symmetrical and other easily defin-able shapes such as circles and rectangles, where you can find the centroid just by looking at it, but on more complex shapes, you may want to use the Selected Point option. The Selected Point option is shown in Figure 8.18.

FIGURE 8.17

Using a sketch-driven pattern

FIGURE 8.18

Using the Selected Point option in a sketch-driven pattern

Selected point corresponds to the
sketch points in the pattern

Table Driven Pattern

A table-driven pattern drives a set of feature locations, most commonly holes, from a table. The table may be imported from any source with two columns of data (X and Y) that are separated by a space, tab, or comma. Extraneous data will cause the import to fail.

The X,Y Origin for the table is determined by a Coordinate System reference geometry feature. The XY plane of the Coordinate System is the plane to which the XY data in the table refers.

You can access the Coordinate System command through the menus at Insert, Reference Geometry, Coordinate System. You can create the Coordinate System by selecting a combination of a vertex for the Origin and edges to align the axes. Like the Sketch Driven Pattern, this feature can use either the centroid or a selected point on the feature to act as the reference point.

The fact that this feature is still in a floating dialog box points to its relatively low usage and priority on the SolidWorks upgrade schedule. The interface for the feature is rather crude in comparison to some of the more high-usage features. This interface is shown in Figure 8.19.

FIGURE 8.19

The Table Driven Pattern dialog box

Fill Pattern

The Fill Pattern feature fills a face or area enclosed by a sketch with a pattern of a selected feature. The type of pattern used to fill the area is limited to one of four pre-set patterns that are commonly used in gratings and electronics ventilation in plastics and sheet metal. These patterns and other options for the Fill Pattern are shown in Figure 8.20.

FIGURE 8.20

Using the Fill Pattern feature

The Pattern Layout panel enables you to control spacing and other geometrical aspects of the selected pattern layout, as well as the minimum gap from the fill boundary. This is most useful for patterns of regularly spaced features with an irregular boundary.

Mirroring in 3D

Because symmetry is an important aspect of modeling parts in SolidWorks, mirror functions are a commonly used feature. This is true whether you work on machine design parts, sheet metal, injection-molded, cast, or forged parts. I discussed sketch-mirroring techniques earlier in this chapter, and now I will discuss 3D mirroring techniques.

Mirroring bodies

Earlier in this chapter, I discussed patterning bodies. I mentioned that the patterning and mirroring tools in SolidWorks do not have adequate functionality when it comes to body management. Neither tool allows the patterned or mirrored bodies to be merged with the main body if the main body is not being patterned or mirrored. Figure 8.21 shows the Options panels for both the Linear Pattern (on the left) and the Mirror (on the right) features. Here you can see that the pattern function has no provision whatsoever for merging bodies. The Mirror appears to have the functionality, but it applies only to bodies that are used or created by the Mirror feature.

In future version of SolidWorks, these features will hopefully be outfitted with more complete merge and feature scope functionality, such as Extrude features.

FIGURE 8.21

Options panels from the Linear Pattern and Mirror PropertyManagers

BEST PRACTICE   Mirroring bodies is the fastest and simplest method when a part has complete symmetry. However, this may not be an option if the part is not completely symmetrical. Also, the decision to mirror must often be made when you are creating the first feature. If the first feature is modeled as a sketch that is built symmetrically around the Origin, then you may need to cut the part in half in order to mirror it. This is an adequate modeling technique, although it is not as clean as it could be.

Mirroring features

Features can be mirrored across planes or flat faces used as the plane of symmetry. If you are mirroring many features, then it is best to mirror them all with a single mirror feature rather than to make several mirror features. You may have to do this by moving the mirror feature down the tree as you add new features. If possible, it is better to mirror bodies than features, but you should not go too far out of your way or model in an unnatural, contrived manner in order to make this happen.

Mirroring entire parts

Often when modeling, you are required to have a left- and a right-handed part. For this, you need to use a method other than body or feature mirroring. The Mirror Part command creates a brand new part, by mirroring an existing part. The new part does not inherit all of the features of the original, and so any changes must be created in the original part. If you want different versions of the two parts, you need to use Configurations, which have not been covered yet in this book.

CROSS-REF Configurations are covered in detail in Chapter 10.

You can use the Mirror Part command by pre-selecting a plane or planar face. You should be careful when choosing the plane because the new part will have a relationship to the part Origin, based on the plane on which it was mirrored.

The Mirror Part command is found in the Insert menu. When mirroring a part, you can bring several entity types from the original file to the mirrored part. These include axes, planes, cosmetic threads, and surface bodies. Sketches and features are two commonly requested items to be brought forward by the Mirror Part command, but this is not possible in the current version of the software.

Tutorial: Creating a Circular Pattern

Follow these steps to get practice with creating circular pattern features:

1. Draw a square block on the Top plane centered on the Origin, 4 inches on each side, .5-inch thick extruded Mid Plane with .5-inch chamfers on the four corners.

2. Pre-select the top face of the block and start the Hole Wizard. (Pre-selection avoids a 3D placement sketch.) Select a counterbored hole for a 10-32 socket head cap screw, and place it as shown in Figure 8.22.

3. Create an axis using the Front and Right planes. Click Insert ➪ Reference Geometry ➪ Axis. Select the Two Planes option, and select Front and Right planes from the flyout FeatureManager. (Click the bar that says Axis at the top of the PropertyManager to access the flyout FeatureManager.) This creates an axis in the center of the rectangular part.

4. Click the Circular Pattern tool on the Features toolbar. Select the new Axis in the top Pattern Axis selection box in the Circular Pattern PropertyManager. Select the Equal Spacing option and make sure that the angle is set to 360°. Set the number of instances to 8.

FIGURE 8.22

Start drawing a plate with holes.

1.50

5. In the Features To Pattern panel, select the counterbored hole. Make sure that Geometry Pattern is turned off.

6. Click OK to finish the part, as shown in Figure 8.23.

FIGURE 8.23

The finished circular pattern

Axis1

Tutorial: Mirroring Features

Follow these steps to get some practice with creating mirror features:

1. Open the file from the CD-ROM called Chapter8 Tutorial2.sldprt.

2. Open a sketch on the side of the part, as shown in Figure 8.24. The straight line on top is 1.00 inch long, and the angled line ends 2.70 inches from the edge, as shown.

FIGURE 8.24

The sketch for the Rib feature

3. Click the Rib tool on the Features toolbar or select it from the menu at Insert ⇨ Features ⇨ Rib. Set the material arrow to go down toward the block, and the thickness setting to go to the inside by .375 inches. The PropertyManager and the preview should look like Figure 8.25.

FIGURE 8.25

Applying the Rib feature

4. Create a linear pattern using the rib, making it go 2 inches into the part.

5. Create a chamfer on the same side of the part as the original rib, as shown in Figure 8.26. The chamfer is an Angle-Distance using 60° and .5 inches.

6. Create a round hole, sized and positioned as shown.

FIGURE 8.26

Additional features on the part

7. Mirror the hole and the chamfer about the Right plane. The parametrics of the chamfer will have difficulty patterning, and so you need to use the Geometry Pattern option. The finished part is shown in Figure 8.27.

FIGURE 8.27

The finished part

Summary

Feature patterns and mirrors are powerful tools, but they require some discipline to benefit from their usefulness. Patterns in particular are extremely flexible, with many types of functions and options available. You should avoid sketch patterns if possible, not only because of performance considerations, but also because complex sketches (sketches with a lot of entities and relations) tend to fail more often than simple sketches.

Chapter 9

Using Equations

Parametric sketch relations are not the only way to drive dimensions with intelligence. You can also use equations, link values, and global variables. Equations help you to create simple or complex mathematical relations between dimensions. Link values are essentially a quick way of making two dimensions equal. Global variables can be used in equations like other dimension names. These three techniques are all very similar and related to one another in the interface, but are used in different ways in different situations.

Equations are a very powerful extension of the set of parametric power tools that SolidWorks offers to users. If you are not accustomed to driving dimensions with equations, then you may find it challenging to get the order of equations correct so that dimensions are not changed multiple times when more than a few equations are involved.

IN THIS CHAPTER

Understanding equations

Link values

Global variables

Expressions

Tutorial: Equations

Understanding Equations

You can find the Equations tool on the Tools toolbar, or through the menus at Tools, Equations. Figure 9.1 shows the Equations main interface along with the Add Equation window. As I have noted with other areas of the interface, Equations still uses a floating dialog box. I would guess that this function is going to be completely revised in the near future, and at least part of this change will involve moving it to the PropertyManager, as is the case with most other commonly used functions.

FIGURE 9.1

The Equations interface

Using the Equations interface, you can turn off equations temporarily by deselecting the Active check box in front of the equation. Equations can also be deactivated by a design table. I will discuss design tables in more detail in Chapter 10, which discusses configurations.

BEST PRACTICE   Although I do not cover configurations until Chapter 10, I will mention this here. Equations and configurations (particularly those that are driven by a design table) should probably not be mixed. This is not because they do not work together, but more for the sake of organization. When controlling dimensions, it can become confusing if the changes are being driven from multiple sources. Also, there is no reason not to bring your equations into Excel rather than using the comparatively limited equation functionality offered by SolidWorks.

Creating equations

Equations are easy to create and useful for many purposes. A common situation where you would use an equation is to space a pattern of holes evenly along an edge, including the gap on both ends, where the gap at the ends is half of the regular spacing. Before you write an equation, you need to take care of a few organizational details.

Naming dimensions

It is not necessary to name every entity in every SolidWorks document, but you should get in the habit of naming important features, sketches, and even dimensions. Dimensions become particularly important when you use equations, configurations, and design tables. Under most circumstances, you do not use or even see dimension names, but with equations, you do.

Named dimensions make a huge difference when you want to recognize the function of an equation by simply reading it. A most obvious example would be the difference between D3@Sketch6 and Length@WindowExtrusionSketch. The first name means nothing, but the second one is descriptive if you are familiar with the part.

To name a dimension, RMB click the dimension and select Properties. At the top of the dialog box shown in Figure 9.2, type the new name for the dimension in the Name text box. You cannot use the symbol @ in dimension names because it is used as a delimiter between the name of the dimension and the feature or sketch to which it applies.

FIGURE 9.2

Renaming a dimension

 You should keep dimension names as short as possible while still making them unique and descriptive. This is because space in the interface is often limited, and when combined with sketch or feature names (and even part names when used in an assembly), the names can become difficult to read.

TIP You can show dimension names as a part of the dimension value itself by accessing the setting at Tools, Options, General, Show Dimension Names.

Building the equation

When creating an equation in SolidWorks, it is often a good idea to write it out on paper first. Examine the part shown in Figure 9.3, where the relevant dimensions have been named and displayed. The behavior to be driven by the equations is that the number of holes—called Instances here—is the driving variable. From that number, the spacing of the holes is calculated over the length of the part. There is also a gap on each end of the pattern of holes. This gap (measured between the center of the last hole and the end of the part) needs to always be half of the spacing between the holes. The sigma symbols to the left of the dimensions indicate that an equation is driving it. Dimensions driven by equations cannot be directly edited.

FIGURE 9.3

Variables for the hole pattern

In this case, more sophistication has not been implemented to account for the diameter of the holes possibly interfering with one another when there are a large number of holes. In other words, because there are two values that need to be calculated (the spacing and the gap), you need to create two equations. Because the gap dimension is always half of the spacing, the spacing needs to be calculated first, as follows:

```
Spacing = Length / ((Instances-1)+1)
```

The *Instances -1* term stands for the number of spacings. If you have two holes, then there is only one spacing. The *+1* term stands for the two half-spacings for the two ends. The second equation is simpler and looks like this:

```
Gap = Spacing / 2
```

The order of the equations is important. SolidWorks solves the equations in the order in which they are listed in the Equations dialog box. Because the gap is dependent on the spacing, the spacing must be calculated before the gap. If it is done the other way around, then you can get into a situation where it takes two rebuilds to finalize a set of equations, or even a situation where in every rebuild, all of the numbers change. This is called a circular relation, and is a common error in order or history dependent functions, not just in SolidWorks, but in any computer application. Figure 9.4 shows the resulting set of equations.

FIGURE 9.4

Equations for the hole pattern

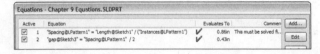

Before beginning to build the equation, you should first display the dimensions that you need to use to create the equation. You can add dimensions to the equation by clicking them from the graphics window. To do this, RMB click the Annotations folder at the top of the FeatureManager, and select Show Feature Dimensions. You should also select the Display Annotations option if it is not already on. When you have done this, all of the dimensions that you need to create every feature are displayed. Also be sure to turn on Tools ➪ Options ➪ General ➪ Show Dimension Names.

> **TIP** For models that have more than a few features, showing all of the dimensions in the entire model may overload the screen with information. In this case, you can double-click a feature from the FeatureManager to show all of the dimensions on that feature.

To build the equation, first use the Equation button on the Tools toolbar to open the Equations dialog box. Then press the Add button to display the Add Equation dialog box. To add dimensions to the equation section, just click the dimension. You can use the keypad on the dialog box or on your keyboard to add operators and syntax. All standard rules of syntax apply for the order of operations, use of parentheses, and driving versus driven sides of the equation.

Using comments

Notice the comment to the right of the first equation in Figure 9.4. Comments can be very useful for annotating equations for yourself or others. Two important reasons to annotate are to remember the significance of variables or dimensions, and to add special notes about the logic of the equation.

You can make comments for equations by using a single quote after the end of the equation, or by using the Comment button in the Add Equation dialog box. In the following example,

```
"Spacing@LPattern1" = "Length@Sketch1" / ("Instances@LPattern1") 'This must be
solved first
```

the comment, "This must be solved first," is applied to the equation using the single quote before the comment.

Adding to the earlier discussion about projected changes to the Equation interface, several standard selection functionalities do not work in the Edit Equation dialog box. These include triple-clicking to select all (although double-clicking works to select a single word) and pressing Ctrl+A to select all.

> **TIP** You can make general comments for the model in the Design Journal, a Microsoft Word document that is embedded into the SolidWorks file. The Design Journal is found in the Design Binder folder near the top of the FeatureManager.

> **ON the CD-ROM** You can find the part used in this section on the CD-ROM with the filename Chapter 9 Equations.sldprt.

Using driven dimensions

Sometimes it is more convenient to use a driven (reference) dimension in an equation. This is particularly true when using geometry is the best way to calculate a number. For example, if you are manufacturing a helical auger in 90-degree sections from flat steel stock, then you need to design the auger in 3D, but begin to manufacture it in 2D.

What is the shape of the auger when flat? The best way to figure this out (aside from lofted bends, which are discussed in Chapter 29) is to use a little high school geometry, a construction sketch, and some simple equations.

Figure 9.5 shows a 90-degree section of an auger blade. The outside diameter is 12 inches, and the blade width is 3 inches. The overall height is 4 inches. In this case, the auger is represented as a surface because the thickness is ignored. Surface features can be useful in situations like this and are discussed in Chapter 27.

FIGURE 9.5

Representation of the auger

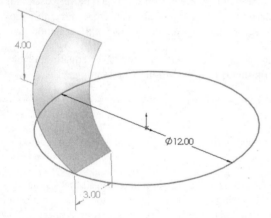

ON the CD-ROM   You can find the part for Figure 9.5 on the CD-ROM with the filename Chapter 9 Auger.sldprt.

With this information, we can calculate the lengths of the 3D edges using a sketch and a simple equation. In Figure 9.6, the hypotenuses of the triangles represent the helical edges of the helices. By making the triangles the same height as the auger section, and by making the horizontal side of the triangle the same length as a quarter of the inside or outside diameter by using simple equations, the geometry and sketch relations calculate the flat lengths of the inside and outside edges of the auger (length of triangle side = diameter of circle × pi / 4). In this way, the triangle is used to simplify the calculation, and give it a visual result.

FIGURE 9.6

Triangles calculate the length of the helical edge.

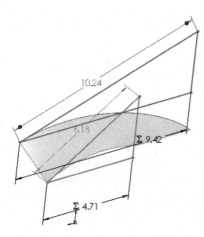

From this point, the flat pattern can be calculated again, using SolidWorks' sketch-solving capabilities as the calculator. Think of the auger as being the cardboard tube inside a roll of paper towels. If you examine one of these tubes closely, you see that it is simply a straight and flat strip of cardboard that has been wound around a cylinder. What was the flat, straight edge of the original board is wound into a helix. This method is simply reversing that process.

This example requires the little-used arc-length dimension to drive the size of the arc. The hypotenuse dimensions are shown by driven or reference dimensions, and these are used to drive the arc-length dimensions, as shown in Figure 9.7. Remember that you can create arc length dimensions by using the Smart Dimension tool to click both endpoints of the arc and then the arc itself. Arcs driven by arc length dimensions often do not react to changes predictably, since the radius and center or end point locations are not necessarily defined.

The reasoning behind this example may be a little difficult to grasp, but the equations and the sketches are certainly simple.

CAUTION Using reference dimensions on the driving (independent, or right) side of the equation can in some situations require more than one rebuild to arrive at a stable value (meaning a value that does not change with the next rebuild). SolidWorks issues a warning when it sees that you are using a reference dimension in an equation, but it does allow it.

Equations are listed in the Equations folder in the FeatureManager. You can edit or delete them through the RMB menu.

FIGURE 9.7

Figuring the flat pattern of the auger

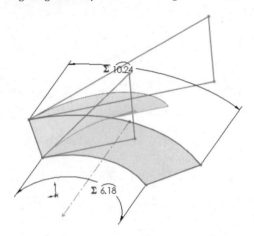

Equation tricks

Some functions that are allowed in SolidWorks equations are often viewed as parlor tricks, but they actually do have some practical applications. The two functions that fall into this category are IIF and SWITCH. If you are familiar with a programming language, you may already be familiar with these two functions. If not, then they are described below.

IIF

In words, this is how an IIF statement is used:

If some relationship is fulfilled, then the IIF function returns a value. If the relationship is not fulfilled, then it returns a different value.

A more technical description is

```
IIF(expression, value if true, value if false)
```

In practice, you could use it like this:

```
IIF(x>5, x-1, x+1)
```

which reads, "if x is greater than 5, then subtract 1 from x; if not, then add 1 to x." One of the reasons why this is considered a parlor trick is that this function causes the value of x to oscillate between two numbers (depending on the number that it starts with) with each rebuild. It may be difficult to imagine an application where this sort of behavior would be desirable, but when you combine it with a macro that simply rebuilds a model a number of times, you can use it to create a certain animation effect.

ON the CD-ROM A simple example of the `IIF` function can be found on the CD-ROM with the filename Chapter 9 Oscillate.sldprt. The equation is shown in Figure 9.8.

FIGURE 9.8

An equation using `IIF`

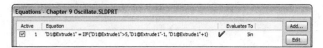

TIP You can find some great examples of this function at www.mikejwilson.com, along with many other extremely creative examples of SolidWorks modeling. The model on this site called Ship in a Bottle.sldprt also includes a macro that will rebuild the model a certain number of times, which is useful for animations that are created in this way.

SWITCH

The `SWITCH` function enables you to have a list of relationships with associated values. The value of the first relationship in the list that is satisfied is returned by the `SWITCH` function. For example,

```
switch (x>2, 1.5, x>1, .5 x<1, 2.5)
```

reads as follows: "if x is greater than 2, then the answer is 1.5; if x is not greater than 2 but greater than 1, then the answer is .5; if x is not greater than 1 but less than 1, then the answer is 2.5."

As you can see, this function does not cover all situations, but it does create a condition where the value cycles through three different numbers in a specific order. Is this useful? Possibly. Again, the main application for this function would be a simple animation for changing the size or shape of SolidWorks components that cannot be done in other more conventional ways.

Using Link Values

Link values are simply a way to link several dimensions together. A link value is not exactly like an equation that sets the dimensions equal, because it does not depend on order like an equation does. All dimensions are set to the same value simultaneously.

Link values are available by RMB clicking the dimension. Unfortunately, they are not available from the RMB menu when the dimension tool is active. To apply a link value to a new dimension, you must place the dimension, exit the dimension tool, RMB click the dimension, and select Link Value.

Link values are listed under the Equations folder in the FeatureManager. Figure 9.9 shows the link values in a listed part, and the drop-down list from which you can select them or type them. Notice again that the Link Values feature also operates from a dialog box instead of the PropertyManager. I would predict that the Link Values and Equations would be redesigned to function more in sync with one another in a future version of SolidWorks.

FIGURE 9.9

Link values listed in the FeatureManager, and the Shared Values interface

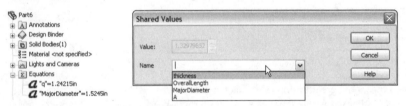

The first link value that is assigned in a part must be manually typed in. After you add the first one, you can link other dimensions to this link value by using the scroll arrows shown in Figure 9.9. You cannot edit link values. In order to change the value to which a dimension is linked, you must first unlink the value and then relink it. The Unlink function is available from the RMB menu in the same way that you assign link values. Dimensions that have a link value have the small chain symbol displayed to the left of the dimension.

TIP   There is one link value name that has a special significance. If you use the name *thickness*, then a Link To Thickness option appears in all extrude dialog boxes. This is intended to reflect sheet metal functionality, but it is useful for models of various manufacturing techniques.

To take this one step further, you can save a part template with a *thickness* link value; all of your new parts will also have this functionality right from the start. To save the template with a link value, you must create at least one dimension to assign the link value, and then delete the geometry (and the dimension); however, the link value will remain.

Link values of different types are not necessarily interchangeable. You cannot use angular dimension link values on radius, diameter, or linear dimensions. You can use linear and diameter link values interchangeably, but not angle link values.

Using Global Variables

Global variables are assigned in the Equations dialog box as simply the variable name equaling the value. Figure 9.10 shows a list of equations, link values, and global variables. When you are typing in the name of the variable, you do not need to add the quotation marks; they are added automatically.

FIGURE 9.10

Equations, link values, and global variables

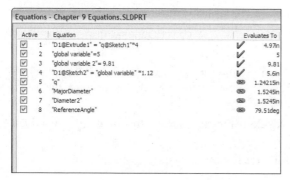

Despite the word *variable* in the name global variable, the values are not variable. They are fixed, and only changeable through the Equations dialog box. The only place where you can use global variables is in equations. You cannot directly enter them into dialog boxes for dimension values.

Using Expressions

Expressions, unlike all of the previous variables, values, and equations, can be entered directly into dimension dialog boxes. The expressions have to be composed of numbers and mathematical operators. An expression such as

    2.375+(4.8/3) -1.1

is perfectly acceptable, as is

    1+1/2

or

    1 1/2.

In the second case above, the plus symbol is understood.

Other types of operations are also available, such as changing units in a dimension box. For example, if you are editing a part in inches, and enter 40mm, then SolidWorks does the conversion for you. You can even mix units in a single expression such as 4.875+3.5mm, where the inch part is assumed.

Tutorial: Using Equations

Follow these steps to get some practice with using equations:

1. Start from the part on the CD-ROM with the filename Chapter9 Tutorial Start.sldprt.

2. Show the dimension names. This setting is found at Tools ➪ Options ➪ General ➪ Show Dimension Names.

3. Double-click the Circular Pattern feature to display the angle and number of instances of the feet and related features. You may have to move the angle dimension to see the pattern instance number.

4. RMB click the instance number, and select Properties. Change the name of the dimension to # (pound or number sign).

5. Double-click the first feature, which is the revolve, and rename the 3.60-inch dimension to **CapRad**.

6. Write an equation that drives the number of legs by CapRad/7.

   a. Open the Equations dialog box at Tools ➪ Equations.

   b. Click Add to add an equation.

   c. Double-click the Circular Pattern and click the # dimension. Make sure that the name of the dimension is listed in the equation box, and type an equal sign.

   d. Double-click the Revolve feature and select the CapRad dimension; then type the characters /7.

   e. Add a comment to the equation to reflect which dimension is driving which dimension.

7. Click Rebuild, press Ctrl+B or Ctrl+Q to rebuild the model, and observe whether any update takes place.

8. Rename the 6.00-inch dimension for the height of the revolved feature to **DomeHt**.

9. Create a second equation that drives the DomeHt dimension at the current ratio of the height to the radius.

   a. Create a global variable called Ratio = 6/3.6 (1.66667) in the Equations dialog box.

   b. Create the equation. The equation will take the form of DomeHt = (Ratio) × CapRad.

10. Use a link value to make the radii of Fillet1 and Fillet2 the same.

11. Double-click Extrude2. Change the .75-inch dimension to .05+20mm (.79").

12. Save and close the part with a new name, including your initials or the date.

Summary

SolidWorks equations and related dimension-management tools are powerful, but often leave you wishing for a little more flexibility and control. The interface is not up-to-date with the rest of the SolidWorks interface, and so I would look to see an updated equation interface soon that integrates dimension input, link values, and global variables.

If you want to encourage SolidWorks to revise certain features, then you can go to the SolidWorks Web site and submit an enhancement request. They do look at customer input when developing or updating functionality.

Chapter 10

Working with Part Configurations

onfigurations, also known as simply *configs*, are variations of a part in which dimensions are changed, features are suppressed (turned off), and other items such as color may also be controlled. Configurations enable you to have these variations within a single part file, which is both convenient and efficient.

This chapter deals only with part configurations, but you should be aware that assemblies can also have configurations. Assembly configurations can use different part configurations, among other things. This will mean more to you as you learn about part configurations.

CROSS-REF   Assembly configurations are discussed in Chapter 14.

One example of the use of configurations is Toolbox. By default, Toolbox uses configurations to create many sizes of hardware within a single part file. For example, the Socket Head Cap Screw is a single part in Toolbox that contains hundreds of sizes. You can change the size by simply varying the dimensions of the existing features. Toolbox parts also have features that you can turn off and on (suppress and unsuppress, respectively), particularly those related to thread representation (swept versus revolved versus cosmetic). Changing dimensions and suppressing or unsuppressing features are the most commonly used techniques that are available through configurations.

IN THIS CHAPTER

Manually controlling items with configurations

Using design tables

Tutorial: Working with configurations and design tables

Controlling Items with Configurations

With every new release of SolidWorks software, it seems that there are new items that become "configurable," that is, able to be driven by configurations. Configurable items for parts include the following:

- Feature dimensions, driving/driven state
- Suppression of features, equations, sketch relations, and end conditions
- Which sketch plane is by a sketch
- Configuration-specific custom properties
- Part, body, feature, and face colors
- Derived configurations
- The ability to assign properties such as mass and center of gravity
- Configuration of base or split parts

You can work with configurations in one of two ways: either manually or through a design table. I describe the manual method first, to give you a good understanding of how to intervene with configs the manual "old-fashioned" way when you need to. Design tables are a fantastic way to organize and manage config data and options, but they also require a bit of syntax, and so I will describe them in a separate section later in this chapter.

Finding configurations

You can handle configurations in the ConfigurationManager. This is the third tab in the FeatureManager/PropertyManager interface.

TIP   You can split the FeatureManager interface into two by dragging the splitter bar at the top of the panel. This is a very useful function that allows you to see the FeatureManager in the upper panel and the PropertyManager or ConfigurationManager in the lower panel.

Deleting configs

Each part has a default config named "Default." There is nothing special about this config; you can rename it and even delete it. There must always be at least one config in the tree, and you cannot delete the current configuration. If you would like to remove a config, then you need to switch to another config first, and then delete it.

In relation to assembly configurations, you cannot delete a config if it is being used in an assembly that is open and resolved. In order to delete a config such as this, you need to either close the assembly or change the part config used in the assembly.

If you try to delete a configuration being used by an open assembly, SolidWorks simply gives the message "None of the selected entities could be deleted" without explanation.

If you delete a configuration of a part that is used in an assembly, but the assembly is not currently open, the next time the assembly is opened it issues the message "The following component configurations could not be found . . . . If the configuration was renamed the same configuration will be used, otherwise the last active configuration will be substituted for each instance."

As you can see, a configuration that is simply renamed is dealt with differently than a configuration that is deleted. In any case, you need to be careful when dealing with parts with configurations that are used in an assembly.

NOTE Many users get into the habit of clicking out of any error, warning, or message box that comes up, often without reading what it has to say. It is important to read error and warning messages when they come up. Some of them, such as the configuration message shown previously, are vitally important to the integrity of your design data. They are sometimes actually useful.

You can delete groups of configs by window select, Shift-select, or Ctrl-select in the Configuration-Manager. You can also use the RMB menu, much like regular features in the FeatureManager.

Sorting configs

In the ConfigurationManager, configs are listed alphabetically, not in the order in which they are created. This has several advantages, especially when you have a large number of configs. For example, if configs are named by size in a part that you are working with, then when selecting a configuration, you can type in a number, and the selection scrolls to that place in the list of configs. This makes it easier to select the one you are looking for, much the same as it works in Windows Explorer.

Alphabetization

This alphabetized order is significant because many other sections of the SolidWorks interface are not alphabetized, which causes problems when you are searching for items in larger lists. Sections that are not alphabetized include Help/Contents, Files Of Type lists in Open and Save dialog boxes, and the Tools/Options/File Locations, Entity Color list. If you are inclined to send in an Enhancement Request, alphabetization is one topic that would benefit everyone and should be fairly easy for SolidWorks to implement.

Naming configs

In order for this sorting and alphabetization to work, you must first name the configs properly. For example, if you have a list of sizes or config names from 1 to 100, then you should use 001, 002...100 as your syntax. This makes the config names easier to browse and type in. Syntax becomes most important when you place a part with many configs into an assembly, because you must select a config from the list, and typing in the first few numbers is often faster and easier than scrolling to it.

ON the CD-ROM The CD-ROM contains a part called Chapter 10 Config Names.sldprt, which illustrates proper naming and alphabetization.

To understand this technique better, you can open the part called Chapter 10 Config Names.sldprt from the CD-ROM, split the FeatureManager area, and change one of the panes to display the

ConfigurationManager. Click one of the configuration names, and type in a number between 001 and 100. The highlight scrolls to the number that you typed in. Thoughtful selection of the configuration names can save you and your coworkers a lot of time when you need to insert select configs into an assembly. Figure 10.1 shows this arrangement.

FIGURE 10.1

The split FeatureManager, displaying the ConfigurationManager

CROSS-REF The splitter bar and other portions of the FeatureManager interface appear in Chapter 2.

Activating configurations

Within a part file, to change the display from one configuration to another, you must first switch to the ConfigurationManager panel, and then either double-click the desired config or RMB click it and select Show Configuration.

Alternatively, you can RMB click the config in the ConfigurationManager and select Show Preview, as shown in Figure 10.2. A small preview thumbnail displays in the PropertyManager panel. However, not all configurations will have previews. For example, in a part with many configs that have been generated automatically by a design table, the configurations may not have previews because the config itself has never actually been rebuilt. Previews exist only when the configuration has been activated once, the image on the screen generated, and the part then saved. SolidWorks stores both the body (geometry) and the preview image of the part so that next time you access the configuration, the software does not have to rebuild everything again.

FIGURE 10.2

Showing a configuration preview

You can even select a configuration while opening a file. This allows you to save time by avoiding two model rebuilds. To take advantage of this option, you must use the File ⇨ Open interface, which is shown in Figure 10.3. You can select the config from the lower-right list window, using the same technique of typing in the first few characters of the config name.

FIGURE 10.3

Selecting a configuration from the Open dialog box

Creating configurations

You can create configs manually or through Excel-driven design tables. Design tables are extremely useful for situations where there are more than a few configs, or more than a few items are being controlled. You should use design tables because they keep things very organized within the spreadsheet grid.

For now, I am going to focus on creating and manipulating configs manually so that you can become familiar with them without also worrying about Excel and design table syntax.

Making a new config

 To make a new config, you can RMB click the top-level icon in the ConfigurationManager, which displays a part symbol and the name of the part, and select Add Configuration. Figure 10.4 shows the RMB menu and the Properties dialog box that you can use to set up the new config.

FIGURE 10.4

Creating a new configuration

Configuration properties and options

The name of the config is important mainly for quick access and organization purposes. The configuration description is also important, because it can display in the ConfigurationManager, and even in the Assembly tree. This is important when the name of the config is numerical rather than descriptive, and you would like to also have a description but not include it in the name. The config description can also appear in place of the filename in the Assembly tree display. I discuss this in more detail in Chapter 12. Config descriptions can be driven manually through the Configuration Properties dialog box or through a design table if you have many configs to manage. You can display config descriptions through the RMB menu, as shown in Figure 10.5.

FIGURE 10.5

Enabling configuration descriptions

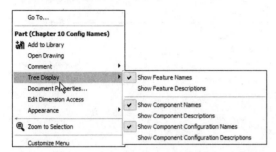

I discuss the Bill Of Materials options in Chapter 24, but the option is set in the Configuration Properties to use the filename, the configuration name, or a custom name that the user specifies. You can save this setting with a template. Control over configurations is achieved through the combination of the Configuration Properties and the Advanced Options, which are discussed next.

BEST PRACTICE Although you can change the preferred settings at any time, it is definitely a best practice to make a template early on when you are using SolidWorks to model parts. SolidWorks remembers the Bill of Materials options and Advanced options that you set for the Default configuration and uses them in document templates. This is true for both part and assembly templates.

Advanced options

The two advanced configuration options are found in the bottom panel of the Configuration Properties PropertyManager. Suppress Features and Use Configuration Specific Color are the two options available. While the second option is self-explanatory, the first one is not, and often catches new and even experienced users off guard.

Suppress Features refers to how inactive configurations should handle new features. For example, if you have two configs, 1 and 2, and config 1 is active and you add a new Fillet feature, then what happens to that feature in config 2? If this option is turned on, then the new features are suppressed. If it is turned off, then the new features will be unsuppressed when the inactive configs are activated. This creates a much bigger challenge for manually created configurations than for design table-driven configs because changing suppression states for several features across multiple configs is much easier in a design table than in manual config management.

Derived configurations

Derived configurations are configs that are dependent on other configs. You can create them from the RMB menu on a configuration instead of on the top level in the ConfigurationManager, and they appear indented underneath the parent config. Figure 10.6 shows the RMB menu and the position of the derived config in the tree.

FIGURE 10.6

Creation and placement of the derived config

Derived configurations maintain the same values and properties of the parent config unless you break the link to the child config by explicitly changing a value in the child config. For all other values, the child config value changes when the parent config value changes.

One very nice application of derived configs is to use them for simplified configurations, and set the properties so that any features that are added to the parent config are also added to the derived config. You can do this by setting the Advanced Option Suppress Features to Off. This causes the derived config to inherit *only* features that are added to the parent, and not to other configs. The simplified configs are used for FEA, making drawings of models where all of the edge breaks have actually been modeled. They are also used for the reverse (a complex config rather than simple) to have a config that includes fillets for rendering purposes that are otherwise not there. You can also create and maintain derived configs using design tables, which are discussed in the next section.

File size considerations

A long-standing dispute has raged over the effects of file size on speed. Here are the facts: When SolidWorks creates a configuration, it stores information about the 3D geometry and a preview thumbnail of the configuration inside the part file. This makes it faster to access the configuration the next time because it has only to read the data, rather than read other data and then recalculate the new data. As a result, saving the stored data allows you to avoid having to recalculate it.

CROSS-REF   Appendix A contains a section on Data Management that has several options for dealing with data and large file sizes.

File size has a negative effect on speed when you are sending data across the Internet or working across a network. If the data is on your hard drive, then storing data instead of calculating it offers a big benefit.

NOTE SolidWorks 2007 Service Pack 1 has a fix associated with it that takes advantage of a new hotfix from Microsoft that removes shadow data from files, and may reduce the size of SolidWorks files to one-half or even one-quarter of their original size. See the SolidWorks Customer Portal and the Microsoft support site for details regarding Microsoft Knowledge Base article 919880. The Microsoft hotfix files can be found on the SolidWorks support site. Files with many configurations are supposed to derive the most benefit from the combination of this service pack and hotfix.

Controlling dimensions

Controlling dimensions with configurations is simple. You need only three things to start: one dimension and two configurations. Because you already know how to create these elements, you are ready to start. Configurations require that you spend some time developing "design intent" for parts. Configurations drive changes in models, and if they are improperly modeled, then configurations will cause feature or sketch failures.

I will start with the example of a simple block. A fully dimensioned block has three dimensions. Make sure that you have manually created at least two configurations. Double-clicking the model brings up all of the dimensions, and double-clicking one of the dimensions brings up the familiar Modify dialog box. Or *almost* familiar, I should say; Figure 10.7 shows that there is a small difference in the new Modify dialog box. It now has a drop-down list where you can specify whether this change applies only to this config, to all configs, or to specified configs. If you select specified configs, then the dialog box on the right in Figure 10.7 appears, where you can select which configs this dimension change applies to.

FIGURE 10.7

Making simple changes to a configuration

First config   Second config

Once you are finished, you can toggle back and forth between the configs by double-clicking each of the configs in the ConfigurationManager. Although this is simple, if you forget to change the drop-down list from the All Configurations setting to either the This Configuration or the Specify Configuration(s) setting, then you apply the change to all of the configurations. This example shows that building a configuration manually is fine for a few simple changes, but it can become unwieldy if you are changing more than a few dimensions in this way. You would then have to remember which dimensions were changed to what. As you can see, using design tables is a better method for multiple dimensions.

Controlling suppression

Suppressing a feature is just like turning it off; the feature appears as grayed-out text in the FeatureManager. With configurations, you can suppress a feature in one config and unsuppress it in another. When dealing with manual configuration techniques, there are two methods for controlling suppression: manually suppressing features, and creating configurations with the appropriate options for the inclusion of new features that I discussed previously in this chapter.

In addition to the Suppress toolbar button, you can also use the Unsuppress and Unsuppress with Dependents features. When you suppress a feature, any feature that is dependent on it is also suppressed. If you then use the Unsuppress feature, it unsuppresses only the feature itself. However, Unsuppress with Dependents brings back all of the dependent features, as well.

PERFORMANCE **Suppressing complex features is a great way to improve performance. Experienced users often create a configuration of a part that they use as a simplified config, where patterns, fillets, and extruded text features are suppressed. This becomes more important as you start working with assemblies.**

Generally, SolidWorks users employ a combination of these methods, mainly because configurations are not usually started on a complete model; they are often added when the model is still in progress, and so features are added after the users create the configurations.

Figure 10.8 to the left side of the image shows a feature that is both unsuppressed and suppressed in the tree. The text and icon for the suppressed feature are grayed out. You can suppress features from the RMB menu on the feature, from the Edit menu, or through a tool on a toolbar. The Suppress button is not on a toolbar by default, but you can find it in the Tools ➪ Customize ➪ Commands dialog box, along with the other buttons for the Features toolbar. Only the menus offer the options of Unsuppress With Dependents, as well as the This Configuration/All Configurations/ Specify Configurations options for each of the Suppress, Unsuppress, Unsuppress With Dependents functions.

When you control suppression in manually managed configurations, you will often need to switch between configs to ensure that you have applied the correct dimensions and suppression scheme. As a result, manual configuration management is not a desirable method.

Suppressing a feature

Controlling custom properties

Custom properties fall into a category of model data called *metadata*, which is text-based information. This metadata is meant for any text-based data that you would like to accompany the part, such as description, material, vendor, vendor part number, price, or even cost. Several reasons may compel you to use custom properties, including search criteria for a Product Data Management system, automatically filling out drawing title blocks, or adding information to the Bill of Materials.

When you are using custom properties with configurations, you must use the Configuration Specific Custom Properties interface, which enables you to have custom properties that change with each configuration. This is useful for situations such as different part numbers for configurations, and many other situations that are limited mostly by your use of configs.

The interface for managing custom properties manually is shown in Figure 10.9. You can access this dialog box through menus at File ➪ Properties. If you are using a newer version of SolidWorks, then you may notice that the interface has improved drastically in recent versions.

You can also link custom properties to mass properties, model dimensions, link values, and global variables by selecting from the drop-down list under the Value/Text Expression column, which appears when you select a cell in the column, as shown in Figure 10.9. To link a custom property to a model dimension, simply place the cursor in the Value/Text Expression box that you want to populate, and click a dimension in the graphics window. Again, managing this data for a single config or only a few configs is easy enough; however, it can quickly become unwieldy, which is where using design tables can make a huge difference.

FIGURE 10.9

The Configuration Specific tab in the Summary Information dialog box

Controlling colors

Face, feature, body, and part colors as well as materials are also configurable. Just switch to the configuration you want to control, and make the changes.

NEW FEATURE New in SolidWorks 2007 sp1 is a button in the Color Properties dialog box labeled Remove All Colors. You do not need to have anything selected for this function to work, but it only works for the current configuration. It removes all colors that are assigned to anything but the part level (the part needs to have a color assigned to it). In the past, users required a macro to eliminate special colors.

Controlling sketch relations

You can individually suppress or unsuppress sketch relations using configurations. Figure 10.10 shows the Display/Delete Relations PropertyManager interface, at the bottom of which is the Configurations panel. To suppress a relation, select it from the list and select the Suppressed option in the Relations section above the Delete buttons.

FIGURE 10.10

The Display/Delete Relations dialog box for configuring sketch relations

TIP   This is another situation where Delete is not used as an editing option. Using this technique, you can save sketch relations, or activate different sets of relations in different
configs; this technique allows a single sketch to react to changes differently.

Controlling sketch planes

You cannot configure the Offset distance in the From option for extrudes, but you *can* configure
the sketch plane for the sketch that is used in the feature. The Sketch Plane PropertyManager interface expands when configurations are present, as shown in Figure 10.11.

FIGURE 10.11

The Sketch Plane PropertyManager interface for configuring a sketch plane

TIP Another way to change the sketch plane is to put the sketch on an offset plane or a plane that can otherwise be driven by a dimension (for example, using reference sketch geometry). Actually moving a sketch to another plane can cause the sketch to rotate or flip. Moving the plane it is on is a better option that does not cause the sketch to rotate or flip.

CAUTION Changing sketch planes indiscriminately can have serious consequences for your model. "Face/Plane Normals" sometimes point in different directions, and can cause a sketch to flip, rotate, or mirror when you change it from one plane to another. One strange result is that changing it back to the original location can cause the sketch to flip again, but in a different way so that it does not go back to its original location/orientation. As a result, every time you change the configuration, the sketch could appear in a new and unexpected location or orientation.

Controlling configurations of inserted parts

 Inserted parts have a long history in SolidWorks. They have had several names in the past, and some sources (including SolidWorks documentation such as training documents and even help files) still use some of these names out of habit or precedence. For example, you will sometimes hear inserted parts called *derived* or *base* parts.

CROSS-REF Inserted parts are discussed in detail in Chapter 28, which describes master model techniques.

Inserted parts use one part as the starting point for another part. The inserted part sits as a feature in the FeatureManager of the child part. The features of the original inserted part are not brought forward; only the finished solid body or bodies, select surface bodies, planes, and cosmetic threads are brought forward. It is a major point of contention for many people that you should also be able to bring forward sketch data, but this option is not available at this time (however, if you have a bookmark to that enhancement request site, you may want to request this feature).

The role of configurations with inserted parts is that the configuration of the inserted part can be controlled from the child component. For example, you may have designed an engine block for an automobile. This engine block is a casting, and using configurations, you have both the six-cylinder and the eight-cylinder blocks in a single-part file. This model represents the "as cast" engine block. The next step is to make the block with all of the secondary machining operations, such as facing mating surfaces, reaming cylinders, drilling and tapping holes for threaded connections, and so on. As a result, the as-cast part is inserted into the as-machined part, and the configuration is selected before you add the cut features. As the name suggests, you add inserted parts through the menus using Insert ➪ Part.

The interface for assigning the configuration is shown in Figure 10.12. Simply RMB click the inserted part feature and select List External References.

FIGURE 10.12

Assigning the configuration of an inserted part

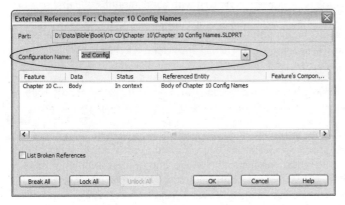

Library features

Library features can have configurations, and they carry those configurations with them into the part in which they are placed. Unfortunately, part configs cannot reference different library feature configs.

CROSS-REF Chapter 17 discusses the Hole Wizard, and Chapter 18 discusses library features.

Configurations for library features are created in exactly the same ways that configurations are created for other parts. The technique for saving the configs to the library feature is discussed in Chapter 18.

Unconfigurable items

As important as it is to know what you *can* do, it is equally important to know what you *cannot* do. The following is a list of items that are not configurable. Although this list is not complete, it contains many of the more relevant items that cannot be configured:

- Hole Wizard holes (although there is a workaround: dimensions can be configured)
- Library feature configs
- Blocks
- Extrude direction or From Offset dimension or direction
- Most of the values in features such as Deform, Freeform, and Twist
- Hide/Show state of a body

Using Design Tables

In addition to describing some of the basic concepts involved with configurations, the first part of this chapter has offered reasons for using design tables. For example, while manual configuration management can be haphazard, and is highly prone to mistakes, design tables lay everything out in an Excel spreadsheet. Although many new users ask whether they can use a different replacement spreadsheet program, you must use Excel.

 The versions of Excel that are supported by SolidWorks for design tables are XP, 2000, and 2003. Although Excel 97 may still work, Microsoft no longer supports that product.

Excel is a format that is easy to read and print out, and even non-SolidWorks users can understand and work with it. Although there is some special syntax that you need to use with design tables, for most uses, SolidWorks can create the syntax automatically for you, and so there is a minimum of manual data entry. If you are careful to name dimensions, features, and configurations properly, design tables should be easy to understand and manage. Excel can also color cells, rows, and columns in such a way that large amounts of tabulated data are easier to sort through. In addition, because design tables use Excel, they can also use Excel's equations.

BEST PRACTICE **When using equations and design tables, it is considered best practice to name dimensions, sketches, features, and other configured items. However, it is not recommended to mix design tables with SolidWorks equations. Besides the fact that Excel equations are far more sophisticated than those of SolidWorks, driving dimensions from too many locations can be confusing when you edit the part after you have forgotten the details of how the part was built.**

It is a great idea to document design intent using comments in the features or the Design Journal. You should also add comments to design tables as needed.

What can be driven by a design table?

Just because something can be configured does not necessarily mean that it can also be driven by a design table. Here is a small list of items that fit into this category:

- Sketch plane configuration
- Suppressed sketch relations
- Suppressed dimensions (suppressed dimensions become driven dimensions)

However, the good news is that there are many items that can be driven by a design table. Table 10.1 lists these items, along with their associated syntax.

TABLE 10.1

Items That Can Be Driven by a Design Table

Item	Syntax (Goes in Column Header)	Possible Values (Goes in Field Cell)	Default Value If Field Is Blank
Configs of Inserted Parts	$configuration@ <part name>	<config name>	not evaluated
Configs of Split Parts	$configuration@ <split feature name>	<config name>	not evaluated
Comment Column	$comment	comment text	blank
Configuration Description	$description	description text	<config name>
BOM Part No.	$partnumber	$d, $document = document name $p, $parent = parent config name $c, $configuration = config name <text> = custom name	config name
Feature Suppression State	$state@<feature name>	suppressed, s unsuppressed, u	present suppression state
Dimension Value	dimension@ <feature name> dimension@ <sketch name>	allowed numerical values	not evaluated
Parent Config (creates a derived config)	$parent	parent config name text	not evaluated
Config Specific Custom Property	$prp@<property name>	property name text	not evaluated
Equation State	$state@ <equation number>@ equations	suppressed, s unsuppressed, u	unsuppressed

continued

TABLE 10.1   (continued)

Item	Syntax (Goes in Column Header)	Possible Values (Goes in Field Cell)	Default Value If Field Is Blank
Light Suppression State	$state@<light name>	suppressed, s unsuppressed, u	unsuppressed
Sketch Relation Suppression	$state@<relation name> @<sketch name>	suppressed, s unsuppressed, u	unsuppressed
User Notes (same as comment)	$user_notes	Text	blank
Part or Feature Color	$color $color@<feature name>	see SolidWorks Help, Colors, Parameters in design tables	0, black
Assigned Mass Mass properties	$sw-mass	allowed numerical values	value from
Assigned Center of Gravity X, Y, Z Coordinates	$sw-cog	allowed numerical values in the format of x, y, z	value from Mass properties
Dimension Tolerance	$tolerance@ <dimension name>	see SolidWorks Help, Tolerance Keywords and Syntax in Design Tables	none

Creating a simple design table

When you prepare to create a design table, you generally need to give appropriate names to dimensions, sketches, and features. Remember that while the feature is the most visible item and the easiest to rename, most of the dimensions probably belong to the sketch, which you may also need to rename. Names should reflect the function or location of the item. It is a good idea to show dimension names when renaming items (remember that you can show dimension names by turning on the option at Tools ➪ Options ➪ General ➪ Show Dimension Names). Figure 10.13 shows the result of renaming the feature and dimension.

You can use one of the following three techniques to add a design table to a SolidWorks part:

- **Insert Blank Design Table:** This method starts from a blank template that contains the underlying framework, but no values.
- **Auto-create Design Table:** This method populates the new design table with any existing configurations and items that are different between the configs.
- **From File:** This method allows you to create a design table externally and then import it.

FIGURE 10.13

Renamed features and dimensions

Although I prefer the Auto-create method, it is most appropriate for when you have existing configurations. The From File method is best when a design table has been exported from another part, saved externally, and brought into the current part. For the following example, I am using the Insert Blank Design Table method.

ON the CD-ROM If you would like to follow along with these steps to create the design table, you can use the part from the CD-ROM with the filename Chapter 10 DTstart.sldprt.

Figure 10.14 shows the results of starting with the new blank design table. You may notice that the window title bar at the top says SolidWorks, but the toolbars look a lot like the Excel interface. This is because Excel is actually running inside of SolidWorks. Clicking outside of the Excel window can cause the Excel window to close, although there are several items outside of the Excel window that you can select without the window closing, such as features in the FeatureManager and dimensions in the graphics window. You can also rotate and pan the view in the graphics window without closing the Design Table window. If you are very careful, you can also drag the thin hatched border of the Excel window to adjust its size or location.

Design Tables also can be edited in a separate window, which makes editing easier, but makes adding dimension and feature names more difficult. To edit the table in its own window, RMB on the Design Table in the FeatureManager and select Edit Table In New Window.

FIGURE 10.14

The interface where you can create the design table, and the resulting blank design table

Figure 10.15 shows a fully developed design table, with some complexity. Although your first design table does not need to be this complex, this example demonstrates what you can do with this feature.

The config names go in the first column, and the feature or property names go in the second row. The first row is reserved for the name of the table. All of this is automatically set up by SolidWorks.

NOTE Because you are actually working in Excel when working with design tables, you can use Excel formatting, which is how the text in Figure 10.15 is rotated 90 degrees for the column headers. (To rotate text in a table, RMB click the cell, group of cells, or row; select Format Cells; and then select the Alignment tab).

In our new design table, the next step is to type in some configuration names. Because you are working in Excel, all of the fill functionality is available. In the example shown in Figure 10.16, I have typed in the first three values of 001, 002, and 003, then window-selected the cells, and dragged the fill handle on the selection window to fill the number pattern to populate a larger area. To find more information about this technique, look for Fill or Automatically Number Rows in the Excel Help files.

FIGURE 10.15

A fully populated design table

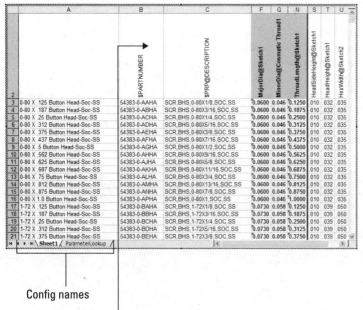

	A	B	C	F	G	N	S	T	U
2		$PARTNUMBER	$PRP@DESCRIPTION	MajorDia@Sketch1	MinorDia@Cosmetic Thread1	ThreadLength@Sketch1	HeadSideHeight@Sketch1	HeadHeight@Sketch1	HexWidth@Sketch2
3	0-80 X .125 Button Head-Soc-SS	54383-0-AAHA	SCR,BHS,0-80X1/8,SOC,SS	0.0600	.046	0.1250	.010	.032	.035
4	0-80 X .187 Button Head-Soc-SS	54383-0-ABHA	SCR,BHS,0-80X3/16,SOC,SS	0.0600	.046	0.1875	.010	.032	.035
5	0-80 X .25 Button Head-Soc-SS	54383-0-ACHA	SCR,BHS,0-80X1/4,SOC,SS	0.0600	.046	0.2500	.010	.032	.035
6	0-80 X .312 Button Head-Soc-SS	54383-0-ADHA	SCR,BHS,0-80X5/16,SOC,SS	0.0600	.046	0.3125	.010	.032	.035
7	0-80 X .375 Button Head-Soc-SS	54383-0-AEHA	SCR,BHS,0-80X3/8,SOC,SS	0.0600	.046	0.3750	.010	.032	.035
8	0-80 X .437 Button Head-Soc-SS	54383-0-AFHA	SCR,BHS,0-80X7/16,SOC,SS	0.0600	.046	0.4375	.010	.032	.035
9	0-80 X .5 Button Head-Soc-SS	54383-0-AGHA	SCR,BHS,0-80X1/2,SOC,SS	0.0600	.046	0.5000	.010	.032	.035
10	0-80 X .562 Button Head-Soc-SS	54383-0-AHHA	SCR,BHS,0-80X9/16,SOC,SS	0.0600	.046	0.5625	.010	.032	.035
11	0-80 X .625 Button Head-Soc-SS	54383-0-AJHA	SCR,BHS,0-80X5/8,SOC,SS	0.0600	.046	0.6250	.010	.032	.035
12	0-80 X .687 Button Head-Soc-SS	54383-0-AKHA	SCR,BHS,0-80X11/16,SOC,SS	0.0600	.046	0.6875	.010	.032	.035
13	0-80 X .75 Button Head-Soc-SS	54383-0-ALHA	SCR,BHS,0-80X3/4,SOC,SS	0.0600	.046	0.7500	.010	.032	.035
14	0-80 X .812 Button Head-Soc-SS	54383-0-AMHA	SCR,BHS,0-80X13/16,SOC,SS	0.0600	.046	0.8125	.010	.032	.035
15	0-80 X .875 Button Head-Soc-SS	54383-0-ANHA	SCR,BHS,0-80X7/8,SOC,SS	0.0600	.046	0.8750	.010	.032	.035
16	0-80 X 1.0 Button Head-Soc-SS	54383-0-APHA	SCR,BHS,0-80X1,SOC,SS	0.0600	.046	1.0000	.010	.032	.035
17	1-72 X .125 Button Head-Soc-SS	54383-0-BAHA	SCR,BHS,1-72X1/8,SOC,SS	0.0730	.058	0.1250	.010	.039	.050
18	1-72 X .187 Button Head-Soc-SS	54383-0-BBHA	SCR,BHS,1-72X3/16,SOC,SS	0.0730	.058	0.1875	.010	.039	.050
19	1-72 X .25 Button Head-Soc-SS	54383-0-BCHA	SCR,BHS,1-72X1/4,SOC,SS	0.0730	.058	0.2500	.010	.039	.050
20	1-72 X .312 Button Head-Soc-SS	54383-0-BDHA	SCR,BHS,1-72X5/16,SOC,SS	0.0730	.058	0.3125	.010	.039	.050
21	1-72 X .375 Button Head-Soc-SS	54383-0-BEHA	SCR,BHS,1-72X3/8,SOC,SS	0.0730	.058	0.3750	.010	.039	.050

Sheet1 / ParameterLookup

Config names

Feature or property syntax from table

FIGURE 10.16

Filling in configuration names

	A
1	Design Table for:
2	
3	001
4	002
5	003
6	
7	
8	
9	

	A
1	Design Table for:
2	
3	001
4	002
5	003
6	
7	
8	
9	

	A
1	Design Table for:
2	
3	001
4	002
5	003
6	004
7	005
8	006
9	007
10	008
11	009
12	010
13	011
14	012
15	013
16	
17	

The next step is to fill in some feature and dimension names in the second row. The first thing that you do is to suppress the HexDrive feature. To make this the first feature in the list, click in cell B2, and then double-click the HexDrive feature in the FeatureManager. The name of the feature and its current suppression state are added to the design table with all of the necessary syntax and correct spelling.

To rotate the text in this row vertically, RMB click row number 2, select Format Cells, click the Alignment tab, and turn the orientation to 90 degrees. The word *unsuppressed* displays with all c apitals and fully spelled out, while all you need is a U or an S. Replace the word with an S, and double-click the line between the column heading letters B and C at the top of the Excel window, to condense column B as much as possible. Alternate the rest of the rows between *U*s and *S*s to either suppress or unsuppress the HexDrive feature in various configurations. Figure 10.17 shows the current state of the design table.

FIGURE 10.17

Building the design table

	A	B	C
1	Design Table for: Chapter 10 (		
2		$STATE@HexDrive	
3	001	s	
4	002	u	
5	003	s	
6	004	u	
7	005	s	
8	006	u	
9	007	s	
10	008	u	
11	009	s	
12	010	u	
13	011	s	
14	012	u	
15	013	s	

Close the Design Table window, and click OK on the message box that lists the new configurations created by the Design Table. Now split the FeatureManager, set the lower pane to the ConfigurationManager, and double-click some configurations. Notice that in the configs where you specified an S, the HexDrive is suppressed, and no longer appears in the model.

You can now add a dimension to the design table. To add a dimension, it is most convenient to display the dimensions on the screen at all times. To show all of the dimensions in the part, RMB click the Annotations folder in the FeatureManager and select Display Annotations. If the dimensions do not display, then you may have to go back and select Show Feature Dimensions. Arrange the dimensions so that you can clearly see them all, as shown in Figure 10.18.

Dimension and annotation display settings

To display the design table again, locate it in the FeatureManager list, just below the Origin, RMB click it, and select Edit Table. Editing the feature changes the settings used for the design table. Edit Table in New Window is an option that we will use later because it simplifies many things; however, for now, the Edit Table option makes it easiest to add new items to the design table.

NOTE If a window appears with the name Add Rows and Columns, just click OK for now. This window lists parameters that have changed in its lower pane, and it is asking you if you would like to add any of the changed parameters to the design table. If you would like to add them, just select the parameter in the lower pane and click OK. If not, just click OK.

If the design table displays on top of your model, you can either move the model or move the design table. Moving the design table is a bit tricky, and involves dragging the striped-line border of the Excel window; remember not to grab it at the corners or midpoints, because this will simply resize it. If you click inside the border, nothing happens. If you click outside of the border, the Excel window closes. Moving the model may be easier. To do this, just Ctrl-drag in blank space in the graphics window; it pans the display so that you can see the part dimensions.

With cell C2 selected, or whatever the next available cell is in the second row, double-click the OverallLength dimension in the graphics window. SolidWorks adds the proper syntax to the design table, along with the current value for the first configuration in the list. Fill in values for the rest of the configurations. These values can then be calculated in Excel using any of the available techniques.

Exit the design table and toggle through the various configurations to see their different lengths. These examples should get you started on more complex configurations and design tables. Any dimensions that are controlled by the design table (and that are therefore locked) display in pink on the screen.

Design table settings

Figure 10.14 shows the PropertyManager for design tables. After you have created the table, you can edit the table settings by RMB clicking the table and then selecting Edit Feature. Edit Feature enables you to edit the settings for the table only; it does not enable you to edit values within the table.

Linked design table

By selecting the From File source option, you can create a design table from an external file; you can also link the table to the external file. When you use the other two options, Blank and Auto-Create, SolidWorks stores the Excel file within the SolidWorks document. Linking to an external file may be useful if you have a non-SolidWorks user who is entering data into the design table, or if a single table controls multiple parts.

Edit control

The Edit Control panel has two options, which act as a toggle. The Allow Model Edits To Update The Design Table option is self explanatory, as is its opposite, the Block Model Edits That Would Update The Design Table option. If the Allow Model Edits option is selected, and you make a manual change to the model, the next time you open the design table, SolidWorks warns you about the change and that it will update the design table. Likewise, if you try to make a manual change and the Block Model Edits option is selected, you receive a warning that the value cannot be changed.

Options

The Options settings determine the behavior when you are using the Allow Model Edits option and a new item has been configured. For example, the design table may already exist, and you manually add a configuration and suppress a feature.

Configurations that have been added manually are displayed somewhat differently from configs that are being managed by the design table. Figure 10.19 shows the two configurations at the bottom of the tree with square symbols, while the design table configs have Excel symbols.

Manually created configs versus design table–created configs

After you manually add the config and suppress the feature, the next time you open the design table, the Add Rows and Columns dialog box appears. Most users are simply annoyed by this, but that may be because they do not understand what it does or why it appears. In the example shown in Figure 10.20, a new configuration has been manually added; it appears in the Configurations box as Manually Added Config, and in the Parameters box, it looks like a feature named BodyChamf has been either suppressed or unsuppressed manually. The appearance of this dialog box means that SolidWorks is asking you if you would like to include these items in the design table. If so, then simply select the items you would like to add to the design table and click OK. If you do not want to include the items in the design table, then simply click OK or Cancel. If you click OK, then you will not be offered these choices again; if you click Cancel, then the next time you open the table, the dialog box with the same choices will reappear. If you never want to see this dialog box again, then make sure that all of the options in the Options panel shown in Figure 10.14 are turned off.

FIGURE 10.20

The Add Rows and Columns dialog box

Editing the design table

As mentioned earlier, when you open the design table inside the SolidWorks window, it can sometimes be difficult to work with. One way to handle this problem is to only edit the design table inside SolidWorks when you want to add new features to the column headers, and when adding new configurations or editing the field values, edit the table in a separate window. This option appears on the RMB menu, as Edit Table in New Window. It allows you much more flexibility in resizing the Excel window, changing zoom scale, and other operations, but it does not allow you to double-click a dimension so that it is added automatically to the column header.

CAUTION   When working on design tables, it is a good idea to avoid conflicts with other sessions of Excel by closing any other Excel windows. The combination of operating Excel spreadsheets inside both SolidWorks and Excel has been known to cause crashes, or the "Server Busy" warning message. If you are diligent about having only one session of Excel active at a time when you are working on design tables (or Excel BOMs), then there is less likelihood of a crash or conflict.

Tutorial: Working with Configurations and Design Tables

Throughout this book, parts that I use for one purpose may also be interesting for other purposes as well. For example, the part used in this tutorial uses a loft with guide curves where both guide curves are created in the same sketch. The guide curve sketch is made from symmetrical splines where I have used the spline handles to change the shape smoothly and in a controlled way. I have also used a curve-driven pattern to go around an elliptical shape.

TIP   If at some point you decide that you have made mistakes from which you cannot recover, or you would simply like to start over again, you can select File, Reload. This is the same as exiting the part without saving, and then reopening the part to start from the beginning.

To start working with configurations and design tables, follow these steps:

1. From the CD-ROM, open the part called Chapter 10 Tutorial start.sldprt. Take a moment to become familiar with this part by using the rollback bar to see how it was made. In particular, look at the two patterns, which need to be parametrically linked. Figure 10.21 shows the part.

FIGURE 10.21

The Chapter 10 Tutorial start.sldprt file

2. Manually create a configuration for the part called Size 1. Remember that to create a configuration, you must show the ConfigurationManager tab in the FeatureManager area, and RMB click the name of the part at the top level. It is better to do this by splitting the FeatureManager window and setting the lower pane to the ConfigurationManager.

3. Set the Advanced option to both Suppress Features and Use Configuration Specific Color (both turned on).

4. Before closing the Add Configuration PropertyManager, click the Color button on the Advanced Options panel of the Configuration PropertyManager and select a different color for the Size 1 configuration. The color does not change immediately. It will change after you close the PropertyManager.

5. Turn on the Tools ⇨ Options setting to Show Dimension Names. (Remember, this the third option on the General page).

6. Double-click the feature CrvPattern1 in the FeatureManager. A number 6 with a D1 under it will appear on one of the holes in the pattern. If you have changed your part to a blue color, then it may be difficult to see, because the text will also be blue.

7. Change the name of the dimension to Hole# by RMB clicking the dimension and selecting Properties.

8. Change the value of the number to 8, and be careful to also change the drop-down setting to This Configuration Only instead of All Configurations. If you forget to do this, then you will have to go to the other configuration and set it back to 6.

9. Click the Rebuild symbol (which resembles a traffic light) to show the changes before exiting the Modify dialog box. Notice that the CrvPattern2 fails after rebuilding CrvPattern1 with eight instances. Click the green check mark icon to exit the Modify dialog box, and then make the same changes to the CrvPattern2, from changing the dimension name and the number of patterned instances to eight (remember to use the This Configuration Only setting). The part should now look like Figure 10.22.

FIGURE 10.22

The model after step 9

10. Double-clicking to change configurations now shows a part with a different color and a different number of holes and ribs. After the first change between configurations, the changes should happen quickly because SolidWorks has stored the geometry.

11. Go to File ⇨ Properties, and select the Configuration Specific tab. Set the Apply To drop-down list to Default, and type a Property Name of **description** and a Value of **Gray Vent Cover**. Now change the Apply To drop-down setting to Size 1 and type a description for the new configuration using the name of the color that you applied to this config. Figure 10.23 shows the two states of the data.

FIGURE 10.23

Setting the Configuration Specific custom properties

12. Exit the Custom Properties dialog box.

13. Now that you have made a few changes manually, the following steps guide you through bringing these changes into a design table and using the design table to make additional changes. From the menus, select Insert ⇨ Design Table. Use Auto-create as the Source, allow model edits, and turn on all three option in the Option panel. Click OK to create the design table. Figure 10.24 shows the design table that you have automatically created.

FIGURE 10.24

The automatically created design table

	A	B	C	D	E	F
1	Design Table for: Chapter 10 Tutorial start					
2		$DESCRIPTION	$COLOR	$PRP@description	Hole#@CrvPattern1	Rib#@CrvPattern2
3	Default	Default	12632256	Gray Vent Cover	6	6
4	Size 1	Size 1	255	Red Vent Cover	8	8

14. Use the striped border to move the window without closing it. This may take some practice. If the window closes, just RMB click the design table in the FeatureManager and select Edit Table. Move the window to a place where you can see the model clearly.

15. If a cell in the second row of the design table is selected, select a different empty cell that is not in the second row (this prevents data from automatically populating cells until you have the correct data). Now double-click the Extrude1 feature in the FeatureManager. Find the .500" (D1) dimension on the screen. RMB click the dimension and rename it BaseThk.

16. Click the next open cell in the second row, and double-click the .500" dimension that you just renamed. You may have to use the handles at the corners and side midpoints to resize the Excel window to see everything. Add another configuration row and the additional values in the cells, as shown in Figure 10.25. The color number is determined by a formula that you can find in the help section under the topic Color Parameter.

FIGURE 10.25

Make additions to the design table.

	A	B	C	D	E	F	G
1	Design Table for: Chapter 10 Tutorial start						
2		$DESCRIPTION	$COLOR	$PRP@description	Hole#@CrvPattern1	Rib#@CrvPattern2	BaseThk@Extrude1
3	Default	Default	12632256	Gray Vent Cover	6	6	0.5
4	Size 1	Size 1	255	Red Vent Cover	8	8	0.8
5	Size 2	Size 2	16711680	Blue Vent Cover	10	10	1
6							

17. Remember that this part needs to have the number of ribs always equal to the number of holes. This is simple to do in Excel. Click in the first row value for the Rib# number. This is cell F3 in Figure 10.25. Type the equal sign, and then click in the cell to the left, E3. You can also simply type =E3 in this cell. This links the Rib# cell to the Hole# cell.

18. Use the Window Fill feature by selecting the dot at the lower-right corner of the selected F3 cell and dragging it down to also include cells F4 and F5, as shown in Figure 10.26.

19. Click in a blank space to exit the design table. Double-click through the configurations in the ConfigurationManager to see the results of your efforts.

FIGURE 10.26

Copying the equation to other cells

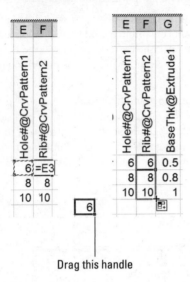

Drag this handle

Summary

Configurations are a powerful way to control variations of a design within a single part file. Many aspects of the part can be configured, while a few cannot. Manually created configurations are useful for making a small number of variations and a small number of configurations, but they become unwieldy when you need to make more than a few variations of either type.

Design tables are recommended because they allow you to more clearly see all of the changes that have been made for all of the configurations. Having the power of Excel available allows you to access many functions that are not shown here, such as using lookup tables and Concatenate functions to build descriptions or configuration names. I will briefly revisit design tables in the section on assembly configurations to expand on the information here, and to incorporate the additional assembly configuration information.

Chapter 11

Editing and Evaluation

I f you work like I do, then you probably create a part once, but edit it many times. As I often say, *design for change* is really at the core of most of the modeling work that you will do in SolidWorks, and deletion is not an editing option.

You do the most good — or the most harm — in the initial stages of modeling when you are setting up parametric relations between features and sketches. For this reason, editing often quickly turns into repair. Granted, some changes are simply unavoidable, but a thorough knowledge of editing — and repairing — can help you to understand the how, what, and why of modeling best practice.

This chapter starts with some very basic concepts of editing, which you may have picked up if you have been reading this book from the beginning. Because this is the last chapter in Part II, and the last that deals strictly with part modeling, it also contains a summary of part-modeling best practice and a set of model evaluation tools that can help you to evaluate the manufacturability and aesthetic properties of parts. I have included these evaluation tools in a chapter on editing because the edit-evaluate cycle is one of the most familiar in modeling and design practice.

Using Rollback

Rolling back a model simply means looking at the results of the design tree only up to a certain point in the model history. In SolidWorks, you can actually change history — that is, you can change the order in which operations are completed. As a result, the chronological order in which features are created is not necessarily related to the order in which these features display in the design tree, or the order in which the operations are completed.

You can use several methods to put the model in this rolled-back state:

- Dragging the Rollback bar with the cursor.

- RMB clicking and selecting one of the Rollback options.

- Editing a feature other than the last one in the design tree (SolidWorks rolls back the model automatically).

- Using the Tools ➪ Options setting that allows you to control the Rollback bar with the arrow keys.

- Pressing Esc during a long model rebuild. This method is supposed to roll you back to the last feature that was rebuilt when you pressed Esc; however, in practice, I have rarely seen it do this, and it usually just rebuilds the entire model anyway.

Using the Rollback bar

The Rollback bar, which is usually found at the bottom of the FeatureManager in SolidWorks part documents, enables you to put the part into almost any state in the model history. This is not the same as the Undo command, but is the equivalent of suppressing everything in the FeatureManager after a certain point. Figure 11.1 shows the Rollback bar in use. Notice how the cursor changes into a hand icon when you move it over the bar.

FIGURE 11.1

Using the Rollback bar

Consumed features

When you use a sketch for a feature such as a Sketch Driven Pattern, the sketch is left in the design tree, in the place where it was created. However, most other features, such as extrudes, *consume* the sketch, meaning that the sketch disappears from its normal order in the FeatureManager and appears indented under the feature that was created from it. Consumed sketches are sometimes also referred to as *absorbed* sketches.

Examining the parent-child relationship

In genealogical family tree diagrams, the parent-child relationship is represented with the parent at the top, and the children branched below the parent. In SolidWorks, parent-child relationships are tracked differently. Figure 11.2 shows the difference between a genealogical family tree and the SolidWorks design tree.

FIGURE 11.2

Different interpretations of the structure of parent-child relationships

You can display the parent-child relations between SolidWorks features as shown in Figure 11.2 by opening the RMB menu on any feature, and selecting Parent/Child. This helps you to determine relationships before editing or deleting, so that you can see which features will be removed or go dangling.

When SolidWorks puts the child feature at the top, it is, in effect, turning the relationship upside down, but long-time users have all somehow learned to look at this without questioning it. In the SolidWorks FeatureManager, the earlier point in history is at the top of the tree, but the children are listed earlier than the parents. Once you look at it this way, you can see that SolidWorks has chosen a very unintuitive method to display the features in the tree. The method SolidWorks has chosen to use stresses the importance of solid features over other types of sketch or curve features.

It appears to be even less intuitive when you think of the order in which features are created. For example, you create an extrude from a sketch, and so the sketches exist before the extrude in the FeatureManager. However, when you create the extrude, SolidWorks places the sketch underneath the extrude. In fact, this restructuring can become more apparent when a sketch (for example, Sketch1) is created early in the part history, and then not used to create a feature (for example, Extrude5) until much later. If you roll down the FeatureManager feature by feature, you arrive a point at the end of the design tree where Extrude5 appears and Sketch1 suddenly moves from its location at the top of the tree to under Extrude5 at the bottom of the tree.

This scenario may cause a situation where many sketches and other features that are created between Sketch1 and Extrude5 are dependent on Sketch1, but where Sketch1 suddenly appears after all of these other features. As this example shows, the more closely you examine how the relationships are depicted, the more counterintuitive they appear.

The only thing that you can do about this relationship structure is to realize that SolidWorks displays many relations upside down, and learn to understand it and not get confused in the process. In some ways, ignorance is bliss, because if you do not know that the relationships are shown in a confusing way, then it might not occur to you that there is anything wrong.

One way to get around difficulties in understanding the chronological order of features when compared against the relationship order of features is to roll back a model tree item by item. This can help you sort through the issues. Also remember that from SolidWorks' point of view, the solid feature is the most important item in the tree and is what the rest of the items in the tree are there to support. SolidWorks has made the solid features easily visible and accessible in the tree.

There is a movement afoot among a group of users to try to convince SolidWorks to enable the tree to be displayed in multiple ways, one of which would be a strictly linear, chronological way. Another option would be graphically showing the hierarchical links between features, and still another would be a traditional "genealogical" tree approach. If you would like to encourage SolidWorks in one of these directions, please fill out an enhancement request.

Rolling back features with multiple parents

Take an example such as a loft with guide curves. If you create the guide curves first, and then you create the loft profiles by referencing the guide curves, then the loft automatically reorders these sketches when they display under the loft feature such that the profiles are listed in the order in which they were selected. The guide curves are also shown in the order that they were selected. This is shown in Figure 11.3. This restructuring can really be confusing, especially if you want to go back and edit any of the relationships between the sketches. It becomes even more so if the sketches have been renamed so that the names do not clearly reflect the natural order of the sketches before they were all consumed by the loft feature. You can find this example on the CD-ROM with the filename Chapter 11 Loftwgc.sldprt.

FIGURE 11.3

Multiple parents and sketch reordering

NOTE In this example, the two guide curves were created as part of a single sketch, and the SelectionManager was used to select them as individual open curves. This is why the Guide Curves sketch is represented with the contour symbol rather than a regular sketch symbol.

Viewing consumed features in their original order

If you want to view consumed sketches in their original order — for example, the sketches in the loft feature in Figure 11.3 — you must first expand the feature so that you can see the consumed sketches, and then rollback between the feature and the first sketch. At this point, a warning message appears, stating that the sketches will be temporarily unabsorbed during editing. You can then move the Rollback bar again to show the sketches.

This maneuver can become complicated when you have two sketches absorbed by a projected curve, the projected curve absorbed by a composite curve, and the composite curve absorbed by a sweep feature. To isolate the original projected sketches, you need to experiment with the placement of the Rollback bar, as shown in Figure 11.4.

FIGURE 11.4

Rollback of nested, absorbed features

To view consumed sketches in their original order, follow these steps:

1. Expand the sweep.
2. Rollback between the sweep and the profile sketch.
3. Answer the prompt that appears.
4. Roll down so that you can see the unabsorbed sketches and curves.
5. Expand the composite curve.
6. Rollback to just after the composite curve.
7. Rollback so that you can see the contents of the composite curve.
8. Expand the projected curve.
9. Rollback to just after the projected curve.
10. Rollback so that you can see the contents of the projected curve.

Enhancement requests

This is a great time to talk about enhancement requests. The SolidWorks Web site (www
.solidworks.com) has a section for users to submit suggestions for adding new features or
changing existing ones in the SolidWorks software. Users have been able to do tricky rollbacks
such as this for the last three releases, but it seems evident that all of the possible ramifications of
this technique have not been considered. Because changes are made on the basis of popularity, I
recommend that if you are interested in seeing this functionality improved, you should submit an
enhancement request for this particular function.

Other Rollback techniques

The Rollback feature is available through the RMB menu. Just RMB click a feature and select either
Rollback or Roll to Previous. If you are already rolled back and you RMB click below the Rollback
bar, then you can access additional options to Roll Forward and Roll to End.

CAUTION If you have a situation with nested, absorbed features as described earlier, then selecting Rollback from the RMB menu can cause the Rollback bar to disappear and for all
the features to gray out. To get out of this mode, where essentially nothing is available, you can either
close out of and reload the part, or simply apply the Undo command.

Editing any feature other than the last feature also serves to rollback the model while you are in Edit
mode. As soon as you rebuild the feature or sketch, SolidWorks rebuilds the entire design tree.

The Tools ⇨ Option setting for Arrow Key Navigation enables you to use the up- and down-arrow
keys to manipulate the Rollback bar. Under normal circumstances, the arrow keys control the view
orientation, but after you have moved the Rollback bar once using the cursor, the up- and down-
arrow keys control the Rollback bar. The left- and right-arrow keys have no effect on the Rollback bar.

CAUTION The one situation where this technique does not work as expected is when you are
working on a part in the context of the assembly, with the design tree rolled back. The
down arrow simply causes the Rollback bar to roll immediately to the end of the design tree.

NEW FEATURE New in SolidWorks 2007, you can save the model while it is still rolled back. In previous
versions, you had to roll to the end of the FeatureManager before saving, and then rollback
to where you were and keep working. This made working in Rollback mode fairly frustrating (if you wanted
to save the model) and dangerous, as crashing without saving means potentially losing a lot of data.

Reordering Features

As you already know, feature order can make a difference in the final shape of a part. For example,
this order:

1. Extrude
2. Cut
3. Fillet
4. Shell

gives you a very different part from this order:

1. Extrude

2. Shell

3. Cut

4. Fillet

The results of these different orders is shown in Figure 11.5 (The part is split and partially transparent for demonstration purposes only). You can view this part on the CD-ROM with the filename Chapter 11 Reorder.sldprt.

FIGURE 11.5

Parts that use a different feature order

On the part in the above example, it is fairly simple to reorder the Shell feature by dragging it up the design tree. As a result, the well created by the Cut feature is not shelled around (to create a tube) if the cut comes after the shell. Also, notice the effect of applying the fillets after the shell rather than before it. The corners inside the box are sharp, while the outside corners have been filleted. When you apply the fillet before the shell, fillets that have a radius larger than the shell thickness are transferred to the inside of the shell.

When you are reordering the features, a symbol may appear on the reorder cursor that says that you cannot reorder the selected feature to the location you want. In this case, you may want to select the Parent/Child option from the RMB menu to investigate. Sketch relationships, feature end conditions, and faces or edges selected for features such shell, patterns, and mirror can cause relationships that prevent reordering.

If two adjacent features are to swap places, it generally does not matter whether you move one feature up the design tree or you move the other one down. However, there are isolated situations that are usually created by the nested, absorbed features discussed earlier, where one feature cannot go in one direction, but the other feature can go in the opposite direction, achieving the exact same result.

Reordering Folders

There are times when, regardless of which features you choose to move and of which direction you choose to move them in, you are faced with the task of moving many features. This can be time-consuming and tedious, not to mention being a potential source for error. To simplify this process, you can put all of the features to be moved into a single folder, and then reorder the folder. Keep in mind that the items in the folder need to be a continuous list (you cannot skip features), and you can only reorder the folder if each individual feature within the folder can be reordered.

BEST PRACTICE Folders are frequently used for groups of features that go together and that may be suppressed or unsuppressed in groups. You can also use folders in assemblies. Folders are frequently used for the mass of cosmetic fillet features that are often found at the end of design trees for plastic parts, or for groups of hole features.

To create a folder, RMB click a feature or a selected group of features and select Add to New Folder. Folders should be renamed to have a name that helps identify their contents. You can reorder folders in the same way as individual features. When you delete a folder, the contents are removed from the folder; they are not deleted.

You can add or remove features to or from the folders by dragging them in or out. If a folder is the last item in the FeatureManager, the next feature that is created is not put into the folder; you must place it in the folder manually. You cannot drag features out of a folder and place them immediately after it, because they will just go back into the folder. If you want to pull a feature out of a folder and place it after the folder, then there must be another feature between the feature that you are moving and the folder. However, you can pull a feature out of the folder and place it just *before* the folder.

Using the Flyout FeatureManager

The Flyout FeatureManager resides at the top-left corner of the graphics window, and was introduced when SolidWorks began to consolidate floating dialog boxes into the PropertyManager window. The PropertyManager goes in the same space as the FeatureManager, and is sometimes too big to allow this area to accommodate both managers in a split window.

The Flyout FeatureManager enables you to select items from the design tree when the regular FeatureManager is not available. It usually appears collapsed, so that you can only see the name of the part and the part symbol. To expand it, either click the title of the active PropertyManager, or click the plus icon next to the name of the part in the Flyout FeatureManager.

If you press the C key after the flyout has been activated by the PropertyManager but is not yet expanded, a set of scroll arrows may appear, so that the flyout can only display a single feature at a time. If the FeatureManager is expanded, pressing the C key causes the Flyout FeatureManager to display right next to the regular FeatureManager. You can use the Flyout FeatureManager in parts or in the assembly. However, you cannot use the Flyout FeatureManager to suppress or rollback the tree.

CROSS-REF Other functionality and limitations of the Flyout FeatureManager that relate to its function in assemblies can be found in Chapters 12 to 15.

You can access the settings for the Flyout FeatureManager at Tools ➪ Options ➪ FeatureManager ➪ Use Transparent Flyout FeatureManager in Parts/Assemblies.

Summarizing Part Modeling Best Practice

This section is a summary of best practice suggestions for modeling parts. Best practice lists are important because they lay the groundwork for conservative usage of the software, which is helpful for new users and users who are trying to experiment with the limits of the software.

I believe that it is only after you respect the rules and understand why they are so important, that you know enough to break them. However, best practice lists should not be taken too seriously. They are not inflexible rules, but conservative starting places; they are concepts that you can default to, but that can be broken if you have good reason.

None of the following best practices applies all of the time, and you have my permission to break any of these rules as long as you can explain why your situation is exempt from them.

- Always use unique filenames for your parts. SolidWorks assemblies and drawings may pick up incorrect references if you use parts with identical names.

- Using Custom Properties is a great way to enter text-based information into your parts. Users can view this information from outside the file by using applications such as Windows Explorer, SolidWorks Explorer, and PDM applications.

- Learn to sketch using automatic relations.

- Use fully dimensioned sketches when possible. Splines are often impractical to fully dimension.

- Limit your use of the Fixed constraint.

- When possible, make relations to sketches or stable reference geometry, such as the Origin or standard planes, instead of edges or faces. Sketches are far more stable than faces, edges, or model vertices, which change their internal ID at the slightest change and may disappear entirely with fillets, chamfers, split lines, and so on.

- Do not dimension to edges created by fillets, or other cosmetic or temporary features.

- Apply names to features, sketches, and dimensions that help to make their function clear.

- When possible, use feature fillets and feature patterns rather than sketch fillets and sketch patterns.

- Combine fillets into as few fillet features as possible; this also allows you to control fillets that need to be controlled separately, such as fillets to be removed for FEA, drawings, and simplified configurations, or added for rendering.

- Create a simplified configuration when building very complex parts or working with large assemblies.

- Model with symmetry in mind. Use feature patterns when possible.

- Use link values or global variables to control commonly used dimensions.

- Do not be afraid of configurations. Control them with design tables where there are more than a few configs, and document any custom programming or automated features in the spreadsheet.

- Cosmetic features — fillets, in particular — should be saved for the bottom of the design tree. It is also a good idea to put them all together into a folder.

- Use the setting at Tools ➪ Options ➪ Performance ➪ Verification on Rebuild in combination with the Ctrl+Q command to check models periodically and before calling them "done." The more complex the model, or the more questionable some of the geometry or techniques might be, the more important it is to check the part.

- Always fix errors in your part as soon as you can. Errors cause rebuild time to increase, and if you wait until more errors exist, troubleshooting may become more difficult.

- Do not add unnecessary detail. For example, it is not important to actually model a knurled surface on a round steel part. This additional detail is difficult to model in SolidWorks, it slows down the rebuild speed of your part, and there is no advantage to actually having it modeled (unless you are using the model for rapid prototype or to machine a mold for a plastic part where knurling cannot be added as a secondary process). This is better accomplished by a drawing with a note. The same concept applies to thread, extruded text, very large patterns, and other features that introduce complex details.

- Do not rely heavily on niche features. For example, if you find yourself creating helices by using Flex/Twist or Wrap instead of Sweep, then you may want to rethink your approach. In fact, if you find yourself creating a lot of unnecessary helices, then you may want to rethink this approach as well, unless there is a good reason for doing so.

- File size is not necessarily a measure of inefficiency.

- Be cautious about accepting advice or information from Internet forums.

If you are the CAD Administrator for a group of users, you may want to incorporate some best practice tips into standard operating procedures for them. The more users that you have to manage, the more you need to standardize your system.

Using the Skeleton or Wide Tree Approach

SolidWorks is not the first parametric modeler to challenge the linear logic of genealogical analysis. The users of software like Pro/ENGINEER are responsible for developing many of the concepts and best practice techniques that SolidWorks users use today.

NOTE The term Skeleton in Pro/ENGINEER has a different significance than the way it is being used here. SolidWorks does not have any feature or function named "skeleton." The term is just being used to refer to a set of sketches, planes, axes, and reference points used to lay out the major faces and features of a part.

The SolidWorks Help files, tutorials, and training curricula have encouraged users in some respects to take a "fast and loose" approach to modeling, which lends itself best to simple models that are not changed frequently. Little thought was given to the structure of the part; the only thing that really mattered was the final shape. The main consideration seemed to be the simplest way to do something, or how it *could* be done rather than how it *should* be done. This mentality fit well with the initial several releases of the SolidWorks software, which at that time was marketed as being simple and fast.

The software has progressed immensely since those days. It is now entirely plausible to create complex castings and plastic parts with many hundreds of features, weaving in and out of surface and solid techniques, multibodies, and external references. This is a far cry from the typical tutorial or training part, which still tend to have fewer than 15 features, half of which may be fillets. With the simpler parts, you hardly give a thought to parent/child relationships, rebuild times, or the consequences of making changes that cause a feature to fail, because the whole part could be rebuilt from scratch in ten minutes anyway. This is because the people who knew the software best were doing brief sales demo vignettes and small models that could be finished before the students fell asleep.

SolidWorks users have traditionally been taught to build each feature linearly, on top of the one that came before. This is the genealogical equivalent of each generation having a single child, and then that child having a single child, and so on. The family tree, or FeatureManager, winds up looking like a long staircase, with each generation related only to the generation immediately before it. In the SolidWorks world, this creates long, linear, daisy-chained relationships between consecutive features.

It turns out that even though this has been hailed as the pinnacle of associative, parametric, history-based modeling, it is not really such a great idea, especially as the parts begin to get more complex. When each feature is dependent upon the one before it, all of the features must be solved in a particular order, and if one feature fails, so do all of the features that come after it. This also slows down the rebuilding process. Especially as we move into the age of parallel multi-threaded processing, a linear set of commands or features must be executed in order one after the other, and there is really no room for parallel processes.

The sophistication of the documentation provided with SolidWorks software has not kept pace with the sophistication of the software itself, which I suppose is why you are reading this book rather than the help files. The documentation is still based on the simple scenarios, and the advanced user is left to figure things out on his or her own.

As the software gets more sophisticated, the models created with the software can get more sophisticated, and our methods used to build the models must also get more sophisticated. We must leave the linear modeling approaches behind.

Rather than using a linear daisy-chain modeling scenario, it is better practice to base features on entities that are less likely to fail or change in such a way that dependent downstream features also fail. In earlier chapters, it has already been suggested that sketch relations should be made to other sketches when possible instead of model edges for this very reason.

Taking that scenario one step further, what if a handful of sketch and plane features were used to centralize control of all of the rest of the features? What if every feature, to the extent possible, related back to these "skeleton" features? Features such as fillets, shell, and draft by design require selections from solid geometry, but other features, such as any feature created from sketches, could be made with only reference to those original skeleton sketches and planes. The parent/child relationship would look very different for a model made in this way. Instead of looking like a long staircase, this tree would look more like a tree that gets wide very quickly. There would be fewer "generations," but each generation would be more populated.

The first thing to notice is that errors in features at the top of the tree do not cascade down the tree as they do in the "stairstep" model. Secondly, it is always much easier to find how a model is constructed, because all the reference geometry used to build it is set up in the first few features. This scenario also has the potential to make better use of multi-threaded processing because the logic is less linear and more parallel.

Using Evaluation Techniques

You can use evaluation techniques to evaluate geometry errors, demonstrate the manufacturability of a given part, or to some degree to quantify aesthetic qualities of a given part, or section of a part. I discuss evaluation techniques here because the design cycle involves iterations around the combination of evaluate-edit-evaluate functions. I discuss the following techniques in this section:

- Draft analysis
- Thickness analysis
- Undercut detection
- Verification on Rebuild
- Check
- Zebra Stripes/RealView/Lights and specularity
- Curvature display
- Deviation analysis
- Tangent edges as phantom
- CosmosXpress
- MoldflowXpress

Many of these techniques apply specifically to plastic parts and complex shapes, but even if you do not become involved in these areas of design or modeling, these tools may help you to find answers on other types of products as well.

Draft analysis

The SolidWorks Draft Analysis tool is a must when working with plastic parts. The part shown below has many of the situations that you are going to encounter in analyzing plastic parts.

The Draft Analysis tool has four major modes of operation:

- Basic
- Gradual Transition
- Face Classification
- Find Steep Faces

Basic draft analysis

The Basic draft analysis (with no options selected) simply colors faces red, green, or yellow. Colors may display transitioning if the draft shifts between two classifications. This transition type is shown in Figure 11.6 in the image to the right. For a clearer view of this method, you can find the part, Chapter 11 Draft Analysis.sldprt, on the CD-ROM.

FIGURE 11.6

Basic draft analysis results

You can perform all types of draft analysis in SolidWorks by selecting a reference flat face or plane, and setting a minimum allowable angle. In Figure 11.6, all walls have at least a one-degree draft, except for the rounded edge shown in the image to the right and the dome. Both of these shapes transition from an angle less than one degree to an angle greater than one degree.

This basic analysis is good for visualizing changes in draft angle, but it also has some less desirable properties, which will become apparent as you study the other types of draft.

Gradual Transition

Although the Basic analysis is able to show a transitioning draft, the Gradual Transition draft analysis takes it a step further. With the Gradual Transition, you can specify the colors. It is also useful because it can distinguish drafts of different amounts by color. It may be difficult to tell in the grayscale image in Figure 11.7, but the ribs, which were created at one degree, have a slightly different color than the floor of the part, and the walls also have a different color. Notice that cavity and core directions have different colors, as well. You may want to open this part in SolidWorks, recreate the settings, and run the analysis so that you can see the actual colors.

FIGURE 11.7

The Gradual Transition draft analysis

Some problems arise when you use this display mode, the first being the flat, non-OpenGL face shading that is used to achieve the transitioning colors. This often makes it difficult to distinguish curved faces, and faces that face different directions. The second problem is that you cannot tell that the boss on top of the dome has absolutely no draft. In fact, there is no way to distinguish between faces that lean slightly toward the cavity and faces that lean slightly toward the core. The third problem is the strange effect that appears on the filleted corners. The corners were filleted after you applied the draft and before the shell, and so the filleted corners should have exactly the same draft as the sides; however, from the color plot, it looks to be a few degrees more.

CAUTION   Software can sometimes interpret things differently from the way that a person does. As a result, any computer analysis must be interpreted with common sense.

Due to this and some of the other problems that I mentioned above, I would use the Gradual Transition draft analysis in conjunction with one of the other tests. Gradual Transition gives an interesting effect, but it is not a reliable tool for determining on its own whether or not a part can be manufactured.

Face Classification

Face Classification draft analysis groups the faces into classifications using solid, non-transitioning colors. You will notice a big difference between the coloration of the Face Classification draft analysis faces and of the Basic or Gradual Transition faces. Face Classification uses OpenGL face shading, which is the same as that used by SolidWorks by default. This allows better shading and differentiation between faces that face different directions. The Basic Analysis coloration looks like all of the faces are painted the same flat hue, regardless of which direction they are facing, which makes shapes more difficult to identify. The non-Open GL alternate shading method makes it possible to display a transition in color. SolidWorks OpenGL shading cannot do this.

Another advantage of using the OpenGL shading is that the face colors can remain on the part after you have closed the Draft Analysis PropertyManager.

Face Classification draft analysis also adds a classification that is not used by the Basic draft analysis. *Straddle Faces* refer to faces that straddle the parting line, or faces that, due to their curvature, pull from both halves of the mold. These are faces that need to be split. On this part, a straddle face is shown in Figure 11.8.

The light bulb icons to the left of the color swatches enable you to hide faces by classification. This is useful when you are trying to isolate certain faces, or visualize a group of faces in a certain way. This can be an extremely useful feature, especially when you have a very complex part with a large number of faces, some of which may be small and easily lost in the mix with other larger faces.

The face counts that appear in the color swatches are a very helpful feature that is absent from the Basic draft analysis.

FIGURE 11.8

Face Classification draft analysis and a straddle face

Straddle face

BEST PRACTICE I prefer Face Classification draft analysis because it is the clearest. If I need additional detail regarding other types of faces, then I may run a Steep Face draft analysis as a supplement. The best practice here is not that you follow my favorite type of draft analysis, but that you understand what you need to know and then use the appropriate tools to find this information. This may include running multiple analyses to collect all of the necessary information.

Find steep faces

A *steep* face is defined as a face that transitions from less than the minimum angle to more than the minimum angle. Steep faces are different from straddle faces in that straddle faces are actually positive *and* negative, while steep faces are either entirely positive or entirely negative. On this part, the dome inside the part is classified as a steep face, as shown in Figure 11.9.

If you click out of either the Face Classification or the Find Steep Faces draft analyses, then you are given the option to save the face colors. I find this useful when I am making edits to add draft or move a parting line on a plastic part. However, the problem comes when trying to switch back to the regular part colors. In the past, the best way to do this was with a macro, although some users would also try to select all of the faces and remove the colors.

A steep face

Steep face

NEW FEATURE   New in SolidWorks 2007 sp1 (it was not available in sp0) is the Remove All Colors option in the Colors and Optics PropertyManager, as shown in Figure 11.10. With nothing selected in the selection box, just click the Remove All Colors button; SolidWorks removes all face, feature, and body colors and sets them back to the part color.

FIGURE 11.10

The Remove All Colors option

Thickness Analysis

Thickness Analysis is part of the SolidWorks Utilities, which are part of SolidWorks Office or higher. After you have activated the Utilities add-in (Tools ➪ Add-ins ➪ SolidWorks Utilities), Thickness Analysis appears under the Utilities menu.

You can run Thickness Analysis in two modes, Show Thin Regions and Show Thick Regions. Of these, Show Thick Regions is the most versatile.

Show Thin Regions

The Show Thin Regions option, or the "Thinness" Analysis, requires you to input a minimum acceptable thickness. Every face with a thickness above this value is turned a neutral gray, and every face with a thickness below this value is displayed on a graduated scale.

Figure 11.11 shows the PropertyManager for this analysis and its result on the same part used for the draft work in the previous sections.

FIGURE 11.11

Results of the Thinness Analysis

One of the things to watch out for here is that some anomalies occur when you apply this analysis to filleted faces. The faces that are shown as colored were created by the Shell feature, and should be exactly .100 inches thick. However, it does correctly represent the undercut on the end of the part and the thickness of the ribs. A nice addition to this tool would be the identification of minimum thickness faces. Perhaps you can submit another enhancement request.

Show Thick Regions

The Show Thick Regions option works a little differently from Show Thin Regions. You need to specify an upper thickness limit value, beyond which everything is identified as too thick. In these examples, the nominal wall thickness of the part is shown as .100 inches, and the thick region limit is set to .120 inches. For this type of analysis, the color gradient represents the thicknesses between .100 inches and .120 inches, while in the Thinness Analysis, the color gradient represents the values between .100 inches and 0 inches.

Figure 11.12 shows how this analysis produces some anomalous results, especially at the corners, and also in the middle. Again, this is a useful tool, if not completely accurate. You can use it to find problem areas that you may not have considered, but you should certainly examine the results critically.

FIGURE 11.12

Results of the Thickness Analysis

The Treat Corners As Zero Thickness option should always be on. I have never seen a situation where turning it off improved the results; in fact, I have found that turning it off has always made corners and fillets behave worse.

This feature can generate a report, which to some extent answers questions about how or why it classifies faces in the way it does. To get a complete picture of the situation, it may be useful to look at the report when you are using the results to make design or manufacturing decisions. A sample of the report is shown in Figure 11.13.

FIGURE 11.13

A sample of a Thickness Analysis report

Summary

Total surface area analyzed	70.019in^2
Critical surface area(% of analyzed area)	3.102in^2 (4.43%)
Maximum deviation from target thickness	0.02in
Average weighted thickness on critical area	0.104in
Average weighted thickness on analyzed area	0.098in
Number of critical faces	27 Face(s)
Number of critical features	9
Minimum thickness on analyzed area	0.007in
Maximum thickness on analyzed area	0.197in

Analysis Details

Thickness range	Number of faces	Surface area	% of analyzed area
0.1in to 0.105in	16	2.253in^2	3.22%
0.105in to 0.11in	5	0.353in^2	0.50%
0.11in to 0.115in	2	0.288in^2	0.41%
0.115in to 0.12in	4	0.208in^2	0.30%

Undercut Detection

 The Undercut Detection tool is conceptually flawed in that it gives incorrect results every time. However, if you think of the labels as being changed slightly, the results become partially usable.

Even if you and your mold builder know that a part has absolutely *no* undercuts, the Undercut Detection tool will nonetheless always identify *all* of the faces to be undercut. In fact, the only faces that this tool will identify as *not* undercut are faces that have no draft on them. The only time it correctly identifies an undercut is when it classifies the undercut as Occluded Undercut. Faces that have no draft and are occluded undercut are improperly identified as simply No Undercut.

You may want to avoid this tool because too much interpretation of incorrect results is necessary; however, if you still want to use it, then here is a translation guide that may help:

- Direction 1 Undercut — should read — Pull from Direction 2
- Direction 2 Undercut — should read — Pull from Direction 1

- Straddle Undercut — should read — Straddle faces
- No Undercut — should read — No draft in the primary draft direction, but may be occluded undercut faces
- Occluded Undercut — should read — Occluded Undercut faces that have draft in the completely irrelevant primary draft directions; does not include occluded undercut faces that have no draft in the primary direction

Figure 11.14 shows the PropertyManager for this function and the results. If you would like to test it for yourself, the part is on the CD-ROM with the filename Chapter 11 Draft Analysis.sldprt.

FIGURE 11.14

The results of the Undercut Detection tool

Verification on Rebuild

Verification on Rebuild is an option that you can access through Tools ➪ Options ➪ Performance ➪ Verification On Rebuild. Under normal circumstances (with this setting turned off), SolidWorks checks each face to ensure that it does not overlap or intersect improperly with every adjacent face. Each face can have several neighbors. This option is shown in Figure 11.15.

FIGURE 11.15

The Verification on Rebuild option

System Options	Document Properties

- General
- Drawings
  - Display Style
    - Area Hatch/Fill
- Colors
- Sketch
  - Relations/Snaps
- Display/Selection
- Performance

☐ Verification on rebuild
☐ Ignore self-intersection check for some sheet metal features

Transparency
☑ High quality for normal view mode
☐ High quality for dynamic view mode

Curvature generation: Only on demand   ▾

With the setting turned on, SolidWorks checks each face with every other face in the model. This represents a slightly better check than with the setting off, and a greatly increased workload. The switch is off by default to prevent rebuild times from getting out of control. For most parts, the default setting is sufficient; however, when parts become complex, you may need to select the more advanced setting.

If you are having geometry or rebuild error problems with a part and cannot understand why, then try turning Verification on and pressing Ctrl+Q. Ctrl+Q applies the Forced Rebuild command, and rebuilds the entire design tree, whether or not SolidWorks determines that it is needed. Ctrl+B, or the Rebuild command, only rebuilds what SolidWorks determines needs to be rebuilt.

If you see additional errors in the design tree that were not there before, then the combination of Verification on Rebuild and Forced Rebuild has worked. If not, then your problem may be elsewhere. You still need to fix any errors found this way.

PERFORMANCE   For speed reasons, it is normal practice to turn Verification On Rebuild off, and to use it selectively to check models with potential errors. The type of speed degradation that you can see is in the 10-percent to 60-percent range. Some of the performance degradation as relates to patterns is documented in Chapter 8.

Check

Check is a tool that checks geometry for invalid faces and other similar geometry errors. It is also often used to find open edges of surface bodies, short edges, and the minimum radius on a face or entity. I usually apply the Check tool before turning on the Verification on Rebuild option. The Check tool points to specific geometry (not features or sketches, but 3D face geometry) that is the cause of the problem. When it finds general faults, the faults are often displayed in threes, and the locations that the Check tool points to may or may not have something obvious to do with a possible fix.

Much of the time, the best tool for tracking down geometry errors is the combination of experience and intuition. It is not very scientific, but you come to recognize where potential problems are likely to arise, such as attempting to intersect complex faces at complex edges. Figure 11.16 shows the Check Entity dialog box.

FIGURE 11.16

The Check Entity dialog box

Reflective techniques

Evaluating complex shapes can be difficult. Subjective evaluation is typically personal, and requires an eye for the type of work you are doing. Objective evaluation requires some sort of measurable criteria for determining a pass or fail, or it enables you to assign a score somewhere in the middle.

One way to subjectively evaluate complex surfaces, and in particular the transitions between surfaces around common edges, is to use reflective techniques. If you look at an automobile's fender, you can tell whether it has been dented or if a dent has been badly repaired by seeing how the light reflects off of the surface. The same principle applies when evaluating solid or surface models. Bad transitions appear as a crease or an unwanted bulge or indentation. The goal is to turn off the edge display and not be able to identify where the edge is between surfaces, for the transition to be as smooth as if the whole area were made from a single surface.

Zebra Stripes

Zebra Stripes can be activated in one of two ways, through the menus at View ➪ Display ➪ Zebra Stripes, or from a toolbar button on the View toolbar. The technique that was really made for analyzing complex shapes is Zebra Stripes. This places the part in a room that is either spherical or cubic, where the walls are painted with alternating black-and-white stripes (although you can change the colors and the spacing of the stripes). The part is made to be perfectly reflective, and the way that the stripes transition over edges tells you something about the qualities of the faces on either side of the edge. Four conditions are of particular interest:

- $c0$ = faces contact at edge
- $c1$ = faces are tangent across edge

- c2 = curvature of each face is equal at the edge and the transition is smooth
- c3 = rate of change of curvature of each face is equal at the edge

The Zebra Stripes tool can only help you identify c0, c1, and c2, and only subjectively. This feature is of most value between complex faces. Figure 11.17 illustrates how the Zebra Stripes tool shows the differences between these three conditions.

FIGURE 11.17

Contact, tangency, and curvature continuity

Original faces
with Zebra Stripes

Original surfaces

Original faces
with the edge filleted
to be tangent

Original faces
with curvature continuous
blend between the faces

Notice how on the Contact-only model, the Zebra Stripe lines do not line up across the edge. On the Tangent example, the stripes line up across the edges, but the stripes themselves are not smooth. On the Curvature Continuous example, the stripes are smooth across the edges. The part shown in Figure 11.17 is a surface model, and can be found on the CD-ROM with the filename Chapter 11 Zebra Stripes.sldprt.

TIP You should rotate the model a lot when you are using the Zebra Stripes tool. Changing the density of the lines can also help, as can increasing the image quality (Tools, Options, Document Properties, Image Quality). Turning off the edge display may also help.

RealView

RealView Graphics display is only available to users with certain types of video cards. To see whether your card supports RealView, check the SolidWorks Web site.

RealView causes reflections that can be used in a way similar to the reflections in Zebra Stripes. Rotate the part slowly and watch how the reflections flow across edges.

Lights and specularity

If the other methods are not working for you, then you can also try to use simple lights with the specularity turned up. This does not work as nicely as the highly reflective Zebra Stripes and RealView techniques, but the bright spots created by the specularity settings for lights can give similar results for evaluating the quality of transitions between faces.

Curvature display

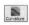
Model curvature can be plotted onto the model face using colors, as shown in Figure 11.18. The accuracy of this display leaves a bit to be desired, but it does help you to identify areas of very tight curvature on your part. Areas of tight curvature can cause features such as fillets and shells to fail.

FIGURE 11.18

Curvature display

Deviation Analysis

Deviation Analysis measures how far from tangent the surfaces on either side of a selected edge actually are. For example, the edges shown in Figure 11.19 are found to be fair, but not very good. I prefer deviations of less than 0.5 degrees. Often with some of the advanced surface types such as Fill, Loft, and Boundary, SolidWorks can achieve edges with less than 0.05-degree maximum deviation.

FIGURE 11.19

An example of Deviation Analysis

While Deviation Analysis helps to quantitatively measure how close to tangent the faces on either side of the selected edge are, you must still run Zebra Stripes to get the complete picture of the flow between faces. Both tests have to return good results to have an acceptable face transition.

Tangent Edges as Phantom

Using the Tangent Edges as Phantom setting is an easy way to evaluate a large number of edges all at once. This feature does not do what the Zebra Stripes tool does, but it gives you a good indication of the tangency across a large number of edges.

Although this is an easy method to use, it is not completely reliable. I have not seen this function deliver false positives (edges displayed as tangent when in fact they were not), but I have seen many false negatives (edges that display as non-tangent when in fact they were). Figure 11.20 shows a situation where the edges are displayed with solid edges, but Deviation Analysis shows them to have a zero-degree maximum deviation.

FIGURE 11.20

Using the Tangent Edges as Phantom setting

COSMOSXpress

COSMOSXpress is a limited version of CosmosWorks that is bundled with SolidWorks to acquaint users with finite element analysis, or FEA. The full version of CosmosWorks does a wide range of analysis, from vibrations to large deformations. COSMOSXpress is a very quick and easy wizard for simple stress analysis on standalone parts with simple constraints. It does simple linear stress analysis on a single part with a single material using only fixed constraints. You can also use COSMOSXpress to do a simple stress/weight optimization based on dimensions that you select to be altered.

You can start COSMOSXpress through the Tools menu. The interface guides you through a very simple wizard. If you have any familiarity with FEA applications, you will find COSMOSXpress easy to understand and use.

Material

The first step in running a simple analysis is to assign a material. The list of materials for COSMOSXpress is limited, compared to the full product. Once you have made your selection, click Apply. Figure 11.21 shows some of the materials selection.

FIGURE 11.21

Assigning a material in COSMOSXpress

The material assigned through the COSMOSXpress interface is applied as a SolidWorks material, complete with RealView, if applicable.

Restraint

You can apply restraints to the part. The restraints are limited to Fixed for the faces that are selected. Figure 11.22 shows the interface and the restraint symbols on the part.

FIGURE 11.22

FIGURE 11.22

Applying restraints

Load

You can apply loads to faces as force or pressure. You can also select multiple faces. Figure 11.23 shows loads that are applied on the sample part.

FIGURE 11.23

Applying a load

Analyze

The analysis automatically takes care of the mesh. An animation plays as the analysis runs. This is shown in Figure 11.24.

FIGURE 11.24

Analyzing the model

Results

The results that can be shown are the stress distribution, the displacement distribution, and the deformed shape of the model. A stress plot is shown in Figure 11.25. You can use a number of good ways to export the results, including as eDrawings, AVI, and HTML.

FIGURE 11.25

A Stress plot for the analysis

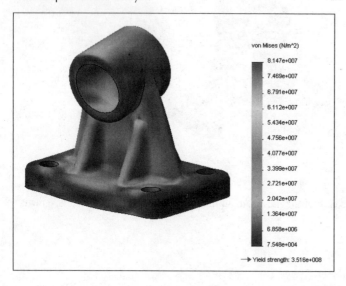

Optimization

Optimization takes a single dimension and varies it to try to achieve the best stress-to-weight ratio. As shown in Figure 11.26, the gussets have been made smaller to reduce weight and to keep the Factor Of Safety above 4.

FIGURE 11.26

Optimization results

MoldflowXpress

MoldflowXpress uses the same concept as COSMOSXpress in that a limited version of the high-end software is bundled into SolidWorks, but it applies to software that predicts moldability of plastic parts, rather than to stress analysis. Also in keeping with the other software, MoldflowXpress is very easy to use, contains a wizard to guide you, and requires no real mold expertise to run.

Although the software is easy to run, in order for you to be able to interpret the results, you have to know a little bit about what you are doing. The two Xpress products do not automatically solve all of your problems regarding FEA and Moldflow analysis. While the wizard interfaces remove most of the expert-level knowledge that is needed to navigate it, setting up the problem and interpreting the results do require some background knowledge.

Injection location

To start a MoldflowXpress analysis, you need to determine the injection location. You are only allowed a single gate, and the analysis is set up to assume that the runner is on the other side of the gate; as a result, this is a single-cavity, single-gate analysis, as shown in Figure 11.27.

FIGURE 11.27

Selecting an injection location

Material

The second step is to establish the material. Again, the Xpress product has a limited selection set, but most of the major families are represented in the selections. Material selection is shown in Figure 11.28.

FIGURE 11.28

Material selection

Conditions

The Conditions tab enables you to adjust the melt temperature and the mold temperature. Default temperatures are probably best, unless you know what you are doing.

Disabling the Automatic Injection Time option can enable you to get a short shot, which is considered a bad thing in real molding; however, in simulation, it can give you some idea of what the flow front is doing — how the liquid plastic is filling the mold, which areas fill first, last, and so on. Figure 11.29 shows this part of the wizard interface.

FIGURE 11.29

The Conditions tab

Analyze and Results

The mold-filling results take a bit longer than the FEA results. MoldflowXpress gives you a general statement about the moldability of your part (in this case, Figure 11.30 shows that it is acceptable), the fill time for the cavity, and a colored fill-time plot showing how long it takes to fill the various areas of the part.

FIGURE 11.30

The Results tab

Tutorial: Making Use of Editing and Evaluation Techniques

Using this tutorial, you make some major edits to an existing part. You use some simple loft and spline commands, and work with the rollback states and feature order, as well as some evaluation techniques. Please follow these steps:

1. Open the existing part with the filename Chapter 11 Tutorial Start.sldprt. Roll the part back and step through it feature by feature to see how it was made. Edit the loft feature to see which sketches were used to create it. This can help you to understand how the part was built. Exit the loft command and move the rollback bar back to the bottom of the tree.

2. Start the Deviation Analysis tool (Tools ⇨ Deviation Analysis). Select the edges, as shown in Figure 11.31.

FIGURE 11.31

Deviation analysis of an existing part

Select

RMB then select tangency

The maximum deviation is about ten degrees, which is far too much. This part needs to be smoothed out, which you can do using splines in place of lines and arcs.

3. The first step is to make the outlet all one piece with the spiral. You can do this with a Fit Spline. You need to create the Fit Spline before the loft profiles and after the spiral.

    Expand the loft, and rollback between the loft feature and the first sketch. Answer OK to the prompt, and then rollback to just after the spiral, as shown in Figure 11.32.

FIGURE 11.32

Rolling back to just after the spiral

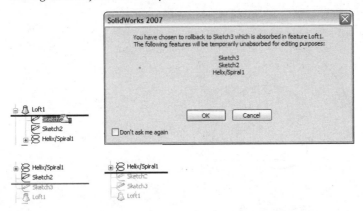

4. RMB click the spiral in the FeatureManager and show it. Open a new sketch on the Top plane.

5. Try to draw a horizontal line from the outer end of the spiral. You will notice that you cannot reference the end of the spiral.

> **TIP** Curves that are absorbed into other features are notoriously difficult to work with. Generally, you need to select them from the FeatureManager to do anything at all with them. Also, if you need to reference an end of an absorbed curve, you are better off using Convert Entities to make it into a sketch entity.

6. Notice that you cannot select the spiral from the graphics window. Even when selected from the FeatureManager, it appears not to be selected in the graphics window. Ensure that it is selected in the FeatureManager, and then click the Convert Entities button on the sketch toolbar.

7. Draw a horizontal line from the outer end of the spiral and dimension it to be three inches long, as shown in Figure 11.33.

8. Select both the converted spiral and the line, and click Tools ⇨ Spline Tools ⇨ Fit Spline. Set the Tolerance to .1 and make sure that only the Constrained option is selected. Click OK to accept the Fit Spline. Test to make sure that a single spline is created by moving your cursor over the sketch to see if the whole length is highlighted.

> **NOTE** The Fit Spline feature fits a spline to a set of sketch entities within the specified tolerance. It can be a useful tool for smoothing out sketch geometry.

> **CAUTION** Do not exit the Fit Spline by pressing the Enter key as you do with other commands, because it simply exits you out of the command without creating a spline.

FIGURE 11.33

Preparing for the Fit Spline

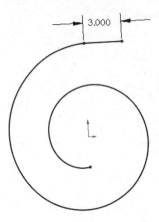

9. Exit the sketch, and create a new plane. Click Insert ⇨ Reference Geometry ⇨ plane.
    Select the Parallel Plane At Point option. Select the Right plane from the Flyout
    FeatureManager and the outer end of the Fit Spline that you have just created. Click OK
    to accept the new plane. This is illustrated in Figure 11.34.

FIGURE 11.34

Creating a new plane

10. Drag the Rollback bar down between Sketch3 and Loft1. If it goes beyond Loft1, then you need to navigate back to this position again.

11. RMB click Sketch3 and select Edit Sketch Plane. Select the newly created Plane1 from the Flyout FeatureManager, and click OK to accept the change.

12. Notice that the loft profile has moved to a place where it does not belong. This is because the sketch has a Pierce constraint to the spiral, and there are multiple places where the spiral pierces the sketch plane.

Edit Sketch3 and delete the Pierce constraint on the sketch point in the middle of the construction line. Create a Coincident relation between the sketch point and the outer end of the Fit Spline, as shown in Figure 11.35. Do not exit the sketch.

FIGURE 11.35

Sketch3 in its new location

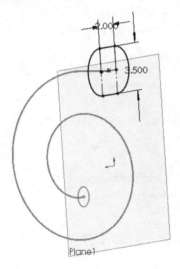

13. One of the goals of these edits is to smooth out the part. Remember that the Deviation Analysis told us that the edges created between the lines and arcs in Sketch3 were not very tangent. For this reason, it would be a good idea to replace the lines and arcs in Sketch3 with another Fit Spline.

RMB click one of the solid sketch entities in Sketch3, and click Select Chain.

14. Create another Fit Spline using the same technique as in Step 8. Exit the sketch.

15. Drag the Rollback bar down one feature so that it is below the Loft. Notice that the Loft feature has failed. If you hold the cursor over the feature icon, the tooltip confirms this by displaying the message, "The Loft Feature Failed to Complete."

16. Edit the Loft feature. Expand the Centerline Parameters panel if it is not already expanded, and delete the Spiral from the selection box. In its place, select the Spiral Fit Spline.

17. If the loft does not preview, check to ensure that the Show Preview option is selected in the Options panel, at the bottom.

18. If it still does not preview, RMB click in the graphics window and select Show All Connectors. Position the blue dots on the connector so that it looks like Figure 11.36.

FIGURE 11.36

Positioning the connectors

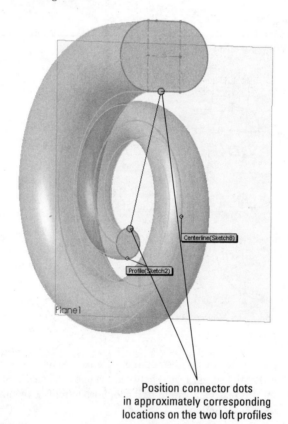

Position connector dots
in approximately corresponding
locations on the two loft profiles

19. Click OK to accept the loft. The loft should be much smoother now than it was before. In addition, the spiral feature should no longer be under the loft, and should now be the first item in the design tree.

20. Drag the Rollback bar down to just before the Shell feature. Notice that Fillet5 has failed. Move the mouse over Fillet5. The tooltip tells you that it is missing some references. Edit Fillet5 and select edges in order to create fillets, as shown in Figure 11.37.

FIGURE 11.37

Repairing Fillet5

Make selections to fillet edges

---

21. RMB click in the design tree and select Roll To End. This causes the FeatureManager to become unrolled all the way to the end.

22. The outlet of the involute is now longer than it should be. This is because the original extrude was never deleted from the end. RMB click the Extrude1 feature and select Parent/Child. The feature needs to be deleted, but you need to know what is going to be deleted with it.

23. The Shell is listed as a child of the extrude because the end face of the extrude was chosen to be removed by the Shell. Edit the Shell feature and remove the reference to the face. (A Shell feature with no faces to remove is still hollowed out.)

24. If you RMB click Extrude1 and select Parent/Child again, the Shell feature is no longer listed as a child.

25. Delete Extrude1, and when the dialog box appears, press Alt+F to select Also Delete Absorbed Features.

26. Edit the Shell feature and select the large end of the loft. Exit the Shell feature. The results up to this step are shown in Figure 11.38.

FIGURE 11.38

The results up to step 26

27. Drag a window in the design tree to select the four fillet features. Then RMB click and select Add to New Folder. Rename the new folder Fillet Folder.

28. Click the Section View tool, and create a section view using the Front plane.

29. Reorder the Fillet folder to after the Shell feature.

30. At this point, you should notice that something does not look right. This is because creating the fillets after the Shell causes the outside fillets to break through some of the inside corners. The fillets should have failed, but have not, as shown in Figure 11.39.

FIGURE 11.39

Fillets that should have failed

31. Go to Tools ⇨ Options ⇨ Performance, and turn on Verification on Rebuild. Then click OK to exit the Tools, Options, and press Ctrl+Q. The fillets should now fail.

32. Click Undo to return the feature order to the way it was.

33. Save the part.

Summary

Working effectively with feature history, even in complex models, is a requirement for working with parts that others have created. When I get a part from someone else, the first thing that I usually do is to look at the FeatureManager, and roll it back if possible to get an idea of how the part was modeled. Looking at sketches, relations, feature order, symmetry, redundancy, and so on are important steps in being able to repair or edit any part. Using modeling best practice helps to ensure that when edits have to be done, they are easy to accomplish, even if they are done by someone who did not build the part.

Evaluation techniques are really the heart of editing, as you should not make too many changes without a basic evaluation of the strengths and weaknesses of the current model.

Part III

Working with Assemblies

Chapter 12

Organizing Assemblies

C hapter 5 offered a brief introduction to the basics of assemblies, how to put parts together, the basics of mating, and so on. The basic process for putting assemblies together remains the same for assemblies of any size, but once the assembly passes a certain point — and this point is likely different for each user or application — the assembly will benefit from some sort of organization or management techniques. This chapter introduces you to the tools and techniques that are available to help you manage performance issues as well as general browse-worthiness or searchability.

Identifying the Elements of an Assembly

From Chapter 5, you know that an assembly has parts and mates. However, the simple tutorial in Chapter 5 did not go beyond this. While this tutorial got you started, it did not provide enough information to make you competent with assemblies. Real-world assemblies can become very complex. As the assembly grows in the number of parts and design requirements, you may need to add some of the following types of assembly elements (you may already be familiar with some of these parts from having worked with part documents):

- Assembly equations
- Assembly layout sketch
- Assembly reference geometry (plane, axis, point, coordinate system)
- Parts

- Subassemblies
- Folders for parts
- Folders for mates
- Mates
- Assembly features (cuts that are made once the parts are assembled)
- Component patterns
- In-context reference placeholders
- Smart Fasteners
- Smart Components
- Hole Series

These elements are shown in Figure 12.1.

FIGURE 12.1

Elements of an assembly

Standard reference geometry items

The three standard planes and the Origin are all familiar to you in the assembly FeatureManager design tree, as are the other standard items, such as the Annotations, Design Binder, and Lights and Cameras folders. These items offer the same standard functionality of their part document counterparts.

Assembly equations

Assembly equations work mainly like part equations, but with some additional complications and considerations. For example, one of the additional features of assembly equations is the ability to drive the dimensions of one part from another part. The syntax is slightly different for this application, as shown in Figure 12.2. Overall, issues with equation order and using driven dimensions on the right side of the equation are the same between parts and assemblies.

 Equations are discussed in detail in Chapter 9.

FIGURE 12.2

An assembly equation driving one part from another

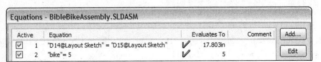

External references

Notice the "->" symbol after the Equations folder in the Assembly FeatureManager. This means that there is an external or in-context reference.

 In-context references are discussed in depth in Chapter 16.

When one part drives another part in this way, the assembly must also be open to drive the relationship. If just the two parts are open individually, then changing the driving part does not update the driven part; because the relationship was created in the context of the assembly, the assembly must also be open to facilitate the change.

Link values and global variables

Link values and global variables also work in assemblies, but they do not work between parts. Local assembly sketches can use these functions, and the parts can use them when edited in the context of the assembly, but they cannot cross any document barriers (links must remain within a single document).

Renaming

In past versions of SolidWorks, assembly equations had a hard time keeping track of parts when they were renamed, but in SolidWorks 2007, equations update regardless of how the part is renamed. This is also true of renaming the assembly. This includes renaming a part using the Save As command, using SolidWorks Explorer, or using Windows Explorer. It also includes redirecting the assembly to the new part name, as well as renaming the assembly using each of these techniques. If the assembly can find the part and recognizes the part as the one that it is looking for, then the equation will work.

The methods named above for renaming parts are not recommended; for testing purposes I was specifically trying to break the relationships in the equations.

Recommendations

While assembly equations are certainly a valid way to control part sizes, I would recommend using assembly or part configurations, possibly with design tables, to accomplish something similar.

CROSS-REF Assembly configurations are discussed in Chapter 14. Design tables are discussed in Chapter 10.

CAUTION You may have unexpected results if a single dimension is controlled from more than one location. For example, if you have a part-level equation and an assembly-level equation, then one of the equations will be automatically set to Read Only and will not be used.

Assembly layout sketch

The layout sketch is a very useful tool for constructing complex assemblies or for laying out a mechanism in an assembly. Sketches in the assembly have the same characteristics as they do in the part environment. In Figure 12.3, the assembly layout sketch is indicated with a heavy, dashed line for emphasis.

FIGURE 12.3

An assembly layout sketch

When combined with in-context techniques, assembly layout sketches can help to determine the shape of parts. You can also use layout sketches to mate assembly components to far more robust and dependable mates, rather than mating part to part. The sketch shown in Figure 12.3 is used for both of these techniques. The shape of the frame and the major pivot points are established in the 2D sketch. The wheels are also mated to the sketch.

When you use an assembly layout sketch for either the in-context part building or simply part positioning, the main advantage that it offers is having a single driving sketch that enables you to change the size, shape, and position of the parts. You can use as many layout sketches as you want, and you can make them on different sketch planes. This enables you to control parts in all directions.

Assembly reference geometry

Planes and axes are frequently created within assemblies to drive symmetry or placement of parts. You can use assembly layout sketches to create the reference geometry entities. When you create reference geometry within the assembly in this way, be aware that the normal history-based parent/child relationships are still followed. The familiar icons for reference geometry entities are also used in the assembly tree.

History-based and non-history-based portions of the assembly tree

Because features such as sketches and reference geometry are history-based and found in the assembly tree, at least a portion of the assembly FeatureManager is history-based. However, not all of it is. For example, the list of parts and subassemblies is not history-based.

Sketches and reference geometry may appear before or after the list of parts, subassemblies, and mates. All of the remaining entity types that can be found in the assembly FeatureManager are also history-based features, and you can reorder them in the tree. However, several situations can disrupt the process. Under normal circumstances, sketches and reference geometry at the top of the assembly FeatureManager are solved, then the parts are rebuilt if required, and then the mates are solved. This ensures that the sketches and reference geometry are in the correct locations so that if parts are mated to them, then all of the components end up being the correct size and in the right position.

Assembly-level reference geometry can be created that references component geometry instead of layout sketches. This creates a dependency that changes the usual order. For example, the planes are usually solved before the part locations, but when the plane is *dependent* on the part location, the plane has to be solved *after* the part. If a part is then mated to the plane, you are beginning to create a dependency loop, such that the plane is solved, followed by the part, then the plane again because the part has moved, and then the mate that goes to the plane has to resolve the part.

BEST PRACTICE If you are a bit confused by all of this, don't worry. You can simply follow this rule: Do not mate to anything that comes after the mates in the assembly FeatureManager tree. This includes assembly planes or sketches that are dependent on part geometry, assembly features such as cuts, in-context features, component pattern instances, Series Holes, or SmartFasteners.

This is probably a lot of information for a new user, but if you remember this rule, then you can avoid creating models with circular references, where A is dependent on B, which is dependent on A — a never-ending loop that causes major problems for large assembly rebuild times.

Parts and subassemblies

Parts and subassemblies are shown with their familiar icons in the design tree. You can reorder and group them in folders, which is covered in the next section.

Folders

`⊞ 🗀 Folder` You can create folders to organize and group both parts and mates. I discuss this technique in detail later in this chapter.

Mates

`⊞ 🗊🗊 Mates` The Mates area remains a constant, single folder, but you can organize it by reordering the mates and grouping them into folders.

Assembly features

In manufacturing, once parts are assembled, secondary machining operations are sometimes applied to them to ensure that holes line up properly, or for other purposes. For example, assembly features can be cut extrudes, cut revolves, or hole features. These features appear only in the assembly, not in the individual parts.

You should not confuse assembly features with in-context features. In-context features are created in the assembly with a reference between parts, but the sketch and feature definition are in the part itself.

Component patterns

`⊞ 🔢 ComponentPattern` Component patterns can pattern either parts or assemblies by creating either a pattern defined in the assembly, or a pattern that follows a pattern feature created in a part. The pattern is listed as a feature in the assembly FeatureManager, and all of the instance parts appear indented from the pattern feature in the design tree. You can hide or suppress each instance, change its configuration, and in most ways control it as if it were a regular part in the design tree.

Because the options for locally defined patterns are comparatively limited, users generally like to use part feature patterns to drive the component patterns when possible.

PERFORMANCE To improve performance, it is best to pattern subassemblies if possible. If it is not possible, then patterning a group of parts is the next best option. Making multiple patterns, one for each part, is an inefficient way to accomplish the same thing.

In-context reference update holders

It is difficult to get a good picture of assemblies in general without including a discussion about in-context references, but to treat the subject properly, it also requires its own section. When you create a reference between parts in an assembly, the assembly needs to remember which parts are involved in the reference. The parts also need to remember which assembly was used to create the relation because the parts are positioned in the assembly, and the reference has meaning only with regard to a particular relative position between the parts.

When you create the relation, a placeholder has to be left behind in the assembly to hold this information. This placeholder is called an Update Holder. The Update Holders do not display by default. To see them, you must RMB click the top level in the FeatureManager and select Show Update Holders. They only exist when in-context references exist in the assembly, and there is one Update Holder for each in-context reference. You cannot do very much with the Update Holders, other than query them for parent/child relations and to list the external relations, but they serve as a reminder that you have in-context references to maintain. Several years ago, they were displayed by default, but they were later hidden by default, presumably because users were confused by the presence of something that you could not do anything with. In-context modeling methods are often scorned by some users, and if you have a list of 50 or 60 Update Holders, then you may be perceived as an overzealous novice. For more information on this feature, see Chapter 16.

Smart Fasteners

 Smart Fasteners are assembly features that automatically select Toolbox parts for use in standard-sized holes, and you can use them in many different ways. The Smart Fastener feature in the assembly FeatureManager is used to edit the definition of the Smart Fastener, which can include adding items such as nuts and washers. You can also use Smart Fasteners in conjunction with the Hole Wizard to place appropriate holes and matched fasteners, all in a single step.

CROSS-REF   Smart Fasteners, Toolbox, and the Hole Wizard are discussed in detail in Chapter 17.

Hole Series

 The Hole Series is a Hole Wizard–type feature that you apply in an assembly. This wizard leaves the feature icon in the assembly, but also adds features directly to the individual parts. It also adds in-context Update Holders to the assembly FeatureManager, as shown in Figure 12.4. The Series Hole is designed to go through a series of parts, placing the appropriate hole type in each part, counterbore, through, threaded, and so on.

FIGURE 12.4

Adding in-context Update Holders

Using Subassemblies

The first tool for organizing assemblies is the subassembly. A subassembly is just a regular assembly that is used as a component in another assembly.

BEST PRACTICE The number of levels of subassemblies is not limited to a specific number, although for different sizes and types of assemblies, I encourage you to establish a best practice for your company. For example, establish a guideline that suggests that subassemblies of 100 parts or less go no deeper than three levels.

You can use several criteria to determine how subassemblies are assigned:

- Performance
- Bill of Material

- Relative motion
- Pre-fabricated, off-the-shelf considerations
- According to assembly steps for a process drawing
- To simplify patterning

The underlying question here is based on the multiple functions of your SolidWorks assembly model. Is it primarily a design tool? A visualization tool? A documentation tool? A process tool? As a design tool, the assembly is used to determine fits, tolerances, mechanisms, complex shapes that span parts, and many other things. As a visualization tool, it simply has to look good and possibly move properly if that is part of the design. As a documentation tool, it is important how the model relates to the Bill of Materials, and the order in which subassemblies are added. As a process tool, you need to be able to show the assembly in various intermediate states of being assembled.

I have seen companies create multiple assembly models for different purposes. Sometimes the requirements between the different methods are contradictory and cannot all be met at the same time with a single set of data. Again, depending on what information you need to be able to extract from your SolidWorks models, you may want to approach assembly modeling and organization differently.

Creating subassemblies from existing parts

You can create subassemblies from parts that already exist in an assembly. To do this, select the parts that you want to add to the subassembly, and then select Form New Subassembly Here from the RMB menu. You are then prompted to assign a name to the new subassembly.

CAUTION When creating a new subassembly from existing parts or when moving parts into or out of a subassembly from the upper-level assembly, some things may be lost. For example, mates are moved from the upper level to the subassembly. If you have in-context relationships, they may be removed. Operations that create subassemblies cannot be undone easily.

Once you have created the subassembly, you can add or remove components using the drag-and-drop method. For example, Figure 12.5 shows the cursor that indicates that the part named Left Crank is being moved into the subassembly named bike crank. To move a part out of a subassembly, simply drag the part into the upper-level assembly.

FIGURE 12.5

Moving parts into a subassembly

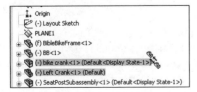

NOTE   When you are dragging a part out of an assembly and into another one, you may again see the cursor symbol that appears in Figure 12.5. If you do not want this to happen, then hold down the Alt key while dragging. The cursor symbol changes to the Reorder cursor (a reversed, L-shaped arrow), and the part is placed after the subassembly rather than within it.

Insert a new subassembly

Along with the RMB menu option Form New Subassembly Here, which takes existing parts and puts them into a newly created subassembly, you can use another option called Insert New Subassembly. The names of these functions do not adequately describe the difference in what they do. Insert New Subassembly inserts a blank subassembly at the point in the design tree that you indicate by right-clicking it. You can place components into the subassembly by dragging and dropping them from the main assembly, or you can open the assembly in its own window, and insert parts by using the usual methods.

Dissolving subassemblies

If you would like to get rid of a subassembly but want to keep its parts, then you can use the Dissolve Subassembly option through the RMB menu. This option has some of the same consequences of the Form New Subassembly Here option in that mates are moved from the subassembly to the upper-level assembly, and you may lose in-context relations and assembly features.

Organizing for performance

Performance in SolidWorks is a euphemism for speed. Subassemblies can contribute to speed-saving modeling techniques by segmenting the work that the software needs to do at any one time.

Solving mates

The mates that contribute to putting the pieces of an assembly together are solved at the level of the top assembly. Under normal circumstances, subassemblies are treated as static selections of parts that are welded together, and their mates are not solved at the same time that the top-level assemblies' mates are solved. This segmenting of the mates leads to improved performance by only solving one set of mates at a time.

Mates are usually solved as a single group unless there is a special situation, such as mates to in-context features, component pattern instances, or an assembly feature, all of which have already been described in this chapter. When one of these situations occurs, the mates have to be divided into separate groups or solved multiple times. This is done transparently behind the scenes so that the user does not have to worry about it.

Flexible subassemblies

When you create subassemblies, the mates for these parts are not solved in the upper-level assembly. This means that if a subassembly is a mechanism, the mechanism does not allow Dynamic Assembly Motion in the upper-level assembly. For example, in Figure 12.6, the front fork is a linkage mechanism, but it is also a subassembly. Without reassembling the parts of the fork in the upper-level assembly, you can allow the mates from the fork subassembly to be solved in the upper-level assembly by using an option in the Component Properties dialog box, which is also shown in Figure 12.6. When you select the Flexible option in the Solve as section, you enable the mates of this subassembly to be solved in the upper-level assembly.

FIGURE 12.6

Creating a flexible subassembly

Solve as flexible or rigid

To access the Component Properties dialog box, RMB click the subassembly and select Component Properties from the menu.

Legacy data

If you have assemblies that were built in older versions of SolidWorks (such as SolidWorks 2001+), mates used to be split up into multiple *mate groups*, which represented the groupings that mates were solved in, which was forced by mating to the history-based features in the assembly FeatureManager. SolidWorks no longer displays mate groups, but the groups are still used in the background to solve mates.

Organizing for the BOM

The Bill of Materials, or BOM, is a table that is placed into a drawing of an assembly. This table shows the parts used in the assembly and includes other information, such as part numbers, descriptions, and custom property data.

CROSS-REF   SolidWorks BOM functionality is discussed in depth in Chapter 24.

Businesses often represent assemblies and subassemblies in various ways by using MRP or ERP software (Manufacturing Resource Planning or Engineering Resource Planning). The methods that accountants and manufacturers use to organize assemblies are not always the same as those that an engineer or designer might choose, but some companies require the BOM on the drawing to match the MRP or ERP Bill of Materials.

BEST PRACTICE When forced into modeling something in an unnatural way to satisfy an outside requirement such as special BOM requirements, it might be best to detach the unnatural part
and model normally. In the situation mentioned here — where MRP is forcing how the assembly is put
together by requiring the BOM to match MRP — I recommend separating the BOM from the assembly
structure. This ensures that the BOM becomes a manually maintained document, rather than building
an assembly that makes other SolidWorks functions difficult. Alternatives to this approach would be
to make configurations or entirely new assembly documents to drive the BOM.

Grouping subassemblies by relative motion

A more natural way to group subassemblies is by considering relative motion. In the bicycle example, each wheel is a separate subassembly because it moves as a unit relative to the rest of the
assembly. Figure 12.7 illustrates where relative motion might be on the bicycle.

FIGURE 12.7

Grouping subassemblies by relative motion

Rear wheel   Drive train   Front wheel

Rear suspension swingarm   Front suspension linkage

Grouping subassemblies by relative motion is great for assembly modeling, but it does not usually reflect product reality very well. Using this method, you often end up with parts in the subassembly that would have to be disassembled in order to actually put the physical parts together. However, if your only consideration is ease of modeling, then this is probably the method to use.

Organizing groups of purchased components

If you are modeling a product that is created from a shopping list of purchased components, then it may make the most sense to organize your subassemblies into groups of parts that are purchased together. In fact, purchased subassemblies are often modeled as single parts, except when relative motion is required in the purchased assembly.

For example, in the bicycle assembly, the sprockets on the rear wheel are purchased as a separate unit, and yet the part that mounts onto the wheel moves relative to the sprockets that are driven by the chain. This is an example of a purchased part that would be modeled as a subassembly to show relative motion. The bicycle chain, another purchased subassembly, has not yet been added to this assembly, and is a more complex model. The desire to show all of the individual links moving through the path may override both the complexity of assembling it and the performance considerations of exercising all of the mates.

Although the BOM method of organizing assemblies sometimes leads to unnatural solutions, you should not discard it altogether. If you can devise concessions in order to make the BOM work automatically, then you should do this.

Depicting an assembly process

Manufacturing and assembly processes need to be documented as well as individual part design. You often need to create exploded-view assembly instructions for manufacturing or service documentation at each step of a multi-step assembly process. Figure 12.8 shows a page of this type of process documentation.

This is certainly a task that is different from the initial design or modeling of the assembly, and it may require an entirely separate model. Generally, you can perform the different steps by using a separate configuration for each process step, with exploded views for each configuration.

Item numbering

Balloons number the parts according to the item number that is used in the BOM, but of course you do not know the item numbers until the BOM is created. You can influence the item numbers by reordering the parts in the assembly (which is discussed later in this chapter), by manually editing item numbers, or by manually numbering the balloons. All of this is discussed in detail in Chapter 24.

Individual steps

Each step corresponds to an assembly configuration (discussed in Chapter 14), and you can place them on a separate sheet of the drawing (discussed in Chapter 21). Each configuration can have multiple exploded views, if necessary, to show all of the steps.

FIGURE 12.8

Assembly process documentation

1. Apply grease to the linkage pivot points on the fork (21)
2. Assemble the linkages (19, 20) to the fork as shown
3. Secure with 1/4-20 Loctite treated screws
4. Test to make sure motion is free and smooth

Bible Bike Assembly

Patterning considerations

The most efficient way to pattern large numbers of components in an assembly is to pattern a single subassembly with all of the components to be patterned in it. While this may not be easily combined with some of the other considerations that were mentioned previously, it is another option that you can use to organize assemblies.

Using Folders

Folders are primarily used in the assembly FeatureManager for grouping parts and mates into either special classifications for easy browsing, or groups that can be easily hidden and shown, or suppressed and unsuppressed, as appropriate. Figure 12.9 shows some examples of these folders.

Creating folders in the FeatureManager

You can add folders to the assembly FeatureManager in one of two ways:

- Add to a new folder
- Create a new folder

FIGURE 12.9

Folders that are used to organize components and mates

Add To New Folder

To use the Add To New Folder tool, RMB click a component or mate (or selection of components or mates) and select Add To New Folder from the menu. This moves the component or mate into the folder. Folders do not affect the assembly in any functional way; they are simply for organization, to speed browsing and selection.

Create New Folder

To simply create a new folder without putting anything into it right away, RMB click either the Mates area or the components list, and select Create New Folder from the menu.

Adding items to existing folders

To move an item into an existing folder, just drag the item (component or mate) onto the folder. If the folder is expanded, showing its contents, then you can also drag the item as if you were reordering a feature in the FeatureManager of a part, and drop it in the list of items where you would like it.

If you are dragging a part or assembly and trying to put it immediately after an assembly, then a cursor may appear, like the one shown in the center in Figure 12.10. This cursor means that the part is going to become part of the assembly. If this is not what you are trying to do, then hold down the Alt key while dragging; the part is placed into the folder immediately after the assembly, instead of being made a part of the assembly. The third image in Figure 12.10 shows the cursor with the Alt key pressed.

FIGURE 12.10

Moving items into folders

Reordering items in the tree

There are times when you may want to reorder items in the assembly tree. For example, you may want to place items close to one another in the tree, or you may be preparing to put items that are next to one another into a single folder.

You can reorder mates simply by dragging them. Mates display in the order in which they are created, but the order is not significant. They can be reordered however you like.

Components also display in the order in which they are added to the assembly, and you can reorder them in any way you like.

BEST PRACTICE It is often useful to have an ordering strategy that helps you to work with the model. I usually try to keep the biggest parts, or the parts that everything else is mated to, or the part that is treated as "ground," as the first part in the assembly. The fasteners and other cosmetic or BOM-driving parts are put at the end of the tree, usually in a descriptive folder.

Working with Tree Display Options

Display options for items in the FeatureManager are often overlooked, but can be useful for displaying data about parts, subassemblies, mates, and features. Figure 12.11 shows the RMB menu options.

NOTE All of these options are available for parts and drawings as well, except for the View Features option and the View Mates and Dependencies option, which are related to assemblies.

FIGURE 12.11

Tree display options in assemblies

Show feature names and descriptions

If you are so thorough that you have added descriptions to your features, then you are doing well. This option refers to the descriptions of features in the parts. The middle image in Figure 12.11 shows a section of the FeatureManager for the bicycle frame part; some of the features have had descriptions added with both of the options for feature names and feature descriptions turned on. The image to the right in Figure 12.11 shows the result of turning off the feature name, with only the feature description option turned on. If no feature description has been created, then the feature name displays. Feature descriptions always appear in double quotes.

Show component and config names and descriptions

The image to the left in Figure 12.12 shows the default arrangement of displaying component and configuration names in the assembly FeatureManager. This example uses the rear wheel assembly from the bicycle assembly. In assemblies, you cannot turn off the component names and the component descriptions. SolidWorks issues a statement when you try to turn off both the name and the description, saying, "You cannot hide both the component name and the file name. At least one must be visible in the tree."

Using names other than the part filename in the assembly FeatureManager

The message in the previous paragraph distinguishes between the *filename* and the *component name* that is listed for individual parts or subassemblies in the assembly FeatureManager. You can specify the component name in the Component Properties dialog box by RMB clicking the component in the assembly FeatureManager and selecting Component Properties.

FIGURE 12.12

Component name options

However, you can assign a component name for a component that is different from the filename only if a special setting is turned off (the setting defaults to on). You can access this setting through Tools ➪ Options ➪ External References ➪ Update Component Names When Documents Are Replaced. What the name of the setting has to do with showing a component name in the FeatureManager is not exactly clear, but these are the steps that you have to go through if you want to change how the part and subassembly names display in the assembly FeatureManager.

After going through the preceding steps, you still receive the warning message about the filename and the component name. This is apparently an "unintended feature," or bug, and should likely say that you cannot turn off both the component name and the component description at the same time.

There may be a situation where you want to show a name other than the filename in the FeatureManager. For example, your company may be using sequential part numbers for the filenames, which are difficult to read, and you want something descriptive in the design tree so that you do not need a cross-reference sheet next to your computer that equates filenames to meaningful descriptions.

If you prefer, you can avoid a lot of problems by just using the part description instead of the filename or the component name. The choice is up to you.

BEST PRACTICE Because the component name options are convoluted, obscure, and will need to be set on each computer where you would like to use them, I do not recommend them. It is simpler and more reliable to use either the default component name (which is the same as the filename) or the component description.

One of the problems with using the component description is shown in Figure 12.13, where the user did not enter proper descriptions for the parts, and SolidWorks used the default description in the templates. The tire and spokes use configurations, which display in the figure.

FIGURE 12.13

An example of what can occur when you do not enter proper descriptions for parts

Viewing features, mates, and dependencies

The last set of options, shown in Figure 12.11, defines what displays under the name of each component. The default setting is for the part's features or the subassembly's components to display, just as if the part or subassembly were open in its own window.

The View Mates and Dependencies option can also show the features, but they are placed into a separate folder. This option makes it very easy to see the mates that are assigned to an individual component. For example, in Figure 12.14, the image to the right shows the mates directly under the BibleBikeFrame part. This often makes troubleshooting much easier because it isolates the mates for a single part. Notice also that the first folder under the part name in the image to the left in Figure 12.14 is the Mates folder. This indicates that, regardless of whether you choose to display mates or features, you always have easy access to the other type.

Another technique for displaying mates is to split the FeatureManager and to show the PropertyManager in one pane. As a result, any parts that are selected show their mates in the PropertyManager pane. If two selected parts have mates in common, then the common mates appear in bold type, as shown in Figure 12.15. This is an extremely useful method for looking at mates.

CAUTION This function does not appear to work in SolidWorks 2007 sp1.0, although it does work properly in sp0.0. Service Pack 1.0 was the latest available service pack at the time that this chapter was written. SolidWorks knows about the bug and has labeled it a "regression," which means that it will receive priority in subsequent fixes. The fix may be available in sp2.0.

FIGURE 12.14

You can view features, as well as mates and dependencies.

FIGURE 12.15

Showing mates in the PropertyManager pane

Tutorial: Managing the FeatureManager

This tutorial uses the BibleBikeAssembly.sldasm file found on the CD-ROM for Chapter 12. Follow these steps to learn about managing the FeatureManager:

1. Create a new subassembly within the existing assembly using the parts BibleBikeFrame and ChainstayBibleBike. Name this new assembly **FrameAssembly.SLDASM**.

2. Reorder the new FrameAssembly to the top of the design tree.

3. Reorder the other parts and assemblies so that the bigger assemblies appear higher on the list, and the parts appear at the bottom. (Remember that the Alt-drag option to prevent a component from being placed into a subassembly.)

4. Drag the part called BB (for Bottom Bracket) into the FrameAssembly (drag without using the Alt key). The assembly FeatureManager at this point is shown in Figure 12.16.

FIGURE 12.16

The starting state, and the state as of step 4

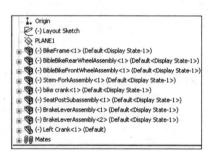

5. Select both wheels and then click Add To New Folder from the RMB menu. Name the new folder **Wheels**, and move it to the bottom of the tree.

6. Expand the Mates folder, select the first four mates, and put them in a new folder (select Add To New Folder from the RMB menu). Name the new folder **Centering Mates**.

Summary

Assemblies are more than simply parts and subassemblies put together with mate relationships; several other types of features and placeholders can also exist in the assembly FeatureManager. Organizing assembly components is fairly straightforward, and can offer benefits for finding parts as well as controlling suppression and display states globally.

The assembly FeatureManager contains several options for the data to display for subassemblies, parts, configurations, and features within. Remember that all of this data that you include in your SolidWorks documents can be accessed and reused later on, and so it is worth the effort. Descriptions can be very important, both at the part level, and also for features and configs.

Chapter 13

Getting More from Mates

In SolidWorks assemblies, mates are the basic units that either make everything work together and function properly, or fill the tree with errors and warning symbols. When properly handled, mates enable your assembly to react predictably to changes in parts in exactly the same way that sketch relations drive changes in part features. As a result, mates and sketch relations often have the same function and even the same weaknesses to watch out for.

This chapter goes one step further with mates, by not just simply putting parts together with Coincident and Concentric mates, but also mating when tolerances, gaps, and symmetry become issues. You will also learn about the more advanced mate types that may be useful for special situations.

One of the assumptions that I make in this chapter is that assembly mates are not just used for positioning parts, but also for motion. Making motion work takes a little more than just establishing the right spatial relationship between parts; it usually also involves analyzing the open degrees of freedom.

From time to time, I have met users who take the "AutoCAD" approach to putting parts together into assemblies, by simply placing parts at the correct X- and Y- coordinates without assigning any relationships to the parts around them. This defeats most of the purpose of creating parametric, associative assemblies in the first place. Assembly mates are an extremely powerful tool for enabling your assemblies to react predictably to change.

Applying Mates

An average assembly of 100 parts would likely have almost 300 individual mates. If you create these parts one at a time, taking perhaps a minute for each mate, then you would spend five hours just applying mates. Any time that you can save applying mates is a benefit to you — assuming you still get the correct results — because it is time that you can spend doing something else. In this section, you will learn efficient mating strategies, as well as speedy techniques.

Mating through the Mate PropertyManager

The Mate PropertyManager is the default method for applying mates, and was used briefly in Chapter 5. The Mate PropertyManager interface is shown in Figure 13.1. You can create mates by pre-selecting entities before applying the Mate command or selecting them after you open the Mate PropertyManager.

FIGURE 13.1

The Mate PropertyManager interface

Mate workflow

If you make a lot of mates, it is important to have an efficient rhythm when working with the interface. The most efficient way to use the Mate interface is as follows:

1. Click the first entity.

2. Click the second entity.

3. Click OK on the RMB cursor icon, which is shown in Figure 13.2.

FIGURE 13.2

The OK option on the RMB cursor

Or, if the automatic default mate type is not the mate that you want to apply, then select it
from the popup list, which is shown in Figure 13.3.

FIGURE 13.3

The Mate selection popup list

4. Click the green check mark icon from the popup list.

5. Repeat steps 1 to 4.

6. After the last mate, press Esc, the green check mark icon, or the red X icon from either the
   PropertyManager or the confirmation corner in the upper-right corner of the graphics area.

CAUTION In SolidWorks 2007 sp0, there is a bug with the distance mate that has been fixed in
sp1.0. In sp1.0, the distance mate defaults to the actual distance between the entities,
but in sp0, it defaults to 1.000 inch, and so you must manually type in a distance.

View and model positioning

Sometimes you will have to rotate the model to achieve the correct view in order to select faces or
edges. There are also times when you will want to *pre-position* so that the model snaps into the correct position automatically. You can rotate individual parts in an assembly by dragging with the
RMB. You rotate the view by dragging with the middle-mouse button, or MMB. You can move
parts by dragging them with the left-mouse button, or LMB. You can pan the view by pressing Ctrl
and dragging with the MMB. When you drag a part with the LMB while the Mate PropertyManager
is active, SolidWorks does not add the selected entity to the Mate Selections list.

To summarize these actions:

- To rotate an individual component in an assembly, drag with the RMB.
- To move an individual component in an assembly, drag with the LMB.
- To rotate an assembly view, drag with the MMB.
- To pan an assembly view, Ctrl-drag with the MMB.

TIP If you have a *Spaceball* or 3D motion controller, you can perform all of these actions more easily and simultaneously using one hand for view rotations and the other hand for selections. You can also use a Spaceball to move parts.

Select Other

The Select Other command enables you to select items that are hidden by other items. It is often used to select faces that are hidden behind other faces without rotating the part. You can apply the Select Other command through the RMB menu. Right-click where the face would be if you could see it. A list of entities displays, and you can select the entity you want from this list or from the graphics window.

Moving your mouse over an entity in the list highlights the entity in the graphics window. Pressing Tab or scrolling the mouse wheel cycles through the entities one by one. Clicking faces with the RMB hides them, which allows you to see further down into the part or assembly. Clicking with the LMB either in the graphics window or the selection list box selects the item. Figure 13.4 shows the Select Other cursor and dialog box.

FIGURE 13.4

The Select Other cursor and dialog box

The item about to be selected turns red in the graphics window.

Although this selection method is also used for other purposes, it is often used for selecting faces for mating.

Multiple Mate mode

 Multiple Mate mode enables you to select one face in order to mate multiple faces from other parts to it. Figure 13.5 shows the interface for this mode, which you can toggle to from the Mate PropertyManager interface. It also shows several small blocks being mated to a single large block. This function works only with the Standard Mate types, not with any of the Advanced Mates, which are discussed later in this chapter.

FIGURE 13.5

The Multiple Mate Mode interface

You can create a special folder for all of the multiple mates by selecting the Create Multi-mate Folder check box in the Mate Selections PropertyManager. You can also automatically link the values for distance and angle mates with link values by selecting the Link Dimensions check box.

SmartMates

SmartMates are mates that you can create automatically by dragging one part onto the other without invoking the Mate command. There are three different methods that you can use to apply SmartMates:

- Alt-dragging the part
- Dragging the part from one window to another
- Using Mate References

Alt-dragging a SmartMate

Probably the easiest way to quickly create a SmartMate is by Alt-dragging. One, two, or even three mates can be applied at once by holding down the Alt key while dragging a face or edge from one part onto a face or edge on another part.

When you are dragging a part while pressing the Alt key, the part is made transparent to allow you to see other part faces that you may want to mate it to. A special cursor appears when a SmartMate is about to be applied. Figure 13.6 shows the cursors that appear for adding Concentric and Coincident mates.

FIGURE 13.6

Applying a SmartMate

When you drop the face onto the mating face to complete the mate, you must use the popup Mate toolbar to accept or alter the mate. In the examples in Figure 13.6, a face is being dragged onto another face. However, you can also drag edges and vertices. Mates are limited to being either Coincident or Concentric.

The *peg-in-hole* mate is actually both a Concentric mate and a Coincident mate. This is the type of mate that is created between a screw and a hole, and is the result of Alt-dragging a circular edge onto a circular edge. When the circular edges are created by the intersection of a cylindrical face and a flat face, the Concentric mate goes between the two cylindrical faces, and the Coincident mate goes between the flat faces. The peg-in-hole mate is illustrated in Figure 13.7. The image to the left shows the state of the parts before the SmartMate. The image in the middle shows the SmartMate orienting the part in the wrong way so that the two parts interfere. In the image on the right, the part to which the SmartMate is applied has been reoriented by pressing Tab before the SmartMate is accepted by dropping the part.

TIP   You can use the Tab key to flip the alignment if a SmartMate tries to put parts together in the wrong way. If you are in the process of Alt-dragging, make sure to release the Alt key before pressing Tab. The Alt-Tab combination shows a list of open applications.

FIGURE 13.7

Using SmartMate to create the peg-in-hole mate combination

Alt-drag this edge

Drag between windows

You can apply SmartMates when dragging a part from one document window to another, or when copying a part within a single window by Ctrl-dragging. The best way to drag a part from one window into another is to tile the windows using the Tile command in the Window menu. Then drag the part using the face or edge that you would like to mate, and bring it near to the face in the assembly to which you want to mate it. The transparent preview should snap into place. Again, if it is backwards, you can just press Tab.

The same is true when copying a part in the graphics window of an assembly. You can simply Ctrl-drag a face of the part to the face of the new location.

Mate references

Mate references are model faces, edges, or vertices that are pre-selected and used in a SmartMate-like fashion when dragging a part in from Windows Explorer or from a library window. Mate References are discussed in Chapter 19 in the course of discussing library parts.

Mating with macros

If all of the confirmations and extra mouse-clicks to open and close windows are not for you, and you are just applying simple mates, then you may want to use macros to mate parts. Macros are not going to give you the same flexibility, but they do improve speed. However, you have to have the parts ready to go when you press the macro button, or you will create the wrong mate.

You can find macros for Coincident, Concentric, Parallel, Perpendicular, and Tangent mates on the CD-ROM. For example, to use the concentric macro, you would need to pre-position the parts so that they are within 90 degrees of the proper alignment, have one of the parts mated in place such that that only one part will move, select the two cylindrical faces, and then run the macro.

CROSS-REF   Macros are discussed in depth in Chapter 32.

To run the macro, pre-position the parts, pre-select the faces, click Tools ➪ Macro ➪ Run, and then browse to the macro. Chapter 32 shows you how to connect macros to hotkeys, which makes this process easier.

Like SmartMates, macros work best for the simpler mate types where you do not need to select any options.

Mating for Motion

Dynamic Assembly Motion is a powerful tool for visualizing the motion of mechanisms in SolidWorks. It works best if there is a single open *degree of freedom*.

Degree-Of-Freedom analysis

When working with motion in SolidWorks, you need to be comfortable with degrees of freedom. When inserted into an assembly, each model has six degrees of freedom:

- Translation in X (tX)
- Translation in Y (tY)
- Translation in Z (tZ)
- Rotation about X (rX)
- Rotation about Y (rY)
- Rotation about Z (rZ)

When applying mates, and especially when troubleshooting motion or overdefinition problems, it is important to look at how each mate translates into degrees of freedom being tied down. For example, a Coincident mate, planar face to planar face, ties down one translation degree of freedom (in the direction perpendicular to the faces), and two rotational degrees of freedom (about directions which lie in the plane of the faces). What remains are two translational degrees of freedom in the plane of the faces and one rotational degree of freedom about an axis perpendicular to the planar faces.

A point-to-point Coincident mate ties down three translational degrees of freedom, and the part can only rotate.

An edge-to-edge Coincident mate ties down two translational and two rotational degrees of freedom. As a result, a part that you mate in this way can only slide along the mated edge and rotate around the mated edge.

TIP　When using face-to-face Coincident mates, it takes three mates to fully define a block type part. When using edge-to-edge Coincident mates, it only takes two mates. You should read through the section on Summary of Mate Best Practices before adopting this approach.

Something to be careful about is that a degree-of-freedom analysis frequently predicts an over-defined mate scenario when SolidWorks does not in fact display any errors or warnings. For example, if one block is mated to another with the simple case of three face-to-face Coincident mates, and each Coincident mate ties down one translational and two rotational degrees of freedom, then the part would be over-constrained by three rotational degrees of freedom.

BEST PRACTICE　This may be an overly cautious approach, but it can mean the difference between an assembly that works and one where errors are frustratingly persistent. If you are careful to approach all parts with the degree-of-freedom analysis in mind such that any newly added mate does not duplicate any of the degrees of freedom that are already tied down, then you will have fewer assembly mate errors and fewer problems with assembly motion.

This means that instead of the traditional three face-to-face Coincident mates, you would have one face-to-face Coincident (one translational degree of freedom, two rotational degrees of freedom), one edge-to-face Coincident (one translational degree of freedom, one rotational degree of freedom) and one point-to-face Coincident (one translational degree of freedom). This accounts for three translational and three rotational degrees of freedom without overdefining any of them.

It is true that SolidWorks internally compensates for over-defined degrees of freedom, but relying on it to do so and then tempting fate by methodically over-defining all assemblies is a risk that you do not have to take, even though it is common practice.

Best bet for motion

The best bet for creating motion in a SolidWorks assembly is to leave open a single degree of freedom. This means that there is only one way the part can move, back and forth, either translation or rotation. Computers in general do not respond well to ambiguity. Dragging an item that may move in several ways is more likely to cause jerky or hesitant motion.

A good example of this kind of problem with motion can be found in one of the sample assemblies that installed with SolidWorks 2007. I have included this example on the CD-ROM for your convenience, and it is shown in Figure 13.8. The filename for the assembly is Plunger.sldasm.

FIGURE 13.8

An assembly displaying best bet for motion

Drag here and the motion is smooth

Drag here and the motion is poor

If you drag the assembly parts from the locations shown in Figure 13.8, the performance varies. This is because when you drag the handle parts, for every position of the handle, there is only one solution for the rest of the parts. However, when dragging the plunger bar, for every position of the plunger bar there are two possible positions for both the links and the handle. This kind of ambiguity causes problems in SolidWorks assemblies such as assemblies that have open degrees of freedom but will not move or move in a jerky fashion.

Another example of difficulties related to open degrees of freedom and motion is shown in Figure 13.9. The grippers at the end of the arm move when the rest of the arm moves, but the grippers cannot be independently controlled. To fix this problem, you may want to either use the Fix/Float option (available through the RMB menu), or use configurations with mates suppressed or unsuppressed. You can open this assembly from the CD-ROM, in the filename called Chapter 13 Robot Assembly.sldasm.

FIGURE 13.9

A robot arm assembly with degree-of-freedom conflicts

Working with Advanced Mate Types

Advanced mate types greatly expand the number of ways that you can put parts together into assemblies. Advanced mate types include the following:

- Symmetric
- Cam
- Width
- Gear
- Rack and Pinion
- Limit
- Belts and Chains

Symmetric mate

The Symmetric mate works a lot like the Symmetry relation in sketches, except that a plane is used as the plane of symmetry instead of a construction line. Figure 13.10 shows a Symmetric mate being applied to the gripper jaws. The Symmetric mate is listed in the Advanced Mates pane of the Mate PropertyManager.

FIGURE 13.10

Applying a Symmetric mate

Cam mate

The Cam mate creates a special instance of either the Coincident or Tangent mate. Four conditions exist with the Cam mate:

- **Coincident:** Vertex on the follower mated to a cam that is created from a single closed-loop face (spline, circle, ellipse).

- **Tangent:** Cylindrical or planar face mated to a cam that is created from a single closed-loop face.

- **CamMateCoincident:** Vertex on the follower mated to a cam that is created from multiple faces. This condition enables the follower to go all the way around the cam, not stopping at the broken faces or following the extension of a single face.

- **CamMateTangent:** Cylindrical or planar face mated to a cam that is created from multiple faces. This condition enables the follower to go all the way around the cam, not stopping at the broken faces or following the extension of a single face.

Figure 13.11 shows both single-face and multi-face cams, along with the Cam Mate interface. The two assemblies are available from the CD-ROM in the file named Chapter 13 Cam.sldasm.

If you open the assemblies and spin the cam plate, you will notice that in both cases, the flat follower does not work very well. In fact, in the single face cam assembly, it does not work at all.

 Barrel (cylindrical) cams cannot use the Cam mate to create cam motion.

FIGURE 13.11

Using Cam mates

Width mate

The Width mate is often used as a replacement for the Symmetric mate in situations where parts are modeled with some tolerance, and have a gap rather than touching face to face. The Width mate requires two pairs of faces to be selected, and works particularly well when a part has to be spaced evenly between two faces and there is no mid-plane, for instance when a square key is placed in a square keyway which is somewhat larger than the key. If a mid-plane is available, the Symmetric mate may be a better option, or at least a faster one to mate since the Symmetric mate only requires two faces and a plane. Figure 13.12 shows a good application for a Width mate as well as the PropertyManager interface for the mate.

FIGURE 13.12

Applying a Width mate

Gear mate

The Gear mate enables you to establish gear type relations between parts without making the parts physically mesh. You can also apply gear ratios and directions without physical connections, so that you can have a shaft in and a shaft out of a black-box transmission. You can open the assembly shown in Figure 13.13 from the CD-ROM. It is named Chapter 13 Gear Mate.sldasm. To see the effect of the mate, open the assembly and rotate the parts. Then edit the mate and change the ratio and direction. The selection for the Gear mate is just two cylindrical faces.

Applying a Gear mate

Rack and Pinion mate

The Rack and Pinion mate takes rotational motion of one part and turns it into translational motion for a second part. Again, the parts do not need to be physically connected and can be simple representations of the actual geometry that is needed to drive the motion in the real world. Figure 13.14 shows an assembly that uses the Rack and Pinion mate. You can find this assembly on the CD-ROM with the filename Chapter 13 RackPinionMate.sldasm.

Limit mates

You can apply limits to distance and angle mates in order to allow the parts to move within a certain range of values. Figure 13.15 shows the PropertyManager interface for the Limit Angle mate. Limit mates accept zero and negative values that are not normally accepted for dimensions in SolidWorks. When used properly, Limit mates can be an extremely powerful tool for creating more realistic motion in assemblies.

FIGURE 13.14

Applying a Rack and Pinion mate

FIGURE 13.15

The Limit Angle PropertyManager

Belt/Chain

The Belt/Chain assembly feature is not technically a standalone mate type, but it uses mates to accomplish its task. The Belt/Chain feature can be used in two ways, to create relationships between sketch blocks or to create relations between parts. This feature also creates a sketch and a solid part representing the belt or chain.

Chapter 4 has a tutorial that discusses the Belt/Chain functionality as it relates to sketch blocks. The functionality using solid parts as pulleys and sprockets is very similar.

Editing and Troubleshooting

You should become proficient with editing and troubleshooting assembly mates. If you are not comfortable with repairing and modifying mates, then you may find assemblies frustrating to work with; as a result, you may avoid making changes to your assemblies. However, once you master the techniques, you will be less afraid of errors, and more confident and willing to experiment with assembly changes.

Editing existing mates

If you are editing just one mate, then you can simply RMB click it and select Edit Feature. Remember that you can find mates in places other than the Mates folder at the bottom of the assembly FeatureManager; most notably, you can find them in folders under the parts that they are mating together.

You can make several types of changes to mates, including changing the selections involved, the mate types being used, and the mate alignment. These types of changes are all shown in Figure 13.16, which displays a mate being edited. The selected faces are highlighted in the graphics window.

To edit multiple mates consecutively without exiting the Mate PropertyManager, it is best if you pre-select the mates. Pre-selected mates are shown in the Mates panel as shown in Figure 13.16. You can switch from editing one mate to another by simply selecting the new mate in the Mates panel. If you select only one mate before clicking Edit Feature, but realize later that you want to edit multiple mates, more mates can be selected through the Flyout FeatureManager.

After the Mates pane has been opened, you can add mates to it by selecting the mates from the Flyout FeatureManager. This technique is somewhat problematic because after selecting a single mate from the flyout menu, it collapses and you have to expand it again.

NOTE   Here is another good place to promote the use of the Enhancement Request forms on the SolidWorks Web site. Editing mates is a function that you will perform frequently, and so it requires a smooth and easy-to-use interface. However, the FeatureManager and the PropertyManager create an awkward workflow when you need to select features from the FeatureManager. An example is when you edit the sketch plane for a sketch; as soon as you select this option, the FeatureManager disappears. This can be frustrating when you just want to select a plane from the FeatureManager that was right next to the sketch, but now you have to manually expand the flyout menu and scroll to find the plane again. I encourage you to suggest improvements to this system directly to SolidWorks through the Enhancement Request forms on the Support Web site.

FIGURE 13.16

Editing a mate

When mate entities are lost, the mate displays a yellow triangle containing an exclamation mark, the text changes to a brown color, and a break appears in the mate icon, as shown in Figure 13.17. You can repair this problem by selecting the Invalid reference in the Mate Selections window and then selecting the correct item from the graphics window.

FIGURE 13.17

Repairing mates with missing references

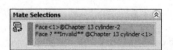

Troubleshooting

It is best to troubleshoot an assembly mate problem as soon as it appears, and not after it has time to become complicated by other issues. Failed mates also cause performance problems because SolidWorks keeps trying to solve the mates that are in conflict with one another.

Assembly problems often appear to be far larger than they actually are. For example, the entire tree may light up with warnings and error symbols when one extra or mistaken mate is applied. You can use several approaches to troubleshoot situations like this. In fact, I sometimes purposefully over-define mates just to locate a left-over mate or a mate that is not supposed to be there.

Two types of symbols may help you to distinguish the kinds of errors that are present in different mate features. The yellow triangle that contains an exclamation point is really not an *error*; it is actually more of a *warning*. It tells you that this mate is in conflict with other mates (this symbol is used for a variety of warnings), but that the mate is still satisfied. One of the other mates with which it conflicts is probably not valid, and so this type of warning is usually accompanied by an actual error symbol where the mate is not satisfied.

The red circle containing the X is a failed mate. This is a mate that is in conflict *and* is invalid. If it is also a Coincident mate, then the two Coincident entities are not coincident.

Distinguishing between the Warnings and the Errors

You can use the following troubleshooting techniques:

- **Last in first out**: When a mate is added that causes warning and error signs to appear throughout the design tree, you can usually correct the problem by removing this last mate.

- **Single elimination**: If you are sure that the last mate added is correct, then you may want to go backwards up the tree starting at the bottom, suppressing individual mates until you find one that causes the warning and error signs to disappear from the tree.

- **Single addition**: It may be easier to take the opposite approach, by suppressing all but the mates that you are sure of, and then gradually unsuppressing mates until the conflict reappears.

- **Suppress a part**: With all of the mates active, try suppressing an individual part to see if this makes a difference. If it does, then unsuppress the part and look at the mates for that part in the Mates folder under the part.

- **Mate Xpert**: The Mate Xpert is an automated routine that creates subsets of groups of conflicting mates. Each subset of mates has one mate that is not satisfied because of the conflict. This may help you to find the cause of the conflict. Figure 13.18 shows the Mate Xpert interface. You can access the Mate Xpert from the RMB menu.

The Mate Xpert interface

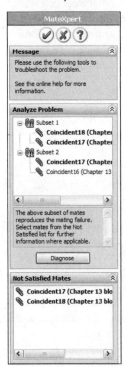

CAUTION In the past several releases, SolidWorks has become increasingly "error-phobic." There are more and more ways to create mate errors that are simply not reported to the user. For example, if geometry goes missing from a part, the mate icon displays with a break on it, but the mate folder is not flagged. This means that you do not know that you have a broken mate until you go looking for it.

Another example is that when a mated part is fixed (using the Fix option), the conflicting mates are automatically suppressed without notifying the user. In addition, when a part is suppressed, the mate is shown as suppressed, but it is also shown as broken. As a result, you are unsure whether the mate is completely invalid or the parent parts are only suppressed.

Examining Mate Options

The Options pane of the Mate PropertyManager is shown in Figure 13.19. Most of the options are self-explanatory, except for the Use For Positioning Only option. This option positions a part but does not apply a parametric mate. Some users make extensive use of this option for various applications where you need the part located precisely, but do not need or want a mate. Positioning parts for Animator animations where the part does not move according to a mate is one example of a use for this option.

FIGURE 13.19

The Options pane of the Mate PropertyManager

Summarizing Mate Best Practices

Sometimes best practice recommendations can contradict one another, and for each best practice recommendation that you find, there are likely several specific situations where the recommendation is invalid. As a result, you should apply the following recommendations carefully.

- Each assembly should have at least one part that is either fixed or fully mated to the standard planes of the assembly so that it cannot move relative to the assembly.

- You should use fixed parts sparingly. One part that serves as a "ground" for the assembly should be fixed. Other than that, the parts of imported assemblies are sometimes fixed to keep them from being moved accidentally.

- Do not mate to time-dependent features in the assembly tree, or to in-context features in parts. You may want to refer to Chapter 12 for a refresher on time-dependent features in the assembly tree. This can create circular references where the assembly must be rebuilt multiple times to fully resolve the positions of all parts and sketches.

- When possible, it is best to mate all parts to the "ground" part. Creating *daisy-chain* mates (where A mates to B which mates to C, and so on) forces the mates to be solved in a particular order, which may take more time to solve than otherwise. If all of the mates relate to established assembly references, the mates may be more stable. Chapter 11 describes using a skeleton in a part to make sketch and feature relations to. The concepts are similar.

- When possible, leave part positions fully defined, especially when other geometry is dependent upon the position of parts. Some examples include in-context features, assembly features, or assembly-level reference geometry, which are dependent on part geometry.

- Constraining the rotational degree of freedom for components such as screws, washers, and nuts is usually considered excessive. At times, open degrees of freedom may cause problems with complex motion, such as a gripper on the end of a robotic arm. SolidWorks functions well when there is a single, well-defined path between two points, but when there are multiple options, the software may become confused.

- Do not leave errors unresolved in the tree.

- Remember to use subassemblies to break up the number of mates that are solved in the top-level assembly.

- Limit the use of flexible subassemblies.

- Do not mate to entities that may be removed later by suppressing or unsuppressing features, especially edges or faces that are created by features such as fillets. For this reason, it is usually best to wait until parts are complete before you use them to create an assembly, although this is rarely practical.

- Use a degree-of-freedom analysis to prevent mates from becoming over-defined.

Tutorial: Mating for Success

In this tutorial, you will put together a model of a robotic arm to better understand some of the mate issues discussed in this chapter. Follow these steps to mate for success:

1. Open the part named Chapter 13 Robot Base.sldprt from the CD-ROM.

2. In the part document window, click the Make Assembly From Part icon, and click the cursor on the Origin of the assembly to place the part Origin at the assembly Origin. The part is automatically fixed in place.

3. Click Insert ⇨ Component ⇨ Existing Part/Assembly. Click the Browse button in the PropertyManager, and find the part called Chapter 13 Robot Tower.sldprt. This part contains a Mate reference to help you mount it to the base. If you bring the cursor near the big circular hole in the base, you can see the transparent preview of the tower snap into place. Click to accept this placement. Figure 13.20 shows this placement in progress. Notice that the cursor appears as a SmartMate cursor for the peg-in-hole mate. When the part is dropped, check the mate list to confirm that a Concentric and a Coincident mate have been applied by the Mate reference.

FIGURE 13.20

A Mate reference being used to SmartMate a component

4. Open the part with the filename Chapter 13 Arm.sldprt in its own window, and click Window ⇨ Tile Vertically. The part and the assembly should be open in adjacent windows.

5. Click the face inside the hole without the chamfer around it in the Arm part, as shown in Figure 13.21. Then drag it into the assembly to the cylindrical face inside the hole at the top of the Robot Tower part. The concentric SmartMate symbol should appear on the cursor.

6. Click the green check mark icon to accept the Concentric mate. Move the part to test that the mates are correct.

7. Click the Mate tool on the Assemblies toolbar. Expand the Advanced Mates panel and click the Width mate.

8. In the Width Selections box, select the two inner faces of the Robot Tower part, and in the Tab selections box, select the outer faces of the Arm part. The selection should look as shown in Figure 13.22.

FIGURE 13.21

Displaying a SmartMate when dragging between windows

Drag the inner face of the hole

9. Open a Windows Explorer window, and select the following parts: Chapter 13 Robot Arm2 and Chapter 13 Robot Gripper. Drag these parts into the SolidWorks assembly window, and drop them in a blank space.

10. Select the chamfered faces of the Arm and Arm2 parts and create a Coincident mate between them. You can make Coincident mates between conical faces as long as the cones are the same angle. This special case acts like a combination of Concentric and Coincident mates. Figure 13.23 shows the selections and the results.

FIGURE 13.22

Creating a Width mate

FIGURE 13.23

Making conical faces coincident

Select these faces

11. Create a copy of the gripper part so that there are two instances of it in the assembly. You can do this by Ctrl-dragging the part within the assembly window.

12. Mate both of the grippers to the Arm2 end using the same mating technique that you used for the previous conical face Coincident part.

13. Once you have applied these parts, try moving the various joints of the assembly. Notice that it is difficult, if not impossible, to isolate the motion of just a single part. This is because there are too many open degrees of freedom, and a lot of ambiguity.

14. Fix Arm2 to allow you to move the gripper parts as you want. Create a Symmetric mate between the indicated faces of the grippers and the Front plane of the Arm2 part, as shown in Figure 13.24.

FIGURE 13.24

Creating a Symmetric mate

Faces for symmetric mate

15. Practice making angle mates, suppressing mates, and fixing parts to limit motion.

16. Save the assembly and exit the file.

Summary

A thorough understanding of mates, and editing and troubleshooting techniques in particular, makes the difference between a real assembly artist and a user who struggles through or avoids certain tasks. There is a lot about mates that is not simply straightforward, but with practice, you can understand and master them. You can put assemblies together quickly, with a focus on rebuild performance and Dynamic Assembly Motion.

Although best practice concepts should not dominate your designs, they are great guidelines to start from. Watch out for the pitfalls outlined in the Summary of Mate Best Practices section in this chapter to avoid making big mistakes.

Chapter 14

Assembly Configurations and Display States

A ssembly configurations enable you to control many things, including part configurations, suppression, visibility, color, and assembly feature sizes. They also allow you to control assembly layout sketch dimensions, mate values, suppression states, and several other items. What you will learn in this chapter about assembly configurations builds on the information in Chapter 10, which discussed part configurations. In this chapter, design tables will also be expanded upon to show how they are used in conjunction with SolidWorks assemblies.

The Display States function was new in SolidWorks 2006. Display States are a better performance alternative to using configurations to control visibility of parts in assemblies. Display State options are discussed at length in this chapter.

IN THIS CHAPTER

Display States

Assembly configurations

Exploded views

Tutorial: Working with assembly configurations

Using Display States

If you are using an older version of SolidWorks, then you may not have access to Display States, which were not introduced until SolidWorks 2006. They are a very useful addition to the software as they allow you to visualize the assembly in various ways. One of the best things about Display States is their ability to show parts in different display modes (Shaded, Wireframe, HLR, Shaded with Edges) simultaneously.

Users have always been able to show parts transparent and shaded at the same time, and a common workaround for combining Shaded and Wireframe modes was to display the parts as Shaded with Edges, but to make some parts completely transparent. This would give the effect of some parts being shown in Wireframe mode. Because of Display States, this workaround is no longer necessary.

Display States and configurations

You can copy Display States between configs. To control the display, you can use the Display pane that flies out from the FeatureManager when you click the double-arrow icon in the upper-right corner of the FeatureManager. This is shown in Figure 2.1 in Chapter 2. Figure 14.1 shows the Display pane in action, along with an assembly showing parts in different Display States.

FIGURE 14.1

The Display pane and an assembly with parts in different Display States

The column symbols for the Display pane are as follows:

	Hide or Show state of the part
	Display Mode options for each component:
	Wireframe
	Hidden Lines Visible (HLV)
	Hidden Lines Removed (HLR)
	Shaded with Edges
	Shaded
	Default Display
	Component/Part Color (see Note)
	Component/Part Texture
	Component Transparency

NOTE The difference between a component and a part in SolidWorks assemblies is that a component is a generic way of identifying any top-level item in an assembly, and may be a single part or a subassembly. It always refers to a specific instance of the part within the assembly. In the case shown in Figure 14.1, the gripper jaw part is used twice, and so there are two instances of the gripper jaw. One instance has its component color set to yellow, and the other instance uses the part color. (The component color is also referred to as an *override* of the part color). The part color is what you see when you open the part in its own window. The component color is only set in the assembly, and you can only see it in that particular assembly; it never affects how the part displays in any other assembly that the part is shown in.

When there is a difference between the part and component properties (when an override exists), the component property appears as the upper-left triangle, in the color column of the Display Pane and the part property appears as the lower-right triangle. You can only see these triangles in the Color and Texture columns.

Color hierarchy is discussed in Chapter 3, but I will briefly summarize it here, showing the lowest priority at the top:

- Part
- Body
- Feature
- Face
- Component

If you override a color, display mode, or texture for a component in a subassembly, and the upper-left triangle appears in the Display pane, then you can remove the override through either the Left Mouse Button (LMB) or Right Mouse Button (RMB) menu. Figure 14.2 shows the LMB menu from a component of a subassembly with overrides.

FIGURE 14.2

You can remove overrides in the Assembly Display pane.

When you select Clear Override, SolidWorks clears any overrides for the currently selected subassembly component. Clear All Top Level Overrides clears all overrides in all subassemblies in the entire top-level assembly. There is no intermediate option to clear all top-level overrides for a particular subassembly; if you want to distinguish between overrides at that level, then you need to clear several individual overrides. The options to remove overrides do not affect top-level components.

The active Display State appears in angle brackets after the configuration name and the filename at the top of the FeatureManager, as shown in the image to the left in Figure 14.3. Display States are created and managed in the ConfigurationManager, in folders under the configuration name, as shown in the image to the right in Figure 14.3. To create a new Display State, simply right-click the Display State folder under the active configuration and choose Add Display State. You can manage Display States in a way similar to the way in which Exploded Views are managed.

FIGURE 14.3

Display States shown in the FeatureManager and the ConfigurationManager

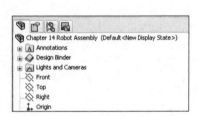

New configurations are always created with a default Display State named Display State-1, just as parts always have a default configuration named Default. To copy the New Display State shown in Figure 14.3 from the Default configuration to Configuration 2, you can Ctrl-drag it from one Display State folder to the other configuration's folder.

PERFORMANCE Display States offer a huge performance gain over configurations when used to control display of parts. The reason for this is that SolidWorks saves some model information for each configuration. In the past, configurations were sometimes created only for display purposes, and changing configurations required reading the model geometry again. When a configuration is created only for the purpose of hiding or coloring a part, this takes up a lot of additional file space and CPU time. Display States change much faster than configurations, almost instantaneously, and they add very little file size to use.

Display States and drawings

Display States can be shown on drawings if you have set the view to a Shaded Display mode. If you set the view to a Wireframe mode, then SolidWorks ignores the Display State, and all of the parts in the view display in that mode. Drawing views are discussed in depth in Chapter 21.

Understanding Assembly Configurations

Assembly configurations are used for many different purposes, including assembly performance, simplified assemblies, variations of assemblies, assemblies in different positions or states, and many others. Like part configurations, assembly configs also have a few best practice type suggestions. Configuration settings for assemblies control how the assembly appears in a Bill of Materials (BOM), what happens to parts, features, or mates that are added to other configurations, and so on. All of these are discussed in this section.

Configurations for performance

One of the best tools to make large assemblies easier to work with is assembly configurations. You can use several techniques to improve the speed of working with assemblies. Although this information is presented in a list of techniques, it is important to select a method that fits the situation.

Suppressing components and features

The most obvious use of configurations for improving assembly speed is to have a configuration or several configurations with suppressed components. One thing to watch out for when doing this is that configurations are not used in the place of subassemblies. If subassemblies are appropriate for the task, then you should use subassemblies. If not, then you should group and suppress parts using configurations.

 Remember that you can use a folder for parts and suppress the folder.

Schemes that you may want to use for suppressing parts are to have configurations that isolate functional areas of an assembly, configs that remove the fasteners or purchased components, configs that remove complex parts, configs that only leave the parts used in in-context relations, configs that suppress patterns and assembly features, assembly configs that use simplified part configs, configs that show the assembly in different positions, or variations of the assembly using different part configurations. So many possible schemes for creating assembly configurations exist that it is pointless to try to list them all. Use your imagination, make sure that it makes sense, and give it a try.

 Avoid using fasteners to locate parts. The relationship should go the other way (fasteners should be located by the holes in parts). You should already have in place any parts that the fastener stack will touch before the fasteners are added. If parts added after the fasteners are either mated to the fasteners or the holes are created from the fasteners using in-context techniques, then suppressing the fasteners also suppresses the mates that locate those parts, and will cause problems with any in-context features.

If you suppress the "ground" part or any part that connects groups of parts, keep in mind that this can cause other parts to float in space, unattached to anything. Obviously this is not a good situation, and you should avoid it if possible. One way to avoid it is to use an assembly layout sketch and mate the parts to the sketch instead of to the ground part.

Aside from components, other items can also be suppressed to improve performance, such as assembly features and component patterns. Do you really need to see all of those parts patterned around the assembly to work on it in a simplified representation? You may be able to suppress the parts. If you feel that you cannot suppress parts, then consider at least using Display States to hide parts that are needed to complete the parametrics but do not need to display.

PERFORMANCE The biggest killer of assembly speed is the dreaded circular reference. You can make circular references in a couple of different ways, but they are usually the result of mixing history-based functions (mates, in-context sketch relations, feature references) with non-history-based functions (parts shown in the Assembly FeatureManager). This allows you to create partial or complete loops of references, where A references B which references A. These are a particular problem with in-context references, which are discussed in more depth in Chapter 16.

Using part configurations for speed

I have discussed simplified part configurations in Chapter 10, and they can consist of configs with cosmetic features such as small fillets and extruded text, or other cosmetic details that are suppressed. Assembly configurations can use different part configurations, which, for example, would enable you to make an assembly config called "Simplified," and in it reference all of the Simplified part configurations.

TIP When opening an assembly through the Open dialog box, the Advanced option enables you to open the assembly and create a new assembly configuration that uses part configurations of a given name, if available. The default part configuration name entered in the text box is, I think, suggestive of how SolidWorks intended for this function to be used. As shown in Figure 14.4, it is "Simplified."

Other special operations for assembly configurations in the Open dialog box include creating a new configuration that has all of the components suppressed. This allows you to see the structure of the assembly without fully resolving all of the components. Another option is to open the assembly with a new configuration, where all of the components are resolved. Beyond that, the Open dialog box also allows you to select a specific configuration to open to so that you do not have to wait for the last saved config to load and then make the change.

NEW FEATURE When you use a part that has several configurations in an assembly, you cannot edit the part in the assembly unless the active configuration is the same as the config used in the assembly. This has always been the case. What is new about SolidWorks 2007 is that if you open the part in its own window from the assembly, SolidWorks automatically makes the config that is used in the assembly the active config. As a result, to change the active config and edit the part in the assembly, all you have to do now is to open the part in its own window and then switch back to the assembly (using Ctrl+Tab).

Advanced Show/Hide

It is curious that this option is not so easily available after the assembly is already open. However, you can use some other techniques to sort through parts. The Advanced Show/Hide Components dialog box is shown in Figure 14.5. You can access this dialog box by right-clicking the configuration name in the ConfigurationManager.

FIGURE 14.4

The Advanced option for assemblies in the Open dialog box

FIGURE 14.5

The Advanced Show/Hide Components dialog box

This tool enables you to establish search criteria and show or hide parts, based on the criteria. Multiple criteria can be used, stored, and retrieved. This tool is generally underused, and in my experience, users are always surprised to find it in the software. It has been there since about 1998.

 A function called Isolate is new to SolidWorks 2007. This works like the inverse of the Show command. If you select multiple parts and click Isolate from the RMB menu, the selected parts remain shown, and everything else becomes hidden. A little pop-up gives you the option of showing the removed components in a Wireframe or Transparent display mode, or of saving the current display as a new Display State. This is a very useful function, as shown in Figure 14.6.

FIGURE 14.6

The Isolate function

SolidWorks Utilities Simplify Assembly

If you have the SolidWorks Office bundle or higher, then you can activate the Utilities add-in. You can do this by selecting Tools, Add-ins, and then turning on Utilities. This displays a Utilities menu with the Simplify option. The Simplify Assembly tool is shown in action in Figure 14.7.

The Simplify Assembly tool can find features in the parts of the assemblies that are under a certain size or that take up less than a certain percentage of the volume of the part. You can then suppress these features in special derived configurations.

FIGURE 14.7

The Simplify Assembly tool

Controlling display performance

Overall, SolidWorks performance is split into two categories: CPU (central processing unit) processing and GPU (graphics processing unit) processing. This is essentially the difference between calculating the parametrics and geometry, as opposed to the graphics and display. Which of these functions your computer performs better can vary widely, depending on your hardware, drivers, and system maintenance, among other factors.

When trying to speed up the performance of an assembly, the biggest impact is obviously made if you can reduce the load on both the CPU and the GPU. You can do this by suppressing a part. When a part is suppressed, it is neither calculated nor displayed, and so the load on each processor for that part is zero.

When you hide a part, its parametric features are still calculated by the CPU; however, because the part is hidden, it creates no load on the GPU. If you have a good main processor and a questionable video card, then you will achieve a greater benefit from removing graphics load from your display.

Lightweight parts

On the other hand, if you want to still show a part but not calculate any of its parametric relations, then you should use Lightweight parts. You can find Lightweight default settings in Tools ➪ Options, on both the Assemblies and Performance pages. You can make parts lightweight through the RMB menu. The opposite of Lightweight is Resolved. Resolved means that the part is fully loaded, its parametrics are loaded and calculated by the CPU, and its graphics display data is calculated and shown by the GPU.

To summarize this section, there is a four-way relationship between the Resolved, Lightweight, Hidden, and Suppressed states, as shown in Figure 14.8.

FIGURE 14.8

The relationship between the Resolved, Lightweight, Hidden, and Suppressed states

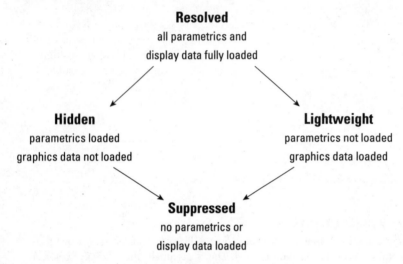

Resolved versus unsuppressed

The terminology becomes a little convoluted here because of the relationship between the four different states. In parts, the feature states are easy to remember because features can be either suppressed or unsuppressed. However, in assemblies, there are four states instead of two, and so *unsuppressed* could mean anything that is not suppressed, which still leaves three states. For this reason, *resolved* is used instead of *unsuppressed* when dealing with components in an assembly.

Configurations for positions

When you use configurations to display an assembly in various positions, you can do this in a couple of ways: by changing mates or by changing a layout sketch. Mates are configurable in two ways: mates can be suppressed and unsuppressed, and angle and distance mate values are configurable in the same way that sketch dimensions are configurable. Although creating a mate scheme that enables you to reposition the assembly using mate suppression states and values is essential to this method, it may not be the best approach.

Using a skeleton or layout sketch to mate parts to may be a better approach, although this also has its drawbacks. If you mate to a layout sketch, you cannot make use of Dynamic Assembly Motion. If you use the mate scheme discussed above, this generally means having a fully defined assembly, and this also does not allow for Dynamic Assembly Motion.

As a compromise, a good way to handle this is by using one configuration for Dynamic Assembly Motion, with one or more open degrees of freedom. You can use other configurations to fully define the mechanism and show it in particular positions using either method. Probably the best way to demonstrate this is with an example using the robot arm assembly.

Positioning with mates

First, let's take a look at positioning with mates. On an assembly such as this one, the goal is to position the grippers. You can do this in a couple of ways, both directly and indirectly. In the assembly used for this chapter, the grippers have been rebuilt as a subassembly, which allows different types of control. Notice that the subassembly has a configuration for the closed position and one that allows Dynamic Assembly Motion. Also, the subassembly is being solved as Flexible. Figure 14.9 shows the assembly and the FeatureManager.

FIGURE 14.9

The assembly used for this example

Driving the position directly

A sketch point has been added to the subassembly to precisely identify the point on the gripper that is to be positioned. Sketch points have also been added to the main assembly to represent parts that need to be picked up by the robotic arm.

 For a better range of motion, this arm should probably have an additional pivot that enables motion out of the plane of the Tower part.

Check the derived configurations under the default config. Notice that when you switch between certain configurations, the parts seem to separate. Moving one of the links causes the parts to snap back together again. This is probably because there are so many options when moving between configurations that the software has difficulty choosing a final position. This is definitely one of the potential problems when using configured mates to show an assembly in various positions.

Notice also that although the grippers are positioned correctly, the arm is still allowed to swivel around the intended target point. You can correct this by defining an orientation for the grippers for each location. If the additional pivot were added to the assembly, then fully defining the parts would become more difficult. The arm would not be able to reach any additional points, but it would not be so limited in orienting the grippers at each point.

Driving the position indirectly

You can also use mates to drive configured positions of the assembly using a series of angle mates. This makes it more difficult because to get to a particular location, you have to do some calculations, but the angle mates appear to be more stable than simply relying on moving the parts to unconstrained positions.

If you cycle through the derived configurations under the Indirect top-level configuration, notice that mates are not suppressed and unsuppressed, rather the values are changed. This makes it somewhat more difficult to precisely position the grippers, but because it is specific about the positions of the individual parts, there is no ambiguity.

Positioning with sketches

Although this technique is still using mates to position the parts, to change the position, you change sketch dimensions rather than mate values. Sketches used to drive parts from an assembly are sometimes called *layout sketches* or *skeletons*. These are also discussed in Chapter 16 for in-context or top-down assembly techniques and Chapter 11 as a way of controlling parent/child relationships. Figure 14.10 shows the same assembly that is used for the rest of this chapter.

FIGURE 14.10

Positioning assembly components with sketches

Position Sketch Plane

This particular assembly is driven by two sketches on different planes to govern the position of the parts. Keep in mind that this assembly has been used for all of the other techniques as well, and so all of these techniques can exist together simultaneously, being controlled by configurations.

Examine the assembly to see how the parts are mated to the sketches. This is important. The first time you create a part such as this, you may be tempted to mate part planes to the sketch lines.

CAUTION Mating planes to sketch lines has a very serious drawback that you must be aware of. Unlike other types of mates, which have an alignment that you can control, plane-to-sketch line mates cannot be aligned. This means that the software is as likely to align elements correctly as incorrectly on any plane-to-line mate.

BEST PRACTICE A better way to mate part planes to sketch lines is to mate the Temporary Axes through the joints with the sketch endpoints. This solves the alignment problem.

Configurations for product variations

In this case, *product variations* means variations in size or part replacement. Some examples are a 4-foot cabinet and an 8-foot cabinet, or a two-button mouse and a three-button mouse.

As a simple example, Figure 14.11 shows the familiar robotic arm assembly, but with a variation: one of the arms has been replaced with a subassembly. The subassembly is made of the original replaced part using configurations, and there are configurations of the subassembly, which is again being used as a flexible subassembly.

FIGURE 14.11

A part that is replaced by a subassembly

Through the course of this chapter, the robot arm assembly has greatly increased in complexity, but it has retained the original information that was in the first version. Maintaining valid assembly data through manually managed configurations is difficult, and all it takes is a simple mistake to wipe out a lot of assembly configuration data. Appropriately, the next section discusses assembly design tables.

Design tables for assembly configurations

Chapter 10 dealt with part configurations and created a good framework for design tables in general. This chapter augments that information with what you need to know to use design tables effectively in assemblies.

Assembly design tables can do everything that part design tables can do, except for selecting configurations of base parts and split parts, which are not valid assembly functions. Assembly design tables can also do some things that a part design table cannot. These include:

- Assigning the Display State for a configuration
- Suppressing the state of a part (R for Resolved or S for Suppressed)
- Assigning the component configuration for the assembly config
- Allowing you to activate the Never Expand in BOM option

If you have been using design tables for a while and are familiar with older versions, then you may have noticed that the $show parameter, which specified whether the part was shown or hidden, has become obsolete due to the new functions of Display States.

Figure 14.12 shows the design table that results from auto-creation using the robot arm assembly. Some of the columns have been hidden to make it small enough to fit on the page. If you want to see the entire table, you need to open the assembly. If you edit the design table, then you will probably want to use the Open in Separate Window option, which is easier to navigate and control.

FIGURE 14.12

An auto-created design table from the robot arm assembly

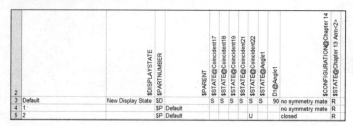

Assembly configuration dos and don'ts

- Avoid using Delete as an editing option when working with configurations. Delete is forever and for all configs.

- Avoid the use of in-context relations to size parts when you are also using configurations to size parts. A non-configured part driven by a configured part only causes confusion.

- Avoid using configurations to represent document control type revisions. I have seen people attempt to do this, but in the end, it limits the kinds of edits you can make to your parts and assemblies, and it is far too easy to make a mistake that wipes out all of your diligence. In the end, this is not a viable technique.

- If you are working with manually created configs, then you should create a new configuration and activate it before making the changes. Otherwise, you will end up trying to set the original config back to the way it was.

- Remember to select the This Configuration Only option for changed dimensions, instead of leaving it at the default All Configurations setting.

Creating Exploded Views

Exploded views enable you to display an assembly taken apart so that you can see all of the parts. They are great for assembly documentation, assembly instructions, and for visualizing assemblies with concealed internal parts.

I have included exploded views in the assembly configurations chapter because, like Display States, exploded views are found in the ConfigurationManager under the configuration. Each config can have multiple exploded views, and you can copy exploded views between configurations.

When you are creating the exploded view of the top-level assembly, and a subassembly already has one, you can include the subassembly's exploded view in the top-level exploded view. While you are creating exploded views, mates are temporarily suspended.

To initiate a new exploded view, switch to the ConfigurationManager, RMB click a configuration name, and select New Exploded View, as shown in Figure 14.13.

Figure 14.13 also shows the Explode PropertyManager interface. This interface includes a helpful How-To section at the top to give you a hint of where to start.

If you are creating assembly instructions or an animation from the exploded view (using Animator or the RMB options, Animate Explode, or Animate Collapse), then you may need to be more careful about *how* the parts are exploded. You can create explode lines that show how the parts go back together.

FIGURE 14.13

Initiating a new exploded view

To begin, you can explode the Base and the Tower down and back, respectively. A single part can explode in multiple directions, or multiple parts can explode in a single direction. These two parts are shown exploded in Figure 14.14. Select the base, and then drag the arrow of the Triad that moves in the direction that you want the part to move.

FIGURE 14.14

Exploding the base

The Tower part is a little more difficult because it is not lined up with the direction in which it needs to be exploded. To remedy this, highlight the Direction box in the PropertyManager and select a face that is normal to the direction that you want to drag, or an edge that is in this direction. Then drag the appropriate arrow on the triad again, as shown in Figure 14.15.

TIP   SolidWorks Help says that you can drag the sphere of the triad onto a face to change the direction, rather than selecting a face in the Direction box. However, it fails to mention that you have to hold down the Alt key while dragging it, in order for it to stick to an entity.

Exploding the Twist Arm subassembly provides the opportunity to show a couple of useful subassembly functions. You can explode the parts of a subassembly either together as a unit or individually. You can even reuse explode steps from the subassembly, which is what you will do here.

FIGURE 14.15

Changing the direction of the explode

Direction box

To explode the subassembly as a single part and then reuse its explode steps from the subassembly file, ensure that the Select Sub-Assembly's Parts option is off, as shown in Figure 14.16.

CAUTION You cannot reuse a subassembly's explode steps if the subassembly is set to Flexible. SolidWorks will tell you that there are no explode steps to reuse if you try to reuse the explode steps of a flexible subassembly. In order to work around this, you can set the subassembly to solve as Rigid, reuse the explode steps, and then set the subassembly back to Flexible. Although awkward, this is an effective workaround to this problem.

TIP While exploding the parts, you should rotate the view from time to time. Unless you are creating the explode for a particular point of view, the explode may look very different if you rotate it a little.

For the final explode step, the grippers will explode individually in opposite directions. Remember that these parts belong to another subassembly. If you create an explode step with the Select Sub-Assembly's Parts option turned off or on, you will not be able to change it later, and so you need to pay careful attention to what you are doing.

Turn on the Select Sub-Assembly's Parts option, select one gripper, Alt-drag the triad to set the direction, and then drag the distance of the explode. If you are in the mood to submit an enhancement request to SolidWorks, then you may want to request a Symmetrical Explode function for situations such as this. Figure 14.17 shows the finished result of the explode.

FIGURE 14.16

Exploding a subassembly

FIGURE 14.17

The finished explode

You may have noticed that each explode step creates a dashed line to show where the explode came from. Unfortunately, these dashed lines cannot be turned into usable explode lines on documentation. You must create explode lines manually, using 3D sketches. Although 3D sketches can be very tricky to use, for this purpose, you can limit their function to simple straight lines. As long as you try for simple results, the Explode Lines feature should work well.

Before I begin to discuss the Explode Lines feature, we should take a minute to look at the terminology, which can be confusing. For example, the opposite of *explode* is *collapse*. Unfortunately, the opposite of *expand* is also *collapse*, and so when the assembly is exploded and you want to collapse it, the RMB menu on the Exploded View displays one entry called Collapse and another called Collapse Items. You must remember that *Collapse Items* refers to expanded ConfigurationManager lists, while *Collapse* refers to un-exploding the Exploded View.

Another example is that the PropertyManager and Tooltips call the function *Route Line* (which can be easily confused with a function of the SolidWorks Routing software), but on the toolbar and menu, it is referred to as *Explode Sketch*. Further, the tool that you use to start the Explode Sketch function is on the Explode Sketch toolbar itself, and does not seem to exist on any other toolbar. You must access it from the Insert menu, by selecting the command called Explode Line Sketch. Figure 14.18 shows some examples of the above-mentioned terminology.

FIGURE 14.18

Interface and terminology inconsistencies in the exploded view and Explode Line functions

To initiate the Explode Line Sketch function, you can select Insert ➪ Explode Line Sketch. This displays the Explode Sketch toolbar and the Route Line PropertyManager interface. Creating nice explode lines takes a little practice, but it is easiest with circular parts, or circular features on parts with other shapes. Selecting circular edges makes the line start from the center of the circle.

If after you have selected two circular edges, the explode line goes the wrong way, you can click the arrow at the start of the line. Notice in Figure 14.19 that the line seems to take an unnecessarily circuitous route. This is because the explode directions were not square to the assembly Origin. To work around this problem to some extent, you can deselect the Along XYZ option in the Route Line PropertyManager. You can move the jogs by bringing the cursor close to the line, and selecting the arrows that pop up.

FIGURE 14.19

Redirecting explode lines

Figure 14.20 shows the difference between using the Along XYZ option (image to the left) and turning it off when the explode was not square to the assembly Origin (image to the right).

FIGURE 14.20

The Along XYZ option, selected and deselected

The completed explode lines are shown in Figure 14.21.

You can animate the explode or collapse from the RMB menu. To do this, right-click the exploded view, and select Animate Explode or Animate Collapse. This method does not offer recording or Photoworks rendering like Animator software, but it is fast and easy.

FIGURE 14.21

Completed explode lines

Tutorial: Working with Assembly Configurations

To begin this tutorial, open the assembly named Chapter 14 Bike.sldasm. This assembly is made from the same parts as the assembly that was used in Chapter 12, but it will be used differently here. This file contains all of the aspects that we need to work with in this chapter, including sub-assemblies, motion, and part configurations.

 NOTE   You can ignore the warning symbols in the BibleBikeFrame part file. These are caused by the Fill feature that is discussed in Chapter 27.

To learn how to work with assembly configurations, follow these steps:

1. Prepare to use configurations by splitting the FeatureManager window into an upper and lower pane. Place the FeatureManager on the top and the ConfigurationManager on the bottom.

2. Before starting to make changes to this assembly, add the top-level configurations that you will need, as follows:

   ▪ Small Tires

   ▪ Motion Configuration

■ Skeleton Driven Positions

■ Mate Driven Positions

The configurations will list alphabetically.

3. Make sure that the Advanced Options of each configuration are set to Suppress New Features And Mates and also Suppress New Components.

4. Activate the Small Tires configuration. Figure 14.22 shows the FeatureManager up to this point.

FIGURE 14.22

The FeatureManager and ConfigurationManager up to step 4

5. Open the Front Wheel Assembly in its own window and switch to the ConfigurationManager. Add a configuration called Small Tires, and change the tire to the configuration called Small Tire, which has already been created.

6. Switch back to the main assembly window (using Ctrl+Tab), RMB click the Front Wheel Assembly in the FeatureManager, and select Component Properties. Select the Default configuration for the Front Wheel assembly, as shown in Figure 14.23.

FIGURE 14.23

Changing the tires in the Component Properties dialog box

7. Repeat steps 4 to 6 for the Rear Wheel assembly.

8. Double-click another configuration from the list and watch the assembly change from small to fat tires.

9. Change to the Motion configuration. RMB click the Stem-Fork assembly, select Component Properties, and set the assembly to be solved as Flexible.

10. Exit the dialog box and check to see that the fork linkage mechanism moves by dragging the fork. Notice that the fork works but that the front wheel does not move with it. The bike design is not yet complete, and so you do not need to worry about that at this point.

11. Switch to the Skeleton Driven Positions configuration.

12. Display the assembly Layout Sketch at the top of the FeatureManager.

13. Create two new derived configurations under the Skeleton Driven Positions configuration, one called Default Position and the other called Compressed Position.

14. Activate the Default Position configuration, and make a coincident mate between the Top plane of the Chainstay part and the sketch line indicated in Figure 14.24.

15. Activate the Compressed Position configuration and make a coincident mate between the same plane and the line that is angled up at 10 degrees.

NOTE   For these configs you also need to set the Advanced options just as you set the top-level configs in step 3. If you do not do this, then you may need to manually suppress the unwanted mates in the appropriate configurations.

FIGURE 14.24

Positioning the rear of the bike

Mate to this line

16. Switch to the Mate Driven Position configuration.

17. Add new derived configurations called 1, 2, and 3. While creating the new configs, ensure that the Suppress New Features and Mates and Suppress New Components options are selected.

18. Make an angle mate between the Bike assembly Top plane and the face of the link, as shown in Figure 14.25.

FIGURE 14.25

Using angles to position the fork

19. Once the mate is complete, double-click the angle dimension (you may have to double-click the angle mate to get it to display and then zoom out to see it), and change the value to 18 degrees.

 You need to set the Fork assembly to solve as Flexible for each configuration. You may also need to control the alignment for the angle mate manually for each configuration.

Summary

Display States in the assembly can save a lot of time because they change faster than configurations and offer more options for visualization, including mixed display modes. You can save and copy multiple Display States between configurations. Assembly design tables can select Display States and drive many other parameters in assemblies.

The Exploded View functionality in SolidWorks has some unusual aspects that you need to work around; however, it is a valuable and useful function, and is worth the extra steps.

Chapter 15

Component Patterns

I n SolidWorks assemblies, the word *component* can refer to either parts or subassemblies at the top level of an assembly. Component patterns can therefore be patterns of parts, subassemblies, or combinations of parts and subassemblies.

PERFORMANCE For best pattern performance, you should use subassemblies as the patterned unit as much as is practical. Multiple patterns of individual components are not as efficient as a single pattern of multiple components. A single pattern of a single component, where the single component is itself a subassembly, is the best choice, if available.

Another performance issue is the fact that component patterns require external references (for the direction or center of the pattern). These external references have the potential to increase rebuild times if you do not choose them carefully.

Although you can experience possible performance problems with patterns, they can also significantly decrease the number of mates in an assembly, which always improves performance.

Component patterns come in two varieties: local patterns, which include linear and circular patterns, and derived patterns, which are driven from a feature pattern in a part. The local patterns are obviously somewhat limited, but because derived patterns follow patterned features, they can also be driven by sketch-driven patterns. Curve-driven and fill patterns cannot be used.

It is possible to focus only on the basics, to simply be able to make patterns that exist in the present moment. However, if you are interested in creating features that will adapt to future changes, then you will find this chapter useful.

Using Local Component Patterns

Local component patterns are limited to linear and circular patterns. The linear pattern directions work just like the linear pattern feature in parts, and must reference a line, axis, edge, and so on to establish the direction. In an assembly, this means that the feature uses model geometry from a part (solid or surface edges, sketches, reference geometry), an assembly sketch entity, or an assembly reference geometry entity (such as an axis). This is important to keep in mind if you are concerned about circular references.

BEST PRACTICE If you have a feature pattern in a part, you should take advantage of it and use a driven pattern instead of a local pattern.

Local pattern references

If you still need to create a local pattern, it is best to use a reference that is not dependent on part geometry. Remember that when part geometry is used for this purpose, the parts must be solved first (sketches and features rebuilt), then the mates must be solved (to position the parts), then any in-context references must be solved (which may change the part geometry), and then any assembly features or component patterns must be solved. As a result, it is best practice to use as pattern direction references, assembly sketches that do not reference anything else. The assembly sketches should sit at the top of the assembly FeatureManager to ensure that they are not picking up references from the history-based features in the design tree (mated components, patterns, assembly features, and so on).

When a local pattern really requires a reference from a part, you have no alternative. However, if you can avoid this by using a sketch assembly skeleton to which the parts are mated and also used for the pattern references, then you should do so. At all costs, you should avoid using in-context features, assembly reference geometry that is dependent on part geometry, and assembly features for the local pattern reference.

Figure 15.1 shows a sample organization of one way that you can set up an assembly to properly control local component patterns. The lines shown can be created in either two 2D sketches or a single 3D sketch. The lines are dimensioned from planes, which allows them to be angled for patterns that are not square to the coordinate system of the assembly, but still lie on its main planes.

In most situations the rebuild time penalty of using model geometry to establish pattern direction is fairly slight. The sketch method is probably most justifiable in large, complex, assemblies, or in assemblies requiring long rebuild times.

Figure 15.1 also shows the PropertyManager interface for the local pattern.

FIGURE 15.1

The Assembly FeatureManager for local component pattern setup

Notice where the pattern is placed in the FeatureManager. You can reorder the pattern feature in the design tree, but you cannot move it above the mates. Interestingly, you can move the sketches after the pattern, even though the pattern is dependent on one of the sketches. Obviously, SolidWorks is working with the order behind the scenes in such a way that the user cannot make mistakes.

Pattern Seed Only

All of the aspects of the interface should be familiar, such as the direction, instances, and spacing. The Pattern Seed Only option is also used in feature patterns.

Patterning the seed only is designed to allow you to create a single pattern in two directions that are separated by 180 degrees, where the internal instances do not overlap one another. For example, if you take a basic two-directional pattern and change the angle between the directions so that they are anti-parallel (parallel but going in opposite directions), then all of the component instances that were between the two legs of the L created by the two directions will come to overlap one another when they are laid out in a straight line.

Figure 15.2 shows how a 5-by-4 pattern with 20 instances becomes a 1-by-8 (the seed is not counted twice) pattern. When this happens, the other 12 instances are overlapping the remaining ones. When you use the Pattern Seed Only option, you are only patterning the two legs of the L, and not the instances in between. This can cause problems with BOMs and mass properties.

When to use the Pattern Seed Only option

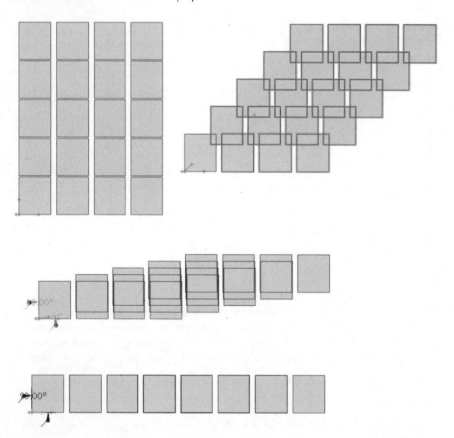

Instances to Skip

The Instances to Skip option for component patterns, shown in Figure 15.3, works just like the equivalent option for features. Click the dots in the graphics window to toggle each instance of the pattern.

FIGURE 15.3

The Instances to Skip option

Using Derived Component Patterns

Derived component patterns have two main limitations: they cannot be driven from either curve-driven or fill patterns. The remaining pattern types that work with derived component patterns are linear, circular, sketch driven, and table driven.

By their very nature, derived component patterns break some of the best practice suggestions in this book, because the pattern is driven by part geometry, and the part must first be solved (by solving features internal to the part) and then placed (by solving mates); only then can the derived pattern be solved. Still, I recommend using derived patterns over local patterns when available because of the parametric link.

NOTE   For the derived component patterns, the location of the initial component is important. You need to match the placement of the initial component with the position of the original feature from which the pattern was created, not one of the patterned instances.

Figure 15.4 shows the PropertyManager interface for a derived component pattern.

The Derived Component Pattern interface

You can nest derived component patterns such that one component pattern is patterned by another component pattern, just like feature patterns. The second pattern can be a local pattern or a derived pattern.

Understanding Other Pattern Options

Figure 15.5 shows the RMB menu for a component pattern.

The component RMB menu

Dissolve Pattern

The Dissolve Pattern option removes the component instances from the pattern feature and puts them in the main part of the assembly FeatureManager. The components just become normal components in the assembly without the intelligence of the pattern feature placing them. The components are left in the assembly without any mates, simply floating in position.

Add to new folder

You can add patterns to folders. If you have a list of patterns at the end of an assembly, it may make sense to group them into related folders for the purpose of organization. This is the same as using folders for features, mates, or components.

Component pattern display options

The individual component pattern instances can have their color and other display options changed individually or collectively as a pattern feature. Figure 15.6 shows the display pane where you can control these display options.

The display pane for controlling display options

Component patterns and configurations

Individual instances of the component pattern also enable you to control configurations. After you create the pattern, you can select individual instances and change their configs. This can be extremely useful if you have a mechanism subassembly shown in various positions, for example, patterned around an indexing dial.

Tutorial: Creating Component Patterns

To learn how to create component patterns, follow these steps:

1. Open a new assembly. Create a new sketch on the Top plane, with two lines from the Origin out at odd angles so that they do not pick up horizontal or vertical automatic relations.

2. Apply dimensions between one of the lines and the Right plane, and set the angle to zero degrees.

3. Apply a second dimension to the other line from the Front plane, again with an angle of zero degrees.

4. Open the part from the CD-ROM named Chapter 15 Pattern Part.sldprt. This part already contains several features so that you can practice using derived component patterns.

5. Insert the part into a new assembly. Locate the part at the assembly Origin such that the part Origin matches the assembly Origin.

6. Open the part called Chapter 15 Patterned Part.sldprt, and place it in the assembly. Remember that it is important to match the part up with the original patterned feature, and not to just place it on any instance of the feature pattern. The original features are colored red in the part.

NOTE   Under normal circumstances, the patterned instances are the same color as the patterned feature because of the Propagate Visual Properties setting, which is turned on by default in all of the pattern feature types. For this part, I turned this setting off for each pattern feature so that the original feature could be a different color than the rest of the pattern.

One notable exception to this is the Table Driven Pattern, which appears to have a bug: if you turn off the Propagate Visual Properties setting and exit the feature, it just turns it back on. In this case, the hole colors were changed by changing face colors rather than feature colors.

7. Place the part on one of the original features. Remember that Alt-dragging the circular edge on the flat side of the part allows you to SmartMate the part to the round holes. It cannot help you with the rectangular or hex holes. For these, it may be best to show the sketch for the holes and place the part with respect to the sketch entities.

8. Create feature driven patterns (Insert ➪ Component Pattern ➪ Feature Driven). Try to use each of the patterns from the pattern part. Notice that the fill pattern gives a specific error that it cannot be used for a derived pattern, but the curve-driven pattern does not. This may mean that in some situations you can use the curve-driven pattern to drive a component pattern, or it may just be another interface inconsistency.

9. Once you have created a few feature-driven patterns and have a better understanding of how it is done, you can create a local pattern (Insert ➪ Component Pattern ➪ Linear Pattern).

10. Select the sketch line that was drawn in the Z direction as the direction.

11. RMB click the top level of the assembly FeatureManager and select Collapse Items. Highlight the Components to Pattern selection box. Select the first part in the FeatureManager and then Shift-select the last pattern feature. This patterns everything in the assembly.

12. Make the spacing four inches with three instances.

13. Create a second direction using another of the sketch lines with six-inch spacing and four instances.

14. Notice how the preview shows 12 instances of the patterned assembly. Click the option for Pattern Seed Only and see how the preview changes to seven instances. Click OK to accept the feature.

15. Change the zero-degree angle in the sketch created in steps 1 through 3, to 30 degrees. You may have to press Ctrl+Q to get the assembly to update properly.

Summary

Performance and best practice are both issues that require compromise. Patterns can cause a performance reduction because of the nature of the references. However, they can also improve performance because the need for extra mates is reduced and it is easier to simplify the assembly by suppressing the pattern feature.

Derived patterns are driven by feature patterns, and transgress more best practice suggestions, but they also add a parametric link, which updates the component pattern automatically.

Chapter 16

Modeling in Context

I n-context modeling offers a gateway to a world of expanded modeling possibilities in SolidWorks. The topic of in-context modeling is often a source of sometimes questionable advice and suggestions from even experienced users. In this chapter, I offer a balanced explanation with each suggestion so that you can evaluate the suggestion for yourself.

If you are well disciplined in your modeling practices, and understand the potential problems of in-context modeling, then you can avoid these problems. After one bad experience, some users focus on this experience, and fail to see the positive side of using in-context modeling. Although dangers *do* exist, they often result from disregarding the rules.

Understanding In-Context Design

In-context modeling is also known as top-down modeling. It is a technique that is used to create relationships between two parts in an assembly, where the geometry of one of the parts is controlled by both the other part and the mates that position them relative to one another.

In-context, or top-down, modeling may be contrasted against *bottom-up* modeling. Bottom-up modeling involves making the parts in their own individual windows and assembling the finished parts into an assembly with mates.

In its most common form, a sketch in one part in an assembly is related to another part in the assembly. The relationship is specific to that particular assembly, and is only relevant *in the context of* that assembly. For example, you may create a box and put it into an assembly. You must then create a lid that is parametrically linked to the size and shape of the box. You can create a lid part in the context of the assembly such that the lid always matches the box. Sketch relationships, dimensions, and feature end conditions from the lid can reference the box. When the box changes, the lid also changes *if the assembly is open*.

The assembly maintains a record of the reference. If the box is changed with both the assembly and the top open, then the top updates, but if the box is changed without the assembly being open, then the lid will not update until the assembly is opened. The record of the reference that the assembly maintains is held in what is called an *update holder*, and in recent versions, it is all but forgotten.

CROSS-REF Chapter 12 discusses in-context reference update holders. These are the pointers in the assembly that hold the reference information. These holders are hidden by default, and do not enable any real functionality, but they do serve as a reminder that the assembly has in-context references, and can be queried to tell you what parts the in-context relations go between.

Advantages of in-context modeling

The advantages of in-context modeling are obvious. I spent the first couple of chapters of this book discussing the strengths of parametric design, and in-context modeling is just an extension of parametric techniques to include parts in the context of an assembly. Making a change to one part and having all related parts update offers indisputable advantages.

Potential problems with in-context modeling

There may also be some issues that arise from this technique of driving changes from a different part model. There are no problems with the *overall concept* of in-context modeling; the problems occur with the *practical application of the technique*. In particular, the biggest problems seem to arise when in-context techniques are combined with other techniques. You must be very careful about file management issues when in-context references exist in your assembly.

Dealing with the Practical Details of In-Context Modeling

Figure 16.1 shows a simple box with the sketch of a simple top for the box. Notice in the FeatureManager that two parts are listed as the Box Top and Box Bottom. The .050-inch offset is creating a sketch in the Top part that is driven by the edges of the Bottom part. This simple assembly demonstrates the in-context process in the sections that follow.

Modeling in Context 16

The top of the box being built in-context

.050

The in-context process

You can perform in-context modeling using one of two basic schemes. You can build parts from the very beginning in the context of the assembly (using the Insert ➪ Component ➪ New Part menu option) or you can start them using bottom-up techniques creating the parts in a separate part window, add them to the assembly, and then add additional in-context features later.

Starting out in-context

To start a new part in the context of an assembly, we will first assume that the assembly contains another part. Creating a new part in a blank assembly is not very interesting. In this case, I am using the assembly shown in Figure 16.1. Once the first part is in the assembly, you must save the assembly before creating a new part in it. This is because the update holder needs to reference a particular filename, and the assembly has no filename until you save it.

To create the new part, click Insert ➪ Component ➪ New Part. This command is also available through a toolbar button that you can place on the Assembly toolbar (it is not there by default). At this point, SolidWorks prompts you to first name the part, and then select a face or plane on which to locate the new part. The selected face or plane actually determines the Front plane of the new part, and a mate is added to the assembly.

The InPlace mate

The mate that you are adding is called an *InPlace* mate. This works like the Fixed option, but is actually a mate that is listed with the other mates and that may be deleted, but not edited.

477

The InPlace mate clamps the part down to any face or plane where it is applied. It is meant to prevent the in-context part from moving. I will explain later in this chapter why it is so important for in-context parts not to move. Although the InPlace mate clamps the part down, I have heard people report bizarre behaviors with the InPlace mate reportedly allowing parts to move unpredictably, but I do not put any stock in these reports. The cause of things such as this usually turns out to be a user who is not paying attention to what is going on.

> **NOTE**   Software is a very deterministic system, where everything happens for a reason. However, if a face on which an InPlace mate has been created is moved by the part changing, then the in-context part could possibly move in a way that you might not predict. The problem is that while the Front plane of the in-context part is defined with respect to the selected face, it is not explicitly defined rotationally about an axis perpendicular to the face, or translationally about axes parallel to the face.

Alternative technique

If you are concerned about using the InPlace mate, then I would suggest an alternative technique. Instead of using the Insert ➪ Component ➪ New Part command, you should simply create a blank part and save it to the desired location. You can then insert the existing but blank part into the assembly and mate the three planes to the assembly or to the part, as appropriate. You can then edit the part in-context, the same as if you had created it in-context. The only difference between parts developed this way and parts created in-context is the InPlace mate. The InPlace mate cannot be edited and does not have relations to other geometry in the usual sense. Many people feel more secure with real mates to real geometry, which can be identified and changed if necessary.

Valid relations

Sketches, edges, and faces from the other parts in the assembly can be referenced from the in-context part as if they were in the same part as the sketch. Most common relations are concentric for holes, and coincident for hole centers. Converted entities (On-Edge relations) make a line-on-edge relation between the parts, and Offset sketch relations are also often used.

Other types of valid in-context relations include in-context sketch planes, and end conditions for extrude features such as Up to Face and Up to Body. Beyond that, you can copy surfaces from one part using the Knit Surface feature, or the Offset Surface feature. I discuss surfacing in more detail in Chapter 27.

Working in-context

When working in-context or using in-context data, visual cues offer information about the part that you are working on. The following topics are all meant to help you understand what is going on.

Text color

When modeling in-context, the FeatureManager text of the part that you are working on turns blue. This should make it immediately obvious first that you are working in-context, and second, which part is being edited.

Part color and transparency

Color and transparency behavior of parts in the assembly where a part is being edited in-context can be controlled through the Tools ⇨ Options ⇨ Colors page. Figure 16.2 shows a detail of this page. Appendix B discusses Tools ⇨ Options settings in more detail. The option at the bottom of the dialog determines whether the colors specified in the list at the top are used or ignored. If they are ignored, the parts retain the same colors as if you were not using in-context techniques.

FIGURE 16.2

Part-color settings for in-context control

An additional setting in Tools ⇨ Options is found on the Display/Selection pane. Here, you can control the transparency of the parts not being edited. Figure 16.3 shows this setting.

FIGURE 16.3

Part transparency for in-context control

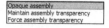

In-context part color transparency control

The options in the Assembly Transparency drop-down list are:

- **Opaque Assembly:** All parts that are not being edited when an assembly component is being edited in-context will turn opaque, even if they are otherwise transparent.

- **Maintain Assembly Transparency:** Leaves all assembly components in their default transparency state.

- **Force Assembly Transparency:** Forces all of the parts, except for the one being edited in the assembly, to become transparent.

These options reflect personal preference more than anything else, but it is useful to have a reminder as to whether a part is being edited in the assembly or the assembly document is being edited in its own window.

 TIP The color selected in the box shown in Figure 16.2 controls both the text color and the color of the part shown in the graphics window.

Edit Component button

 You can use the Edit Component button in two ways. First, after you have created a part in-context, seeing the Edit Component button depressed serves as a reminder that you are editing the part rather than editing the assembly. Along with the part color and transparency displays, this is important because assembly functions such as mates, exploded views, and others are not available when you are editing the part.

The second use of the Edit Component button is to begin or finish editing a part that is already in an assembly. When you are editing a part in the context of an assembly, the title bar of the SolidWorks window reflects the fact that you are editing a part in an assembly, the toolbar changes to a part-editing toolbar, and the lower-right corner of the taskbar displays the words *Editing Part*, as shown in Figure 16.4.

FIGURE 16.4

Indicators that you are editing a part in-context

Editing a component can also mean editing a subassembly in the context of the top-level assembly. You can create in-context assembly features and mates if necessary. This is done far less frequently than editing parts in-context.

NOTE Creating in-context relations is not the only reason to edit a part or subassembly in the context of the top-level assembly. Sometimes it is simply more convenient to do normal editing when you are in the top-level assembly, so that you can see how the part relates to other parts after making changes in the assembly without making relations between the parts.

Editing a subassembly in the context of the upper-level assembly is often useful as well, to see how changing subassembly mates affects the top level.

Probably the most common mistake that users make around the issue of editing the part versus editing the assembly is when they add a sketch. If you intend to add a sketched feature to a part in the context of an assembly, but you fail to switch to Edit Part mode before creating the sketch, then the sketch ends up in the assembly rather than the part; you can only do limited things with a sketch in an assembly. Likewise, if you intend to make an assembly layout sketch, but you do not switch out of Edit Part mode, then you end up with a sketch in a part that cannot do what you want it to do.

External reference symbol

The external reference symbol appears as a dash followed by a greater-than sign. External references do not only indicate in-context features. You can also create external references by using the Split Part command as well as the Insert Part (base or derived part) or the mirrored part functions. Figure 16.5 shows the expanded FeatureManager for a part with an in-context reference in a sketch.

External references can have four states, which are also shown in Figure 16.5. These are:

- In-context
- Out-of-context
- Locked reference
- Broken reference

FIGURE 16.5

The in-context "carrot" on Extrude1 and Sketch1

In-context

I have already discussed the in-context relationship earlier in this chapter.

Out-of-context

Out-of-context means that the document — usually but not necessarily an assembly — where the reference was created is not open at the time. It is indicated by an in-context symbol followed by a question mark. You can open the document where the reference was created through the RMB menu, using the Edit In Context option. Edit In Context opens either the parent part of an inserted part, or the assembly where the reference was created. When you open the referencing document, the out-of-context symbol changes to the in-context symbol.

Locked reference

You can lock external references so that the model does not change. Other features of the part may be changed, but any external reference within the part remains the way it is until the reference is either unlocked or removed. In our Box-and-Top example mentioned earlier, this means that if the Bottom part is changed, and the external reference on the Top is locked, then the Top will no longer fit the Bottom.

One of the best things about locked references is that you can unlock them. They are also flexible and give you control over when updates take place to parts with locked references.

Broken reference

The broken reference is another source of controversy. Some users believe that if you make in-context references, the best way to respond to them is to break them immediately. However, I would argue that using the Break References function is *never* a good thing to do. I believe that you should remove the reference by editing the feature or the sketch or change it to make it useful.

The problem with a broken reference is that it has absolutely no advantage over a locked reference. For example, while locked references can at least be unlocked, broken references cannot be repaired. The only thing that you can do with a broken reference is to use Display/Delete Relations or to manually edit features to completely remove the external reference. Perhaps it would be better for SolidWorks to replace Break References with a function called *Remove References*. Would anyone like to make an enhancement request?

BEST PRACTICE Best practice is to not put yourself in a situation where you are using either locked or broken references. Parametric relations should not change if the driving geometry does not change. Again, as is typical with CAD software, things may happen that you cannot explain, but there is always a reason for it (even if it is not immediately apparent).

You cannot selectively lock or break external relations. For example, all of the external relations in the part can be locked, all of the external relations can be broken, or none of them can be locked or broken. If you need to selectively disable relations, then you should consider suppressing features, sketch relations, end conditions, or sketch planes.

List External References

You can access the locked and broken references through the List External References option on the RMB menu of any feature with an external reference symbol. Figure 16.6 shows the name and path of the assembly where the external reference was created, as well as the part names and entity types.

FIGURE 16.6

The External References dialog box

No External References

The No External References button on the Assembly toolbar is also available through Tools ⇨ Options ⇨ External References ⇨ Do Not Create References External To The Model. As its name suggests, this setting prevents external relations from being created between parts in an assembly. When you offset in-context edges or use Convert Entities, the resulting sketch entities are created without relations of any type.

This lack of references includes the InPlace mate, which is not created when a part is created in-context. As a result, when you add the part to the assembly, if you exit and later re-enter Edit Part mode, then SolidWorks reminds you that the part is not fixed in space by displaying the warning shown in Figure 16.7.

FIGURE 16.7

The dialog box that warns you about adding in-context relations to an under-defined part

This message should remind you that in-context features should be used only on parts that are fully positioned in the assembly.

External reference settings in Tools, Options

The Tools ⇨ Options ⇨ External References pane of settings controls many aspects of the behavior of external references. You can find a full description of all of the options in Appendix B; however, I will discuss two of these options in this section. I have discussed one of these references earlier — No External References — and I discuss the other feature, Multiple Contexts, next. This page in the Tools ⇨ Options dialog box is shown in Figure 16.8.

FIGURE 16.8

The Tools ⇨ Options ⇨ External References pane

In-context best practice suggestions

In-context techniques are most frequently misused by beginning to intermediate users. Many users purchase the software because of the promise of parametric relationships between parts. However, this is a technique that requires a fair amount of discipline, restraint, and judgment.

The potential problems associated with overuse or misuse of in-context techniques primarily include performance problems (speed) and lost references due to file management issues. Users may also experience problems with features or sketches that change with each rebuild. The following section contains best practice suggestions that can help you avoid these situations.

Multiple contexts

Multiple contexts occur when a part has references that are created in multiple assemblies. By default, multiple contexts are prevented from happening. If you place a part that already has external references into a different assembly, a warning appears, as shown in Figure 16.9.

The warning message that appears about multiple contexts

Although SolidWorks displays many warnings about multiple contexts, you may still run into situations where you need to use them. For example, you may have a subassembly where a part, such as a top plate of a stand, has in-context references to locate a set of mounting holes. When you place the subassembly into the top-level assembly and mount another assembly to the top plate, another set of in-context holes is required in the top plate.

Figure 16.10, at the top, shows the first table and points out the in-context relations. At the bottom, the large bracket appears for the other machine that is mounted to the table top using more in-context relations. In Figure 16.11 are the External References dialog boxes for the two different in-context features. Notice that the Assembly fields at the top of the External References dialog boxes are different. You can only achieve this by activating the Allow Multiple Contexts for Parts When Editing in Assembly option shown in Figure 16.8.

FIGURE 16.10

Using multiple contexts

FIGURE 16.11

External References dialog boxes

NOTE   The Tools ➪ Options setting for multiple contexts is a system option. This means that this option is either on or off for every document on a single machine, but when the assembly is used on another machine, the option is off. Rather than always leaving this option on for all documents on a given computer, I think it would be best if it were a document-specific option that traveled with the document, rather than sticking to the machine — another possible enhancement request.

BEST PRACTICE   The best practice is to avoid creating multiple-context references. If you need to do this, then be very careful about naming files, and remember to turn off the multiple-context option when you have finished creating the reference.

If you receive a multiple-context part from someone else, the best thing to do is to determine whether you have all of the files required to make it work. RMB click the external reference symbol and select Edit In Context to determine whether SolidWorks can find the right files.

Aside from doing some programming, the only way to find out whether a part was created as a multiple-context part is to examine the External References list for each in-context feature. This can be very time-consuming. Although multiple-context parts should be very rare, it is impossible to determine ahead of time whether or not a part that you have received is a multiple-context part, at least without programming.

I once worked on a part that had both some in-context and some out-of-context features. Of course, this looks strange when you realize what you are looking at because in most situations, if any references are out-of-context, all references will be out of context. After some examination, I discovered that there were multiple contexts, which were created because of poor file management. The assembly had changed names slightly, and caused the original in-context relations to not be recognized. I will discuss in-context relations and file naming later in this chapter.

In-context with configurations

On the surface, mixing in-context references with configurations sounds like it is combining two powerful techniques that should offer you great control over models. Although this may sometimes be true, I want to caution you about some of the effects that combining these two techniques may cause. In particular, you should be careful about part configurations, particularly configurations of the *referenced* part.

If you are using in-context relations to parts with configurations, then you may want to consider a few things. First, look at the door-hinge part shown in Figure 16.12. At the top are three configurations of one of the hinge plates. The second hinge plate is built in the context of the assembly so that it will always match the first plate. At the bottom are the results of changing the first hinge-plate part configuration in the assembly. This looks like an ideal situation because the second hinge plate always changes to match the first hinge plate. What could be wrong with this?

The problem here is that you can only show the size of the second hinge plate that corresponds to the configuration of the first plate that is active in the assembly. If you had two instances of the hinge assembly in a top-level assembly, then you would be able to show only one size for the second plate.

A second situation where combining in-context references and configurations can cause you trouble is if you have referenced the edges of a part from another part, and a configuration of the referenced part either adds or removes fillets or chamfers, thus breaking the edges. Either of these situations can cause the in-context sketches or other features to fail. This may be a reason to reference the underlying sketches, rather than the model edges or faces themselves.

In some situations, configurations work well with in-context relations. One example of this would be when an assembly has many configurations used for positioning parts. Use one configuration for the sole purpose of creating in-context relations.

FIGURE 16.12

Combining in-context references with configurations

In-context with motion

You should make in-context references between parts where there is no relative motion. The parts themselves can move relative to the rest of the assembly, but they should remain stationary relative to one another. The parts should also be fully defined to ensure that they will not move; you should not simply count on avoiding dragging underdefined parts.

In some cases, such as an assembly of imported parts, it may make sense to fix parts in bulk rather than to mate them. When you are using in-context relations, you need to take extra care to ensure that the parts do not move around. When parts move around, in-context features also move.

Obviously, if the motion is around a hole, and the in-context feature is circular and is not affected by the rotation of the referenced part, then it makes less difference; however, if there is a keyway, that may change things. You need to pay attention when combining underdefined parts and in-context features.

 For best practice, you should avoid in-context relations between parts when relative motion is allowed between these parts.

In-context with multiple instances

Another situation that can cause problems is when multiple instances of an in-context part are being used in the assembly. In cases like this, you need to be careful and consistent, by always using the same instance to create the in-context relations. You can do this by putting parts into folders, or giving the in-context part a special component color.

In-context and file management

Understanding what you are doing with file management is imperative when working with parts that depend on in-context features. Because the references are stored in both the part that is doing the referencing and the assembly where the reference is created, improperly changing the name of either document is bound to cause problems. For example, if you rename an in-context part using Windows Explorer, then the assembly will not recognize the part, as demonstrated in an earlier chapter. This also means that any in-context references will not update.

BEST PRACTICE For best practice, you should use either the SolidWorks Save As command or SolidWorks Explorer to rename parts and assemblies.

In-context and mates

This was mentioned earlier, but a section on in-context best practices would not be complete without issuing the warning against mating to in-context features. Mating parts to in-context features creates a parametric daisy chain, thus establishing an order in which assembly features and mates must be solved. This always creates performance problems in assemblies, especially large ones.

Circular references

Circular references in assemblies are a bigger problem than most people realize. In fact, most people do not realize that circular references *are* a problem, or, for that matter, that they even exist.

A circular reference takes the form of "Part A references Part B, which references Part A." It creates a circular loop that really wrecks assembly rebuild times. Part feature design trees are not susceptible to this sort of looping because the part FeatureManager operates in a linear fashion (at least when it comes to applying relations between sketches or features).

The Assembly FeatureManager is solved in this order, or an order that is very similar:

1. Solve reference geometry and sketches that are listed before parts in order, at the top of the design tree.

2. Rebuild individual parts as necessary.

3. Solve the mates and locate the parts.

4. Solve in-context features in parts.

5. Solve reference geometry and sketches listed after the mates.

6. Solve assembly features and component patterns.

7. Loop to step 3 to solve mates that are connected to anything that was solved after the first round on the mates.

8. Continue to loop until complete.

As you can see, even if you do not have a reference such as "Part A references Part B, which references Part A," it is still possible to get a highly convoluted, if not entirely circular, loop. Many users with smaller assemblies in the hundreds of parts complain about very poor performance. Unfortunately, it is far easier to complain than to really examine what is going on.

Skeletons and layouts

When making in-context references, a technique that can help you avoid circular references is to always create references to parts that are higher in the design tree. You can expand on this idea until a single entity is at the top of the design tree, to which all in-context references are made. This could take the form of an Assembly Layout Sketch, or a skeleton. These concepts are discussed in chapters 11, 12, and 13.

Remember that the layout sketch consists of a single or even multiple sketches that control the overall layout of the assembly, as well as all of the relationships between parts. When you refer all of the relations to a single entity that does not change with part configurations, or lose or gain filleted edges, the inter-part parametrics become much stronger and more stable.

When building a mold for plastic injection molding, a single sketch can control the size and position of the plates, pins, and so on. If all of the 3D parts are mated to the 2D sketch, or use the 2D sketch by converted entities, then the parts will move with the sketch. This same technique is important and useful for any type of die or punch design, along with many other types of design.

In-context and libraries

Library parts should never contain in-context references, especially if the in-context references are out-of-context. Small library assemblies may have in-context references between the parts, but a single part should not have features created in-context. External references may be unavoidable in the form of mirrored or base parts, but in-context references are completely avoidable.

Removing relations

 You can remove relations by using the Display/Delete Relations tool. You can sort the relations by selecting the Defined In Context option, as shown in Figure 16.13.

FIGURE 16.13

Sorting sketch relations by type

If you are considering using the Break Relations tool, then you should either reconsider and use Lock Relations instead, or simply remove all of the in-context relations altogether.

Other types of in-context references are not as easy to remove as sketch relations. When you see the External Reference symbol on a sketch, it could be the sketch relations, or it could be the sketch plane that was in-context. In order to fix this problem, you must redefine the plane locally in the part.

TIP   You can make a local plane from an existing in-context plane (or even just a 3D view) by using the following workaround. Looking normal to the view, open a 3D sketch, and draw three sketch points that do not pick up automatic sketch relations to anything else. Once the points are drawn, select all three of them and make them coincident. Then delete the coincident relation and drag the points apart. The three points come out on a plane that is parallel to the plane of the screen. Next, simply make a three-point plane.

You should also not forget end conditions such as Up To Surface, Offset From Surface, or even From Surface. If an external reference symbol remains on a feature, you can use the Parent/Child option on the RMB menu to locate it. Remember that using an edge or vertex for a plane definition can cause an in-context relation.

Should you use mating or in-context?

You should not become too enthusiastic about in-context relations. This can cause you to do things such as using in-context relations to locate parts, or using in-context instead of mating parts.

In-context modeling is like chocolate: a little is a wonderful thing, but too much can be bad for you. You should only use in-context to locate or size features. In-context is initially so fast and easy to use that it can be addictive, but you need to think before you use it.

Communicating design intent

If someone else needs to use your model after you are done with it and possibly edit it, then you should leave them some clues to help them understand how the model works, and how it is best changed. For example, you can use descriptive feature and sketch names, comments that are associated with features, the Design Binder to add documentation, and the Design Journal to write notes. You can even put HTML links in notes that display in the graphics window.

In-context design intent may not always be obvious, and an impatient user may find it more expedient to delete the in-context references and replace them with either local relations or no relations at all. The more you document your intent, the more likely others will be to follow it.

Other Types of External References

The external reference symbol (- >) indicates in-context features that have been created in the context of an assembly, but it also indicates three other types of external references:

- Inserted parts
- Split parts
- Mirrored parts

Inserted parts

Inserted parts are discussed to some extent in Chapter 10, and in more detail in Chapter 28. In the past, inserted parts have also been called base parts and derived parts, and some users still use those names.

An inserted part is simply an entire part that has been inserted into another part. This is sometimes referred to as a *pull* operation because the data is pulled from the original part into the child part. The part may be inserted at any point in the history of the design tree, and it may create an additional body within the part or be added to the existing one. Additional features can also be added to the inserted part, but you cannot see or change any of the features of the part that has been added from the downstream document. The inserted part becomes much like an imported, or *dumb*, solid.

Items that can be brought along with the inserted part are solid bodies, surface bodies, planes, and axes. You cannot bring features or sketches. You can use a particular configuration of the inserted part in the child part. I discuss this aspect in Chapter 14, dealing with configurations, and also in Chapter 28.

You can use inserted parts for many modeling applications, such as cast parts and secondary operations. You first insert the original cast part into a new blank part. Then, you add cut and hole features until the part resembles the finished part.

Another application for inserted parts is a single part that has been built from several models. For example, I once worked on a large, rather complicated plastic basket, where the basket was modeled as three individual parts, and then reassembled into a single part. Another application may be to insert a part as a body into a mold block to create a mold cavity. To insert a part into another part, you can select Insert, Part.

Split parts

I discuss split parts in detail in Chapter 28, in the section about master models. Inserted and split parts are both master model techniques, as are a few more techniques that I discuss in Chapter 28. Some people also include in-context techniques with the master model tools because this is a way of making several parts update together.

Split parts are sometimes called a *push* operation because the data is pushed from the original part to the children parts. The *split* function takes a single body and splits it into several bodies, optionally saving the bodies out as individual parts. This is done for various reasons, such as creating a single, smooth shape out of several different parts, for example, automobile body panels or the various covers and buttons on a computer mouse. You can use the split parts technique for other applications as well. Sometimes a product is designed as a simple, single solid to keep the modeling simple, and because it is not known how the parts will be assembled or manufactured. When the manufacturing decisions are made, the part can be split into several models that have the engineering details added to them.

Mirror parts

You can mirror a right-handed part to create a left-handed part. To activate the Mirror Part command, you must select a plane or planar face. Then, select Insert ➪ Mirror Part to initiate the Mirror Part command.

Mirror parts can also use configurations, and so if you have one of those "mirrored exactly except for . . ." parts, you can select the configuration of the parent from the child document.

Tutorial: Working In-Context

Follow these steps to get a feel for the workflow of working with parts in the context of an assembly:

1. Open the assembly named Chapter 16 Tutorial Assembly.sldasm.

2. Set the colors that are to be used during in-context editing. Remember that two settings control this — one at Tools ➪ Options ➪ Colors, and the other at Tools ➪ Options ➪ Display/Selection, as shown in Figure 16.14.

FIGURE 16.14

Setting in-context colors

Set the Assembly, Edit Part color to a shade of blue, and the Assembly, Non-Edit Parts to a shade of gray.

Also set the Assembly Transparency for In Context Edit setting to Force Assembly Transparency, with the slider at around 90 percent.

3. Now you are ready to begin. Select the Table Top part, and click the Edit Component button on the Assembly toolbar. This command is also available through both the RMB menu and the drop-down menu as Edit Part. (If you RMB click a subassembly, the Edit Subassembly option becomes available.) Notice that the Table Top part and the FeatureManager text turn the same color.

4. Expand the Table Top part in the Assembly FeatureManager, select the Front plane, and open a new sketch on it. Notice that you cannot select the edges of the transparent parts through the transparency, even if the Select Through Transparency option is turned on (Tools ➪ Options ➪ Display/Selection). This setting applies only to faces, not to edges. Instead, change the display mode for the entire assembly to Wireframe.

5. Now select the 16 hole edges on the legs. It does not matter whether you select the top edges or the bottom, or even a combination of top and bottom. Use the Convert Entities command to project the edges into the sketch plane as circles, as shown in Figure 16.15.

FIGURE 16.15

Converting entities in-context

6. Create a cut that goes Through All. You may have to change the direction of the extrude to get it to work. Save the tutorial assembly.

7. Now open the file named Chapter 16 Tutorial Machine Assembly.sldasm. Notice that the Table Top part in this assembly is using the Wireframe display state, which is assigned in the Display pane.

8. RMB click the part and select Edit Part from the list, or select the part and click the Edit Component button on the toolbar. A warning will display that the part has features that were created in the context of another assembly. You can edit the part, but you cannot add any more external references (in-context features) to it.

9. Toggle off the Edit Component button on the Assembly toolbar to exit Edit Part mode.

10. In Tools ⇨ Options ⇨ External References, select the Allow Multiple Contexts for Parts When Editing in Assembly option. Now try to edit the Table Top part again in the context of the assembly. This time, no warning message displays.

11. Make sure that you are editing the Table Top part. It will not change colors as specified in the Tools ⇨ Options ⇨ Colors settings because it is using the Wireframe display mode. Ensure that the status bar in the lower-right corner displays *Editing Part* rather than *Editing Assembly*.

12. Open a sketch on the Front plane, and convert the four edges of the holes, as shown in Figure 16.16.

FIGURE 16.16

Creating holes in-context

13. Cut the holes using the Through All setting. Again, be aware of the direction of the cuts. Toggle out of Edit Component mode and press Ctrl+S to save the assembly. Figure 16.17 shows the finished assembly.

FIGURE 16.17

The assembly as of step 13

14. Open the Machine Base Bracket part in its own window by selecting Open Part from the RMB menu. The part is shown in Figure 16.18.

FIGURE 16.18

The Machine Base Bracket part, ready for mirroring

15. Select the Front plane and select Insert ⇨ Mirror Part. This creates a new part and opens a new PropertyManager interface, as shown in Figure 16.19.

FIGURE 16.19

The Mirror Part PropertyManager

In this case, you do not need to add any of the items in the list, and so you can deselect any that are selected and click OK.

Figure 16.19 shows the Locate Part panel of the Mirror Part PropertyManager. This panel does not appear when the feature is first created, although it probably should. This screen capture was taken with SolidWorks 2007 sp1.1, 32-bit version.

You can use Locate Part to move the part once it is inserted. If you do not use it, then the part is just positioned using its mirror plane. For this reason, it is best practice to mirror about one of the standard planes.

Also note that the template used for this part was chosen based on the settings at Tools ➪ Options ➪ Default Templates ➪ Always Use These Default Document Templates or Prompt User To Select Document Template.

16. Notice that the new part is indeed a mirrored copy of the original. You can see that the "MADE IN USA" text on the bottom is backwards. Fortunately, a configuration exists specifically for this purpose. Change the configuration by selecting For Mirroring in the Configuration Name drop-down list in the External References dialog box, as shown in Figure 16.20. Notice that this configuration removes the extruded text from the model.

FIGURE 16.20

Selecting a configuration

17. Add your own "MADE IN . . ." extruded text to the bottom of the part. Save the part.

Summary

Although in-context functions are powerful and seductive, you should use them sparingly. In particular, be careful about file management issues such as renaming parts and assemblies. The best approach is to use SolidWorks Explorer or the Save As command with both the parts and assemblies open.

Other external references include inserted parts, split parts, and mirror parts. These types of external references are often used in discussions on master models, which I address in a later chapter.

Part IV

Creating and Using Libraries

Chapter 17

Using Hole Wizard and Toolbox

The Hole Wizard and Toolbox are two applications that go together because of the information they share; they both work from a single database of matching hole and screw sizes. One of the most useful examples of combining these two applications is the ability to automatically place holes through multiple parts and put appropriately sized screws and hardware into the holes, all in one step. The hole knows which fastener or stack of fasteners needs to go together.

IN THIS CHAPTER

Using the Hole Wizard

Understanding Toolbox

Tutorial: Gaining experience with the Hole Wizard and Toolbox

Using the Hole Wizard

The Hole Wizard enables you to place holes for many types of screws with normal, loose, or tight fits. You can create Hole Wizard holes as assembly features in an assembly or as features in individual parts that are built in the context of an assembly using the Series Hole functionality.

This tool is called a *wizard* because it guides you through the process step by step. The process of creating a Hole Wizard hole can be summarized as follows:

- Pre-select the face to put the holes on, although this is not required. This turns out to be an important issue that is related to the type of placement sketch, and I revisit this subject later.

- Select the type of hole, for example, counterbored, countersunk, drilled hole, tapped hole, pipe tap, or legacy.

- Set the standard to be used, such as ANSI inch, ANSI metric, or ISO.

- Select the type of screw. For example, a counterbored hole can accommodate a socket head cap screw or a hex head screw, among others.

- Select the size of the screw.

- Select the fit of the screw into the hole, such as normal, loose, or tight.

- Select the end condition of the hole.

- Select options for clearance and countersinks or edge breaks.

- Alternatively, you can use or assign a Favorite. A favorite is a hole with settings that you use frequently and want to save. These are discussed later in this chapter.

- You can use Custom Sizing when you need a hole with non-standard dimensions.

- Locate the center of the hole or holes. You can place multiple holes in a single Hole Wizard feature, even on different faces and curved faces. I address the specifics of this step later in this chapter.

- Click OK to accept the type, size, and placement of the hole.

The Hole Wizard PropertyManager interface is shown in Figure 17.1.

FIGURE 17.1

The Hole Wizard PropertyManager Interface

Anatomy of a Hole Wizard hole

Hole Wizard holes are made of two sketches: a center placement sketch and a revolved cut profile. Figure 17.2 shows a simple part with an expanded Hole Wizard feature. Notice that the feature is named for the size and type of the hole.

FIGURE 17.2

A design tree containing a Hole Wizard hole

> **NOTE**   Another useful aspect of naming the hole feature is that if you change the type or size through the Hole Wizard interface, the name changes to match.

If you create a Hole Wizard feature with more than one hole, there is still just a single revolved sketch. A multiple-hole Hole Wizard feature works similar to making a revolved cut and using a Sketch Driven feature pattern to create the multiple instances.

Placement sketch

The placement sketch is listed first under the Hole Wizard feature. It has one or more sketch points marking the hole centers. It may also contain construction geometry with relations and dimensions to fully locate the hole centers. Placement sketches are discussed in more detail in the next section, 2D versus 3D placement sketches.

Hole sketch

The revolve profile sketch is not on an identifiable sketch plane that you can reuse for other features, although that would be useful. You can change the sketch dimension outside of the wizard interface, and if you later use the wizard to edit it, then the changes appear in the Custom Sizing panel. Figure 17.3 shows the Custom Sizing panel with the changed counterbore diameter highlighted.

If you select any of the choices from the Options panel, then the revolved sketch profile is altered to accommodate the change. For example, the sketch changes to add a line for the countersink; a separate chamfer feature is not added.

FIGURE 17.3

The Custom Sizing panel

2D versus 3D placement sketches

Possibly one of the most difficult aspects of the Hole Wizard for new users to grasp is the use of 2D and 3D sketches to place the centers of the holes. There is a condition that is not immediately obvious, which is that if you *preselect* a flat face, then the placement sketch is 2D, and if you do not pre-select a flat face (meaning that if you just start the Hole Wizard without having selected a flat face), then the placement sketch is 3D.

Advantages and limitations of the 2D sketch

The main advantages of the 2D sketch method are the simplicity and completeness of the available tools. Everyone knows how to manage 2D sketches, sketch planes, dimensions, and construction geometry. I have argued for years that the 2D placement sketch should be the default sketch used, because of its universal nature.

A limitation of the 2D sketch is that the holes that you create through this method are limited to a single planar face. Sometimes this creates a great limitation, while other times it does not matter.

Advantages and limitations of the 3D sketch

The obvious advantage of the 3D placement sketch is that it can put a set of holes on any set of solid faces, regardless of whether they are non-parallel or even non-planar. This function offers multiple holes, multiple faces, and multiple directions. In situations where that is what you need, then nothing else will do.

A limitation of the 3D sketch is that if you have never used 3D sketches, they can be fairly cumbersome. Also, several relation types that are familiar in 2D sketches are not available in 3D sketches.

Dimensions work very differently in 3D sketches compared to 2D sketches. For example, to create and place a hole in a specific position on a cylinder, you need to follow these steps:

1. Begin with a circle with a diameter of one inch, drawn on the Top plane, and extruded using the Mid-plane option one inch.

2. Start the Hole Wizard without any preselection, either through the Features toolbar or by selecting Insert ➪ Features ➪ Hole ➪ Wizard.

3. Set the interface to use an ANSI inch, one-quarter-inch, counterbored hole for a socket head cap screw. Use Through All for the End Condition, and a Normal fit, with a .100-inch head clearance (in the Options panel), and no custom sizing changes. These settings are shown in Figure 17.4.

FIGURE 17.4

The Hole Wizard settings for the socket head cap screw

4. Click the Positions tab, which is located at the top of the PropertyManager window. The interface automatically changes to a 3D sketch with the Point tool turned on. This means that wherever you click, you create a point.

NOTE Be careful about clicking when the Point tool is turned on. For example, if you click in a blank space, then the Point tool places a point off the part. SolidWorks will try to use the point later to create a hole in empty space, which usually causes an error.

5. Click the cylindrical surface of the part. The surface appears red when you move the cursor over it to indicate that an OnSurface sketch relation will be created between the sketch point and the cylindrical surface.

6. The hole should be positioned from one end of the cylinder. Using the SmartDimension tool, click one flat end face of the cylinder and the sketch point. Place the dimension and give it a value of .300 inches, as shown in Figure 17.5.

Locating the point angularly around the cylinder is more difficult. You can use several methods to do this, but this example shows one using construction sketch geometry.

FIGURE 17.5

Dimensioning the 3D Placement sketch point

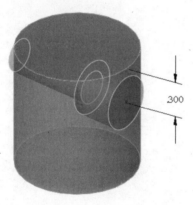

TIP To force a 3D dimension to have a certain orientation, dimension from a plane or planar face rather than from an edge, vertex, or sketch entity. A dimension from a plane is always measured in a direction perpendicular to the plane, but a dimension from a line or point is always measured by the shortest distance between the entities. Two-dimensional sketches can force dimensions to be horizontal or vertical, but 3D sketches cannot.

CAUTION 3D sketches have the ability to make planes within the sketch, without leaving the sketch environment. Planes that are made in this way cannot be referenced from outside the sketch, are not created using the same methods as regular planes, and do not follow documented techniques reliably. They have been removed from the SolidWorks Corporation training manual examples, and for this reason, I recommend finding other more reliable methods to do the same things.

7. With the Line tool activated while still in the 3D sketch, Ctrl-click the flat end face that the previous dimension referenced. This moves the red "space handle" origin to the selected face, and constrains any new sketch entities to that face. You are still in the 3D sketch, but are constrained to the selected plane, and still must play by all of the 3D sketch rules. The elements of 3D sketches are described in detail in Chapter 31.

8. Turn on the Temporary Axes view by selecting View ⇨ Temporary Axes.

9. Place the cursor near the center of the activated end face; a small, black circle appears, indicating that the end point of the line will pick up a coincident relation to the temporary axis. Draw the line so that it picks up an AlongX sketch relation. The cursor shows the relations about to be applied, just like in a 2D sketch.

10. Draw a second line again from the center, but this time do not pick up any automatic relations. This line should also be on the flat end face.

NOTE Although you can set these lines to display as construction lines if you like, this is not required in order for the feature to work; they also work as regular solid lines.

11. Put an angle dimension between the lines, and change the angle to 30 degrees. To be thorough (which is always recommended in 3D sketches, which have a tendency to handle underconstrained sketch geometry unpredictably), constrain the ends of the lines to the circular edge of the cylinder. At this point, the part looks like Figure 17.6.

FIGURE 17.6

The example part at the end of step 12

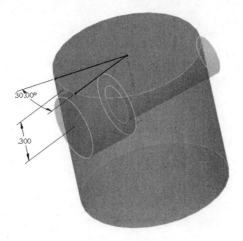

30.00°

.300

12. Create an AlongY sketch relation between the points indicated in Figure 17.7. The hole centerpoint on the cylindrical face is one of the points, as well as the endpoint of the angled line. Change the angle dimension to ensure that it is controlling the sketch point as expected.

FIGURE 17.7

Control the placement of the 3D sketch point around the cylinder.

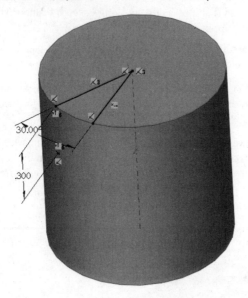

The finished part from this example is on the CD-ROM, and is called Chapter 17 3D Hole Placement.sldprt.

Making and using Favorites

Hole Wizard Favorites store types of holes that you use frequently so that you can simply recall a favorite, rather than manually making all of the changes every time you use the same hole. Favorites are saved to a database named Default.mdb as you create them, and are immediately available from all other part documents. You can also save favorites to a special file type, with the extension *.sldhwfvt. You can then load these files and add them to other Default.mdb databases.

Creating a Hole Wizard Favorite

To create a Hole Wizard Favorite, set up a Hole Wizard hole as you normally would, and then use the Add Favorite button to add it to the Favorites database. The Hole Wizard Favorite panel contains five buttons:

Apply Defaults/No Favorites: Removes favorite settings from the current interface, setting all values back to their defaults.

Add or Update Favorites: You can use this button to either add a new favorite to the database or change the name or other settings for an existing favorite.

Delete Favorite: Removes a favorite from the database.

Save Favorite: Saves a favorite to an external file with the extension, *.sldhwfvt, which can be loaded by other users and added to their databases.

Load Favorite: Loads a saved favorite file.

Storing custom holes

You can use Hole Wizard Favorites to store custom holes. Create the hole with its custom sizes, and then add the favorite and give it a recognizable name. The custom hole will now be available to anyone who connects to the same database file.

Administering Hole Wizard Favorites

The database file is typically found in the Data subdirectory of the SolidWorks installation directory, but an option in Tools ➪ Options ➪ File Locations theoretically enables you to move the file to somewhere else.

Further, the *.sldhwfvt files do not have an entry in the File Locations list, but seem to always default to the lang\english subdirectory of the SolidWorks installation directory. Neither this location nor the Data directory makes sharing among multiple users very convenient, but both file types can be copied to other installations.

BEST PRACTICE It is a best practice to create a folder for library type files that you want to save and use with a future version of SolidWorks. You can specify the locations for these files through Tools, Options, File Locations. I recommend a location such as D:\Library. This moves the file off of the same drive as the operating system, in case you need to reformat, and it keeps it out of the Program Files area to prevent it from being lost or overwritten when SolidWorks is installed, uninstalled, upgraded, or changed in other ways. Even for files that need to remain in the SolidWorks installation directory (such as macros) it is best to also have these backed up in a library location.

Favorites quirks

Hole Wizard Favorites seem to have a couple of quirks that are possibly "sub-optimal," as they say. First, you can only see the favorites for a specific type of hole when that type of hole is activated in the interface. For example, if you have a number of favorites for countersunk holes, but you currently have the counterbored hole icon activated, then you will not be able to see the countersunk favorites until you switch to the countersunk icon.

If you have a lot of favorites, then this may be beneficial, but if you have only a few favorites, or you do not use favorites frequently, then it may be confusing, and can create some unnecessary steps to find all of your favorites.

A second quirk occurs when you allow SolidWorks to name the favorites and you have fractional values such as ¼ — which happens now and then in hole sizes — and then try to save the favorites. Each favorite is saved as a separate file, using the name that was automatically assigned to it by SolidWorks as the filename. Unfortunately, the character "/" is not allowed in a filename, and so it fails.

Fortunately, you can change favorites names by using the Add Or Update Favorites button on the Favorites panel of the Hole Wizard PropertyManager.

When saving Hole Wizard Favorites, SolidWorks has no way to establish a default folder for these files, although it seems to always go to the lang\english subdirectory of the SolidWorks installation directory. You need to determine a folder to put them into and load them from, and browse to that location every time, especially if you are using a shared network. Also, remember to copy any favorites files to a backup library location.

Using the Hole Series

 The Hole Series enables you to make a series of in-context hole features in individual parts that are connected by a Hole Series assembly-level feature. It is intended for a stack of parts where, for example, the top part has a counterbored hole, the middle part has a clearance through hole, and the final part has a blind threaded hole. You can also do this by using an existing hole to align the rest of the series.

Hole Series interface

The Hole Series used to be part of the Hole Wizard, but has since been exported as a separate tool. It is now a four-step, wizard-based feature. Figure 17.8 shows the interface for the various steps.

Notice in the first panel that there is an option to add a Smart Fastener. The Toolbox feature, which I discuss in the next section, is required to be able to add Smart Fasteners.

Basic Hole Series steps

When using the Hole Series feature, you must follow these basic steps:

1. Have an assembly open with two or more parts in it that need to be fastened together.
2. Initiate the Hole Series tool by selecting Insert ➪ Assembly Features ➪ Hole ➪ Hole Series. It is also available as a toolbar button, but it is not on the toolbar by default. The Hole Series also depends on pre-selection to decide whether it uses a 2D or 3D sketch for the placement sketch. You should always pre-select a flat face before creating a Hole Series feature.
3. If the Hole Series is to be started from an existing hole, then select it in the Hole Position panel. If not, then use sketch points, construction geometry, dimensions, and sketch relations to locate the hole centerpoints.

FIGURE 17.8

The Hole Series interface

4. Use the blue arrow at the top of the PropertyManager to advance from one panel to the next.

- The Start Hole Specification is referring to the part where the series of holes starts.

- The Middle Hole Specification is for all parts between the first part and the last part.

- The End Hole Specification is the last part and is either a through clearance hole or a threaded hole.

The finished feature leaves an in-context feature in each part, with the Hole Series part in the assembly, as shown in Figure 17.9.

FIGURE 17.9

The finished Hole Series

Comprehending Toolbox

 I recommend that you read this section through, from beginning to end. If you read a paragraph out of context, then you may not understand the point that I am making. With Toolbox, it is vital that you know what you are doing, to ensure the quality of your production data regarding fasteners and hardware.

 Improper installation, maintenance, or management of Toolbox can cause the loss of all useful information about fasteners and hardware in your assemblies.

Toolbox is an add-in that requires SolidWorks Office or higher, although you can also purchase it separately. In this book, I typically avoid talking about add-ins because the amount of material simply becomes overwhelming at a certain point; however, Toolbox is the cause of much consternation among users and CAD Administrators, and so it deserves some attention.

Toolbox is an application that creates fasteners and other hardware components, on the fly or reuses existing parts when possible. Technically, Toolbox is not a library, but a *configurator*. Libraries store existing components, while configurators build them on the fly from information supplied by the user.

One advantage of configurators is that the parts start out very compact because there is only the default size, and the sizes are efficiently stored in a database, and created as needed.

The advantage of a library is that it allows you to simply plug in the parts and they work. No mess, no fuss. This is not how Toolbox works, but it is good to remember the fact that what Toolbox really needs to do for users is provide a library of parts. Anything more than that is only beneficial if it offers some improvement over a simple library of existing parts without introducing any risks or setbacks.

How Toolbox works

Because Toolbox is not a library, and is not passive the way a library is, there is a component of it that is active. To make an analogy, no one asks how a staircase works, because it does not work, it simply exists, and people use it. An escalator, however, is a different issue. With an escalator, there is a complex installation, and then to operate it, you have to know how to get on and get off, and what to do if it stops working. The end results of using the staircase and using the escalator are the same (you start at the bottom and arrive at the top), but the complex automation is supposed to save you some effort.

That is one of the ways in which you can look at Toolbox. The end product is supposed to be the same as using a static library of parts, but there is some mechanism behind the scenes that has to be set up and maintained properly in order for it to work in the way you expect. Most SolidWorks books, tutorials, or training materials are going to ask you to accept what happens inside Toolbox as a "black box" and just assume that the end results are exactly what you need and intend. Here, I supply you with information about how it works, because it is important.

The database

When Toolbox is installed, it starts as a set of SolidWorks parts with named features and dimensions, some suppressed features (depending on settings), some dlls (executable programs), and a database. The parts have a single Default configuration, which is typically one of the size extremities, either the largest or smallest. The database starts out about 65MB, and includes all of the size information for all of the parts, as well as all of the standards information.

If you create a *custom standard* in Toolbox, it actually replicates a section of the database. By doing this, the database file can easily double in size.

Later, you will see that a network installation of Toolbox requires the database to be on the network, and every time you create a new fastener, it has to open the database. As a result, simply placing a screw in an assembly can mean that even if your assembly is located on your local hard drive, you still have to open a very large database file across the network. The first rule about performance with SolidWorks is to work locally rather than across a network.

By default, the database is located at C:\Program Files\Common Files\SolidWorks Data\Browser\ lang\English\SWBrowser.mdb. You can open this file with Microsoft Access or Excel.

> **NOTE**   When specifying network paths, it is best to specify a universal naming convention, or UNC, path rather than a mapped address. A UNC address follows the format, \\Server\Shared Folder. The advantage of the UNC over the mapped drive is that mapped drives do not always connect immediately, but the UNC should be able to find its link as long as the network is working. Also, mapped drives can vary from one computer to another, but the UNC is always the same.

The Configurator application

If you have just installed Toolbox the way that most, if not all, new users do, then you will accept all defaults, and trust the software that you just purchased to not give you bad advice. In this situation, the database is installed locally and Toolbox is set to use configurations for sizes.

When you put a Toolbox part into an assembly, you do not even notice anything other than the part going into the assembly, although it may hesitate while the large database is opened. If you check the part configurations, you may notice that there is a Default config and a new one that represents the size that you just created. Every new size that you create makes another new configuration. Figure 17.10 shows a Toolbox part with the FeatureManager and ConfigurationManager open.

Next, you may receive an assembly from a client. Often, because Toolbox parts are located in an area where you would not necessarily look for parts, users send assemblies and parts, but do not send Toolbox parts. You may think that this is okay; after all, you have Toolbox on your system, and so it should pick up your toolbox parts. The truth is that when receiving an assembly from someone else, you are better off if one of the parties does not have Toolbox on their system. Here's why:

FIGURE 17.10

A Toolbox part showing the FeatureManager and ConfigurationManager

Huge screws

If both you and the client who sent the assembly have Toolbox, then you should be okay, right? Well, yes and no. Yes, your client's assembly will pick up your Toolbox parts, but no, it will not work properly because you do not have all of the same configurations and sizes that your client has. In cases like this, you will experience what I have come to refer to as the Huge Screws syndrome. When SolidWorks finds the right file but cannot find the right configuration, it uses another configuration, usually the Default, which is generally the biggest size. This is where the Huge Screws name came from.

Part of the really bad news is that if you save your assembly with the Huge Screws, SolidWorks has no way of knowing that the huge screws are not the correct screws, and the problem can be solved only by manually going through the assembly and reassigning sizes to the huge screws.

You can work around this by opening an assembly that has not yet been saved with the Huge Screws, by using the Advanced option in the Open dialog box, and selecting the New Configuration Showing Assembly Structure Only option. With this option, all components are suppressed. You can unsuppress any non-Toolbox parts and continue working. Ask your client to send you his Toolbox parts and then unsuppress those parts in the assembly, making sure that it finds the right parts, which is probably best done by having the correct parts already open before you open the assembly. These options are shown in Figure 17.11.

FIGURE 17.11

Opening an assembly with all parts suppressed

If you replace your Toolbox parts with the Toolbox parts from the client, then you may experience the same problem in reverse if you had configs that your client did not. In the end, it would be great to be able to merge the two parts to combine all of the available sizes into a single file. There is a way of doing that, which I will describe later. Files that have the same names and different content are at the top of the list of things you shouldn't do in file management, and yet the SolidWorks Toolbox system frequently creates this very situation.

A slight retraction

To be fair, SolidWorks has fixed the Huge Screws problem in the 2007 version, by coming up with a clever method for figuring out which size is missing and building it on the fly when the assembly is opened. Additional information about the Toolbox parts is now stored in the assembly, which helps identify the missing parts. Unfortunately, the fix only works for assemblies that use the parts from the new 2007 library and assemblies that have been built in SolidWorks 2007. To sum up, if you have assemblies built in an older version of SolidWorks, and your Toolbox library becomes corrupted or lost, or you are sent an assembly that uses a different Toolbox library, even if you are working in SolidWorks 2007, you cannot benefit from this fix.

This is disappointing in many respects because anyone who has existing Huge Screws problems will continue to have them until they rebuild the assembly or manually repair the configurations. It is doubly disappointing because the information needed to recreate the correct configuration has always been stored in the assembly — the filename and the configuration name are enough — but SolidWorks has missed an opportunity to really fix this problem.

Before the Summary at the end of this chapter, I have some recommendations if you are still interested in using Toolbox.

Toolbox organization

Toolbox parts can be organized in a number of ways. The raw parts are organized as follows:

- Standard and Units (for example, ANSI Inch or ANSI Metric; most standards do not include multiple units, they assume metric).

- Hardware Type (such as bearings, bolts, and bushings).

- Each type is organized differently, but bolts and screws are organized by drive or head type (for example, you have socket head screws, hex head, and thumb screws).

- Filenames look like Socket Button Head Cap Screw_AI.SLDPRT, where the "AI" represents ANSI Inch.

Figure 17.12 shows this organization in part.

FIGURE 17.12

Toolbox content organization

Configurations or parts?

By now you are probably unsure about the use of configurations in general. If so, that is not the impression I am trying to convey. Configurations in themselves are not the problem; the problem here is in the file management practice of having files with the same names but different content. Mixing that with the practice of trying to treat "configurator" software like a "library" exacerbates the problem.

That said, you have two options regarding how you create different sizes. The default option is that sizes are created as configurations within a single part. The other option is that sizes are created as individual files.

The best time to make this choice is before you install SolidWorks. Unfortunately, before you install SolidWorks, you probably do not have any idea that these issues exist. The reason for making this decision not just early, but immediately, is that if you start using the default setting (configurations), and make a few configurations for some parts, and then switch to using the Save Parts setting, the parts that are saved out will all have the pre-existing configurations, and thus different sizes.

If you find yourself in this situation, it is better to reinstall Toolbox, or simply to copy over a new default library with no configurations.

You can access the option to either Create Configurations or Create Parts by selecting Toolbox ➪ Configure ➪ Settings, as shown in Figure 17.13. I will discuss the other settings in this dialog box later in this chapter.

Which is better?

The following list contains some pros and cons of each option.

Configurations are better for:

- Controlling data across several sizes. For example, a design table can drive custom properties that are added to all configurations. Doing this with many individual parts would be very messy.
- The interface to select configurations from a list is easier to work with than the interface to select a part from a list.
- File management organization is somewhat easier for configured parts.

Separate parts are better for:

- Keeping the file size small.
- Replacing all of one size part with another.
- A guarantee that you will never have the Huge Screws problem.

FIGURE 17.13

Toolbox settings for the Create Configurations or Create Parts options

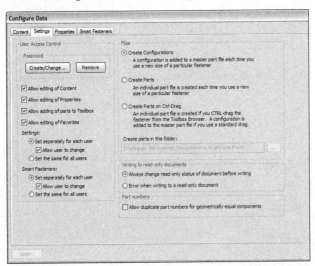

Materials or custom part numbers in Toolbox

Maybe your company uses screws of different materials or finishes in your products. Toolbox, in its default arrangement, does not have an option to deal with this directly. If you ask a tech support person whether materials and custom part numbers can be used in SolidWorks, they will tell you "of course, simply enter in the desired quantity when making the part." The implication here is that you do them one at a time, and that whoever creates the part uses the same syntax as everyone else.

Figure 17.14 shows the PropertyManager interface for adding a Toolbox part to an assembly. You can access this interface by dragging a Toolbox part from the Design Library window into the assembly graphics window. The materials assignment is usually intended to be done as part of the Description. You can access this interface and the Part Number fields through the Add Favorite button in the upper-left corner of the Favorites panel.

FIGURE 17.14

Adding a part number and description to a new Toolbox part

The way that SolidWorks expects you to work with materials and custom part numbers is simply not practical unless you have one person doing all of the work, and you do not have many parts to create. SolidWorks does not provide any direct way to mass-populate data of this type.

One method to work around the lack of a mass-population tool is to first create all of the sizes for a part using configurations. Then auto-create a design table and you can use Excel techniques to build descriptions, custom part numbers, materials, and whatever custom property you want to have.

Another method to do this is to create a custom standard for materials. A custom standard essentially copies a high level in the database such as ANSI Inch. You can specify a name such as Company X Stainless Hardware, or Company X Black Oxide Hardware.

I have already mentioned that adding custom standards greatly increases the size of the database, and contributes to the delay in adding the Toolbox parts to an assembly. If this is not a handicap for you—and you should at least try it—then it may be a more viable way to incorporate materials and finishes.

Toolbox in a multi-user environment

There are a few ways in which you can make Toolbox work the way it is intended to. The most reliable way is to remove your computer from the network, and to not bring in any assemblies from external sources that were created referencing Toolbox parts. That sounds like an extreme measure, but it is necessary, as Toolbox's weaknesses come from sharing Toolbox data.

Unfortunately, most SolidWorks users do not have this luxury. They generally share files with other users across a network, in a PDM system, or across the Internet through FTP, e-mail, or VPN. If each user has their own Toolbox installation locally, as happens with the default installation, then you could run into the same problems as described above when receiving an outside client's files. As a result, you must somehow share Toolbox.

Sharing Toolbox

Keep thinking to yourself "Toolbox is just a library, Toolbox is just a library . . ."

You can share Toolbox by redirecting the Common Files part of the SolidWorks installation to a shared network location. This part of the installation is shown in Figure 17.15.

FIGURE 17.15

Locating the Toolbox library during installation

Sharing an existing Toolbox library

This is fine for the first installation, but for any installation where a version of the software already exists on your computer, the shared files also already exist. There is no installation option to accommodate this situation, and so you have to either install over the shared documents or install to a dummy location and redirect SolidWorks to the shared files manually. You have to go through this installation, even the dummy installation, because it is installing the *application* part of Toolbox. Remember that a Toolbox installation has three components: the empty default library part files, the database with all of the information in it that is used to populate the library, and the application dlls that make everything work.

This is particularly important to pay attention to if the library has been changed. If you overwrite the database, that is not really important unless, for example, standards have been changed, or custom properties added. However, if the library has been changed (for example, by adding configurations) and a later installation overwrites it, then you can cause yourself or someone else a lot of difficulties.

For this reason, you need to know how to manually redirect Toolbox to a different location. A file called Toolbox.ini is located in the Toolbox subdirectory of the SolidWorks installation directory, as shown in Figure 17.16.

Finding the Toolbox.ini file

When you edit this file with a text editor such as Notepad, the file contains the path of the SolidWorks Data folder. The database that controls both Toolbox and the Hole Wizard is located in the \lang\English (or appropriate language) folder, and is called SWBrowser.mdb. The Toolbox library parts are in the \browser folder, under the appropriate folders, as displayed in the Design Library. Figure 17.17 shows the Toolbox.ini file open in Notepad.

FIGURE 17.17

The Toolbox.ini file displayed in Notepad

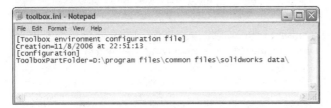

Toolbox administration

If you have only one user, you can do what you like — even use the default installation — and Toolbox should work for you. If, however, you are administering an installation with more than one user, you need to be informed of the issues involving setting up and using Toolbox mentioned above, and a few more mentioned below.

Read-only setting

If a Toolbox is shared, is it possible that multiple people can access the same files at the same time? This is one of the most frequently asked questions about Toolbox administration. If two people need to write to a file at the same time, then that can cause problems. In order to remedy this, SolidWorks plays referee between multiple users who are accessing the same Toolbox files.

You need to apply the following settings to share Toolbox files on a network:

- Toolbox ➪ Configure ➪ Settings ➪ Always Change Read-only Status of Document Before Writing; this option should be on.
- The Windows users should have full permissions to access the SolidWorks Data directory, and the SolidWorks Data\Browser directory should be set to Read-only for all users.

Upgrading SolidWorks with Toolbox

It is time to upgrade. You have your SolidWorks 2007 disks, and SolidWorks 2006 is installed. You can now go ahead and install SolidWorks 2007, but when it comes to the part in the installation shown in Figure 17.15, take notice again of what you are doing. The installation may default to the SolidWorks 2006 Toolbox location. If you overwrite this location, then you will not be able to use Toolbox with SolidWorks 2006 (because the library will be a future version). If you intend to use multiple versions, then you also need to maintain multiple Toolbox installations.

You should also consider what would happen if you make a mistake and completely overwrite the SolidWorks 2006 library that contains all of the configuration data that you have worked hard to create. When upgrading, you do not want to overwrite your existing library. The following is a set of steps to help you upgrade safely and effectively:

■ Install the new version with Toolbox in a new location, for example SolidWorks 2007 Data or a directory name that helps to distinguish this library from another.

■ Copy the old SolidWorks 2006 data (containing the correct configurations) over the top of the new SolidWorks 2007 data.

■ Browse to the Toolbox\data utilities subdirectory of the SolidWorks installation directory and run UpdateBrowserData.exe. The interface for this program is shown in Figure 17.18.

FIGURE 17.18

The UpdateBrowserData.exe interface

■ Select the Updating Database field and use the ellipsis button to browse to Toolbox\data utilities\lang\English\updatedb.mdb in the SolidWorks installation directory.

■ Select the Database To Update field and browse to SWBrowser.mdb. You can find this file by following the ToolboxPartFolder path in the Toolbox.ini file, and looking in the \lang\english subdirectory.

■ Click Update.

This prevents you from overwriting your old version, while still copying the old version to the new installation and avoiding the Huge Screws syndrome.

Adding custom Toolbox parts

If you have been using SolidWorks and Toolbox for a few releases, then you may recall that Toolbox had a function called the Add My Parts Wizard, which added user-created parts to the Toolbox libraries. The parts were limited in that you could not use them with Smart Fasteners, but the interface would work if the part had configurations.

In SolidWorks 2007, the Add My Parts Wizard has been removed. However, you can still add your own parts to Toolbox by simply dragging-and-dropping them. Drag-and-drop is available in third-level folders. Levels are counted from the Standard folder, which is level 1.

Adding folders to Toolbox

You can add folders to Toolbox through the RMB menu. Just RMB click a first- or second-level folder, and select New Folder. You can create a new level-1 folder by RMB clicking the Toolbox icon, as shown in Figure 17.19.

Adding a new folder

Merging Toolbox libraries

You can merge Toolbox libraries by simply copying or moving one folder in with the existing library folders. Another type of merging may be less successful. If you have two Toolbox parts from different sources and they have different sets of size configurations, these are things you may want to merge to get the benefits of both sets of sizes.

Unfortunately, there is no direct way of doing this in Toolbox. The best way would be to auto-create design tables in both parts, and then to copy the configurations from one design table to the other design table. This should effectively copy configurations between parts, although you may need to remove any duplicate configuration rows.

Toolbox and PDM

This topic could be a chapter on its own, but I will not delve too deeply into it here because it goes beyond the intended scope of this book. A discussion of Toolbox requires some mention of how it may be used in conjunction with a PDM product.

Toolbox and PDMWorks Workgroup, or any other PDM product for that matter, can be a challenge to combine. Generally, it is useful to be able to see the fasteners in PDM because of the BOM capabilities, quantities, Where Used options, and complete searches. Some users choose not to put library parts in the vault because they are not revision-managed documents. All the same, revision management is not the only reason to put items in the vault.

Looking at it from the Toolbox point of view, Toolbox cannot work with its parts in the vault, and if changes were allowed to the parts (sizes add configurations), then you would need to check in the part every time you added a size. This is not necessarily a problem, but it does become awkward.

Some PDM products allow files to exist outside the vault, while pointers to the files exist within the vault. This is one very good option for using Toolbox with a PDM product.

Another good option is to simply use the Create Parts setting. This creates individual files that are easier to manage. It may also be important for a different reason: some PDM products, such as PDMWorks Workgroup, do not distinguish configurations as separate controllable or separately identifiable documents.

Toolbox settings

You can find Toolbox settings in the Toolbox menu, by selecting the Configure option. The Configure Data dialog box has four tabs: Content, Settings, Properties, and Smart Fasteners.

Content tab

The Content tab shows all of the standards. If you are not using certain standards, then you can turn them off by deselecting their check mark. You can do the same for folders and even specific parts within the standard. If you have added folders or custom parts in the Design Library window, they appear here.

As you expand the standard, and then the fastener type and the specific head types, you can select individual parts. The Countersunk Bolt is selected in the list shown in Figure 17.20.

FIGURE 17.20

The Toolbox Configure Data Content tab

Several tabs contain different types of information for Toolbox parts:

- You can use the General tab to offer alternate filenames.
- You can use the Size tab to disable specific sizes.
- The Finish tab is not available for all fasteners, but you can use it to remove parts of the description.
- You can use the Length tab to limit the available lengths.
- You can use the Thread Display tab to limit the available thread types. Available thread types are shown in Figure 17.21.

FIGURE 17.21

Available thread display options

Schematic   Simplified   Cosmetic

- The All Configurations tab enables you to create all of the configurations that are available for a particular Toolbox part. It will also export the database data to an Excel spreadsheet, and import a spreadsheet that is created in this way.

Creating all of the configurations for a single part can take a couple of hours, and in the few times I have done it, I have never seen the SolidWorks interface recover from starting the command, although it seems to finish. Having all of the configurations is very useful, especially if you are being plagued by the Huge Screws.

Settings tab

The Settings tab is where you can set the config and part options. If you choose to create parts, then you also need to specify a location for the parts to be kept. If you choose a network location, it is best to use the UNC path, rather than a mapped drive because mapped drives may not reconnect on start up and may be mapped to different letters from computer to computer, but the UNC always points to the same location from any point on the network.

The Settings tab also enables the Administrator to establish a password for Toolbox data configuration changes. The Settings tab is shown in Figure 17.22.

FIGURE 17.22

The Settings tab

Properties tab

The Properties tab enables you to set up properties that appear in the PropertyManager. For example, you can enable fill-in or drop-down lists for values. Properties can be enabled for specific items, as shown in Figure 17.23.

Smart Fasteners tab

The Smart Fasteners tab controls Smart Fasteners, which are discussed later in this chapter. The tab is shown in Figure 17.24. As an example of the types of settings you can use here, you can control which screw types are used with which types of Hole Wizard or non-Hole Wizard holes.

FIGURE 17.23

The Properties tab

FIGURE 17.24

The Smart Fasteners tab

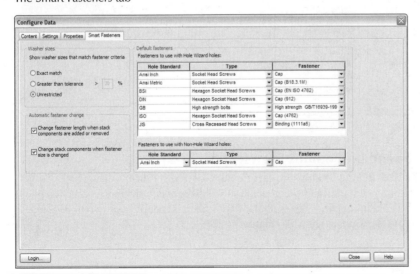

Using Toolbox

Up to now in this chapter, we have looked at Toolbox mainly from the administrative point of view; now, we will look at it from the user's point of view. Toolbox has two components: Toolbox and Toolbox Browser. In practice, the *Toolbox* component is actually ignored, and the *Toolbox Browser* component is generally referred to as Toolbox.

The Toolbox Browser is the Task pane interface, and is found on the Design Library tab, as shown in the image to the left in Figure 17.25. The Toolbox component is found in the Toolbox drop-down menu. It includes structural steel shapes, grooves, cams, and beam and bearing calculators.

FIGURE 17.25

Toolbox and the Toolbox Browser

Turning Toolbox and the Toolbox Browser on

You can turn on Toolbox and the Toolbox Browser through the Tools, Add-Ins dialog box. The column of check boxes on the left indicates that the add-in will be active for the current session of SolidWorks only. The column of check boxes on the right indicates that the add-in will be active every time the software starts up, as shown in Figure 17.26.

FIGURE 17.26

Turning Toolbox on in the Tools, Add-ins interface

Once the Toolbox Browser is turned on, you can use it by expanding the Task pane at the right of the SolidWorks graphics window and clicking the Design Library, which looks like a stack of books. In this panel, you will see the Toolbox screw symbol. Expand icons until you find the fastener or other hardware that you are looking for, and then drag the part into the assembly.

Populating holes

Holes can be populated in several ways, such as dragging-and-dropping, populating multiple holes at once, and using feature-driven component patterns. I discuss manual and patterning options here, and Smart Fasteners in the next section.

Drag-and-drop

The simplest way to bring Toolbox parts into an assembly is to drag-and-drop them. Position the part that the fastener goes into so that you can see the edge of the hole where the screw head will go. Then browse to the correct fastener, and drop the fastener onto the edge, as shown in Figure 17.27.

Because of the use of Mate References in Toolbox parts, they know that they are supposed to snap into holes on flat faces. When dropping the fastener into the hole, the Smart Mate icon momentarily appears. A Smart Mate of this sort applies two mates, one that is concentric between cylindrical faces, and one that is coincident between two flat faces.

FIGURE 17.27

Dropping a fastener onto a hole

Populating multiple holes at once

Figure 17.28 shows the progression from a plate with holes in an assembly. In this example, you would select the edges of the holes, then select a fastener, and then choose Insert Into Assembly from the RMB menu, to fully populate the part.

FIGURE 17.28

Populating multiple holes at once in an assembly

Feature Driven component patterns

Chapter 15 discussed Feature Driven component patterns (also known as derived patterns), where a pattern of parts in an assembly is driven by a feature pattern in a part. You can find this assembly feature in the assembly menus under Insert ⇨ Component Patterns ⇨ Feature Driven.

Smart Fasteners

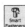 Smart Fasteners are Toolbox parts that know what holes they go into automatically. The database that holds all of the information for Toolbox part types and sizes also holds the information for the sizes of the holes. It is only natural that SolidWorks try to combine this information and use it to its best advantage. You can use Smart Fasteners in two ways:

Smart Fasteners with Hole Series

One way to use Smart Fasteners is in conjunction with Hole Wizard Hole Series. Hole Series creates the holes through multiple parts at once, creating the appropriate type of hole through each part, and then Smart Fasteners automatically places fasteners in the holes, even including nuts and washers. To do this, you can select the option on the first panel of the Hole Series PropertyManager interface, as shown in Figure 17.29. If you are planning on using Smart Fasteners, using them in conjunction with the Hole Series is your best bet, using them in conjunction with the Hole Series holes.

FIGURE 17.29

The Hole Position interface

The Smart Fasteners with Hole Series is a function that you should be careful when using. It is very effective, but it may cost you some performance (speed). The Hole Series is an Assembly Feature (sketch) that drives several in-context features (holes), and then parts are mated to those in-context features (fasteners).

Smart Fasteners Populate All

Smart Fasteners functionality also has an automatic component. Once an assembly has parts mated into place, you can place fasteners into parts with appropriate holes by face, by part, or for the entire assembly at once.

CAUTION   You may not want to spend a lot of time trying to use this type of the Smart Fasteners functionality. I have tried to find examples where Smart Fasteners works well and predictably, but to no avail. I have searched through training examples, tutorial files from SolidWorks, and I have even made some of my own example files. I have looked for presentations from user groups and SolidWorks World that use Smart Fasteners, but no one appears to be talking about this functionality. Although in theory, it offers interesting functionality, in reality, it receives very little attention — definitely a warning sign.

The one assembly that I did find where Smart Fasteners worked surprisingly well (in fact, almost perfectly) was from the sample files that installed with SolidWorks. Upon closer examination, the reason this worked well was because it used assembly features for the holes, and so the holes did not appear in the individual parts. If that is the price that you have to pay just to get fasteners to populate automatically, then I would rather put them all in manually.

The limitations of Smart Fasteners

Smart Fasteners have some documented limitations where you should not expect them to work:

- Holes in single parts
- Holes created by extruding a nested loop
- A mirrored hole or cut features
- Holes in mirrored, imported, or derived parts
- Misaligned holes
- Holes with a large difference in diameter
- Holes with large gaps between them (a large gap in the axial direction)
- Holes made using different techniques (such as sketch pattern versus feature pattern)

If you would like to try out Smart Fasteners, then you can use the assembly included on the CD-ROM called Chapter 17 Smart Fasteners.sldasm. In this assembly, half of the holes are done correctly, and in the other half, the screws are put in either backwards or head-first. The documented method for flipping the fasteners is to expand the Smart Fastener, RMB click the series, and select Flip. In this case, my attempts resulted in success about half of time, which was somewhat higher than my attempts with other assemblies. In some cases, screws were put in the ends of shafts without holes, on filleted edges, and unfortunately missed most of the places that I *did* want the screws to go.

Organizing Toolbox parts in an assembly

Assembly FeatureManagers are hard enough to manage when they become full of parts; they become even more unmanageable when they also need to include the many types of fastener parts. As a result, I recommend that fasteners, as well as any other type of part that is found in large quantity in the assembly, be organized into folders, as shown in Figure 17.30. You should also group parts of the same size or function together.

FIGURE 17.30

Organizing Toolbox parts into folders

Recommendations

After spending almost an entire chapter saying what you *should not* do, it is finally time to say what you *should* do. Toolbox can be downright dangerous if you install and use it improperly; however, the following recommendations work in most situations.

The simplest setup that works

If you are a single user who does not share files over a network with other users, then installing SolidWorks and Toolbox with the default settings should work for you. This appears to be the arrangement that the developers had in mind when they programmed the tool, because it is the only scenario in which it works as expected.

Be careful if you ever receive an assembly from another Toolbox user, because this is the one situation that can cause immediate trouble. If they also send their Toolbox parts, then I recommend that you open all of their Toolbox parts before you open their assembly, so that the assembly is certain to access their Toolbox parts instead of yours.

If you need to include materials and mass-populate custom properties, then I recommend that you go through the exercise of building all of the configurations of all of the parts, and then use an auto-created design table to drive the properties.

If you have more than one user, then this technique will not work for you, unless both users work independently from one another.

A complete setup that works

If you have multiple users that share assemblies, then you need to also share the Toolbox library. If you share assemblies only among yourselves, meaning only with other users who are also sharing Toolbox, then sharing Toolbox should be good enough. However, if you share assemblies with Toolbox users who do not share your Toolbox library, then you should probably go through the exercise of populating all of your parts with all of the available configurations. Setting your library to use the Create Parts setting cannot help you to avoid the Huge Screws problem when you receive an assembly from outside your group. If the originator has used parts with configurations, then you must also use configurations.

If you do not receive assemblies from outside of your group with Toolbox parts in the assembly and you have network performance problems, then it may be a good idea to install Toolbox locally, but to set it to use the Create Parts setting, where the parts are on a shared network location.

If you use a PDM system, then I would definitely install Toolbox locally, and use the Create Parts setting. The sharing occurs through the PDM system.

The least problematic technique is to turn Toolbox off altogether and either buy or make your own library of static parts. You can then distribute these files internally in your organization, as well as to any other people upstream or downstream from you who also share files with you. You can build this type of library by using Toolbox's config population tool; materials or other custom properties are then dealt with the way you want, probably using auto-created design tables.

Tutorial: Gaining Experience with the Hole Wizard and Toolbox

Figure 17.31 shows a section view of the assembly used for this tutorial. Notice that there is a gasket under the Sensor part.

FIGURE 17.31

A section view of the tutorial assembly

This tutorial assumes that you have a working copy of Toolbox running on your computer. If you do not have Toolbox, then you can proceed to the next chapter. This tutorial also assumes that your Toolbox is using the default Create Configurations setting, although it can also work with the Create Parts setting. To get some experience using this tool, follow these steps:

1. Open the assembly from the CD-ROM called Chapter 17 Tutorial.sldasm.

2. Make sure that the Toolbox Browser is turned on by selecting Tools ⇨ Add-Ins ⇨ Toolbox ⇨ Toolbox Browser.

3. Expand the Task pane, found on the right side of the graphics window, and display the Design Library panel, which contains the Toolbox icon. Expand the ANSI Inch standard, and the Bolts and Screws folder, and finally click the Hex Head bolt, as shown in Figure 17.32 on the left. Drag-and-drop the hex head bolt into the indicated hole. It snaps into place because of the Mate Reference that is used on the Toolbox part. Use the settings shown in the PropertyManager to size the bolt.

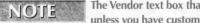 The Vendor text box that displays in the PropertyManager above will not be available to you unless you have customized the Properties tab in the Configure Data Settings dialog box.

4. Add a flat washer and nut to the bolt, as shown below in Figure 17.33. The washer is Plain Washer Type A, Preferred - Wide Flat Washer.

    The nut used is Hex Nut, Heavy Hex Nut.

FIGURE 17.32

Select and place a fastener.

Drop hex head bolt here

FIGURE 17.33

Specifying the washer and nut

5. Notice that the bolt is too short, as shown in Figure 17.34. RMB click the bolt, either in the graphics window or in the FeatureManager, and select Edit Toolbox Definition, toward the bottom of the menu. Change the length of the fastener to 1.625 inches.

FIGURE 17.34

The bolt is too short.

TIP   Use the Dynamic Preview option at the bottom of the Toolbox PropertyManager. After you select a new size, the bolt in the graphics window immediately updates to reflect the new size.

TIP   The selection of which hole the first fastener was positioned in could be arbitrary on this assembly because it uses a circular pattern, but if it had been a rectangular pattern, then the order would have mattered. When preparing to use a Feature Driven component pattern, it is important to put the components in the seed feature (the original feature that the pattern was created from).

NOTE   If you try to apply Smart Fasteners to the hole, then you will notice that the fastener is placed incorrectly. This is another situation where Smart Fasteners are a problem.

6. Create a Feature Driven component pattern (Insert ⇨ Component Pattern ⇨ Feature Driven) using the circular pattern of holes on either the Top or Base parts. Pattern the bolt, washer, and nut all in the same component pattern.

7. Zoom in on the sensor on the top of the assembly. There is a gray gasket between the orange sensor and the blue top parts. Click one of the flat ends of the sensor part and then click the Hole Series toolbar button, or select Insert ⇨ Assembly Feature ⇨ Hole ⇨ Hole Series.

 Remember that the pre-selection of a flat face is important so that you can use a 2D placement sketch, rather than a 3D placement sketch.

8. Make sure that you select the Add Smart Fastener option, as well as the Create New Hole option.

9. Make three sketch points and use construction geometry and dimensions to locate the holes, as shown in Figure 17.35. The size and types of holes are determined in a later step. (This is from the reverse of the normal Hole Wizard, where you first determine the type and size of hole, and then you establish the positions.)

FIGURE 17.35

The positions of holes in step 9

10. Click the Next button (the blue arrow pointing right) to move to the First Part hole specification. Set it to a counterbored hole, for a #10 binding head screw, with a head clearance of .025 inches, as shown in Figure 17.36 in the image to the left. Click the Next button to advance to the Middle Parts hole sizing.

11. In the Middle Parts PropertyManager, make sure that the Auto Size Based On Start Hole option is on, as shown in Figure 17.36 in the middle image. This creates a normal fit clearance hole for the gasket part. Click Next to advance to the hole definition for the Last Part.

12. In the End Hole Specification panel, make sure that you select the Hole rather than the Tap option, as well as the Auto Size Based on Start Hole option. This is shown to the right in Figure 17.36. When this step is complete, click the OK button (the green check mark icon).

FIGURE 17.36

Sizing the holes

NOTE The interface here looks unfinished. Notice that the Fit text box is available for the End Hole, even if you use the Auto Size Based on Start Hole option, but it was not available for the Middle Part. Also notice the lack of drop-down arrows for the Fit and Size text boxes.

13. The Smart Fasteners PropertyManager appears. Expand the Binding Head Screw header in the Fasteners panel, and notice the warning icon on Series1, as shown in Figure 17.37. When you click this warning icon, a message displays in the Information panel at the top of the PropertyManager window. This particular flag suggests that there may be an interference; however, there is no interference. This warning disappears when the feature is finished.

FIGURE 17.37

The Smart Fastener PropertyManager

14. Add a washer and a nut to the bottom stack of the binding head screws. This is easy to do, and almost makes up for the rest of the Smart Fasteners shortcomings. To do this, RMB click the Bottom Stack entry at the bottom of the Fasteners panel and select the Bottom Stack option that pops up.

15. A dialog box appears, enabling you to add a washer and a nut, as shown in Figure 17.38. You may want to roll the model over so that you can see the components being added to the underside of the screw. You can add other properties to the parts using the Properties button. Notice that the screw has been lengthened to accommodate the added components.

 If you add a washer to the top stack, the hole does not automatically become larger, and it may cause an interference. Be careful about your choice of top-stack washers.

FIGURE 17.38

Adding washers and nuts

NOTE   You may have noticed that this time, Smart Fasteners worked almost flawlessly and certainly saved you some time. Although this tool is not applicable to other purposes, when used with the Hole Series, it is quite useful.

16. You may want to group the fasteners and even the fasteners' mates into folders, as shown in Figure 17.39.

CAUTION   The version of the assembly labeled Finished on the CD-ROM may open up on your computer with Huge Screws if you open it before completing the tutorial. This is because the configurations used in the assembly are on *my* computer. Although you have the same parts, before doing this tutorial, you may not have the same configurations, and so they cannot be found and come in Huge instead. This was intentional; it is a practical reminder of this problem and how easily it can happen to you. If you are using SolidWorks 2007, you should be able to tell Toolbox to simply recreate the sizes and continue on. If the assembly provided on the CD-ROM had been made prior to SolidWorks 2007, that option would not exist.

FIGURE 17.39

The finished Assembly FeatureManager interface

Summary

The Hole Wizard can make holes based on 2D or 3D sketches. The type of hole that you create depends on whether or not you have pre-selected a flat face before clicking the Hole Wizard tool. Two-dimensional sketches are far easier to use than 3D sketches.

I have met people who claim to have had good success with Toolbox even in a shared environment, but since the problems with the tool are so easy to demonstrate, these people are either extremely disciplined or extremely lucky. For all users except those who work alone and do not share files with other Toolbox users, Toolbox can cause a number of major problems. You can develop techniques to prevent you from experiencing Huge Screws, for example, either not sharing assemblies with other Toolbox users or pre-populating all of your configurable parts with all possible configurations. Further, Smart Fasteners that you use in conjunction with Hole Series violate any best practice guidelines that you could name when it comes to assembly performance and circular references; however, if you can work with that, then it is a really sophisticated technique.

Chapter 18

Working with Library Features

L ibrary features are features that you create once and re-use many times. They are intended to be parametrically flexible to fit into many types of geometry, but they can also be of a fixed size and shape. All of the information that you have learned in previous chapters about designing for change, and design intent, will be used here, and you will also learn how to create, use, and store library features in this chapter.

Using Library Features

Library features reside in the Design Library, which is located in the Task pane to the right of the graphics window.

TIP You can actually detach the Task pane from its docking location and move it wherever you want, leave it undocked, or even dock it to the left side of the screen.

If you are a long-time SolidWorks user, then you may still know the Design Library as the Feature palette. Another change to the old library features and palette features is that they have been combined, thus removing some of the limitations of the old palette features.

You can use library features for snap rings, grooves for o-rings, custom holes (you can even customize a Hole Wizard hole and put it in the library), mounting bosses for plastics, mounting hole patterns, electrical connector holes, and so on.

One very useful aspect of library features is that they can be driven by configurations and design tables. Once the feature is in the part, the configurations are still available, and so you can change the config of an applied library feature at any time.

You can also link a library feature to an external file. This enables you to change a feature or set of features in several parts at once, if they are all externally linked to the file.

Getting started with library features

Library features are simple to use, but difficult to set up. For that reason, this chapter discusses using them first, so that you know what kind of behavior you are trying to create. As a result, setting them up should make a little more sense.

To use a library feature, you just drag and drop it onto the appropriate geometry. You are then prompted to select references in the new part that match the base geometry that the library feature is attached to. You can be fairly creative with references, but one of the goals is to make the library feature work with as few references as possible, in order to make it easy, fast, and reliable to use.

SolidWorks software installs with several sample library features in the Design Library. The following demonstration uses some of these standard library features. Later, you can add library features from the CD-ROM to the Design Library.

The Library Feature interface

Library features work best if they go from a certain type of geometry to a similar type of geometry, for example, from rectangular to rectangular, or from circular to circular. This is because the relations or dimensions that link the feature to the rest of the part tend to be dimensions from straight edges or concentric sketch relations. Of course, there are other ways of applying library features, but these are the most prevalent. Library features can be applied unconstrained and then constrained, or moved later, but the process is cleanest when it all just falls together correctly the first time.

Task pane

You do not have to save the part or do anything special before applying the library feature. All you need to do is find the Task pane. The Task pane is the window that flies out from the right when you open SolidWorks. You may have turned it off and forgotten about it, in which case you can turn it back on by selecting View ⇨ Task pane.

The Task pane automatically closes when you click outside of it unless you pin it open using the push-pin icon in the upper-right corner of the window. When you do this, any toolbars that appeared on the right side of the Task pane control tabs are moved out and positioned between the graphics window and the Task pane, which now remains open by default.

You can also detach the Task pane by dragging the bar at the top of the pane. Figure 18.1 shows the Task pane docked to the right side of the SolidWorks window.

FIGURE 18.1

FIGURE 18.1

The Task pane docked to right side of the SolidWorks window

> **TIP** If you are using dual monitors, you can drag the detached Task pane onto the second monitor, which allows you to use the Task pane, and at the same time gives you more room in the graphics area. This must be done each session; the Task Pane does not remember positions on a second monitor.

Design Library

 The Design Library tab displays an image of a stack of books. It is the overall library area for all sorts of elements in SolidWorks, which I will discuss later in this chapter. The only part of the Design Library that concerns us right now is the Features folder. If you expand this folder, you can see that it is populated with some sample features.

Open a new part and create a cylinder using any method you want (for example, extrude, revolve). Make the diameter three inches, and the length a little more than one inch.

In the Inch features folder, click the folder called o-ring grooves. The first feature in the list is called *face static – gas*. Drag-and-drop this feature onto the end flat face of the cylinder. As shown in the image to the left in Figure 18.2, the PropertyManager displays a yellow information panel explaining the process.

The next step is to select the configuration, as shown in the image to the right in Figure 18.2. Not all library features have multiple size configurations, but these ones do. The configs in this case are driven by design tables. Select configuration 330.

FIGURE 18.2

Placing the feature and selecting the configuration

When you select the configuration, the interface changes. In this case, only a sketch relation locates the feature; it is not located by dimensions. Notice that in the References panel shown in Figure 18.3, there is an Edge entry with a question mark. This means that the library feature needs a circular edge to locate it. Notice that a small window appears, displaying the library feature. You may not be able to distinguish it in Figure 18.3, but the circular edge around the face that the library feature is on is highlighted in green. This indicates that you need to select an edge that has the same relation to the library feature as the highlighted edge. Pick the circular edge of the part on the end of the cylinder where you want to place the library feature.

Next, use a rectangular part where the library feature is located by using dimensions rather than sketch relations. Create a rectangle, 1.5 inches by 2 inches, and extrude it to about 2 inches in depth.

FIGURE 18.3

Locating the library feature

Next, in the Design Library, browse to features, then inch, and then the fluid power ports folder, and drag the sae j1926-1 feature onto the end of the extruded rectangle. Select the 38-24 size from the configurations list. A window appears, prompting you for reference selections, as shown in Figure 18.4.

> **TIP** It is often helpful to orient the part that is receiving the library feature in the same way as the part shown in the preview window. This helps you to visualize which edges to select.

After the locating edges have been identified, the Locating Dimensions box becomes active, and you can change the values of the dimensions to locate the feature. Further, in the Size Dimensions pane at the bottom of the PropertyManager, clicking the Override Dimension Values option allows you to change dimensions of the feature itself.

When you use a library feature with a design table, the design table is not brought into the part with the library feature. If the part already had a design table, this would cause multiple tables, which is not currently possible in SolidWorks.

FIGURE 18.4

Placing a library feature with dimensions

If you override the feature dimensions when feature configurations already exist, then a new configuration is created in the list of feature configurations called Custom Configuration. It appears that multiple custom configurations are not allowed, and so if you have to make changes, then you must ensure that they are right before you use the library feature in a part.

Other Design Library functions

The Design Library has other functions besides library features. For example, you can use it as a repository for other items that you use frequently.

Annotations

You can store commonly used annotations in the Design Library. If you look at the Annotations folder with the default sample annotations, you see a combination of symbols and blocks. You can use symbols and notes in 3D models, but you can only use blocks in sketches or 2D drawings. Keep in mind that not all annotation types can be used in all places.

Annotations can be stored in the library as favorites or blocks. Many file extensions are used for different types of favorites, but they typically begin with *.sld* and end with *fvt*, as in *.sldweldfvt. Figure 18.5 shows the default location of the Design Library, and the Thumbnail view of the favorites and blocks in the Annotations folder.

The Annotations folder in Windows Explorer

Location of the Design Library folder

If you frequently work with different types of annotations, then you should organize the library into sub-folders to separate symbols, annotations, and blocks, and move these folders to a different location. By default, the Design Library folders are found at <SW install dir >\data\design library\. You should store them to another location, not in the SolidWorks installation directory, but in an area that you have selected to maintain SolidWorks data between releases. For example, I have a folder at D:\Library that contains folders for macros, templates, library features, library parts, favorites, and so on. You can easily back up or copy these files from one computer to another, although you must quit SolidWorks before making these changes.

After moving the library, you have to point SolidWorks to the new location. To do this, select Tools ➪ Options ➪ File Locations ➪ Design Library. Delete the old location and browse to the new location. You should move other items in this list and redirect any items that you use, such as the templates and any other items you use frequently. Once you have specified the settings, they should be retained when you install service pack upgrades or future versions.

Library Parts

The Design Library can also store commonly used library parts. One of the advantages of using the library for parts is that on placement into the assembly, if configurations are available in a part, then a window pops up, enabling you to select which configuration to place into the assembly.

NOTE In many cases, using the Design Library for Library Parts is thought to be an acceptable replacement for the automated function of Toolbox. If you use Toolbox to make the parts and populate them with configurations, and then save the parts out of Toolbox and into the Design Library, many options, including naming conventions, and more flexible use of custom properties become available that are not available through Toolbox.

Figure 18.6 shows the configuration selection window. Note that this is alphabetically listed, and you can type in the box to go to the configuration that you want.

FIGURE 18.6

Inserting library parts with configurations

Parts inserted from the library parts folder can also take advantage of the Mate References functionality in the same way as Toolbox, by allowing parts to snap into place.

Sheet metal forming tools

Sheet metal forming tools are only mentioned here as a part of the library. They work much like other library features, but they do so within the specialized functions of sheet metal parts in SolidWorks. Sheet metal forming tools are discussed in Chapters 29 and 30.

Assemblies

You can use library assemblies in SolidWorks in the same ways that you use library parts, because they are inserted into the top-level assembly as a sub-assembly. For sub-assemblies that require motion, such as universal joint sub-assemblies, you can set the sub-assembly to solve as flexible.

 When saving assemblies to the library, it is recommended that you put the parts in a separate folder to segregate the parts of different assemblies.

Routing

Routing is a separately purchased add-in that is included with SolidWorks Office Premium. It includes piping, tubing (rigid and flexible), and wiring. Routing makes extensive use of libraries and automation, but is not part of the scope of this book.

Smart Components

Smart Components are components that resize by automatically selecting configurations, depending on the size of the geometry onto which they are being dropped. For example, a clamp with many sizes driven by configurations would select the correct config when dropped onto different sizes of cylinders. This is a very useful tool. Smart Components are discussed in Chapter 19.

Creating Library Features

When you save library features to the library, they use the file extension, *.sldlfp (library feature part). They must contain some base geometry, which simulates the part onto which the feature will be dropped. The base geometry is not transferred to the new part; only features that are marked with the "L" in the FeatureManager (for Library) are transferred to the new part. Figure 18.7 shows the FeatureManager of a library feature part.

FIGURE 18.7

The FeatureManager of a library feature part

Creating a library feature

When creating a library feature, the first problem that you need to solve is how the feature will be located on a new part. Does it need to be placed on cylindrical parts, rectangular parts, other types of shapes, or does this matter at all? Will the feature be located by using dimensions or sketch relations, or will it just be placed underdefined and later fully defined manually rather than automatically?

You may have noticed in one of the earlier examples that the sample fluid power ports had two versions of the same feature. One version is intended for the feature to be placed on the flat end of a cylinder, and the other version is intended to be placed on a rectangular face.

A few limitations

Library features can contain multiple features of different types. They may add and remove material, even within a single library feature. However, a few limitations exist. For example, they require a base feature, and multibody features and external references are not allowed, nor are sheet metal, weldments, or molds. In addition, you cannot add scale features to the library, nor can you apply library features to an assembly.

Creating a new library feature

To start a new feature, the first decision that you need to make is what shape to make the base. Is the feature a type that is usually going to go onto a single shape or multiple shapes? Regardless of your decision, you or whoever ends up using the feature will have the flexibility to change, or simply not use, the relations when you place the feature.

For this example, I use a rectangular base. The library feature that I want to create consists of two boss extrudes, a cut extrude, and several fillets. Here is how it works:

First, you need to create a rectangular extrusion. The size should be bigger than the feature that goes on it, and representative of the face of the end part onto which this feature will typically be placed.

Next, in beginning to create the features that you want to reuse, it is very important that you pay attention to any references outside of the sketch; these include absolutely *anything* outside the active sketch, such as the sketch plane, references to edges, the Origin, other planes, other sketches, and axes. Although these references are allowed, each reference to anything that is not already part of the library feature must be reconnected when you place the feature on the part. The ideal situation is obviously a single drag-and-drop, but generally speaking, at least one other step is usually needed. The initial drag-and-drop determines the face for the feature to start from, and from there, you usually need to locate features, either by using relations or dimensions. A concentric dimension locates the feature in a single reference selection of a circular edge (although it may also need to be rotated), and dimensions typically require a dimension in the X dimension, and another one in the Y dimension.

Figure 18.8 shows the base feature and the first feature of the library feature. The only relations between the sketch of the library feature and the base feature are the sketch plane and the two dimensions.

> **NOTE**   Notice that names have been assigned to all of the dimensions, sketches, and features. This is because the dimension names all display in the interface. If you look back to Figure 18.4, in the Size Dimensions pane, dimension names make it easy to know which dimension to change, whereas the D1 dimension leaves you guessing as to what it applies to.

FIGURE 18.8

Creating a library feature

You should ensure that subsequent features after the first one reference only the first feature of the library feature (which is the second feature in the part). This is not a mandatory requirement, but a helpful guideline. You can make additional references, but they should be limited to the same items that were already referenced, if possible. Users who model carelessly or do not pay attention to what they are doing, typically have trouble making library features that function and are easy to use.

Now you can add the second extruded feature, being careful to reference only geometry that is going to move with the library feature. Figure 18.9 shows the newly added feature. If you would like to follow along with the building of this feature, you can open the part from the CD-ROM under the filename Chapter 18 First Library Feature.sldprt.

FIGURE 18.9

Adding the next feature to the library feature

Notice that a plane has been added. The plane is made to only reference geometry that is internal to the library feature; it is perpendicular to an edge at the midpoint, which simultaneously locates and orients the plane correctly to enable it to be used to mirror the Ear feature.

Also notice that the EarSketch uses the same face reference from the base feature. This will appear in the Reference list as a single reference.

NOTE SolidWorks has made some changes that affect library features in two ways that may not be immediately obvious. First, before SolidWorks allowed multibody parts, the first feature of the part was always called the *base feature*. This terminology remains, even though the concept of a base feature is obsolete. (The first feature in a part may be reordered so that a different feature becomes first.)

Second, SolidWorks used to distinguish between palette features and library features. Palette features were limited to a single reference, and library features were a bit less user-friendly but more powerful. They have been combined and improved to what we have today.

Saving the library feature

You can use two methods to save a library feature. You can either drag-and-drop into a Design Library folder, or use the Save As method. Because Save As is a little more common, I will describe it first.

The first step in saving the library feature is to select all of the features in the FeatureManager that are intended to be a part of the library feature. Collapse the features first so that the sketches belonging to features are not selected. If the sketches are selected you may get a warning message saying that all of the selected features cannot be used in the library feature. Do not worry; the sketches still will be included.

> **TIP**   Remember that you can Ctrl-select individual features, Shift-select a range, or click-and-drag a box in the FeatureManager to select multiple features. Also keep in mind that if you do not select a feature (other than the base feature), then it will not be placed into the part when you insert the library feature. If there were any relations to the omitted feature, they may display as errors or warnings when you place the feature.

With the features selected, click File, Save As, and under Files of Type drop-down list, select the *.sldlfp file type. Browse to the Design Library folder, and save the part. Figure 18.10 shows the FeatureManager of the finished library feature.

FIGURE 18.10

The finished library feature part

Display of the Library Feature icon

During the Save As process, a new folder was added to the Design Library named Bosses, as shown in Figure 18.10. Notice the new icon for the library feature in the lower window. You may notice that some of the default library features saved in the Design Library have a bluish background. This occurs because of the SolidWorks viewport background color, which you can set in Tools, Options, Colors. Even if you never see that color because you are using a gradient background, SolidWorks still uses the color specified by that setting as the background when saving thumbnails and previews. I always set this color to white for this reason, so that document backgrounds in previews do not have the blue color.

You may want to orient and zoom the library feature before saving it, so that it displays clearly in the panel. One of the techniques that I like to use is to make the base feature a different color than the library feature itself; this helps you to more easily determine what is the geometry that will be transferred and what is just dummy material.

TIP Figure 18.11 shows various settings for displaying the icons in the Design Library. Which one you select will depend on your screen resolution, the number of icons that you want to display, and the quality of the preview images.

FIGURE 18.11

Display modes for the Design Library

The real test for a library feature comes when you actually use it. This feature is recreated perfectly on the new part, but I noticed one problem. When the feature was placed, it was 90 degrees away from the orientation that I wanted it to be in. It seems that the only way to make the feature rotatable is to create it with parallel and perpendicular relations rather than horizontal and vertical ones, so that one of the references can act as a rotation reference.

Figure 18.12 shows the completed library feature placed on a part.

FIGURE 18.12

The completed library feature placed on a part

Once you place a library feature on a part, it can be edited, unless you select the Link To Library Part option in the Configuration pane, in which case the feature is driven externally from the *.sldlfp file.

One of the available options is to dissolve the library feature so that all of the constituent features become regular features in the main part.

Creating a library feature from an existing part

When creating a library feature from an existing part, you use essentially the same process, but it is actually somewhat more difficult to achieve the correct results. It is best to remove all of the features that do not either form the base feature or go into the library feature itself. This can cause a lot of broken references. It may be better to use a different technique such as creating a new part with only the base feature. You can then Ctrl-drag the desired features from the existing part to the new part, set up the rest of the library feature, and save it with a *.sldlfp extension.

You can also create a library feature by dragging and dropping, although there are some limitations with this technique that seem to override the convenience. However, there is a workaround for the biggest limitation. If you select faces from features and drag them into the lower Design Library window, then an Add to Library PropertyManager interface appears to enable you to start creating a library feature. The Add to Library PropertyManager interface is shown in Figure 18.13. You must select the features from the flyout FeatureManager. This is the source of one of the limitations. In our example, the plane cannot be selected by this method. The workaround for this is to complete the feature without the plane, RMB click the icon in the Design Library window, and then select Open. With the library feature open in its own window, RMB click the plane feature and select Add to Library; that individual feature is then added.

FIGURE 18.13

The Add to Library PropertyManager interface

Adding folders to the library

You can add folders to the library in two ways, either by RMB clicking in the Design Library window and selecting New Folder, or by using the Windows Explorer interface. Another RMB menu option is Add Existing Folder, which enables you to add a folder from another location to the library. The folder is not moved or copied, but a shortcut is added to the Design Library, and the contents appear in the lower pane.

> **TIP**   After a library feature has been edited, or folders or documents have been added to the library using Windows Explorer, you can press F5 in either the lower or the upper window to update the display for that window, or by using the Refresh icon located at the top of the Task pane.

Tutorial: Working with Library Features

This tutorial guides you through customizing a Hole Wizard hole to use as a specialty library feature, then storing it in the library, editing it, and placing it in a part. Follow these steps:

1. Open a new part, and create a rectangular base feature, about three inches high by three inches wide, and three inches deep.

2. Pre-select a flat face and start the Hole Wizard.

3. Create a counterbored hole for a Heavy Hex Bolt, ½-inch, Normal Fit, Blind, 1.2 inches deep. Locate the hole with dimensions from two perpendicular edges, as shown in Figure 18.14. Click the green check mark icon to accept the hole settings.

FIGURE 18.14

Placing a hole

4. Select Tools ➡ Options ➡ General, and turn on Show Dimension Names.

5. Double-click the counterbored hole feature in the FeatureManager to show the dimensions. RMB click one of the dimensions that you created to locate the center of the hole, and select Properties.

6. Rename the dimension using different names, so that they will have meaning when you place the dimension, such as XDir, or YDir. Do this for both dimensions.

7. Edit the second sketch of the hole. Figure 18.15 shows what the sketch should look like before and after the edit.

CAUTION Do not delete any of the named dimensions in a normal or revised Hole Wizard hole. SolidWorks has a checking mechanism that looks for these names, and it will display an error if the named dimension is not there. If there is no use for the dimension, it still has to be there, although it does not need to be used for its original use. You could rename another dimension with the name or simply dimension the centerline or an otherwise unused construction line. It does not matter about the function of the dimension, as long as there is a dimension with that name in the sketch.

TIP You should also name any new dimensions that you may want to change. These dimensions will have more meaning when you are placing the feature if they have names.

FIGURE 18.15

Reconfiguring the hole

TIP Remember that to get the diameter dimensions shown in Figure 18.15 (instead of radius dimensions), you must use the dimension tool to select the centerline (construction line) and the line or endpoint on one side, and then move the cursor to the other side of the centerline to place the dimension (the order of selection does not matter). When the cursor crosses the centerline, the dimension will display as a diameter instead of a radius.

8. When you are done editing the sketch and renaming dimensions, exit the sketch.

9. Click the CBORE feature twice, or click it once and press F2, to rename it as SpecialHole.

10. Pre-select the same flat face that the first hole feature was placed on, and start the Hole Wizard again.

11. Place a #8-32 tapped hole, accept the default depth, and specify a center-to-center distance of .75 inches between it and the SpecialHole. Rename the radial dimension as MountRad.

12. Using the temporary axis through the center of the SpecialHole, make a circular pattern of the new tapped hole, creating a total of four instances of the tapped hole. Make the SpecialHole Feature red, and the tapped hole and pattern yellow.

13. Split the FeatureManager window into two by using the splitter bar at the top. Change the lower panel to the ConfigurationManager.

14. Rename the Default configuration to Size1.

15. Create a new configuration called Size2. Double-click the SpecialHole feature and change the dimension named C'Bore Dia to 1.5 inches. Be sure to change to This Configuration Only, using the drop-down menu.

16. Make a dimension change for the MountRad dimension to 1 inch. The results to this point are shown in Figure 18.16.

FIGURE 18.16

The results after step 16

17. Auto-create a design table by selecting Insert ➪ Design Table, and then selecting the Auto-Create option. Edit the design table to look like Figure 18.17.

TIP Remember that to fill the first two columns up to Size5, you can make the two-by-two selection of the Size1 and Size2 entries in the first two columns, and pull down the handle in the lower-right corner of the selection box until the appropriate boxes are filled.

FIGURE 18.17

The design table for the SpecialHole feature

18. Manually fill in the C'Bore Dia values, but in cell D3, type the equation **=C3/2+.25**. Then use the same Fill technique to populate cells D3 to D7.

19. Test the configurations to make sure that they all work.

20. In the Design Library, browse to a folder where you would like to put this library feature. (Make sure that it is not used by assemblies or sheet metal forming tools.) Click a face created by the SpecialHole feature, and drag the feature into the lower pane of the Design Library. The Add to Library PropertyManager should appear on the left.

21. Although you selected a feature and dragged it into the library, the Items to Add field appears blank. Select the SpecialHole, tapped hole, and circular pattern features, either through the split FeatureManager or the flyout FeatureManager. Selecting the features from the graphics window does not work.

22. Position and zoom the view of the part so that when it is saved, you see a good preview of the library feature. Also, if you have not changed your background color from blue to white, this would be a good time to do so.

23. In the Save To pane, make sure that you select the correct folder, then fill in a filename, and click OK. Figure 18.18 shows the completed PropertyManager interface for this function.

TIP You may notice that there are two library entries in the window. This is because an additional path has been added in Tools ⇨ Options ⇨ File Locations ⇨ Design Library.

24. If the new library feature does not appear in the Design Library, then click in the Design Library and press F5. If you do not like the way that it displays, then RMB click in a blank space inside the lower library window and select one of the other three options.

25. To edit the preview image of the feature, RMB click the feature in the Design Library window, select Open, reposition or zoom the view, and save it. Click in the Design Library and press F5 again.

FIGURE 18.18

Saving the library feature

> **TIP**   It is recommended that when placing a library feature, you should close the original
> library feature window. The workflow proceeds much more smoothly if the part is
> closed before you use it.

26. Open the part from the CD-ROM called Chapter 18 Tutorial Blank.sldprt. If you would like to examine the version of the SpecialHole part that I created, it is stored with this data as well.

27. Drag the SpecialHole library feature from the Design Library onto the face of the blank part. Place the feature near the squared-off end. Select a configuration from the list in the PropertyManager.

> **TIP**   Although there is no prompt, when the Library Feature interface hesitates and there are
> configurations in the library feature, it is waiting for you to select a configuration. A
> prompt actually does exist, but it appears in the lower-left corner of the screen on the status bar in a
> tiny font, and most users probably do not notice it.

28. Try to orient the part in the same way that it appears in the preview window, as shown in Figure 18.19.

568

FIGURE 18.19

Orienting the part and selecting references

29. Select edges on the Blank part that correspond to the preview window. Click OK to accept the placement of the feature.

30. Double-click the SpecialHole feature and change the X and Y placement dimensions to place it one inch from the edges in both directions.

NOTE You may remember from Chapter 10 that library feature configurations cannot be controlled by part configurations. In order to show different library feature configurations in different part configurations, you need to suppress one library feature and insert another. This is the best available workaround. It may be time to visit that enhancement request site again.

31. Place another library feature onto the blank part. Select a configuration, and click the green check mark icon, without selecting edges for the references.

32. Notice that the feature in the FeatureManager appears with an exclamation mark. If you investigate the cause of this, then you can see that the two dimensions that should be attached to edges are dangling because you did not select the references while placing the library feature. This was done on purpose to show a different technique.

33. Expand the library feature and the SpecialHole feature, and edit the first sketch in the Special Hole. This is the placement sketch. Delete the two dimensions that appear in dangling colors.

34. Add a concentric sketch relation between the placement point and the arc edge of the Blank part. Exit the sketch. The error message should now be gone and the hole should now be placed in the center of the arc.

35. RMB click the second library feature and select Dissolve Library Feature.

NOTE   When you dissolve a library feature, you lose any access to any configurations. Some users insist on dissolving every library feature, so that they can see regular features in the FeatureManager. This technique may also be useful if you would like to reorder some of the individual features within the library feature.

36. Figure 18.20 shows the finished part and FeatureManager. Good job!

FIGURE 18.20

The finished part

Summary

Library features are very useful in automating frequent design tasks. They are easy to create, easy to store, and easy to apply. Setting up the features for the most flexibility often takes careful planning and attention to the detail of the references that you use.

Chapter 19

Using Smart Components

Smart Components are one of the better design automation tools to come from SolidWorks in the last several releases. This is functionality that can save you a lot of time; the more standard items that you insert into your assemblies, the more time it can save you.

Smart Components are parts or assemblies that you can place into an upper-level assembly and that carry with them mounting features and hardware (cut-outs, mounting holes, and even fasteners). Smart Components are configurable, and can automatically size themselves on cylindrical parts.

Understanding Smart Components

A Smart Component can comprise several elements:

- A single part or an assembly that may use size configurations
- A configurable library feature that usually serves as mounting holes or a viewing window for the Smart Component
- Associated hardware that may also be driven by sizes
- A training assembly that is used to define the Smart Component

Some minor limitations exist, as you might expect:

- A Smart Component part cannot have references that are external to the Smart Component group of which it is a member
- When placed in the assembly, the associated library feature can only affect one component

■ The associated library feature is limited to one of several feature types:

   ▪ Extruded or revolved cuts or bosses

   ▪ Hole Wizard holes

   ▪ Simple hole features

The setup time for Smart Components can be significant for the first one or two that you create, especially if you choose the auto-size option. The complexity of setup depends mainly on the number of configurations and configured parts that you use. The auto-sizing function takes the most time to set up because it requires matching configurations, and the auto-size table takes a while to manage, especially for multiple parts. Still, if you end up placing a given part with associated features and other components many times manually, this is a technique that can save you a lot of time.

Using Smart Components

 Figure 19.1 shows a simple assembly. It took approximately 20 minutes to model all of the parts, set up the Smart Component, and test it in an assembly. This example does not use auto-sizing, but it does use an in-context feature and two instances of a single hardware piece. This is an excellent example of Smart Component functionality because it is fast to create and fast to apply, and saves you some time whenever you use it.

FIGURE 19.1

A simple Smart Component

Getting started with a simple Smart Component

In this assembly, you first place the electrical connector part in the assembly, mate it in place, and then apply Smart Components. You can apply Smart Components by clicking the Smart Component icon that appears on the part in the graphics window when you select it. SolidWorks then prompts you to select the inside and outside faces of the sheet metal part (the hardware references the outside, and the cut-out feature references the inside). SolidWorks then creates the cutout as an in-context feature that it places in the sheet metal part.

 This in-context feature is why the Smart Component is limited to affecting a single part.

When you create the Smart Component, a new folder is added to the FeatureManager of the component. This folder contains all of the required information about the other elements, such as the in-context feature, any other parts that go with the Smart Component, the "training assembly" location, and the face references to locate everything. Figure 19.2 in the image to the left shows this folder in the connector part that is used in this example. The image to the right shows what is added to the assembly FeatureManager when you add a Smart Component. The only thing that existed in the design tree shown in Figure 19.2 before the Smart Component was the Test Box sheet metal part.

FIGURE 19.2

The Smart Component folder in the connector part

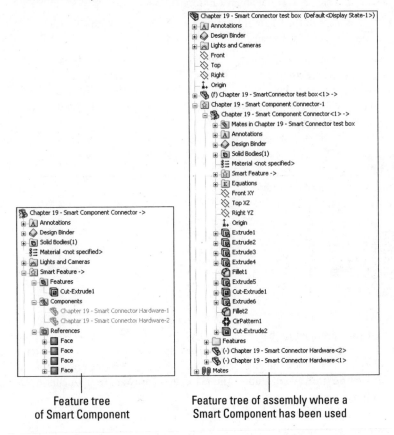

Feature tree
of Smart Component

Feature tree of assembly where a
Smart Component has been used

A star appears on the part symbol at the top of the FeatureManager, indicating that the part is a Smart Component.

You can place this Smart Component by following these steps:

1. Create an assembly, and add the target part to it. The target part is the one that the Smart Component will be mated to, and the one that will have the in-context cut-out inserted into it.

CAUTION   It is a good idea to save the assembly *before* you add the Smart Component to it. If the Smart Component is placed before the assembly is saved, the assembly has a tendency to forget that it has not been saved, and bumps the in-context feature to out-of-context when the name is changed from whatever the default name is (for example, Assem1.sldasm) to the name that you assign to it.

2. Put the Smart Component into the assembly. You can do this in the same way that you would add any normal part, including from the Design Library. If you use a part frequently enough to make it into a Smart Component, then you are probably going to want to have it in the Design Library for quick access. In fact, you can add a Smart Component to an assembly without using any of the Smart Component options.

3. Mate the Smart Component in the assembly. In this case, it was done with a face-to-face coincident mate and a pair of distance mates.

4. Next, apply Smart Components by clicking the Smart Component symbol on the part. If this symbol does not appear, then select the part in the FeatureManager. Figure 19.3 shows the Smart Component symbol on the part. If you have inserted many instances of a Smart Component, then each instance has the option to apply the Smart Component features and associated components.

FIGURE 19.3

The Smart Component symbol on a part

5. At this point, an interface similar to that of the Library Feature interface appears, with the small prompt window and a box for selecting references, as shown in Figure 19.4. After you select the references, and click the green check mark icon, the Smart Component, as well as the Smart Feature (in-context feature) and associated hardware components, are placed, and the job is done.

FIGURE 19.4

The interface for adding the Smart Feature and additional components of the Smart Component

Auto-sizing Smart Components

Auto-sizing is the ability of a Smart Component to select a size from a list of configurations, based on the size of geometry onto which it is being dropped. At this time, the only shape that can be auto-sized is the cylindrical shape.

Figure 19.5 shows the effects of auto-sizing. Notice the two shaft holders. These are two instances of the same part, using different size configurations. When you drag the Smart Component over the small end of the stepped shaft, the configuration corresponding to that size appears. As you drag the part along the shaft and the shaft diameter increases, the next-larger Smart Component configuration appears. This is part of the functionality of Smart Components. Each configuration of the Smart Component is set up to fit onto a range of shaft diameters. If the diameter of the shaft is outside of the range or between sizes, then the Smart Component is not applied.

FIGURE 19.5

A Smart Component with auto-sizing

Sizes are governed by a configurator table, which looks similar to a design table, but works somewhat differently. The configurator table relates the configurations of the Smart Component to configurations of the individual components, which may also change size with the Smart Component. This serves as a subset of the function of a design table in an assembly, assigning part configurations to assembly configurations. Figure 19.6 shows a sample configurator table made for the following assembly.

FIGURE 19.6

A configurator table

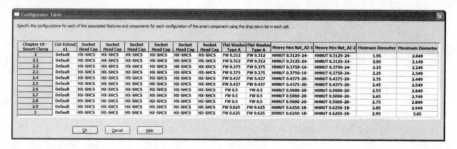

When you look at this table, you begin to understand why creating auto-sizing Smart Components is much more involved than in the previous example. The configurations of the Smart Component are listed to the left, and the individual part configs can be selected in each cell from a drop-down list of all available configs for that part. There is no way to set configs for multiple components at once, nor is there a copy-and-paste function. These shortcomings combine to make this format somewhat less user-friendly than an Excel-based design table.

Most notable are the Minimum and Maximum Diameter columns to the right. These columns supply the parameters that make the auto-size function work. While the range of sizes used here is too large for real-world design (+/– .050 inches), it serves to convey the idea. More importantly, SolidWorks understands that mating sizes are not always exactly equal, and the ability to use a range rather than exact values accommodates this very nicely, although it can be tedious to set up.

Another aspect of the setup shown here is that it uses Toolbox parts. If you want to use the auto-size functionality, then you need to be using configurations for Toolbox parts. You should pre-build all of the needed configurations, and ensure that the configurations are always available.

Making Smart Components

The most important point to remember about Smart Component setup is that you need to do it only once for each Smart Component. The second most important point is that the first setup is the most difficult. After that, subsequent setups become much easier to create. Adding components to the Smart Component is not so time-consuming unless the additional components are also configured and also auto-sized.

Smart Components must contain at least one associated component and one in-context feature, or have the configurator table filled out and functional. If you try to create a Smart Component from a standalone part, then nothing happens; the Smart Component interface simply closes. You may combine all three elements (associated component, in-context feature, and auto-size), but you must have at least one element.

Getting started with a simple Smart Component

Because the electrical connector shown in Figure 19.1 has already been used to demonstrate the insertion of a Smart Component, it is used here to demonstrate how to create one.

All that you need to make a Smart Component with an associated Smart Feature (in this case, a cut-out and mounting holes) and mounting hardware (in this case, two stand-off screws) is the part itself. The part can even be an imported part (a Smart Component made from dumb geometry).

From the CD-ROM for Chapter 19, open the file named Chapter 19 – Connector Start.sldprt. This part is shown in Figure 19.7.

There is nothing special about this part. I modeled it in SolidWorks using standard features, and there are no configurations or special features. It represents an electrical connector that may be mounted in a sheet metal electrical enclosure.

FIGURE 19.7

An electrical connector part

The first step in setting it up is to create a mock assembly with a dummy part representing the sheet metal box. The part does not need to be complex or even sheet metal for that matter; it just needs to be close to the thickness that you would expect it to be mounted to. The assembly is called a *training* assembly, not because you are learning how to make a Smart Component, but because you are training the Smart Component to be *smart*.

1. Make a simple rectangular part, approximately 4 inches square and about .06 inches thick. Save the part to your hard drive. Give a name to the part so that it is clear that it belongs to this training assembly.

2. Place the rectangular dummy part into a new assembly, with a name that is both unique and identifiable.

3. Put the connector into the assembly. Mate the part so that the flange is flush with the rectangular piece. Also use distance mates to locate the connector planes from the edges of the part, similar to Figure 19.8 in the image to the left.

4. Next, edit the dummy part in context, and offset edges of the connector part to extrude a cut, as shown in Figure 19.8 in the image to the right. Offset the two mounting holes and the area around where the connector will stick through the sheet metal by about .02 inches.

FIGURE 19.8

Placing the connector on the dummy part

5. Exit Edit Component mode and add two instances of the part named Chapter 19 – Smart Connector Hardware.sldprt to the assembly. Mate the hardware part to the in-context hole, making sure that it goes to the outside thickness of the dummy sheet metal part.

NOTE I have spent a fair amount of time trying to convince you that it is a best practice to *avoid* mating parts to in-context features, and yet here I tell you to do exactly that. Another thing I have tried to stress is that best practice suggestions are more like guidelines. If you are having performance problems with an assembly, then this may not be a great technique to use. However, sometimes there is a price to pay for sophisticated functionality, and if you think that your design can afford the price and will benefit from this functionality, then you should use it.

6. Now that everything is in place, click the Make Smart Component tool on the assembly toolbar. If the button is not there, you can add it to the assembly toolbar by selecting Tools ➪ Customize menu, or by selecting Tools ➪ Make Smart Component. The resulting interface is shown in Figure 19.9.

7. In the Smart Component selection box, select the connector part.

8. In the Components selection box, select the two hardware components.

9. In the Features selection box, select the in-context feature from the dummy part.

10. You are now finished setting up the Smart Component. Click the green check mark icon to accept the changes and exit out of the PropertyManager, and save the file.

FIGURE 19.9

The Smart Component PropertyManager interface

Creating an auto-sizing Smart Component

The simple Smart Component took about 20 minutes to model and set up. That is not too bad for a feature that you will probably use a lot. The benefits are somewhat modest, placing three components and a feature.

However, when it comes to the auto-sizing example that is shown next, the benefits are more extensive. A total of seven individual parts are placed (including Toolbox parts) — three of which are automatically sized, depending on the geometry into which the Smart Component is dropped — and an in-context feature is added.

To begin, open the part from the CD-ROM named Chapter 19 – Clamp Start. Notice that this is a multibody part. There is no special knowledge that you need to have about multibody parts to complete this task. Multiple bodies are discussed in detail in Chapter 26.

1. With the Clamp Start part open, notice that several configurations already exist. If you click through the configurations or examine the design table in the part, you can see that various dimensions change. The primary dimension that changes is the diameter of the hole, and this change drives the diameter of, and distance between, the mounting holes.

NOTE In SolidWorks 2007, you can only drive auto-sizing by cylindrical geometry.

2. Part of the Smart Component definition includes applying a Mate Reference to the part, so that the big hole automatically snaps to cylindrical geometry. Another aspect is that it adds in-context holes that match the mounting holes on the clamp. Figure 19.10 shows the assembly that this part is meant to go into. The clamp snaps onto the stepped shaft and adds holes to the plate.

FIGURE 19.10

The assembly where the Smart Component will be used

3. Open the file named Chapter 19 Autosize Training Assembly.sldasm. This has been prepared to help you get started with the Smart Component training.

NOTE The shaft is not necessary in the training assembly. The training assembly is intended to create the in-context Smart Feature and to create the configurator table. The shaft part has been added here for visualization only.

4. Insert the clamp part into the assembly, and mate it concentric to the shaft and coincident to the blue plate. It does not matter where the clamp sits along the shaft, but it should be fully mated into the location so that it does not slide back and forth.

5. Edit the plate in the context of the assembly, and convert entities from the mounting holes in the clamp to create holes in the plate that align with the holes in the clamp.

6. Exit the Edit Component mode.

7. Activate Toolbox, select the four holes, as shown in Figure 19.11, and insert Socket Head Cap Screws, ⅜ by 24 by ⅝ inches. If you do not have Toolbox or choose not to use it, then a part with the correct name and sized configurations is provided on the CD-ROM.

FIGURE 19.11

Inserting four screws at once using Toolbox

Pre-select these four edges

8. Use the same fastener to place in the mounting holes, using the correct size for the hole. The length will be set later. Use a default length of 2.25 inches for both mounting holes.

> **NOTE**   Working with the length of the fasteners is not a clean operation in Smart Components. The length is dependent on the thickness of the plate, which is not controlled by the Smart Fastener, nor can the Smart Fastener account for it, except through mates. (Remember that auto-sizing is driven only by a diameter.) Later in this chapter, you will see how the washers and nuts are put in place on the underside of the plate, but the screw length cannot be automatically calculated (unless the screw itself had an in-context relation to the nut).

9. Place washers and nuts on the screws on the backside of the plate.

10. This is where the process becomes a little convoluted. When the shaft diameter changes, the hole in the clamp changes to match (within the ranges that will be established). As the clamp becomes bigger, bigger screws are needed to secure the clamp and the holes grow further apart. Bigger screws mean additional configurations for the screw, washer, and nut parts. Remember that the configurations do not necessarily exist. I would not count on a Smart Component working if this meant that Toolbox had to create new configurations.

To create this example, I have pre-populated the Toolbox parts with all of the configurations needed for the range of sizes involved with this Smart Component. When you make your own Smart Components, you will have to do the same thing if you intend to use auto-sizing with Toolbox parts. The difficulty here is that the configurations include the diameter size of the screw as well as the length, which is unknown until you place the part.

All you have to worry about in this step is to make sure that the configurations are available and that the screws are placed properly.

11. Up to this step, you have just assembled the parts as if this were the only time you were going to do it. The automation of the process comes next. Figure 19.12 shows the training assembly to this point. The shaft and plate are shown in wireframe because they are external to the Smart Component.

FIGURE 19.12

The training assembly up to step 11

12. This is the point in the previous example where the Make Smart Component command was used, and it is no different here. Click the Make Smart Component tool on the assembly toolbar.

13. Figure 19.13 shows the filled in Smart Component PropertyManager. Activate the Smart Component selection box and pick the clamp part.

In the Components selection box, select the six screw instances, the two washers, and the two nuts.

In the Features selection box, select the in-context feature or features that are associated with the Smart Component.

FIGURE 19.13

The Smart Component Property Manager

Although the in-context feature can affect only a single part, this does not mean that you are limited to a single in-context feature. In most cases, only one feature is needed, but I am sure that there are situations where more than one would be useful. Also, remember that the in-context features are limited to extruded and revolved bosses and cuts, Hole Wizard holes, and simple hole features.

14. The configurator table is simply a table that enables you to select which component configurations are to be used with which Smart Component configuration. It looks and works very much like an assembly design table, but it is not Excel-based, and every cell must be set explicitly rather than using techniques for mass population or assigning properties to a range of configs, such as you can do with a real design table.

Each cell has a drop-down list of all of the available configurations for that component. If you have four instances of a single component, then you have to set each instance of each component.

Figure 19.14 shows the configurator table for this example.

FIGURE 19.14

The configurator table for the Clamp Smart component

NOTE If the configurator table were to ever be as easy to use as, for example, an Excel design table, then Smart Component complexity could increase significantly. The configurator table could even ideally be created *from* an assembly design table. Instead of a single component with its associated hardware and mounting features, think of larger-scale sub-assembly attachments. This sort of work is possible now, but with configurator tables as cumbersome as they are, it is difficult to do more than a handful of parts.

15. Click OK. You are now done creating the auto-sizing Smart Component!

File management with Smart Components

You may expect that with the training assembly, there is an extra burden of file management with Smart Components. This may seem counter-intuitive, but in fact, the only file that you need to worry about is the Smart Component itself.

This is not explained very well (or at all) in any of the documentation, but the Help and every reseller demonstration that I have seen on the topic all recommend that you simply *delete* the training assembly once you are done with it because it is not needed any more. This seems like saying that you should delete all of the mates in an assembly or the sketch relations in a part. How do you edit the Smart Component if you delete the assembly in which it is created?

It turns out that all of the information to recreate the training assembly is stored in the Smart Component itself. This includes the in-context feature (which is stored as a library feature), and the locations of any associated components, as well as the configurator table. Figure 19.15 shows a part of the FeatureManager of a Smart Component. As you can see, the in-context feature, the associated components, and the face references are all listed there.

FIGURE 19.15

Part of the FeatureManager of a Smart Component

I was skeptical of this originally and had to test it thoroughly to ensure that deleting the training assembly would not cause any data to be lost, and so I can assure you that it works. Go ahead and delete the assembly.

Editing Smart Components

Expanding somewhat on the discussion about whether or not to keep the training assembly file, here is a little exercise that you can try. Make a Smart Component by going through the preceding steps, by using the following tutorial, or by creating one of your own. Just make a simple one with perhaps one associated component and an in-context feature. Then go ahead and delete the training assembly.

With the defining assembly gone, there appears to be no way to edit the setup of the Smart Component. RMB click the Smart Feature folder in the FeatureManager of the Smart Component, and select Edit in Defining Assembly, as shown in Figure 19.16. What happens next is that SolidWorks recreates the defining assembly from the data that is stored in the Smart Component. This assembly is saved in a system temp folder using the name <Smart Component name>_ta.sldasm. If the Smart Component uses an in-context feature, it is saved to the temp directory as a library feature file using the name of the dummy part, and appending "_lf" to the filename, for example, Dummy_lf.sldlfp.

Selecting the Edit in Defining Assembly command

The Edit Definition button appears in the upper-right corner of the graphics window. If you click this button, the Smart Component PropertyManager interface appears again, enabling you to change the selection of associated components and in-context features, to change the auto-size setting, or to edit the configurator table.

Thus, all of the settings are preserved, and the training assembly exists only as a phantom in a temp directory. Although this appears to be counter-intuitive, it works.

Tutorial: Working with Smart Components

This tutorial guides you through creating a Smart Component that only uses the auto-sizing feature. This enables you to manually create parts that snap to size like Toolbox parts, but without using Toolbox functionality. Follow these steps:

1. Open the part from the CD-ROM that has the filename Chapter 19 – Tutorial Start.sldprt. This part originally came from Toolbox, and already contains a few configurations.

2. Make an assembly that contains *only* this part.

3. Make the part into a Smart Component, and turn on the option to auto-size.

4. Select the small diameter of the part as the concentric mate reference. Figure 19.17 shows the selection.

FIGURE 19.17

Selecting the concentric mate reference face

Concentric mate reference face

5. Click the Configurator Table button, and fill the table in so that it looks like Figure 19.18. Some configurations are blank. This is because only the rows that have minimum and maximum values are used by the auto-size function. The rest are overlooked.

6. Close the configurator table, and save the assembly.

7. Exit the assembly and, in the part file, save it to a folder in your Design Library. If you do not know where your Design Library is located, then select Tools ⇨ Options ⇨ File Locations ⇨ Design Library.

8. Display the part in the Design Library panel of the Task pane.

9. Open the part from the CD-ROM with the filename Chapter 19 Tutorial Plate.sldprt. Place this part into a new assembly.

10. Drag the Tutorial Start (Smart Component) from the Design Library into the assembly, and move the part over the holes in the plate. As you drag the part up and down the row of holes, the part changes sizes to match each hole. Figure 19.19 shows all of the holes that are populated with the matching Smart Component sizes, as driven by the configurator table.

11. To edit the configurator table, open the Smart Component part in its own window. Then RMB click the Smart Feature folder and select Open In Defining Assembly.

FIGURE 19.18

Filling in the configurator table

Chapter 19 Tutor	Minimum Diameter	Maximum Diameter
Default		
HX-SHCS 0.138-3		
HX-SHCS 0.19-32		
HX-SHCS 0.19-32		
HX-SHCS 0.19-32	0.1	0.199
HX-SHCS 0.25-20		
HX-SHCS 0.25-20		
HX-SHCS 0.25-28	0.2	0.249
HX-SHCS 0.3125-		
HX-SHCS 0.3125-		
HX-SHCS 0.3125-		
HX-SHCS 0.3125-		
HX-SHCS 0.375-2		
HX-SHCS 0.375-2		
HX-SHCS 0.375-2		
HX-SHCS 0.375-2		
HX-SHCS 0.375-2	0.25	0.449
HX-SHCS 0.4375-	0.45	0.469
HX-SHCS 0.4375-	0.47	0.479
HX-SHCS 0.4375-	0.48	0.499
HX-SHCS 0.5-20x	0.5	0.529
HX-SHCS 0.5-20x	0.53	0.549
HX-SHCS 0.5-20x	0.55	0.579
HX-SHCS 0.5-20x	0.58	0.599
HX-SHCS 0.625-1	0.6	0.629
HX-SHCS 0.625-1	0.63	0.659
HX-SHCS 0.625-1	0.66	0.699
HX-SHCS 0.75-16	0.7	0.8
HX-SHCS 0.875-1	0.801	1.109
HX-SHCS 1.25-12	1.11	2
PreviewCfg	0.801	1

FIGURE 19.19

Smart Component parts match holes in the part.

12. An assembly opens that was created from the data stored in the part. Click the Edit Definition button that appears in the upper-right corner of the graphics window.

13. Reassign the minimum and maximum diameter values for the ³/₁₆-inch and ¼-inch configurations to the shortest lengths. For example, the chart shows the ³/₁₆-32x.75-inch configuration to be assigned to a minimum of .1 and a maximum of .199. Move the .1 and .199 values up two cells to the ³/₁₆-32x¼-inch configuration. Do something similar for the ¼-28x1-inch configuration. The edited part of the chart now looks like Figure 19.20.

FIGURE 19.20

The edited configurator table

Chapter 19 Tutor Default	Minimum Diameter	Maximum Diameter
HX-SHCS 0.138-32x0.5x0.5-N	0.1	.199
HX-SHCS 0.19-32x0.25x0.25-N		
HX-SHCS 0.19-32x0.4375x0.4375-N		
HX-SHCS 0.19-32x0.75x0.75-N		
HX-SHCS 0.25-20x0.625x0.625-N	.2	.249
HX-SHCS 0.25-20x1.375x1.375-N		
HX-SHCS		

TIP You may have difficulty expanding the width of the column that contains the configuration names, thus making it difficult or impossible to read the ends of the long config names. However, like Excel, you can expand the height of the rows, which causes the config names to wrap, as shown in Figure 19.20.

Summary

Smart Components can automate the placement of a main component, as well as associated mounting features and components. It can also offer automatic resizing options, depending on the geometry to which they are mated. The setup for Smart Components varies from simple to complex, with auto-sizing causing most of the complexity.

Part V

Creating Drawings

Chapter 20

Automating Drawings: The Basics

IN THIS CHAPTER

The difference between templates and formats

Creating drawing formats

Creating drawing templates

Creating blocks

Engineering drawings include a lot of repetitious information from one drawing to the next. The information is not always exactly the same, but it is usually in the same format and of the same type. For example, part drawings always include information about who made the drawing, when they made it, what the material and surface finish of the part are, and some basic notes that depend on the use of the drawing (manufacturing, assembly, or inspection).

All of this information needs to appear consistently on each drawing, every time. However, humans are not always good at following dull routines, which is why we have computers, to help with these boring or difficult tasks.

The Difference between Templates and Formats

Even experienced users sometimes cannot tell the difference between templates and formats in SolidWorks. I have mentioned this before, but it is worth mentioning again. Simply put, *templates* are collections of document-specific settings and default views, saved in the *.prtdot (part template), *.asmdot (assembly template), and *.drwdot (drawing template) formats.

Formats, more formally called "sheet formats," are exclusive to drawing documents, and contain the sheet size, the drawing border-line geometry, and the text/custom property definitions that go with the text in the drawing border. Formats can also include company logo images.

You can save formats in templates; in fact, this is the method that I both use and recommend. Using SolidWorks' default settings, you specify the size and the format when creating a new drawing from a blank template; however, when the format is already in the template, the size is taken care of ahead of time, and so the templates end up being saved as sizes. Of course, you can change formats later if you need to use a larger drawing sheet.

Can templates be changed?

No. This is one of the most common questions from new users. Perhaps if SolidWorks received enough enhancement requests on this topic, they would be willing to change the software to enable the user to transfer the settings from an existing template to one or more existing documents.

Currently, once you create any kind of a document, you cannot change the underlying template. However, you can change all of the settings, which is for the most part equivalent. There are macros available on the Web that you can use to copy the settings from one document to another or to apply settings to a document or group of documents. In particular, there is a spreadsheet available that has a list of settings and options that you can copy to a given document. You will need to search around for these utilities, but they should be easy to find through the newsgroup comp.cad.solidworks, by using Google Groups if you do not have a newsreader.

Why have different templates or formats?

Different formats must be maintained for different sheet sizes. If you do contract design or detailing work, then you may need to maintain separate formats for different customers. Some people also choose to have different formats for the first sheet of a drawing and a simplified format for the remaining sheets.

Why you should maintain different templates is an easier answer. First, if you put formats on the templates, then you are making separate templates for various sizes. Also, separate templates are frequently created for different units or standards, because templates contain document-specific settings. I also keep a blank template with no format on it just to do conceptual scribbles or to make an informal, scalable, and printable drawing without the baggage that typically accompanies drawings.

CAUTION SolidWorks can install with default document templates that use different standards. Be careful of the difference between drawings with ANSI and ISO standards, or more importantly, the use of third-angle projection versus first-angle projection. Figure 20.1 shows the difference between a third- and first-angle projection. Third angle is part of the ANSI standard used in the United States, while first angle is part of the ISO standard used in Europe.

If you work for a company that does a lot of international work, then you may have to deal this issue more frequently. The setting that controls the projection angle is not in Tools, Options (where you might expect it to be), but in the Sheet Properties, which you can access by RMB clicking anywhere on the blank drawing sheet and selecting Properties.

FIGURE 20.1

Third-angle versus first-angle projection

Creating Drawing Formats

Drawing formats can be either simple or difficult; the good news is that you can choose which one you want to use.

Customizing an existing format

The simple solution is to customize an existing format for your own use. This generally works well, and you can usually finish the task in a few minutes, depending on your requirements. Some options exist for sources. The easiest option is to take the existing SolidWorks sample formats and add a few things such as a company name, logo, and tolerance block to them. You can also use formats from other drawings, editing and saving out as your own.

Sample formats

The sample formats that installed with SolidWorks are located in the Data folder in your SolidWorks installation directory. They include ANSI sizes A to E, and ISO sizes A0 to A4. You can probably find enough space on the formats to place a company logo and some standard notes.

You cannot open a format directly — it must be on a drawing — and so to get a closer look at the format, you must make a new drawing using the format.

NOTE Templates that have been saved with a format already on them skip the step of prompting you to select a format, which allows you to create drawings quickly. If you select one of the default SolidWorks templates, these do not have formats on them and so you are prompted to select one. Figure 20.2 shows the interface for selecting a format that displays after you have selected the template for a drawing.

FIGURE 20.2

Selecting a format

Editing a format

The SolidWorks drawing environment frequently gives new users trouble. Once you understand how it is organized, it is not so bad, but you may make several mistakes while getting used to it. In the drawing, you are either editing the sheet or editing the format. You can think of the sheet as being a piece of transparent Mylar over the top of the drawing border format. In order to get to the format, you have to peel back the Mylar layer. Drawing views go onto the sheet, and so when you edit the format, any drawing views that may be there disappear. (Of course, drawing views — except for maybe some Predefined views — should not be on a drawing when you are creating a format.)

To peel back the sheet and gain access to the format, RMB click a blank area of the sheet and select Edit Sheet Format. This RMB menu is shown in Figure 20.3. Be careful of the terms here, which include Sheet and Sheet Format. The sketch lines of the format light up like a sketch becoming active, and at the lower right-hand corner, on the status bar, a message appears, saying Editing Sheet Format.

The lines in the format border are just like regular SolidWorks sketch entities, but they display a little differently. Also, sketch relations are sometimes not used in formats because solving the relations causes the software to be a bit sluggish. Typically, Trim and Extend functions are the best tools for editing lines.

Images that you add to the format work best as bitmaps. Be aware of the file size of the bitmap when you put it into the format, as bitmap images can be large, and all of that extra information will travel around with each drawing that you create from the format. Figure 20.4 shows a bitmap placed in the format.

You can resize the bitmap by dragging the handles in the corners, and move it by simply dragging it. The image to the right in Figure 20.4 shows the Print Preview window. I included it here to show that the outline around the bitmap that displays while you are working in SolidWorks does not print out.

FIGURE 20.3

Selecting the edit sheet format

FIGURE 20.4

Placing an image

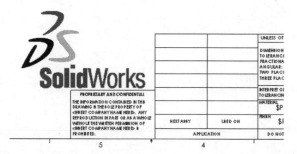

Managing text

One of the newer functions in SolidWorks is the ability to make a text box of a specific size that causes text to wrap. This is particularly useful in drawings. The image in the center of Figure 20.5 shows a new annotation being added. The image to the right shows the same text box after the corner has been dragged.

FIGURE 20.5

Adding an annotation, and wrapping the text

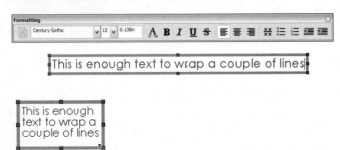

> **TIP**   When dragging the text box, it may seem intuitive to drag the middle handle on the end, thinking that shortening the box will cause it to wrap. However, that only works if the box has some space on the bottom to wrap to; SolidWorks does not automatically expand the text box down the way PowerPoint does. You are better off dragging a corner to get the wrap to work.

Custom properties

The most important part of the drawing format is the custom properties. While the rest of the format is just for display, custom properties use automation to fill out the title block automatically from matching custom properties in the model document. Custom properties can pull items such as filenames, descriptions, materials, and other properties from the model associated with the sheet, or they can pull data from the drawing itself, such as the sheet scale, filename, sheet number, and total sheets. Figure 20.6 shows the existing custom property formatting in the default format being used for this example.

FIGURE 20.6

Custom property formatting in the title block

Property link display

The syntax $PRP or $PRPSHEET indicates that the property that follows the syntax is to be pulled from either the current document (drawing) or from the model specified in the Sheet Properties, respectively. This is an important distinction to make. Most of the time, custom properties are typed in at the part or assembly level so that the data can be reused by drawing properties, BOM, or even design tables.

Notice that all of the notes in the format that are showing raw syntax are pulling data from the model. This is because there are no properties being pulled from the drawing, "Draw2," and the Scale notes are driven by the drawing. When no value exists for the property to display, you have an option of what to show. Figure 20.7 in the image to the left shows the settings in the View menu that control the display of syntax of the custom property links. In general, it is common to turn off the error display, and to show the link variables.

FIGURE 20.7

Link variable display options and effects

Errors and link variables

The errors in Figure 20.7 are caused by links to the local document for which there is no corresponding property. For example, the "ERROR!: COMPANYNAME" message is linked to "$PRP: COMPANYNAME," but the local custom property "COMPANYNAME" does not exist. If it existed, but had a null or space value, the error would disappear.

Likewise, with the option to display link variables turned on, the syntax that calls model custom properties displays until there is some value for it to pull from. If a part is put onto the drawing, then some of the properties are filled in because properties and values exist to pull from, and the rest of the properties simply disappear to make space. Notice in Figure 20.8 that the Material property has been filled in, but the Finish property has not. This is because there is either no Finish property in the part on the drawing or a null value in the Finish property.

FIGURE 20.8

Custom properties filled in by a part

UNLESS OTHERWISE SPECIFIED:		NAME	DATE	Dezignstuff		
DIMENSIONS ARE IN INCHES	DRAWN	Matt	1/8/2007			
TOLERANCES: FRACTIONAL±	CHECKED	You	1/10/2007	TITLE:		
ANGULAR: MACH ± BEND ± TWO PLACE DECIMAL ± THREE PLACE DECIMAL ±	ENG APPR.	None	1/12/2007	Cast Clamp		A
	MFG APPR.	Prelim	1/12/2007			
INTERPRET GEOMETRIC TOLERANCING PER:	Q.A.	None	1/13/2007			
	COMMENTS:					
MATERIAL Cast Iron				SIZE	DWG. NO.	REV
FINISH ERROR:Finish				B	Chapter 19 - Smart Clamp	B
DO NOT SCALE DRAWING				SCALE: 1:1	WEIGHT: 0.814 SHEET 1 OF 1	

> **TIP**   When initially setting up the format, it can be useful to have a dummy model already on the drawing. You should delete the views containing the dummy model before saving the format or the template. The dummy model should have all of the custom properties in it that you intend to use in your drawings. This prevents the blank fields or error messages during setup.

> **NOTE**   If you drag-and-drop a part onto a drawing while editing in the Sheet Format, the views may appear for a split second and then disappear again. This is because you cannot display drawing views while editing the Sheet Format. Once you exit the Sheet Format and go back to editing the sheet, the views can display once more.

Creating linked properties

It is easy to create annotations that are linked to properties. Begin as if you are creating a note:

1. Click the Note toolbar button on the Annotations toolbar, or click Insert ➪ Annotations ➪ Note.

2. Place the note on the drawing. The Formatting toolbar appears.

3. Click the Link To Property button in the Text Format pane of the Note PropertyManager. This displays the Link to Property dialog box, as shown in Figure 20.9, which gives you the option of linking to a custom property in the current (drawing) document or in the model (part or assembly) that is on the drawing.

4. If the desired custom property is not in the drop-down list shown to the right, then you can type it into the text box or click the File Properties button to edit the properties. This button is not available for the model if there is no model on the drawing, in which case you must type in the name of the property manually.

FIGURE 20.9

The Link to Property dialog box

Creating a format from a blank screen

There is no graceful way to say this, and so I'll just say it: SolidWorks is not really good at manipulating a lot of 2D sketch-line data such as what you find in drawing title blocks. I have gone through the process of making my own formats, as well as the process of importing data from which to create one. By the time you have everything centered, in the right color, and on layers if you are using them, and the text aligned, you have used up more than a couple of hours. If you choose to custom build one size and then use it to create the rest of the sizes, you need to be patient. SolidWorks typically turns off the most useful parametric sketch functions when working with a format (what SolidWorks considers a large sketch) because of speed problems. If you would like to turn these settings back on, they are located at Tools ➪ Sketch Settings.

SolidWorks is not the best program for making a nice-looking drawing border. If you insist on creating your own, set aside some time for it, and have an idea of what you are trying to achieve, maybe sketched out by hand or in a printout of a title block that you would like to replicate.

The Modify Sketch tool may be useful in moving entities around the screen, and even scaling them. You can also access a useful hidden command by RMB clicking the name of the drawing in the FeatureManager, and selecting Move from the menu, as shown in Figure 20.10. A small dialog box appears that enables you to move the entire format by a specified distance.

TIP If you need to use construction geometry to help you size or locate objects or text while manually creating your Sheet Format, then you do not need to delete the geometry when you are done. You can put all of the construction geometry on a specially created drawing layer and turn the layer off.

FIGURE 20.10

The Move Drawing dialog box

Creating a format from an imported DWG/DXF file

If you still think you want to create your format from an imported DWG or DXF file, then locate the file that you would like to import, and open it from the File, Open dialog box. The DXF/DWG Import screen appears, as shown in Figure 20.11.

FIGURE 20.11

The DXF/DWG Import screen

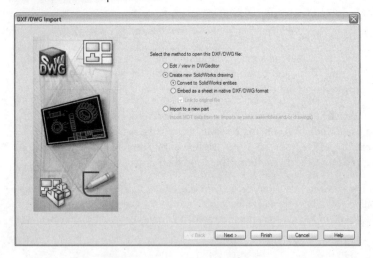

The sample file used for this example can be found on the CD-ROM for Chapter 20 if you are interested in following along. To make a drawing format, you can select the Create New SolidWorks Drawing and Convert To SolidWorks Entities options. Although one of the other options contains the word *format*, it is not being used in the same sense, so do not be misled. When this selection is complete, click Next. Figure 20.12 shows the next screen.

FIGURE 20.12

The Drawing Layer Mapping screen

Select the Layers Selected For Sheet Format option. Select the TB layer, leaving the other layers off. Every imported file will be different in this respect, because layers used by title blocks vary widely. Click Next when you have made these selections. Figure 20.13 shows the Document Settings screen.

FIGURE 20.13

The Document Settings screen

The important features in the Document Settings screen are the Document template selection and the Geometry positioning options.

Document template selection is only important if you plan to save the format with a template. Be sure to select a template that does not already have a format saved in it. In the Geometry positioning section, if you can get the software to center the title block for you, definitely take advantage of this functionality and use the Center In Sheet option. Once you are happy with these settings, click Finish. The resulting format is shown in Figure 20.14.

FIGURE 20.14

The finished imported format

From here, you can add the links to custom properties as described earlier, as well as logo images, loading favorites, and blocks. You can now save the format as described in the next section.

TIP   Using the Color Display Mode button on the Line Format toolbar toggles the display from using the layer color to using the SolidWorks sketch colors. Another setting that affects sketch display in drawings is found at Tools ➪ Options ➪ System Options ➪ Drawings ➪ Display Sketch Entity Points, which shows endpoints and arc center points in the same way that they are shown in feature sketches.

Saving the format

You can save drawing formats in two ways, either with the template, or separate from the template. You cannot edit formats separate from a template, but they do have their own file type, *.slddrt.

If you are wondering how the extension *.slddrt relates to a sheet format, what is now known as *sheet format* used to be called a *drawing template* (thus, the *drt* of slddrt). What is now called a template did not exist in 1997. The shift in architecture and, more importantly for users, the shift in terminology has left many people a bit confused.

Saving templates is covered in the next section. To save a format, select File ⇨ Save Sheet Format. This can be done with or without the format being active. Save the format into a location with other formats, and give it a descriptive but unique name. If you have not yet done so, this is a good opportunity to create a separate folder, outside of your SolidWorks installation folder, that contains your most frequently used files. Remember also to tell SolidWorks where this library location is through Tools ⇨ Options ⇨ System Options ⇨ File Locations ⇨ Sheet Formats.

Second sheet formats

When you have multi-sheet drawings, it is often important to have a simplified or specialized format for the second sheet. Figure 20.15 shows sample page-one and page-two formats side by side.

FIGURE 20.15

First and second sheet formats

Adding new sheets

You can add sheets to a drawing through the RMB menu of the sheet tab at the lower-left corner of the drawing window. If you RMB click the first sheet tab, the sheet that is added gets the format that is used on the first sheet. If you RMB click the second sheet tab, the added sheet gets the second sheet format.

Reloading formats

If a format has been changed, and you would like to update a drawing to the new format, this option is available in the Sheet Properties, as shown in Figure 20.16.

FIGURE 20.16

Updating a format through the Sheet Properties

Creating Drawing Templates

Document-specific settings are an important part of the template, and it is probably best to get one size drawing completely set up the way you want it, and then create the other sizes from this drawing. This helps to ensure that the settings, such as bent leader length, font, and line weight, are the same for all of the templates. Uniform settings on drawings give them a consistent look, and make them easier to read. An in-depth discussion of document-specific settings at Tools ➪ Options ➪ Document Properties can be found in Appendix B.

Using predefined views in drawing templates

When I use drawing templates, one of my favorite techniques to get to a multi-view drawing quickly is to put one Predefined view on the template along with appropriate views projected from the Predefined view. A Predefined view establishes an orientation and location on the drawing sheet. You can add multiple Predefined views and align them with one another on the drawing sheet so that a drawing is automatically populated by the model, but this is not recommended because if you decide to change the orientation of the drawing, you have to change each Predefined view independently. If you set up a single Predefined view and make the rest of the views with projected views, changing the orientation of the Predefined view causes all of the projected views to update associatively. You cannot directly change the orientation of a projected view. Predefined views and views projected from Predefined views appear blank until they are populated with model geometry. The *predefined* part of a Predefined view is the orientation and placement of the view.

Figure 20.17 shows a template using Predefined and projected views. You can access Predefined views on the Drawings toolbar; although it is not there by default, you can place it on the toolbar through the Tools ⇨ Customize ⇨ Commands interface. You can also access Predefined views through Insert ⇨ Drawing Views ⇨ Predefined. Projected views are also accessed from the Drawings toolbar.

FIGURE 20.17

Predefined views on a template

Once a Predefined view has been placed, you can select an orientation for it from the PropertyManager. Figure 20.18 shows the Drawing View PropertyManager. The orientation for a view is set in the top Orientation panel. In addition to orthogonal views, you can also create isometric and other custom views as Predefined views.

Once the view has been oriented, you may want to create more views on the drawing that also become populated by model geometry. This is where the projected views are used. Make sure that the drawing properties are set to the correct projection angle.

Because the rest of the views have been created relative to the Front view, none of the views needs to be rotated as they would if, for example, the Top view were placed above the Back or Right views.

FIGURE 20.18

The Drawing View PropertyManager

Although it is not on this drawing, many drawing templates include a third-angle projection symbol as a part of the Title Block, which is in the format. Figure 20.19 shows first- and third-angle projection symbols. These are included as blocks with the sample data in the SolidWorks 2007 installation. Blocks are discussed in more detail in Chapter 22.

FIGURE 20.19

Projection angle symbol blocks

Aligning predefined views

You can align views to one another through a view's RMB menu, as shown in Figure 20.20. Projected views are aligned to one another automatically, but if you chose to use a Predefined view rather than a projected view to one side of the original Predefined view, you can use the Align Vertical by Origin or the Align Horizontal by Origin command. This ensures that the parts in each view are aligned. Aligning by center should not be used for projected views on an engineering drawing, because it is not guaranteed to line up edges in adjacent views.

FIGURE 20.20

Alignment options

Populating a drawing with Predefined views

Four methods exist to populate a drawing with Predefined views:

- **Drag-and-drop:** Drag a part or assembly from the FeatureManager and drop it in the drawing window. All Predefined views are automatically populated.

- **Insert Model:** RMB click a view and select Insert Model. From the interface, browse for the model to be displayed in all of the related (projected) views.

- **PropertyManager:** Select a predefined view, and from the PropertyManager, select Browse in the Insert Model panel.

- **Make Drawing from Part/Assembly:** Click the Make Drawing From Part/Assembly button in the Standard toolbar and select a template that uses Predefined views.

Predefined views and sheet scale

When Predefined views are created, they are set to follow the sheet scale by default; however, you can manually set them to have a custom scale. If you are using the automatic scaling option (found at Tools ➪ Options ➪ System Options ➪ Drawings ➪ Automatically Scale New Drawing Views), the sheet scale is automatically changed when the drawing views are populated to make a nice fit of the model geometry on the drawing. The scales used by the automatic feature are all standard multiples of two, and so you do not have to worry about odd scale factors on your drawings.

Predefined view limitations

The function and expectations of Predefined views are fairly straightforward, although there are a few things that could be improved. For example, SolidWorks does not allow you to create predefined section or detail views. Also, the View Palette does not preview the populated Predefined views.

Using favorites and blocks in templates

Favorites function like styles and formatting in Microsoft Word, or other word-processing software, by adding underlines, bold formatting, and even items such as tolerances and symbols. Hole Wizard Favorites are described in Chapter 17, and work similarly to Dimension and Note Favorites (described in Chapter 22). This chapter is concerned with the fact that favorites can be saved to files, and loaded to documents. In particular, they can be loaded to documents that can be saved as templates, thus maintaining the loaded favorites. Several types of favorites can be loaded into and saved with drawing templates, including dimension, note, GD&T, weld, and surface finish symbols.

When a favorite is loaded into a template, any document that you create from that template can use any of the loaded favorites. The many file types for favorites exist mainly to transfer favorites from one document to another, but they are not needed once the favorite is loaded. As a result, before saving a template, you should gather together your favorites into your library folder and load them into the template.

You can load favorites by going to the interface for the type of favorite, for example, dimensions or notes. Figure 20.21 shows the top of the Note PropertyManager interface, which contains the Favorites panel.

FIGURE 20.21

The Favorites panel for the Note PropertyManager

The buttons in the Favorites panel of the Note PropertyManager interface have the following functions:

[icon]	Apply the default attributes to the selected notes
[icon]	Add or update a favorite
[icon]	Delete a favorite
[icon]	Save a favorite
[icon]	Load a favorite

This section is concerned with the last function, Load a favorite. After clicking this button, you can load multiple favorites at once by Shift-selecting them through the Open dialog box that appears.

Even symbol types that can be applied by dragging-and-dropping from the Design Library can also be loaded as favorites. However, I prefer dragging from the Design Library because you get a preview of the symbol; with the favorites, you just see a text tag.

Blocks can also be loaded into a template or used from the Design Library as drag-and-drop items.

Custom properties in templates

Part of the usefulness of templates is that you can do work once, and have it replicated many times. This is an excellent example of process automation. One of the ways that you can take advantage of this feature is by putting default custom properties in your templates. In many cases, simply having a default value for something is better than no value, and a default value may even prompt you to put a value with real significance in the property. For example, the Description of a document is extremely important, especially if you are using sequential part numbers for your filenames. A custom property named Description can be added to your template, and the default value is used unless it is changed when the template is used in a document.

You have already seen how custom properties used in parts can be instrumental in filling out a title block on a drawing. Custom properties in part and assembly documents work exactly the same as they do in drawings. The custom properties interface is shown in Figure 20.22.

FIGURE 20.22

The custom properties Interface

Saving a template

Drawing templates are saved through the Save As menu, by selecting Drawing Templates in the Files of Type drop-down list. This automatically takes you to the folder for the templates, as specified in Tools ⇨ Options ⇨ File Locations ⇨ Templates.

In the case where a template and format have been saved together and are being saved together, but the format also needs to be saved to its own file, saving the template with the changed format only changes the format for documents that are made from that point forward with that template.

You may also save out the format to its own file from the edited template. Formats are needed in their own file (in addition to existing within a template) for situations when you have an existing drawing and want to change the size of the sheet, and then need a format to put on the sheet. Another situation is when a drawing may come in to your organization from an outside contractor, and they have not used your format; in this case, you can simply replace their format with yours, or you can send them your format (and template, for that matter), from which the contractor can create all drawings for you.

Separate formats are important for when you have multi-sheet drawings. When adding a sheet, you also need to add a format. You can save multi-sheet drawing templates in which the first and second sheets have different formats on them.

Creating Blocks

Blocks are an important aspect of automating drawing creation. They enable you to combine text and sketch geometry and to annotate common features on drawings. Blocks are discussed in Chapter 4 (sketch blocks) and also in Chapter 22 (creation, editing, and placement). Blocks can be used for many purposes, including the following:

- Tolerance blocks on drawings that might change with the process (if you do not have separate formats that already contain this information).

- Electrical or pneumatic schematic symbols that can be snapped together.

- Flowchart type symbols.

- Fluid flow-direction arrows.

- Special markers calling attention to a specific detail.

- Sheet formats that can be created as a block, enabling you to move it around as a single entity much more easily.

You can create blocks by selecting a group of sketch entities, annotations, or symbols and then clicking Tools ⇨ Block ⇨ Make.

 For more information on the creation, editing, management, and placement of blocks, see Chapter 22.

Summary

Getting your templates and formats correct creates an excellent opportunity to save some time with drawings by automating many of the common tasks through the use of templates, Predefined views, multiple formats, blocks, favorites, and linked custom properties. Setup becomes more important when you are administering a larger installation, but is also important if it is just for yourself. One of the most important things that you can do is to establish a file library and direct your Tools ⇨ Options ⇨ File Locations paths to the files. There is nothing quite as productive as having something that works right the first time, and every time.

Chapter 21

Working with Drawing Views

Ten years ago, when I first moved from AutoCAD to SolidWorks, one of the most difficult concepts to understand was that in SolidWorks you do not create lines in the drawing view, and in fact, you cannot move any of the lines in the view at all. The drawing view was in effect a snapshot of the 3D model from a particular point of view. The snapshot could be updated, but it could not be manipulated manually.

At first, this seemed a little bit confining. However, once I understood it, the concept was liberating rather than confining. It meant that I did not have to worry about the drawing views being inconsistent or incorrect. All I had to worry about was the 3D model being correct.

If you are a new user, then you should feel confident that SolidWorks properly maintains the views better than you could do it manually. Any type of view from any point of view of even the most complex model or assembly geometry can be updated perfectly.

To be fair, there are some things that SolidWorks has difficulties with, but knowing this now means that you will be ready for these issues and know how to deal with them when or if they occur. One issue arises from assemblies that contain parts that interfere. HLR (hidden line removed) display of interfering parts can show extra lines or hide lines that should be shown. At other times, you may have issues with lightweight parts. When possible, it is best to work with model geometry that is fully resolved as well as high-quality drawing views.

Creating Common View Types

The previous chapter discussed Predefined views in templates. Predefined views make it faster to automatically create drawings with consistently placed, simple views. However, sometimes you may need to create views on templates that do not have Predefined views, or you may need a special arrangement of views. SolidWorks has a good assortment of view types to make practically any type of view that you may need.

NOTE When creating or changing either the geometry or the settings that control how a view is displayed, the view may become cross-hatched, indicating that the model needs to be rebuilt. To resolve this problem press Ctrl+Q, to update the view.

Using the View palette

The View palette is shown in Figure 21.1. It is activated automatically if you use the Make Drawing From Part tool, unless the drawing template that you select has Predefined views on it. In this case, the Predefined views are populated, and the View palette is not activated.

FIGURE 21.1

The View palette

The View palette contains all of the standard named views, the current view of the model, and any annotation views (views that the model was in when annotations were added to it). You can drag-and-drop these views on the drawing.

 To activate the View palette without using the Make Drawing From Part tool, simply create a new drawing document, ensure that the Task Manager panel is available, and click the View Palette tab in the Task Manager. Then use the ellipse button (. . .) to browse to a part. After you select a part, the palette window is populated with views of the model. This method has the advantage of enabling you to see the views before you put them down. It does not link views in the same way that the Predefined and projected views are linked, however. I find this interface somewhat difficult to use, and prefer to set up the Predefined views or to use the Multiple Views option in the Model Views PropertyManager, which is shown later in this chapter.

Named

 Named views are one of the few types of views that are not dependent on another view. Everything has to start from somewhere, and most drawings have to start with either a named or Predefined view.

You can place named views by using the Model View button on the Drawings toolbar or by clicking Insert, Drawing View, Model. Using the Model View PropertyManager is a two-step process, and is shown in Figure 21.2. In the first step, you select the model, and in the second step, you set the options for the view.

Open documents

The large selection box in the Part/Assembly to Insert panel displays any models that are open in SolidWorks at the moment. If the model that you are looking for is not in the list, then you can use the Browse button to look for it.

I find this part of the interface to be clumsy because an extra step is involved that was not there before. It used to be that when you chose to place a named view, you would open the Browse dialog box directly, but now there is an intermediate step. For this reason, I try to use a workflow that avoids this dialog box. I typically use the Create Drawing From This Part/Assembly if the part is open, and if not, I drag-and-drop the part onto a new drawing template with Predefined views on it. This combination saves a lot of work.

One of the annoying quirks of this interface occurs in the first step when you are using the PropertyManager (the image to the left in Figure 21.2). If you click in the drawing window for some reason (for example, if you are expecting it to simply place a view), then a prompt appears, stating that you are not paying attention. (Obviously this happens to me very frequently.)

Thumbnail Preview

This is a nice option that shows the part that you selected in the Open Documents window. It is a useful feature, but, because it is collapsed by default, it is easy to miss. After it is used the first time, it retains the setting.

FIGURE 21.2

The Model View PropertyManager

Options

This should just say "Option," as there is only one. In any case, the Start Command When Creating New Drawing option causes this PropertyManager to open up immediately when a new drawing is created. If you click in the drawing window, then the prompt appears, telling you that you are not paying attention.

Cosmetic Thread Display

Cosmetic threads can display in either high or draft quality. The distinction is made for perform-ance reasons. The difference in terms of display is that in high-quality mode, hidden cosmetic threads (cosmetic threads that are behind a face) do not display in shaded mode.

Number of Views and Orientation

This is the one function that almost redeems the Model View PropertyManager for me. In Single View mode, you select the view that you want to place from the Orientation panel, place the view, and then move on. In Multiple Views mode, you select all views that you want to be displayed, including choices such as Current Model View and any named views that are created in the model interface. These views are indicated on the drawing as boxes (representing view borders), as shown in Figure 21.3.

FIGURE 21.3

Placing multiple views

This is really useful functionality. It makes view selection and placement very easy and is visually clear. Unfortunately, the Single View setting is the default setting, and the PropertyManager does not remember the last setting that was used. Still, the combination of Multiple Views and Orientation is far better, in my opinion, than the View Palette, which I find visually confusing and non-intuitive.

Options

The one option in the Options panel is Auto-Start Projected View, which, on the placement of a view, automatically enables you to place more views. This option only works when you have selected the Single View option in the Number of Views panel.

Display Style

You can set the default display style in Tools ⇨ Options ⇨ System Options ⇨ Drawings ⇨ Display Style. This panel provides an override for views being placed. This panel also allows you to control High or Draft Quality views, which are described later in this chapter.

Scale

SolidWorks drawings always default to showing views at the overall sheet scale, unless the System Option on the Drawings page called Automatically Scale New Drawing Views is turned on. If this setting is on, the sheet scale saved with the drawing template is overridden. For example, a 1:1 sheet scale can be changed automatically to 1:4 by the setting.

You can change the sheet scale through the sheet properties, which were discussed in Chapter 20. Controlling views with the sheet scale makes it much easier to change the size of a drawing and to scale all of the views together. Individual views can be displayed at the view scale, and detail views are typically created at a different scale automatically. The scale setting is found at Tools ⇨ Options ⇨ System Options ⇨ Drawings ⇨ Detail View Scaling. Detail views, covered later in this chapter, automatically get a note showing the custom scale for the view. You can create a note that functions in the same way as the automatically created "Scale" text manually from a note and a link to a custom property for views where the link to the sheet scale has been broken manually.

 A note that automatically links to the scale of a drawing view is something you could consider creating a note favorite or block for.

Dimension Type

Even in non-orthogonal (isometric) views, true dimensions should be used for most drawing views. Projected dimensions depend on the angle of the edge to the view plane.

Cosmetic Thread Display

If something is worth having, it is worth having twice. This panel appears in both steps, just in case you missed it in the first step.

Projected view

 The Projected view type simply makes a view that is projected in the direction that you dragged the cursor from the selected view. Be aware that first-angle and third-angle projections result in views that are opposite from one another. For example, if you drag at a 45-degree angle, the result is an isometric view. When placing an isometric view that you have created in this way, SolidWorks constrains the new view to a 45-degree-angle line through the Origins of the two views. To place the view somewhere other than along this line, press the Ctrl key while placing the view to break the alignment. The PropertyManager for the Projected view is shown in Figure 21.4.

When you use the push-pin on the Projected View PropertyManager, you can place multiple projected views from the originally selected view, or select a new view to project views from. Display properties and scale of the projected views are taken from the parent view.

FIGURE 21.4

The Projected View PropertyManager

Standard 3 view

 The Standard 3 View tool on the Drawings toolbar can also be accessed at Insert ⇨ Drawing View ⇨ Standard 3 View. This places a Front view, and projects Top and Right views for third-angle projection drawings.

Detail view

 The Detail view is activated from the Drawings toolbar or at Insert ⇨ Drawing View ⇨ Detail. Either way, you can use the function in two different ways, one that is fast and easy and the other that gives you more control but is not quite as fast.

Pre-drawn detail circle

The detail "circle" can be drawn before you initiate the Detail View command. When you pre-draw a detail circle, you must ensure that you are sketching in the view and not on the sheet. To draw in the view, the view must be activated. You can activate a view by clicking in the view or by bringing a sketch cursor over the view. When you activate a view, the status bar in the lower-right corner of the SolidWorks window displays the message, "Editing Drawing View," as shown in Figure 21.5.

The dotted border in the image to the left shows that the view is selected, and the status bar shows that it is activated. The image to the right with the solid corners indicates that the view has "Locked Focus." You can lock focus on a drawing view by double-clicking it or by right-clicking and selecting Lock Focus from the menu.

If a view is not activated or the focus is not locked on the view, then any sketch elements that you draw will be placed on the drawing sheet. While sketching in a drawing view, it is a good practice to watch the status bar.

The point of all of this is to sketch a closed loop in the view so that it can be used for a Detail view. The closed loop can be a circle, ellipse, spline, series of lines, or any other shape, as long as it is a closed loop. The closed loop is called a *circle* for the purposes of the Detail view in SolidWorks terminology.

FIGURE 21.5

Activated drawing views

A setting controls how the circle displays, in particular whether it displays as drawn or as an actual circle. This setting is found at Tools ⇨ Options ⇨ System Options ⇨ Drawings ⇨ Display New Detail Circles as Circles. The name of this setting sounds strange — after all, what else would you call a circle? If the setting is turned on, regardless of what closed-loop shape you draw, it will display as a circle. If the setting is off, then SolidWorks will display whatever shape you draw. The different results are shown in Figure 21.6.

FIGURE 21.6

Drawing a closed loop, with the Display Detail Circles as Circles option both on and off

Once you create the loop, you can click the Detail View toolbar button and place the view. The view is automatically scaled by the factor set at Tools ➪ Options ➪ Drawings ➪ Detail View Scaling.

Detail circle drawn in-line

A faster way to complete the Detail view is to simply click the Detail View toolbar button without pre-selecting or pre-drawing the loop. This activates the Circle sketch tool immediately, which activates the view as soon as you bring the cursor over the view, so that when you draw the circle, it is sure to be in the view rather than on the sheet.

Alternatively, you could swap the circle tool for an ellipse or spline; this works just as well, but offers more flexibility. Regardless of the sketch tool, when you close the loop, SolidWorks prompts you to place the view. The workflow for this in-line method is better than the old-school pre-drawn loop technique.

Editing a Detail view

You can edit a Detail view by dragging the circumference of the detail circle to a new diameter, dragging the center of the detail circle to a new location, or by selecting Edit Sketch from the detail circle RMB menu. This method enables you to edit sketch relations or otherwise edit the sketch that you used for the detail. When you are done with the sketch, you can use the Confirmation Corner to click OK.

You can delete Detail views by selecting and deleting the detail circle. Unlike older versions of SolidWorks, in SolidWorks 2007, deleting the detail circle gives you the option to delete the resulting view as well as the original sketch. Also, deleting the detail view gives you the option to delete the detail circle and the original sketch.

Section view

Section views in SolidWorks offer many options.

Default Section view

The default Section view has the same in-line and pre-drawn optional techniques as the Detail view, as well as the same advantages and disadvantages.

Section views have the possibly unique distinction that they often use a straight line, and that straight line often goes through the center of a cylindrical feature. Even though you are in a drawing and not in a model sketch, you may still benefit from model sketching techniques. For example, to draw a straight vertical line through the model shown in Figure 21.7, in the images on the left, you can hover the cursor over a circular edge to wake up the center, and then pick up the inference lines to the center. Another technique is to show the temporary axes (using the View menu), just sketch the line, and then assign a sketch relation in the same way that you would in a feature sketch. This technique is shown in the images on the right.

FIGURE 21.7

Aligning a line in a Section view sketch

You can also use jogged section lines with the default section tool. Similar sketch relation techniques are more common in jogged sections because there are more sketched lines. The results are shown in Figure 21.8.

FIGURE 21.8

Default and jogged Section views

SECTION A-A

SECTION B-B

Partial Section view

A Partial Section view is created when the section line does not cut all the way across the model. In Figure 21.9, the line that is drawn to create the Partial Section view was the vertical section line. The prompt that appears enables you to confirm that you intended to create a partial section cut. If you answer No to the prompt, the result is an error, with the new view displayed in the dangling color.

FIGURE 21.9

A Partial Section view

Sketched line

You can use another technique to create a section that looks like a partial section, but is not considered a partial section by SolidWorks. You can create it by drawing perpendicular lines, and selecting the line to be used as the projection direction for the section before clicking the Section View tool. This differs from a true partial section in that it shows half of the model unsectioned. It is also similar to the Aligned Section view, but it does not unfold the second sectioned side. When the prompt shown in Figure 21.9 displays, clicking Yes causes the resulting view to look like the view on the left in Figure 21.9. Clicking No causes the view shown in Figure 21.10 to appear.

FIGURE 21.10

Another Section view

SECTION D-D

Selected line

Sketched lines

Aligned Section view

The Aligned Section view takes two separate sections at right angles to one another and lays them out flat on the page. It is essentially two partial sections that display side by side. The section lines look identical to those shown in Figure 21.10, but the resulting view is different, as shown in Figure 21.11. The finished view aligns with the selected sketch element.

FIGURE 21.11

The Aligned Section view

SECTION E-E

Editing a Section view

Section views are edited in the same way as detail views. You can edit the section lines directly by dragging, or the section line sketch through the RMB menu. You can use the Edit Sketch command through the section line RMB menu to edit sketch relations, or to add or remove sketch elements to the sketch.

Section views are also deleted in the same way as detail views, with the option to also delete the underlying sketch for the section. When you delete one segment of the section line, the resulting view, as well as the underlying sketch, is also deleted.

Creating Other View Types

SolidWorks is able to create any type of view that you need. If you can define what the view should look like, then SolidWorks can create it. The only limit is your creativity.

Crop view

The Crop view is simply a view that looks like a Detail view without requiring a parent view. This feature allows you to reduce the number of views on a sheet, and save some room. However, a cropped view may be confusing if it is not clear which area is being detailed in the cropped view.

Crop views have some limitations, including the inability to crop an assembly exploded view, a Detail view, or the parent of a detail view.

Unlike Detail views, in Crop views, the closed loop must be sketched in the view before you invoke the command. To make the Crop view, draw the closed loop as shown in Figure 21.12 in the image to the left, and then click the Crop View button on the drawing toolbar or access the command at Insert ⇨ Drawing View ⇨ Crop.

FIGURE 21.12

A sketch loop and a Crop view

Editing a Crop view

To edit a Crop view, RMB click the view, expand the arrow next to Crop View, and select either Edit Crop or Remove Crop. Removing the crop does not delete the sketch that the crop was created from.

Broken-out Section view

 The Broken-out Section view is another view type that alters an existing view rather than creating a new view. It also requires a closed loop sketch. The Broken-out Section view is very useful in assembly views where parts are obscured by other parts, in particular when a set of parts are inside a housing and you want to show the inside parts without hiding the housing. Of course, you can also use Broken-out Section views on parts with internal detail.

Broken-out Section views act like a cut that is created from the drawing view. Any faces created by the cut are hatched. Figure 21.13 shows a simple assembly view using a Broken-out Section view. On the left is the view with the driving sketch (in this case, a closed loop spline), and on the right is the finished view.

You cannot create Broken-out Section views using existing detail, section, or alternate position views.

FIGURE 21.13

A Broken-out Section view

Drawing the closed loop

Broken-out Section views are initiated from an existing view either with or without a pre-drawn closed loop. If the loop is pre-drawn, then you must select it before clicking the Broken-out Section toolbar button on the Drawings toolbar or accessing the command at Insert ➪ Drawing View ➪ Broken-out Section.

If the view has no pre-drawn, pre-selected loop, then initiating the function activates the spline sketch tool. It is not necessary to use a spline as the closed loop for this view type, but Broken-out Section views are traditionally created with a freehand sort of boundary, even when drawn manually.

If the loop is closed in an uninterrupted workflow, then after the last spline point is drawn, joining the spline back to itself, the Section Scope dialog box appears. This enables you to select any parts that are not to be sectioned. It is customary to avoid sectioning shafts, screws, or other cylindrical components. Using the Section Scope, the image on the right in Figure 21.13 would be altered to look like the image on the right in Figure 21.14.

The recommended workflow is to initiate the function from the toolbar, use the spline to create the closed loop, and to not pre-draw a loop. This makes everything flow more smoothly, and you create the view surprisingly quickly. If you must use a sketch tool other than the spline, then you must pre-draw it. Even if you simply change sketch tools when the Broken-out Section view automatically activates the spline, because the workflow has been broken, creating the closed loop does not automatically display the Section Scope interface.

FIGURE 21.14

Using the Section Scope

Selecting the depth

After you make the Section Scope selections, the next step is to set the depth of the cut. You can do this in one of several ways. Broken-out Section views are usually applied to the center of a hole if available, or in other ways that show the view as cleanly as possible. If you know the depth of the cut that you want to make, then you can type it in as a distance value. Of course, that raises the question "Distance from *what*?" to which the answer seems to be "from the geometry in the view that would come the farthest out of the screen toward the user." Users most often choose the distance when it does not matter *exactly* how deep the cut goes or exactly *where* it cuts, but to give a relative position.

In situations when you want to cut to the center of a particular feature or up to an edge, it is far easier and less bothersome to simply select the geometry from a drawing view. For example, Figure 21.15 shows the PropertyManager interface where the depth of the cut is set. In this example, the edge of the shaft in the view to the right has been selected. This tells SolidWorks that the cut should go to the center of the shaft. Another possibility is to show the temporary axes, as shown in Figure 21.15, and to select an axis through the center of the shaft.

FIGURE 21.15

Setting the depth of the Broken-out Section view

Editing the view

At this point the view is finished. Now you may choose to edit the view in some way, such as by changing the sketch, the depth, the section scope, and so on. Figure 21.16 shows how the Broken-out Section view is positioned in the Drawing FeatureManager. It is listed as a modification to an existing drawing view. The Broken-out Section RMB menu is also shown. Selecting Edit Definition displays the PropertyManager, shown in Figure 21.15. Selecting Edit Sketch enables you to change the section spline shape. Selecting Properties displays the dialog box shown to the right in Figure 21.16. This contains options for the underlying original view as well as the Broken-out section modification to the original view. Only the Section Scope tab is added by the Broken-out Section view. The rest of the options are for normal view properties.

FIGURE 21.16

Editing the Broken-out Section view

631

Break view

Break views are typically used to display parts that are very long in one dimension on a drawing in such a way that you can see both ends, or other important features. You can break views more than once in the same direction, or even in opposite directions. Figure 21.17 shows the full view of a part and a view that was broken twice. Notice that the dimensions are correct, and any dimension that includes a broken length has a special dimension line.

FIGURE 21.17

Dimensions on a Break view

The PropertyManager in Figure 21.17 shows a bit of a discrepancy in terminology. Using "Break" as the name of the view seems a little awkward, and I much prefer it as it is shown here in the PropertyManager as "Broken View." It is inconsistent, but you get the idea anyway.

To create a Break view, click the Break toolbar button on the Drawings toolbar, or select it at Insert, Drawing View, Break. You need to place break lines in pairs, and you can choose from one of four break symbol styles, as shown in Figure 21.18. You can change the style from the RMB menu or from the PropertyManager.

The Break command is a bit awkward to finish. If you press Esc, then all of the breaks that you placed are removed. There is no green check mark icon on the cursor RMB symbol as there are for many other functions in SolidWorks. As a result, the Confirmation Corner is probably the best way to exit this function and save your work.

If you have worked with previous versions, then you may find that the current interface and functionality are vastly improved. In previous versions, you had to choose between Vertical Break and Horizontal Break. I could never tell the difference — were the break lines vertical or was the shortened distance vertical in a vertical break? In SolidWorks 2007, the icons display with tooltips, which clears up the confusion.

FIGURE 21.18

Selecting the break symbol

The Broken View PropertyManager also enables you to set the gap size and the style of the break. The gap refers to the gap between the break lines in the finished broken view. The setting here overrides the default for this view only. The default setting is a template setting found in Tools ➪ Options ➪ Document Properties ➪ Detailing. Other options that you can set in this location are the break line extension (the distance the lines extend past the model edges) and the break line font (on the Line Font page of the Document Properties tab). The setting that enables the broken symbol on a dimension is found on the Dimensions page, and is named Show Dimensions As Broken In Broken Views.

You can remove individual breaks in a broken view by selecting one of the break lines and pressing Delete. You can add breaks by applying the Break command and adding more breaks to a view. You can alter breaks by simply dragging the break lines. In past versions, it was possible to get the view very confused by dragging one set of breaks to interfere with another set of breaks. That problem has been fixed by not allowing break lines to be dragged past one another.

Auxiliary view

 An Auxiliary view is a view that is projected from a non-orthogonal edge. This type of view is often necessary to view features (such as holes drilled at an angle) square on, so that they appear circular in the view rather than foreshortened and elliptical. An auxiliary view is shown in Figure 21.19 in the image to the left. If the edge that the view was created from is updated, then the auxiliary view will reorient itself. The image to the right shows an auxiliary view projected from an arbitrarily drawn sketch line. The line or edge used to project an auxiliary view cannot be reselected; however, if a sketch is used to project the view, then the Edit Sketch option is available through the view arrow RMB menu.

FIGURE 21.19

Two Auxiliary views

Alternate Position view

The Alternate Position view is only available for views of an assembly, and shows the assembly in two different positions (not from different viewpoints; this requires an assembly that moves). This is another view type that does not create a new view, but alters an existing view. Figure 21.20 shows the PropertyManager interface for this view type, a sample view that it creates, and the way that it is represented in the drawing FeatureManager.

FIGURE 21.20

The Alternate Position view

To create an Alternate Position view, ensure that you have an assembly on the active drawing that can have multiple positions, and click the Alternate Position View button from the Drawings toolbar, or select the same tool at Insert ➪ Drawing View ➪ Alternate Position.

Next, click in the drawing view to which you want to add the alternate position. The PropertyManager shown in Figure 21.20 prompts you to select an existing configuration for the alternate position or to create a new configuration. If you choose to create a new config, then the model window appears, a new config is created, and you are required to reposition the assembly. The alternate position is shown in a different line font on the same view, from the same orientation as the original.

> **TIP** The best way to create this view is to either create two configurations that are used exclusively for the Alternate Position view, or to have two configurations where you know that parts will not be moved, suppressed, or hidden. The main idea is that you need to ensure that these configurations remain in the same position or are changed intentionally, knowing that it will alter this drawing view.

To delete an Alternate Position view, select it in the drawing FeatureManager, and press Delete.

Predefined view

Predefined views are discussed in depth in Chapter 20.

Empty view

Empty views are just that — empty. The reasons for creating an Empty view can include making a view from a sketch, or a schematic from blocks, or combining several elements — such as blocks, sketches, imported drawing geometry, annotations, and symbols — into an entity that can be moved as a group on a drawing.

Custom view

You can create Custom views by orienting the view in the model document, and saving the view. Remember that views can be saved in the View Orientation window, which you can access by pressing the spacebar. Custom views are placed on the drawing using the Named View functionality.

While not appropriate for showing dimensions, views using perspective are most useful for pictorial or illustrative views. The only way to get a perspective view on a drawing is to save a custom view in the model with perspective turned on. You can access the Perspective option at View ➪ Display ➪ Perspective, and you can edit the amount of perspective at View ➪ Modify ➪ Perspective.

Relative view

The Relative view enables you to create a view that does not necessarily correspond to any of the standard orthogonal views or named views. This type of view is very similar to using the Normal To tool. First select the face that is to be presented square to the view, and then select the face that represents the top of the view. When this view type is initiated, SolidWorks opens the 3D model window to allow you to select the faces needed to define the view.

This type of view is particularly useful when a part has a face that is at an odd angle to the standard planes of the part. It is in some ways similar to the Auxiliary view, except that in the Auxiliary view you cannot select which face is the top.

The Relative view has a special function that is important for drawings of multibody parts. If both faces used to establish the view are from the same body, then all of the rest of the bodies in the part can be hidden with an option in the Relative View PropertyManager, which is shown in Figure 21.21. This functionality is particularly useful in Weldments and is covered in more detail in Chapter 31. Multibody modeling is covered in Chapter 26.

FIGURE 21.21

The Relative View PropertyManager

3D Drawing View Mode

3D Drawing View Mode is not technically a drawing view type. It is a mode that enables you to select faces or edges of the model that may need to be selected for some purpose, but cannot be seen from the orientation of the drawing view. You can invoke the 3D Drawing View Mode from the 3D Drawing View toolbar button, which is on the View toolbar and can be accessed via the menus at View ⇨ Modify ⇨ 3D Drawing View.

Ironically, this mode does not work for the Relative view, which would be a perfect application for it. It is intended for views such as the Broken-out Section view where a depth must be selected for the cut.

In Figure 21.22, notice the small toolbar above the drawing view. This toolbar is available while the 3D Drawing View Mode is turned on. Clicking OK on the small toolbar turns off the mode and returns the view to its previous state.

FIGURE 21.22

3D Drawing View Mode

View orientation and alignment

Although you may have selected the Top view, and it displays the correct geometry, you may want to spin the view in the plane of the paper, or orient it in a particular way. You can do this using two methods. The easiest way to reorient the view is to use the Rotate View tool on the View toolbar. This rotates the view in the plane of the paper much like it rotates the model in 3D.

Another option is to select an edge in the view and assign the edge to be either a horizontal or vertical edge. Figure 21.23 shows how a view can be re-oriented using this tool, which is located at Tools ➪ Align Drawing View ➪ Horizontal or Vertical Edge.

Another option for view alignment is to align it relative to another view; this involves stacking one view on top of another or placing them side-by-side. You can do this by selecting the second pair of options in the menu shown in Figure 21.23, Horizontal to Another View and Vertical to Another View.

Situations may arise where a view is locked into a particular relationship to another view, and you need to disassociate the views. The Break Alignment option, which is grayed out in the menu in Figure 21.23, serves that purpose.

Default Alignment resets a view to its original orientation and alignment if it has been altered.

FIGURE 21.23

Rotating a drawing view to align an edge

Selected edge

Using Display Options in Views

Some important display options and settings are not listed in Tools, Options, but are only available through the menus. You can find more information about the display options and settings that are available through Tools, Options in Appendix B.

Display States

Display States can be used in drawing views, but they only have an effect when a drawing view is set to Shaded Display mode. You can control Display States for drawing views in the View Properties tab of the Drawing View Properties dialog box. RMB click inside the view but away from any geometry, and select Properties. The Drawing View Properties dialog box appears, as shown in Figure 21.24.

One of the limitations of the Display States functionality in drawing views is that when wireframe display is used, the drawing edges appear black rather than using the color settings to show wireframe in the same color as shaded.

FIGURE 21.24

The Drawing View Properties dialog box

Display modes

With even the 2D drawing world becoming less and less black-and-white, SolidWorks drawings have the ability to apply shaded views to drawings. This is probably most useful in isometric, perspective, or pictorial views on the drawings. The shading and color may be distracting for dimensioned and detailed views, but it can also be indispensable when you need to show what a part actually looks like in 3D. Not everyone can read engineering prints, and even for those who can, nothing communicates quite like a couple of shaded isometric views.

The more standard 2D drawing display modes are Wireframe, HLR (hidden lines removed), and HLV (hidden lines visible), which work in the same way as they do in the model environment. Unless you override it, the Display mode is set for all of the components in the view.

Component Line Font

Individual components within an assembly can be shown in different fonts, similar to the display in the Alternate Position view. You can access this function through the component RMB menu, by selecting Component Line Font. Figure 21.25 shows the Component Line Font dialog box, along with a drawing view in which a couple of part line fonts have been changed. The part can only be changed in the view where it was selected, or it can be changed across the board in all views in the active drawing where it appears. This is useful if you want to emphasize or de-emphasize certain parts in the assembly view.

FIGURE 21.25

The Component Line Font dialog box

Layers

Yes, SolidWorks drawings *can* use layers. No one likes to admit this, but it is nonetheless true. You can place individual parts onto layers, and the layers can have different colors and fonts. Most entities can be put into layers, including edges, annotations, and sketch items. Hidden layers are often used for reference information or construction entities on a drawing.

Edge display options

SolidWorks drawings and models offer some options for displaying tangent edges. Many users find it distracting when tangent edges (which in a physical part are not edges at all) are given as much visible weight as the sharp edges of, say, a chamfer. These settings are found at View ➪ Display, as shown in Figure 21.26. The Tangent Edges Removed option may be appropriate for parts with few fillets, but it causes a part to look over-simplified and makes details of the shape difficult to distinguish.

FIGURE 21.26

Edge display options

Tangent edges visible

Tangent edges with font

Tangent edges removed

View quality settings

View quality is one of those issues that keep users confused because it has changed so many times in recent releases. If you look for view quality settings, then you may be looking for some time. Are the settings with the view, the sheet, system options, document properties? Where are they?

You have the choice between two options for drawing view quality: high quality and draft quality. The quality that you choose influences the performance of the software. Draft quality views are noticeably rough when viewed closely, but from a distance, they are at least recognizable. However, Draft quality is becoming less accessible, and so I would not recommend relying on this option. Although new Draft Quality views can be created, once they are set to High Quality, they cannot be set back to Draft Quality.

In SolidWorks 2007, all views are created as High Quality unless the view quality setting is overridden. This setting is found at Tools ➪ Options ➪ System Options ➪ Drawings ➪ Display Style ➪ Display Quality For New Views. The only other way that you can create Draft Quality views in this version is if you open a drawing from an older version of SolidWorks that used draft quality views.

In Figure 21.2 earlier in the chapter, the image to the right shows the Display Style pane. This PropertyManager has been taken from a High Quality view. A Draft Quality view enables you to toggle between Draft and High quality, as shown in Figure 21.27. This means that you can switch a view from Draft to High, but not from High to Draft. Also notice in Figure 21.27 that the cursor over a Draft Quality view displays a lightning bolt symbol, indicating draft quality.

FIGURE 21.27

The Draft Quality options and cursor

You can access the Cosmetic Thread Display setting in both the Step 1 PropertyManager and the Step 2 PropertyManager. However, you need to be careful not to misread the interface, by thinking that either of these interfaces controls the View Quality. The best advice for using the view quality settings is to forget about them. It looks like this function is being phased out or at least discouraged.

Distinguishing Views from Sheets

It is sometimes difficult for new users to understand the difference between being *in* a sketch and being *out of* a sketch, or the difference between editing the *sheet* as opposed to the *sheet format*. In the same way, confusion frequently surrounds the difference between sketching in a view and sketching on a sheet. The easiest way to determine if a sketch will be associated with a view or with the drawing sheet is to look at the prompt in the lower-right corner of the SolidWorks window, on the status bar, which displays the message, Editing Sheet, Editing Sheet Format, or Editing View.

This issue becomes especially important when you want to do something with a sketch entity, but it is grayed out and unavailable. This means that whatever entity is active is *not* the one that the sketch entity is on. Drawing views expand to contain all of the sketch entities that are associated with the view, and so if you see a view that is extended on one side, larger than it should be, then it could be extended to contain the grayed-out sketch entity. Activate the sheet and the suspected views; when the sketch entity turns from gray to black, you have found the place where it resides.

Tutorial: Working with View Types, Settings, and Options

This tutorial is intended to familiarize you with many of the view types, settings, and options that are involved in creating views. To begin, follow these steps:

1. From the CD-ROM, open the part called Chapter 21 – Tutorial Part.sldprt.

2. Move the drawing template named Inch B Bible Template.drwdot, also found on the CD-ROM, to your templates folder. If you do not know where your templates are located, go to Tools ⇨ Options ⇨ System Options ⇨ File Locations ⇨ Document Templates.

3. From the window with the open part, click the Make Drawing from Part button from the toolbar. The drawing becomes populated with three standard views and an isometric view, as shown in Figure 21.28.

4. In the drawing document, turn on the display of the Origins. This will help you to align a section view. Origins can be displayed through the menus at View ⇨ Origin.

5. Click the Section View tool on the Drawings toolbar. This activates the Line sketch tool.

FIGURE 21.28

Using a template with Predefined views

6. In the Top view (in the upper-left section of the drawing), draw a line that picks up the inference from the Origin. You may have to run the cursor over the Origin to activate the inference lines. Make sure that the line goes all the way through the model geometry in the view, as shown in Figure 21.29. When you finish the line, the section view is ready to be placed. Place it to the right of the parent view.

FIGURE 21.29

Creating a section view

When sketching, remember to make sure that you are sketching in the view rather than on the sheet. A section view cannot be created from a sketch entity if it is not in a view. A glance at the status bar in the lower-right corner of the window lets you know if you are in Editing View or Editing Sheet.

To change the letter label on the drawing, click the section line and change the label in the top panel of the Section View PropertyManager.

7. Bring the cursor over the sharp bend in the section line until the cursor looks like the image to the left. Double-click the cursor; the section arrows flip to the other direction, and the drawing view becomes cross-hatched. The cross-hatching indicates that the view needs to be updated.

8. Press Ctrl+Q; the view updates, removing the cross-hatching.

9. Click the section line and press Delete. Answer Yes to the prompt. If you are familiar with older versions of SolidWorks, then you may notice that the original sketch is also deleted with the section line and the view, so that you do not have to delete separate elements individually.

10. Create a new section view using a jogged section line, as shown in Figure 21.30. In order to do this, you must pre-draw the jogged section line, and press the Section View button with the part of the line that you want to use to project the new view.

FIGURE 21.30

Creating a jogged section view

11. Next, click the Detail View button on the Drawings toolbar. This activates the Circle sketch tool.

12. Sketch a circle in the Front view, located in the lower-left section of the drawing. Try not to pick up any automatic relations to the center of the circle. One way to prevent this is to hold down the Ctrl key when creating the sketch.

13. Place the view when the circle is complete. Note that the view was created at a scale of 1:2. The sheet scale is 1:4, and so the detail is two times the sheet scale. The Detail view is shown in Figure 21.31.

FIGURE 21.31

Creating a Detail view

DETAIL B
SCALE 1 : 2

14. Drag the circumference of the circle and watch the view dynamically resize.

15. Leave the Detail circle selected so that the center of the circle is highlighted. Drag the center of the circle around the view. The effect is like moving a magnifying glass over the part. If you drag the center with the Ctrl key pressed, then you will not pick up any automatic sketch relations when you drop it somewhere.

16. Click the Broken-out Section View tool on the Drawings toolbar. Draw a spline similar to the one shown in the image to the left in Figure 21.32. Splines take a little practice.

FIGURE 21.32

Creating a Broken-out Section view

17. Click inside the view border but outside of the part in the Top view (in the upper-left section of the drawing). Press Ctrl+C.

18. RMB click the tab in the lower-left corner of the drawing that says Sheet1, and select Add New Sheet. If you used the template that I provided, a message may appear, saying that SolidWorks cannot find the format. This is because I only supplied you with the template file, not the format as a separate file. In any case, switch to the B size format and accept.

19. Click any spot inside the sheet and press Ctrl+V. SolidWorks pastes the copied view from the other sheet. Delete the section line.

20. Click the Projected View tool from the Drawings toolbar, and then click the pasted view. Practice making a couple of projected views, including dragging one off at a 45-degree angle to make an isometric. Make sure that one of the views is a side view showing the angled edge, as shown in Figure 21.33. Once you create the views, click model edges in the views and drag them around to a better location.

FIGURE 21.33

Projecting views

Create at least one of these views

21. Select the angled edge from one of the side views and click the Auxiliary View toolbar button. While placing the view, press and hold the Ctrl key to break the alignment. You can resize the view arrow by selecting the corners and dragging. If you drag the line itself, then you can move it between the views. Alternatively, with the view arrow selected and the PropertyManager displayed, you can deselect the green check mark icon in the Arrow panel at the top of the window to turn off the arrow.

22. Create a new drawing from the New dialog box. If the automatic Model View interface appears in the PropertyManager, click the red X icon to cancel out of it.

23. Expand the Task pane and activate the View palette (the tab that looks like a drawing icon). Click the ellipse button (. . .) and browse for the assembly named Chapter 21. SF casting assembly.sldasm. This is shown in Figure 21.34.

FIGURE 21.34

The View palette

24. Drag the Back view onto the drawing. Notice that when you use this technique, the views do not resize automatically, regardless of the setting at Tools ⇨ Options ⇨ Drawings ⇨ Automatically Scale New Drawing Views.

25. Delete any view that you have created using this method. Open Windows Explorer, browse to the assembly, and drag it into the drawing. The views that you create using this method are equivalent to the Standard 3 View tool. This time, the views auto-size.

26. Select the Front view and change it to the Back view. Notice that the rest of the views change to reflect the new parent view.

27. Zoom in on the Back view. Change the view to show Tangent Edges With Font through View ⇨ Display.

28. Click the Alternate Position view toolbar button. Type a name in the PropertyManager for a new configuration and click the green check mark icon. SolidWorks opens the assembly model window.

29. Rotate the handle 90 degrees and click the green check mark icon. SolidWorks returns to the drawing and shows the new position in a dashed font, as shown in Figure 21.35.

30. Place an isometric view on the drawing. Change the Display Mode to make it a shaded view.

FIGURE 21.35

Creating an Alternate Position view

31. RMB click inside the view but away from the parts, and select Properties. The dialog box appears, as shown in Figure 21.36. Make sure that the view is set to use the Default configuration, and also select the Show in Exploded State option.

FIGURE 21.36

The Drawing View Properties dialog box

Summary

SolidWorks has the capacity to make many different types of views of parts and assemblies. In addition to the tools for projecting views, custom views saved in the model document can be saved and used on the drawing. The associative nature of the drawing to the model helps ensure that drawing views, regardless of how unusual the section angle or view orientation, are displayed in the correct size, location, and geometry.

It is sometimes better to create some of the views that require sketches by pre-sketching. Make use of workflow enhancements when possible; for example, the Broken-out Section automated workflow works well, but forcing it to be a manual process makes it awkward to use.

Chapter 22

Using Annotations and Symbols

Annotations and symbols are a major component of communicating a design through a drawing. SolidWorks has several options available to help you manage these entities to make engineering drawings look good and communicate effectively.

Using Notes

Notes are the workhorse of SolidWorks annotations. You can use notes in many different configurations, and mix them with links to custom properties, hyperlinks, and text wrapping boxes. You can also use them with favorites, leaders, balloons, and symbols.

The workflow for placing notes

Sometimes users have difficulty working through some of the interfaces in SolidWorks. This is not necessarily the fault of the software, but is often because users may not fully understand how the workflow of a particular feature is supposed to function. The Model View interface from the last chapter is one that can be confusing until you have been through it a few times and gain a more intuitive feel for how it works.

Understanding the workflow is paramount to being able to use the software efficiently. I sometimes find myself using the Annotations clumsily, and sometimes wind up with blank notes, double notes, or extra lines at the ends of notes. After using the tool a few times, I get back in the groove.

For these reasons, I have added some step-by-step suggestions here to help you establish expectations that will enable you to use a fast workflow with annotations.

IN THIS CHAPTER

Using notes

Using blocks

Using symbols

Using center marks and centerlines

Tutorial: Using annotations

Follow these steps to create a note:

1. Click the Note toolbar button on the Annotations toolbar.

2. Click in the graphics window where you want to create the note *or* click an entity that you want the note leader to point to, and *then* click where you want the note.

3. Type the note. Press Enter at the end of a line, or, if you intend to force the note to wrap, just allow the line of text to be as long as it wants to be. While you create the note, the text box expands to the right until you press Enter, and it expands down every time a line is added.

   At the end of the last line of the note, *do not* press Enter again (this creates extra lines) and *do not* press Esc (this causes the entire note to disappear).

4. To finish the note, click the mouse outside of the text box. After that, if you are done, press Esc. If you want to continue with another note, click again to place it, and start typing. If you want to place the same note as the first one again, the text is already there, so click a second time.

Fonts

SolidWorks uses any TrueType fonts that Windows will accept. This includes symbol, non-English, and Wingding fonts. SolidWorks does not use true monofonts like AutoCAD, because they do not have width information. Some look-alike fonts are installed with SolidWorks that do have a very narrow width, and are shaped like some of the monofonts.

If you are a long-time SolidWorks user, you will be pleased to know that in recent versions of the software, different pieces of text within a single note can be formatted with multiple fonts, multiple sizes, bold, italics, underline, and so on.

The Fonts toolbar displays with two different names. If you use it in the CommandManager, it displays with the Fonts name, with the icon shown at the beginning of this Fonts section. In Tools, Customize, the Fonts toolbar displays as the Formatting toolbar. The Formatting toolbar also appears in the graphics area immediately over your text every time you either insert a new note or edit an existing note, unless the toolbar is already docked somewhere. The Formatting toolbar is shown in Figure 22.1.

FIGURE 22.1

The Formatting toolbar

Text boxes and wrapping

Text boxes are a more recent addition that enables the user to limit the size, particularly the width, that a note can occupy. This enables notes to wrap in tight spaces on title or revision blocks, as well as other places.

You can size text boxes immediately after placement, even while they are blank; the text then wraps as you type it. The text box expands downward automatically. Blank text boxes can be left on the drawing to provide a placeholder for future text. The blank text box has a rectangular border that contains an X, both of which are removed when you add text. If spaces are added to a text box, the text box becomes invisible, although you can select it if you know where it is. When you move the cursor over the text box, the cursor displays the note symbol. Text boxes do not highlight when window selected.

While typing a note, it is not possible to resize the note using the middle handle on the right end of the box; you should use the lower-right corner handle, as shown in Figure 22.2.

FIGURE 22.2

Resizing a text box using the lower-right corner handle

If a custom property is used to populate a note, and the value of the property is long, you may have difficulty getting the text of the property to wrap. One way to accomplish this is to make the font of the note very small, then size the box to the appropriate size, then set the note font back to the original size. The text now wraps to fit the box.

Notes and leaders

When you start to place a note, a preview shows the text box with or without a leader depending on the position of the cursor. If the cursor is over a blank section of the drawing, the note is placed without any leader. If the cursor is over a face, edge, or vertex, then a leader is added using the arrow controlled by the settings at Tools ➪ Options ➪ Document Properties ➪ Arrows ➪ Attachments. By default, a leader attached to a face uses a dot as an arrow, and a leader attached to an edge, sketch entity, or nothing at all uses a regular arrow. You can change these defaults at the options location mentioned above, and you can change individual note leaders in the PropertyManager that becomes available when you select a note.

Figure 22.3 shows the preview that is displayed by the cursor when you place a note over a face, over an edge, and over blank space on the drawing.

You can also change settings for bent leaders in the Tools ➪ Options ➪ Document Properties area. It is recommended that you use the same bent leader lengths for all annotations, and save them in the templates that you use.

FIGURE 22.3

Placing a note with a leader

Some minor but basic functionality appears to be missing from notes in SolidWorks. Single-clicking inside an active text box places the cursor between letters, as expected. Double-clicking inside an active text box selects the entire word that you click, again as expected. Triple-clicking in Microsoft applications such as Word and PowerPoint generally selects the whole paragraph or the contents of the text box. However, the triple-click option is not available in SolidWorks notes. Ctrl+A does work to select all of the text inside a text box. To format the entire note, do not activate the text box; instead, only select the note, and apply the setting to the entire note rather than to selected text within the note.

You also cannot drag-and-drop selected text to move it within a text box. However, you can Ctrl+C, Ctrl+X, and Ctrl+V the text.

Adding a leader to a note

To add a leader to a note that was created without a leader, click the note and select the leader options in the Leader panel of the PropertyManager, as shown in Figure 22.4. After you add the leader, you can reposition the handle at the end of the leader to attach it to an entity on the drawing.

FIGURE 22.4

Adding a leader to a note

Note Without Leader

Note With Leader

Multiple leaders

You can also attach multiple leaders to notes. To create a new note with multiple leaders, preselect the entities that the leaders are to be attached to, and then click the Note toolbar button.

To add a leader to an existing note, first click the note, and then Ctrl-drag the handle on the end of the leader to the second location. A note with multiple leaders is shown in Figure 22.5. To remove one of multiple leaders from a note, click the handle at the end of the arrow and press Delete.

FIGURE 22.5

A note with multiple leaders

Jogged leaders

Jogged leaders have come a long way since their introduction many releases ago. You can switch a regular leader to a jogged leader by selecting an option in the PropertyManager. In Figure 22.4, the middle icon in the top row is the Jogged Leader icon. The icon to the left simply turns on the default leader, and the icon to the right turns off leaders altogether.

Once you activate the jogged leader option, you can add a jog from the leader RMB menu. Notice in Figure 22.6 that two options give you control over the jogged leader.

FIGURE 22.6

Jogging a leader

Add Jog Point

Selecting the Add Jog Point command adds a new handle to the leader that you can move around.
You can add multiple jog points to the leader.

Insert New Branch

The Insert New Branch command enables you to create a new jogged leader that ends in another
arrow from the selected point. This arrangement with multiple branches in a jogged leader is
shown in Figure 22.7.

FIGURE 22.7

The results of adding a new branch to a jogged leader

Favorites

For notes, a favorite can apply a font, an underline or bold formatting, or any other setting from
the Formatting (Fonts) toolbar.

To create a note that uses the favorite setting from another existing note, pre-select the existing
note before starting the Note command; SolidWorks applies the favorite to the new note.

CAUTION   Sometimes adding a favorite to a note can make other changes that you may not expect,
such as turning off the leaders if a note has multiple leaders. In particular, if the favorite
is made from a note with a jogged leader, then it turns off leaders for regular multiple leaders.
Favorites that are created from regular leader notes do not turn off jogged leaders.

Making a change to the leader of a note after you apply the favorite removes the favorite from the
note, although the formatting remains. This does not apply to adding multiple leaders, only to changing the type of leader.

Applying a favorite may also remove the ability of the text to wrap, as well as any changes to the text
box shape. You cannot move the corner of a text box of a note to which you have applied a favorite.

Favorites exist only in the document in which they were created, but they can be shared to other
documents by saving the favorite out as a separate file. Note favorites use the extension, *.sldnote-
fvt. Once you save the favorite, you can load it into other documents. The Favorites panel of the
Note PropertyManager interface is shown in Figure 22.8.

FIGURE 22.8

The Favorites panel of the Note PropertyManager interface

The Favorites panel contains the following buttons:

    Apply Defaults/No Favorites: Removes favorite settings from the current interface, setting all values back to the defaults.

    Add or Update Favorites: This can be used to either add a new favorite to the database or to change the name or other settings for an existing favorite.

    Delete Favorite: Removes a favorite from the database.

    Save Favorite: Saves a favorite to an external file (*.sldhwfvt), which can be loaded by other users and added to their databases.

    Load Favorite: Loads a saved favorite file.

Favorites can be loaded into document templates so that for every document created from the template, those Favorites will be available.

Linking notes to custom properties

You can link notes to custom properties. The custom properties can be from the drawing, or from the model that is referenced by the drawing. This kind of link is also mentioned briefly in Chapter 20, but I discuss it more thoroughly here.

Figure 22.9 shows a note on a drawing with custom property links pulling data from the model shown on the drawing. To add these links, driven by the syntax $PRPSHEET:"material", click the icon indicated in the image to the right in Figure 22.9.

In this case, text has been combined with custom properties, but custom properties can also appear alone. The Custom Properties interface is found at Tools, Properties.

Hyperlinking text

Hyperlinking text is sometimes useful on drawings to provide a link to reference documentation, specification, test results, and so on. The first button in the Text Format panel enables you to add a hyperlink to text in the note. Either copy the URL to the hyperlink dialog box that appears, or browse to it from the dialog box.

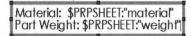

FIGURE 22.9

Linking notes to custom properties

Link to
Custom Properties

Hyperlink text   Add symbol

Notes and symbols

Notes and symbols are regularly combined in SolidWorks. Symbols are discussed more fully later in this chapter, but are mentioned here because of the frequency with which they are used with notes. The image to the right in Figure 22.9 shows the Text Format panel, which contains a button to the interface where you can add symbols.

Using Blocks

Blocks in SolidWorks can contain sketch elements and notes. When used in drawings, blocks have several common uses, including the following:

- Standard note blocks for tolerances, disclaimers, or default requirements
- You can put together a mechanism in 2D where each block represents a part
- Flow direction for fluid systems
- Drawing stamps such as "Not For Release," "Preliminary," "Obsolete," and so on
- Symbols for schematics which can be snapped together
- You can save drawing templates as blocks to make them easier to place as a single entity

Like favorites, blocks reside in the document in which they are created, but you can save them out to a *.sldblk file, load them into other documents, and save them as a part of a document template.

Inserting blocks

You can apply blocks in several ways, including by dragging from Windows Explorer and by using the menus at Insert ⇨ Annotations ⇨ Block. However, the most efficient way is to access them from the Design Library. Library folders can be established specifically for blocks. Check the settings at Tools ⇨ Options ⇨ File Locations ⇨ Blocks, and redirect this setting to a library area outside of the SolidWorks installation directory. Figure 22.10 shows the Design Library with a folder containing blocks that are selected. The blocks do not show previews in the window, but the tooltip displays large previews. You can drag blocks from the Design Library onto the drawing sheet.

FIGURE 22.10

Blocks in the Design Library

Each block has an insertion point, which snaps to any sketch entity endpoint, even if it is in another block. This makes schematics easy to snap together. If the default insertion point is not the point that you need to snap to the other geometry, then you can place the block anywhere on the drawing and drag the point that needs to snap.

Once blocks are snapped together, to detach them from one another, you can click the point at which they touch; a Coincident sketch relation displays in the PropertyManager. Deleting the sketch relation enables you to drag the block away from the other geometry.

When blocks are inserted, you can control several options in the PropertyManager. This function may be somewhat hidden because it does not appear automatically when you place the block. After you place the block, SolidWorks wants you to place another copy of the block. If you press Esc to cancel out of placing additional blocks, then the first placed block is not selected, and so the PropertyManager does not display. Figure 22.11 shows the Block PropertyManager.

FIGURE 22.11

The Block PropertyManager

Existing Relations

This panel lists the sketch relations that are linked to the block. These may cause the block to not move properly when you drag it. This feature is most helpful when the block is being used as a representation of a part in a simulated 2D mechanism.

Definition

Blocks can be linked to an external file, which enables all linked instances of a block to be updated at once, even if they are being used in other drawing documents. The path box for the Link to File option only displays if you select the check box.

The Edit button refers to editing the block. A toolbar button also exists for editing blocks. The Leader & Insertion Points button enables you to edit both of the controls. You can use the For Construction option to change any sketch entities in the block to construction entities.

Parameters

The top field with the two circles to the left controls the scale of the block. This number affects the entire block, including the text. You also have the option to scale dimensions.

The Lock Angle option refers to the rotation of the block. If the Lock Angle option is not selected, then you can rotate the block if one point on it is coincident to a stationary object, such as a vertex in a drawing view.

Leader

You will recognize these options from the Notes leaders. The leader is attached to the block where the angled black handle was placed when you created the block.

Text/Dimension Display

The Display Dimensions option controls whether or not any notes and dimensions in the block are displayed or hidden.

Layer

You can assign most entities on drawings to layers, which in turn have controls for items, such as line type, color, and visibility.

Creating blocks

 You can create blocks by selecting the sketch and annotation elements and clicking the Make Block toolbar button from the Blocks toolbar, or by accessing the command through the menus at Insert ⇨ Annotations ⇨ Block.

CROSS-REF   Sketch Blocks have been covered in some detail in Chapter 4. The current chapter is limited to a discussion of blocks that may be found on drawings rather than those used in model sketches.

By default, when you create a block, the Insertion Point panel of the PropertyManager does not expand. If you expand this panel, the blue Origin symbol represents the insertion point that is attached to the cursor during block insertion, as shown in Figure 22.12. The angled line hanging off of the left side of the block is the leader attachment point for the block. You can also drag this line around the block and snap it to sketch geometry. By default, this block does not use a leader, but if one is required, then you can turn it on when you place the block.

FIGURE 22.12

Creating a block

Editing blocks

 Although you do not have many options when creating blocks, many more options become available when you edit them. You can access editing options for a block from four locations:

- The Edit Block toolbar button on the Blocks toolbar
- The Edit button in the Block PropertyManager
- Through the menus at Tools ⇨ Block ⇨ Edit
- From the RMB menu of the block in the Blocks folder in the drawing FeatureManager

The standard edit function gives you access to the sketch and note elements that make up the block.

Add/Remove Entities

 While you are editing the block, the Add/Remove Entities button on the Blocks toolbar becomes available. This enables you to add or remove sketch or note entities from the block definition.

Rebuild

 When you are finished editing the block, and you need to leave Edit mode, you can use the Rebuild button to do so.

Explode

This is not technically an edit option, but it certainly does change things. Explode is available when you are not editing the block, but when it is selected. Explode returns the contents of that particular instance of the block to the drawing, removing them from the block. This removes any leaders that are attached to the block, as well as sketch relations.

Using Symbols

SolidWorks symbols are different from symbols that are a part of a font family. SolidWorks symbols fall into several categories including, weld, surface finish, hole, modifying symbols, GD&T, and several flag symbols. You can also construct custom symbols.

Where can you use symbols?

You can use symbols in notes and dimensions. They also are an intrinsic part of weld symbols and surface finish symbols. Hole Callouts use symbols extensively, as do GD&T (geometric dimensioning and tolerancing) frames.

Figure 22.13 shows the Text Format panel from the Note PropertyManager and the Dimension Text panel from the Dimension PropertyManager. Both of these interfaces give you access to the symbol library.

FIGURE 22.13

Accessing symbols and the symbol library

Custom symbols

You can create custom symbols in SolidWorks, but creating them may not be as simple as you expect. In the lang\english subfolder of the SolidWorks installation directory is a file called Gtol.sym. This is the file that stores the representations of all of the SolidWorks symbols. This is also the file where you can create symbols of your own. You can edit the file in Notepad.

As a warning, unless you enjoy writing scripts for the command line, or you are a fan of DOS 5.0, then you may not want to create custom symbol projects. The format for creating symbols is simple enough, but it is what you might call somewhat arcane. It is effective at creating line-art symbols that can be used with text and can even be used to contain text. If you are a little inventive with this, then you can create interesting shapes that integrate with your notes and dimensions.

Keep in mind that this topic does not appear in the Help files, but all of the instructions you need are inside the file itself. You may have to experiment a little to discover what the rules are in terms of making shapes outside of the limits of the 1X1 matrix.

Using Center Marks and Centerlines

You can apply center marks either manually or automatically to edges that appear circular in the drawing view. The settings to control automatic insertion are found at Tools ➪ Options ➪ Document Properties ➪ Detailing ➪ Auto Insert on View Creation. The size of the mark at the center and the use of lines extending to the actual circular edge are also controlled on this tab, in the Center Marks section.

NEW FEATURE Starting with 2007, there is now an option in Tools ➪ Options ➪ Document Properties to exclude center marks from arc edges created by fillets.

Figure 22.14 shows some of the options that are available for center marks.

Center marks propagate well to patterns, and you can dimension to them individually. You can rotate center marks in views where they need to be referenced from an edge that is not parallel to horizontal. You can also place center marks into layers.

You can apply centerlines to any geometry that has a temporary axis that is perpendicular to the drawing sheet. Centerlines can also be placed automatically when you place the part into the drawing. You can create centerlines by selecting a face or a pair of parallel lines or concentric arcs. Centerlines may be displayed improperly on parts that are created by mirroring, as shown in Figure 22.15.

FIGURE 22.14

Options that are available for center marks

Select symbol to propagate
center mark to pattern

FIGURE 22.15

Centerlines can display improperly on a mirrored part.

Tutorial: Using Annotations

This tutorial shows you how to use some of the tools that were discussed in this chapter. It does not cover every feature, and so you should explore a little on your own, and not necessarily follow the instructions exactly. Start here:

1. From the CD-ROM, open the file named Chapter 22 – Tutorial.slddrw. This is a drawing file with views of the part from Chapter 21, but it does not contain dimensions or annotations.

2. Click the Center Mark tool on the Annotations toolbar. (If the button is not there, then use Tools ➪ Customize ➪ Commands to place it on the toolbar, along with the Centerline tool.) Click one of the holes in the pattern of three, and click the Propagate symbol to propagate the center marks to all three holes in the pattern. The view should look like Figure 22.16 when you are done.

3. Activate the Centerline tool to add two centerlines to the right view, in the lower-left area. Select the cylindrical faces for each feature to place the centerlines. Click the vertical centerline and drag the ends past the edges of the part.

4. Select the edge that is indicated in Figure 22.17, and initiate a note from the Annotations toolbar. Type the text shown, all in one line. You can place the degree and diameter symbols from the symbol library, which you can access using the indicated button in the PropertyManager. Both symbols are in the Modifying Symbols library, also shown in Figure 22.17. Drag the lower-right corner of the text box to make the text wrap as shown.

5. Draw an arrow with a text note inside it, as shown in Figure 22.18. Make the sketch and text into a block by window-selecting all of it and clicking Make Block from the Blocks toolbar, or by selecting Tools ➪ Block ➪ Make. Make sure that the end of the arrow is its insertion point. You have to expand the Insertion Point panel in the PropertyManager to access this option. When the block is set up, accept it by clicking the green check mark icon. When the block is created, delete it from the drawing.

6. Place the block using the Insert Block function, so that the block is to the right of the right view. Once you place it, press Esc to cancel the placement of more blocks. Then select the block to activate the PropertyManager. Deselect the Lock Angle option, and set the angle to 270 degrees.

FIGURE 22.16

Center marks and centerlines on a part

Add centerlines by clicking cylindrical faces

FIGURE 22.17

Placing symbols in an annotation

3 HOLES PLACED 120° APART ON Ø2.750" B.C.

Access the symbol library

FIGURE 22.18

Creating a block

Summary

Annotations and symbols in SolidWorks have many options for connection, creation, and display. Recent releases have brought major improvements to text box–driven annotations. Custom properties and hyperlinks allow the user to populate drawing annotations with content and links to content. Sharing favorites in templates is a great idea for readily available note styles.

Blocks have several flexible uses and can be updated from external files across many documents. Their use for simulating mechanisms, piecing together schematics, and annotating drawings, in addition to the Belts and Chains functionality discussed in Chapter 13, make blocks one of the most flexible functions available.

Chapter 23

Dimensioning and Tolerancing

IN THIS CHAPTER

Putting dimensions on drawings

Dimension options

Adding tolerances

Using dimension favorites

Tutorial: Working with dimensions and tolerances

In years past, dimensioning and tolerancing was an art form and a science. People did, and still do, become very passionate when discussing the right way of performing these tasks. In truth, the techniques are probably not so black and white, but are highly dependent on the industry, the means of manufacture, and the purpose of the drawing. For example, the drawing could be used for quotes, manufacturing, inspection, assembly, testing, and so on, and the drawings for each of these purposes would be somewhat different.

While it is important to follow standards and use manufacturing drawing conventions properly, this is not an argument that I want to reignite here. In this chapter, I will focus on how to apply the available tools in SolidWorks.

Putting Dimensions on Drawings

Drawings are typically not one of the hotter topics that SolidWorks users become excited about, but a few issues still ignite heated discussions. How to put dimensions onto drawings is one of these topics. This is much like the "tastes great/less filling" debate. Each side of the issue has valid points, and the question is not likely to be resolved any time soon.

At the center of this debate is whether the dimensions that you use to create the model should be placed directly on the drawing, or whether a dimensioning scheme specifically for the drawing is better. In the following sections, each method is examined for its benefits and drawbacks.

Insert Model Items

Insert Model Items takes all of the dimensions, symbols, annotations, and other elements that are used to create the model, and puts them onto the drawing. Because these dimensions come directly from the sketches and features of the model, they are *driving* dimensions. This means that they can be double-clicked and changed in the same way that sketch and feature dimensions can be changed, and with the same effect. As a result, changing these dimensions even from the drawing causes the parts and assemblies in which they are used to be changed.

You can insert the model items on a per-feature basis, either only bringing the items that are appropriate into the current view, or bringing items into all views. Insertion can be further broken down by type of item, and it can become as specific as pattern counts, Hole Wizard items, specific symbol types, and reference geometry types. You can select Insert ➪ Model Items, or you can access this command from the Annotations toolbar. The Model Items PropertyManager interface is shown in Figure 23.1.

FIGURE 23.1

The Model Items PropertyManager interface

Usually, the dimensions need to be rearranged, although SolidWorks does try to arrange them so that they do not overlap. Figure 23.2 shows the result of bringing dimensions into all views for the part. The part is on the CD-ROM in the Chapter 21 materials.

FIGURE 23.2

The default placement of dimensions into all views

Figure 23.2 contains duplicate dimensions, overlapping dimensions, unnecessarily long leaders, radius dimensions pointing to the wrong side of the arc, and a lot of awkward placement. This is what you can expect from using the automatic functions. At best, these dimensions require rearranging, and at worst, they probably require that you delete and replace some of them, or move them to new views where they make more sense.

To move a dimension to another view, you can Shift-drag it from one view to the other (make sure that the dimension is appropriate in the destination view). To copy a dimension, you can Ctrl-drag it. If you cannot place the dimension in the view that you have dragged it to, then the cursor will indicate this with a special cursor symbol.

If you approach this task by placing dimensions on a per-feature or per-view basis, then that does not change the number of dimensions that you will have to move; it just means that they have to be inserted more often. Keep in mind that if you choose this method, there is a significant amount of cleanup and checking that you must do. The convenience of having the dimensions put into the views for you, and the ability to actually change the model from the drawing are quite useful, but you may not save very much time or effort by doing things this way.

Using reference dimensions

The alternative to automatically inserting model dimensions is to manually place reference dimensions. At first, this appears to be simply recreating work that has already been done, and this is somewhat true.

However, in several important ways, these dimensions are not merely duplicates of the model items. In fact, the reference dimensions that you manually place on the drawing are quite different from the dimensions that are used in the model, unless either the dimensioning scheme of the model or the drawing is changed in some extreme way. The dimensions serve completely different purposes in the two settings, and could only be the same through some odd coincidence.

When modeling, I tend to dimension symmetrically, but only on one side, which would not be shown on a manufacturing or inspection drawing. I frequently use workarounds that force a different modeling-dimensioning scheme than I would prefer to use. Often, a feature is located from the midpoint of an edge, which involves no dimensions whatsoever. Sketch entities may have Equal relations, which also leave sketch elements undimensioned. Beyond that, when draft is involved, as is the case with plastic or cast parts, the dimensions of the sketch that you used to create the feature often have little to do with the geometry that is dimensioned on a print for inspection or mold building. Dimension schemes in models reflect the need for the model to react to change, while dimension schemes in drawings reflect the manufacturing or inspection methods, in order to minimize tolerance stack-up, and to reflect the usage of the actual part.

Although there are strictly technical reasons for dimensioning drawings independently from the way the model was dimensioned, there are other factors such as time, and the neat and orderly placement of dimensions. Time is an issue because by the time you finish rearranging dimensions that were inserted automatically from the model — checking and eliminating duplicates and then manually adding dimensions that were left out or that had to be eliminated because they were inappropriate for some reason, as well as ensuring that all of the necessary dimensions are on the drawing — it would have been much quicker to manually dimension the drawing correctly the first time using reference dimensions. Inevitably, manually inserting dimensions leads to a different scheme than would be imposed on you by using the Insert Model Items method.

It is my opinion that inserting model dimensions into the drawing is in most cases impractical for manufacturing or inspection drawings. This is because of the amount of time required to rearrange and check the dimensions, the need to ensure that you have placed the necessary dimensions, and the simple fact that the dimensioning and sketch relations needed for efficient modeling are usually very different from the dimensioning needed for manufacturing or inspection.

It is recommended that you use the manual dimension placement option, which works much in the same way as when dimensions are added to sketches. Dimensions that you place in the drawing in this way are called *driven* or *reference* dimensions. Technically, reference dimensions are "extra" dimensions that you place to ease calculations, and you usually create these dimensions with parentheses around them. You can find the setting that controls the parentheses around reference dimensions at Tools ⇨ Options ⇨ Document Properties ⇨ Dimensions ⇨ Add Parentheses By Default.

Annotation views

Annotation views are views in the model in which annotations have been added. These are generally used by people who are using model dimensions on drawings. Annotation views are accessed from the Annotations folder in the model FeatureManager. They are created automatically when dimensions or notes are added to the part. The annotation view can be used in the model to show the note or dimension in the view in which it was created, or on the drawing to help parse the dimensions into views where they are easily read.

Annotation views can be inserted manually or automatically. You can access the settings for annotation views through the RMB menu of the Annotations folder, shown in Figure 23.3.

FIGURE 23.3

The Annotations folder RMB menu

Driven dimension color

Driven dimensions on the drawing display in gray, and this can be a problem when the drawing is printed out. There are two methods that you can use to deal with this printing problem. The first method is to set the Page Properties of the drawing to force it to print in black and white. You can find the Page Properties at File ⇨ Page Setup. The Page Setup dialog box is shown in Figure 23.4.

The second method is to set the color for driven dimensions to black rather than gray. This color setting is found at Tools ⇨ Options ⇨ Color ⇨ Dimensions Non-Imported (Driven).

FIGURE 23.4

The Page Setup dialog box

Ordinate and baseline dimensions

Ordinate and baseline dimensions are appropriate for collections of linear dimensions when you have a number of items that can all be dimensioned from the same reference. Flat patterns of sheet metal parts often fall into this category. When you apply ordinate dimensions, a zero location is selected first, followed by each entity for which you want a dimension. When dimensions become too tightly packed, SolidWorks automatically jogs the witness lines to space out the dimensions adequately. You can create jogs manually by using the RMB menu. Once you create a set of ordinate dimensions, you can add to the set by selecting Add To Ordinate from the RMB menu.

Baseline dimensions are normal linear dimensions that all come from the same reference, and are stacked together at a defined spacing. The default settings for baseline dimensions are found at Tools ➪ Options ➪ Dimensions ➪ Offset Distances.

TIP   Baseline dimensions work best either when they are horizontal or when the dimension text is aligned with the dimension line (as is the default situation with ISO standard dimensioning). Vertical dimensions where the text is horizontal do not usually stack as neatly because the dimension text runs over the dimension line of the adjacent dimensions.

Figure 23.5 shows ordinate and baseline dimensions in the same view.

You can access ordinate and baseline dimensions from the Dimensions/Relations toolbar (although they are not there by default, you must place them there with the Tools ➪ Customize dialog), or by RMB clicking in a blank space, selecting More Dimensions, and then selecting the type of dimension that you want to use.

FIGURE 23.5

Ordinate and baseline dimensions in the same view

Autodimensioning

 If the Insert Model Items feature is not likely to produce dimensions that are usable in a manufacturing drawing, then the Autodimension feature is even less likely to do so. However, if you use autodimensioning in a controlled way, in the right situations, then it can be a valid way to create selected dimensions. The Autodimension PropertyManager is shown in Figure 23.6.

The Autodimension function can fully dimension the geometry in a drawing view. This is best for ordinate or baseline dimensioning where many dimensions are derived from a common reference, as is often the case with sheet metal parts or a plate with many holes drilled in it. You should limit the use of this option to cases where that type of dimensioning is what you would choose, having the choice of all available types of dimensions — do not allow the software to dictate the dimensioning scheme for your drawing.

NOTE The Autodimension function is different from the Fully Define Sketch function, which is new in SolidWorks 2007. Autodimension works in the drawing, only adding dimensions. Fully Define Sketch works in the model sketch mode, adding dimensions and sketch relations. In previous versions, these functions were consolidated in a single function called Autodimension.

FIGURE 23.6

The Autodimension PropertyManager interface

Reference sketches

For some types of dimensions, you may need to create additional reference sketch entities. For example, with angle dimensions, it may be desirable to add construction lines to help define the angle. You can add centerlines as separate axis-like entities, as discussed in Chapter 22, but you can also sketch in centerlines manually if needed. This type of sketch is most often attached to the view rather than the drawing sheet.

TIP   Remember that, if necessary, you can create angle dimensions by selecting three points (vertex of the angle first) instead of two lines. When you do this, sketch lines are typically drawn to indicate the vertex of the angle.

Dimension Options

The Dimension PropertyManager contains settings, default overrides, tolerances, favorites, and several other important settings for use with dimensions. The PropertyManager for driven dimensions is shown in Figure 23.7. Favorites and tolerances are covered in their own sections later in this chapter, but the other panels of the Dimension PropertyManager are described in the following paragraphs.

FIGURE 23.7

The Dimension PropertyManager interface

Dimension Text

The Dimension Text panel enables you to add text to the dimension. You can add lines of text both before and after the dimension value itself, and you can also add text before and after the DIM value on the same line. The DIM field is what places the actual value; if this syntax is somehow deleted, then you can just type it back in and the dimension will still work.

The Dimension Text panel includes some formatting tools, such as justification and a setting for the position of the dimension line. The last two rows of buttons include the more commonly used symbols, with access to the complete library, such as any custom symbols that you may have made for the library.

Primary Value Override

Among SolidWorks users, one of the biggest and most common mistakes made by former AutoCAD users is the override of dimension values. Apparently due to popular demand, the Primary Value Override is now available in SolidWorks 2007 drawings, in the Dimension PropertyManager as shown in Figure 23.7. This option was added to the software mainly to enable the creation of dimensions with words instead of numbers, as shown in Figure 23.8.

FIGURE 23.8

Using the Override Dimension value

Display Options

You can control the default setting for parentheses around driven, or reference, dimensions in Tools ➪ Options ➪ Document Properties ➪ Dimensions ➪ Add Parentheses By Default. The option in the Display Options panel controls the override of the default for the current dimension.

Although you can also control dual dimension defaults in Tools ➪ Options, you can turn them on and off from this interface for individual dimensions. When you enable the Dual Dimension option, SolidWorks uses the settings from Tools ➪ Options.

 NOTE   If it has been a few releases since you examined the Dual Dimension options, then you may find that SolidWorks 2007 has improved placement options for the dual dimensions.

The foreshortened radius is only valid for individual radial dimensions. A foreshortened radius is shown in Figure 23.9. Foreshortened radius dimensions are typically used for large radii when dimensions to the center point are not important.

The inspection dimension is shown in Figure 23.9 with an oval around the dimension.

FIGURE 23.9

A foreshortened radius

Witness/Leader Display

This panel enables you to set the arrows and dimension lines to be placed inside the witness lines. You can perform this function more easily by using the handles on the arrowheads. From this panel, you can also change the display type of individual arrowheads.

Break Lines

When you select the Use Document Gap option in this panel, the witness, or extension, lines of the selected dimension are broken by other crossing dimension lines, witness lines, or arrows. This is shown in Figure 23.10.

Layer

Layers are discussed in detail in Chapter 25.

More Properties

The More Properties button displays the older Dimension Properties dialog box, which has some duplicate settings, but also contains some less commonly used options that are only available through this interface. Examples of these settings include units, dimension font, control over individual arrow style, and the ability to turn arrows and extension lines on or off. The remaining settings are duplicates of settings in the PropertyManager interface. The Dimension Properties dialog box is shown in Figure 23.11.

FIGURE 23.10

Broken witness lines

FIGURE 23.11

The Dimension Properties dialog box

Adding Tolerances

You can add dimension tolerances in the Dimension PropertyManager, which you can activate by selecting the dimension that you want to modify. Available tolerance types include:

- Basic
- Bilateral
- Limit
- Symmetric
- MIN
- MAX
- Fit
- Fit with tolerance
- Fit (tolerance only)

NOTE You can also add tolerances to dimensions in models; the tolerance is brought in with the dimension if you use the Insert Model Items feature.

The Tolerance/Precision panel is shown in Figure 23.7. The appropriate number entry fields are activated when you assign the corresponding tolerance type to the dimension. The tolerance types that are available in SolidWorks are shown in Figure 23.12.

FIGURE 23.12

The available tolerance types in SolidWorks

Basic

Bilateral

Symmetrical

Limit

Max

Min

Fit Tolerancing

Precision

In SolidWorks, *precision* means the number of decimal places with which dimensions are displayed. Typically, SolidWorks works to eight places with meters as the default units. You can create templates that use up to that number of places as the default setting, and then change the number of places for individual dimensions as necessary. The first of the two boxes under Precision is used for the dimension precision, and the second is used for tolerance precision.

You can change Precision values for individual dimensions in the PropertyManager for the dimension, and for the entire document at Tools ➪ Options ➪ Document Properties ➪ Units.

Geometric Tolerancing

The full range of Geometric Tolerancing symbols are available for control frames, datums, datum targets, and so on. You can use the Geometric Tolerance dialog box to build control frames. This dialog box is shown in Figure 23.13. For commonly used Geometric Tolerance symbols, you may want to create and use favorites.

FIGURE 23.13

The Geometric Tolerance settings

Using Dimension Favorites

You can use dimension favorites to apply many items to dimensions. Unlike notes, this is not limited to fonts and formatting. Some of the most common uses of dimension favorites are:

- To add standard tolerances to dimensions
- To set precision values for dimensions
- To add text, such as TYP, to a dimension
- To add a commonly used GD&T reference

You can save favorites from one document and load them into another document, even between document types. For example, you can load part dimension favorites into a drawing.

When an external favorite is updated, any document that it is linked to also updates. In addition, you can break links to external favorites (with the appropriate button on the Favorites panel). Otherwise, dimension favorites have very similar functions to the other types of favorites; the functions of all of the buttons on the Favorites panel are the same.

Tutorial: Working with Dimensions and Tolerances

In this tutorial, you can use a single part in several different ways to demonstrate different dimensioning and tolerance functions. Follow these steps to learn more about these topics:

1. Open the part from the CD-ROM called Chapter 23 Tutorial.sldprt.

2. Open the drawing from the CD-ROM called Chapter 23 Drawing.slddrw.

3. Tile the windows using Window ⇨ Tile Vertically, and drag the part from the top level of the FeatureManager into the drawing window. This automatically populates the four drawing views.

4. Delete the Top view, leaving the views as shown in Figure 23.14.

FIGURE 23.14

The drawing after step 4

5. Click Insert ➪ Model Items, and ensure that the Select All option is selected for Dimensions and Annotations. Also make sure that the Source/Destination drop-down menu is set to Entire Model. Click the green check mark icon and watch the drawing populate.

6. The resulting drawing is quite cluttered. Delete and move dimensions so that the drawing looks like Figure 23.15.

FIGURE 23.15

The drawing after dimensions have been deleted and moved

7. Shift-drag the surface finish symbol to the Right view, and do the same with the 1.900-inch dimension. You may have to first Shift-drag it into the other view, and then drag it again to correctly attach or position it.

8. Create a set of horizontal ordinate dimensions from the left end of the part, and dimension the X position of each column of holes. Do the same for rows of holes, using the bottom edge of the Front view as the zero reference. Remember that you can create ordinate dimensions by starting a normal Smart Dimension, then RMB clicking to display the More Dimensions list, and then selecting your choice.

9. If necessary, add center marks and centerlines to the view for clarity.

10. Select the .188 diameter dimension, and in the Dimension Text box, type **TYP** after the <DIM> text, and add a bilateral tolerance of +.003, -.005. Save this as a favorite by clicking the Add Favorite icon.

11. Apply the newly created dimension favorite to the R.100 dimension. The results up to this step are shown in Figure 23.16.

FIGURE 23.16

Dimensions and tolerances after step 11

12. Make one of the dimension leaders for either the .188 or the R.100 dimensions cross the extension lines of the 4.500 dimension. Then select the 4.500 dimension and in its PropertyManager, select the Use Document Gap option in the Break Lines panel.

13. Place a B datum marker on the circumference of the smaller arc on the left end of the part. Create a Geometric Tolerance control frame, as shown in Figure 23.17.

FIGURE 23.17

Creating a Geometric Tolerance control frame

Summary

The argument about how to set up and use dimensions on drawings is as old as the process of creating geometrical plans from which objects are built. It is often difficult to separate fact and best practice from opinion. Although I leave it up to you to decide these issues for yourself, this chapter is intended to help you understand how to create the type of drawing that you want.

The biggest conflict in this subject arises over whether to place live model dimensions on the drawing or to allow the requirements of the drawing to specify which dimensions are placed where. I am by no means impartial when it comes to this question, but again, you must make the choice for yourself.

Chapter 24

Working with Tables and Drawings

SolidWorks enables you to place several types of tables on drawings, such as the Bill of Materials, or BOM. Design Tables that are used in parts and assemblies can also be shown on the drawing to create a tabulated type drawing. Hole Tables enable you to chart the center locations and sizes of holes for easy access to manufacturing data. Revision Tables can work with PDMWorks or by themselves to help you document the revision history of a drawing. General Tables are also available for any specialized items that are not covered by the other table types.

Driving the Bill of Materials

The Bill of Materials, or BOM, is one of the most frequently used types of tables that are available in SolidWorks. BOMs are intended for use with assemblies, but can also be used with individual parts for specialized applications. The types of information that you can expect to see on a BOM are item number, filename, quantity used, description, and any other custom property that you would like to add to it. A typical BOM is shown in Figure 24.1.

BOMs are made in one of two ways. The default BOM is made from a special SolidWorks table, while an Excel-based BOM is driven by Excel. While Excel has advantages and disadvantages, many users appear to prefer the default BOM. The reason for this preference is that little is perceived to be given up, except for the stability (crash-worthiness) compared to Excel and the options to keep manual edits.

If you plan to use anything other than the standard SolidWorks BOM templates, then you need to make your own BOM templates. If you plan to create either Excel- or SolidWorks table-based templates, then you must choose one of them.

FIGURE 24.1

A sample BOM

ITEM NO.	PART NUMBER	DESCRIPTION	QTY.
1	Saddle	Vice Base Casting	1
2	lower plate	Tie Plate	2
3	upper plate	Upper Tie Plate	2
4	cap screw	1/4x.80" Round Head Screw	5
5	tool holder	Vice Tool Holder	1
6	handle shaft	Locking Handle Shaft	4
7	locking handle	Locking Handle	4
8	compound center member	Multipivot Member	1
9	upper compound member	Upper Half Pivot	1

SolidWorks table-based BOM

The BOM shown in Figure 24.1 is a default SolidWorks table-based BOM. The differences between the displays of the two types of BOM are mainly cosmetic; the bigger differences lie in the functionality. The PropertyManager interface for the SolidWorks Bill of Materials is shown in Figure 24.2.

Table-based BOM templates

Like other types of data, the SolidWorks table-driven BOM starts from a template. The BOM in Figure 24.1 was created from the default BOM template. When a BOM is initiated, you can select the template in the Table Template panel at the top of the PropertyManager, as shown in Figure 24.2.

Table-based BOM templates are created in much the same way that other templates are created:

- Specify the settings
- Delete the document-specific data
- Save the template

To save the template, right-click the BOM and select Save As. In the Files of Type drop-down list, select Template (*.sldbomtbt, which stands for "SolidWorks Bill Of Materials Table Template"). Any of the settings, additional columns, links to properties, and so on are saved to the template, and reused when you create a new template from it.

FIGURE 24.2

The PropertyManager for a table-driven BOM

BEST PRACTICE   Put the BOM template in your library area outside of the SolidWorks installation folder. Then identify the path in the Tools ➪ Options ➪ File Locations area.

Table Anchor

A table anchor locks a corner of the table to a selected point on the format. If no point is selected in the format, then the table is placed at a corner of the sheet. To specify a point in the format to act as the anchor, you must be editing the format (RMB click the sheet and select Edit Sheet Format). Then right-click a sketch endpoint in the format, select Set As Anchor, and specify which type of table the anchor is for. You can set different anchor locations for different types of tables. Figure 24.3 shows the selection and menus for this option.

FIGURE 24.3

Setting a BOM table anchor

   You should save the format and drawing template with these table anchors specified so that you do not need to re-specify them for each new document.

BOM Type

As the name suggests, the Top Level Only BOM only shows components on the top level. It treats subassemblies as a single entry. As a result, if the top-level assembly shown on the drawing is made up of five subassemblies and two individual parts, and you select the Top Level Only option, then only seven items are shown in the BOM.

The Parts Only BOM ignores subassembly structure, and only displays parts in an unindented list.

The Indented Assemblies BOM shows the parts of subassemblies in an indented list under the name of the subassembly. This is the most complete list of SolidWorks documents used because it includes all parts and assemblies.

The Show Numbering option for indented assemblies is only activated after the Indented Assemblies option is checked, and you have placed the table. When you use this option, it causes subassembly parts to be numbered with an X.Y number system. For example, if item number 4 is a subassembly, and it has three parts, then those parts receive the item numbers 4.1, 4.2, and 4.3.

Configurations

The Configurations panel of the BOM PropertyManager displays slightly differently for Top Level Only BOMs compared to the other types. The Top Level Only BOM type enables the option to show multiple assembly configs and display the quantities for top-level components in separate columns, as shown in Figure 24.4. This figure shows that the configuration named "D" has some suppressed parts, including some parts that are now not used in the "D" configuration, and that therefore have a zero quantity. Notice the available options for dealing with zero-quantity parts.

FIGURE 24.4

Configuration options with the BOM

ITEM NO.	PART NUMBER	DESCRIPTION	Default/QTY.	d/QTY.
1	Saddle	Vice Base Casting	1	1
2	lower plate	Tie Plate	2	2
3	upper plate	Upper Tie Plate	2	2
4	cap screw	1/4x.80" Round Head Screw	4	4
5	Assem1	inch assembly description	1	1
6	handle shaft	Locking Handle Shaft	4	2
7	locking handle	Locking Handle	4	2
8	compound center member	Multipivot Member	1	-

Keep Missing Items

When you are making changes to a model, parts are often either suppressed or deleted altogether. Some company documentation standards require that parts that are removed from a Bill of Materials remain on the bill, and display with strikethrough formatting, although this may be a relic from days gone by when it was more difficult to remove items from hand drawings.

Zero Quantity Display

The Zero Quantity Display settings are only used for configurations where some components are not used in some configurations. The three options that are available are:

- **Quantity Of Dash:** Substitutes a dash for the quantity value
- **Quantity Of Zero:** Uses a zero for the quantity value
- **Blank:** Quantity value is blank

Item Numbers

Item numbers for components listed in the BOM can start at a specific number and be given a particular interval. The Do Not Change Item Numbers option means that even when rows are reordered, item numbers stay with their original components.

The Follow Assembly Order option, which is also available through the RMB menu, means that the order of the components in the BOM follows the order of the components in the Assembly FeatureManager. If the order is changed in the assembly, it also updates in the drawing.

BOM Contents

The BOM Contents button at the bottom of the Bill of Materials PropertyManager opens the dialog box shown in Figure 24.5. This dialog box enables you to reorder as well as hide or show rows of the BOM. If you created the BOM using the Indented Assemblies option, then assemblies can also be expanded and collapsed from this interface.

FIGURE 24.5

The BOM Contents interface

You can also group and ungroup components in this interface, to reorder them as a group that is handled differently from the way that a subassembly is handled.

Table Format

Below the BOM Contents button is a button that allows you to access the Table PropertyManager. The Table PropertyManager interface is shown in Figure 24.6. The options in this interface are self-explanatory, and help you to visually format the table.

The Table PropertyManager interface

Controlling the appearance of the Table-based BOM

If you are already familiar with formatting an Excel-based BOM, then it may take some getting used to formatting the SolidWorks table-based BOM. Figures 24.7 and 24.8 show some of the cursor feedback and selection methods for selecting a column, a row, and a single cell, and moving the entire table.

FIGURE 24.7

Selecting a column, row, cell, and table

To move the table, click above and to the left of the upper-left corner and drag the table to a new location. When the table is selected, a border appears around the table that is not normally visible, and is not printed with the drawing. You can change the properties of a row or a column by selecting just outside of the row or column to the top or the left.

You can establish spacing and width of rows or columns by dragging with the split cursor shown in Figure 24.7 or by typing a value for the column width in the Column Properties panel.

Adding rows or columns

To add a column, right-click near where you want to add the column, and select Insert. Then select whether you are adding a row or a column, and whether you are placing it above or below where you right-clicked.

If the column goes in the wrong location, then you can move it by selecting the column and using the arrows in the Column Properties panel to move it left or right.

FIGURE 24.8

Column, Row, and Cell properties

The next thing you will want to do with a column is to assign what kind of data goes into the column. You can use a custom property such as Part Weight or Vendor, as shown in the Column Properties panel in Figure 24.8. The Title box in the panel enables you to put a header at the top of the column. You can also use equations in the SolidWorks table-driven BOM.

If the Custom Property option is checked in the Column Properties panel, then a custom property can be selected to populate the cells of that column for each part in the assembly.

NOTE   If you create a BOM with the columns and properties that you like, then you can save it to a template as described earlier in this chapter.

Excel-based BOM

 In previous releases, the Excel-based BOM was the only way to add a BOM to a drawing. This feature has been replaced in most respects by the table-driven BOM, but many people still use the Excel-based BOM either out of habit or to comply with legacy standards. Figure 24.9 shows the interface for the Excel-based BOM.

BEST PRACTICE   Unless you have a compelling reason to do otherwise, I recommend that you use the SolidWorks table-based BOM, as it is the function that will be best supported in future versions of SolidWorks software.

FIGURE 24.9

The interface for Excel-based BOMs

Using Design Tables

Design Tables that are used to drive configurations of parts and assemblies can be shown on the drawing. This is often called a tabulated drawing, and is typical of parts that have a basic shape that is common among several sizes or versions of the part. The sizes are shown by a symbol on the drawing, with a column headed by that symbol showing the available dimensions and the corresponding size (configuration) names.

You can insert a Design Table into a drawing by selecting Insert ⇨ Tables ⇨ Design Table or through the Design Table button on the Tables toolbar. In either case, you must pre-select a drawing view of a part or assembly that contains a Design Table before the menu selection or toolbar button become activated.

Design Tables that are displayed in this way are often formatted visually to some extent. It is necessary to hide columns and rows unless you want the dimension or feature name syntax to display on the drawing as well as the values. Extra columns and rows are often added to make the design table readable. The image to the left in Figure 24.10 shows a design table that is formatted to be placed on a drawing. The image to the right shows the same design table with all of the information shown. The first column and the first row are hidden to make the table more readable on the drawing, and the second column and second row use the $user_notes header to format the names.

FIGURE 24.10

A design table prepared to be placed on a drawing

Worksheet in Chapter 24 - DT Part.SLDPRT

	$user_notes (Pipe Thickness)	PipeThickness@Sketch1 (Pipe Thickness)	Length@Sketch1 (Length)	FlangeThickness@Sketch1 (Flange Thickness)	ID@Sketch1 (Inside Diameter)	FlangeDia@Sketch1 (Flange Diameter)	BoltCircle@Sketch2 (Bolt Circle Diameter)	HoleDia@Sketch2 (Hole Diameter)
$user_notes		Pipe Thickness	Length	Flange Thickness	Inside Diameter	Flange Diameter	Bolt Circle Diameter	Hole Diameter
Size1	Size1	0.25	3	0.275	0.8	3.6	2.7	0.25
Size2	Size2	0.25	3.5	0.275	0.9	3.7	2.8	0.25
Size3	Size3	0.25	4	0.275	1	3.8	2.9	0.25
Size4	Size4	0.3	4	0.3	1.1	3.9	3	0.25
Size5	Size5	0.3	4.5	0.3	1.2	4	3.1	0.25
Size6	Size6	0.3	5	0.3	1.2	4.1	3.2	0.25
Size7	Size7	0.35	5	0.35	1.3	4.1	3.2	0.38
Size8	Size8	0.35	5.5	0.35	1.4	4.2	3.3	0.38
Size9	Size9	0.35	6	0.35	1.5	4.3	3.4	0.38

Figure 24.11 shows the drawing with the table inserted. To display the table properly, you have to edit the table in the window of the parent document and adjust the border of the table to be exactly how you want it to appear on the drawing. The adjusted table is shown in Figure 24.11.

The labeled dimensions were created by simply making reference dimensions and overwriting the <DIM> value in the Dimension Text panel of the Dimension PropertyManager. If you would like to examine this data more closely, the drawing and part are included on the CD-ROM. The drawing is named Chapter 24 – DT.slddrw.

This drawing uses a part Design Table, but you can also place assembly Design Tables onto the drawing. This type of drawing is often called a tabulated drawing.

FIGURE 24.11

A drawing with the Design Table inserted

If you need to place something on your drawing such as a Design Table, but it does not appear that the Design Table is going to meet your needs, then you may want to simply copy the data out of the Design Table and recreate it in a static Excel spreadsheet. The Design Table that you place on the drawing updates if it is changed in the part or assembly, just like the drawing geometry, but you must manually update an Excel spreadsheet that is created from copied data. Again, you must answer the question about whether the automatic functions make up for the cost of setting them up to work for you. In many cases they do, but in other cases they require more work than they save.

Using Hole Tables

 You can place Hole Tables on drawings to include information such as the size, position, and number of holes of a given size on a drawing. Only circular holes are recognized, although they do not have to be Hole Wizard or simple hole features. The position is given relative to a selected reference position, and the holes are labeled.

Like other table types, Hole Tables can use templates. As with other templates, you should locate Hole Table templates in a library area outside of your local SolidWorks installation folder. You can then direct SolidWorks to this location using the path settings at Tools ➪ Options ➪ File Locations.

Hole Tables use anchors in exactly the same way as BOMs. For more information, see the Table Anchors subsection in the Bill of Materials section earlier in this chapter.

You can find the options for hole tables at Tools ⇨ Options ⇨ Document Properties ⇨ Tables. These settings are discussed in detail in Appendix B.

Figure 24.12 shows the PropertyManager for a hole table. Figure 24.13 shows the resulting Hole Table on a drawing with a part that contains holes. The table incorporates holes from multiple views, using a different zero reference for each view.

FIGURE 24.12

The PropertyManager for the Hole Table

To initiate the Hole Table function, you must first select a view. You can access the Hole Table function through Insert ⇨ Table ⇨ Hole Table.

To specify the datum, either select an edge in each direction to serve as the zero mark for the X and Y directions, or select a vertex or point to serve as the Origin in both directions.

FIGURE 24.13

A Hole Table combining holes in different views

TAG	X LOC	Y LOC	SIZE
1	.25	.24	
2	.25	5.69	
3	1.61	2.92	
4	.74	.34	Ø .201 THRU ALL
5	.74	5.17	⌴ Ø .375 ▼ .190
6	8.55	.34	
7	8.55	5.17	
8	.71	.78	
9	.71	1.67	
10	.71	2.49	
11	.71	3.46	
12	.71	4.29	Ø .177 THRU ALL
13	.71	5.15	∨ Ø .332 X 82.00°
14	2.41	2.21	
15	3.45	5.26	
16	6.46	2.21	
17	7.49	5.26	
18	2.48	4.24	
19	3.56	4.24	
20	4.95	4.24	Ø.265 THRU
21	6.07	4.24	
22	9.37	1.90	
23	9.37	5.31	Ø .136 ▼ .411
24	10.99	1.90	8-36 UNF - 2B ▼ .328
25	10.99	5.31	

To select the holes to be included in the table, activate the Holes panel selection box, and either select the hole edges directly, or select the faces on which the holes are located. Once you place the table, you can add holes or change the datum information. To do this, use the RMB menu of the Hole Table entry in the Drawing FeatureManager, and select Edit Feature. The RMB menu is shown in the middle image of Figure 24.12. If you simply select a Hole Table that has already been created, the Properties interface displays, as shown in the top-right image. You can resize columns and rows in the same way as for BOM tables.

In the table in Figure 24.13, the Combine Same Sizes option is used, which causes several of the cells of the table to merge. If you use the Combine Same Tags option, then the hole locations are not displayed—only the hole callout description and the quantity appear. Figure 24.14 shows this arrangement.

FIGURE 24.14

The Combine Same Tags option used with a Hole Table

TAG	SIZE	QUANTITY
1	Ø .201 THRU ALL ⌴ Ø .375 ▼ .190	7
2	Ø .177 THRU ALL ∨ Ø .332 X 82.00°	10
3	Ø.265 THRU	4
4	Ø .136 ▼ .411 8-36 UNF - 2B ▼ .328	4

You can control the hole callout description used in Figure 24.14 by using the file named callout-format.txt, which is found in the lang\english subdirectory of the SolidWorks installation directory. Again, if you customize this file, then you should keep it in a library external to the installation directory and list it in the Tools ⟹ Options ⟹ File Locations area. This text file enables you to specify how hole callouts are specified for different types of holes.

Using Revision Tables

 Revision Tables in SolidWorks can be used in conjunction with PDMWorks Workgroup, but this integration goes beyond the scope of this book. The Revision Table uses a Table Anchor, which is used in exactly the same way as the BOM table. Revision Tables also use templates in the same way as the other table types, and it is recommended to move customized templates to a library location and specify the location in Tools ⟹ Options ⟹ File Locations.

Figure 24.15 shows the Revision Table PropertyManager interface where you can create and control the settings for the table. You can find the default settings for Revision Tables at Tools ⟹ Options ⟹ Document Properties ⟹ Tables. These settings are described in more detail in Appendix B.

The image in the upper left of Figure 24.15 is the PropertyManager interface that displays when you initially create the Revision Table, and the rest of the Figure 24.15 images are for editing or adjusting the table. The properties for columns, rows, and cells can be controlled in much the same way as other table types.

You can initiate the Revision Table function through the menus or the Tables toolbar. However, this function simply creates the table, it does not populate it. You must set the table anchor in the format in order for the Table Anchor to work. Additional columns may be added or formatted to accept other data. Once you have created the columns or formatting, you can save the changes to a template, which is also available through the RMB menu.

You can add a revision to the table by right-clicking the table and selecting Revisions ⟹ Add Revision. The settings for Revision Tables are controlled through Tools ⟹ Options ⟹ Document Properties ⟹ Tables. These settings are shown in detail in Appendix B. This includes control over whether the revision uses numerical or alphabetical revision levels, but does not provide for more complex revisioning schemes.

FIGURE 24.15

The Revision Table PropertyManager interface

Immediately after you have created the revision, if the option is enabled, you are prompted to place a balloon that contains the revision level to identify what has been changed. To finish placing symbols, you can press Esc or click the green check mark icon in the Confirmation Corner or the

PropertyManager. When you are finished placing the balloons, you can fill in the description of the revision by double-clicking in the Description cell where you want to add text. Figure 24.16 shows a Revision Table with balloon symbols placed on the drawing.

FIGURE 24.16

A Revision Table with balloon symbols

		REVISIONS		
ZONE	REV.	DESCRIPTION	DATE	APPROVED
	A	ADDED CHAMFER AROUND ANGLED PORT	8/6/2005	
	B	ADDED THROUGH HOLE	11/19/2006	

Revision Tables work by creating a Revision custom property in the drawing document, and by incrementing this revision each time a revision is added to the table. Additional columns that are linked to custom properties can be added to Revision Tables and Revision Table templates.

Using Gauge Tables and Bend Tables

Gauge Tables and Bend Tables are specific to sheet metal parts, and are covered in detail in Chapters 29 and 30.

Using Weldment Cut List Tables

 Weldment Cut Lists are a special type of table that closely resembles a BOM table in many ways. These are discussed in Chapter 31, which covers Weldments.

Using General Tables

General Tables can be used for any type of tabulated data. Column headers can be filled with either text labels or custom property links. Regular Excel OLE objects can also be used for the same purpose, and depending on the application, you may prefer this.

The General Table uses the filename extension, *.sldtbt. It can be created without a template, as a simple block of four empty cells, or you can use a template that has a set of pre-created headers.

Tutorials: Using Tables

Rather than having tutorials for every table type, this chapter has tutorials only for the BOM, Hole Table, and Revision Table. The skills used with these types are transferable to the other types.

Using BOMs

This tutorial guides you through the steps that are necessary to prepare an assembly for the drawing and BOM. Configurations and custom properties are used in this example. Remember that if a drawing view is cross-hatched and you cannot see the geometry, then you may have to press Ctrl+Q to rebuild it. Follow these steps:

1. Begin this tutorial with SolidWorks closed and Windows Explorer open.

2. If you have not already done so, create a folder for a library that is not in your SolidWorks installation folder. Call it D:\Library\ or something similar. Make a folder inside this folder called Drawing Templates. Copy the file from the CD-ROM named inch B.drwdot to this new folder.

3. Launch SolidWorks and go to Tools ⇨ Options ⇨ File Locations ⇨ Document Template. Click the Add button and add the new library path to the list. Shut down SolidWorks and restart it.

4. Open the assembly Chapter 24 – BOM Assy.sldasm from the CD-ROM.

5. Using the Make Drawing From Part/Assembly button, make a new drawing of the assembly from the drawing template.

6. Delete the isometric view, and in its place make a new drawing view using the named model view "exploded."

7. Edit the sheet format. Right-click the sketch point at the location indicated in Figure 24.17. In the pop-up menu that appears, select Set As Anchor and then select Bill of Materials.

FIGURE 24.17

Setting the Table Anchor

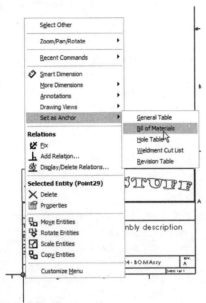

RMB on this point

8. Exit Edit Sheet Format mode by selecting Edit Sheet from the RMB menu.

9. Select the new view and click Insert ➪ Table ➪ Bill of Materials, or click the Bill of Materials button from the Tables toolbar. Use the default selections, except in the panels shown in Figure 24.18.

10. Click inside the exploded view, but off of any part geometry, and then select the Autoballoon tool from the Annotations toolbar. Toggle through the available options to see whether any of the possible autoballoon configurations meets your needs. If not, use the standard Balloon tool to select the part and place the balloon. This gives you more control over the attachment points and placement of the balloons.

FIGURE 24.18

Creating the Bill of Materials

ITEM NO.	PART NUMBER	DESCRIPTION	Angle 1/QTY.	Angle 2/QTY.
1	Bracket Angle 1	description	1	-
2	Chapter 24 - Pin Block	description	1	1
3	Clevis Male	description	1	1
4	Long	Long Pin	1	1
5	Clevis Female	description	1	1
6	Short	Short Pin	2	2
7	Bracket Angle 2	description	-	1

11. Change the balloon for the short pin to be a circular split-line balloon (do this by clicking the balloon, and then switching the style in the PropertyManager). Notice that the quantity appears in the bottom of the balloon. The drawing view and the BOM should now look like Figure 24.19.

12. Notice that several of the parts use a default description of "description." Edit each of these parts by right-clicking the part's row in the BOM table and selecting Open *<filename>* from the menu. Change the custom property called Description in each part. Keep in mind that this may be handled differently for configured parts.

NEW FEATURE New in SolidWorks 2007 is the ability to open a part directly from its entry in the BOM.

13. The Bracket part is listed twice using the configuration name because of the way the configurations are set up for the parts. To list the bracket only once using the filename, open the bracket, RMB click one of the configuration names in the ConfigurationManager, and select Properties. In the Bill of Materials Options panel, select Document Name from the drop-down list. Do this for the other configuration, as well.

Notice also that the Description field holds the configuration-specific custom property for Description, which is used in the BOM.

FIGURE 24.19

The drawing view and the BOM after step 11

ITEM NO.	PART NUMBER	DESCRIPTION	Angle 1/QTY.	Angle 2/QTY.
1	Bracket Angle 1	description	1	-
2	Chapter 24 - Pin Block	description	1	1
3	Clevis Male	description	1	1
4	Long	Long Pin	1	1
5	Clevis Female	description	1	1
6	Short	Short Pin	2	2
7	Bracket Angle 2	description	-	1

14. Toggle back to the drawing (using Ctrl+Tab), select anywhere on the BOM table, and then select Table Properties from the PropertyManager. Expand the Part Configuration Grouping panel, and select the Display All Configurations Of The Same Part As One Item option. This changes how the bracket displays, as well as the pins.

15. In this step, you will add a column to the BOM that calls on an existing custom property that is already in all of the parts. Place the cursor over the last column on the right and RMB click it. Select Insert ⇨ Column Right. This places a new column to the right of the last one and displays the Column Properties panel of the Insert Column Right PropertyManager, as shown in Figure 24.20.

16. In the first drop-down selection box, select the Weight custom property. Click the green check mark icon to accept the changes.

17. The BOM with the additional column can be saved as a BOM template by right-clicking anywhere in the BOM and selecting Save As. You can then set the type to a BOM template, and the directory to the library location for BOM templates.

If you would like to compare your results against mine, the finished drawing is called Chapter 24 – BOM Tutorial Finished.slddrw.

FIGURE 24.20

Adding a column to the BOM

 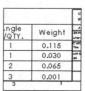

Using Hole Tables

This tutorial guides you through the creation and setting changes that are common in SolidWorks Hole Tables. The part for this tutorial is the part from which the figures for the section on Hole Tables were made. Follow these steps:

1. Create a new drawing from the template that was used for the BOM tutorial. If you have not done the BOM tutorial, then move the drawing template named inchB.drwdot from the Chapter 24 materials on the CD-ROM to your library location for drawing templates. Then create the drawing from the template.

2. Click the Model View button on the Drawings toolbar, and browse to the part named Chapter 24 – Hole Table Part.sldprt.

3. Place a Front view and project a Left view and an isometric view. Then press Esc to quit the command. Finally, delete the four predefined views.

4. There is not an anchor in this template for a Hole Table. If you would like to create one, this would be a good time to do so. Follow the steps in the BOM tutorial for specifying the anchor point.

5. From the Tables toolbar, click the Hole Table button.

6. Figure 24.21 shows a section of the Hole Table PropertyManager with the selections that you need to make for this Hole Table.

7. Once you have completed the selections, press the Next View button at the bottom of the PropertyManager, and make similar selections in the Left view. The holes for both views are added to a single Hole Table.

FIGURE 24.21

The Hole Table PropertyManager and selections

Select these two faces
to go into the Edges/Faces box

Select this vertex
to go into the Origin box

8. The table is created using the default settings established in Tools ⇨ Options ⇨ Document Properties ⇨ Tables, but you can change them here for this specific table. Click anywhere in the table, and then select Table Properties at the bottom of the PropertyManager. Changing from numerical to alphabetical assigns a letter to each hole type, and a number to each instance of the type. Make this change and update the table. Figure 24.22 shows the table before and after the changes.

FIGURE 24.22

Using numerical and alphabetical hole tag identification

TAG	X LOC	Y LOC	SIZE
1	.25	.24	
2	.25	5.69	
3	1.61	2.92	Ø .201 THRU ALL
4	.74	.34	⌴ Ø .375 ▼ .190
5	.74	5.17	
6	8.55	.34	
7	8.55	5.17	
8	.71	.78	
9	.71	1.67	
10	.71	2.49	
11	.71	3.46	
12	.71	4.29	Ø .177 THRU ALL
13	.71	5.15	∨ Ø .332 X 82.00°
14	2.41	2.21	
15	3.45	5.26	
16	6.46	2.21	
17	7.49	5.26	
18	2.48	4.24	
19	3.56	4.24	Ø.265 THRU
20	4.95	4.24	
21	6.07	4.24	
22	9.37	1.90	
23	9.37	5.31	Ø .136 ▼ .411
24	10.99	1.90	8-36 UNF - 2B ▼ .328
25	10.99	5.31	

TAG	X LOC	Y LOC	SIZE
A1	.25	.24	
A2	.25	5.69	
A3	1.61	2.92	Ø .201 THRU ALL
A4	.74	.34	⌴ Ø .375 ▼ .190
A5	.74	5.17	
A6	8.55	.34	
A7	8.55	5.17	
B1	.71	.78	
B2	.71	1.67	
B3	.71	2.49	
B4	.71	3.46	
B5	.71	4.29	Ø .177 THRU ALL
B6	.71	5.15	∨ Ø .332 X 82.00°
B7	2.41	2.21	
B8	3.45	5.26	
B9	6.46	2.21	
B10	7.49	5.26	
C1	2.48	4.24	
C2	3.56	4.24	Ø.265 THRU
C3	4.95	4.24	
C4	6.07	4.24	
D1	9.37	1.90	
D2	9.37	5.31	Ø .136 ▼ .411
D3	10.99	1.90	8-36 UNF - 2B ▼ .328
D4	10.99	5.31	

9. Change the number of decimal places used in the Hole Table from two places to three. You can do this in the Table Properties window, in the Hole Location Precision panel.

10. Deselect the Hide Hole Centers option in the Visibility panel.

Using Revision Tables

In this tutorial, you create a basic Revision Table, and make a template. Follow these steps:

1. Using a drawing that you completed in one of the previous tutorials, make sure that a Revision Table Anchor has been placed in the upper-right corner of the Sheet Format. You must edit the Sheet Format to do this by RMB clicking the point that you want to use for the anchor. Remember to select Edit Sheet from the RMB menu to exit Edit Sheet Format mode.

NOTE Ideally, the anchors for all table types should be set in templates and formats, but here it is set up to ensure that you get some practice with creating the anchors.

2. Click the Revision Table button on the Tables toolbar. Be sure to select the upper-right corner that you want to be anchored, and select the Attach to Anchor option in the PropertyManager. Click the green check mark icon to accept the table. Figure 24.23 shows the initial stub of the Revision Table.

FIGURE 24.23

The initial stub of the Revision Table

TIP Drawing templates can be saved with the Revision Table stub if it also has a format. The revision table is not saved with the format because it has to go on the drawing sheet.

3. To initiate a new revision level in the Revision Table, RMB click the table and select Revisions ➪ Add Revision.

4. Depending on the default settings in Tools ➪ Options ➪ Document Properties ➪ Tables, the first revision will be either A or 1. If you are using PDMWorks Workgroup, then you may have other options.

5. Depending on your options settings, you may immediately be prompted to place a balloon that contains the new revision level. You can place balloons with or without leaders. The balloons are meant to indicate areas of the drawing that are affected by the revision. Press Esc or click the green check mark icon when you are finished placing the balloons.

You may want to be careful using balloons on assembly drawings or other drawings that already have balloons that are used for other purposes. For this reason, it may be a good idea to use a distinctively shaped balloon for Revision Tables.

6. To add text to the Description field, simply double-click in the field and start typing. The text automatically wraps to fit the box.

7. Practice by adding a couple of revisions, balloons, and descriptions.

8. After you have added a couple of revisions, check the custom properties by going to File ➪ Properties ➪ Custom. Notice that a revision property has been added, and the latest revision is represented by the value of the custom property.

The number of revisions kept in the Revision Table is no longer an option as it was in previous releases, but in its place you can now control how revision tables interact with multiple sheets. For more information, see Appendix B.

9. You can add columns in the same way that they were added to the BOM. You can merge and unmerge cells, and link properties to cells. With the cursor over the last column (Approved), RMB click and select Insert ➪ Column Left. In the Column Properties, select Custom, and from the Properties drop-down menu, select DrawnBy. Accept the changes by clicking the green check mark icon.

10. Save the template by right-clicking anywhere in the Revision Table and selecting Save As ➪ Rev Table Templates. Then save it to the appropriate location outside of the SolidWorks installation directory.

Summary

SolidWorks enables you to work with both tables that are highly specialized for particular uses, and the General Table, which is available for any type of tabulated data. The most frequently used types are BOMs, Hole Tables, and Revision Tables. Design tables that drive part and assembly configurations can also be placed on a 2D drawing, but in these cases, some formatting is usually necessary to make the Design Table presentable and the information on it easy to read.

Other types of tables, such as Gauge and Bend tables and Weldment Cut Lists, are specialized for sheet metal and weldment parts, respectively, and are discussed in chapters that cover those topics.

Chapter 25

Using Layers,
Line Fonts, and Colors

Most SolidWorks users have used AutoCAD at some point in their careers. AutoCAD is the Microsoft of CAD. Regardless of what you think of the company, the software, or the 2D world in general, AutoCAD has left its mark on CAD users of all kinds in the form of certain default expectations that people have about CAD software. A few common preconceptions are that layers, the Command Line, paper space/model space, and printing should be really difficult.

Given the ubiquity of AutoCAD in the market, it is not surprising that a few AutoCAD-like functions have found their way into the SolidWorks software. SolidWorks users, and even the SolidWorks Corporation, become a little defensive when you start talking about AutoCAD, or AutoCAD-like functionality. Maybe that is because we consider ourselves more highly evolved, having understood that 3D parametric design is a more sophisticated plane of existence than flatland 2D design.

When former AutoCAD users make the switch to SolidWorks, the questions start: Where is the Command Line, How do I put parts on layers, How do I change the background color to black, and my personal favorite, Where is the zero-radius trim?

This chapter addresses a couple of AutoCAD-like functions in the SolidWorks drawing environment. The goal is not to make the functions look or work or compare in any way to AutoCAD, but to simply to make them useful in the context of SolidWorks.

Controlling Layers

Layers are arguably one of the most visible differences between AutoCAD and SolidWorks. Layers are not available in SolidWorks 3D modeling at all—only in the 2D drawing environment—and even there, they do not see a lot of use. However, this is not to say that there is no need for them.

Layers in imported 2D data

When you import data through DXF or DWG format files, the layers that exist in the original data are brought forward into SolidWorks, and you can use them in a similar way to the original AutoCAD usage. For example, you can turn layers on or off (visible or hidden), and you can change layer names, descriptions, color, line thickness, and line style.

The way you intend to use the imported data determines how you should open the file. If you only intend to view and print the drawing, then I would suggest using DWG Editor, which is installed with SolidWorks and enables you to do almost anything you can do with basic AutoCAD. It also has the advantage of having a familiar interface for the AutoCAD user (it even has a black background!). DWG Editor is available from the Start menu, by selecting Programs ⇨ SolidWorks ⇨ DWG Editor.

If you need to integrate data from the imported document into a native SolidWorks drawing, then you can open the DWG file from the normal Open dialog box in SolidWorks.

TIP   If you want to make a 3D part from the 2D data in the DWG file, then you may want to import the drawing into the part sketch environment. This usually leads to some speed issues. If you prefer, sketch entities can also be copied from the drawing to the model sketch. You can even copy entities from DWG Editor to the SolidWorks part sketch. The sketch needs to be open in order to paste the sketch entities. In the case where imported 2D data is brought into the model sketch, you lose all of the layer information, because part and assembly documents do not allow layers.

The colors assigned to layers are often based on a black background, and so they can be difficult to see on a white background. The two ways of dealing with this are to change the SolidWorks drawing sheet color to something dark or to change the individual layer colors to something dark. Either method is easy, although if you have to send the 2D data back to its source, it may be best to temporarily change the drawing sheet color.

Figure 25.1 shows the layer interface with an imported drawing in the background. The colors have been changed here to improve visibility. The Layers dialog box is activated by the Layer Properties toolbar button, which is found on both the Layer and Line Format toolbars.

Be aware that many items in an imported drawing may come into SolidWorks as blocks. These items may need to be exploded before you can work with them. This is often the case with the drawing border, title block, or format.

FIGURE 25.1

The Layers dialog box and the Layer toolbar

Layers on the sheet format

One of the most obvious uses of layers is on the sheet format. The sketch lines used to create the border often have a heavier line weight and a different color that easily distinguishes them from model geometry.

You can assign layers in one of three ways:

- Select existing items, and then select a layer from the drop-down list on the Layer toolbar.

- Set the active layer and create new items.

- While creating items such as sketch entities and annotations, select the layer for the new entity directly from the PropertyManager.

To set a layer to the active layer, double-click it from the Layers dialog box, as shown in Figure 25.1, or change it from the drop-down list on the Layer toolbar. When you assign an active layer, other newly created entities are also placed on the layer, not just sketch entities. Symbols, annotations, blocks, and other elements can also be put onto layers. If you are not particular about the layering scheme on a drawing, then it may be advisable to set the active layer to None, which is a valid option in the Layer toolbar drop-down list.

Another option when building a sheet format, or any other drawing function that requires sketching, is to use a special layer for construction geometry. This enables you to hide the layer when it is not being used, but it still maintains its relations. Hidden layers can be used in several other ways, for example, as standard notes on the drawing, and they can be easily turned on or off.

Dimensions and notes on layers

SolidWorks drawings have a tendency to be drab black-and-white drawings, in contrast to AutoCAD drawings, which often seem to take on a plethora of contrasting colors. Still, drawings do seem a little easier to comprehend when different types of items are colored differently, but in order for this to work, you must apply the coloring scheme consistently. Dimensions and annotations can also be placed on layers in the three ways described in the previous section (active layer, from the PropertyManager during creation, and through the drop-down list on the Layer toolbar). However, the line styles do not affect dimensions and notes, only the color and visibility settings.

Components on layers

Assembly drawings probably suffer the most from the monochromatic nature of most SolidWorks drawings because individual components can be difficult to identify when everything is the same color. This is why SolidWorks users typically color parts in the shaded model assembly window. It only makes sense that as users, we would want to do the same thing on the drawing.

An intuitive and easy workaround for this problem would seem to be to simply turn the drawing view to a wireframe mode in the same way that changing a drawing view to a shaded mode shows the parts in color. Unfortunately, wireframe on drawings always defaults to black edges. Even if you set a Display State using some wireframe parts where the wireframe displays in the same color as the shaded part in the assembly window, this still appears in black and white on the drawing.

All that is left to display the components of an assembly in different colors while using a wireframe display mode is to set the Component Line Font options. (Line Fonts are covered in the next section.) The Component Line Font dialog box contains a Layer setting, which you can use to put a part on a layer. If the layer is set up with a color, then the part displays with that color in all views of the drawing, or in just the current view, depending on your settings. While it does take a little time to set up the individual layers for each part and then to set the parts to the layers, it is better than the alternative, which is to do nothing.

You can access the Component Line Font dialog box by right-clicking a component in a drawing view. The Component Line Font dialog box is shown in Figure 25.2.

In normal use, the Use Document Defaults option is selected and all of the settings in the dialog box are grayed out. To gain access to these settings, you must deselect the Use Document Defaults option, as shown in Figure 25.2.

FIGURE 25.2

The Component Line Font dialog box

Controlling Line Format

The Line Format feature is composed of three different settings, Line Color, Line Thickness, and Line Style. These settings can be controlled separately from layers, and so they can be used in model sketches as well as on drawings. In the model, the line font can only be displayed for inactive sketches. Any sketch that is both closed and shown can be displayed with the Line Format settings.

CROSS-REF For more information on using line styles in the model, see Chapter 6.

Figure 25.3 shows the Line Format toolbar along with the interfaces for Line Color, Line Thickness, and Line Style.

FIGURE 25.3

The Line Format toolbar and related interface options

The term *line font* refers to a combination of style, end cap, and thickness. Line fonts are set in the document-specific settings at Tools ➪ Options ➪ Document Properties ➪ Line Font. These settings are described in detail in Appendix B.

Using the Line Format settings

You can specify the Line Format settings using two different methods. In the first method, you can set them with nothing selected, in which case they function like System Options (the new setting takes effect for all documents that are opened on the current computer). In the second method, if they are set with sketch entities or edges selected, then the settings apply only for the selected entities.

CAUTION   If you change these settings with nothing selected, then the Line Format settings for color, thickness, and style function as system options.

End Cap Style

Another option for the Line Font settings is the End Cap Style. This offers an important option, especially for thick lines. The three options are flat, round, and square, although the square style is usually appropriate. In the past, flat was the default setting, and there were no other options.

NEW FEATURE   The End Cap Style settings in Tools ➪ Options are new for SolidWorks 2007.

Figure 25.4 shows the difference between the three options of End Cap Style.

FIGURE 25.4

The End Cap Style setting options

Line Thickness settings

The Line Thickness settings are thin, normal, thick, and thick (2) to (6). Figure 25.5 shows the Line Weights dialog box, and the Print dialog box.

This is an area where the Help file will not only be little actual help, but may also steer you in the wrong direction. The Help does not appear to point to a location where you can set up the actual dimensional widths of printed lines assigned to the 9 thicknesses. The easiest to find direct mention of "line thickness" points to an obscure PhotoWorks setting. Other mentions of "line thickness" point to either the Layers or Line Format functions.

The correct information in the help is cleverly hidden, listed under "lines, weights." The settings for the line widths used to be on the Page Setup dialog box—the help for Page Setup still has a line thickness entry, even though the setting is no longer found there — but are now found in the Print dialog box.

Figure 25.5 shows the Print dialog box and the Line Weights dialog box.

FIGURE 25.5

The Line Weights settings in the Print dialog box

> **CAUTION** The Line Weights settings are system options, and are not document-specific. As a result, if drawings are printed from two different computers, and one of them has been customized, then the drawings may look different.

Line Style setting

You can create custom line styles using the syntax shown on the Tools, Options, Document Properties, Line Style page. This is a document-specific setting, and so if you make a custom line style and want to use it in another document, then you have to save it out (as a *.sldlin file) and load it into the other document. Also, if you save your templates with this line style loaded, then you will not have to load the styles for any document made from that template. For more information about line styles, see Appendix B.

Color Display mode

Color Display mode toggles between the display of assigned colors and sketch colors. This is primarily used in drawings when you are making sketches where sketch relations are important.

Hiding and Showing Edges

Sometimes, for illustrative purposes, it is desirable to hide certain edges in drawing views. The Hide Edge and Show Edge toolbar buttons are associated with the Line Format toolbar, although they may not be on the toolbar by default. You can use Tools ➪ Customize to put them on a toolbar.

To use the Hide Edge tool, simply select the edges that you would like to hide, and click the Hide Edge toolbar button. To show the edges, click the Show Edge toolbar button; the cursor will now be able to select the hidden edges.

Tutorial: Using Drawing Display Tools

Some of the functions described in this chapter are difficult to understand until you actually use them. This tutorial guides you through the functions step by step so that you can see them in action. Start here:

1. From the CD-ROM, open the drawing called Chapter 25 – Tutorial.slddrw. Make sure that the Layer and Line Format toolbars are active and that the Hide Edge and Show Edge buttons are available on the Line Format toolbar.

2. RMB click a blank space and select Edit Sheet Format from the menu.

3. Window-select everything on the format and use the drop-down list on the Layers toolbar to assign the selection to the Border layer. Notice that this changes the color and the thickness of the sketch lines.

> **NOTE**   Selection filters are inactive when you are editing drawings or formats; they are active only at odd times, such as when you edit a note.

4. RMB click a blank space and select Edit Sheet.

5. Click the Layer Properties button on either the Layer or Line Format toolbar. Add new layers for each of the part groups, bracket, clevis, pins, and blocks, assigning different colors to each layer. Figure 25.6 shows the Layers dialog box with these layers created.

FIGURE 25.6

The Layers dialog box

CAUTION Be aware that creating new layers leaves the last layer that you created active, as indicated by the yellow arrow in Figure 25.6. There is no way to set the active layer to None from the Layers dialog box, and so this has to be done using the drop-down list in the Layer toolbar.

6. Set the active layer to None in the Layer toolbar drop-down list.

7. RMB click the Bracket part in one of the views and select Component Line Font. Deselect the Use Document Defaults option, and select the Bracket layer from the drop-down list in the lower-right corner of the dialog box, as shown in Figure 25.7. Make sure that the Drawing View option is set to All Views.

FIGURE 25.7

The Component Line Font dialog box

8. Repeat Step 7 for all of the components, assigning each component to its own layer. Notice how this makes the parts easier to identify.

NOTE Alternatively, you could simply change the line style and weight (thickness — note the terminology inconsistencies here) for each component. This saves you creating the layers, but you lose the color settings.

9. Open the Component Line Font dialog box for the Bracket part again. This time, set the Line Weight to Thick (6), and then click OK. You may have to rebuild the drawing to show the change (Ctrl+B or Ctrl+Q). Figure 25.8 shows a detail of the corners that are created by the thick lines. Notice the notches created at the corners.

FIGURE 25.8

Applying thick edges

10. These notches are supposed to be fixed using a new setting in SolidWorks 2007. In the menus, go to Tools ⇨ Options ⇨ Document Properties ⇨ Line Font, and set the End Cap Style to Square. Click OK to exit the Document Properties. In the drawing, select inside the view where you are working, and make sure that it is set to High Quality. (The setting is found in the PropertyManager for the view in the Display Style panel. If it is already set to High Quality, then there will be no other view option; if it is not, then there will be an option that is set to Draft Quality.)

The image to the left in Figure 25.8 is the old setting with the draft quality view, and the image to the right is the new setting with the high quality view.

11. In the Component Line Font dialog box, set the Line Weight setting back to Default for the Bracket part, but keep it on the Bracket layer.

12. In the isometric view, Ctrl-click all of the tangent edges on the Bracket part, as shown in Figure 25.9. Click the Hide Edge toolbar button on the Line Format toolbar.

13. Click the Show Edge toolbar button. The PropertyManager message changes to indicate that you can now select hidden edges, and the hidden edges are shown. Ctrl-select the hidden edges and RMB click when you are done.

FIGURE 25.9

Hiding edges

Before   After

Summary

While SolidWorks is not primarily built around the strength of its 2D drawing functionality, it offers more capabilities than most users take advantage of. Layers in SolidWorks offer adequate functionality, but could be improved by some automation to put parts on layers automatically; this would enable SolidWorks to show the parts in wireframe with the same colors assigned to the solid.

Other line and edge display functionality is sometimes difficult to find or access, or may have obscure functions. Creating drawings that use color to make them easier to read should be easier in SolidWorks than it is in AutoCAD.

Part VI

Using Advanced Techniques

Chapter 26

Modeling Multibodies

J ust a few releases ago, SolidWorks software did not allow what were then called *disjoint solids*. Feature trees began with a base feature that could not be changed or reordered, and every part had to contain a single contiguous solid. Most SolidWorks users accepted this situation as good enough, mainly because most of the arguments for the need to use more than one solid within a single part were simply not convincing.

However, as the usage of surfacing techniques in SolidWorks became more prevalent, it became apparent that surfaces and solids were not handled in the same ways. Users coming to SolidWorks from other high-end systems, such as Unigraphics, Pro/Engineer, Catia, and SDRC, already had some experience with the more complex techniques. Surfacing techniques resulted in surface geometry that was not contiguous. SolidWorks grouped the surface functions in with the reference geometry functions, such as planes and axes.

With the advent of what became known as multibody modeling, a world of possibilities opened up. If you remove the constraint that all of the geometry in a part must be linked into a single solid body, and see the surface features also being created as independent bodies, then many more options become available.

This created a best-practice crisis for some users. For years, the SolidWorks Corporation preached the doctrine that multiple bodies were not necessary, and indeed were somehow evil, and some users bought into that point of view. This was mainly preached by the sales side simply because SolidWorks lacked the functionality, and sales has a need to put a positive spin on technical issues.

Now that the functionality exists, how should conservative users look at this new functionality? What are the drawbacks and advantages, uses and limitations? When multibody modeling was first introduced in SolidWorks, adventurous users just used the new modeling tools because they could, and some actively went in search of the limits to see how far they could be taken, and in which directions.

By the release of SolidWorks 2007, four or five releases have now offered multibody functionality, and have sorted through some of the first-generation issues that arose with multibody modeling. Some of the issues discussed here are general organizational issues with the broad concept of multiple bodies within a single part. Other issues are specific to SolidWorks, special quirks, tools, and tips.

With Great Power Comes Great Responsibility

Multibody functionality provides the user with great power. Power can be wielded for the good or for the bad. I find myself using the same responsible-modeling speeches when discussing multibodies as I tend to use for in-context modeling. This is because multibodies present some of the same issues as in-context modeling. The first similarity is that on the surface, both techniques appear to be all-day-every-day types of design tools. The second similarity between them is that neither tool is what it appears to be on the surface.

The responsibility part arises when thinking about other users who will use the multibody parts once they are created, even including yourself in that list. It is not always easy to remember how you executed a particular project six months and 100 models ago. Other users may have to edit your work, and if errors happen, then you have to be able to navigate the design intent without destroying the relationships in the FeatureManager or completely rebuilding it. This is the reason for trying to standardize best-practice issues, particularly in larger organizations where more users may work with the data.

If you are an independent contractor and do not share your models with other SolidWorks users, then you have more flexibility to model how you like. As long as you can come back to the model and change it when you need to, more power to you.

Multibody modeling is not assembly modeling

Multibody modeling is not assembly modeling. This concept is important, and so I will repeat it: Multibody modeling is not assembly modeling. Many times when new users are introduced to the capabilities of multibody modeling, the first thought that comes to mind seems to be, "This is far easier than making assemblies." However, it should not be treated as a replacement for assembly modeling.

Several assembly type functions are missing from multibodies. They include the following:

- Interference detection
- Dynamic assembly motion

- BOM for drawings
- Exploded views
- Configs for separate parts
- Display States
- Center-of-gravity calculations for individual parts
- Mass property calculations for individual parts

To say that these functions are missing from multibodies does not imply that they should or will be there someday. In fact, I believe that the distinction between multibody and assembly design techniques should be kept as clear as possible. Simply because a technique is easier does not make it *better*. Above all, remember that modeling multibody parts puts *all* of the data for *all* of the bodies in a *single* part file, in a *single* FeatureManager; there is no easy way to separate the parametric features out into individual parts later on, regardless of how complex the part becomes.

Further, creating drawings of individual bodies of a multibody part is *far* more difficult than creating drawings of individual parts. Also, editing the features of individual bodies is not as easy as if the individual body were an individual part. When you create several bodies in a single part, you constantly have to carry the feature and design intent overhead of *all* of the features used to create *all* of the bodies to edit any individual body.

Appropriate multibody uses

Obviously, I am trying to alarm you a little. You need to have a healthy respect for the problems that you can create for yourself and others by using multibody modeling in inefficient or inappropriate ways. Still, appropriate uses for multibody modeling do exist. You may hear people recommend that at the end of the FeatureManager, only a single solid body should remain, with the rest of them either absorbed or deleted. For others, anything goes. I recommend that if you decide to use multibodies, then you are at least able to articulate *why* you have chosen to do so in a way that does not sound like you are making excuses for careless work.

Appropriate uses for multibody modeling include (but are not limited to):

- As an intermediate step on the way to a single-body solid
- As multiple or inserted bodies for reference (reference bodies may be deleted at the bottom of the FeatureManager)
- As over-molded parts
- As parts that need to be assembled into a single, smooth shape, such as a computer mouse or an automobile body where the shape is impossible (or at least far more difficult) if done in-context
- When the end shape of the finished product is known, but the part breaks due to manufacturing methods, and materials have not been decided yet, multibody techniques can save a lot of time compared to modeling an assembly
- As captive fasteners and purchased inseparable subassemblies

- When SolidWorks weldments result in a single multibody part
- When the Mold tools result in a single multibody part representing the plastic part and the major mold components

If you are administering a SolidWorks installation of multiple users, then you may be looking for a "bright line" test to clearly define for users which types of multibody modeling are allowable and which are not. So many possibilities exist that it is difficult to say definitively what really *should not* be done, but here is a short list that you can modify for your needs:

- Do not use multibody modeling simply to avoid making an assembly — you must be able to cite a specific reason for using the technique.
- Do not leave a part in a multibody state that should be joined together into a single body.
- Hiding a body is sometimes appropriate, and deleting a body is sometimes appropriate — understand the difference.

Okay, the lecture is over. The message that you should take from all of that is not to use multibody techniques just because you can; you must have a reason for it. I do not say this because I am the *design police*; I say this because it is the criterion that I use for my own modeling, and what I would like to see in models that I inherit from other SolidWorks users, and I think that this philosophy will serve you well if you are conscientious about it.

Understanding Multibody Techniques

To complicate the issue somewhat, nearly all surface modeling is also multibody modeling. In this chapter, I am referring to solids, unless I specifically state otherwise. Surface bodies are discussed in Chapter 27.

Multibody techniques cover a wide range of functionality, and as soon as someone creates a list of what you can do with them, someone else will come up with a new technique. Still, here is a short list of techniques where multibody functionality makes things either easier or simply possible:

- Complex shapes across multiple parts
- Tool bodies/Boolean operations
- Local operations
- Patterning
- Simplifying very complex parts
- As a bridge between solids
- Undetermined manufacturing methods
- Manipulating imported geometry

In the remainder of this chapter, each technique is illustrated using an example model, and the positives and negatives of each technique are discussed.

Complex shapes across bodies

When creating a part such as a computer mouse, you encounter complex shapes that span several parts. It makes the most sense to model the entire shape as a single part, and then to break it up into separate bodies, making parts from the bodies, adding detail to individual piece parts, and then bringing the parts back together as an assembly.

CROSS-REF This method also uses the Master Model techniques discussed in Chapter 28.

A part that uses this technique is shown in Figure 26.1. This part seems to contradict what I said earlier about not being able to use exploded views with multibody parts, but this part uses the Move/Copy Bodies feature to move bodies within the part. This function remains in the part as a history-based feature in the FeatureManager, and is much more labor-intensive to create than an assembly exploded view because each body is moved by a separate feature.

FIGURE 26.1

A multibody part with a complex shape across bodies

The part shown in Figure 26.1 is not complete, but the starting point for each part has been formed. This part was created from surface features that are discussed in detail in Chapter 27. The part is named Chapter 26 – Mouse Base Part.SLDPRT and is located on the CD-ROM. You may find it interesting to open the part to see how it has been modeled.

From here, each body is saved out to individual parts to complete the detailing, and then the parts are brought back together to create an assembly. The separate bodies in this case were created using the Split feature, which enables you to use surfaces or sketches to split a single body into multiple bodies. This is described in more detail later in this chapter.

The entire process for creating a finished assembly of finished parts is detailed in Figure 26.2. This flow chart shows conceptually how the overall shape created as a single part has moved from a single part/single body to a single part/multiple body to individual parts to an assembly of individual parts.

FIGURE 26.2

Master Model workflow

The image to the left in Figure 26.3 depicts how this part was modeled. The first step was to create the shape as a single body within the part. As shown in the FeatureManager, this is all contained inside the Overall Shape Features folder. This folder is presented here as a *black box* because surface features were used to create the part, and these features are not discussed until Chapter 27.

The image to the right in Figure 26.3 shows transparent surface bodies that were used to split the model into separate bodies using the Split features shown in the tree. Using this technique, you can create the overall shape as a single piece and then split it into separate parts. It is also possible to apply this technique in the context of an assembly, but this method is far more direct.

To go from the multibody part created here to a set of separate parts uses a Master Model function, which is described in Chapter 28.

FIGURE 26.3

Splitting the part into bodies

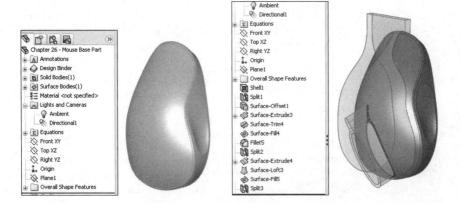

Tool bodies and Boolean operations

Some features require multiple bodies within a part, such as the Indent and Combine features, among others. Using one body to create a shape in another is a common use for bodies within a part.

Indent feature

The Indent feature was covered briefly in Chapter 7 before multibodies were introduced, and so it is fitting that I revisit it here so that the multibody aspect of its use is better understood. The Indent feature *indents* the *target* body with the *tool* body. It can also use another part in the context of an assembly as the tool. The indentation can exactly fit the form of the tool, or there can be a gap around the tool. You can also control the thickness of the material around the indent. A further option is to simply cut the target with the tool instead of indenting.

Figure 26.4 shows the target part as transparent, and the tool as opaque, before and after the Indent feature has been applied. The Indent PropertyManager is also shown.

FIGURE 26.4

The Indent feature using a tool body

The Indent feature can be problematic if it breaks into multiple areas as it does in this part, due to the ribbing on the underside of the target body. Notice that in the PropertyManager in Figure 26.4, two selections were made in the Tool Body Region selection box. The tool body is selected on either side of the rib that bisects the tool. This concept is not very intuitive, and you may have to play with the part and the options to understand what it is doing.

The Keep Selections and Remove Selections options are equally unintuitive, but they determine which side of the target body is indented. For example, if the part of the tool body that is outside of the target body (flat side) were selected instead of the two inside regions, then the resulting part would look as it does in Figure 26.5, where the tool body has been hidden. You can achieve the same result by toggling the Keep Selections and Remove Selections options. These options exist because sometimes it is difficult or impossible to select the correct areas of a body that is embedded in another body.

FIGURE 26.5

Using the Keep and Remove Selections options

 TIP Also notice that toggling the Keep and Remove Selections options means that only one region of the tool body would need to be selected to create the original result shown in Figure 26.4.

Move/Copy Bodies and Combine features

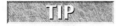 The Move/Copy Bodies and Combine features can be demonstrated using the same part. The body that was used in the previous example to indent the main body is moved and then added to the main body in this example.

Figure 26.6 shows the starting and ending points of the process, as well as the PropertyManagers of the two features that are used to get from one point to the other. Keep in mind that both the Move/Copy Bodies and the Combine features are history-based features that are listed in the FeatureManager.

FIGURE 26.6

Using the Move/Copy Bodies and Combine features

Multiple bodies

Repositioned and combined into a single body

In this case, the Move/Copy Bodies feature uses mates. These mates enable you to locate bodies in a way similar to the way they are used in assemblies. One important difference is that with bodies, you must use the actual body geometry of the body that is moving; you cannot use reference geometry such as planes. By clicking the Translate/Rotate button at the bottom of the PropertyManager, you can also position bodies using distances and angles.

By looking at the Combine PropertyManager, you will notice that common Boolean operations, such as union (add), difference (subtract), and intersection (common), are available through this interface.

> **TIP**   You can use an interesting technique in this part. The features creating the smaller tool body and the Move/Copy Bodies and Combine features can be put together into a folder, and the folder itself reordered before the Shell feature. This means that the combined body is also shelled out, and the rib goes down inside of it. This produces an odd error message and unexpectedly places several features into the folder, but it does work.
>
> You may want to open this part in SolidWorks to see exactly how all of this was done instead of relying on the figure illustrations. The part used for Figure 26.7 is on the CD-ROM and is named Chapter 26 – Move Body.SLDPRT.

FIGURE 26.7

Reordering features

Local operations

If you have ever had a modeling situation where you needed to shell out a portion of a part but not the entire part, or you had a fillet that would work if only certain geometry were not there, then you may have been able to benefit from multibody techniques to accomplish these tasks.

Flex feature

The part shown in Figure 26.8 was first seen in Chapter 7 to demonstrate the Flex feature. In order to make one side of the part flex without flexing the other side, multiple bodies were used. The part was split into two bodies using the Split feature and a plane. One side of the part was then twisted, and the two bodies were combined back together. The Features folder contains the features that were used to build the original part geometry, which could just as easily have been either native or imported.

FIGURE 26.8

Splitting a part to perform a local operation

Shell feature

The Shell feature hollows out one solid body in a part at a time. If there are multiple solid bodies, then you must select one to be shelled. Any face of the solid that you select will be removed during the shelling. You can select a body without selecting a face by using the small Solid Body selection box under the larger Faces To Remove selection box in the PropertyManager. If you do not select any faces to be removed, then the body will be hollowed out with no external indication that the part is hollow, unless you view it in section view, transparency view, or wireframe view. Single or multiple faces can be removed. This feature works by offsetting the faces of the outside of the model, and the feature may fail if this causes problems with the internal geometry.

The Multithickness Shell option enables you to select faces that will have a different thickness from the overall shell thickness. This is one method that you can sometimes use to limit the scope of the Shell feature to a certain area of a body, but it is somewhat limited. Faces with different thicknesses cannot be tangent to one another.

There is a lot more that can be said about creating and troubleshooting the Shell feature, but I am discussing it here mainly to show another local operation that can be handled using multibody parts.

Because the Shell feature only works on one body at a time, splitting a part into multiple bodies can be an effective way to limit the scope of the feature. The part shown in Figure 26.9 has been split in half, and one-half has been made transparent for visualization purposes; as a result, you can see that the part is shelled on the bottom on one end and on the top on the other end. The Shell feature has no option for doing this with existing geometry. The only ways that you can do this are either through feature order or by using multibodies.

FIGURE 26.9

Shelling locally

To shell the part this way with feature order, you would create one block and shell it, and then create the other block and shell that. In order for this technique to work, the second shell needs to be as big as, or bigger than, the first shell. If it is smaller, then it will (or may) hollow out areas that are not intended to be hollow.

To shell the part with multibodies, you can use two methods. One method is to build the first block, and then build the second block, but to turn off the Merge option. This creates bodies that are side by side. You then shell one block on the bottom and the other on the top. To avoid a double-thickness wall between them, the end face can be removed along with either the top or bottom face. If you edit the part, then you may notice that one of the Shell features has two faces removed.

The second method is to build a single block, then split it using a sketch line, a plane, or a surface, and then proceed in the same way as the first method.

Patterning

Patterns of bodies are fast, powerful, and commonly used alternatives to patterning features. Chapter 8 discussed feature patterns and mirroring, and examines, at least in part, how different types of patterns affect model rebuild speeds. When appropriate, patterning bodies can also be a big rebuild time saver. When patterning a body, none of the parametrics or intelligence is patterned with it, but you must pattern the entire body. Another odd thing about patterning bodies in SolidWorks is that there is no option to join the bodies either to one another or to a main body. This requires an extra step that involves adding a Combine feature. Mirroring is the same, except that it does have an option to merge bodies, but it only merges the original body to the mirrored body. It will not merge either the original or the mirrored body to a central main body.

In this example, an imported part has a "feature" that needs to be reused around the part. The technique used here is to split away the feature as a separate body and then pattern the body around the part and joint it all back together. This function can be used with native geometry as well as imported. This process is shown in Figure 26.10. This function does use a simple planar surface. A plane could have been used to split off the body to be patterned, but the plane would have also split off a part of the globe at the top, so a planar surface (which can be limited in extent where a plane can not) was used.

The image on the left in Figure 26.10 is the raw imported part. The middle image shows a planar surface created on the face of the part, where the planar surface has been used with the Split feature to cut the leg off of the part. The image on the right shows the split leg patterned around an axis that was created from the intersection of two planes.

FIGURE 26.10

Splitting away a body and patterning it

If you would like to practice with this part, it is on the CD-ROM for Chapter 26; the imported Parasolid file is named Chapter 26 – Pattern import.x_t.

PERFORMANCE In some situations, patterning bodies is a performance advantage, and in some situations it is not. You get an advantage from patterning bodies when the geometry used to create the pattern seed is complex, uses many features, or does not work or does not work well for a feature pattern.

On the other hand, if you repeat the experiments from Chapter 8 using a small body with a hole in it instead of patterning a hole feature, you find that the body pattern is far slower than the feature patterning.

Simplifying very complex parts

Certain types of parts lend themselves very well to being built in sections. For very complex parts with a lot of features, this sometimes makes sense from the point of view of segmenting the rebuild times for parts with hundreds of features. The example used to demonstrate this technique is a large plastic part built entirely from ribs, and making use of literally hundreds of solid bodies.

This part is molded using pulls in five directions. Two of these directions are symmetrical, and the core block pulls in a single direction; as a result, in the end, the modeling has to account for three directions.

The rebuild time for a model like this can easily reach several minutes, depending on your hardware. To minimize the rebuild time, a different workflow was established for this part. First, the major inside and outside faces were created with surfaces. Next, the surfaces were saved into several other parts (using Master Model techniques that are discussed in Chapter 28), and each of these parts represents the part geometry that will pull in a particular direction from the mold. Enough information exists in the Master Model to align the features in each part.

The ribs on this part were created by making a single extrusion (the Rib feature could not be used because there was no geometry to serve as a boundary for the ribs), and then the extrusion was patterned and the pattern was mirrored. After all of the ribs were created, they had to be shaped, and so the surfaces from the Master Model were used to cut the ribs to shape.

The ribs could not be extruded with a draft or with fillets because the outer and inner surfaces were non-planar. The draft had to be built as a Parting Line draft for the same reason, and the fillets had to be applied after the draft. Further, draft and fillets can only be applied to a single body at a time; as a result, a separate draft feature and a separate fillet feature had to be applied to each body, and each rib was a separate body. Once the draft and fillets were applied, the bodies were joined into a single body.

Figure 26.11 shows two of the separate pull direction parts being separated from one another in the same way that the mouse part was shown exploded in the previous example. Here the frame is also modeled as a separate part, again because it was not so intimately related to the other parts, and was easily separated out.

Once this was complete for each direction, the separate parts were put together as bodies into a single part and again joined together using the Combine feature. Having all of those features in separate parts enables you to segment the rebuild time. This is the opposite of building all of the parts of an assembly in a single part, where you are simply compounding your rebuild time. Figure 26.12 shows bodies joined together as a single body.

FIGURE 26.11

A complex model created as separate parts and brought together as bodies in a single part

FIGURE 26.12

Bodies all joined together as a single body

This is probably a technique that you will not use very often, but when you do, it can save you a lot of rebuild time. I use it whenever I have a model that takes more than 20 to 30 seconds to rebuild and I know that I am going to be working on it a lot; it must also lend itself to segmenting in the way that this one did.

Bridge between solids

Often when modeling, you "build what you know" and "fill in as you go." An example of this would be modeling a duct between end connections that are well defined. The duct in between is defined only by the ends, which must exist first. Another example is a connecting rod where you know the diameter of each end and the distance between the ends, and the connection between them is of secondary importance.

Figure 26.13 shows a connecting rod made in this way. In this case, the bearing seat at one end was created, and the other end was created by copying the body of the first one. From there, the link between bearing seats was created, which joined the separate bodies together into a single solid body.

FIGURE 26.13

Connecting disjoint bodies

This part contains some interesting features. First is the Thin Feature extrude that is used to make the first bearing seat, which is combined with a Mid-plane extrude to make it symmetrical at the same time. Then comes the Move/Copy Bodies feature, which copies the body in the same way that the feature in previous examples has moved bodies. Next is the use of the Extrude From option, which extrudes from a face, and then the end condition Up To Next ends the feature neatly. The part also incorporates fillets that use faces and features to form the selection.

If you are not familiar with these options, then I recommend that you open up the part from the CD-ROM and have a look at it. It is a simple part that takes advantage of nice but simple productivity-enhancing options that have been available for some time in the SolidWorks software. The part filename is Chapter 26 – Bridge.

By default, Solid features have the Merge option turned on, and they automatically combine with any bodies that they touch. At the same time, they do not display errors if the Merge option is on but the new body does not touch any existing bodies.

Undetermined manufacturing methods

Sometimes you must start a design before you know exactly how the product will be manufactured. This is an example of where the geometry of the finished product exists first, and is then broken up into manufacturable parts. The initial model, shown in the image to the left in Figure 26.14, is created as a single part as a result of input from marketing, but when it comes time for manufacturing input, the part count and processes keep changing. Where the parts break from one another keeps changing as well. When that kind of change is happening, having the parts created as individual parts is a big liability because it is difficult to change. Changing which bodies are merged together is much easier.

FIGURE 26.14

A towel rack, modeled as a single part, and broken into individual parts in an assembly

It is worth•mentioning two potential difficulties that you may run into with methods like this. The first is that if you have people making drawings from parts that have been derived from bodies in a single part, then they are forced into the Reference Dimension scheme of dimensioning parts because the feature dimensions do not survive being moved from the multibody part. This may or may not be an issue, depending on how the people doing the drawings are accustomed to working.

The second potential issue is what you do in situations where there are multiple instances of a part that has been modeled this way. If you notice the towel rack in Figure 26.14, there are several finials, spacers, rails, and other parts that are duplicated. This requires some manual assembly modeling. You can make the assembly directly from the multibody part, but if you need to make multiple instances of particular parts, then you need to do this manually rather than automatically.

Creating Multibodies

In the first section in this chapter, I raised the questions of *if* or *when* multibodies should be used, and in the second section, I raised the question of *why* multibodies should be used. In this section, I simply ask, or rather answer, *how* they should be used.

Disjoint sketches

The easiest way to create multiple bodies is to simply create what SolidWorks classifies as multiple disjoint closed contours. What that means is simply two circles or rectangles that do not touch or overlap. If these are created in the same sketch, then when extruded, they will create as many bodies as there are closed loops in the sketch.

If the part has an existing solid, then creating a sketch that does not touch the solid can also create a separate body. You cannot make Multiple Thin features in a single sketch. This is presumably because the interface has no way to identify different thickness directions for different open profiles. This holds true whether or not the Multiple Thin features create multiple bodies.

If a solid feature other than a mirror or pattern touches a solid body, then the new and the old bodies will be merged into a single body.

Merge Result option

You can prevent a feature from automatically combining with other bodies by turning off the Merge Result option. This holds true between features, but not across all bodies in a part. For example, if an extrude feature uses the Merge Result option, all of the bodies that it touches become merged together, but if the original extrude feature does not touch a body it will not be merged. This option is shown in Figure 26.15, and is found on all features that create new solid bodies except for the Patterns, Rib, and Move/Copy Bodies features.

FIGURE 26.15

The Merge Result option

Feature Scope

The Feature Scope used for multibodies is not the same as the Feature Scope used for assembly features, but it does function in a similar way. In assemblies, the Feature Scope identifies which parts are affected by the current assembly feature. In parts, it only applies to bodies, and can be used for features that add material as well as features that remove material (assembly features can only remove material).

The Feature Scope is a way to make the Merge Result option more selective. The Merge Result option does not discriminate; it causes the feature to merge with any other solid body that it touches. However, the Feature Scope enables the user to select which bodies to either merge with or otherwise affect. Feature Scope also applies to additional feature types such as cuts. The Feature Scope becomes available in the PropertyManager whenever there are multiple bodies in the part and an eligible feature is used. The Feature Scope panel is shown in Figure 26.16.

FIGURE 26.16

The Feature Scope panel

The default setting for the Feature Scope is to use the Selected Bodies option with the Auto-select option. The All Bodies option is essentially the same as using the Merge Result option. When the Selected Bodies option is on and Auto-select is off, as is shown in Figure 26.16, you must select bodies for the current feature to affect them. New bodies that are added to the model are not automatically added to the list; you need to manually edit the feature and add additional bodies to the list as appropriate.

Rib feature

The Rib feature is hyper-sensitive to the presence of multiple bodies. A rib only automatically merges with a body if it is the only body in the part. If a rib is created and then the model is rolled back and an additional body is created before the rib, then the Rib feature will fail when the tree is unrolled. The error that this causes reads, "The rib is not bounded properly. The extension of the rib does not intersect the part model." Technically speaking, this is true, but like other SolidWorks error messages, that does not make it helpful. The cause of the error is that suddenly, the body that the rib is supposed to merge with is no longer identified. The Rib feature has no Auto-select option. You can fix this problem by going to the Feature Scope to select a body for it to merge with. The Rib feature does not use the normal Feature Scope, because the Feature Scope is intended to select multiple bodies, and the Rib feature requires a single body. There is a simple Selected Body box in the Rib PropertyManager.

After you have selected the target body, deleting the new bodies that caused the problem in the first place, thankfully, does not make the problem reoccur. However, if the body that the rib is merged with is split using the Split feature, then that *does* cause a problem. As a result, the two things that cause the Rib feature problem are rolling back and either adding bodies or splitting the body to be ribbed.

CAUTION As you encounter more specialized situations with multibodies and dependencies, you may notice more quirks in the SolidWorks internal body management. The next section on Managing Bodies addresses some of these quirks directly.

Delete Body feature

If you have created many ribs in a casting or plastic part, then it may be tedious to go through and repair them all every time the body count changes. This sort of thing happens even if the other body is just a reference body or an unused leftover.

In cases like this, you can use the Delete Body feature. Delete Body removes the body from the body folder (discussed in the Body Folders section). This is a *history-based delete*, which means that before the Delete Body feature in the tree, the body exists, and after the Delete Body feature in the tree, the body does not exist. This feature has no effect on file size, because the data for the body must still exist, and it has little, if any, effect on rebuild time. What is happening is that the body is still there; you just cannot see it and have no access to it.

Delete Body is often used for other purposes as well, primarily to clean up a model at the end of the tree. The reasoning is that multiple bodies in a part confuse people. My view on this is that if multiple bodies confuse people, then just think what a *feature* called *Delete Bodies* does for them. In either case, they have a bit to learn. My recommendation here is to remove bodies if they are getting in the way, either for a hyper-sensitive feature like the Rib feature or if they are causing visualization problems.

Cut feature

A Cut feature may create multibodies, either intentionally or unintentionally. When it does happen, the Bodies To Keep dialog box appears to enable you to select which bodies you intend to keep. The Bodies To Keep dialog box is shown in Figure 26.17. This dialog box was formerly called Resolve Ambiguity, which was not as descriptive as Bodies To Keep.

The Bodies To Keep dialog box

Notice that the Bodies To Keep settings are also configurable, and so different bodies can be kept in different configurations, which is very useful.

Split feature

Of all of the features in SolidWorks, the Split feature is one of the most contentious and controversial. In some situations, it is positively dangerous, and can cause a lot of data loss if you are not aware of the workarounds to make it work properly. Endless forum discussions are devoted to this one feature that most SolidWorks users probably do not even use.

The Split feature has essentially three functions:

- To split a single solid body into multiple solid bodies using planes, sketches, and surface bodies
- To save individual solid bodies out to individual part files
- To reassemble individual part files that are saved out into an assembly where the parts are all positioned in the same relative position as their corresponding bodies

The last two functions of the Split feature are addressed in Chapter 28, and these are the most controversial areas of its functionality.

The part of the Split feature that concerns this chapter is the first function mentioned, which is splitting a single solid body into multiple bodies using a sketch, a plane, or a surface body.

Splitting with a sketch

When using a sketch, the Split process works like this:

1. Create a sketch with an open or closed loop; even a mixture of open and closed profiles will work. If it is open, then the endpoints have to either be on an exterior edge or hanging off into space; they cannot actually be inside the boundaries of the solid.

2. Initiate the Split feature from the Features toolbar or from the menus at Insert ➪ Features ➪ Split. You can do this with the sketch active, with the sketch inactive but selected, or with nothing selected at all.

3. Click the Cut Part button. This does not actually cut anything; it only previews the split. When this is done, the resulting bodies appear in the window below, and callout flags are placed on the part in the graphics window. These flags are often useless because they tend to point to the borders between two different bodies in such a way that it is completely ambiguous as to which body they are indicating. However, in the example shown in Figure 26.18, the result is very clear.

FIGURE 26.18

Using the Split feature

Check marks next to the body in the list indicate that the body will be split out. The lack of a check mark does not mean anything. For example, in Figure 26.18, notice that two boxes are checked, but this will result in a total of four bodies. Body 3 and Body 4 are free. If only Body 1 were selected, then the result would be only two bodies.

The callout flags and the bodies list where <None> is shown are looking for a path and filename to save the body out to a file. Again, this functionality is covered in Chapter 28 with the Master Model information.

The Save All Bodies button simply puts check marks in all of the boxes. If the Resulting Bodies box contains more than ten bodies, then the interface changes slightly, as shown in the image to the right in Figure 26.18. In past releases, the list box did not contain the slider bar; only the Next 10 button appeared, and it was easy to miss, not being a usual interface technique for accessing lists that were longer than the box in which they appeared.

The Consume Cut Bodies option removes, or consumes, any of the bodies that have a check mark. If you used the Split feature a couple of releases ago, the default was for it to consume all bodies. The current situation is a big improvement.

Splitting with a plane

Splitting with a plane gives the same type of results and uses the same options as splitting with a sketch. However, you never have to worry about the plane being extended far enough, because the cut is made from the infinite planar extension of the plane. The only thing you have to worry about with a plane is whether it intersects the part.

Splitting with a surface body

Surface bodies are used to split solid bodies for a couple of reasons. In the part shown in Figure 26.10, a surface body was used to make the split instead of a sketch or a plane, because both of those entities split everything in an infinite distance either normal to the sketch plane or in the selected plane. A surface body only splits to the extents of the body. If you look closely at the part, you will notice that a plane or sketch would lop off one side of the sphere on top of the object, but the small planar surface is limited enough in size to only split what is necessary.

Another advantage to using a surface body is that it is not limited to a two-dimensional cut. The surface itself can be any type of surface, such as planar, extruded, revolved, lofted, or imported. Taking this a step further, the surface is not limited to being a single face, or a body resulting from a single feature; it could be made from several features that are put together as long as it is a single body and all of the outer edges of the surface body are outside the solid body. If you examine the mouse part shown in Figure 26.1, you will notice that it has splits made from multi-feature surface bodies.

Splitting with surface bodies is mentioned here because this is where the Split function is discussed, even though the surfacing functions have not been covered yet. It may be useful to read parts of this book out of order; because of the interrelatedness of all of the topics, it is impossible to order the topics in such a way that nothing ever refers to a topic that has not yet been covered.

CROSS-REF For more information about surface bodies, see Chapter 27.

Insert Part feature

 The Insert Part button can be found on the Features toolbar, or you can access this feature through the menus at Insert, Part.

Insert Part enables you to insert one part into another part. When inserting the part, you have the option to also insert axes, planes, cosmetic threads, and surface bodies. All solid bodies from the selected part are automatically brought into the current part. The PropertyManager interface for the Insert Part feature is shown in Figure 26.19.

FIGURE 26.19

The Insert Part PropertyManager

This feature has two major functions: inserting a body as the starting point for a new part, and inserting a body to be used as a tool to modify an existing part. Notice that the basket part shown in Figure 26.11 and Figure 26.12 also uses Insert Part to put together bodies to form a finished part.

When you use Insert Part, there is no Insert Part feature that becomes part of the tree. Instead, a part icon is shown with the name of the part being inserted.

Also notice in Figure 26.19 that the Launch Move Dialog option displays at the bottom, and is on by default. This option launches the Move dialog box after you insert the part. This Move feature is the same as the Move/Copy Bodies feature, with the same options (translate or rotate by distance or angles, or use assembly-like mates to position bodies).

Insert Part is used in many situations, some of which are covered in Chapters 11 and 28 in the section on Master Model and Skeleton techniques.

Secondary operations

One of the commonly used techniques has to do with secondary operations. For example, you may have designed a casting that needs several machining operations after it comes from the foundry. The foundry needs a drawing to produce the raw casting, and the machine shop needs a different drawing to ream and tap holes, spot face areas, and so on.

Although you can use configurations to do this, using Insert Part is another way. This has nothing to do with multiple body techniques, but this is the only place where Insert Part is covered in much detail. One of the advantages of using Insert Part is that you no longer carry around the overhead of all of the features in the parent part. It is as if the inserted part were imported. The configurations method forces you to carry around much more feature overhead. Of course, the downside is that now there is an additional file to manage, but this can be an advantage because many companies assign different part numbers to parts before and after secondary operations.

Starting point

Looking back to the mouse shown in Figure 26.1, the main part has been split into several bodies. You can use Insert Part to insert the whole mouse into a new part where all of the bodies except one are deleted, and then the remaining body serves as the starting point for a new part. Many additional features are needed on all of the bodies that make up the mouse, such as assembly features, cosmetic features, functional features, and manufacturing features.

Managing Bodies

Managing bodies in SolidWorks is not as clean a task as managing parts in an assembly. As you work with bodies, you will discover some real surprises in how bodies are managed. Hopefully in this section, I can prepare you for some of the more problematic surprises.

Body folders

The top of the FeatureManager includes a pair of folders, one called Solid Bodies, and the other called Surface Bodies. These folders are only there if you have solids or surfaces in the model, and they reflect the state of the model at the current position of the Rollback bar. As a result, the folders can change and even disappear as you roll the tree back and forth in history. Figure 26.20 shows the top of a FeatureManager that has both solid and surface body folders. Notice that the number in parentheses after the name of the folder shows how many bodies are in that particular folder.

An odd fact about these folders is that you are allowed to rename the folders, but the name changes never remain. If you go back to rename the folder again, the name that you assigned is displayed; you cannot name another feature with the name that you assigned, but it is never displayed as the name of the folder.

FIGURE 26.20

Body folders in the FeatureManager

By right-clicking either of the bodies folders, you can select the Show Feature History option, which shows the features that have combined to create the bodies. This view of the FeatureManager is shown in Figure 26.21. This option is very useful when you are editing or troubleshooting bodies.

FIGURE 26.21

Using the Show Feature History option

Figure 26.21 also shows the other options in the RMB menu. All of the bodies in the folder can be alternately shown or hidden from this menu, as well as deleted. While the Hide or Show state of a body does not create a history-based feature in the tree, the Delete feature does, as discussed previously.

The Insert Into New Part feature and the Save Bodies feature are discussed in Chapter 28.

You can expand the Display pane in parts, in order to show display information for bodies. In Figure 26.22, the Display pane shows the colors assigned to the solid bodies, as well as the fact that several surface bodies exist but are hidden.

The Display pane showing information about solid and surface bodies

The folders also make bodies easier to identify, especially when combined with the setting found at Tools, Options, Display/Selection, Dynamic Highlight From Graphics View. This setting quickly turns the body outline red if you move the mouse over the body in the body folder.

Hide or show bodies

You can hide or show bodies in one of several ways. I have already described the method of using the bodies folders to hide or show all of the bodies at once, but you can also RMB click individual bodies in the folders to hide or show from there as well. Also, if you can see a body in the graphics area, then you can RMB click the body and select Hide under the Body heading. This works for both solids and surfaces.

When you are hiding or showing bodies from the FeatureManager, and not using the bodies folders, but rather using the features themselves, things get a little complicated. If you want to hide or show a solid body, then you can use any feature that is a parent of the body to hide or show the body. For example, you can use the Shell feature in the mouse model to hide or show all of the bodies of which it is a parent.

Although this technique works well for solid bodies, surface bodies are a different story. In order to show or hide a surface body using features in the FeatureManager, you have to select the *very last* feature that was used on that particular body. For example, in the mouse model, Fillet 5 was the last feature to touch that particular body, but Surface-Offset1 was the first feature of that body, and it cannot be used to hide or show anything. This is an example of the inconsistency that causes confusion with managing bodies in SolidWorks.

Other facts that you need to know about bodies and their hide or show states are that the Hide or Show feature is both configurable and dependent on the rollback state. As a result, if you hide a body, and then roll back, it may appear again, and you will have to hide it. Then, if you roll forward, the state changes again. Also, a body can be hidden in one configuration, and then when you switch configurations, it remains hidden. This makes it rather frustrating to work with bodies. To me, it would be nice if bodies had simple on/off toggles that were neither intelligent nor tricky.

CAUTION Some features exclude bodies if the bodies are hidden when you edit the feature. Be careful of this, and be sure to show all of the bodies that are used in a particular function before you edit it. For example, if a body is hidden, and you create a new extrude that touches the hidden body, then the new body does not merge with the hidden one *even if the Merge option is on.* If the hidden body is then shown and you edit the second body, then the bodies will merge upon the closing of the second body.

Deleting bodies

 I have already mentioned that you can delete bodies using the Delete Bodies feature, and that this feature sits in the tree at a specific point in the history of the part.

Delete Bodies does not affect file size or rebuild speed. In fact, I find it difficult to come up with examples of when you should use it, other than the situation already mentioned with the Rib feature, or if a throwaway body somehow remains in the part. Some people use this feature to clean up the organization of the tree, which could be useful if there are many bodies in the part. Other users insist on keeping the tree free of extraneous bodies, and so they immediately delete bodies that have been used. To me, this technique replaces one kind of clutter with another, and means that tools that should be available to you (solid or surface bodies) are not available unless you reorder the Delete Body feature down the tree and/or roll back. In any case, this is really a matter of personal working style, and not of any great importance.

Renaming bodies

Notice that the bodies that you see in the folders have been named for the last feature that touched that body. That naming scheme is as good as any, except that it means that the body keeps changing names. Even if you deliberately rename a body, the name will change with the next feature that is added to it. This is particularly true when a feature results in a body being split into multiple features or when the feature combines bodies. This means that body names are also rollback state-dependent, like body colors, and the Hide or Show feature.

Tutorials: Working with Multibodies

This tutorial contains various short examples of multibody techniques in order from easy to more difficult.

Merging and local operations

This tutorial gives you some experience using the Merge Result option and using features on individual bodies to demonstrate the local operations functionality of multibody modeling. Try these steps:

1. Start a new part, and sketch a rectangle on the Top plane, with the Origin at the midpoint of the line at one end of the rectangle. Size is not important for this exercise.

2. Extrude the rectangle to roughly one-third of its smaller dimension.

3. Open a second sketch on the Top plane. Hide the first solid body by right-clicking it in either the FeatureManager or the graphics window.

4. Show the sketch for the first feature, and draw a second rectangle on the far side of the rectangle from the Origin. Make sure that the second rectangle gets two coincident relations to the first sketch, at two corners so that the rectangles are the same width. When the sketch is complete, hide the sketch that was shown.

5. Extrude the second rectangle to about two-thirds of the depth of the first rectangle.

NOTE   Notice that the Merge option was not changed from the default setting of On for the second extrude, but because the first extrude was hidden, the second extrude did not merge with it. Be careful of subsequent edits to either of the features if the first body is shown, because this may cause the bodies to merge unexpectedly.

In this tutorial, the bodies are later merged intentionally. In this case, the tutorial uses a bug in the software as an advantage, but ideally what you should do (in case the bug is fixed at some point) is to deselect the Merge option of the second extrude.

6. Shell out the second extrusion by removing two adjacent sides, as shown in Figure 26.23. One of the sides is the top and the other is the shared side with the hidden body. The body that should be hidden at this point is shown as transparent in the image for reference only. The body was made transparent to make it easier to select the face of the second body.

FIGURE 26.23

Shelling two sides of a block

7. Show the first body either from the Solid Bodies folder at the top of the tree or from the RMB menu of the first solid feature in the tree.

8. Shell the bottom side of the first body, so that the cavities in the two bodies are on opposite sides.

9. Combine the two bodies using the Combine tool found at Insert ⇨ Features ⇨ Combine. Select the Add option and select the two bodies. Click OK to finish the feature. Figure 26.24 shows the finished part.

FIGURE 26.24

The finished part

Splitting and patterning bodies

This tutorial guides you through the steps to delete a pattern of *features* from an imported body, separate one of the features, and then pattern it with a different number of features. This introduces some simple surface functions, in preparation for Chapter 27. Follow these steps:

1. Open the Parasolid file from the CD-ROM called Chapter 26 – Bonita Tutorial.x_t.

2. Using the Selection Filter set to filter Face selection (the default hotkey for this is X), select all of the faces of the leg. You can use window selection techniques to avoid clicking each face.

3. Click the Delete Face button on the Surfaces toolbar, or access the command through the menus at Insert ⇨ Face ⇨ Delete. Make sure that the Delete And Patch option is selected. The selected faces and the Delete Face PropertyManager should look like Figure 26.25. Click OK to accept the feature.

FIGURE 26.25

The Delete Face PropertyManager

4. Repeat the process for a second leg, leaving the third leg to be separated from the rest of the part and patterned.

5. After the two legs have been removed, click the outer main spherical surface, and then from the menus, select Insert ➪ Surface ➪ Offset. Set the offset distance to zero. Notice that a Surface Bodies folder is now added to the tree, near the top.

 TIP   A zero distance offset surface is frequently used to copy faces.

6. Hide the solid body. You can do this from the Solid Bodies folder, from the FeatureManager, or from the graphics window.

7. Hiding the solid leaves the offset surface, and there should be three holes in the surface. Select one of the edges of the hole indicated in Figure 26.26 and press the Delete key. The Choose Option dialog box appears. Select the Delete Hole option rather than the Delete Feature option. The Delete Hole operation becomes a history-based feature in the model tree.

FIGURE 26.26

Using the Delete Hole option

NOTE   Delete Hole is really a surface feature called Untrim. Untrim is discussed more in Chapter 27, but you can use it to restore original boundaries to a surface.

8. Once you delete the hole from the surface body, change the color of the surface body in the same way that you used to change colors of parts, faces, and features.

9. This is not a necessary step, but many people choose to use it. Click the surface body in the Surface Bodies folder and either press the Delete key, or select Delete from the RMB menu. Then click OK to accept the feature. This places a Delete Body feature in the tree. It keeps the body from getting in the way when it is not needed.

TIP   If you delete a body in this way and then need it later down the tree, you can delete, suppress, or reorder the Delete Body feature later in the tree.

10. Now show the solid body. You will notice the color of the surface conflicting with the color of the solid. This mottled appearance is due to the small approximations made by the rendering and display algorithms.

11. Initiate the Split feature through the menus at Insert ➪ Features ➪ Split, or on the Features toolbar. Use the surface body to split the solid body. Click the Cut Part button, and select the check boxes in front of both bodies in the list. Click OK to accept the feature. Notice now that the Solid Bodies folder indicates that there are two solid bodies.

12. From the View menu, turn on the display of Temporary Axes. Initiate a Circular Pattern feature, selecting the temporary axis as the axis, and the split-off leg in the Bodies To Pattern selection box. Set it to four instances, as shown in Figure 26.27.

FIGURE 26.27

Patterning a body

13. Use the Combine feature to add together all five bodies. You can access this feature through the menus at Insert ➪ Features ➪ Combine.

Summary

Beginning to understand how to work with multiple bodies in SolidWorks opens a gateway to a new world of design possibilities. However, like anything else, not everything is perfect. Like in-context design, multibody modeling is definitely something that you have to go into with your eyes open. You will experience difficulties when using this technique, but you will also find new possibilities that were not available with other techniques. The key to success with multibodies techniques is discipline and circumspection.

When using a model with the multibody approach, make sure that you can identify a reason for doing it this way rather than using a more conventional approach. Also keep in mind the list of applications or uses for multibody modeling that are mentioned in this chapter.

Chapter 27

Working with Surfaces

From a CAD point of view, a *solid* is defined as the volume enclosed by a surface boundary. To enclose a volume, the boundary must have no gaps or overlaps. The skin or surface of the boundary itself is infinitely thin, and has no volume, although it has a surface area. In this way, surfaces are one of the building blocks of solids.

In many respects, there are no real differences between a solid model and a surface model. If you export a SolidWorks part to IGES format and read it into another capable modeler, or even back into SolidWorks, then that file can be read in as either a solid or a surface. There is no way to distinguish which it was when it left the originating modeler. The real difference between the two is how the modeler handles the data internally.

It is possible to drive a car without knowing how the engine works, but you cannot get the most possible power out of the car by only pressing harder on the gas pedal; you have to get under the hood and make adjustments. In a way, that is what working with surfaces is really all about.

Surface modeling can start from a blank screen, from imported geometry, from native SolidWorks solid and surface features that have been built side by side, or from a native or imported solid that has been deconstructed into surfaces.

The goal of most surface modeling is to finish with a solid. In the same way in which we learned to refer to solids as "solid bodies," surface features can also be knitted together into a single contiguous body. This does not happen by default, however. By default, solid features are automatically merged into a single body if they touch one another and can form a single body. Surface features do not do this automatically; in fact, most surface features do not even have the option to be knitted (the surface equivalent of the solid "merge") together, but require an additional Knit feature to do this.

Why Do You Need Surfaces?

In the end, you may never really *need* surfaces. It is possible to perform workarounds using solids to do most of the things that most users need to do. However, many of these workarounds are very inefficient and cumbersome. Although you may not look at some typical things that you now do as being inefficient and cumbersome, once you see the alternatives, you may change your mind. The goal for this chapter is to introduce surfacing functions to people who do not typically use surfaces, and for everyday modeling. Here I am not trying to show how surfaces are used in the context of creating complex shapes, although the same techniques can be used, regardless of the complexity of the shape.

The word *surfacing* has often been used (and confused) synonymously with the creation of complex shapes. Not all surface work is done to create complex shapes, and many complex shapes can be made directly from solids. Many users think that because they do not make complex shapes, they never need to use surface features. This chapter shows mainly examples that are not complex shapes, in situations where surfaces make it easier, more efficient, or simply possible to do the necessary tasks.

While some of the uses of surfaces may not be immediately obvious, by the end of this chapter, you should have enough information and applications that you can start experimenting to increase your confidence.

Understanding Surfacing Terminology

When dealing with surfaces, different terminology may often be used that is not typically used with solid modeling. It is important to understand the terminology, which makes the techniques easier to understand. This special terminology also often exists for surfaces because of important conceptual differences between how solids and surfaces are handled.

These terms are fairly universal among all surfacing software. The concepts underlying surface and solid construction are generally uniform between the major software packages. What varies from software to software is how the user interacts with the geometry through the software interface. You may never see some of these terms in the SolidWorks menus, Help files, training books, or elsewhere, but it becomes obvious as you use the software that the concepts are relevant.

Knit

 Knit is analogous to the solid feature Combine in that it joins multiple surface bodies into a single surface body. Unlike Combine, Knit does not perform the subtract or intersect Boolean operations.

It also has an option to create a solid if the resulting surface body meets the requirements (a fully enclosed volume without gaps or overlaps). However, unlike the solid bodies in Combine, which may overlap volumetrically, surface bodies must intersect edge to edge, more like sketch entities.

Knit is also sometimes used in the same way that the zero-distance offset is used, to copy a set of solid faces to become a new surface body.

One nice option that enables you to quickly see where the boundaries of a surface body lie is found at Tools ⇨ Options ⇨ Display/Selection ⇨ Show Open Edges Of Surfaces In Different Color. By default, this color is a medium blue, and you can change it at Tools ⇨ Options ⇨ Colors ⇨ Surfaces ⇨ Open Edges.

Trim

 The Trim function in SolidWorks is analogous to the solid Cut. Also much like the Cut, internally, Trim simply creates an additional boundary for the surface. The underlying surface is defined by a two-dimensional mesh, and for this reason, it is usually four-sided, but may be other shapes. When the underlying surface is trimmed, the software still remembers the underlying shape, but combines it with the new boundary, which is typically how face shapes (especially non-four-sided shapes) are created.

Untrim

 Untrim is predictably the opposite of Trim. All it does is remove the boundary from a surface. It can remove the boundary selectively (one edge at a time, interior edges only, and so on) or remove all of the edges at once. Untrim even works on imported geometry, as described in the tutorial in Chapter 26. Figure 27.1 shows how Untrim works.

FIGURE 27.1

Untrimming a surface

Untrim works on native and imported geometry. It is not truly like feature history in imported geometry, but it does help to uncover the underlying original shape of the face.

Hybrid modeling

Modeling software has long divided itself along Solid/Surface lines with products such as Rhino (strictly surface modeling) and early versions of SolidWorks (strictly solid modeling). However, in the last several years, modelers are increasingly enabling both methods, and allowing them to interact. This hybrid modeling is a combination of solid and surface modeling. These days, very few mechanical designers or engineers model exclusively in surfaces. Surface modeling is slow because you model each face individually, and then manually trim and knit. Cutting a hole in a surface model is much more involved than cutting a hole in a solid. Solid modeling is faster because it is essentially highly automated surface modeling; however, as any software user knows, automation almost always comes at the expense of flexibility, and this situation is no different.

Solid modeling tends to limit you to a type of parts with square ends or a flat bottom because solids are creating all sides of an object at once. For example, think about an extrusion: regardless of the shape of the rest of the feature, you have two flat ends. Even lofts and sweeps typically end up with one or two flat ends. Surfaces enable you to create one side at a time. Another way of looking at it is that using surfaces *requires* you to create one side at a time.

You will find times when, even with prismatic modeling, surfacing functions are extremely useful, if not complete indispensable. I do not propose that you dive into pure surface modeling just to benefit from a few of the advantages, but I do recommend that you consider using surface techniques to help define your solids. This hybrid approach is sensible and opens up a whole new world of capabilities. I have heard people say after taking a SolidWorks surfacing class that they would never look at the software in the same way again.

NURBS

NURBS stands for Non Uniform Rational B Spline. NURBS is the technology that most modern mechanical design modelers use to create face geometry. NURBS surfaces are defined by curves in perpendicular directions, referred to as U and V directions, which form a mesh. The fact that perpendicular directions are used means that the surfaces have a tendency to be four-sided. Of course exceptions exist, such as three-sided or even two-sided patches. Geometry of this kind is referred to as *degenerate*, because one or more of the sides has been reduced to zero length. Degenerate geometry is often, but not always, the source of geometrical errors in SolidWorks and other CAD packages.

Figure 27.2 shows some surfaces with the mesh displayed on them. You can create the mesh with the Face Curves sketch tool.

FIGURE 27.2

Meshes created with the Face Curves sketch tool

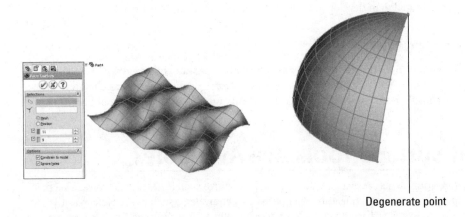

Degenerate point

An example of a competitive system to NURBS surface modeling is point mesh data. This comes from systems such as 3DSMax, which create a set of points that are joined together in triangular facets, and can be represented in SolidWorks as an STL (stereolithography) file. When displayed in SolidWorks, this data looks very facetted or tessellated into small, flat triangles, but when viewed in software that is meant to work with these kinds of meshes, it looks smooth. Many advantages come with this type of data, especially when it comes to applying colors and motion. However, the main disadvantage is that the geometrical accuracy is not very good, and most of all, the data is not parametric, feature-based data that lends itself to changes in the definitions of features. Point mesh data is typically used by 3D graphic artists, animators, and game developers.

By using a SolidWorks extension such as ScanTo3D, it is possible to take point mesh data and create a NURBS mesh over it. This feature is not completely automatic, but it offers capabilities where none previously existed. ScanTo3D is beyond the scope of this book, but you should find it useful if you are interested enough to read about NURBS and point meshes.

Developable surface

Developable surfaces are surfaces that can be flattened without stretching the material. These include planar, cylindrical, and conical shapes. It is not a coincidence that these are the types of shapes that can be flattened by the Sheet Metal tools.

Ruled surface

Developable surfaces are a special type of a broader range of surface called ruled surfaces. SolidWorks has a special tool for the creation of ruled surfaces that is described in detail in the next section. Ruled surfaces are defined as surfaces on which a straight line can be drawn at every point. A corollary to this is that ruled surfaces may have curvature in only one direction. Ruled surfaces are far less limited than developable surfaces, but are not as easily flattened.

Gaussian curvature

Gaussian curvature is not referred to directly in SolidWorks software, but you may hear the term used in more general CAD or engineering discussions. It can be defined simply as curvature in two directions. As a result, a sphere would have Gaussian curvature, but a cylinder would not.

What Surface Tools Are Available?

Surface feature equivalents are available for most solid features such as extrude, revolve, sweep, loft, fillet, and so on. Some solid features do not have an equivalent, such as the Hole Wizard, shell, and others. Several surface functions do not have solid equivalents, such as trim, Untrim, Extend, Thicken, Offset, Radiate, Ruled, Fill, and Boundary.

The surface features are listed here in the order in which they appear in the Tools ⇨ Customize ⇨ Commands list for the Surfaces toolbar. This is not a comprehensive guide to complex shape modeling, but it should serve as an introduction to each feature type and some of the details about how it operates.

Extruded Surface

 The Extruded Surface works exactly like an extruded solid, except that the ends of the surface are not capped. It includes all of the same end conditions, draft, contour selection, sketch rules, and so on that you are already familiar with. Figure 27.3 shows the PropertyManager for Extruded Surface.

You can also create extruded surfaces from open sketches, and, in fact, that is probably a more common situation than creating a surface with a closed sketch.

When two non-parallel sketch lines are joined end to end, the result of extruding the sketch is a single surface body that is made of two faces. If the sketch lines were disjoint, then the extrude would result in disjoint surface bodies. If the sketch lines were again made end to end, but done in separate sketches, then the resulting surface bodies would be separate bodies; the second body would not be automatically knit to the first one as happens with solid features. This is an important quality of surfaces to keep in mind. If you create surfaces in different features and want them knitted into a single body, then you will have to do that manually.

FIGURE 27.3

The Extruded Surface PropertyManager

Revolved Surface

The Revolved Surface functions like its solid counterpart, right down to the rules for how it handles entities that are touching the axis of revolution; nothing can cross the axis. A single sketch entity is allowed to touch it at a single point, but multiple sketch entities cannot touch it at the same point.

Swept Surface

Swept surfaces work much like their solid counterpart, and the sketch rules and available entities are the same. The main difference here is going to be that swept surfaces usually use an open contour for the profile, while swept solids use closed contours.

Lofted Surface

The main difference between lofted surfaces and lofted solids is that the surfaces can use edges and curve features to loft, rather than simply sketches and faces.

Boundary Surface

The Boundary Surface feature is new to SolidWorks 2007. It most resembles a loft, but also has elements of the fill surface. It is limited to a four-sided patch, and requires you to select edges or sketch elements in two different directions, directly relating to the NURBS scheme that was discussed earlier in this chapter. This feature works with only one set of edges selected.

If several edge or sketch segments combine to form one side of a direction, then you must use the SelectionManager to form the edge segments into a group. This works like the former Smart Selection, but the SelectionManager is somewhat better.

The interface for the Boundary Surface is shown in Figure 27.4.

FIGURE 27.4

The Boundary Surface PropertyManager

I find it difficult to feel enthusiastic about this feature, especially considering that the Fill feature works so much better. The interface is busy (a cacophony of colors), the selection sets cannot be selected with a single loop, it is limited to four-sided patches, the feature delivers bewildering error messages, and, most of all, it often does not work in situations where the Fill feature works far more quickly and easily.

The types of models where you end up using the Boundary Surface are highly curvy models that are modeled mainly with surface features, and require a four-sided patch.

Still, I expect to see this feature improve in future releases. I have run into one situation where Boundary Surface created a better-looking patch than any other feature that does roughly the same thing when analyzed with the various tools for evaluation such as Deviation Analysis and Zebra Stripes. The main advantage of Boundary Surface over Loft is that Boundary Surface (in theory) can apply a Curvature boundary condition all the way around, while Loft cannot apply curvature on the guide curves. Fill surfaces also can apply a Curvature boundary condition.

For this release, if Loft cannot do what you need it to, then try Fill first, with Boundary Surface as a last resort before moving on to more drastic workarounds.

Offset Surface

The Offset Surface has no solid feature counterpart, but it does in 3D what the Offset Sketch function does in 2D; it may also fail for the same reasons. For example, if you offset a .25-inch radius arc by .3 inches to the inside, it fails because it cannot be offset up to or past a zero radius. The same is true of offsetting surfaces. Complex surfaces do not have a constant curvature, but are more like a spline in having a constantly changing curvature. If the offset is going in the direction of decreasing radius, and is more than the minimum radius on the face or faces being offset, then the Offset Surface feature will fail.

One of the ways to troubleshoot a failing Offset Surface is to use the Check tool to check for minimum radius. Remember that minimum radius is only a problem if the curvature is in the same direction as the offset. If a small radius will increase when it is offset, then that small radius is not the problem. The problem comes from the other direction where you are offsetting to the inside of a small radius.

Unlike the Sketch Offset function — and as was shown in Chapter 26 — you can offset surfaces by a zero distance. This is usually done to copy either solid or surface faces to a new surface body. Zero-distance offset and Knit are sometimes used interchangeably, although Knit causes a problem if you are selecting a surface body that is composed of a single face. Knit assumes that you are trying to knit one body to another, and so, by default, it selects the body, and then fails with the message that you cannot knit a body to itself.

Knit does have two functions that Sketch Offset does not. One of these is the option to create a solid from the knit body if it forms a closed body. The second option is somewhat more obscure, offering the ability to select all faces on one side of a Radiate surface. This option is discussed in more depth later in this chapter in the Knit Surface section.

For at least one common situation Knit does not work, but Sketch Offset often requires that you actually set the offset distance to zero. However, with a zero-distance offset, you can change your mind later if you want to, changing the number from zero to something else. With Knit, you do not have this option.

When talking about copying surface bodies, you must also consider the Move/Copy Bodies feature, which is described in Chapter 26. When simply copying a body without also moving it, this feature issues a warning that asks whether you really intend to copy the body without moving it. This is an annoying message. Also, the Move/Copy Bodies feature does not enable you to copy only a part of a body (selected faces) or to merge multiple bodies into one like the Knit and Sketch Offset features.

All things considered, I recommend using the zero-distance Sketch Offset feature to copy bodies or parts of bodies unless your goal is to immediately make a solid out of it (in which case you should use the Knit feature) or when using a Radiated surface (typically in a mold-building application).

Radiate Surface

The Radiate Surface is not one of the more commonly used surface features. It has been largely superseded by the Ruled Surface. This is because Ruled Surface does the same sort of thing that Radiate Surface does, as well as a lot more, and is also more reliable. Radiate works from an edge selection, a reference plane, and a distance. The newly created surface is perpendicular to the selected edge, parallel to the selected plane, and the set distance wide. It is probably most commonly used in creating molds or other net shape tooling such as dies for stamping and forging, blanks for thermoforming, and so on.

Figure 27.5 shows the PropertyManager and selection for creating a Radiate Surface.

FIGURE 27.5

The Radiate Surface PropertyManager

The Radiate Surface feature does not give you a preview of the finished surface, only the small arrows that indicate the direction in which the surface will radiate. At times, you may need to switch the arrows to the other side, which you can do by using the arrow button next to the plane selection.

When creating a Radiate Surface, the use of a loop in the edge selection always causes an error, because the feature only uses the initial edge that was selected for the loop. As long as individual edges are listed in the selection box, you should be okay.

The one application where the Radiate Surface has a very interesting usage is when you combine it with the Knit function, as mentioned earlier. Figure 27.6 shows a part surrounded by a Radiate Surface in which the Knit feature is being used to select all of the faces to one side of the radiated surface. The second smaller selection box in the PropertyManager that contains Face<1> is called a *seed face* and causes the Knit to automatically select all the faces on the same side of the model as the selected seed face. The requirement here is that the Radiate goes completely around the model and separates the faces into faces on one side of the Radiate and faces on the other side of the Radiate. The use of the Radiate with the Seed Face selection is extremely useful for mold creation.

FIGURE 27.6

Using Radiate Surface with Knit

Seed face selection

Radiated surface selected

Knit Surface

 The Knit Surface functionality has been discussed in the terminology section and also in the Radiate Surface section.

The one function that remains is the Try To Form Solid option. In previous versions, when this option was turned on, SolidWorks did not notify you if it did not work. If the selection could not be knit into a solid, then it would simply turn off the option. You would have to look into the bodies folder to see if it was turned into a solid or remained as a surface. In SolidWorks 2007, this problem has been fixed, and failure to knit a solid results in an error (as it should). To fix the error, you can fix the model, fix the selection, or turn off the option.

You can also make a solid from a surface using two other functions. The Fill Surface has an option to merge the fill with a solid or to knit it into a surface body; if the knit surface body is closed, then it gives you the option to make it a solid. This is very nice, complete interface design, with options that save you many steps. The Fill Surface feature is described in more detail later in this chapter.

The other function that also creates a solid from a surface is the Thicken feature. If a surface body that encloses a volume is selected, then an option, Create Solid From Enclosed Volume, appears on the Thicken PropertyManager, as shown in Figure 27.7. You can access the Thicken feature from the menus at Insert ⇨ Boss/Base ⇨ Thicken.

FIGURE 27.7

The Thicken PropertyManager

Planar Surface

Planar surfaces can be created quickly, and are useful in many situations, not just for surfacing work. Because they are by definition *planar*, you can use them to sketch on and for other purposes that you may use a plane for, such as mirroring. Further, you can create a planar surface in a way that many users have long wanted to use, by selecting two co-planar edges or sketch lines.

However, more commonly, planar surfaces are created from a closed sketch such as a rectangle. You can create multiple planar surfaces at once, and the surfaces do not need to all be on the same plane or even parallel. This is commonly done to close up holes in a surface model, such as at the bottom of cylindrical bosses on a plastic part, using a planar circular edge. A good example of this is the bike frame part in the material for Chapter 27 on the CD-ROM, named Chapter 27 – bike frame.SLDPRT.

Remember that a planar surface was used in Chapter 26 with the Split feature to split the leg off of an imported part. This was more effective than a sketch or a plane because the split was limited to the bounds of the planar surface, and not infinite like the sketch or the plane.

The planar surface does not knit itself into the rest of the surface bodies around it automatically, and so you have to use the Knit feature to do this.

Extend Surface

 The Extend Surface feature functions much in the same way that the Extend function works in sketches. Figure 27.8 shows the PropertyManager interface and an example of the feature at work.

FIGURE 27.8

The Extend Surface PropertyManager

The only item here that requires explanation is the Extension Type panel. The Same Surface option means that the extended surface will simply be extrapolated in the selected direction. A planar surface is the easiest to extend because it can go on indefinitely without running into problems. A cylindrical surface can only be extended until it runs into itself. Complex lofted or swept surfaces are often difficult to extend. Extrapolating a complex surface is not easy to do, and often results in self-intersecting faces, which causes the feature to fail.

When the Same Surface setting works, it creates a nice result because it does not create an edge where the extension begins; it smoothly extends the existing face.

The Linear option is more reliable than the Same Surface option because it starts tangent to the existing surface and keeps going in that direction, working much like a Ruled surface, which is covered later in this chapter. This option creates an edge at the starting point of the new geometry.

Trim Surface

The Trim Surface feature is described briefly earlier in this chapter, but it warrants a more complete description here. Surfaces can be trimmed by three different types of entities:

- Sketches
- Planes
- Other surfaces

When you use surface bodies to trim one another, you must select one of two options: Standard or Mutual Trim. The Standard option causes one surface to act as the Trim tool and the other surface to be trimmed by the Trim tool. When you select the Mutual Trim option, both surfaces act as the Trim tool, and both surfaces are trimmed.

For an example of trimmed surfaces, open the mouse example from Chapter 26 and step through the tree. This shows examples of a couple of types of trimmed surfaces, as well as extended surfaces and others.

Fill Surface

The Fill Surface is one of my favorite tools in SolidWorks. I often refer to it as the "magic wand" because it is sometimes amazing what it can do. It is alternately referred to as either Fill or Filled, depending on where the reference is made. You will find it listed as both in the SolidWorks interface.

The Fill Surface is intended to fill in gaps in surface bodies. It can do this either smoothly or by leaving sharp corners. You can use constraint curves to drive the shape of the fill between the existing boundaries. It can even knit a surface body together into a solid, all in one step. Beyond this, you can use the Fill Surface directly on solid models and integrate it directly into the solid automatically (much like the Replace Face function which is described later in this chapter).

Several rather complex examples of the Fill Surface are found in the bike frame example that was originally shown in Chapter 12. One of these fills is shown in Figure 27.9.

The first thing you should notice about the Fill Surface is that it is creating an oversized, four-sided patch and trimming it to fit into the available space. This is one of the reasons why I consider this to be such a magical tool. The four-sided patch referred to earlier in the section on NURBS is shown very clearly in this feature preview. Also, the trimmed surface concept is illustrated nicely by this feature. Not surprisingly, if you Untrim the fill surface, then you return to the surface that is previewed here. In this one function, SolidWorks gives us some useful insight about what is going on behind the scenes.

FIGURE 27.9

The Fill Surface PropertyManager and the results of applying it

When using the Fill Surface, it is best to have a patch completely bounded by other surfaces, as shown in Figure 27.9. Fill Surface can work with a boundary that is not enclosed, but it works better with a closed boundary.

You can set boundary conditions as Contact, Tangent, or Curvature. Contact simply means that the faces touch at an edge. Tangent means that the slopes of the faces on either side of the edge match at all points along the edge. Curvature means curvature continuous (or C2), where the fill surface matches not only tangency, but also the curvature of the face on the other side of the boundary edge. This results in a smoother transition than a transition that is simply tangent.

When you select the Optimize Surface option, SolidWorks tries to fit the four-sided patch into the boundary. Notice that on this part, even though the Optimize Surface option is on, it is clearly being ignored because the boundary is a six-sided gap, and cannot be patched smoothly with a four-sided patch. It is not necessarily an improvement to make a fill surface optimized, even when it works.

Constraint curves can influence the shape of the fill surface. An example of this is shown in Figure 27.10. The construction splines shown on the faces of the part were created by the Intersection Curve tool, and enabled the spline used for the constraint curve to be made tangent to the surface.

FIGURE 27.10

The Fill Surface feature with constraint curves

Mid-surface

 The Mid-surface feature is not used very often. It is intended to be used on parallel faces of a solid. If the faces have opposing draft (such that a wall is wider at the bottom than at the top), then the Mid-surface will not work. It works on linear walls and cylindrical walls, but not on elliptical or spline-based shapes. The PropertyManager for the Mid-surface is shown in Figure 27.11.

The intended application for this feature is to create a model for mid-plane type stress analysis using 2D elements.

Similar to the Planar Surface, you can also use the Mid-surface to create a surface that can be used like a plane. No plane type can create a symmetrical plane, but using a Mid-Surface, you can create a symmetrical planar surface between parallel walls.

FIGURE 27.11

The Mid-surface PropertyManager

Replace Face

 The Replace Face feature does not create new surface geometry, but it does integrate surface geometry into the solid. It replaces selected faces of a solid with a selected surface body. Replace Face is one of the few tools that can add and remove material at the same time with a single feature.

If you were to manually perform the functions that are done by Replace Face, then you would start by deleting several faces of the solid, then extending faces, and then trimming surface bodies, and finish by knitting all the trimmed and extended faces back into a single solid body.

This is a very powerful and useful tool, although it is difficult to tell which situations it will work in. Figure 27.12 shows a part before and after a Replace Face feature has been added. The surface used to replace the flat face of the solid has been turned transparent. The first selection box is for the solid face or faces, and the second selection box is for the surface body. The tool tips for each of the boxes are Target Faces For Replacement and Replacement Surface(s), which seem a little ambiguous. I like to think of them as Old (top) and New (bottom).

FIGURE 27.12

Using Replace Face

Untrim Surface

 The Untrim Surface is discussed in the terminology section of this chapter. You can use it either selectively on edges or on the entire surface body.

Parting Surface

The Parting Surface is part of the SolidWorks Mold Tools. The Mold Tools are beyond the scope of this book.

Ruled Surface

Ruled surfaces are discussed in general in the section on terminology. Here I discuss the topic in more detail, and specifically with regard to the SolidWorks interface for creating Ruled surfaces.

The Ruled Surface feature in SolidWorks is one of those features that you may never have missed until you see it in action. It is extremely useful for constructing faces with draft, extending faces tangent to a direction, making Radiate surface types, building molds, and many other applications.

Figure 27.13 shows the PropertyManager interface for the Ruled Surface.

FIGURE 27.13

The Ruled Surface PropertyManager interface

The Ruled Surface works from the edge of a solid or surface body. The feature has five basic types of operation that it can perform:

- Tangent to Surface
- Normal to Surface
- Tapered to Vector
- Perpendicular to Vector
- Sweep

The part in Figure 27.13 was created with a five-degree taper at the edge where the Ruled surface has been created. The Tangent to Surface setting is self-explanatory. The Alternate Face option would be available if the base shape had been a solid, with a face filling the big elliptical hole. This would make the ruled surface tangent to the bottom face instead of the side.

Using the Normal to Surface setting, because the surface is lofted with a five-degree draft angle at the big end, making a Ruled surface that is normal to the surface means that it tilts up five degrees from the horizontal. Be careful of using this setting because it looks close to what you may be hoping that it is, but it is slightly off. One of the other options may be a better choice, depending on what you are looking for.

The Tapered to Vector setting needs a plane or axis selection to establish a direction, and then the Ruled surface is created from that reference at the angle that you set. With a combination of the Alternate Side button and the arrow direction toggle button next to the plane selection, you can adjust the cone created by this setting. The interface to make the changes is not exactly clear unless you use this function often, but it does work.

The Perpendicular to Vector setting is a better option than the Normal to Surface setting when the surface has been created with some sort of built-in draft angle. This is also the setting that looks most like the Radiate Surface feature, although it works much better than Radiate Surface.

The Sweep setting makes a face that is perpendicular to the surface created by Perpendicular to Vector. It is as if a straight line were swept around the edge. This is actually a great way to offset an edge or 3D sketch, by using the edge of the surface as the offset of the original.

The Ruled Surface is useful in many ways, including for construction geometry, reference geometry, draft for complex surfaces, and more. I discuss it in the next section of this chapter, which concerns techniques and applications where these tools are useful.

Using Surfacing Techniques

I am not pretending that this section can even begin to do justice to the topic of surfacing techniques. I can give you a few basic ideas, but you will find as many surfacing techniques as you will find surfacing designers. The topic for this section could be the topic for an entire book on its own.

Instead, what I show here are a few broad categories of techniques that you can apply to particular situations.

Up to Surface/Up to Body

Some situations seem to require elaborate workarounds until you think of doing them with a combination of solid and surface features, such as the part shown in Figure 27.14. This geometry could be made with solids, but it would be more difficult. In this case, a surface is revolved, representing the shape at the bottom of the hole, and the cut is extruded up to it.

CROSS-REF Chapter 5 contains more information on end conditions such as Up To Surface and Up To Body.

FIGURE 27.14

Using the Up to Body setting

Another familiar situation is when you have a feature to place and you want to use an Offset from Surface end condition, but the feature spans two faces. In that situation, you can knit the necessary faces together (or use offset), and then extrude offset from that surface body.

TIP Using Up to or Offset from Body rather than Face often avoids the common error message, "The end face cannot terminate the extruded feature," especially if the feature that is extruded spans more than one face.

Figure 27.15 shows a part using an offset surface to extrude text up to where the text spans more than a single surface. This is a very common application, even if it is not text that is being extruded. The part that was used in Figure 27.15 is on the CD-ROM in the materials for Chapter 26, and is called Chapter 26 – Up To Body.SLDPRT.

FIGURE 27.15

Extruding text

Cut With Surface

Sometimes you may need to make a cut that is more complex than what a simple extrude can do. For example, the cut may need to have shape in multiple directions. You could make the cut with multiple cut features, or even with a surface. Figure 27.16 shows a part that is cut with a surface.

FIGURE 27.16

Using the Cut With Surface feature on a part

When cutting with a surface, the edges of the surface must be outside of the body that is being cut. With sketches, it is advisable to have more sketch than you need so that you are not trying to cut line-on-line. The same applies to cutting with a surface, where it is advisable to have more surface than you need to make the cut.

Replace Face

The Replace Face feature can be used on imported or native geometry. You can use it to add or remove material from a part. When it adds material, it must be able to extend faces adjacent to those that are being replaced, which can be a limitation. A face or faces do not need to be replaced with the same kind or same number of faces, but the entire face that is being replaced must be removed. If you only want to replace a part of a face, then you can use a Split line to scribe the face, and then replace the part you want.

Figure 27.17 shows that the multiple faces of the letter U on this part have been replaced with a surface from an inserted part. Replace Face is a fantastic tool that you can use in a number of situations, although it is a little particular sometimes and you cannot always predict when it will or will not work.

FIGURE 27.17

Using Replace Face

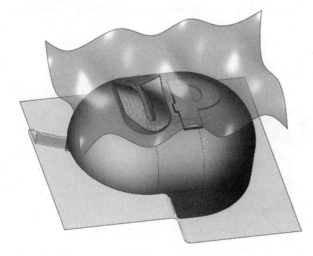

Fill Surface in action

The Fill Surface is by far the most complete surface function in SolidWorks. It was a good tool before, but has become even better. With SolidWorks 2007, this feature is even more predictable, meaning that:

- It works more often.
- It does what you asked it to do more often.
- It includes more options than before.

NOTE The Fill Surface is an advanced surfacing function. Sometimes, when talking about advanced surfacing functions, or indeed any software function, users have a tendency to sound a little cynical. This is because the tool is often expected to work on very complex geometry. It is not always the software's fault when it cannot perform a particular task, or does not do what you imagine you want it to do. Sometimes, the tool is simply not meant to perform certain tasks, there may be an unseen flaw in the geometry that prevents it from working, or the user does not understand the settings completely. The more complex the work, the more frequently you need to find workarounds to get something done. Avoiding problems does not make them go away, and it does not help you as a user to know how to handle them when they happen. In this book, I have chosen to take a realistic look at most of the features, and if there are problems, then I tell you.

Figure 27.18 shows the Fill Surface blending an intersection between tubes. The image to the left shows the before condition with the tubes coming together at an edge. The center image shows the edge trimmed out using the Trim feature, and the right image shows the hole blended over by the Fill Surface feature.

FIGURE 27.18

Blending with the Fill Surface

In Figure 27.19, a solid starts with a Split line on the surface. A sketch is then added, and a fill surface is created using the sketch as a constraint and the Split line as the boundary. The Merge Result option in the Fill PropertyManager has a different significance than it does in a solid feature PropertyManager, but the end result is the same. Remember that this is a surface function, and if it does not merge, then it is left as a surface feature.

FIGURE 27.19

The Fill PropertyManager for merging a fill surface directly into a solid

Notice that this fill is also adding and removing material at the same time. If you had to go through these steps manually, then you would use the Replace Face feature to integrate the surface into the solid.

Memory surface

A *memory surface* is not another new type of feature that you can select from the menu or a toolbar; it is just the name that I gave to a technique that I use from time to time. A memory surface is just a Knit or Offset surface that is made at one point in the feature tree when a particular face is whole, and reused later when the face has been broken up, but you still need to reference the entire original face. An example of this technique is shown in Figure 27.20. In this case, extra material is created around the opening, and a surface that was created in a Rollback state is used to remove it.

FIGURE 27.20

Using the memory surfaces technique to cut away unwanted geometry

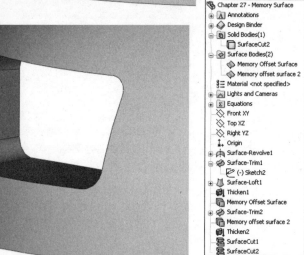

Molds

The Mold Tools functionality in SolidWorks depends heavily on surfacing. Unfortunately, the most important feature in the Mold Tools arsenal, Parting Surface, only gives acceptable results for planar parting lines. The Shutoff Surfaces are also only good for planar shutoffs. The rest of the Mold Tools procedure works acceptably, but with these two major components not being used, it leaves you with a lot of manual modeling to do.

The steps that follow are a very brief overview of one technique that you can use to create mold splits in SolidWorks without using the Mold Tools functionality.

The first step is usually a draft analysis. This enables you to correctly place the parting surface between the faces that are pulling from opposite directions. It is also important to scale the plastic part before creating the mold block inserts to compensate for plastic shrinkage.

You can create the parting surface in several ways, by extruding a surface, or by using Radiate or Ruled surface. If you use one of these last two methods, be sure to carefully monitor changes in the level of the parting line, because the surface may go in the wrong direction, and this may be difficult to see. This is what causes problems for the SolidWorks Mold Tools.

Once you create the parting surface, select all of the faces on one side of the part. It does not matter much whether it is the cavity or core side; select whichever is easier. You can do this by orienting the part into a top or bottom view, and window-selecting the faces. Knit them together with the parting surface.

Close off any pass-throughs (shutoffs) in the part with a surface. For complex shutoffs, this may take some time and effort. Simple shutoffs can be done with a Delete Hole, Planar Surface, or Fill Surface. Knit any shutoffs into the surface body.

The rest of this process can be done either in the context of an assembly or as a multibody arrangement. Either way, the parts will likely need to be shown as individual part files in the end, and so an assembly may be a better choice (although SolidWorks Mold Tools use the multibody approach, and so the rest of this short technique description also uses the multibody approach).

Make a block around the part representing the mold insert blocks. Center the block in the way that you want the part cavity to be centered in the actual mold insert block. Make sure that the Merge option is turned off when the block is created.

Use the knitted-together parting surface with the Split feature to split the block in two. At this point, one side of the split should be correct, and the other should still contain the plastic part impression. Use the Combine feature with the Subtract option to remove the plastic part from the second block.

This technique is used on the part shown in Figure 27.21. Again, I realize that this is a very simple part and does not account for the normal complexities that are found in most molded parts. However, it does demonstrate the beginning of the technique that may be extended to include more complex mold features. If you are interested in this technique, you can open the part from the CD-ROM in the Chapter 27 folder. The filename is Chapter 27 – Mold.SLDPRT.

FIGURE 27.21

Creating mold insert blocks

Tutorial

This is another chapter that contains many important ideas, and yet there is only so much space for tutorials. The best way to learn is to experiment. I recommend that you closely follow the tutorial steps once, and then, when you understand the concepts involved, that you can go back and experiment.

Using Cut With Surface

Follow these steps to gain some experience with the Cut With Surface feature:

1. Start by creating a new part and drawing a rectangle centered on the Origin, about 4 inches by 6 inches.

2. Extrude the rectangle Mid-plane, by 2 inches.

3. From the Surface toolbar, select Lofted Surface, and select one 4-inch edge as a loft profile. Then select a second 4-inch edge diagonal from the first one. This is shown in Figure 27.22.

FIGURE 27.22

Lofting a surface from the edges of a solid

Select for lofted surface

4. Expand the Start/End Constraints panel, and set both ends to use the Direction Vector setting, selecting the plane that is in the middle of the long direction in each case. In the part shown, the Right plane is used. Click OK to accept the feature.

5. From the menus, click Insert ➪ Cut ➪ With Surface. Select the surface from the flyout FeatureManager, and toggle the arrow direction so that the top is cut off. (The arrow points to the side that is cut off.)

Using Offset Surface

Follow these steps to gain some experience with the Offset Surface:

1. Open the part from the CD-ROM called Chapter 27 – Offset Tutorial.SLDPRT.

2. Right-click a curved face of the part and click Select Tangency in the menu.

3. From the Surfaces toolbar, click Offset Surface, and set the surface to offset to the outside of the part by .060 inches. You can tell when the surface is offsetting to the outside when the transparent preview appears. If you do not see the transparent preview, then toggle the Flip Offset Direction arrow button. Click OK to accept the feature when you are satisfied.

4. Look in the Surface Bodies folder at the top of the FeatureManager tree, expand the folder, and select the offset surface. Then use the Edit Color toolbar button to change the transparency of the surface body to about .75. This is done so that you can see the part underneath the surface, without mistaking the surface for the actual part.

> **TIP**
>
> It is a common practice to change surface colors to something that contrasts with the part color. I usually use a color like yellow, which suggests temporary status or construction. Some users take this a step further, and set the template colors for surface types at Tools, Options, Document Properties, Colors. These settings do not always work; in some cases, they turn surface features to a different color, and in other situations, they do not.

> **CAUTION**
>
> When changing transparency, SolidWorks automatically also changes the color to whatever the default color is. Unfortunately, the default color is not the same as the part color. This is one of those annoyances for which it is worth sending in an enhancement request.

5. Select Sketch2, and select Extruded Boss/Base from the Features toolbar. Do not mistake the extruded surface for an extruded solid. Set the end condition to Up To Surface, activate the Face/Plane selection box, and select the transparent offset surface. The result is shown in Figure 27.23.

FIGURE 27.23

Extruding with the Up To Surface setting

790

TIP It is preferable to select the surface from the Surface Bodies folder, rather than the feature list or the graphics window. In this case, you want to extrude up to a body. If you make the selection from the feature list, then you are likely to select a feature (which is okay in this situation, but not in all situations). If you make the selection from the graphics window, then the selection is likely to be interpreted as a face. It is best to be as explicit as possible when making selections because SolidWorks may interpret your selection literally.

In this case, it is probably a better idea to use Up To Body for the end condition than Up To Surface, because the goal is really to use the surface body as the end of the feature.

6. To invert the lettering so that it sits below the surface rather than above the surface, you can make a few simple changes. First, edit the offset surface feature and flip the direction of the offset so that the surface is now inside the solid rather than outside the solid. You will not be able to see it unless the solid is either transparent or in wireframe mode.

7. Next, delete the extrude that you created to extrude the text. There is no way to change an extrude into a cut directly.

8. Recreate the extrude as an extruded cut. Use the From settings at the top of the PropertyManager window. The settings and results are shown in Figure 27.24.

FIGURE 27.24

An extruded cut

Using Fill Surface blend

Sometimes fillets do not meet your needs. Blends, such as those shown in the bike frame example, are smoother and can blend just about anything. However, the technique is not exactly straightforward. Follow these steps to gain familiarity with this technique:

1. Open the part from the CD-ROM for Chapter 27 called Chapter 27 – Blends.SLDPRT.

2. Draw a square 2 inches on a side, and centered on the Origin.

3. Use the Split Entities tool found on the Sketch toolbar or through the menus at Tools ➪ Sketch Tools ➪ Split Entities. Divide each line of the rectangle into three pieces, with the two outer pieces of each line being .6 inches (use an Equal sketch relation). The sketch should be fully defined when you are done. This arrangement is shown in Figure 27.25. This is done because the edges of the tubes need to be broken into sections.

FIGURE 27.25

Using split entities to split lines

4. Use Delete Face to delete the ends of the four tubes. Set the option to Delete, not the default option of Delete And Patch. This converts the solid into a surface body.

5. Use the sketch with the split entities to trim out the center section of the tubes, keeping the outer section, and leaving four surface bodies. This leaves each tube end, where they have been trimmed, divided into four segments, as shown in Figure 27.26.

FIGURE 27.26

Split ends after trimming

6. Initiate the Lofted Surface feature, and select the nearest edge segments from adjacent tubes. If the loft preview twists, then use the light-blue handles to straighten it out, or deselect and reselect one of the edges in approximately the same location as the other edge was selected. Expand the End Conditions panel and set each edge to use the Curvature setting. You may adjust the End Tangent Length option if you want, but keep in mind that this may make the part asymmetrical.

7. Create lofted surfaces all the way around the part, linking all of the tubes. Figure 27.27 shows the part with three of the lofts already completed, and the last one in progress.

FIGURE 27.27

Adding lofted surfaces

8. Start a Planar Surface feature, and select the open ends of each tube where the faces were deleted in step 4.

> **NOTE**   Not all features allow you to operate from multiple bodies, but the Loft and Planar Surface features do. Features such as Fillet and Draft restrict you to creating features that are associated with one body at a time.

9. Start a Knit Surface feature, and Shift-select all of the bodies in the Surface Bodies folder (select the first body in the list and Shift-select the last body). When you click OK to accept the feature, notice that the number of surface bodies changes to one. Selecting bodies in this way is much faster for large numbers of bodies than selecting them one at a time from the graphics window.

> **NOTE**   Notice that the open edges of the surface body are shown in a different color. At this point, there are two open edges around the holes at the intersection of the tubes.

10. This is a situation that the Fill Surface is really meant for. In fact, this technique was created specifically to take advantage of the Fill Surface capabilities. Right-click any of the open edges and click Select Open Loop. Initiate the Fill Surface. Change the Edge Setting option to Tangent, and make sure that the Apply To All Edges option is on. Turn the Merge Result option on, but leave the Try To Form Solid option off. The model at this point is shown in Figure 27.28, along with the PropertyManager settings that are used.

> **NOTE**   The Optimize Surface option is ignored for this part because the opening is eight-sided rather than four-sided.

11. Click OK to accept the feature.

12. Start another fill surface, turning the part over to use the same selection on the back and the same settings as the first fill; however, on this one, also use the Try To Form Solid option. Click OK when the selections and settings are complete.

13. For the last feature, apply a Shell feature, selecting the flat ends of the tubes, and shelling to .100 inches. The final state of the model is shown in Figure 27.29.

FIGURE 27.28

Creating a fill surface patch

FIGURE 27.29

The finished model

Summary

Surface functions have a wide range of uses other than for complex shape parts, but thinking about your models in terms of surface features requires a slightly different approach. Becoming comfortable with the terminology, and the similarities and differences between solids and surfaces, is the first step toward embracing surfacing tools for everyday work.

Of course, I would be remiss if I did not mention some of the complex tools, of which Loft and Fill are certainly the most useful. Whether or not you use the Mold Tools techniques, surface modeling figures into the modeling of any mold, die, cast, or other net shape type application.

Chapter 28

Master Model Techniques

The term *master model* may be used in several different ways. In this book, it is used to refer to a technique where an entire assembly is laid out or has its major faces constructed by a single part, and that part is then placed into other files from which the individual parts are created. Master model techniques are usually used in situations that are beyond the ability of in-context design to deal with, or where in-context design is cumbersome.

You can use in-context techniques with a master model concept, especially when you use the skeleton concepts discussed in Chapter 16. These concepts are used primarily to centralize driving geometry, minimize errors, and prevent circular references.

As an example of a multibody master model technique, a computer mouse is a complex shape, and the shape flows smoothly between parts. This is not conducive to in-context design, but works perfectly as a multibody master model. In-context design works best for replicating the locations of edges and holes, not the flow of a face. The multibody master model technique entails building the entire mouse as a single part, and then splitting it up into bodies that are in turn sent to different part files to have the detail features added.

Master model techniques are a product of four separate features or functions that have some similarities and some differences, and rely heavily on your knowledge of multiple bodies and surface functions. The four features are Split, Save Bodies, Insert Part, and Insert Into New Part. In turn, these four features can be categorized into Push and Pull type functions.

As an example of master model technique, consider the mouse model shown in Figure 28.1 which should be familiar by now. The overall shape is modeled as a single part, and is split into several bodies using multibody methods. Then, using these master model techniques, the individual bodies are used to create individual part files where detail features are added.

FIGURE 28.1

A mouse master model

Using Pull Functions

Pull functions are initiated from the child document and pull data from the master model (parent document) into the child. These functions insert a feature into the child that points to the parent, but do not insert a feature into the parent that points to the child.

The features that fall into this category are Insert Part and Insert Into New Part.

Insert Part

Insert Part is initiated from the child document, through the menus at Insert ⇨ Part or from the Features toolbar using the Insert Part button (which may not be on your toolbar by default). As the name suggests, this feature pulls one part into another. All of the solid bodies in the inserted model are brought forward by default, with the option to also bring forward all surface bodies, planes, or axes. The Insert Part PropertyManager interface is shown in Figure 28.2.

FIGURE 28.2

The Insert Part PropertyManager

Figure 28.3 shows the FeatureManager of a part where the first feature is an Insert Part feature. All of the solid bodies are listed both under the normal Solid Bodies folder, and also under a second Solid Bodies folder under the inserted part icon. Other inserted items, such as surface bodies, planes, and axes, are also listed under the inserted part icon.

FIGURE 28.3

The FeatureManager showing items inserted with an inserted part

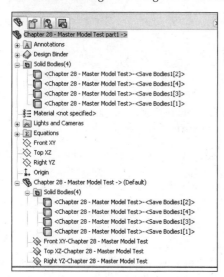

You cannot be selective about which bodies are pulled forward, but you can delete unwanted bodies once they have all been brought in. You can set configurations of the parent document in the External References dialog box, which is available through the RMB menu of the feature that is

inserted into the child document FeatureManager. The External References dialog box is shown in Figure 28.4. If the overhead of bringing many bodies forward only to be deleted is an issue for you, then you can use parent part configurations to delete the bodies first; then, from the child using List External References, you can select which configuration to insert.

FIGURE 28.4

The External References dialog box

As the original inserted bodies are modified, and the names change, they are removed from the folder under the inserted part, and only appear in the body folders under the top level.

File management is a real issue with all of these master model functions; in fact, it may not be an exaggeration to say that it is the *biggest* problem that arises with them, although you could say the same thing about overall body management (for example, what happens when the number of bodies increases or decreases, when the bodies are split differently or change names, and so on).

One of the issues caused by not having some sort of a marker in the parent document is that if the parent is renamed, there is no way of knowing whether any children will be affected by the change. Further, a very dangerous situation exists when the child cannot find the parent (because the parent has been renamed or moved), the List External References dialog box cannot help you locate references. At that point, the parent cannot find the child (because of the way the feature works), and the child cannot find the parent (because of a user file management error combined with a bug); as a result, you do not even know where to look to fix the problem unless you just happen to know what went wrong.

Insert Into New Part

Insert Into New Part qualifies as a Pull function because it does not create a feature in the FeatureManager of the parent file, even though it is actually initiated from the parent rather than from the child. This function does not have a drop-down menu location, nor does it have a toolbar button. You can initiate it from the RMB menu from either the Solid or Surface Bodies folders or from the individual bodies within the folders.

This gives Insert Into New Part both advantages and disadvantages over Insert Part. The advantages are that it can *selectively* insert *either* solid or surface bodies, *or even selections of both types*. You can Ctrl-select multiple bodies (solid or surface) to bring only the bodies forward that you need. However, it cannot bring forward planes or axes, or change the selection of what is brought forward after the feature is created. This is definitely a good news/bad news situation, but with this information, you can make a more informed decision about which function to use.

When Insert Into New Part is used to place bodies into a part, the bodies are not shown in the same way that the Insert Part function shows them. Figure 28.5 shows that the Stock feature symbols are used rather than the Inserted Part symbol since individual bodies are being placed rather than entire parts.

FIGURE 28.5

Bodies placed in a part using Insert Into New Part

Using Push Functions

Push functions are initiated from the master model (parent document) and push data from the parent part out to a child part. The parent part is the master model, and the child part is the detail part file. A feature in the tree of the parent identifies the point at which the model is pushed out to the child, and the child file can be found from the parent.

The first feature in the child part is a Stock feature, and contains a reference back to the parent, so that the parent can be found from the child. The features that fall into this category are Split and Save Bodies.

Split feature

It has already been mentioned that the Split feature has three functions, two of which are plainly visible, and one that is hidden. The Split PropertyManager is shown in Figure 28.6.

FIGURE 28.6

The Split PropertyManager

Split

The primary function of the Split feature is to split a single body into multiple bodies. This can be done with sketches, planes, or surface bodies, and is discussed in depth in Chapter 26.

Save All Bodies

There is not really an official name for this function, and so the name of the button, Save All Bodies, will do for our purposes. The Split feature can save both the pre-existing bodies and any bodies that result from the split as individual part files, using the Stock feature as the initial feature in the part.

The ability to save bodies out from the Split feature is a very convenient option, but there are some major drawbacks to working this way. If the number of bodies changes, or the method of creating those bodies changes, and the Split feature is edited, then the list of names of all of the files being saved to is reset. If the same names are entered into the PropertyManager, then the existing files are overwritten when you click the green check mark icon. This is not a problem if the overwritten parts do not have any dependent features within the part. However, it is a huge problem if there are dependent features. Dependent features are part of the end goal of using the Save All Bodies function, saving out the unfinished bodies, and finishing them with additional dependent features in their own files.

Fortunately, there is a workaround. It is clumsy, but so is redoing a lot of modeling work. The workaround involves temporarily moving the affected files to another folder before redefining the files in the Split feature's Save All Bodies function, and then moving the files back to overwrite the overwritten files. This retains all of the dependent features, and allows the Split feature to update.

Create Assembly

After the Split feature has been created and you have saved bodies out of the Split feature, the RMB menu displays an option, Create Assembly, which puts all of the parts created from the bodies in the original part back together in the correct positions. Parts within the assemblies created this way are fixed in space with the same relationship to the assembly origin that they originally had as bodies to the part origin.

Save Bodies

The Save Bodies feature is another function in SolidWorks that does not have a menu location, or toolbar button, but is accessed only from the RMB menu from the bodies folders. Save Bodies works similarly to giving path and filename information in the Resulting Bodies selection box of the Split feature. However, Save Bodies enables you to create an assembly right in the PropertyManager for the feature, rather than as a hidden feature with no record of the assembly name created by the feature. The PropertyManager for Save Bodies is shown in Figure 28.7.

FIGURE 28.7

The Save Bodies PropertyManager

Tutorial: Working with Master Model Techniques

Some of the concepts presented in this chapter may not make much sense until you see them applied to a specific situation. The goal of this tutorial is to demonstrate the strengths and weaknesses of the various functions, as well as to give you some practical experience with the file management issues that you will encounter. The mouse multibody part is used by each of the four tools so that you can become familiar with the differences in functionality by using the same starting point for each. To get some experience with these techniques, follow these steps:

Insert Part

To work with the Insert Part function, follow these steps:

1. Make sure that you have access to the material from the CD-ROM for Chapter 28. Create a new part, and insert the part named Chapter 28 – Mouse Base Part.SLDPRT. You can access Insert Part through the menus at Insert ➪ Part. After issuing the command, SolidWorks attaches the part to your cursor and prompts you to specify a location for the

inserted part. Drop the part at the Origin of the child part. There is no need to use the Move dialog box; if it appears, then turn off the option that enables it, and accept the feature. For this part, do not transfer any of the optional items, only the solid bodies.

2. Once the feature is accepted and in the tree, RMB click it and select List External Refs from the menu. The External References dialog box is shown in Figure 28.8, with the list of configurations displayed.

FIGURE 28.8

The External References dialog box

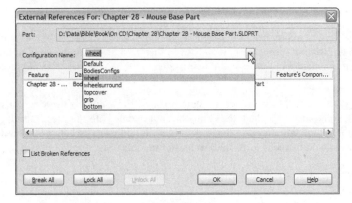

3. Select the Wheel configuration from the list.

4. Save and name the part file in such a way that it has the name of the technique used to create it (Insert Part) and the name of the body that it represents (such as Wheel).

NOTE   A little bit of preparation work has been done on your behalf to make this tutorial flow more smoothly. If you ever choose to do modeling in this way, then you will need to know what this preparation work entails.

In the mouse master model, a separate configuration was made for each body, and in that configuration, a Delete Body feature was created that deleted all of the bodies except one.

The alternative to this approach is to bring all of the bodies into each new part, and use a Delete Body feature in each child part that deletes all but the one body that is needed. The advantage to using configurations is that bringing in a single body theoretically decreases the overhead for the individual part files.

5. Repeat steps 1 through 4 for each of the five bodies in the master model.

6. If the mouse master model (Chapter 28 – Mouse Base Part) is open, then close it. In any of the child parts, the inserted part feature shown in the tree should have the Out Of Context symbol on it (- >?). RMB click the inserted part feature and select Edit In Context, which opens the master model.

   Notice that from the master model, you have no way of knowing where the child parts are or even *if* any child parts exist. Notice also that there is no easy way to create an assembly.

7. Create a new assembly document.

8. Drop all of the individually created parts into the assembly by selecting them in Windows Explorer and dragging them onto the assembly Origin. This is probably the easiest way to create an assembly using the Insert Part feature.

NOTE There is no link from the parent to the child, and so if the child part is renamed, the parent will not lose track of it. However, there is a link from the child to the parent, and so if the parent is renamed without the child being open at the same time, the child loses track of the parent.

If the parent is changed, the child does not update unless the symbol is showing In Context (->). If it is out of context, broken, or locked, the child does not update with the parent. Both documents need to be open at the same time to make the update happen (although they do not both need to be open when the original edit happens to the parent master model).

9. Save and close all of the parts and assemblies.

Insert Into New Part

To work with the Insert Into New Part function, follow these steps:

1. For this feature, start from the master model. Open the part Chapter 28 – Mouse Base Part.SLDPRT. Make sure that the part is set to the Default configuration. If it is set to a different configuration, the insertion of bodies will not go as smoothly as it could.

2. Expand the Solid Bodies folder in the FeatureManager. RMB click the first body in the list (Wheel), and select Insert Into New Part from the menu.

NOTE You could select multiple bodies and even combine solid and surface bodies to insert using this technique.

3. When prompted, name the new part using the same convention used in the previous tutorial, which was to use the name of the technique (Insert Into New Part) and the name of the body. In this part, leave the configuration setting in the External References dialog box to the Default configuration.

4. Repeat steps 1 through 3 for each of the bodies.

5. Right-click the Stock feature in the tree, and select Edit In Context. SolidWorks opens the master model part.

Once again, there is no way back to the child document from the master model using the Insert Into New Part feature.

6. Create a new assembly document and use the same technique from the previous tutorial to put all of the parts in the assembly located from the Origin. Again, no automated assembly creation tool exists for this method.

7. Save all documents and close them.

Split

To work with the Split function, follow these steps:

1. This time, start from a copy of the master model part. The Split feature makes additions to the model, and because you have already created assemblies based on the original, any additional features should be created using a copy of the part rather than the original. Copy it using the Copy and Paste feature in Windows Explorer, and rename the copy as Chapter 28 – Split Tutorial.

 It is best to copy and rename this document before continuing with the rest of the tutorial. Otherwise, you may encounter problems with the file references, from which it is difficult to recover.

2. With the newly copied and renamed document open, initiate the Split feature from Insert ➪ Features ➪ Split.

3. Because the bodies already exist, there is no need for the Trim tools or Cut Part functions in the Split feature, only for the resulting bodies. To save the bodies to individual files, you must give each one a unique name. You can click the Save All Bodies button to automatically name them with generic names. The callout flags have a tendency to be difficult to discern where they are pointing. Once the names are all satisfactory, click OK to accept the feature.

 The Consume Cut Bodies option deletes the bodies of any bodies involved in the Split feature. For most purposes, you should turn this option off.

4. To automatically create an assembly with all of the components located in the proper location, right-click the Split feature in the Master Model FeatureManager, and select Create Assembly. Multiple Split features can be included in this command if bodies have been created by multiple Split features. Use the Browse button to locate and name the assembly. Click OK when you are done. Completing this step opens the assembly that you just named and located.

5. RMB click one of the parts in the assembly to open it. Notice that a Stock feature is used in the tree, and so it is possible to access the parent part and to change the parent part configuration used in the current part. RMB click the Stock feature and select Edit In Context.

6. With the master model open, RMB click the Split feature and select Edit Feature. From here, it is possible to see where each of the child parts is located.

7. If you rename any of the documents, then you should do this either by using SolidWorks Explorer or the Save As command with the other documents open as well. If you want to rename the parent part (master model), then make sure that all of the child parts are open as well (you can easily do this by opening the assembly; although the assembly was created from the master model, there is no direct link between the Split feature and the assembly).

> **NOTE**   If the scheme by which the bodies are split changes in such a way that additional bodies are created, the Split feature may fail and need to be redefined. When this happens, the parts that were previously created will be overwritten. If features of the detail parts have been created within those files, then they will be overwritten as well. As mentioned earlier, the best workaround for this problem is to copy the files with the detail features in them out to another location, allow the Split feature to overwrite the files, and then move the copied files back to the original directory. This essentially overwrites the overwritten files, and all is well again.
>
> You can also try this by rolling back before the final split and splitting another body off.

8. Save and close all of the files before proceeding.

Save Bodies

To work with the Save Bodies function, follow these steps:

1. As before, create a copy of the original master model part and rename the copy Chapter 28 – Save Bodies Tutorial.

2. Open the renamed copy, and RMB click the Solid Bodies folder. Select Save Bodies from the menu. This function does not appear on a drop-down menu or toolbar, although it is slightly different from the other functions that do not appear on a toolbar or drop-down menu (Save Bodies does have its own icon that is used to denote the placeholder feature in the FeatureManager).

3. The Save Bodies PropertyManager is nearly identical to the lower section of the Split PropertyManager. The major addition in the Save Bodies dialog box is that of the Create Assembly function directly within the PropertyManager. The primary benefit of this addition is that it retains the name and path of the assembly in this interface so you can look it up later if necessary, remedying one of the weaknesses in the Split feature.

> **NOTE**   In both the Split/Create Assembly and Save Bodies features, when an assembly is created, SolidWorks may rebuild the tree of the part as many times as you have bodies to save out. This may take some time for a complex model with a lot of bodies.

4. After finishing step 3, you are left in the reconstructed assembly. RMB click one of the parts and select Open Part to open it in its own window. Notice that the Stock feature has again been used to push a single body into the part.

5. RMB click the Stock feature, and select Edit In Context, which takes you back to the master model.

6. Save and close all of the files.

Summary

Each of these four functions has strengths and weaknesses. Because of this, there is no one feature that is clearly superior to the others. Most of the weaknesses have to do with file management, the types of data that they can work with, the ease of creating an assembly, and access to children from the parents. Unfortunately, I cannot offer a single solution that addresses all of the problems and retains each of the strengths.

I look to this area of the software being improved in a future release. If I were responsible for the functionality, I would consolidate the four flawed functions into a single feature that would be primarily used as a Push type master model function. This feature would have the ability to pre-select which bodies, reference geometry, and even sketches would be pushed out to the child part, and it would make every piece of it redefinable without losing existing data.

Part VII

Working with Specialized Functionality

Chapter 29

Using the Base Flange Method for Sheet Metal Parts

Many releases ago, SolidWorks changed the way that the software dealt with sheet metal parts. In the old way, the model was created through normal modeling features, mainly centered around thin feature extrudes, but also including shell features. It did not matter *how* you got the geometry, as long as it had a consistent thickness and the edge faces were sheared perpendicular to the material. Once the geometry existed, an *Insert Bends* feature was applied that turned the part into sheet metal and enabled bends to be flattened. In this method, you had to be proficient with working in Rollback states, because most changes to the model had to be done this way. Certain types of features had to go in certain places in the feature tree, corresponding to either a flat or formed state of the model. Although it was possible to do this, SolidWorks was very particular about the details.

The new way uses a functional feature approach, which greatly simplified the feature order requirements, and at the same time added some powerful and easy-to-use feature types. This new way is what we now call the Base Flange method, and is the main tool for sheet metal creation that we use today.

The Insert Bends method is still viable, but it is typically relegated to being used with imported parts and special uses such as creating rolled conical sheet metal parts.

Although I am primarily a plastics designer, the sheet metal tools in SolidWorks work so well and intuitively that I often wish that I did more sheet metal modeling work.

Understanding the Big Picture

The basic concept with the Base Flange method is that when you insert a Base Flange feature, SolidWorks identifies that part as a sheet metal part. The Base Flange feature is not *required* to be the first feature in the tree, but it is difficult to imagine why it would not be. You can create multi-body sheet metal parts, but you can only insert one Base Flange for each part document, and so only one body can be sheet metal. If you try to create a second Base Flange feature, then SolidWorks interprets it as an attempt to add a tab, which is the alternate function of the Base Flange tool.

When you add the Base Flange feature, a Sheet Metal placeholder feature is also automatically added before the Base Flange feature. The Sheet Metal placeholder is described later in this chapter.

Another feature is added automatically when you add the Base Flange. This one is called the Flat Pattern feature. Sheet Metal is added before the Base Flange and Flat Pattern are added at the bottom of the tree. This feature has a couple of special properties that are not found with other features. The first property is that it *remains* at the bottom of the tree when you add other sheet metal features, and the second property is that it is added as a *suppressed* feature. The Flat Pattern feature is discussed in more detail later in this chapter.

Bends may be flattened individually, or the whole part may be flattened at once. Configurations are often created with various bends flattened to show the part in various stages of the manufacturing process.

Bend Allowances can be specified by Bend Table, K-Factor, Bend Allowance, or Bend Deduction. These items are all listed in the Sheet Metal feature that is inserted as the first feature with a Base Flange.

Auto Relief has three options, which you can also set in the Sheet Metal feature. These three options are Rectangular, Tear, and Obround. Auto Relief and Bend Allowance settings are described in detail later in this chapter.

One of the general ideas about SolidWorks sheet metal is that some of the functions must create visual approximations of what the parts are going to look like, especially in the formed part, because the area where two bends run into one another is difficult to model. For this reason, the flat pattern may be easier to depict than the formed geometry. Many users become annoyed when the software simplifies the 3D model, but this is how the software works, and the very fine detail is probably not really needed anyway.

Other limitations that users often encounter when working with sheet metal in SolidWorks occur when they want to depict weld beads, spot welds, or other types of welds on finished parts. There is currently no defined way of doing this, but you can add extruded features to the model that approximate welds. Welds can be created in assembly, and in parts that are designated Weldment parts, much in the same way that parts can be designated Sheet Metal parts. At this time, Sheet Metal and Weldment parts cannot be combined in SolidWorks, although in shop practice that is done frequently. This may be another great enhancement request topic.

I find that when expectations of the software are reasonable, users tend to be more successful and satisfied with the results. I do not mean to make excuses for the software; I am very impressed with the functionality in the sheet metal features in SolidWorks, but it does not do *everything*, and users still need to use some imagination.

Using the Base Flange Features

The features used in the Base Flange method are easy to grasp conceptually, although they have many individual controls that may be confusing at first glance. Many of the tools can be changed by pulling handles, by using spin arrows, or by typing in specific numbers or dimensions. Maybe best of all, SolidWorks knows to change the thickness for the entire part at once.

The Sheet Metal features are all available from the Sheet Metal toolbar or through the menus at Insert, Sheet Metal, and by selecting the appropriate tool.

Base Flange /Tab feature

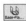 The Base Flange and Tab tool has three functions:

- By drawing an open contour in the first feature, the Base Flange creates a feature-like extrusion that includes the rounded corners of the bends.

- By drawing a closed contour in the first feature, the Base Flange creates a flat sheet that is shaped like your sketch for you to start from.

- When used at any time other than the first feature, it functions as a tab.

Figure 29.1 shows these three functions of the Base Flange/Tab feature.

Notice that the sketch of the part at the left of Figure 29.1 shown in preview has all sharp corners, and that the bend radius is added to each corner. SolidWorks automatically adjusts when bend directions are combined to make sure that the inside radius is always the same regardless of bend direction.

The bends are shown as BaseBend features in the FeatureManager. You can change individual bend radii from the default setting by editing the BaseBend feature, as well as by assigning custom bend allowances on a per-bend basis. You cannot change the bend angle for these particular bends because the angle is controlled through the sketch. However, for other types of bends (such as those created by Edge Flanges), you can adjust the bend angle through the feature PropertyManager.

If you need to, you can reorder all of the bends from a list that you can access from the RMB menu selection, Reorder Bends on the Flat Pattern. This dialog box is shown in Figure 29.2.

FIGURE 29.1

The three functions of the Base Flange and Tab feature

FIGURE 29.2

The Reorder Bends dialog box

The BaseBend features can be suppressed, but the only effect that this has is to prevent the associated bend from flattening when the Flat-Pattern feature is unsuppressed.

Sheet Metal feature

The FeatureManager is shown for the Base Flange with all of the bends below in Figure 29.3. The Sheet-Metal1 feature is automatically added to sheet metal parts as a placeholder for default sheet metal settings such as material thickness, default bend allowance settings, and Auto Relief options, as well as the default inside bend radius.

FIGURE 29.3

The FeatureManager after the Base Flange is added

Bend order

The Bend Order setting shown does not appear to have any effect when you are using the Base Flange method. In the Insert Bends method, a warning appears if the part intersects itself during bend operations, as determined by the bend order. This function may have been removed from more recent versions of the software, but the Bend Order options remain.

Gauge Table

Gauge Tables enable you to assign a thickness and available inside-bend radii, which limit the choices that the user can make to those in the table. Each K-Factor has a separate table, and the choices listed in the table appear in the drop-down lists in the Sheet Metal PropertyManager. Figure 29.4 shows the top few lines of a sample Gauge Table, and a Sheet Metal PropertyManager when a Gauge Table is used.

FIGURE 29.4

A sample Gauge Table and Sheet Metal PropertyManager

Type:	Aluminum Gauge Table	
Process	Aluminum - Coining	
K-Factor	0.5	
Unit:	Millimeters	

Gauge No.	Gauge (Thickness)	Available Bend Radius
Gauge 10	3	3.0; 4.0; 5.0; 8.0; 10.0
Gauge 12	2.5	3.0; 4.0; 5.0; 8.0; 10.0
Gauge 14	2	2.0; 3.0; 4.0; 5.0; 8.0; 10.0
Gauge 16	1.5	1.5; 2.0; 3.0; 4.0; 5.0; 8.0; 10.0

If necessary, you can override the values that are used in the Gauge Table by using the override options in the thickness, bend radius, and K-Factor fields.

The Bend Allowance options (Allowance, Deduction, and K-Factor) are explained in more detail later in this chapter.

Fixed Face or Edge

The Sheet Metal feature is also used in the Insert Bends method, and Fixed Face or Edge selection box is used in that method, but not in the Base Flange method. For information on how to use the setting in the Insert Bends method, see Chapter 30.

Bend Radius

This option specifies the default inside bend radius for all bends in the part. You can override values for individual bends or individual features.

Thickness

The part thickness is grayed out in the Sheet Metal PropertyManager. You can change the value by double-clicking any face of the model. The thickness displays as a blue dimension rather than a black dimension. It is easier to identify if you have dimension names turned on, because it is assigned the name Thickness.

All features in sheet metal parts that use the thickness value use a link value to link all of the feature thicknesses. This makes it easy to globally change the thickness of every feature in the entire sheet metal part.

To save these settings to a template file, you can create a Sheet Metal feature, specify the settings, delete the Sheet Metal features, and then save the file to a template with a special name that represents the settings that you used.

TIP When a link value is named Thickness, the Extrude dialog box always shows a Link To Thickness option to link the depth of an extrusion to the Thickness link value. If you save a template where Thickness has been created as a link value, then the option is always available to you, regardless of whether or not you are making sheet metal parts.

Bend Allowance

You can control the Bend Allowance by using one of four options:

- Bend Table
- K-Factor
- Bend Allowance
- Bend Deduction

Bend Table

Two general types of Bend Tables are available, text-based and Excel-based. The first few rows of each type of table are shown in Figure 29.5. Each table can use K-Factor, Bend Allowance, or Bend Deduction.

FIGURE 29.5

Sample text- and Excel-based Bend Tables

```
Bend Allowance Tables
---------------------
# Available types are Bend Allowance/Bend Deduction/K-Factor
# Keywords (Type:, Unit:, ...) must start at the beginning of the line.
Type: Bend Allowance
Material: Steel
Unit:   meters

Thickness: 0.0005
Bend Radius (read across)    0.0000  0.0005  0.0010  0.0015  0.0020  0.0025  0.0030  0.0040  0.0050
Opening Angle (read down)
                       5     0.0002  0.0002  0.0002  0.0002  0.0002  0.0002  0.0002  0.0002  0.0002
                      10     0.0002  0.0002  0.0002  0.0002  0.0002  0.0002  0.0002  0.0002  0.0002
                      20     0.0002  0.0002  0.0002  0.0002  0.0002  0.0002  0.0002  0.0002  0.0002
```

Unit	Inches												
Type:	Bend Allowance												
Material:	Soft Copper and Soft Brass												
Comment:	Values specified are for 90-degree bends												
Radius	**Thickness**												
	1/64	1/32	3/64	1/16	5/64	3/32	1/8	5/32	3/16	7/32	1/4	9/32	5/16
1/32	0.058	0.066	0.075	0.083	0.092	0.101	0.118	0.135	0.152	0.169	0.187	0.204	0.221
3/64	0.083	0.091	0.1	0.108	0.117	0.126	0.143	0.16	0.177	0.194	0.212	0.229	0.246
1/16	0.107	0.115	0.124	0.132	0.141	0.15	0.167	0.184	0.201	0.218	0.236	0.253	0.27
3/32	0.156	0.164	0.173	0.181	0.19	0.199	0.216	0.233	0.25	0.267	0.285	0.302	0.319

Sample Bend Tables can be found in the lang\english\Sheetmetal Bend Tables subdirectory of the SolidWorks installation directory. While the values may not be what you need, the syntax and organization is correct. You may want to contact your sheet metal fabrication shop to see what they are using for a table or equations.

K-Factor

When sheet metal is formed from a flat sheet, bending the metal causes it to stretch slightly on the outside part of the bend, and to compress slightly on the inside part of the bend. Somewhere across the thickness of the sheet is the Neutral Plane, where there is no stretching or compression. This Neutral Plane can be at various places across the thickness, depending on the material, tooling, and process. The ratio of the distance from the inside bend surface to the Neutral Plane, to the thickness is identified as the K-Factor, where .5 means halfway, 0 means on the inside face, and 1 means on the outside face. Typically, you can expect values between .5 and .3.

Bend Allowance and Bend Deduction

Bend Allowance and Bend Deduction are specific length values, not a ratio like the K-Factor. The Bend Allowance is essentially the arclength of the Neutral Plane through the bend region.

The three values are related, as shown in Figure 29.6. The dark rectangle represents the bend area. Material outside of the bend area really does not matter, although it is usually shown and used in the generally accepted formulas about bend calculations for sheet metal.

FIGURE 29.6

Calculating the Bend Deduction from the Bend Allowance and K-Factor

$$K = t/T$$
$$BD = 2X - BA$$

The ratio t/T (the K-Factor) is usually used from a published table or by asking your sheet metal vendor what values they typically use. The values from the tables have been developed experimentally by bending a piece of metal of known length, and then measuring the arclength of the inside of the bend and the arclength of the outside of the bend. By comparing these numbers to the original linear length of the bent area, you can find the t value and thus the K value. From the K value, the BA (Bend Allowance) value can be calculated and from that, the BD (Bend Deduction) value is easy to find.

The specific formulas for finding these numbers are not as important as an intuitive grasp of what the numbers mean, and how they are used, at least in relation to using SolidWorks to model sheet metal parts. The numbers used to fill out Bend Tables using K, BA, or BD values are typically taken from experimentally developed tables.

Auto Relief

Auto reliefs were formerly called Bend reliefs. You can specify three different Auto relief options to be applied automatically to bends that end in the middle of material. These options are illustrated in Figure 29.7.

The three Auto relief configurations: Rectangular, Tear, and Obround

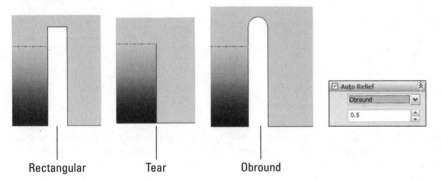

Rectangular   Tear   Obround

For the Rectangular and Obround types, you can control the width and the distance past the tangent line of the bend through the Relief Ratio selection box, which is immediately below the type selection box in the Sheet Metal PropertyManager. This ratio is the width of the relief divided by the part thickness. For the Rectangular relief, a ratio of .5 and a thickness of .050 inches means that the relief is .025 inches wide and that it goes .025 inches deeper into the part beyond the tangent line of the bend. The Obround relief goes slightly deeper because it has a full radius after the distance past the tangent line of the bend, and so it essentially goes a total of one full material thickness past the tangent line.

The Tear relief is simply a face-to-face shear of the material with no gap.

Flat Pattern feature

The Flat Pattern feature is added automatically to the end of the tree when the Base Flange feature is added. This feature is used to flatten the sheet metal part when the feature is unsuppressed. The Flatten toolbar button acts as a toggle to unsuppress or suppress the Flat Pattern feature in the tree. As mentioned earlier, the Flat Pattern has a couple of special properties that are not seen in other features. The first is that it remains at the *bottom* of the FeatureManager when other Sheet Metal features are added.

The second property of the Flat Pattern feature is that it is added in the *suppressed* state. When it is unsuppressed, it flattens out the sheet metal bends.

By editing the Flat Pattern feature, you can set a few options. The Flat Pattern PropertyManager is shown in Figure 29.8.

FIGURE 29.8

The Flat Pattern PropertyManager

The Fixed Face parameter determines which face remains stationary when the part is flattened out. Generally, the largest face available is selected automatically, but if you want to specify a different face to remain stationary, you can do that here.

When the Merge Faces option is on, it causes the flat pattern to form a single face, rather than being broken up by the tangent lines around the bends. This does a few things. First, selecting the face of the flattened part and clicking Convert Entities (found on the Sketch toolbar) makes an outline of the entire flattened part, which is easier to use for certain programming applications. Second, the edges around the outside are not broken up. Third, the tangent edges around the bends are not shown. The differences between flat patterns with this option on and off are shown in Figure 29.9.

FIGURE 29.9

The Merge Faces option, on and off

Merge faces on   Merge faces off

Bend lines are shown in both examples in Figure 29.9.

When you turn on the Simplify Bends option, it simplifies curved edges that are caused by flattening bends to straight lines from arcs or splines. When the option is off, the complex edges remain complex. Simple edges can be cut by standard punches, and do not require CNC-controlled lasers or jets.

The Corner Treatment option controls whether or not a corner treatment is applied to the flat pattern of a part. The corner treatment is illustrated in Figure 29.10. The model used to create this corner used a Miter Flange around the edges of a rectangular sheet.

FIGURE 29.10

Using the Corner Treatment setting in the Flat Pattern PropertyManager

Corner treatment on

Corner treatment off

Edge Flange feature

 The Edge Flange feature is very flexible and can be changed in several ways. If you have not kept up with the changes to Edge Flange for the last couple of releases, then you may find some surprises.

Edge Flange is intended to turn a 90-degree flange from a selected straight edge in the direction and distance specified using the default thickness for the part. The default process for this feature is that you select the tool, select the edge, and then drag the distance, click a distance reference such as a vertex at the end of another flange of equal length, or type a distance value manually. You can select multiple edges, from a part which do not necessarily need to be consecutive. That is all there is to a simple default flange, although several options give you some additional options for angle, length, and so on. Figure 29.11 shows the Edge Flange PropertyManager, as well as a simple flange.

FIGURE 29.11

The Edge Flange PropertyManager and a simple flange

Edit Flange Profile

The Edit Flange Profile button in the Edge Flange PropertyManager enables you to edit a sketch to shape the flange in some way other than rectangular, or to otherwise edit the shape of the flange. Notice in Figure 29.11 that both of the flanges made by a singe flange feature have been edited. You can do this by selecting the flange for which you want to edit the profile before clicking the Edit Flange Profile button.

NOTE If you have added dimensions to the sketch, as shown in Figure 29.11, then you will no longer be able to use the arrow to drag the length of the flange. To edit the length, you will need to edit the sketch or double-click the feature, and then double-click the dimensions that you want to change.

You can add holes to the flange profile as nested loops. This allows you to avoid creating additional hole features, but does not allow you to control suppression state independently from the flange feature.

You can make flanges go only part of the way along an edge by pulling one of the end lines back from the edge. This works even though the end lines appear black, and fully defined. A situation where the sketch has been edited this way is shown in the image to the right in Figure 29.11.

Use Default Radius

This option enables you to override the default inside bend radius that is set for the entire part for this feature. The bend radii for individual bends within an edge flange that has multiple flanges cannot be set; the only override is at the feature level. If you need individual bends to have different bend radii, then you need to do this using multiple Edge Flange features.

Gap Distance

The gap distance is illustrated in Figure 29.12. The Gap Distance selection box is only active when you have selected multiple edges in the main selection box for this feature. The gap refers to the space between the inside corners of the perpendicular flanges.

FIGURE 29.12

Specifying the gap distance

Gap

Angle

Because the Edge Flange is not dependent on a sketch for its angle like the Base Flange is, you can set the angle in the Angle panel of the PropertyManager. The values that this selection box can accept range from any value larger than zero to any value smaller than 180. Of course, each flange has practical limits. In the flange shown in Figure 29.13, the limitation is reached when the bend radius runs into the rectangular notch in the middle of the flange to the right, at about 158 degrees. The angle affects all of the flanges that are made with the feature. To create a situation where different flanges have different angles, you need to create separate flange features.

FIGURE 29.13

Establishing the limit of the flange angle

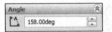

Flange Length

As mentioned earlier, if you have edited the Flange Profile sketch and a flange length dimension is applied in the sketch, then the flange length is taken from that sketch dimension. If this dimension has not been added to the profile sketch, then the options for this setting in the PropertyManager Flange Length panel are Blind and Up To Vertex. Using Up To Vertex is a nice way to link the lengths of several flanges.

Flange Position

The small icons for Flange Position should be fairly self-explanatory, with the dotted lines indicating the existing end of the material. The names for these options, in order from left to right, are:

- Material Inside
- Material Outside
- Bend Outside
- Bend From Virtual Sharp (for use when an angle is involved)

Trim Side Bends

In situations where a new flange is created next to an existing flange, and a relief must be made in the existing flange to accommodate the new flange, you can turn this option on to trim back the existing flange. Leaving this option off simply creates a relief cut, as shown in Figure 29.14.

FIGURE 29.14

Using the Trim Side Bends option

Trim Side Bends off   Trim Side Bends on

Curved Edges

Edge Flanges can be created on curved edges, but the curved edge must be on a planar face. For example, if the part were the top of a mailbox, then an Edge Flange could not be put on the curve on the top of the mailbox. The flange would have to be made as a part of the flat end of the mailbox, instead.

Figure 29.15 shows Edge Flanges used on a part. Notice that reliefs are added to the ends of the bends, although they are not really needed.

All of the edges that you select to be used with a curved Edge Flange must be tangent. This means that in Figure 29.15, neither of the Edge Flanges could have been extended around the ends of the part. You would need to create separate Edge Flange features for those edges.

Because these Edge Flanges are made in such a way that they are developable surfaces, they can be (and are) flattened in such a way that they do not stretch the material of the flange when the flat is compared to the formed shape. Doubtless there is some deformation in between the two states in the actual forming of this flange, and so its manufacturing accuracy may not be completely reliable.

FIGURE 29.15

Curved Edge Flanges on a part

Notice bend reliefs where they are not needed

Miter Flange feature

The Miter Flange feature can create picture frame–like miters around corners of parts, and correctly recognizes the difference between mitered inside corners and mitered outside corners. The PropertyManager and a sample Miter Flange are shown in Figure 29.16.

FIGURE 29.16

The Miter Flange PropertyManager and a sample part

A Miter Flange feature starts off with a sketch that is perpendicular to the starting edge of the Miter Flange feature.

> **TIP** A quick way to start a sketch for a Miter Flange that is on a plane perpendicular to a selected edge is to select the edge, and then click a sketch tool. This automatically creates a plane perpendicular to the edge at the nearest endpoint.

Miter Flange sketches may have single lines or multiple lines. They may even have arcs. Still, remember that just because you can make it in SolidWorks does not mean that the manufacturer can make it. It is often a good idea to check with the manufacturer to ensure that the part can be made. Also, you usually learn something from the experience.

> **TIP** When selecting edges for the Miter Flange to go on, be sure to remain consistent in your selection. If you start by selecting an edge on the top of the part, then you should continue selecting edges on the top of the part. If you do not, then SolidWorks prompts you with a warning message in a tooltip that says that the edge is on the wrong face.

Some of the controls in the Miter Flange PropertyManager should be familiar by now, such as Use Default Radius, Flange Position, Trim Side Bends, and Gap Distance. You have seen these controls before in the Edge Flange PropertyManager.

The Start/End Offset panel enables you to pull a Miter Flange back from an edge without using a cut. If you need an intermittent flange, then you may need to use cuts or multiple Miter Flange features, as shown in Figure 29.17.

FIGURE 29.17

The Start/End Offset settings for a Miter Flange

End Offset

Sketch for
Miter Flange

Start Offset

Hem feature

The Hem feature is used to roll over the edge of a sheet metal part. This feature is often used to smooth over a sharp edge or to add strength to the edge. You can also use it for other purposes, such as to capture a pin for a hinge. SolidWorks offers four different hem styles — Closed, Open, Tear Drop, and Rolled — which are shown as icons on the Hem PropertyManager. The PropertyManager for the Hem feature is shown in Figure 29.18.

FIGURE 29.18

The Hem PropertyManager and a sample hem

One of the limitations to keep in mind with regard to hems is that SolidWorks cannot fold over a part so that the faces touch perfectly line-on-line. Doing this would cause the two sections of the part to merge into a larger piece, thus removing the coincident faces. SolidWorks, computers, and mathematics in general do not always handle the number zero very well. In reality, you can often see light through these hems, and so a perfectly flush hem may not be as accurate as it seems.

Jog feature

The Jog feature puts a pair of opposing bends on a flange so that the end of the flange is parallel to, but offset from, the face where the jog started. The Jog PropertyManager and a sample jog are shown in Figure 29.19.

FIGURE 29.19

The Jog PropertyManager and a sample jog

The Jog feature is created from a single sketch line on the face of a sheet metal part. The geometry to be jogged should not have any side bends; it should be a simple tab-like flange, as shown in Figure 29.19. The line to create the jog can be drawn at an angle, causing the jog to also be angled.

The three icons on the Jog Offset panel illustrate what dimension is being controlled by that setting.

Fixed Face

Like most sheet metal features, the Jog feature bends faces on the part, and when it does so, although it may be obvious to you as the user, it is not obvious to the software which face should remain stationary and which faces should be moved by the bend. The Fixed Face selection box enables you to select a face, or in this case, a part of a face, that you want to remain stationary as the rest of the faces move. The black dot on the face identifies it as stationary.

> **TIP** Problems can sometimes arise when using configurations that change sizes, because these markers for fixed faces can be pushed onto other faces. This can cause problems with assemblies and drawings, and in general makes visualization difficult. In cases like this, it may be advisable to select a larger face or one that has fewer changes, if possible, to be used as the fixed face.

Jog Offset

You can control the direction of the jog by using the arrow button to the left of the end condition selection box.

You can control the jog distance by selecting the end conditions, Up To Surface, Up To Vertex, or Offset From Surface. The default setting is Blind, in which you simply enter a distance for the offset, in exactly the same way that end conditions are controlled for features such as extrudes.

Fix Projected Length

One setting that may not be obvious is the Fix Projected Length. This refers to the length of the flange that the jog is altering. In Figure 29.19, you can see that the height of the jogged feature is the same as the height of the original feature. The jog obviously requires more material than the original, but the Fix Projected Length option is turned on, and so the height is maintained. If you turned this option off, then the finished height of the flange after the jog is added would be shorter, because the material is used by the jog, and additional material would not be added. For comparison, the image to the right in Figure 29.19 shows this situation.

Jog Position

The Jog Position selection establishes the relationship between the sketched line and the first bend tangent line. The Jog Position icons have tooltips with the following names, from left to right: Bend Centerline, Material Inside, Material Outside, and Bend Outside.

Jog Angle

The Jog Angle enables you to change the angle of the short perpendicular section of the jog. You can angle it to smooth out the jog (angles of less than 90 degrees) or to curl back on itself (angles of more than 90 degrees). Again, be careful to check with your manufacturer's capabilities.

Sketched Bend feature

 The Sketched Bend works in some respects like half of a jog. It requires the sketch line, and the Fixed Face selection. You define a bend position with the same set of icons that you used in the jog, and you assign a bend angle in the same way.

TIP You can use the Sketched Bend feature to "dog ear" corners. You do this by drawing a line across the corner at an angle and setting the angle to 180 degrees and then overriding the default radius with a much smaller one, such as .001 inches.

Unlike Jog, the Sketched Bend feature does not show you a preview. The Sketched Bend PropertyManager is shown in Figure 29.20.

FIGURE 29.20

The Sketched Bend PropertyManager

Closed Corner feature

The Closed Corner feature extends flanges on the sides to meet with other flanges. It is typically used when corners leave big open gaps, in order to create a corner that is more easily welded shut (although welds cannot be created in sheet metal parts in SolidWorks). The image to the left in Figure 29.21 shows a part where angled flanges have been applied. This creates big gaps in the corners. Although a Miter Flange may have been better, these were created using regular Edge Flanges. The image to the right shows the Closed Corner PropertyManager, as well as a preview of the corner being closed.

Faces To Extend

You must select the thickness face of one of the flanges in order to extend it. Selecting one face automatically selects the matching face from the other flange that you also want to extend. The Corner Type selection icons depict the selected face as red, and the three icons display tooltips: Butt, Overlap, and Underlap.

Gap

The Gap setting enables you to specify how close you want the closed corner to be. Keep in mind that you cannot use the number zero in this field. If you do, then SolidWorks reminds you to "Please enter a number greater than or equal to 0.00003937 and less than or equal to 0.86388126." It is good to know your limits.

Overlap/Underlap ratio

The Overlap/Underlap ratio setting controls how far across the overlapped face the overlapping flange reaches. Full overlap is a ratio of 1, and a Butt condition is (roughly) a ratio of zero. This ratio is only available when you have specified Overlap or Underlap for the corner type.

FIGURE 29.21

Applying the Closed Corner feature

Open Bend Region

The Open Bend Region option affects how the finished corner looks in the bend area. If Open Bend Region is turned on, then a small gap is created at the end of the bend. If the option is turned off, then SolidWorks fills this area with geometry. Figure 29.22 shows the finished model with this option on and off, as well as the resulting flat patterns for each setting.

FIGURE 29.22

The Open Bend Region option, both on and off, and the resulting flat patterns

Open Bend
Region on

Open Bend
Region on –
flat pattern

Open Bend
Region off

Open Bend
Region off –
flat pattern

Corner Trim and Break Corner features

 The Corner Trim feature is available only when the sheet metal part is in its flattened state. The Corner Trim PropertyManager also has the Break Corner interface built right into it. However, the Break Corner feature is only available when the sheet metal part is in its folded state. Figure 29.23 shows the combined interface. Both functions are included here, and SolidWorks treats them as if they are part of a single function.

When finished, the Corner Trim feature places itself after the Flat Pattern feature in the FeatureManager. It similarly follows the suppress/unsuppress state of the Flat Pattern feature. When the Break Corner feature is used on its own, it is placed before the Flat Pattern feature. With this in mind, it seems best to use Break Corner as a separate feature unless it is being used specifically to alter the flat pattern in a way that cannot be done from the folded state.

Break Corner on its own is primarily used to remove sharp corners using either a chamfer or a rounded corner. This tool is set up to filter edges on the thickness of sheet metal parts, which is useful, because these edges are otherwise difficult to select without a lot of zooming. Break Corner can also break interior corners.

One of the main functions of the Corner Trim feature is to apply bend relief geometry to the flat pattern. The three available options are Circular, Square, and Bend Waist. These options are shown in Figure 29.24.

FIGURE 29.23

The Corner Trim PropertyManager, including the Break Corner panel

FIGURE 29.24

Applying the Corner Trim Relief options

Forming Tool feature

Forming tools in SolidWorks enable you to place features that are not formed on a brake press. These are features that are not straight-line bends, but rather punched, drawn, formed, lanced, sheared, or otherwise deformed material.

One of the important things to understand about forming tools is that they do not stretch the material in the SolidWorks part in the same way that happens in a real-life forming operation. In real life, material is thinned when it is punched, stamped, or drawn. In SolidWorks, the thickness of a sheet metal part remains the same, regardless of what happens to it. For this reason, you need to be careful when using mass properties of sheet metal parts or doing stress analysis of parts that have formed features.

SolidWorks installs with a library of fairly simple forming tools that you can use as a starting point for your own personal customized library. You can also examine some of these tools to see how they create particular effects. The library is found in your Design Library in the Task pane. Some of the more interesting forming tools are the lances and louvers.

Creating forming tools

Forming tools are essentially a part that is used to form another part. One flat face of the forming tool part is designated as a Stopping Face, which is placed flush with the top face of the sheet metal part. You can move and rotate the tool with the Modify Sketch tool, and you can use dimensions or sketch relations to locate it.

Creating forming tools is far easier than it used to be, and with a little creativity, it can give good results. This section of the chapter gives you the information that you need to effectively create useful forming tools, and a couple of hints for more complex forming tool creation.

To create a forming tool, you can use the Forming Tool button on the Sheet Metal toolbar. Figure 29.25 shows the PropertyManager interface for this tool.

FIGURE 29.25

The Form Tool PropertyManager and a sample tool

The Stopping Face turns a special color, and so do any faces that are selected in the Faces To Remove selection box. Faces To Remove means that those faces will be cutouts in the sheet metal part.

Another aspect of the forming tool is the orientation sketch. The orientation sketch is created automatically by using Convert Entities on the Stopping Face. If you have used this function in any of its previous versions, then you know that this latest iteration is far easier to create than before. However, to me, it looks like the orientation sketch has taken a step backwards. The orientation sketch cannot be manually edited, and so for forming tools where *footprints* are symmetrical, but other features in the tool are not, you cannot tell from the sketch which direction the forming tool should face. Orientation could be managed more easily in earlier versions of forming tools because the placement sketch was just a manually created sketch.

When creating a forming tool, you must remember to build in generous draft and fillets, and not to build undercuts into the tool. Also keep in mind that when you have a concave fillet face on the tool, the radius becomes smaller by the thickness of the sheet metal; as a result, you must be careful about minimum radius values on forming tools. If there is a concave face on the tool that has a .060-inch radius and the tool is applied to a part with a .060-inch thickness, then the tool will cause an error. Errors in applied forming tools cannot be edited or repaired, except by changing dimensions.

Once the forming tool is created, special colors are used for every face on the part. For example, the Stopping Face is a light blue color, Faces To Remove are red, and all of the other faces are yellow. Figure 29.26 shows the small addition that is made to the FeatureManager when you make a part into a forming tool. This feature did not exist in older versions of the tool.

FIGURE 29.26

The FeatureManager of a forming tool part

Forming Tool Library

The folder that the forming tools are placed into in the Design Library must be designated as a Forming Tool folder. To do this, right-click the folder that contains the forming tools and select Forming Tool Folder (a check mark appears next to this option).

Placing a forming tool

To place a forming tool on a sheet metal part (forming tools are only allowed on sheet metal parts), you can drag the tool from the library and drop it on the face of the sheet metal part. Forming tools are limited to flat faces.

From there, you can use the Modify Sketch tool to move and rotate the forming tool. It may be difficult to orient it properly without first placing it, seeing what orientation it ends up in, and then reorienting it if necessary.

Configurations cannot be used with forming tools like they can with library features, although you can change dimensions by double-clicking the Forming Tool icon in the sheet metal part FeatureManager.

Forming tools are suppressed when the part is flattened.

Special techniques with forming tools

One application of forming tools that is asked for frequently is the cross break to stiffen a large, flat sheet metal face. SolidWorks does not have a tool to deal with this directly, and it is clearly not something that SolidWorks can do using straight bends, but a forming tool can do it.

You can create the forming tool by lofting a rectangle to a sketch point on a plane slightly offset from the plane of the rectangle. This creates a shallow pyramid shape. Open the part from the material on the CD-ROM for Chapter 29, called Chapter 29 – Cross Break.SLDPRT, to examine how this part was made. Figure 29.27 shows the Cross Break tool applied to a sheet metal part.

FIGURE 29.27

The Cross Break tool applied to a part

A second special technique is a gusset or a form that goes across bends. This can be adapted in many ways, but here it is shown going across two bends. I cannot confirm the practicality of actually manufacturing something like this, but I have seen it done.

The technique used here is to call the single long flat face of the forming tool the Stopping Face. The vertical faces on the ends and the fillet faces must be selected in the Faces To Remove selection box. The fillets of the outside of the forming tool also have to match the bends of the sheet metal part exactly. You may need to edit this part each time you use it, unless it is applied to parts with bends of the same size and separated by the same amount.

When you place the tool on the sheet metal part, you must place it accurately from side to side to get everything to work out properly.

This part is in the same location as the Cross Break file, and is called Chapter 29 – Form Across Bends.SLDPRT. Figure 29.28 shows the tool and a part to which it has been applied.

FIGURE 29.28

Forming across bends

Stopping face

Faces to remove (both ends)

Lofted Bends feature

The Lofted Bends feature enables you to create transitions between two profiles. The range of functionality available through the Loft feature is not available with Lofted Bends; it is limited to two profiles with no end conditions or guide curves. Both profiles also need to be open contours, in order to allow the sheet metal to unfold.

Lofted Bends is not part of the Base Flange method, but it is part of the newer set of sheet metal tools that are available in SolidWorks.

Figure 29.29 shows what is probably the most common application of this feature. The bend lines shown must be established in the PropertyManager when you create or edit the feature. Bend Lines are only an option if both profiles have the same number of straight lines. For example, if one of the profiles is a circle instead of a rectangle with very large fillets, then the Bend Lines options are not available in the PropertyManager.

FIGURE 29.29

The Lofted Bends PropertyManager, a sample, and a flat pattern with bend lines

Like the forming tools, you can also use Lofted Bends in situations for which they were probably not intended. Figure 29.29 shows how lofting between 3D curves can also create shapes that can be flattened in SolidWorks. In this case, a couple of intermediate steps were required to get to the 3D curves, which involve surface features.

Unfold and Fold features

 Unfold is a feature that unfolds selected bends temporarily. It is typically used in conjunction with a Fold feature to re-fold the bends. This combination is used to apply a feature that must be applied to the flat pattern, for example, a hole that spans across a bend.

Figure 29.30 shows the FeatureManager of a part where this combination has been applied, as well as the part itself, showing the bend across a hole, and the PropertyManager, which is the same for both features.

FIGURE 29.30

Applying the Unfold and Fold features

Both the Unfold and Fold features make it easy to select the bends without zooming in, even for small bends. A filter is placed on the cursor when the command is active, which allows only bends to be selected. The Collect All Bends option also becomes available. This feature also requires that you select a stationary face to hold still while the rest of the model moves during the unfolding and folding process.

Flatten command

 The Flatten command is different from the Unfold feature in a few important ways. First, Flatten is not a feature; it is just a command that unsuppresses the normally suppressed Flat Pattern feature. The Flat Pattern feature keeps track of the bend lines for a part. The individual bends are listed under the Flat Pattern feature, and when the feature is unsuppressed, the individual bends can be suppressed. This enables you to establish configurations that can show bend processing order on the drawing or in an assembly. You can duplicate the Flatten command by manually suppressing or unsuppressing the Flat Pattern feature.

Tutorial: Using the Base Flange Sheet Metal Method

SolidWorks Base Flange method sheet metal is fun and easy to use as you will see in this tutorial:

1. Open a new part using a special sheet metal template if one is available.

2. On the Top plane, draw a rectangle centered on the Origin, 14 inches in X by 12 inches in Y (or Z).

3. Initiate the Base Flange tool, accept the default thickness of .029 inches, and change the K-Factor to .43. Notice that the default inside bend radius is not shown. This setting is made in the Sheet Metal feature that is placed before the Base Flange feature in the FeatureManager.

4. After the Base Flange has been created, edit the Sheet Metal feature, and change the default bend radius to .050 inches.

5. Click one of the 12-inch edges and then select the Line tool from the Sketch toolbar. This is a shortcut to creating a plane perpendicular to the end of the edge and opening a new sketch on the plane. This is useful in other situations in addition to working with sheet metal. Draw a sketch similar to that shown in Figure 29.31. The arc overrides the default inside bend radius setting, and directly controls that particular bend.

FIGURE 29.31

The sketch to start a Miter Flange

6. With the sketch still active, press the Miter Flange button on the Sheet Metal toolbar. Use the settings shown in the image to the right in Figure 29.32. Select three edges as shown. Remember to select the edges on the same side of the Base Flange. In particular, notice the Start/End offset settings. Click OK when you are satisfied with the settings.

FIGURE 29.32

Specifying the Miter Flange settings

7. Select the remaining edge that is not touched by the Miter Flange, and click the Edge Flange tool on the Sheet Metal toolbar. Double-click the top point of one end of the Miter Flange to establish the flange length, using the Up To Vertex end condition.

8. Press the Edit Flange Profile button in the PropertyManager, and manually pull the sketch back from the ends of the flange. Add dimensions to make the flange 3 inches from the corner on the left side, and 5 inches from the corner on the right side, as shown in Figure 29.33; otherwise, use the default settings for the flange. Click OK to accept the feature when you are satisfied with the settings.

FIGURE 29.33

Creating an Edge Flange

9. Select the inside edge of the top of the Edge Flange that you have just created, and initiate a Hem feature. Use the settings Material Inside, Closed Hem, with a length of .25 inches, and make the material go toward the inside of the box. The settings and preview of the feature are shown in Figure 29.34.

FIGURE 29.34

Creating a hem

10. Create a second Edge Flange the same height as the first, just to the right of the first flange, as seen from the point of view used in Figure 29.33. Edit the flange profile and pull the new flange away from the existing flange. Add a dimension to make the new flange 2 inches wide. Click OK when you are satisfied with the settings.

11. Open a sketch on the inside face of the new Edge Flange and draw a line across the flange .75 inches from the end.

12. Create a Jog feature with the settings shown in Figure 29.35. Make sure to set a custom bend radius by deselecting the Use Default Radius option and entering .025 inches. If you do not set the custom radius, then you may get a warning that the jog distance is less than a minimum jog value.

FIGURE 29.35

Creating a jog

13. From the CD-ROM, in the folder for Chapter 29, find the part named Chapter 29 – Cross Break.SLDPRT. Copy this file to a folder in the library that you have established outside of your SolidWorks installation folder, called Forming Tools.

14. Make sure that this folder appears in the Design Library. You may have to press F5 or the Refresh button at the top of the Task pane. When the folder appears, RMB click the folder and activate the check mark next to Forming Tools Folder.

15. When the file has been copied and the folder has been assigned as a Forming Tool folder, drag the Chapter 29 – Cross Break part from the folder and onto the big flat face of the sheet metal part. You will be put into a sketch that looks like Figure 29.36.

FIGURE 29.36

Placing a forming tool

Position form feature

Please use dimensioning and sketch modify tools to place the form feature. Note that the sketch moves as a whole when dimensions or other actions are applied to it.

< Back   Finish   Cancel   Help

16. Once you have dropped the feature into the sketch, drag the Origin of the sketch onto the Origin of the part, and then click Finish. Notice that the cross break is in the middle of the part, but is too small.

17. Double-click the new feature in the FeatureManager; a set of dimensions appear on the screen. Change the 4-inch dimension to 13.9 inches, and the 6-inch dimension to 11.9 inches. The cross break should now look like Figure 29.37.

18. Create a new configuration named Flat. In this configuration, suppress the forming tool that you just placed, and unsuppress the Flat Pattern feature at the bottom of the tree.

FIGURE 29.37

Resizing the cross break

Summary

The newer set of sheet metal tools that are available in SolidWorks is known as the Base Flange method. These tools are extremely powerful, and in most cases are very easy to use and understand. The setup of defaults is kept in the initial Sheet Metal feature, and all of the bends and bend lines are contained in the final Flat Pattern feature.

Chapter 30

Using the Insert Bends Method for Sheet Metal Parts

I n Chapter 29 on the Base Flange method, I explained the co-existence of two conceptual models for the creation of sheet metal parts in SolidWorks. The Base Flange method is the newer and more powerful of these two functions. However, some functionality is available only through the Insert Bends method, and the two methods may be combined to some extent. This shows that the older method is by no means obsolete.

One of the reasons for creating a new method was that the old method was very convoluted, and required certain types of features to be put into specific locations in the FeatureManager order; this meant that the user was frequently working in Rollback mode. In the days before being able to save in Rollback mode (which is new in SolidWorks 2007), this was not only tedious but dangerous, as well. This is because without the ability to save while the model was rolled back, users were more likely to lose their work.

One of the advantages of the old method was that you were able to just use the same old SolidWorks features that you were accustomed to using for regular modeling. Of course, this same advantage frequently turned out to be a disadvantage, as well because the standard features by definition did not have any specialized sheet metal functionality.

Today, the Insert Bends method is used for specific situations. For example, it is used for parts that have been created as generic SolidWorks models and that need to be flattened, imported parts that need to be flattened, and conical rolled sheet metal parts.

Architecture of Insert Bends

In Chapter 29, it was shown that a part created with the Base Flange method had as its first feature a Sheet Metal feature, which was a placeholder for sheet metal defaults for the current part. The Base Flange feature came next, followed by additional Sheet Metal features, and the list of specialized features was completed with a suppressed Flat Pattern feature.

The structure of parts created with the Insert Bends feature is somewhat different. Figure 30.1 shows a comparison of the two methods' FeatureManagers for simple parts.

FIGURE 30.1

A comparison between default features for Base Flange and Insert Bends

Base flange

Insert bends

The most notable difference is that the Insert Bends part starts off with non-sheet metal features. The Rip feature also stands out, but the Rip feature is not exclusive to sheet metal. Although you can use Rip on any model, it is found only on the Sheet Metal toolbar.

The Sheet Metal feature is found in both the Base Flange and Insert Bends methods, and has the same PropertyManager function in both methods.

The new features in the Insert Bends method are the Flatten Bends and Process Bends features. The way the Insert Bends method works is that the model that is built with the sharp-cornered non-sheet metal feature is flattened by the Flatten Bends feature. The model is then reconstructed with bends by the Process Bends feature.

In earlier versions of SolidWorks, the Flat Pattern did not exist, and so to create a flat of your model, you suppressed the Process Bends feature. This is where the implications of the feature order became apparent. To build a cut across a bend (which you can do with the Unfold and Fold features in Base Flange parts), the cut had to be put between the Flatten and Process Bends features. Changes to the overall shape, and especially new bend geometry, had to be added before the Flatten Bends feature. Features could also be added after the Process Bends, but they would not appear on the flat pattern; this was reserved for secondary machining operations, and other features of that type.

With this brief explanation of the feature-order sensitivity of the Insert Bends method, you begin to get a sense of why a new architecture was created.

Making Sheet Metal from a Generic Model

At least two basic rules are enforced by SolidWorks for all sheet metal parts: the parts must have a constant wall thickness, and the thickness faces must be perpendicular to the face of the part (edges are not sheared at a non-perpendicular angle). When all of the geometry is made from the beginning as a sheet metal part (using the Base Flange method), these issues rarely arise. However, when the part is modeled from thin features, cuts, shells, and so on, there is no telling what may happen to the model.

If you perform an Insert Bends operation on a model that does not have a consistent wall thickness, then the Flatten and Process Bends features fail. If a thickness face is not perpendicular to the main face of the part, then the software simply forces the situation.

Normal Cut

If a Cut feature is placed before the Sheet Metal feature, then as far as SolidWorks is concerned, the part is not a sheet metal part. However, if the cut feature is created after the Sheet Metal feature, then the model has to follow a different set of rules. The "normal shear" mentioned above is one of those rules. In Figure 30.2, the sketch for a cut is on a plane that is not perpendicular to the face that the cut is going into. Under a normal modeling situation, the cut just goes through the part at an angle. However, in SolidWorks sheet metal, a new option is added to the PropertyManager for the cut. This is the Normal Cut option, and it is turned on by default. You could be modeling and never even notice this option, but it is important because it affects the geometrical results of the feature.

As shown in Figure 30.2, when the Normal Cut option is on, the thickness faces of the cut are turned perpendicular (or *normal*) to the face of the sheet metal. This is also important because if the angle between the angled face and the sketch change, the geometry of the cutout can also change. This setting becomes more important as the material becomes thicker and as the angle between the sketch and the sheet metal face becomes shallower.

FIGURE 30.2

Using the Normal Cut option

Normal cut off   Normal cut on

Rip feature

When building a sheet metal part from a generic model, a common technique that is used to achieve consistent wall thicknesses is to build the outer shape as a solid, and then shell the part. The only problem with this method is that it leaves corners joined in a way that cannot be flattened. You can solve this problem by using the Rip feature. Rip breaks out the corner in one or both directions in such a way that it can be unfolded. Bend reliefs are later added automatically by the Process Bends feature.

Figure 30.3 shows the Rip PropertyManager and the results of using this feature. The model was created to look like a Miter Flange part.

FIGURE 30.3

Using the Rip feature

Notice also in Figure 30.3 that after the Rip, the edges of the material are still sheared at an angle. Because the top of the part was shelled, the thickness of the part is not normal to the main face of the sheet metal. You can fix this by using the Flatten Bends feature, which lays the entire part out flat, calculates the bend areas, and corrects any discrepancies at the edges of the part.

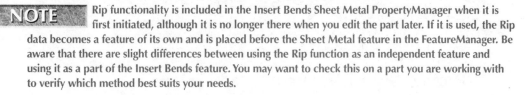 Rip functionality is included in the Insert Bends Sheet Metal PropertyManager when it is first initiated, although it is no longer there when you edit the part later. If it is used, the Rip data becomes a feature of its own and is placed before the Sheet Metal feature in the FeatureManager. Be aware that there are slight differences between using the Rip function as an independent feature and using it as a part of the Insert Bends feature. You may want to check this on a part you are working with to verify which method best suits your needs.

Sheet Metal feature

 The Sheet Metal feature used in the Insert Bends method is very similar to the one used in the Base Flange method. However, two main differences exist: Insert Bends Sheet Metal requires the user to select a Fixed Face, and the Base Flange Sheet Metal allows the use of Gauge Tables. Both features function as placeholders and otherwise contain the same information, use the same name and icon, and are inserted automatically when a different feature is created.

Flatten Bends feature

The Flatten Bends feature is added automatically by the Insert Bends tool. As mentioned earlier, it takes the model with sharp corners and lays it flat, adjusting the material in the bend area and normalizing the thickness faces around the flat pattern. A Merge Faces option is not available in the Insert Bends method except in the Flat Pattern feature, and so the flat pattern created by the Flatten Bends feature always has edges created by the tangent lines of the bends.

Notice in Figure 30.4 that the Flatten Bends feature has a sketch and several Sharp Bend features under it. The Sharp Sketch is simply an account of the bend lines, and you cannot edit it manually. The Sharp Bend features can be suppressed, in which case they are not re-formed in the Process Bends feature. You can also edit Sharp Bend features to change the default radius, bend allowance, and relief type.

FIGURE 30.4

Using the Flatten Bends feature

Process Bends feature

The Process Bends feature takes all of the flat pattern information, the bend information, and entities in the Flat Sketch, and rebuilds the model with the formed bends. The Flat Sketch under the Process Bends feature is the Insert Bends method version of a sketched bend. You can add sketch lines here to bend panels of the part. After you add lines to this sketch, exiting the sketch causes the part to be created with a default 90-degree bend corresponding to the line. Of course, all of the Sketched Bend rules exist, such as that the line has to extend at least up to the edges of the part, the lines cannot extend across multiple faces, and construction lines are ignored.

For every bend created by a sketch line in the Process Bends Flat Sketch, a Flat Bend feature is added to the list under Process Bends. You can control the angle and radius of each of these Flat Bends by editing the Flat Bend feature. This is all illustrated in Figure 30.5.

FIGURE 30.5

Using the Process Bends feature

Bend lines drawn in Flat Sketch
to add bends to part

Bends added to part
by bend lines

Added by bend lines
added to the Flat Sketch

No Bends

The No Bends tool on the Sheet Metal toolbar is simply used to roll back the model before the Flatten Bends feature in the tree with a single button click. This is primarily to add new geometry that is turned into bends through the Flatten and Process Bends features.

Flat Pattern

The Insert Bends method uses the Flat Pattern feature as well as the Base Flange method. However, it was not part of the original scheme, being added at some point after the new tools had proved their value. This enables you to make use of the new features as well, as discussed later in this chapter in the section Mixing Methods.

857

Working with Imported Geometry

Working with imported geometry starts at the point where you use the Rip feature. While imported geometry can be geometrically manipulated to some extent in SolidWorks, that is beyond the scope of this chapter. The need for a model with walls of constant thickness still exists, even if the imported model has filleted edges showing bend geometry already in the model.

FeatureWorks may be used to recognize sheet metal features or to fully or partially deconstruct the model by removing bend faces as fillets. While FeatureWorks is not covered in this book, the technique may be useful when editing imported parts with overall prismatic geometry that is common to sheet metal parts.

When a sheet metal part is imported, whether it meets the requirements immediately or must be edited in one way or another, to make a sheet metal part of it, you can simply use the Insert Bends feature.

Making Rolled Conical Parts

One of the reasons for maintaining the legacy Insert Bends method is to have a way of creating rolled conical parts. You can create cylindrical sheet metal parts by drawing an arc that almost closes to an entire circle, and creating a Base Flange from it. However, no equivalent technique for creating tapered cones exists with the Base Flange method.

With the Insert Bends method, a revolved thin feature does the job nicely. You simply revolve a straight line at an angle to the centerline, so that the straight line does not touch or cross the centerline; the revolve cannot go around the full 360 degrees, as there must be a gap. Sheet metal parts are not created by stretching the material (except for Forming Tools).

When creating a rolled sheet metal part, a flat face cannot be selected to remain fixed when the part is flattened. Instead, you can use a straight edge along the revolve gap, as shown in Figure 30.6.

> **NOTE**   When a conical sheet metal part is created, it does not receive the Flat Pattern feature at the end of the FeatureManager. This is because none of the new Base Flange method features are allowed on this type of part.

FIGURE 30.6

Selecting a straight edge for a conical part

Select one of these edges in the
Fixed Face/edge selection box

Mixing Methods

Once you have used the Insert Bend tool on a part, it is not automatically excluded from using some of the more advanced tools that are available through the Base Flange method, unless it is a cylindrical or conical part. A Flat Pattern feature is added to the bottom of most feature trees, and the presence of this feature is what signifies that the current part has now become a sheet metal part to the Base Flange features.

However, it is recommended that you avoid mixing the different techniques to flatten parts, for example, suppressing bends under Flatten and Process Bends, as well as using the Flat Pattern.

Tutorial: Working with the Insert Bends method for sheet metal parts

The Insert Bends method has been relegated mainly to duty for specialty functions. Gain an understanding of how this method works by following these steps:

1. Create a new blank part.

2. On the Top plane, open a sketch and sketch a rectangle centered on the Origin 12 inches in the Horizontal direction and 8 inches in the Vertical direction.

3. Extrude the rectangle 1 inch with 45 degrees of draft, Draft Outward, in Direction 1, and in Direction 2 extrude 2 inches with no draft. The two directions should be opposite from one another.

4. Shell out the part to .050 inches, selecting the large face on the side where the draft has been applied. The part should now look like Figure 30.7.

FIGURE 30.7

The part as of step 4

5. Use the Rip feature to rip out the four corners. Allow the Rip to rip all corners in both directions. The part should now look like Figure 30.8.

FIGURE 30.8

Ripping the corners

Completed rip

6. Draw a rectangle on one of the vertical faces of the part, as shown in Figure 30.9.

FIGURE 30.9

Adding a sketch for the cut

7. Use the sketch to create a Through All cut in one direction. Notice that the Normal Cut option is on by default. Examine the finished cut closely; notice that it is different from the default type of cut because it is not made in a direction normal to the sketch, but rather in a direction normal to the face of the part. Details of this are shown in Figure 30.10.

FIGURE 30.10

Using the Normal Cut option

8. Click the Flatten button on the Sheet Metal toolbar. Notice that the Flat Pattern feature becomes unsuppressed and that the Bend Lines sketch under it is shown. This works just like it did in the Base Flange method. The finished part is shown in Figure 30.11.

FIGURE 30.11

The finished part with the Flat Pattern feature unsupressed

Summary

The Insert Bends method was convoluted, requiring a lot of jumping around between rollback states, and reordering to place features in the proper order so that everything appears on the flat pattern where it belongs. The new tools are far easier to use, but do not replace all of the functionality of the old technique.

Chapter 31

Using Weldments

Weldments in SolidWorks are built on driving structural profiles along sketch entities in a multibody part environment. Weldment members can be curved, you can make them using standard or custom profiles, and you can build them from both 2D and 3D sketches. A Cut list within the part keeps track of how much of each profile is needed to fabricate the weldment. Weldments are specialized parts that are similar in some ways to sheet metal parts.

You can use weldments for round or rectangular tubular structures, structures made from channels, flanged sections, standard or custom shapes, gussets, and end caps, and they can also represent weld beads in the part. You can also use weldments to create structures that are bolted together, structural aluminum extrusion frames, and vinyl window frames, and you can put them into assemblies with other parts such as castings, sheet metal, and fabricated plate.

Sketching in 3D

 Three-dimensional sketching is important for creating weldments in SolidWorks. Structural frames are a large part of the work that is typically done using weldment functionality in SolidWorks, and frames are best represented as 3D wireframes. You can do this with a combination of 2D sketches on different planes, with a single 3D sketch, or with a combination of 2D and 3D sketches. If you have confidence in your ability to use 3D sketches, then that is the best way to go. Three-dimensional sketches can be challenging, but they are certainly manageable if you know what to expect from them.

Earlier chapters discuss the tools that are available for 3D sketches; this chapter covers techniques for 3D sketching.

Navigating in space

When working in a 3D sketch, the cursor and Origin initially look as shown in Figure 31.1. The large red Origin is called the *space handle*, with the red legs indicating the active sketching plane. Any sketch entities that you draw lie on this plane. The cursor also indicates the plane to which the active sketching plane is parallel. The XY graphic shown in Figure 31.1 does not mean that the sketch is going to be *on* the XY plane, just parallel to it.

FIGURE 31.1

The space handle and the 3D sketch cursor

Pressing the Tab key causes the active sketching plane to toggle between XY, YZ, and ZX. The active sketching plane indication does not create any sketch relations; it just lets you know the orientation of the sketch entities that are being placed. If you want to create a skew line that is not parallel to any standard plane, you can do this by sketching to available endpoints, vertices, Origins, and so on. If there are not any entities to snap to, then you need to accept the planar placement, turn off the sketch tool, rotate the view, and move one end of the sketch entity.

An excellent tool to help you visualize what is happening in a 3D sketch is the Four Viewport view. This divides the screen into four quadrants, displaying the Front, Top, and Right views in addition to the trimetric or isometric view. You can sketch in any of the viewports, and the sketch updates live in all of the viewports simultaneously. This arrangement is shown in Figure 31.2. You can easily access the divided viewport screen by using buttons on the Standard Views toolbar or the view selector in the lower-left corner of the graphics window. You can also manually split the screen by using the splitter bars at the lower-left and upper-right ends of the scroll bar areas around the graphics window. These window elements are also described in Chapter 2.

When unconstrained entities in a 3D sketch are moved, they move in the plane of the screen. This can lead to unexpected results when viewing something at an angle, moving it, and then rotating the view, which shows that it has shot off into deep interplanetary space. This is another reason for using the Four Viewport view, which enables you to see what is going on from all points of view at once.

FIGURE 31.2

The Four Viewport view

Sketch relations in 3D sketches

Sketch relations in 3D sketches are not the same as in 2D sketches. Although vast improvements have been made by the addition of relations such as Midpoint and Equal, other relations are missing, such as Symmetric and Pierce. Pierce is replaced by Coincident, because in 3D sketches, there is no difference between Pierce and Coincident; this is because relations are not projected into a plane the way they are in 2D. The Symmetric relation, however, is sorely missed.

On the other hand, several other relations are available in 3D sketches that are not found in 2D sketches, such as AlongX, AlongY, AlongZ, and OnSurface.

As mentioned earlier, relations in 3D sketches are not projected like they are in 2D sketches. For example, an entity in a 2D sketch can be made coincident to an entity that is out of plane. This is because to make the relation, the out-of-plane entity is projected into the sketch plane, and the relation is made to the projection. In a 3D sketch, Coincident means Coincident, with no projection.

As a general caution, keep in mind that solving sketches in 3D is more difficult than it is in 2D. You will see more situations where sketch relations fail, or flip in the wrong direction. Angle dimensions in particular are notorious in 3D sketches for flipping direction if they change and go across the 180-degree mark. When possible, it is advisable to work with fully defined sketches, and also to be careful (and conservative) with sketch relations.

For example, the sketch shown in Figure 31.3 cannot be fully defined without also overdefining the sketch. The main difficulty is that the combination of the tangent arc and the symmetric legs of the end brace cannot be located rotationally, even using the questionable reliability of 3D planes that are discussed next. The only workable answer to this is to create a separate 2D sketch on a real 2D sketch plane, where the plane is defined by the elements of the 3D sketch. If you are interested in examining this part in detail, then you can find it on the CD-ROM. The filename is Chapter 31 – Cant Define.SLDPRT.

FIGURE 31.3

Three-dimensional sketches may be difficult to fully define.

This set of sketch entities
cannot be located rotationally
within the 3D sketch

Planes in space

Starting with SolidWorks 2006, it has been possible to create planes directly in 3D sketches. These planes function in some respects like sketch entities, by following sketch relations. Sketches can be created on these planes, and move with the planes. Having planes in the sketch also enables planar sketch entities such as arcs and circles in 3D sketches.

Unfortunately, there is a lot to watch out for with 3D planes, as they are called. The first thing to watch out for is that they do not follow their original definition like normal Reference Geometry type planes. Figure 31.4 shows the PropertyManager interface for creating 3D planes; however, keep in mind that the plane does not maintain the original relation to these initial references. The parent-and-child relations that SolidWorks users are used to are suspended for this one function, or work in the reverse from what you normally expect.

The three-dimensional planes PropertyManager

Three-dimensional planes cannot be fully defined unless there is some sketch geometry on the plane that is in turn related to something else. Relations cannot be applied directly to the plane itself, only other entities on the plane. Horizontal and Vertical relations of entities on the plane are relative only to the plane and not to the rest of the part, and so making a line horizontal on the plane does not mean anything when the plane rotates (which it is free to do until it is somehow constrained to prevent this).

Beyond this, when a plane violates a sketch relation, the relation is not reported, which severely limits the amount of confidence that you can place in planes that are created in this way.

The basic recommendation on this tool is to either use it at your own risk, having been warned, or simply to leave it alone. The preference is to use reference planes that are created in the familiar and reliable way. Although this requires that the planes be made beforehand, it guarantees that the planes will stay where you put them, or move in controllable ways.

If you choose to use these planes, to activate the plane for sketching, then you can double-click the plane with the cursor, or select the plane and press the 3D Sketch On Plane button on the Sketch toolbar. The plane is activated when it displays a grid. You can double-click an empty space to return to regular 3D Sketch mode.

Planar path segments

Some path segments that are allowed in 3D sketches can only be used if they are sketched on a plane. These entities include circles and arcs, and can include splines, although splines are not required to be on a plane. It has already been mentioned that to sketch on a 3D Plane (a plane created within the 3D sketch), you can simply double-click the plane.

To sketch on a standard plane or reference geometry plane, you can Ctrl-click the border of the plane with the sketch entity icon active or double-click on the plane. The space handle moves, indicating that newly created sketch entities will lie in the selected plane.

CAUTION When sketching a rectangle, you are accustomed to getting horizontal and vertical relations on the lines of the rectangle, which orient it in space. When sketched on a selected plane in a 3D sketch, the elements of a rectangle are given relations similar to those of a parallelogram, where parallel and perpendicular relations are used instead of horizontal and vertical ones.

This is due in part to the nature of the 3D sketch, where horizontal and vertical relations are replaced by AlongX, AlongY, and AlongZ.

Dimensions

Dimensions in 2D sketches can represent the distance between two points, or they can represent the horizontal or vertical distance between objects. In 3D sketches, dimensions between points are *always* the straight-line distance. If you want to get a dimension that is horizontal or vertical, you should create the dimension between a plane and a point (the dimension is always measured normal to the plane) or between a line and a point (the dimension is always measured perpendicular to the line). For this reason, reference sketch geometry is often used freely in 3D sketches, in part to support dimensioning.

Using the Weldment Tools

Like the Sheet Metal tools, the Weldment tools in SolidWorks are specialized to enable you to create weldment-specific features in a specialized environment. Everything starts from a sketch or set of sketches representing the wireframe of the welded structural members.

Weldment

The Weldment button on the Weldment toolbar simply places a Weldment placeholder in the FeatureManager. This placeholder tells SolidWorks that this part is a special weldment part, much in the way that the Sheet Metal feature in sheet metal parts is a placeholder, and denotes a special part type. The Weldment feature moves to the top of the tree, regardless of when it is created in the part history. If you do not create a Weldment feature manually, then one is automatically created for you and placed at the top of the tree when the first Structural Member feature is created. Structural Members are discussed next in this chapter.

This feature does not offer any special default settings, except for the ability to set custom properties that transfer to all Cut list items that are created in the current part, and the fact that the Merge Result option is turned off by default in Weldment parts. The former is important when multiple weldments go together to make an assembly. You can access the custom properties interface, shown in Figure 31.5, through the Properties option on the Weldment feature RMB menu.

FIGURE 31.5

The Weldment Properties interface

Structural Member

A Structural Member is the basic building unit of weldments in SolidWorks. You can create a Structural Member by extruding a profile along one or more path segments, and it may result in a single body or multiple bodies. The path segments may be in the form of 2D or 3D sketches. A Structural Member may use path segments from multiple sketches, and each selected sketch entity must touch another selected sketch entity, although they do not need to touch end to end.

NOTE A single Structural Member feature may create multiple bodies, with each body corresponding to a single cut length of stock. In other words, the feature name "Structural Member" does not necessarily refer to a single piece of the weldment, although it may.

One limitation of the use of sketches in Structural Member features is that only two selected sketch entities may intersect at any one location. For example, at each corner of a cube, three path segments intersect, and so you can only select two of those elements at one time to create a Structural Member feature. Because each of the path segments requires a piece of metal, the leftover path segments may be used by a second Structural Member feature.

When creating the sketch for the weldment, it is important to decide what the sketch represents. For example, does it represent the centerline of the structural elements, or does it represent the closest that the elements can be to one another or to something else? You can orient and position structural shape profiles relative to the frame sketch in several ways, with positioning at the shape centroid being probably the most intuitive for closed shapes, and a corner being most intuitive for angle channels.

Figure 31.6 shows a single 3D sketch of a simple frame and a Structural Member feature in the process of creation. You must select the standard first, then the type, and finally the size. A limited number of profiles come with the software, and although it is very likely that you will need to create some custom profiles; fortunately, they are very easy to create.

To access a large number of weldment profiles in various standards, open the Design Library and select the SolidWorks Content icon. Under that, the Weldments folder has several zip files containing weldment profiles. Ctrl-click an icon to down load the file, and then extract the contents of the zip file to the library location you have established for your weldment profiles.

FIGURE 31.6

A 3D sketch of a frame

Locating and orienting the profile

When you apply a profile to a path segment in a Structural Member feature, the profile must have some relationship to the path segment. The default point where the path "pierces" the profile is at the sketch Origin. To change the pierce point, you can click the Locate Profile button at the bottom of the Structural Member PropertyManager, which zooms the view to present the profile sketch so that you can select another sketch point to use as the pierce point. You can select any sketch point on the profile, including endpoints, sketch points, and virtual sharp points if they are present in the sketch.

Profile sketches are generally surrounded by several sketch points, which may seem unnecessary until you consider that you can use any of the points to position the profile. The Settings panel at the bottom of the Structural Member PropertyManager is shown in Figure 31.7, and displays a profile sketch with the interface.

FIGURE 31.7

Locating the profile

In addition to locating the profile sketch, you can also rotate the profile using the Angle field in the Settings panel. This rotates all of the bodies that are created by the Structural Member feature at the same time. In the example of the four-legged frame, if the legs are rectangular or circular, they can all be created in the same Structural Member feature because they are all rotated in the same way. However, if the legs were made from an asymmetrical shape such as an angle, then each leg would need to be made using a separate Structural Member feature, with each leg rotated differently.

Disjoint sketch segments

You can select disjoint sketch segments in a single Structural Member feature if they are parallel to the first segment and use the same location and orientation. For example, in Figure 31.6, notice the four angled supports in the corners attaching to the legs. Because they are parallel in pairs, all four of these supports could not be made in a single Structural Member feature; however, they could be made in two features or by one feature and a mirror. Later in this section, when those path segments are actually used to place Structural Members, the additional requirement of using an angle profile means that the profiles each need to be rotated differently from one another, and thus cannot be used in a single Structural Member feature. Ultimately, the way to accomplish this is by using one Structural Member feature and two Mirror features, thus mirroring the body that is created.

Custom profiles

Most of the custom profiles that you will need may be simply new sizes of existing profiles. You can easily create a custom profile by opening an existing profile, editing it, and saving it under a different name using the Save As command. It is important to note that when creating a weldment profile, a sketch must be selected prior to initiating the Save As command. Weldment profiles are Library Features, and use a *.sldlfp filename extension. Each size must be saved as a separate library feature in order to appear in the selection list. While library features are configurable, the configurations are not selectable for weldment profiles.

Other sources for custom profiles include 3D Content Central, which has a large number of erector-set aluminum extrusion profiles and the accessory hardware for those systems. Toolbox also has a Structural Steel sketch generator, shown in Figure 31.8, which allows you to generate most standard shapes. If you have Toolbox installed on your system, then you can find this tool in the Toolbox menu.

FIGURE 31.8

The Structural Steel sketch generator interface

As I have said throughout this book, weldment profiles are a great candidate for storing in your special library folder, separate from the SolidWorks installation directory. To establish this library location, you can go to Tools ➪ Options ➪ File Locations ➪ Weldment Profiles. Also keep in mind that if you share design duties with other users, then the library location should either be shared among users on a network, or the libraries should be copied to each user's local library. You can also share library data through a Product Data Management, or PDM, program.

If you are creating completely new custom profiles, then remember that when locating the profile relative to the path segments, you can use any sketch point. As a result, you should provide ample selections for pierce points. Virtual sharps function well around filleted corners, as well as sketch points at the centroid of a shape.

In addition to sketch geometry, the library part files should also contain custom property information about the structural shape, such as part number, supplier, material, and so on. This information propagates to the Cut list.

Corner treatments

Any intersection of sketch lines at mutual endpoints within a single Structural Member feature, except as noted in this section, creates a situation that requires that the corners be cut to match. Figure 31.9 shows an example of the three options that are available when lines meet at right angles.

FIGURE 31.9

Corner treatment options

To access the toolbar with the Corner Treatment options, you can click the pink dot at the intersection of the path segments. Default corner treatment settings are made in the Structural Member PropertyManager, but they may need to be adjusted individually.

Two situations do not require corner treatments. The first situation is when a line intersects another line at some location *other* than an endpoint in the same Structural Member feature, for example, a support meeting the main member in the middle. In this situation, the member that ends in the middle of the other member is trimmed to a butt joint. The second situation is when an intersecting member is created by a later Structural Member feature. This situation is dealt with by using the Trim/Extend function, which is described later in this chapter.

NOTE   You may encounter a situation where it seems like a good idea to create collinear sketch segments. In a typical extrusion, the faces created from collinear lines are simply merged together as one. However, in a weldment, this does not work when it is done in a single feature. In order to create Structural Members on collinear sketch lines, you must either extend one line to encompass the length of both lines or do the work in two separate Structural Member features.

Arc segments

When arc sketch segments are part of the selection for a Structural Member, a Merge Arc Segment Bodies option displays after the selection box in the Selections panel. This means that any *tangent* arc segment will be joined to the entities to which it is tangent, but any non-tangent entities will create separate bodies.

A tangent arc is illustrated in the curved leg brace shown in Figure 31.10, along with the Merge Arc Segment Bodies option in the PropertyManager.

FIGURE 31.10

A tangent arc segment used in a Structural Member feature

If the Merge Arc Segment Bodies option is not selected, then a separate body is created for arc segments. The Merge Arc Segment Bodies option applies to the whole feature, and cannot be set selectively for individual arc segments within the selected sketch entities; it is either on for all or off for all. If some arc segment bodies should be merged and others should not, then you should create separate Structural Member features.

It is also a curious limitation that only one arc may be selected if the selected path segments are disjoint. For example, the two arcs for two J shapes that do not touch could not be selected in the same Structural Member feature. The obvious workaround is to create two separate Structural Member features.

Patterning and symmetry

Bodies created by the Structural Member feature can be patterned and mirrored. Remember that there is a difference between patterning *features* and patterning *bodies*. The Move/Copy Bodies feature is also appropriate for creating bodies to be used in the weldment, although the Structural Member feature does not create them directly.

I mention this to emphasize the point that sketching with symmetry is still important, although it is far more difficult with 3D sketches than with conventional 2D sketches. This is due to the lack of the Symmetry constraint and the ability to mirror sketch entities in 3D. I also mention this because in larger weldments (or when using slower computers), performance may be an issue, and mirroring or patterning bodies is certainly a performance enhancement over building parametric features.

Configurations

When you start creating a weldment, SolidWorks automatically creates a derived configuration. Both configurations are named Default, but they have different descriptions. The parent configuration description is As Machined, and the derived, or indented, configuration description is As Welded.

This arrangement holds true for any additional top-level configurations that you create in the part; they will all get the description As Machined and inherit an identically named derived configuration with the description As Welded. These configurations are meant to help you create drawings where the raw weldment is distinguished from the weldment after it has been machined, ground, and drilled.

Trim/Extend

 In situations where you must create multiple Structural Member features, thus creating intersecting bodies, the interferences must be dealt with using the Trim/Extend feature. An example of this is shown in Figure 31.11. The legs and braces shown are all being trimmed by a single face on the bottom side of the rectangular section of the frame, where the small arrow appears.

Bodies may be trimmed by planar faces or other bodies. Bodies may also be trimmed before they are mirrored or patterned. Although trimming with faces gives better speed results, it may not give the same geometrical results.

The Extend option enables either trimming or extending, as appropriate. If the Extend option is not selected, then trimming is the only action available.

FIGURE 31.11

Using the Trim/Extend feature

Trim with
planar face

Body to
be trimmed

End Cap

The End Cap feature closes off an open-ended Structural Member. You can add multiple end caps without re-initiating the feature by using the push-pin icon in the PropertyManager. The PropertyManager and the end product are shown in Figure 31.12.

FIGURE 31.12

Using the End Cap feature

The end cap sits on the outside face of the member, and overlaps the thickness of the member by the inverse of the Thickness Ratio that is applied in the Offset panel. If the Use Thickness Ratio option is turned off, then it functions as an offset from the outer faces of the member from which it is created. When this option is turned on, the thickness ratio can range from zero to one. For a value of zero, it is flush with the outer faces of the member, and for a value of one it is flush with the inner faces of the member.

Gusset

The Gusset feature creates a three- or five-sided gusset in a corner between Structural Members, as shown in Figure 31.13. You can place the gusset at specific locations along the edge in the corner, or offset it by a specific dimension in a specific direction by using the settings in the Parameters panel. You can control the size and thickness of the gusset in the Profile panel. There is no sketch for this feature type; it is simply created from the parameters that you enter in the PropertyManager interface. Again, if you need to make multiple Gusset features in succession, then you can use the push-pin icon to keep the interface displayed until you close it by clicking the red X icon.

FIGURE 31.13

Using the Gusset feature

Fillet Bead

The Fillet Bead feature is somewhat limited in its ability to make realistic weld beads on a weldment part. To start with, it is limited to fillet welds, and does not weld around commonly found situations such as that shown in Figure 31.14. It works best where flat faces butt up against one another cleanly, with enough space all the way around them for the weld bead. It is often suggested that for drawings, you are better to leave the Fillet Bead feature off of the model and simply to use weld symbols or caterpillars to represent the weld bead.

FIGURE 31.14

Using the Fillet Bead interface

Using Non-Structural Components

Non-structural components are frequently needed in weldments, and include items such as feet, plates, brackets, mounting pads, castings, and other items. Simpler items that can be easily modeled in place can be placed directly into the weldment part. You can also insert parts into the weldment using the Insert Part feature, and move them into place by using dimensions or mates. In general, if any item is actually welded into the weldment, then you are recommended to place it in the weldment part; however, items that are bolted on should probably be placed into an assembly. Of course, this probably depends more on your company's documentation standards, part-numbering standards, and assembly processes than on software capabilities.

When adding a plate such as the footplate shown in Figure 31.15, the geometry is added using the standard Extrude feature, except that the Merge option is turned off by default. This ensures that non-structural components that are manually modeled, such as this part, are created as separate bodies, and not merged together with the existing structural items.

FIGURE 31.15

A foot plate added to the weldment

NOTE It is recommended that similar elements of the weldment be grouped together. For example, you can create the tubular members in a group, and the angle members in another group, as well as non-structural components, gussets, weld beads, and end caps in groups or folders of their own. This can help to keep a busy part organized.

Using Sub-Weldments

From a modeling point of view, sub-weldments are generally used for either organizational or performance reasons to group together elements of a weldment or to break a larger weldment into more manageable pieces. This is in much the same way that subassemblies are created for the same purposes within larger assemblies. From a fabrication point of view, sub-weldments are also used to break a large weldment into pieces that can be transported or handled.

To create a sub-weldment, you can select several bodies from the Cut list, and then select Create Sub-Weldment from the RMB menu. (You can also select the bodies from the graphics window if you use the Select Bodies selection filter.) This creates a separate folder for the sub-weldment bodies. You can then RMB click the sub-weldment folder and select Insert Into New Part.

Using Cut Lists

The Cut list that is maintained in the model FeatureManager is simply a replacement for the Solid Bodies folder. It has most of the same functionality as the Solid Bodies folder, as well as a few additional items. The two symbols shown before the Cut Lists title show the folder symbol for the folder when it requires an update (top) and after the update has been performed (bottom). Cut lists are updated automatically when a drawing that uses the Cut list is accessed.

You can access the Update command from the RMB menu of the Cut List folder. Figure 31.16 shows the result of the update. The weldment solid bodies are broken down further into subfolders that reflect quantities of identical bodies. Notice that the weld beads at the bottom of the list are not in a folder.

FIGURE 31.16

The Cut list in the model FeatureManager

Custom properties

Custom properties that come from profile library features, and the Weldment feature in a part, contribute to the information that can appear in a Cut list on a drawing. You can access custom properties for individual Cut list items from the Cut List Item's RMB menu, as shown in Figure 31.17.

FIGURE 31.17

The Cut List Custom Properties interface

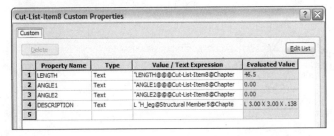

Make Weld Bead

To exclude a feature in the FeatureManager from the Cut list, you can select Make Weld Bead from the feature's RMB menu. The next time the Cut list is updated, the members that were created by that feature will be listed at the bottom of the Cut List folder with the weld beads. You can set back a feature to be included in the Cut list by selecting Make Non-Weld Bead from the feature's RMB menu and updating the Cut list again.

Creating Weldment Drawings

Weldment drawings have a couple of special features that distinguish them from normal part drawings. The first is obviously the Cut list. Like a BOM in an assembly, you can place the weldment Cut list on a drawing by selecting Insert ⇨ Table ⇨ Weldment Cut List. Figure 31.18 shows a sample Cut list on a drawing. In this case, the blank rows represent non-structural components, being the foot plates and the gusset. You can manually add data for these parts either directly into the table or by adding it to the properties of the corresponding folder in the Cut list in the model document.

FIGURE 31.18

A Cut list on a drawing

ITEM NO.	QTY.	DESCRIPTION	LENGTH
1	2	L 3.00 X 3.00 X .138	32.929
2	2	L 3.00 X 3.00 X .138	32.929
3	1	TUBE, RECTANGULAR 3.00 X 2.00 X .25	68.793
4	1	TUBE, RECTANGULAR 3.00 X 2.00 X .25	60
5	4	L 3.00 X 3.00 X .138	46.5
6	1		
7	4		
8	2	TUBE, RECTANGULAR 3.00 X 2.00 X .25	118
9	2	TUBE, RECTANGULAR 3.00 X 2.00 X .25	62
10	1	TUBE, RECTANGULAR 3.00 X 2.00 X .25	58

Also shown in Figure 31.18 is an auto-ballooned isometric view of the entire weldment. This works the same way that assembly auto-ballooning works, and it also corresponds to the Cut list in the same way as the assembly corresponds to the BOM.

Weldment drawings can also include views of individual bodies. You can do this by making a Relative view, selecting both faces from the same body, and then using the PropertyManager of the Relative view in the window of the solid model to control whether the view shows the entire part or just selected bodies. The Relative View PropertyManager is shown in Figure 31.19.

FIGURE 31.19

The Relative View PropertyManager

To access the Relative View PropertyManager interface, follow these steps:

1. Click the Relative View button on the Drawings toolbar or select Insert ➪ Drawing View ➪ Relative To Model.

2. RMB click a blank space on the drawing sheet and select Insert From File. Browse to the part file.

3. Identify the faces to be shown in the particular orientations, and specify whether the entire part or the selected bodies should be shown in the view.

Tutorial: Working with Weldments

This tutorial guides you through building a section of a tubular truss support. You can create many different types of weldments, from simple small gauge frames to large architectural designs such as this one. This tutorial also helps you to navigate successfully through some 3D sketch functionality for creating fully defined sketches.

Follow these steps to learn about working with weldments:

1. Open a new part. If you have Toolbox, then activate it by selecting Tools ⇨ Add-Ins ⇨ SolidWorks Toolbox. If you do not have Toolbox, then simply draw two concentric circles on the Front plane of a new part. The circles should have diameters of 10.02 inches and 10.75 inches. Alternatively, you can copy the library feature from the CD-ROM for Chapter 31 to the location specified at the end of step 5.

2. If you have Toolbox, then select Toolbox ⇨ Structural Steel.

3. Select ANSI Inch, P Pipe, P10. This profile has an inside diameter of 10.02 inches and an outside diameter of 10.75 inches. Click the Create button, and then click Done.

4. Use Custom Properties to add any properties that you would like to have automatically added to the Cut list.

5. Remembering the technique from Chapter 18 on library features, first close any open sketches, then select the sketch from the FeatureManager, and then save the part as a Library Feature Part file to a path such as D:\Library\Weldment Profiles\Custom\Pipe\ P-Pipe10in.SLDLFP.

NOTE   The Custom folder (located in the first level under the Weldment Profiles) will be recognized as the Standard, similar to ANSI or ISO. The next folder down, Pipe, will be recognized as the Type, and the name of the file will be recognized as the Size, in the same way as shown in Figure 31.6.

6. Go to Tools ⇨ Options ⇨ File Locations ⇨ Weldment Profiles, and add your non-installation directory location to the list of folders. Alternatively, you can remove the Program Files location from the list, and copy the files from that location to your own library location.

7. Open another new part, and open a new 3D sketch in the part. Press the Tab key until the space handle (large red Origin) indicates the ZX or Top plane.

8. Draw a rectangle around the Origin, and draw a construction line from the midpoint of one line across to the midpoint of the opposite line. Then assign a Midpoint relation between the Origin and the new construction line. The sketch should now look like Figure 31.20. Apply an Equal relation to two adjacent sides of the rectangle, and dimension any of the lines as 120 inches.

FIGURE 31.20

A centered rectangle in a 3D sketch

9. Select one of the lines of the rectangle, Ctrl-select the Top plane, and assign an OnSurface sketch relation.

10. Activate the Line sketch tool and press Tab until the cursor indicates the XY plane.

11. Draw a line from one corner of the square down, trying to avoid any automatic relations such as coincident relations to other points and any AlongX, Y, or Z relations. Connect the other three corners of the square with the free endpoint of the new line, as shown in Figure 31.21.

FIGURE 31.21

Adding lines

12. Rotate the view slightly. Notice that the first line that you drew in step 10 and one other line are on a plane. Drag a selection box around the point where the four lines converge, and assign an Equal relation to all of the lines. This makes the shape into an upside-down pyramid shape.

13. Drag the point. Notice that it moves up and down, although it seems a little erratic. Place a dimension between the point and the part Origin. Notice that the sketch becomes overdefined and turns red and yellow. Theoretically, this combination should work, but for some reason SolidWorks does not accept it.

14. Using the Display/Delete Relations tool, delete all of the Equal relations that you just added to the part (it may be faster to use Undo or Ctrl+Z).

15. Draw a vertical construction line from the part Origin to the point where the four lines meet, and assign this line an AlongY relation. Notice that the point drags much more smoothly. This is a good reason for using simpler relation schemes when possible. The four equal relations in this case that had to be solved simultaneously are now replaced by a single relation that is easier to solve when you drag the sketch. Apply a dimension of 80 inches to the new construction line.

16. Draw a new line from the point where the four lines come together AlongX in the positive X direction. Dimension this new line as 120 inches. The sketch should now look like Figure 31.22.

FIGURE 31.22

The sketch after step 16

17. Exit the sketch. Click the Structural Member toolbar button on the Weldments toolbar. In the Standard drop-down list in the Structural Member PropertyManager, select Custom. In the Type drop-down list, select Pipe. In the Size drop-down list, select P-Pipe10in. This is the name that corresponds to the way the library feature part was saved in step 5.

18. In the Path Segments selection box, select the original four sides of the rectangle. In the Settings panel, make sure that the Apply Corner Treatment option is turned on and that the End Miter icon is selected. This is shown in Figure 31.23.

FIGURE 31.23

The sketch and the Structural Member PropertyManager after step 18

19. Expand the Structural Member feature. Notice that the four bodies are listed under it. Expand the Cut List folder. The bodies should also be listed there.

20. Open the 10-inch pipe library feature that you created at the beginning of this tutorial. Edit the two dimensions to subtract 2 inches from each dimension, and add a custom property description called "Support Leg." Use the Save As command to save the library feature to the same location as the original, but with the filename P-Pipe8in.SLDLFP.

21. Initiate another Structural Member feature, this time selecting the 8-inch size of pipe from the Custom folder. In the Path Segments selection box, select two of the angled lines that go to opposite corners.

NOTE   Remember that three intersecting Structural Members cannot be created with a single feature. To create material on all four lines, you need two Structural Member features.

22. Make a second Structural Member feature with the other pair of angled lines. The model should now look like Figure 31.24.

FIGURE 31.24

The model after step 22

23. Apply another Structural Member feature to the 10-foot (120-inch) section, again using the 10-inch-diameter pipe. Notice that this member is not long enough to cut through the peak of the pyramid.

24. Edit the 3D sketch and draw a 12-inch extension to the original line past the peak of the pyramid. Use an additional line rather than extending the existing one. Exit the sketch.

25. Edit the Structural Member feature to add the new line.

NOTE You will have to turn off the Apply Corner Treatment option to get this technique to work. If this option is on, then SolidWorks tries to miter or otherwise create a corner treatment between the bodies, which fails when the parts are parallel.

26. The four angled members need to be trimmed on both ends because they extend to the ends of the sketch entities rather than stopping at intersecting members. Initiate the Trim/Extend feature. Select the four angled members in the Bodies To Be Trimmed selection box. Select the four members created by the original rectangle as the Trimming Boundary, and make sure that the option is set to Bodies (as opposed to Planar Face), as shown in Figure 31.25. Accept the feature when you are done.

27. Create another Trim/Extend feature. This time, trim off the point end of the four angled members, using the 10-inch horizontal pipe and the small segment as the trimming boundary.

28. Half of the support structure has been modeled to this point. You can create the rest of it by mirroring the existing bodies. Create a Mirror feature, using the free end of the 10-foot-long member as the mirror plane, and selecting all of the bodies in the Bodies To Mirror selection box. Do not use the Merge Solids option, as you will need to do this manually. Click OK to accept the feature when it is set up properly. The PropertyManager for the Mirror feature is shown in Figure 31.26.

FIGURE 31.25

The model after step 26

FIGURE 31.26

The PropertyManager for the Mirror feature in step 28

An easy way to select all of the bodies is to use the flyout FeatureManager, select the first body in the list, and Shift-select the last body.

29. Start the Combine feature (Insert ➪ Feature ➪ Combine), and set it to Add. Select the two 10-foot sections and the two smaller 1-foot sections to combine them into a single continuous body. Click OK to accept the feature. Also hide the 3D sketch.

30. Right-click the Cut List folder, and select Update. Figure 31.27 shows before and after images of the Cut List folder.

FIGURE 31.27

The Cut List folder in step 30

31. RMB click the folder for the large cross member and select Properties. Change the Description field to read Support Pod Members.

32. Use the Create Drawing From Part/Assembly button on the Standard toolbar to make a drawing. Place Front, Bottom, and isometric views, and then press the Esc key to quit placing views.

33. Select one of the views and then select Insert ➪ Table ➪ Weldment Cut List. When the PropertyManager displays, select the options that you want and click OK. Then place the table.

34. Click inside the Bottom view, and from the Annotations toolbar, click Auto-Balloon. The finished drawing looks like Figure 31.28.

FIGURE 31.28

The finished drawing

ITEM NO.	QTY.	DESCRIPTION	LENGTH
1	8	Support Pad Members	130.75
2	1	Support Leg	110.374
3	1	Support Leg	110.374
4	1	Support Leg	110.374
5	1	Support Leg	110.374
6	1	Support Leg	110.374
7	1	Support Leg	110.374
8	1	Support Leg	110.374
9	1	Support Leg	110.374
10	1	Cross Beam	264

NOTE Relative views are difficult to create with round pipe rather than rectangular tube, although starting with 2007, planes can be used as references for relative views.

Summary

Weldments are based on either a single 3D frame sketch or a set of 2D sketches, usually denoting the centerlines or edges of the various structural elements. This creates a special type of part in the same way that the Sheet Metal commands create a special type of part. Structural profiles are placed on the frame sketch to propagate and create individual bodies for the separate pieces of the weldment. Custom profiles are easily created as library features, and you can add custom properties to the library features, and the custom properties then propagate to the Cut lists.

Chapter 32

Creating and Using Macros

M acros can be an important source of productivity enhancements that are not offered directly by SolidWorks software. Being able to create your own macros can make you more valuable at your place of work. Macros can do anything from centering a rectangle on the Origin, to setting all face colors back to the part color, to changing the decimal places of a selected dimension, to creating a spline from an equation. You do not have to be a programmer to follow the information in this chapter. However, you should have a general understanding of Visual Basic.

Visual Basic is a common programming language. Visual Basic for Applications, or VBA, is included in SolidWorks in the same way that it is included in Word and Excel. If you have programming skills with these other common applications, then those skills are largely transferable to working with SolidWorks macros.

Application Programming Interface, or API, refers to the available SolidWorks functions that can be called programmatically (numbered in the hundreds) from VB, VBA, VB.NET, C++, C# (c sharp), or macro files that have the filename extension of *.swp or *.swb.

NOTE   The *.swb filename extension type is a legacy macro. You can edit and save these files into the newer SWP format, or you can run them as they are. Also keep in mind that *.swp is the filename extension that is used by the Windows Swap file.

This chapter is a quick overview of how to create simple macros, and how to connect them to hotkeys and custom toolbar buttons. It guides you through the creation of an intermediate-level macro to show some of the capabilities that are available to combine with Excel and SolidWorks at the same time.

IN THIS CHAPTER

Recording macros

Creating a macro with a user form

Finding macro help

This chapter is *not* a comprehensive how-to guide for API programming. That would be a book unto itself. However, the end of this chapter does offer some useful resources for help with macros.

Recording Macros

Everything has to start somewhere, and macros start from one of three places:

- As a completely new macro
- From another copied and edited macro
- From a recorded macro

Recorded macros do not always do everything that you want them to do, but they usually offer a good starting place and direction. When recording a macro, SolidWorks lists the SolidWorks API commands that are used to create the action that is being recorded. The macro recorder does not always capture all of the actions, and it does not always record the latest versions of the functions, but again, it is a starting place.

Recording a rectangle-sketching macro

Before getting started, you need to become acquainted with the Macro toolbar. This is shown in Figure 32.1.

FIGURE 32.1

The Macro toolbar

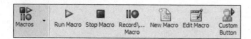

The first macro in this chapter is a simple one that is used frequently: sketching a rectangle and centering it on the Origin. When you start to make a new macro, you have to think about where you want it to start and finish. What exactly do you want to automate? Do you want the macro to always create a rectangle on the Front plane, or just on a *selected* plane? Does it always center on the Origin or on a selected point?

The macro in this example needs to do the following:

- Create a rectangle on a selected plane
- Center the rectangle on the part Origin
- Add dimensions and allow the user to enter values as the macro plays

This means that the selection of the sketch plane needs to be either not recorded or edited out afterward. Because this section discusses recording rather than editing, the macro will be recorded without the reference.

To prepare for recording the macro, you need to turn off PhotoWorks if it is turned on. Macros record some PhotoWorks settings, which are not needed unless you are doing something that is specific to PhotoWorks. You can turn it off at Tools ➪ Add-Ins ➪ PhotoWorks.

Also, when recording a macro, be careful not to make a lot of extra mouse-clicks or keyboard strokes. These may record unnecessary data to the macro, which requires additional editing.

Recording the macro

To record the macro, follow these steps:

1. Open a new part and select a plane.
2. Click the Record Macro button on the Macro toolbar.
3. Open a sketch on the selected plane and sketch the rectangle around the Origin.
4. Sketch a construction line either from corner to corner or from midpoint to opposite midpoint.
5. Select the construction line and the Origin, and assign a sketch relation of Midpoint.
6. Apply a dimension to a horizontal line and accept the default dimension.
7. Apply a dimension to a vertical line and accept the default dimension.
8. Click the Stop Macro button on the Macro toolbar, and save the macro with a name such as Rectangle.swp.

The Macro Editor appears and shows the recorded macro:

```
'*****************************************************************
****
' C:\DOCUME~1\MATT~1.SON\LOCALS~1\Temp\swx3696\Macro1.swb - macro
_ recorded on 12/05/06 by matt
'*****************************************************************
****
Dim swApp As Object
Dim Part As Object
Dim SelMgr As Object
Dim boolstatus As Boolean
Dim longstatus As Long, longwarnings As Long
Dim Feature As Object
Sub main()

Set swApp = Application.SldWorks

Set Part = swApp.ActiveDoc
Set SelMgr = Part.SelectionManager
```

```
Part.SketchRectangle -0.04490775510204, 0.02713176870748, 0, _
0.06081258503401, -0.02806734693878, 0, 1
Part.ClearSelection2 True
Part.CreateLine2(-0.04490775510204, -4.677891156463E-04, 0, _
0.06081258503401, -4.677891156463E-04, 0).ConstructionGeometry =
True
Part.SetPickMode
Part.ClearSelection2 True
boolstatus = Part.Extension.SelectByID2("Point1@Origin", _
"EXTSKETCHPOINT", 0, 0, 0, False, 0, Nothing, 0)
boolstatus = Part.Extension.SelectByID2("Line5", "SKETCHSEGMENT",
_ 0.007328696145125, -6.237188208617E-04, 0, True, 0, Nothing, 0)
Part.SketchAddConstraints "sgATMIDDLE"
Part.ClearSelection2 True
boolstatus = Part.Extension.SelectByID2("Line1", "SKETCHSEGMENT",
_ 0.009355782312925, 0.02759955782313, 0, False, 0, Nothing, 0)
Dim Annotation As Object
Set Annotation = Part.AddDimension2(0.0057694, 0.039918, 0)
Part.ClearSelection2 True
Part.Parameter("D1@Sketch6").SystemValue = 0.0898155
boolstatus = Part.Extension.SelectByID2("Line4", "SKETCHSEGMENT",
_ 0.04490775510204, 0.009667641723356, 0, False, 0, Nothing, 0)
Set Annotation = Part.AddDimension2(0.0661142, 0.0057694, 0)
Part.ClearSelection2 True
boolstatus =
Part.Extension.SelectByID2("D1@Sketch6@Part2.SLDPRT", _
"DIMENSION", 0, 0, 0, False, 0, Nothing, 0)
Part.Parameter("D2@Sketch6").SystemValue = 0.0551991
Part.ClearSelection2 True
End Sub
```

Understanding what was recorded

A few pieces of macro syntax and terminology need to be covered first, especially for those who are not familiar with programming, or who need a refresher.

A single quote in front of a line of text is a way to *comment out* a line, which means that anything after the single quote is not processed, but may be used for reference, explanation, or troubleshooting.

A space followed by an underscore at the end of a line means that the line is continued to the next line. You do not see this in the recorded macro, but it is used here because the lines are too long for the page and must therefore wrap.

At the beginning of the macro, the line with the file path between two rows of asterisks is only added to make a record of who created the macro and when they did so. The name is taken from the user's Windows login name. It is common practice to leave this information in the macro, and even to edit it as various people update the macros. This is one way of giving credit to the original author when macros are shared among users.

The six lines of `Dim` statements are establishing the different types of variables that are often used in macros. Just because a variable has a `Dim` statement does not necessarily mean that it is used in the macro. You can remove some of these if you want. The first two, `swApp` and `Part`, must remain; in fact, these are used for almost all SolidWorks macros. In this case, you can leave all of the `Dim` statements in.

The line starting with `Part.SketchRectangle` is placing the two corners that are used to describe the rectangle. These dimensions are in meters. SolidWorks macros all work in meters, and to use other units, you have to work with conversion factors as appropriate. In more sophisticated macros, the document units are determined, and any user input is filtered through that setting. The corner coordinate data is given in the form X1, Y1, Z1, X2, Y2, Z2, with the 1 and 2 representing the first and second corners. To clean up the macro, you could change some of the numbers to round them out to whole numbers in the unit system of your choice. However, if you do that, then you will need to make other changes, such as changing the endpoint coordinates of the construction line that is sketched later at the `Part.CreateLine2` command.

Going through the rest of the macro in this way helps you to understand what each of the functions does. It helps even more if you keep the SolidWorks API Help file open and look up functions as you go through the macro, such as the `Part.ClearSelection2 True` line. Searching the Index on just the `ClearSelection2` code brings you to an entry that also indicates what the True option does. You can access the API Help from the main SolidWorks Help menu, under SolidWorks and Add-Ins API Help Topics. This help file has a lot of detailed information about specific methods.

Replaying the macro

The first step in using your new macro is to see what the recording contains. Exit and delete the sketch. As an experiment to see how the macro reacts, do not pre-select a plane. Return to the macro editor window, and press the Run Macro button.

The rectangle is drawn, the construction line is drawn, the sketch relation is applied, and the first dimension is applied, but when you enter a value for the dimension, there is an error. The error originates from the `Part.Parameter` line. In this short chapter, there is not enough space to discuss troubleshooting API functions; in this case, it is acceptable to comment out the offending line. The error message enables you to debug the problem. After you click the Debug button, the editor highlights the problem line of code, and if you put a single quote in front of the line and press Run Macro again, the same error occurs for the second dimension at an almost identical line. You can comment out the second line as you did with the first line. This is shown in Figure 32.2.

FIGURE 32.2

Commenting out offending lines in the code

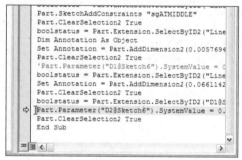

Clear the sketch and run the macro again. This time, with the two lines of code commented out, it works perfectly. Also notice that if no plane is pre-selected, then it goes to the Front plane by default; however, if a plane is pre-selected, then the rectangle is built on that plane.

You may notice some irregularities, for example, that the sketch overdefines if multiple rectangles are built in a single sketch, or a that new rectangle may pick up automatic relations to existing geometry. You can either live with these shortcomings or learn more sophisticated programming techniques to overcome them.

So with a simple recording operation and some minor revisions, you have a simple yet functional and highly useful macro that draws a centered rectangle around the Origin. Many of the tutorials in this book start with the instruction to "sketch a rectangle centered on the Origin," and this is a macro that I use frequently.

Storing your macro

Out of necessity, I usually store macros in two locations. One location is in the SolidWorks installation directory in a folder called *macros*. It is important for this folder to exist with the name spelled just that way so that certain functions with the Tools ⇨ Customize dialog box will work properly, including assigning hotkeys and menu selections to the macros.

Of course, the other location is not in the SolidWorks installation directory so that when you uninstall the software, you do not lose all of your macros. When you do this, remember to also set the Tools ⇨ Options ⇨ File Locations ⇨ Macros setting. Telling SolidWorks where the macros are only affects where SolidWorks looks when you press the Run Macro button on the Macro toolbar; it does not affect the need for the macros folder in the installation directory that is required by the Tools ⇨ Customize dialog box mentioned previously.

Connecting to a hotkey

You can connect a macro to a hotkey through the Tools ⇨ Customize ⇨ Keyboard interface. This interface has been greatly improved in SolidWorks 2007. In order to connect a macro to a hotkey, you require the *macros* folder mentioned previously. You may need to restart the software if you have just created the macros folder, or if you have added new macros in the current session. Scrolling to the bottom of the list shows the macros in the folder, as shown in Figure 32.3.

FIGURE 32.3

The Tools ⇨ Customize ⇨ Keyboard interface

Notice that some of the listed macros already have shortcuts, or hotkeys, assigned. Hotkey assignments are discussed in Chapter 2.

Connecting to a custom toolbar button

Connecting a macro to a custom toolbar button is far easier than it sounds. You can place custom toolbar buttons onto your toolbar from Tools ⭢ Customize ⭢ Commands ⭢ Macro. When you drop them onto a toolbar, the Customize Macro Button dialog box appears, as shown in Figure 32.4.

FIGURE 32.4

The Customize Macro Button dialog box

Type a Tooltip and a Prompt. You can select a custom image for the button. The custom image must be 16 pixels square, in a bitmap format using 256 colors. In the Macro selection box, click the Ellipse button (. . .) to browse to the macro location. You can even assign a shortcut, or hotkey, here; however, I would recommend one or the other, but not both a custom toolbar button and a hotkey. You will end up using one technique or the other, but not both.

Creating a Macro with a User Form

The rectangle macro is a very simple macro that performs a set operation using standard SolidWorks input forms for the dimensional data. While that was a very simple macro, the macro in this section is an intermediate-level macro; it is still not highly complex, but it may take more than an hour to put together. The interface, or user form, is shown in Figure 32.5.

FIGURE 32.5

The user form for the macro

This macro creates a spline from an equation, using Excel to evaluate points in the equation. It allows the user to enter an equation in the form Y = <expression>, where the expression can use quadratic or periodic functions. The user then specifies a first and a last value, and then tells the macro to create the spline.

You can open this macro using the Edit Macro tool on the Macro toolbar. The macro can be found on the CD-ROM for Chapter 32, with the filename Chapter 32 – User Form.swp.

Building the Form

Whenever an interface is created, specific actions are assigned to specific controls in the interface. The most obvious control that performs an action here is the Create Spline feature. In the macro editor, you can double-click the Create Spline button to display the code for the form.

Each of the controls that accept user input drives a particular variable, which is then used to calculate another value or to set a part of the interface. You should have enough controls to do what needs to be done, but not so many that the interface becomes confusing. For example, the Spin Increment is an unnecessary control, and could be removed to make the interface a little less confusing.

You can build the form visually by using the tools on the Toolbox toolbar. The properties for each control are found in the Properties window, which you can access through the View menu. The Properties window and Toolbox toolbar are shown in Figure 32.6.

FIGURE 32.6

The Properties window and Toolbox toolbar

After the user fills out all of the boxes and presses the Create Spline button, the subroutine called CommandButton1_Click takes over. This is the code that you can see by double-clicking the Create Spline button in Design mode.

The macro starts by checking to see if there is an active SolidWorks document:

```
Set swApp = CreateObject("SldWorks.Application")
Set Model = swApp.ActiveDoc
If Model Is Nothing Then                       ' If no active doc
found
    swApp.SendMsgToUser "No active doc found!"   ' Warning to the
user
    Exit Sub                                     ' Exit this
app
End If
```

Then, based on user input, the last X value of the spline is either calculated or used directly. The first X is entered explicitly by the user.

```
first = firstval.Value
last = rangeInt.Value
If rangeInt1.Value = True Then last = first + rangeInt.Value
```

```
If rangeInt2.Value = True Then last = first + (howMany - 1) *
rangeInt.Value
```

Then the step interval is calculated, based on the range and number of data points.

```
step = Abs((last - first) / (howMany - 1))
```

In macros, you find yourself checking for situations that you may normally assume to be the case, and having the macro make a decision, based on the results of the check. For example, this macro checks for an open sketch, and if it does not find one, then it creates one.

```
Set activeSketch = Model.GetActiveSketch
If (activeSketch Is Nothing) Then    ' If a Sketch is not active,
then
    Model.InsertSketch              ' insert a new sketch for our
spline
End If
```

The real functional part of the macro exists in the next few lines.

```
For row = 1 To howMany

'Rebuild user input equation

strlen = Len(equation.Value)   'length of equation string
neweq = "=" & equation.Value   'put an "=" in front of the eq
repl = "A" & row
neweq = Replace(neweq, "X", repl, 1)'step through string and find
"X"
neweq = Replace(neweq, "x", repl, 1)   'replace "X" with "a(row)"

ws.Cells(row, col).Value = xvalue     'write values to excel
ws.Cells(row, col + 1).Value = neweq

yvalue = ws.Cells(row, col + 1).Value 'read Y value from excel

    Model.SketchSpline (howMany - row), xvalue * unitconv, yvalue
* unitconv, 0# ' Draw the sketch thru it

xvalue = xvalue + step ' read X value from excel

Next row
```

This macro writes an equation in each cell with the appropriate X value, and then draws a spline point using the matching X and Y values. It then steps to the next row and does it again until all of the values have been calculated and all of the points drawn. This has the additional benefit of being able to leave you with an Excel spreadsheet that contains the values.

Finding Macro Help

SolidWorks has some excellent on-line resources with a lot of sample code for many applications. If you are creating a completely new macro with programming, then it is probably best to start out by taking a class in Visual Basic or getting a book on the topic. This will give you a general foundation in programming with Visual Basic.

Beyond Visual Basic programming, you need to know some things that are specific to programming for SolidWorks; the best solution is probably to take an API class from your local reseller. This class is not as popular as other classes, and so you may need to wait until the class is offered, or you may be able to find the class available from another reseller. This class can be very useful when taught by someone who knows the material well. I advise checking into the instructor's credentials before taking the course.

SolidWorks has a Web site with a lot of great information that is dedicated to API help: `www.solidworks.com/pages/services/APISupport.html`. If you know what you are looking for, then this is an excellent resource.

Also keep in mind that the Web is a great source of free information. A simple search reveals many personal Web sites of individuals who share or trade SolidWorks macros. In addition to using search engines, check the major forums, including comp.cad.solidworks, eng-tips, and the SolidWorks Discussion Forums.

Summary

The SolidWorks API is extremely powerful, enabling you to create useful macros that range from simple to very complex. However, macro programming is not a casual pursuit, and some basic programming knowledge is a definite prerequisite. Fortunately, you do not need to be an expert, as many macros are put together by cut-and-paste programming, and by incorporating parts of useful macros from many different sources.

Part VIII

Appendixes

Appendix A

Implementing SolidWorks

This appendix is intended to help anyone who is getting started with SolidWorks, or who needs to rescue an existing but poorly implemented system. Everyone, from a single user to the CAD Administrator of a large installation, can benefit from reading this appendix.

Your success with SolidWorks does not only depend on the functionality and quality of the software, or even on how thoroughly you know the software. It also depends on how you maintain the system, license it, install it, and manage the design data, as well as how well your methods are accepted in the rest of the organization. SolidWorks becomes the interface between the engineering department and the manufacturing, IT, project management, and documentation departments. All of these issues come together to describe the overall implementation and integration of SolidWorks into your business processes.

Licensing

Depending on how and where you buy SolidWorks, there may be different licensing options available to you.

Home license

The SolidWorks license agreement allows the primary user of a license at work to also use the license at home or on a laptop, providing that both are not in use at the same time. There are some complications when it comes to network licenses or licenses that require dongles. Your reseller or support organization should be able to give you more details.

Network license

A network license works by running an application on a central server (this could be any computer, not necessarily a real server) that knows how many licenses it can dispense from a license file that SolidWorks provides to you. Each time you start SolidWorks on a computer connected to the server application, it takes one license away from the total available. This system can manage the different levels of SolidWorks, including add-ins. When you shut down SolidWorks, the license is added back to the available list.

A network license offers a fairly simple and straightforward way to install and manage SolidWorks. It is a convenient way for users to share licenses when there are fewer licenses than users. Assuming most of the users are not full-time users, this can be a good solution. If a user wants to run SolidWorks, but there are no available licenses, then the user receives a message saying so, and must wait until a license becomes available. You can add licenses to the network license by getting a new license file.

Dongle

A dongle is a hardware key that plugs into your computer, and allows software to run. In the past, dongles attached to the parallel port, but because many new computers do not have parallel ports, newer dongles are attached through the USB port. Non-U.S. licenses of SolidWorks require dongles.

Standalone license

A U.S. standalone license requires only a 16-digit serial number and an 8-character registration code to install and run. Starting with SolidWorks 2007, this will begin to change to a new process called *activation*. Activation works like activating Windows XP over the Internet.

Levels of SolidWorks

SolidWorks comes in three levels: SolidWorks, SolidWorks Office Professional, and SolidWorks Office Premium. Figure A.1 shows a detailed list of the functionality available in each level.

FIGURE A.1

Add-ins that are available with each level of SolidWorks software

	SolidWorks	SolidWorks Office Professional	SolidWorks Office Premium
SolidWorks 3D CAD Software	✓	✓	✓
DWGeditor	✓	✓	✓
COSMOSXpress	✓	✓	✓
MoldflowXpress	✓	✓	✓
eDrawings Professional		✓	✓
SolidWorks Utilities		✓	✓
SolidWorks Animator		✓	✓
Toolbox		✓	✓
FeatureWorks		✓	✓
PhotoWorks		✓	✓
SolidWorks Task Scheduler		✓	✓
3D Instant Website		✓	✓
SolidWorks Design Checker		✓	✓
PDMWorks Workgroup		✓	✓
SolidWorks Routing			✓
COSMOSWorks Designer			✓
COSMOSMotion			✓
ScanTo3D			✓

Training Options

After the purchase of a new CAD system, training is extremely important. A lack of training often indicates the lack of an implementation plan, and generally leads to far lower productivity and a longer ramp-up time. Although training is valuable, you should try to get the best training possible for a reasonable price.

To make the best use of training, it is best to immediately after the training get the trainees involved in projects using the software. The biggest waste of time and money that most companies commit is to put the trainees back on the old software to finish another project after the training. It is best if your planning can take project scheduling into account so that they have a new project ready to go when they finish the training, especially if it is classroom training with an instructor.

Here are some options for SolidWorks training.

Reseller training

When the reseller sells you the software, they are going to try to bundle in or simply add on the standard training. If you buy the training, make sure that the trainees are prepared for it. Make sure their schedules are cleared for the period of training, and that there are no conflicts with important deadlines or company meetings. Most importantly, make sure that the trainees all go through the SolidWorks tutorials before going to the class. They will get far more out of the class if they have some basic idea of what is going on before they get there. There is a lot to be said for being able to ask intelligent questions beyond the basic, "how do I start the software?" I taught SolidWorks at resellers for about seven years, and the difference between a student who has done his homework and one who has not is immediately obvious.

Before signing up for the training, here are a few ideas.

Training as evaluation

If you are reading the appendix of this *SolidWorks Bible*, then it is probably too late for this suggestion, but taking training as a part of the software purchase evaluation is a terrific way to help you make an informed decision about which software package to buy. Because of the time commitment involved, this is generally only an option if you come from a larger organization with a dedicated CAD Administrator. Training as evaluation is also best done with two people rather than one so that they can trade and share ideas instead of relying on one person's opinions. Make a deal with the software resellers that as a part of the evaluation, you will get training on all of the software packages being considered, and if you buy their software, you will pay for the training. I have also seen this work the other way, where you pay for the training up front, and if you buy the software, then the cost of the training is treated as a credit toward the software.

However you negotiate it, this option is sometimes acceptable to the resellers because they see that you are willing to invest in the learning process, and are serious about the purchase plans.

Using training as evaluation helps you to evaluate more than just the software; it also helps you to see what doing business with a particular reseller is like. If they have to send you to another facility for training, then this is something that you will want to take into account. If the trainer is exceptionally knowledgeable, then that is an obvious benefit to you. If you get to meet the support people, then that is another benefit.

Quality of trainers

In the software reseller world, the sales department is given the highest priority. This means that the best technical people are generally devoted to sales demonstrations and contact with prospective customers. Following this line of thinking, any post-sales activity is usually a lower priority. For example, training and tech support are considered post-sales activity. Because sales organizations often see any technical function as pure overhead (even though it is the only thing on which the customer places value), they may cut corners when hiring technical staff.

Although you may be very impressed with the knowledge and abilities of the application engineer who does your initial software demonstration (which is typically a scripted and highly practiced performance), you should ensure that you become acquainted with the person who will be doing the training. This is because they may be different, depending on the size of the reseller organization.

There is a training certification test given by the SolidWorks Corporation, and you should make sure that your trainer has been certified for training as a Certified SolidWorks Instructor (CSWI). Other certifications that the trainer should have include the Certified SolidWorks Professional (CSWP), and Certified SolidWorks Support Technician (CSWST). Of these, the CSWST is the most difficult to achieve.

Beyond knowledge of clicking buttons and making menu selections, it is also useful if the trainer has some experience in manufacturing or design in the real world, in order to put the software examples into context and understand your questions more completely.

To sum up, before getting training from your reseller, make sure that you are comfortable with the instructor. The main advantage of training with a live instructor is the ability of the instructor to react to your questions meaningfully.

SolidWorks training materials

The SolidWorks training materials generally get high marks for covering what you need to know. The Advanced Assembly Modeling book was always my favorite. Well illustrated and in color, the books are meant to be used in a class with an instructor, but are generally written in a tutorial format, giving the instructor the steps to guide you through the demonstration. As a result, they could conceivably be used for self-paced learning.

Unfortunately, these books are not available to the general public except through the reseller. You can try to buy the books through your reseller without taking the class, (a $100 book versus a $1,500 class), but most resellers will not do this. Of course, there is eBay, but books related to recent versions may be difficult to find through this venue.

Hiring a consultant

Reseller training fees are usually charged on a per-seat basis, and average approximately $300 per day per student. One user for one charge, two users for two charges, and so on. Hiring a consultant may give your company some flexibility, and yet still enable you to get a live instructor, and a flat rate. If you have a large SolidWorks installation and a number of users to train, then this option could save you a significant amount of money. Consultants also offer other advantages, such as coming to your location, as well as the ability to customize material to include only the topics that you need, and to add new material not covered by the standard SolidWorks books.

Specialty topics

Consultants are more likely to be specialists in a certain discipline such as machine design, plastics, or mold design, and so you stand a better chance of getting higher-quality information. If your company has special design practice requirements, it may be worthwhile to have a specialist consultant develop custom material for you. For example, if your company develops mixing equipment, and auger design is important to you, but the SolidWorks software does not have tools that apply directly to your design or manufacturing needs, then a consultant who has developed a process or an add-in custom application will be a worthwhile investment. High-end surfacing is another area where a consultant could do you some good, because there is a general lack of documentation on this topic for SolidWorks.

On-site training

On-site training generally sounds attractive to managers because you do not have to pay for a room, travel, or move computers. It seems more efficient, you have access to your people all day, and they can still reply to e-mails and phone calls. I have done a fair amount of on-site training, and have mixed opinions about it. While it is undoubtedly more convenient and less costly for the host company, the trainees are often far more distracted. I even had classes that were put on hold because most of the class was called away to other tasks.

If you choose to do on-site training, try to set the class up in an area where there are a minimum of interruptions, and plan for it to be as if the trainees were not available for their normal duties at all.

On-line or CD-based training

There are several vendors available that sell on-line or CD-based training. Check the SolidWorks Web site in the Partners area for links to specific suppliers. The advantages of this type of training are that you can go through them again and again, and then give the CDs to other users to go through at their leisure. Compared to reseller training, the cost is very low, and does not require driving to the location, staying in a hotel, or clearing your schedule for a week. It is often well indexed, with searches and hyperlinks, and animated screen shots that demonstrate functions. Some of these also have available self-testing for evaluation.

However, digital media cannot respond to questions in the same way that a live instructor can. A user must also be self-motivated to get much out of this kind of self-paced training.

Train the trainer

The *train the trainer* method can be a good option to help you save some training money and develop some in-house talent. This is particularly true if you have a strong SolidWorks user who is also inclined to being an instructor. The biggest challenge with this training scenario is finding materials for the trainer to teach from. The SolidWorks materials are not available for public sale, and developing your own curriculum is a daunting task.

If you are not familiar with this method, it usually works by sending a couple of people to the formal retail training, and then have them come back and train the rest of the users.

Local colleges

Local colleges may offer courses on SolidWorks. You can contact SolidWorks directly to get a list of the colleges in your area that are using SolidWorks software. Keep in mind that one of the difficulties with using a local college is that the educational version of the software is always one version behind the commercial software. This may or may not be a limiting factor for you. Generally there is not a big difference between the versions.

User groups

I am personally a huge proponent of user groups as a great way of disseminating SolidWorks knowledge. However, I would not rely on user groups for training. The meetings are a couple of hours a month at most, and usually only cover a single topic at each meeting. As a method of training, it would take years to get through the software in this way, but it is still a great source for information.

CROSS-REF See Appendix C, "Finding Help," for a larger listing of general help sources.

Implementation Schemes

Choosing an implementation scheme that best fits your company is one of the first steps after making a new CAD purchase. How you choose to transition from one design software to another depends on many factors, including the skill of your users, how you manage your data, if you work on distinct projects or use teams, and if you do design or manufacturing, or both. The size of your company and the nature of how you work are likely to be the most influential factors.

Implementing something new is usually a painful experience. Software in general, and CAD software in particular, tends to create a dedicated following, and switching allegiance is unthinkable for many users. Also, if you have a lot of time invested in learning a particular software, then making a change can be a daunting and frustrating task. Different personalities deal with change differently, and as a CAD Administrator, although psychologist is not necessarily part of your job description, you need to be able to handle the resistance to change.

In any implementation scheme, it is imperative to have the backing of management, not just one level up, but often much higher than that, depending on the size of your organization. The directive that a change is going to be made needs to come from high enough up the ladder that there is no question about the commitment of the whole organization. End users will think harder before crossing senior management than they will before crossing the CAD Administrator. If the owner of the company has made the decision to buy the software, then you should also enlist him or her to help ensure that the implementation is successful. A failed design system implementation is much more costly than simply throwing away expensive software.

Recognizing that there is an infinite number of combinations of types of projects, sizes of organization, and so on, you may have to use your imagination to apply one of these scenarios to your situation. The following are some of the typical implementation schemes that I have worked with or helped develop at companies where I have worked or consulted with.

Planning

If you are responsible for a multi-seat installation of CAD software, then you need to plan any new software implementation. A Gantt chart, a flow chart, a timeline, or even a simple checklist is a good place to start with planning the implementation, depending on the size of your organization and the size of the task that you face. You should establish goals and dates, and try to understand the prerequisites and criteria for judging success at each step. You should also plan the costs associated with each step. Costs can include training, learning curve, consulting, data conversion or archiving, new hardware, new infrastructure, or associated software.

Pilot project

If your organization tends to have several projects a year where a small number of users are involved in each project and the project has a finite length of perhaps a few months, then a pilot project may be a good option for your implementation scheme.

In the pilot project implementation scheme, you assign a small number of users (usually one to three) to a new project. The end of their training should coincide closely with the beginning of the project. Too often, users go to training and have a gap until their first project with the new software begins, and they forget much of what they have learned.

The users selected for the pilot project should be users who can adapt easily to change, and who learn new software quickly. It may be useful to include a younger, enthusiastic user with an older, more experienced designer. Generally, having two people to encourage one another is a good tactic when setting up a team for this sort of project. One person can develop bad habits or become bogged down easily, while two people can work together to solve problems and learn from one another.

At the end of the pilot project, you have the opportunity to learn from difficulties and mistakes, to tweak the process for the next project, or to expand the project to the rest of the organization.

Phased approach

The phased approach works best when the company has several groups for different product lines (such as motors, brakes, and transmissions), or different disciplines (such as New Product Development, Production Engineering, Manufacturing Engineering, and so on). This approach tackles individual departments separately, by segmenting the immediate task. In the case where work between departments is sequential (passing from Development to Engineering to Manufacturing), the implementation process should obviously start at the top of the organization, and flow through the organization at the same speed that the newly created data flows through the organization.

One thing that the phased approach is *not* meant to do is to phase out the use of one CAD product while another is being phased in on the desktops of individual users. When changing CAD packages, it is best for each user to move completely to the new package. While there are always questions of practicality, such as what to do with unfinished projects or fix-up jobs in the old software, the company should move forward as quickly and cleanly as possible. Looking back or keeping the old software active can cause a lingering stagnation, which always puts an emphatic question mark at the end of the implementation. From an efficiency point of view, it is better to have a single user dedicated to changes and cleanup with the old software, rather than have several users splitting their time between the old and the new.

The phased approach allows you to learn from small mistakes and address the task in small pieces. Getting in over your head is a classic mistake of over-enthusiastic, poorly planned implementations.

This is also a good way to plan when there is more than just a CAD package being implemented. For example, when Product Data Management, or PDM, software is also being implemented, the complexity increases significantly. PDM software is arguably more complex to implement than CAD software, mainly because PDM affects your business processes on top of the large amounts of data that can be affected by the change. PDM is beyond the scope of this book, but it is related to the general discussion and cannot be completely avoided. Implementation of general Data Management practices is covered later in this chapter.

Typical phases used in the phased implementation can include the following:

- **Information Gathering:** What was your condition when you started the implementation? If you ask five people in your organization to write down your documentation process, you may be surprised at how little they agree on what is currently happening. Getting everyone to agree on the initial state of affairs is key to agreeing on an improved process.

- **Process Development:** Write the new process down. If you have flow-charting software, it is a good idea to use it and let people know what to expect, particularly management and IT (if you require desktop hardware/operating system support).

- **Pilot:** Run a live test partially to demonstrate that the process works, and partially to work the problems out of the new process.

- **Rollout by Department or Discipline:** The software is rolled out according to the plan.

- **Evaluation:** Often called a *post mortem*, this involves evaluating how you did, and the strength of the new process.

Cold turkey

Cold turkey as an implementation scheme is probably not very useful unless you have a small group of users. Using the Cold Turkey method means that one day you just turn off the old software and turn on the new. It is probably best if it is planned in conjunction with the beginning of a new project, the hiring of a new employee, or some other culture-changing event. It is not a very sophisticated method, but in smaller groups it may make more sense than an involved schedule. It is advisable to have the training completed before you require the user to be productive with the software.

Hardware Selection

Hardware changes so quickly that my suggestions here will have to be general rather than specific. Still, the overall requirements for SolidWorks have been about the same for several years. Basically, you need to get as much computer as you can afford.

Primary components

The main aspects of a new computer that you want to pay particular attention to are:

- CPU
- Video card
- Memory

CPU

The CPU is on top of the list because it is the least upgradeable. It is certainly possible to upgrade the CPU, but it is rarely economical to do so, because a new CPU in an otherwise old computer will not use the new CPU to its best advantage. Purchase the fastest CPU that you can afford. This is really the heart of your computer. The more complex your parts or assemblies, or the more intense computing that you do (such as FEA or photo rendering), the faster the CPU needs to be.

Multi-processor or multi-core

In the newer higher-end computers, it is difficult to avoid buying multi-core processors, and from all indications, they are only going to become more prevalent. You may hear people say that SolidWorks is not multithreaded (this basically means that it can only do computations serially — one after another), but this is not necessarily true. The response of SolidWorks to multi-core processors varies greatly, depending on what types of work you are doing. For loading assemblies, drawings, stress analysis, rendering, and some of the more complex multi-body solid or surface modeling operations, multi-core is extremely helpful.

If you use your computer for more than one task at a time, then multi-core will be useful to you. For example, while you are waiting for SolidWorks to do an operation on a long FeatureManager or large assembly, you can also check your e-mail or fill in an Excel spreadsheet. This kind of multi-tasking definitely benefits from a multi-core processor. Drawings also benefit from multiple processors, as well as some advanced feature types. I suspect that multibody parts are able to take advantage of the technology as well. This includes most surfaced parts, since most surface models are also multibody models. However, if you are simply calculating a list of features in a single part, and each feature is dependent on the feature before it, then a multi-core processor may be of little advantage to you.

AMD versus Intel

Many years ago, there were problems with AMD processors and SolidWorks. However, in the last several years, AMD has created processors that are far superior to those made by Intel. It was only in mid-2006 that Intel caught up on the highest-end processors. Of course, this changes monthly, and between the time that I write this and the time that the book is published, things may change back and forth four or five times. In any case, for what it is worth, I use all AMD processors on my SolidWorks computers — a desktop (single-core) and a laptop (dual-core).

32x versus 64x systems

If you are getting a computer that you hope will last three years or more, then you will probably want to get a 64-bit-compatible processor. New 64-bit operating systems are available, and SolidWorks is now also available as a 64-bit application. The main reason to move to the 64-bit system is to increase the available RAM. If you are working with very large assemblies or drawings, and you have problems with SolidWorks, or even with Windows shutting down because the memory limits of the system are exceeded, then you are a good candidate for a 64-bit system. All AMDs are 64-bit compatible, as are the newer Intels.

Vista Compatibility

Microsoft is beginning to prepare people for the new version of Windows, called Windows Vista. SolidWorks already has a special beta version of the software to run on this operating system. Most new computers will have a Vista certification, but you need to check for this. Not all new hardware is compatible with Vista, so check it out before you buy.

At some point, new computers will begin shipping with Vista loaded on them. When you buy a new computer, you need to be aware of the operating system and the availability of the Vista version of SolidWorks. At the time of this writing, SolidWorks is only commercially available for Windows XP. There is likely to be substantial overlap between SolidWorks compatibility with XP and Vista, as well as 32 and 64 bit.

Video card

For the past several years, it has been a safe bet to recommend an nVidia Quadro video card, something higher than the 500 model. The nVidia geForce cards also work but have some limitations. You should check the SolidWorks Web site, which has a link on the front page to video card test results. It all boils down to "Red is bad, Green is good." I have run into some users who have an unexplainable obsession with particular brands, and cannot accept that they work great for Doom4 but not for SolidWorks. The bottom line is that for SolidWorks, you should avoid the ATI Radeon, although the ATI FireGL works just fine.

Engineering and game applications use different graphic languages. SolidWorks uses Open Graphics Language, or GL, and works best with video cards that have good Open GL drivers. Game cards use Direct X.

Older video cards and computers use Accelerated Graphics Port, or AGP, slots on the motherboard to mount the card. Newer computers use Peripheral Component Interconnect express, or PCIe. The two types are not compatible, and so if you replace a card, make sure that you have the right kind.

If you have to save some money on one of the three major components, then it may be okay to save on the graphics card. You can replace graphics cards on better computers much more easily than replacing the CPU. Also, graphics cards range greatly in price from a couple of hundred dollars for a functional CAD card to a couple of thousand for bragging rights.

Memory (RAM)

For almost any purpose in SolidWorks, you need to start out with 1GB of RAM. Do not even try to settle for less than that. For complex parts and assemblies, you may need to go to 2 or 3GB. Windows cannot make use of more than 3GB of RAM unless you are running the 64-bit version of Windows. At this point, the memory limit is the only real reason for a SolidWorks user to move forward to 64-bit operating systems and applications.

Memory is a relatively easy and inexpensive component to upgrade. If you buy too little RAM, then your computer uses the hard drive like RAM. However, the hard drive accesses data much more slowly than RAM, and so this causes speed problems.

Secondary components

Secondary components that affect a computer's speed (although not as much as the primary components) are:

- Hard drive
- Network card
- Motherboard

Hard drive

There are two main distinctions in hard drives that affect performance:

Drive speed

Drive speeds are measured in RPM, with the most common speeds being 5400, 7200, and 10000. The faster the drive spins, the faster it can access and write data.

RAID configuration

Redundant Array of Independent Disks, or RAID, can be configured in several ways for speed or for backup use. RAID0 (striped) writes data alternately between two physically separate disk drives, which essentially doubles the write speed. The downside of this option is that if either drive goes bad, then your data may be inaccessible.

Network card

While it is recommended to work with local files, the network card speed does affect file transfer speeds. Network cards are commonly available in 10-, 100-, or 1000-Megabit-per-second transfer speeds.

Motherboard

Motherboards have many components and transfer-rate specs, such as Front Side Bus, or FSB, and Scalable Link Interface, or SLI, which allows you to use two video cards for increased performance.

Installation

The various types of installations of SolidWorks are fairly straightforward and easy enough for the average user to accomplish. You need to observe some general conditions before installing.

Before installing

The following points are really important, and (although reading and following instructions is not thought of as necessary by engineers and IT people) you really need to incorporate them.

Before installing SolidWorks, you need to make sure that you have Administrator rights on your computer.

Next, you need to make sure that your Windows installation is up to date. You can save yourself a lot of problems if you do this before installation. Also make sure that your computer has been scanned for viruses and defragmented before you start.

Finally, disable your anti-virus software and any application that may block access to the registry, such as anti-spyware and firewall software. Blocking applications such as these often prevent SolidWorks from changing system files or accessing the registry to make needed changes or additions.

In particular, Norton AntiVirus seems to be the worst culprit when it comes to getting in the way. Do a search for Norton or Virus on the SolidWorks customer portal, and you will see many references where Norton is specifically blamed for all sorts of strange things happening in SolidWorks.

If you happen to make a mistake and install with your anti-virus application running, and you notice strange messages and crashes, then you can just disable the anti-virus application, and reinstall using the Repair option on the installation. SolidWorks is not supposed to act strangely or crash randomly. If this is happening to you, then there is a problem, because the software does not ship with massive and obvious problems immediately after installation. In my experience, most crashes and strange behaviors are the result of installation or system maintenance problems, not directly attributable to coding bugs in the software.

Installation Manager

The SolidWorks Installation Manager automatically takes care of several things. First, it checks your serial number and determines the software that you are entitled to. It then checks what is installed and displays a screen with the option to select or deselect software or service packs to download from the SolidWorks Web site. Finally, it initiates the installation of the downloaded data.

Installation Manager is installed as a separate application, and you can run it whenever you need to. You can also set it to automatically and periodically check for service pack updates. Installation Manager works on regular disc installations or on administrative image installations, which are discussed later in this appendix.

Installing from discs

Starting with SolidWorks 2007, SolidWorks can be installed either from a set of six CD-ROMs or a single DVD. Installation from the DVD is far easier because you only have to handle one disc instead of several CD-ROM discs, depending on what level of SolidWorks and add-ins you are installing. The six CD-ROMs are necessary for 32- and 64-bit versions, along with all of the add-ins, including libraries for Toolbox and the Routing package. This includes COSMOSXpress, COSMOSWorks, COSMOSMotion, PDMWorks, MoldflowXpress, and so on.

> **NOTE**   As a late addition before this book goes to press, it looks as if SolidWorks will be supplying only DVD format installation media. If you have a computer without a DVD drive, it is time to install one. This alleviates one of the biggest installation headaches for me, which has been swapping out the disks during installations and upgrades.

Pay attention while installing

It is so easy to simply run the installation automatically and click Next, Next, Next . . . when installing, but you really need to pay attention. Read the notices as they come up, particularly the one about the Common Files location. This has to do with Toolbox installation and could have a big impact on how Toolbox works on your system.

New installation or upgrade?

Definitely do a new installation. Most people want to have access to the old version as well as the new one for at least a period of time. Upgrading overwrites the existing old version. However, the best reason for doing a new installation is to simply perform the clean install, with no legacy software.

Level to install

Even though SolidWorks Office is no longer sold, it is still available as an installation option because many users have this level of the software. The only difference between Office and Office Professional is the installation of PDMWorks Workgroup Client. Select the level that you purchased, which should be shown on the original box.

Customize

Customizing the components to install allows you to simply turn off certain files. For example, if you do not have a RealView-capable graphics card, then it probably does not make sense to take up the extra 460MB on your hard drive, and so you can turn this option off. If you have the space, then you may want to install all of the software that you are entitled to. For example, you never know when you may need to use ScanTo3D to surface a point cloud.

Installation folders

This is where you really need to be paying attention. By default, SolidWorks installs to your C:\ drive. However, I like to partition my drive so that C:\ is for operating system files and D:\ is for program files and data. When installing SolidWorks, I always append the version to the end of the folder name; for example, instead of just *SolidWorks*, it says *SolidWorks 2007*. This helps me to keep things organized when I have three versions on my computer and I need to add a Macros folder to one of them, or edit a particular symbols file.

The part where you *really* need to pay attention is with the second folder path. It just says "Install SolidWorks 2007 SP0 common data to:" which sounds innocuous. However, if you are not careful with this setting, you can overwrite all of your existing Toolbox data, which means that all of the assemblies where you used Toolbox parts will lose the size information.

CAUTION Overwriting the common data overwrites all of your size information for Toolbox parts. It is best to install this data to a completely new folder, and then redirect it later to the original folders. If you are sharing the Toolbox library with multiple versions, then you may want to copy the old library to an area where it will be used by the new version. If you try to overwrite the Toolbox data, a message displays and tells you that you are overwriting files that will no longer be compatible with the older version, as shown in Figure A.2. If you have IT people who install software for you, then make sure that they either know *exactly* what they are doing or have a SolidWorks-savvy person available to help them.

FIGURE A.2

A warning message displays, telling you that you are about to overwrite your Toolbox data.

Starting with SolidWorks 2007, Toolbox does have some new options for recovering lost size data like this, but in order to use it, the assembly must have been created in 2007 from a 2007 Toolbox library, and you have to successfully access SolidWorks 2007. It will not repair lost data between an older version and SolidWorks 2007.

 More information about the potential problems of using Toolbox is available in Chapter 17.

Serial number and license server

With the standalone license, you must input a serial number. With the network license (sometimes called SNL for SolidWorks Network License) you must enter a name for a license server. If you are using a network license, the server application should be installed on the license server prior to installing the clients.

SolidWorks Search

If you perform many searches on your computer for SolidWorks files, then SolidWorks Search can save you some time. However, if you do not typically do this, then I would not recommend installing SolidWorks Search. My experience with it has been that it slows down everything else, and can even interfere with shutting down your computer.

SolidWorks Search is based on Windows Desktop Search, which indexes files on your computer to make searches faster and more complete.

Performance feedback

If you choose to participate in the Customer Experience Feedback Program, the software will periodically send information back to the SolidWorks Corporation. This includes information on the features used and the frequency of use, the cause of crashes, system, processor, memory, and OS version, SolidWorks version and serial number, active add-ins, video card and driver, and which commands you have used. This information is meant to help SolidWorks evaluate problems such as random crashes, and understand how users use the software. This is likely the source of information for which features are used the most and which are used the least.

Other software

After the SolidWorks installation, other software is also installed, such as eDrawings, SolidWorks Explorer, and DWG Editor. A reboot may also be required, and after the reboot, some of these additional applications may try to install themselves. It is best to let SolidWorks do what it needs to do to install all of the goodies.

Administrative Director

The SolidWorks Administrative Director creates the installation in a central location so that computers on the network can install from the central location without the discs. You can also apply standardized settings to each installation. The first step is to create an administrative image. This is similar to doing a normal installation. If you require detailed instructions on creating the administrative image, search the SolidWorks customer portal on the SolidWorks Web site.

The second step is to create the initialization file. This contains the settings used for the administrative image installation. The settings can be taken from an existing installation of SolidWorks, or a registry file created by the Copy Settings Wizard.

CAUTION Be careful when editing the registry or individual registry files. Deleting or changing settings in the registry can cause hardware failure or result in the need to reinstall the operating system. When you double-click registry files, they may enter information into the registry that may or may not belong there.

The result of this process is an HTML file with a button that you click to start the installation. The HTML file needs to be sent to each user to run on the local computer, so that SolidWorks can be installed.

No options are available through the administrative image to automatically grant users Administrator rights or to disable anti-virus software.

Configuration and Standardization

Setting up the options in SolidWorks is covered in detail in Appendix B. Standardization can be achieved through use of the Administrative Director (administrative image installation) or by using the Copy Settings Wizard.

Data Management

Data Management is one of the most hotly debated topics in SolidWorks. However, little question exists that using a Product Data Management (PDM) or Product Lifecycle Management (PLM) system is the best way to go if you can afford it. PDM or PLM systems are beyond the scope of this book, but I will discuss manual file management techniques. Manual file management just means using Windows Explorer and any built-in functions in SolidWorks, such as SolidWorks Explorer.

Managing SolidWorks files is not like managing AutoCAD or Microsoft Office files. The external references in SolidWorks need to be maintained, and so you can rename the files, but it has to be done in very specific ways. The most important rule is: *Do not use Windows Explorer to rename your files*. A secondary rule is that if you are creating assemblies of parts or drawings that reference parts or assemblies, *you should not put revision levels in your filenames*.

Of course, the main reason to understand rules like this is so that you know how and when to break them. Both of these rules can be broken without harming your data, but only if you really know what you are doing. The beginning or casual user should adhere scrupulously to these rules. The best way to tell if you are a beginning or casual user is as follows: if you do not know *why* the two rules are so important, then the rules apply to you.

Filenames

When you model something round that rolls, it is very tempting to call it Wheel.SLDPRT. It is also tempting to call something that sits on the bottom, Base.SLDPRT, or something on top, Cover.SLD-PRT. This turns out to be poor practice. Descriptive names have the tendency to be duplicated the next time you make a similar part with a similar function. This kind of carelessness has caused me many problems. For example, I used to work for resellers, and had a lot of demonstration files on my computer. The demonstration files came from a variety of sources: some I had built, some were from customers, and some were from the SolidWorks Corporation. Once, during a file management presentation, I did a search on my computer for all of the parts named Cover. I found about 150 parts.

One session of SolidWorks cannot have two different files with the same filename open at the same time. You can have two different Base parts open at once, but they have to be in two different sessions of SolidWorks. If they are in different subassemblies that are used in the same top-level assembly, the first one to load is going to be used in both instances.

Rules of file management

The preceding example leads to the first rule of SolidWorks File Management:

1. Always use unique filenames.

Most people can see the logic of this, but when it comes to the next rule, many people cringe:

2. Never use descriptive filenames.

Descriptive filenames are what intuitively come to mind when naming a part. The problem is that the same type of function in a similar part tends to create an identical descriptive filename. There is no way to guarantee that a purely descriptive filename will also be unique, and so we come to the third rule:

3. There should always be at least a sequential part of the filename.

I cannot tell you how many times I have heard people argue with fervor that they cannot read numbers, and the only way that they can tell this part from that one is to have a descriptive file-name. I assure you that there are good reasons for these rules; I do not make them up.

You will notice that even the files that are on the CD-ROM for this book have a sequential part in their filename, in that they are preceded by the chapter number, and then followed by the descrip-tive section of the name. This obeys the rules that I have just described.

The filename is really meant for the computer to be able to keep track of the file; it is not intended primarily for human reference. A description of the part is for people to read, and nothing is harmed if two parts have identical descriptions. Descriptions can be displayed in the assembly FeatureManager, in fact, they can be displayed instead of the filename.

The most controversial rule of file management is:

4. Do not put the revision level in the filename.

While this is common practice when files do not have external references, SolidWorks documents are very intolerant of this method. Changing the names of files breaks associative relationships between documents. You can do this if you are not building assemblies, or if you are not making drawings. For example, I may use a part called Part1 on Drawing1 and Assembly1. If I revise Part1, and rename it as Part1A using Windows Explorer, then the next time I open the drawing, it will not be able to find the part. The same goes for the assembly.

There are two ways to fix this simple problem:

- With both Assembly1 and Drawing1 open, use the Save As command from SolidWorks to save Part1 as Part1A. In this case, the references to the assembly and drawing will be updated.

- Use SolidWorks Explorer to rename Part1 to Part1A, and make sure that it updates the references.

These techniques make renaming the part possible, but if you have to do it on a larger scale, then it quickly becomes impractical. For example, if you revise a bracket that is used in ten assemblies, then you are going to spend a lot of time renaming parts.

Beyond filenames, there is the question of how, or indeed whether, files should be grouped into folders. Does it really make sense to break the files into folders simply to group them into smaller groups? The answer to that is ultimately reduced to a network speed issue. If Windows Explorer can refresh the screen in a reasonable amount of time with a thousand files, then there is no reason to break it down into smaller groups. If you use the Thumbnails views, then the refresh may be slower.

When doing PDM implementations, I recommend that you determine folder structure by one of two issues: permissions and searchability. Other than that, why do you really need to break up the files?

Compromise methods

If you find that strictly sequential numbers will not work for you or your company, then a few compromise methods may work:

Intelligent numbering systems

Intelligent numbering systems have many drawbacks, but I have seen them work for companies. The intelligence usually breaks down at some point, and the system becomes more of an encumbrance than an improvement over a strictly sequential system.

Typically, intelligent or semi-intelligent numbering systems work by using some sort of a prefix to signify a defined type of document or part. The prefix may also signify a department for larger companies. Drawing numbers and part numbers are not always the same, because a part may require more than one drawing; for example, a casting that gets machined requires two drawings. Some companies will also change the part number of the machined casting. For example, you may have a number XX-YYYYY-ZZ, where XX denotes what type of part the number is documenting, such as electrical, sheet metal, casting, purchased, secondary operation, process flow document, and so on. YYYYY is a sequential number, assigned from a database or custom application. ZZ may be used as a dash number to signify secondary operations, components of an inseparable assembly, or versions of the same basic part number.

Hybrid naming system

Many people absolutely insist on a numbering system that allows them to scan a column of numbers and read some sort of descriptive language that has some significance. These are the people who often lack the imagination to understand that separating the filename (part number) and description can be both useful and beneficial.

If you accept that a descriptive name does not guarantee unique filenames, and at the same time insist that the filename contain descriptive information, then you are forced into a hybrid naming convention. This combines a sequential number and a descriptive name (or worse yet, a semi-intelligent number and descriptive name), and it has some detrimental effects. The first challenge from this method is determining how you structure the descriptive name so that anyone who makes a new descriptive name uses the same structure. Using the same structure is important for sorting (alphabetizing) and for scanning or keyword searching. Syntax structure governing descriptive names is notoriously (even hilariously) complicated.

The second real challenge from this method is that it makes the filename twice as long as it needs to be. We all know that space inside the SolidWorks window is limited, and having filenames with 20, 30, or more characters makes for some very inefficient use of space and time that you will spend expanding and shrinking windows.

Revision control

The issue of revision in the filename is so contentious and so many people have had to confront it, that several methods exist to deal with it:

- **The current revision is left without the revision in the filename.** When you create a new revision, you save the old revision using the Save As Copy command, and the revision is added to the filename. If you send any files out of the company, they are sent as an eDrawing with a revision in the filename. This has the advantage that the assembly will never reference the wrong part file. The downside of this method is the same as any other manual file management technique: the method is only as good as the discipline of the people using it. This is my preferred method of manual file management.

- **Only archive drawings, not models.** This can easily be done with either eDrawings or PDF documents. This works if you make drawings of your parts, and you are making drawings when you start the revision scheme on the models.

- **Configurations.** I have seen people use this method, although I cannot imagine how they made it work without losing a lot of current or past work, besides the fact that drawings do not have configurations. I do not recommend this method.

- **Use a PDM system.** Almost every objection that you can come up with for any of these manual techniques is resolved by a using a PDM system. In the end, that is the only answer that can give you a high level of confidence. The purchase of a simple PDM application is less expensive than a single documentation mistake.

Network files

If you are not using a PDM system and you are working with other SolidWorks users, then you are almost certainly working with files across a network. Opening files across the network with SolidWorks is not a recommended practice, for three main reasons:

- **Performance:** Speed of working with files across the network can be incredibly slow. Just test it some time with a network file and a local file. Better yet, do it with a drawing or an assembly that references a lot of parts. Besides the speed of the network itself, there are other things such as firewall and anti-virus applications that can significantly contribute to this problem. If an anti-virus program is scanning your SolidWorks files, then you are probably losing 40 to 60 percent of your open and save time just to that.

- **File corruption:** When working across a network, your SolidWorks files are more likely to become corrupted. Search the knowledge base on the SolidWorks Web site for more specific information on this issue. I mention it here to discourage you from working across the network, if possible.

- **Undo:** The network does not have an Undo command for Delete or Move functions. Unless your IT department has provided for this, mistakes on the network can be permanent, requiring a time-consuming backup recovery.

If you have to share files with other users, then how do you do it if working across the network is not recommended? The ultimate solution is to manually imitate what PDM software automatically does. The best way to work on files is to work on them locally. PDM applications know this, and that is how they work. Copy the files locally to work on them. You gain all of the benefits of working locally, but you give up the ability to lock the network files so that other users cannot make changes to the files that you are already changing. This is automatically taken care of by the PDM system, and aside from changing permissions or physically moving files, there may not be a good manual equivalent.

Using a PDM application

Basically, everything under the File Management heading says that you should be using a PDM system to manage your files. It can be either inexpensive and easy to learn, or complex and powerful. Any PDM application is better than trying to manage SolidWorks files manually. If you own SolidWorks Office Professional, then you own PDMWorks Workgroup, which is a perfectly adequate tool for basic file management and revisioning. It is easy to learn, relatively easy to administer, and highly cost-effective.

The details of PDMWorks Workgroup and Enterprise are beyond the scope of this book.

System Maintenance

SolidWorks users use their computers harder than other office workers. For example, SolidWorks puts more stress on your computer than Excel, and COSMOSXpress puts more stress on a computer than Photoshop. This can mean that SolidWorks users need to be more computer savvy than other office workers. Engineers are more likely to exceed the limits of their computer than almost anyone else, and so they need to be able to handle any problems that arise.

I have found that companies that are large enough to have dedicated IT personnel, have varied experiences. In some cases, the IT department realizes that they are a support group that helps other people to do their jobs, which helps to bring in money for the company to pay everyone's salaries. In other companies, the world revolves around the IT department, and it is more about control than enabling others. It has always been my policy when consulting and playing intermediary between IT and engineering to get IT to concede a little control or at least to develop an engineering department liaison who has enough access to the necessary people, places, and things to prevent engineering from losing work time due to IT system issues.

Here are some things that you need to do to maintain your system. Most of these are recommended anyway for general maintenance, but with the extra resources required by SolidWorks, maintenance is more critical for SolidWorks users.

- If you run anti-virus software, then turn it off when installing software. Real-time scanning can also be extremely detrimental to performance, particularly when working across a network. Take a sensible approach to using anti-virus software. If running anti-virus software according to rigid company standard practices is costing you 20 to 50 percent of your SolidWorks work time, then you need to look at a different solution.

- Make sure that your video driver is approved on the SolidWorks Web site.

- Clear out the Windows temp folder locations regularly.

- Regularly defragment your computer, as well as network locations of SolidWorks files.

- Back up your SolidWorks data, including libraries and customized files in your SolidWorks installation directory. Off-site backups are generally recommended in case of disasters such as fire or flood.

- Periodically make sure that the fan on your computer is functioning properly and is not clogged with dust or other debris.

- Keep the Microsoft updates current. Whether you do it manually or automatically does not matter as much as that you do it.

- Use System Restore and the emergency repair disk. This is basic computer maintenance common sense.

- If at all possible, keep your SolidWorks computer off of the Internet, or at least limit its exposure to the Internet. If you need to have the weather updates running on your taskbar or you just cannot live without a dancing dinosaur cursor, then do all of that on a separate computer that is older, cheaper, and less critical to how you make a living.

- If at all possible, avoid installing semi-professional software on your SolidWorks computer. Every time you install or uninstall software, something is added to, and possibly not removed from, the registry. This accumulates over time. There are ways to clean the registry, but the best way to clean it is to not clutter it up in the first place. This is a great use for your older multi-media computer.

- iTunes is a great application, and I love listening to music while I am working as much as anyone. You can already hear what I am going to say next. I use a retired home computer to play music, access the Internet, and install any questionable software on. This kind of computer can be purchased new for $500, and used for next to nothing. Use a KVM (keyboard, video, mouse) switch to share all of the peripherals between the two computers.

Appendix B

Tools, Options

A program with the complexity of SolidWorks is going to have a lot of settings. You can access most of these settings in the Tools ⇨ Options menu. These include system settings that affect only your local computer and document settings (template-based) that are saved with the file. You will not likely need to know all of the settings unless you are doing CAD administration or consulting work, or writing a *SolidWorks Bible*, but this reference will familiarize you with the most important settings. All settings shown in the figures are the recommended settings for general use. Recommendations always change with the situation, and so you should only use these recommendations as starting points.

 In this appendix, the star icon denotes features that are new in SolidWorks 2007, and the rabbit icon denotes features that affect performance.

IN THIS APPENDIX

System Options

Document Properties

System Options

System Options apply only to your local computer, but they apply to every document that you open. The settings are not saved with the files, so be aware that when changing the System Options, other users on different computers will not necessarily see things the way that you see them.

Settings that are saved with the file and used on other computers are called Document Properties, and are discussed later in this appendix.

General Settings Page

The General System Options are for items that affect all of the software. One of the most used settings on this page is showing the dimension names, but several others are important. Figure B.1 shows the list of options on this page.

The System Options ⇨ General page

- **Open last used document(s) at startup:** The options are Never or Always. If you select Always, then when you start SolidWorks, it automatically opens the last document that you had open.

- **Input dimension value:** When you place driving dimensions in model sketches, the Modify dialog box appears so that you can change the dimension immediately, as shown in Figure B.2.

FIGURE B.2

The Modify dialog box

- **Single command per pick:** This option is often overlooked. It allows only one application of a tool for each selection, after which the tool is automatically turned off. For example, if you turn on the Single Command Per Pick option and you click the Line tool, then after you draw one line, the Line tool turns itself off. If you double-click the Line icon from the toolbar, then you can draw multiple lines as usual. For selections from the RMB menu and drop-down menus, the setting is always followed and cannot be overridden.

 This double-clicking function also works in other Windows applications such as PowerPoint, in various functions such as drawing figures, and in text boxes.

- **Show dimension names:** This option displays the dimension name in parentheses below the actual dimension. It is most useful when you use Design Tables, Link Values, or Equations. See Figure B.3.

FIGURE B.3

Using the Show Dimension Names option

- **Show errors every rebuild:** Every time the model rebuilds, if any errors exist, then SolidWorks displays error messages, as shown in Figure B.4.

FIGURE B.4

A warning message for a sketch error

■ Warn before saving documents with update errors: This is particularly noticeable in assemblies, but also in individual parts. When you save a document with an error, SolidWorks asks whether or not you really want to save it, as shown in Figure B.5.

FIGURE B.5

The Update Error warning

SolidWorks 2007

C:\Documents and Settings\matt\Desktop\Part1.SLDPRT has one or more update errors. Save anyway?

OK   Cancel

☐ Don't ask me again

TIP   The Don't ask me again toggle is a nice option if you find these messages annoying. The one caveat to this is that the setting often only pertains to the current session of SolidWorks. After SolidWorks is closed down and restarted, you will see the same prompt again.

■ **Maximize document on open:** This option causes all of the new windows in SolidWorks to be maximized within the SolidWorks window, even if the actual SolidWorks window is not maximized.

■ **Use shaded face highlighting:** When the model is shaded, any selected face turns entirely to the selection color (green by default). If this option is turned off, then only the edges of the face are highlighted.

■ Show thumbnail graphics in Windows Explorer: This setting turns the small SolidWorks icons in front of the filename shown in the Windows Explorer detail view into a very small preview of the part. This option creates a performance issue because the thumbnails take longer for Windows to process than the standard file type icons. See Figure B.6.

FIGURE B.6

Thumbnail graphics in Windows Explorer

Name ▲
cover.sldprt
gear.sldprt
housing.sldprt
inner rotor.sldprt
oil_pump.sldasm
outer rotor.sldprt
pin.sldprt
retaining ring.sldprt
shaft.sldprt

TIP   If you want to display the preview of the part in Windows Explorer, then it is probably better to use the Views ↻ Thumbnail setting in Windows Explorer rather than the SolidWorks setting. The SolidWorks setting creates small icons that are barely distinguishable, while the Windows Explorer setting shows icons that are clearly visible, as shown in Figure B.7.

FIGURE B.7

Using the Windows Explorer setting in Windows Explorer

TIP   You can set the size of the Windows Thumbnail icons in the Windows Registry at [HKEY_CURRENT_USER\Software\Microsoft\Windows\CurrentVersion\Explorer]

ThumbnailSize = 32

Use a value between 32 and 256. Larger sizes will affect load time.

CAUTION   Editing the registry can be dangerous to your operating system and potentially to your hardware. Undertake this sort of change with extreme care and only if you understand what you are doing.

- **Use system separator for dimensions:** This setting establishes the character used to separate decimal values from whole number values. In Europe, a comma is most frequently used, while in the United States, a period is used. This setting depends on the Windows setting that is found in the Windows Control Panel.

    When the setting is on, SolidWorks uses the default Windows setting, and the box to the right where you enter the separator character is disabled. When the setting is off, the box to the right is enabled.

- **Use English language menus:** This setting is active only when SolidWorks has been installed in a language other than English. English is always available, regardless of what language was installed.

- **Use English language feature and filenames:** Again, this setting is active only when a language other than English has been installed. This setting does not change the displayed names of existing documents and features; it only controls the default names assigned to new documents and features.

- **Enable Confirmation Corner:** All SolidWorks functions that use the Confirmation Corner (triangular area of the upper-right corner of the graphics window containing the green check mark and the red X) should also have a green check mark icon in the

Property Manager or on the RMB menu. Turning this option off could save some interface space, although it is not recommended. See Figure B.8.

FIGURE B.8

The Confirmation Corner

 ■ **Auto-show PropertyManager:** This option automatically shows the PropertyManager for items such as sketch entities and dimensions. If this setting is off, then you need to manually select the PropertyManager tab to access settings for these items.

■ **Automatically edit macro after recording:** This setting saves you from manually opening macros so that you can edit them immediately after recording them.

■ **Enable FeatureXpert:** This option enables the Mate, Fillet, and Draft Xperts. The Xperts are intended for two purposes, either for novice users or for situations where a large number of entities are involved and you want the system to sort out errors automatically.

 ■ When rebuild error occurs: The available options are Continue, Stop, or Prompt. Continue is the default behavior, and simply continues to rebuild the part to the end, with or without errors. Stop causes the rebuild to stop at the first error and allows you to correct the error before moving down the tree. Prompt asks you what to do if there is an error.

■ **Custom property used as component description:** The available options are any custom property. This setting affects which custom property is used in the Save As and Open dialog boxes. You can use the drop-down menu to replace the word Description and the value that follows it with any custom property name and value, as shown in Figure B.9.

 This does not apply to the Description used in the BOM.

■ **Enable performance feedback:** Performance feedback is data about how you use SolidWorks, how often it crashes, and what was happening when it crashed. This feedback is in the form of an e-mail, and works best with Outlook.

The Description custom property is shown in the Save As dialog box.

Drawings page

The Drawings page has many general settings that affect the display and default settings used on your computer. If you want to affect specific geometry or data types, then you may want to look on the Document Properties page. Figure B.10 shows the Drawings page of settings.

- **Automatically place dimension inserted from model:** When using the Insert Model Items function, this option allows SolidWorks to automatically rearrange dimensions to minimize overlap.

- **Automatically scale new drawing views:** This option automatically scales new drawing views, based on the size of the view geometry relative to the size of the sheet.

- **Show contents while dragging drawing view:** When moving drawing views, it is often useful to see the view geometry. The downside of this option is obviously system performance, particularly on large assembly views. The alternative is to only show the rectangular view border when dragging.

- **Smooth dynamic motion of drawing views:** This option pertains to the view geometry when zooming or panning. Again, this is a display quality versus performance issue.

- **Display new detail circles as circles:** No, you are probably not the only one to whom this sounds like double-speak. A detail circle refers to any closed loop that is used to create a detail view. This option displays the loop as a circle, regardless of whether it is drawn as a hexagon, rectangle, ellipse, spline, or any other closed profile.

- **Select hidden entities:** This option allows you to select edges that have been manually or automatically hidden by moving the cursor over them, and using the RMB menu.

FIGURE B.10

The System Options ⇨ Drawings page

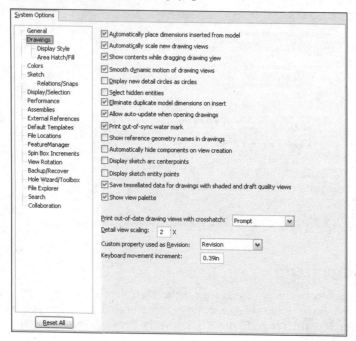

- **Eliminate duplicate model dimensions on insert:** Prevents duplicate dimensions when you use Insert, Model Items. You can override this setting before dimensions are placed by using the Eliminate Duplicates toggle in the Model Items PropertyManager.

- **Allow auto-update when opening drawings:** This option rebuilds drawings and associated models when you open the drawing.

- **Print out-of-sync water mark:** Detached drawings that have not been updated since the model was last changed, can be printed with a watermark to make sure that users know that what was printed was not the latest available version.

- **Show reference geometry names in drawings:** Reference geometry, such as planes and axes, may be assigned names that are important, or may just have generic default names such as Plane1. This option allows you to control whether or not these entities are shown on drawings.

- **Automatically hide components on view creation:** If an assembly component is not visible when a view is created, then it will be set to hidden. This helps to reduce drawing rebuild times.

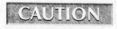 This option can leave parts hidden when they should be shown, for example, when using exploded and section views.

- **Display sketch arc centerpoints:** This is the same as the setting under the Sketch heading. Sketched arc centerpoints (not edge centerpoints) can be shown or hidden using this setting.

- **Display sketch entity points:** This refers to endpoints, ellipse, parabola, and spline control points. When these points are off, it can be difficult to tell where the ends of sketch entities are in a chain of entities. Troubleshooting sketches can also become more difficult when the points are turned off. However, some people find the display of the points to be distracting.

BEST PRACTICE Best practice for this setting is to turn it on. Being able to see the relations on the endpoints can save you a lot of frustration.

- **Save tessellated data for drawings with shaded and draft quality views:** You can use tessellated data in View-only mode and in eDrawings. If this data is not saved, then the viewer and eDrawings will show blank views where shaded or draft quality views are called for. The setting has no effect on high-quality drawing views. Tessellated data increases drawing file size significantly.

BEST PRACTICE Best practice for this setting is to turn it on. There is a constant trade-off between file size and performance (speed). Reading large files is slow compared to reading small files, but reading data is faster than re-computing the data.

- **Show view palette:** The View Palette is located in the Task Pane, and you can use it to quickly drag-and-drop drawing views onto the drawing. See Figure B.11.

FIGURE B.11

The View palette

- **Print out-of-date drawing views with crosshatch:** The available options are Prompt, Always, and Never. Out-of-date drawing views happen when a model changes, but the drawing has not yet been rebuilt to reflect the changes.

- **Detail view scaling:** This option controls the default scale at which detail views will be created. This is most commonly set as shown.

- **Custom property used as Revision:** This option controls which custom property is used to drive the Revision Table.

- **Keyboard movement increment:** You can nudge drawing views and annotations by pressing an arrow key on the keyboard. This setting controls the distance.

 TIP SolidWorks tends to display many default values as ".39 in" or some multiple variant. This is because SolidWorks thinks in metric units, and .39 inches corresponds to 10 millimeters.

Display Style

The Display Style page sets the defaults for display style, tangent edge display, and display quality, as shown in Figure B.12. These values apply only to newly created views, not views that already exist.

FIGURE B.12

The System Options ⇨ Drawings ⇨ Display Style page

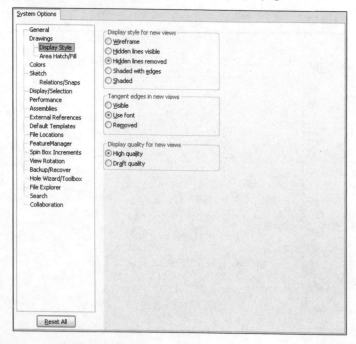

- **Display style for new views:** This setting applies to newly created views. It does not affect existing views.

- **Tangent edges in new views:** Edges between tangent faces display using the selected style. The Removed option does not typically work well with parts without sharp edges, although it would be a good way to display an image of only the silhouette outline of a part.

- **Display quality for new views:** Draft quality views are created when the model is lightweight, and are typically used for large or complex assemblies to improve performance.

Area Hatch/Fill

This page allows you to set the defaults for hatching and area fills, as shown in Figure B.13.

FIGURE B.13

The System Options ⇨ Drawings ⇨ Area Hatch/Fill page

- **Area Hatch/Fill:** This setting determines the default hatch, scale, and angle for newly created hatch fills.

Colors

You can establish color schemes for various items on the interface by using the settings shown in Figure B.14.

FIGURE B.14

The System Options ⇨ Colors page

- **Current color scheme:** By default, SolidWorks installs with several color schemes, and you can make your own custom schemes and save those as well. You can use this drop-down menu to select a color scheme.

- **Object colors:** Figure B.15 shows the list of entity colors that you can change. Some colors stand for multiple objects that may not be listed.

CAUTION   If you change the background to the same color as another object, then you may not be able to see the object. SolidWorks does not automatically change text color if it set to the same color as the background.

- **PropertyManager Color:** The PropertyManager window is treated separately from the FeatureManager window.

FIGURE B.15

List of entity colors that can be changed

Viewport Background	Drawings, Paper Color	Sketch, Over Defined
Top Gradient Color	Drawings, Background	Sketch, Fully Defined
Bottom Gradient Color	Drawings, Visible Model Edges	Sketch, Under Defined
Dynamic Highlight	Drawings, Hidden Model Edges	Sketch, Invalid Geometry
Highlight	Dimensions, Imported (Driving)	Sketch, Not Solved
Selected Item 1	Dimensions, Non Imported (Driven)	Sketch, Inactive
Selected Item 2	Dimensions, Dangling	Grid Lines, Minor
Selected Item 3	Dimensions, Not Marked for Drawing	Grid Lines, Major
Selected Item 4	Dimensions, Controlled by Design Table	Construction Geometry
Selected Face, Shaded	Text	Assembly, Edit Part
	Sketch. Over Defined	Assembly. Hidden Lines of Edit Part

Assembly, Hidden Lines of Edit Part	Temporary Graphics, Shaded
Assembly, Non-Edit Parts	Active Selection Listbox
Inactive Entities	Surfaces, Open Edges
Inactive Handles	Edges in Shaded With Edges Mode
Temporary Graphics	Feature Tree, Normal Item
Temporary Graphics, Shaded	Feature Tree, Selected Item
Active Selection Listbox	Annotations, Imported
Surfaces, Open Edges	Annotations, Non Imported
Edges in Shaded With Edges Mode	Assembly Interference Volume
Feature Tree, Normal Item	Hidden Edge Selection Show Color
Feature Tree. Selected Item	

■ **PropertyManager Skin:** A PropertyManager skin includes a background image for the PropertyManager, as well as a set of buttons for OK, Cancel, Detailed Preview, and Help, as shown in Figure B.16. You can create custom skins using your own images for the background and the buttons. Button images require both an unpressed and pressed version of each button.

FIGURE B.16

Extrude PropertyManager using a skin

■ **Background appearance:** You can select from a plain color, a gradient color, or an image file background. Background images must be in one of the following formats: BMP, GIF, JPG, JPEG, TIF, WMF, and PNG. Not all compression formats are allowed.

> **TIP** A free image application, such as IrfanView (www.irfanview.com), can be very helpful in changing formats, cropping images, or editing colors or resolutions.

> **TIP** When you save SolidWorks files and preview them using thumbnail images, for example, through the Windows Explorer thumbnails, the Viewport Background color will be used as the image background, regardless of the Background Appearance setting. As a result, if the Background Appearance is set to Gradient using a grey top to a white bottom, and the Viewport Background is set to blue, then the thumbnail displays with a blue background. The default SolidWorks setting is a bright blue background. For this reason, I prefer to use white as a Viewport Background setting, although I normally use a gradient background.

- **Match graphics area and FeatureManager backgrounds:** While the PropertyManager and FeatureManager cannot be linked in appearance, the FeatureManager and the graphics window can be linked. This applies for plain, gradient, or image file backgrounds.

- **Reset All To Defaults:** If you create a visual mess that you cannot repair, then you can easily return the settings back to their defaults.

- **Save As Scheme:** If you have multiple users on one Windows login or you just like a change of pace from day to day, then you can save your schemes. I use a scheme with a white background for capturing screen images, and a gradient background for working.

- **Use specified color for Shaded With Edges mode:** The Shaded With Edges display mode can use either a single color for edges on all models (black is the default), or a contrasting shade (the same hue, but either lighter or darker).

> **TIP**   When displaying an assembly in Wireframe mode, it is most useful for each component to be displayed in its own color, rather than having all of the parts use the same color. The wireframe color can be related to the shaded color for a part through a document-specific setting, Document Properties, Colors, Apply Same Color to Wireframe, HLR, and Shaded.

- **Use Specified colors when editing parts in assemblies:** When editing parts in the context of an assembly, you can specify that the colors of parts being edited and parts not being edited to the colors specified in the object color list for Assembly, Edit Part and Assembly, Non-Edit Part.

> **TIP**   You can change the transparency of the parts by selecting System Options ⇨ Display/Selection ⇨ Assembly transparency for in-context edit.

Sketch

You can control the default sketch behavior and display by using the settings shown in Figure B.17.

- **Use fully defined sketches:** If this setting is turned on, then you cannot exit a sketch or create a feature from a sketch unless the sketch is fully defined.

- **Display arc centerpoints in part/assembly sketches:** Arc centerpoints can be useful to select for relations or dimensions, but they can also clutter your screen if there are too many of them.

- **Display entity points in part/assembly sketches:** *Entity points* means endpoints for all sketch entities, as well as control points for splines, ellipses, and parabolas. Endpoints are important to display because without them, you cannot know whether or not the length of the sketch entity has been defined. Figure B.18 shows a line segment with and without this setting. While the display looks cleaner without the big endpoints, the information conveyed by the color of the entity point is important.

FIGURE B.17

The System Options ➪ Sketch page

FIGURE B.18

Showing sketch entity points

- **Prompt to close sketch:** If an open sketch profile can be closed using model edges, then SolidWorks prompts you to allow it to automatically convert edges to sketch entities as shown in Figure B.19. The software closes the sketch in the direction of the arrow, and allows you to reverse the direction in which to close the sketch.

- **Create sketch on new part:** If you create a lot of new parts, then this may be a useful option.

CAUTION   The Create Sketch on New Part option has been known to cause problems with third-party add-ins that create new parts automatically.

FIGURE B.19

A prompt appears, allowing you to automatically close the sketch.

- **Override dimensions on Drag/Move:** This is a great option for concept work. It allows you to drag fully defined sketches as if they were underdefined. It is also available through the menus at Tools ➪ Sketch Settings ➪ Override dims on Drag/Move.

TIP   You can use the Override Dimensions on Drag/Move setting in conjunction with the Move/Size Features tool. This enables dragging sketches and blind extrusion depths without editing sketches or features.

- **Display plane when shaded:** When you are editing a sketch and the model is displayed in a shaded mode, the sketch plane is translucent. This is often an aid that is used when training new users to help them visualize when they are in Sketch mode and which sketch plane they are using. The setting is often used with grid display, as shown in Figure B.20.

FIGURE B.20

A shaded sketch plane with grid display

- **Display virtual sharps:** In the versions from SolidWorks 2007 pre-release to SP 2.0 when this appendix was written, this option did nothing. According to tech support, it is supposed to control the display of virtual sharps in the sketch.

- **Line length measured between virtual sharps in 3D:** When you apply a dimension to a line in a 3D sketch with fillets on the ends of the line, the dimension goes to the virtual sharps rather than the endpoints of the line.

- **Enable Spline Tangency and Curvature handles:** This setting makes the handles visible.

- **Show spline control polygon by default:** The spline control polygon is the set of gray straight lines and dots that surround a spline. This control polygon is helpful in getting a smoothly shaped spline.

- **Ghost image on drag:** This setting enables a ghosted image of where your sketch was originally placed when dragging. The ghost disappears when the sketch entity is dropped. Figure B.21 shows a sketch ghost. This is useful on all kinds of sketches, particularly complex sketches and splines.

FIGURE B.21

A sketch ghost

- **Prompt to set driven state:** When adding a dimension that overdefines a sketch, SolidWorks prompts you to set the dimension to a driven or reference dimension state (gray). The alternative is to leave it overdefining (red or pink).

- **Set driven by default:** This setting automatically makes a dimension driven if it overdefines the sketch.

Relations/Snaps

The settings shown in the Relations/Snaps page control sketch snapping behavior. Most of the Sketch Snaps can also be accessed using the Quick Snaps toolbar. Other snapping and automatic relation settings can also be accessed in the menus at Tools ➪ Sketch Settings or Tools ➪ Relations. See Figure B.22.

- **Enable snapping:** This option toggles all automatic relations, snapping, and inferencing. Items that are snapped to are controlled by the items selected in the Sketch snaps area.

- **Snap to model geometry:** If this setting is off, then sketching does not interact with model geometry, such as edges and vertices, but it does interact with other sketch entities.

■ **Automatic relations:** If this setting is turned off, then no automatic relations are created, although the inference symbols and relations still appear.

FIGURE B.22

The System Options ➪ Relations/Snaps page

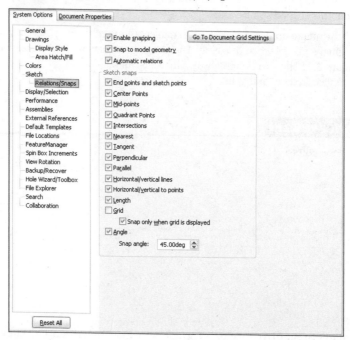

> **TIP**   It is easy to tell which cursor symbols will result in an automatic sketch relation being applied. If the background of the symbol turns yellow, then the relation will be applied. If the background remains white, then no relation will be applied. For example, in Figure B.23, the horizontal relation will be applied, but the vertical relation is only implied.

FIGURE B.23

The horizontal relation is applied, but the vertical relation is only implied.

■ **Sketch snaps:** By default, all of these options are selected except for Grid. You can easily change the snap behavior through the Quick Snaps icon on the Sketch toolbar, as shown in Figure B.24. A sketch tool must be active for this icon to be activated.

FIGURE B.24

Quick Snap filters

Display/Selection

The Display/Selection page allows you to set up your edge and in-context transparency settings, as shown in Figure B.25.

FIGURE B.25

The System Options ⇨ Display/Selection page

- **Hidden edges displayed as:** This setting refers to edges that are not visible through the part.

- **Allow selection in wireframe and HLV modes:** This option enables you to select hidden edges in display modes where they can be seen. HLV is short for Hidden Lines Visible.

- **Allow selection in HLR and shaded modes:** This option enables you to select hidden edges in display modes where they *cannot* be seen. On simple models where you want to be able to select edges without rotating the model or changing to Wireframe mode, this option can be useful. However, on complex models and assemblies, you may want to turn this option off.

NEW FEATURE ☆ In releases prior to SolidWorks 2007, the Fillet feature automatically but temporarily *enabled* the Allow Selection in HLR and Shaded Modes option, even if it was turned off. This often made it extremely difficult to select edges or faces on a model with a lot of edges in the background (you were likely to get a hidden edge that you could not see). In SolidWorks 2007, the Fillet feature has a toggle to enable or disable this setting for that particular feature. See Figure B.26.

FIGURE B.26

The Fillet feature's Select Through Faces option for hidden edge selection

- **Part/Assembly tangent edge display:** Edges created by fillets and other tangent features follow this display setting. There is a similar setting on the Drawings ➪ Display Style page for new drawing views.

NEW FEATURE ☆ New in SolidWorks 2007 is the display of tangent edges in phantom line font for shaded models. Prior to 2007, tangent edges could only be shown in phantom line font if they were visible.

TIP This is a simple analysis technique that is often employed to see which faces on a model are really tangent. Deviation Analysis is a more detailed method, but simply showing tangent edges in a font shows most of what you need to know at a glance. Edges that are not tangent can also be analyzed separately in more detail.

■ **Edge display in shaded with edges mode:** This setting hides edges that lie behind the solid or displays all edges in Shaded with Edges display mode, as shown in Figure B.27. HLR stands for Hidden Lines Removed.

Edge display in Shaded with Edges mode, showing the Wireframe option (left) and the HLR option (right)

■ **Assembly transparency for in context edit:** This setting forces either assembly transparency or opacity, or leaves transparency as-is when editing parts or assemblies in-context. In-context colors are controlled on the Colors page. Transparency often has a negative impact on graphics performance.

■ **Highlight all edges of features selected in graphics view:** If this option is turned on, then all of the edges of a feature will be highlighted. Selected faces are highlighted according to the Use Shaded Face Highlighting setting on the General page.

■ **Dynamic highlight from graphics view:** When the cursor is over an entity such as a face, edge, or sketch element, the entire entity is highlighted and the cursor changes to show what type of entity would be selected if you clicked at that instant.

■ **Show open edges of surfaces in different color:** Open surface edges are edges that are not shared by two faces. The default color for this setting is medium blue by default and is driven by the Surfaces ➪ Open Edges object type from the Colors page.

■ **Anti-alias edges/sketches:** Model edges, and most noticeably shaded model edges, can be anti-aliased to display more smoothly. Anti-aliasing means that angled lines, which typically display as jagged stair-steps, appear smoother. Sometimes this results in a slight blurring or even thickening of the edges.

  In SolidWorks 2007, sketches can be anti-aliased as well as edges.

■ **Display shaded planes:** When planes are displayed, they appear translucent — typically green from one side and red from the other. Colors are controlled in Document Properties ➪ Plane Display. This setting may slow down some graphics cards.

■ **Enable selection through transparency:** Transparent parts in an assembly are invisible to the cursor if there is a shaded part under the cursor. If there is nothing under the cursor except for the transparent part, then it can be selected. You can override this setting by holding the Shift key while selecting the part.

■ **Display reference triad:** This refers to the reference triad in the lower left area of the screen. See Figure B.28.

FIGURE B.28

The reference triad

 ■ **Display dimensions flat to screen:** The alternative is to show the dimensions parallel to the sketch plane in which they were applied, as shown in Figure B.29.

FIGURE B.29

Dimensions flat to screen and flat to the sketch plane

■ **Projection type for four view viewport:** The options are Third Angle or First Angle. This setting does not refer to drawings, only to viewports in the model or assembly window. See Figure B.30.

FIGURE B.30

Third and First Angle projection viewports

 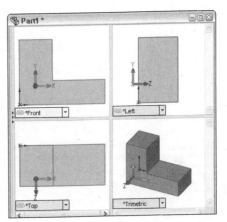

CAUTION This setting is not linked to dimensioning standards or the country in which the software is installed. Third Angle projection is used in the United States and is part of the ANSI standard, while the First Angle projection is used in Europe and is from the ISO standard. Sending a Third Angle drawing to a manufacturer where the standard is First Angle may at least cause some confusion, and could potentially cause incorrect parts to be manufactured.

Performance

All of these settings, shown in Figure B.31, affect an item's rebuild time, file size, or load time.

 ■ **Verification on Rebuild:** When SolidWorks rebuilds a model, it checks the geometry for errors. To save on checking time (when the Verification on Rebuild option is off), each face is checked only against adjacent faces (faces with which it shares an edge). This is adequate for about 90 percent of models. When the Verification on Rebuild option is turned on, each face is checked against every other face in the model, which takes more time. The advantage of using this option is that you do not unknowingly create bad geometry. The rebuild time penalty varies, depending on the model, but adds between 5 percent and 60 percent to the rebuild time. The number of faces obviously affects the verification time (the number of faces is often greatly affected by the existence of small fillets), as does the state of the model with respect to solid and surface bodies. The more bodies, the longer the verification takes. Aside from longer rebuild times, a result of having this option turned on will be failed features when SolidWorks finds face errors.

BEST PRACTICE Best practice for the Verification on Rebuild option is to turn it on until it becomes too much of a burden. You should then only turn it on to check the model after critical points and when the model is complete. To make full use of this tool, turn it on, press Ctrl+Q, and run a Tools ⇨ Check analysis.

FIGURE B.31

The System Options ⇨ Performance page

- **Ignore self-intersection check for some sheet metal features:** Sheet metal parts sometimes have an edge-on-edge condition that causes a self-intersection warning message to appear. This option suppresses the warning message when appropriate.

- **High quality for normal view mode:** When a transparent model is not being rotated, zoomed, or panned, it is displayed in high quality transparency. For reference, low quality transparency causes a coarse "screen door" effect. This option is generally only turned off for low-end graphics cards and large assemblies.

- **High quality for dynamic view mode:** When a transparent model is being rotated, zoomed, or panned, it is displayed in high quality transparency.

TIP   Some graphics cards may exhibit slowdowns if shaded (transparent) planes are in use (System Options ⇨ Display/Selection ⇨ Display Shaded Planes) with the high-quality transparency settings.

- **Curvature generation:** The options are Only on Demand and Always. This should always be left at its default setting, which is Only on Demand. Curvature can be displayed on a per-model or per-face basis. Because curvature display can slow down system performance, you should use this it sparingly, only when it is needed. The Always option generates the curvature display information behind the scenes, and makes it available more quickly, but at the expense of system memory and CPU time.

■ **Level of detail:** Depending on the complexity of the assembly, and the performance of your graphics card, the *Less* end of the slider will cause small parts to be simplified into blocks when you rotate the view. Moving the slider toward *More* will prevent the simplification of parts, but may result in more choppy rotation. The label O in the interface for this setting is conspicuously misplaced. The Help information for it is also misleading. Off refers to the decimation of detail being turned off, so that all of the detail is displayed (Help says that none of the detail is displayed). Figure B.32 shows a view with detail settings of More and Less.

FIGURE B.32

A high level of detail compared to a low level of detail

 ■ **Automatically load components lightweight:** Assembly components are loaded lightweight. This includes parts and subassemblies, unless the Always Resolve Sub-assemblies option is turned on. For a discussion on lightweight, see Chapter 14.

 ■ **Always resolve sub-assemblies:** When a top-level assembly is opened lightweight, subassemblies are resolved, although subassembly components are still lightweight.

 ■ **Check out-of-date lightweight components:** The options are Don't Check, Indicate, and Always Resolve. Out-of-date lightweight components are parts or assemblies that have changed since the last time they were resolved in the upper-level assembly. When they are in this state, they appear like the last version of the part or subassembly that was resolved. Obviously the Don't Check option is the most vulnerable to this kind of error, and Always Resolve is the most conservative approach.

 ■ The Indicate option will put a special symbol on the components in the tree, indicating that the component is out of date.

■ **Resolve lightweight components:** The options are Prompt and Always. Some operations require data that, in turn, requires that lightweight components be resolved. In these cases, this option determines whether the user is prompted to approve the resolve or whether components are just resolved automatically.

 ■ **Rebuild assembly on load:** The options are Prompt, Always, and Never. Sometimes when an assembly is opened, rebuild symbols will appear on some of the parts or features because referenced components have changed while the assembly was not open. In these cases, the assembly needs to be rebuilt to correctly represent the design. The best option for this setting will be determined by assembly size or complexity.

 ■ **Mate animation speed:** When parts are mated in an assembly, it is a visualization aid to have them move into place so that you can see how the parts fit together. Pushing the slider all the way to the left turns off the animation.

 ■ **Update mass properties while saving document:** Solid mass properties take some time to compute, and can slow down rebuilding and saving times, particularly for larger assemblies with many parts. However, if you have BOMs or notes on drawings linked to part or assembly mass properties, then you may want to use this option.

 ■ **Use shaded preview:** Most features allow a preview of the geometry. Although this can reduce performance on a marginal system, in most cases, it is a good way to visualize the finished feature, and it is also useful for troubleshooting. Loft and Sweep features allow a mesh preview in addition to the shaded preview.

 ■ **Use Software OpenGL:** OpenGL, where GL stands for Graphics Language, is the standard that SolidWorks uses to drive the display of shaded 3D geometry. If your graphics card is not OpenGL compatible, then SolidWorks emulates the hardware acceleration with software. Software emulation is much slower than hardware acceleration. You can only change this option when there are no documents open. If your graphics card is not OpenGL compatible, then SolidWorks will turn on this option, and you will not be able to turn it off. The Use Software OpenGL option is often used for troubleshooting. If you are having trouble with SolidWorks crashing, then selecting the Use Software OpenGL option will either eliminate or indicate the graphics card or driver as the cause.

 ■ **No preview during open (faster):** When opening documents, SolidWorks displays a preview that can be panned, rotated, and zoomed. Disallowing this preview speeds up opening the documents.

Assemblies

Figure B.33 shows the settings for assemblies, and is mostly comprised of large-assembly settings.

The System Options ➪ Assemblies page

- **Move components by dragging:** Without this option, you need to use the Move Component tool from the Assembly toolbar to move parts. The default setting (on) allows you to move underdefined components in an assembly by just using the Select cursor.

- **Use Large Assembly Mode . . . :** Large Assembly Mode, or LAM, automatically initiates when the number of components in the active assembly exceeds the number that you enter here. You can also initiate LAM manually by selecting Tools ➪ Large Assembly Mode. LAM is saved with the document, and so the next time an assembly is opened, it is opened with the LAM settings.

- **Automatically load components lightweight:** This is the same setting as on the Performance page, but it activates only when LAM is active.

- **Do not save auto recover info:** This option overrides the Auto-recover setting on the Backup/Recover page.

■ **Hide all planes, axes, sketches, curves, annotations, etc.:** This option is the most frequent cause of confusion with LAM because it turns off all of the items in the View menu. To get the items back, just deselect Hide All Types in the View menu.

 ■ **Do not display edges in shaded mode:** This setting disables Shaded With Edges mode, using simple Shaded mode instead. This is because displaying edges reduces graphics performance.

 ■ **Suspend automatic rebuild:** In assemblies with many mates, patterns, or in-context features, rebuilding the assembly can take a fair amount of time. Suspending automatic rebuilds can save that time, but it may cause other problems if you are not careful such as out of date references. You can manually rebuild the assembly or override the setting by using the RMB menu at the top of the assembly tree.

External References

The External References page, shown in Figure B.34, contains some settings that you should be familiar with, particularly if you deal with assemblies, in-context relations, or other more involved assembly reference functions.

FIGURE B.34

The System Options ⇨ External References page

■ **Open referenced documents with read-only access:** If you open an assembly, then all of the parts and subassemblies are opened with read-only access. If you open a drawing, then whatever is referenced by the drawing is also opened read-only. This option is typically used when many users are sharing files from folders directly over a network, especially if one user is working mainly on drawings, and another user is working on parts or assemblies. Using the Reload function allows you to change from read-only to read-write access, and vice versa. For more information, see the section of this appendix on Collaboration settings, as well as Appendix A.

■ **Don't prompt to save read-only referenced documents (discard changes):** If you open a large assembly as read-only, it is possible for changes to occur just in rebuilding the assembly, which, in turn, makes SolidWorks think that the parts have changed. In this case, when you exit the assembly, SolidWorks will prompt you to save the parts, even though they are read-only and cannot be saved. There is no way out of the loop, other than to just answer No to each prompt to save. This option can help keep you to avoid getting into that loop.

■ **Allow multiple contexts for parts when editing in assembly:** This option allows in-context references from one part to more than one assembly. Although it is usually considered very bad practice to use this option, there are times when you will need to. An example of an appropriate use for this option is if a plate has in-context references in both a subassembly and the top-level assembly. Remember that this is a System Option, and does not follow the document. In-context references are a major source of assembly performance problems.

 Best practice for in-context references calls for moderation and avoiding circular references. For more information, see Chapter 16.

■ **Load referenced documents:** The options are Prompt, All, None, and Changed Only. In this case, referenced documents refer to base parts, mirror parts, and so on. For example, if you open a part called Right Shoe, and Right Shoe was made by mirroring Left Shoe, and this option is set to All, then Left Shoe will automatically be opened as well.

■ **Warn about saving referenced documents:** When saving an assembly, this option enables or disables the prompt to save referenced documents. If you turn this option off, then referenced documents are automatically saved without prompting the user. This eliminates a dialog box that is usually unnecessary.

■ **Search file locations for external references:** The file locations referred to in this case are listed in System Options ⇨ File Locations ⇨ Referenced Documents. The Referenced Documents paths come first in the references search order. For more information on references search order, see Appendix A and the section of this appendix that discusses the System Options ⇨ File Locations page.

- **Update out-of-date linked design tables to:** The options are Prompt, Model, and Excel File. This setting refers to linked design tables in two situations: design tables on drawings linked to model tables, and external design tables linked to the model.

- **Automatically generate names for referenced geometry:** When you turn this option on, it creates names for geometry used in mates, and thus requires write access to the parts being mated. The default setting is off, which is best unless you plan to replace parts using named entities. Naming is done through the Properties for each entity, such as face, edge, vertex, and so on.

- **Update component names when documents are replaced:** This option should remain with the default setting (on) unless you use Component Properties to assign names to parts that are to be used in the assembly tree.

- **Do not create references external to the model:** This option applies to in-context references such as converted edges and feature end conditions. When you select this option, offset or converted sketch entities will be created without relations, and extrude "up to" features and offset surfaces will be created with broken references.

Default Templates

The default templates settings, shown in Figure B.35, help to determine how templates are used for automatically created files.

- **Default template paths:** You can specify the path to the template folder in the System Options, File Locations page.

- **Always use these default document templates** and **Prompt user to select document template:** These two options are actually a single toggle (one of them will always be on). When the system has to create a new document, this toggle determines how it will know which template to use. Situations where the system has to create a new document include imported parts, split parts, and mirrored parts. The Always Use these Default Document Templates option means that the above listed templates will be used automatically. If they are not available, then automatically generated default templates will be used (these are the original templates that exist with a new installation of SolidWorks). The Prompt User to Select Document Template option means that in those situations, the user will be prompted to select a template for each part that is generated. In imported assemblies with a lot of parts, it may be wise to opt for the automatic setting unless you need to specify different templates for different parts.

BEST PRACTICE Create a Library folder that includes items such as templates, blocks, library parts, and features, forming tools, and so on. This folder should be separate from your installation directory. This allows you to access the library between computers or multiple SolidWorks installations.

FIGURE B.35

The System Options ⇨ Default Templates page

File Locations

Use the File Locations settings shown in Figure B.36 to establish libraries of different types of files, stored from version to version.

■ **File Locations:** The list of file types for which SolidWorks can specify a specific library location is fairly extensive.

BEST PRACTICE Best practice for File Locations is to create a library folder somewhere other than the default SolidWorks installation folder. When you upgrade SolidWorks, change computers, change jobs, or share data with coworkers, this data is portable. File types that you can store this way include document and table templates, formats, logos, blocks, Design Library parts, library features, forming tools, special fonts, gauge tables, customized symbol files, material libraries, macros, and basically anything else on the list that you have improved from its default, installed state.

FIGURE B.36

The System Options ⇨ File Locations page

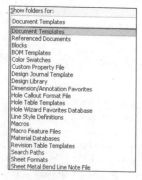

FeatureManager

The FeatureManager settings, shown in Figure B.37, determine how the FeatureManager reacts to various actions.

FIGURE B.37

The System Options ➪ FeatureManager page

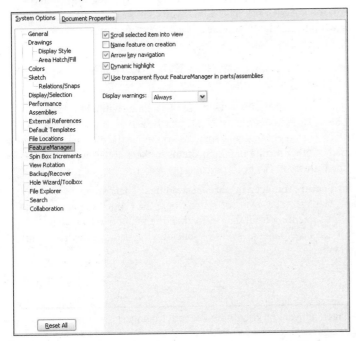

- **Scroll selected item into view:** When something is selected in the graphics window, the FeatureManager scrolls to display the selected feature. Of course, this happens only if the number of features in the FeatureManager is greater than the available window space can accommodate.

- **Name feature on creation:** Although you may seldom want to rename *every* new sketch and feature as it is created, when you want to do so, this is the option to select. Immediately upon creation of a feature, you are put into Edit mode on the feature name. When I tried using this option, I found that I ended up with a lot of features named zzzz because I usually wanted to zoom out after creating a new feature.

BEST PRACTICE It is certainly best practice to name key features and sketches with names that will be easy to identify later. Renaming features is not just for your own convenience, but is also useful if anyone downstream from you will need to edit your work.

TIP In addition to renaming features, you can use the Go To function in SolidWorks. Available from the RMB menu, this function searches the FeatureManager for text that you enter.

■ **Arrow key navigation:** Under normal usage, the arrow keys rotate the model by an angle specified in System Options ➪ View Rotation. However, when the Rollback bar in the FeatureManager has been selected and arrow key navigation is turned on, the up- and down-arrow keys control the Rollback bar. This allows you to more easily step through the features. One caveat with this is that if you are editing a part in-context, the down arrow will roll to the end in one keystroke.

On the topic of rollback management, the RMB menu has several rollback options, such as Rollback, Roll to End, and Roll to Previous.

■ **Dynamic Highlight:** This is not to be confused with the Dynamic Highlight from Graphics View option, found at System Options ➪ Display/Selection. This option highlights faces, edges, vertices, sketch entities, and so on as you move the mouse over them in the graphics window. The other setting highlights items in the graphics window as you move the mouse over the features in the FeatureManager.

■ **Use transparent flyout FeatureManager in parts/assemblies:** There are many situations where the PropertyManager takes over the space where the FeatureManager should be, and you need to select something from the tree. When the flyout is activated, as shown in Figure B.38, it can be expanded by double-clicking the name of the feature at the top of the PropertyManager.

FIGURE B.38

The flyout FeatureManager, activated through the PropertyManager

An alternative to displaying the flyout FeatureManager is splitting the FeatureManager, as shown in Figure B.39.

FIGURE B.39

Splitting the FeatureManager

- **Display warnings:** The options are Always, Never, and All But Top Level. Never and All But Top Level may be options that you want to use when your boss is looking over your shoulder, but for real-world work, you should select the Always option so that you know when there is a problem.

BEST PRACTICE Best practice for displaying warnings is to set it to Always. Another best practice is to repair errors as soon as you can. Errors may cause more errors down the line, and they affect performance adversely because SolidWorks keeps trying to resolve the error.

Spin Box Increments

Figure B.40 shows the settings for the spin box increments. Spin boxes enable you to increase values by clicking on the arrows. Some spin boxes, such as the Dimension Modify spin box, also have a button that enables you to select from a list of increment values. The +-? symbol shown in the Modify box in Figure B.41 does this.

FIGURE B.40

The System Options ⇨ Spin Box Increments page

■ **Length increments:** Whenever you click one of the spin arrows on a dimension or number setting, it increments by this value. The exceptions are features such as the tolerance for Fit Splines, where the increment values are determined by the scale of the geometry.

NEW FEATURE ⭐ SolidWorks 2007 has new functions for incrementing values. The Modify dialog box shown in Figure B.41 contains a spin wheel below the number field. By clicking this wheel and dragging right or left, you can increase or decrease the value in the number field. Holding the Ctrl key while dragging increases the increment by a factor of ten. Holding the Alt key while dragging decreases the increment by a factor of ten.

FIGURE B.41

A Modify dialog box with a spin wheel below the number field

View Rotation

The View Rotation options, shown in Figure B.42, are discussed below. View rotation can be done with the mouse, with the keyboard, and automatically by certain functions. The speed of rotation or increment of rotation is controlled by the settings on this page.

The System Options ⇨ View Rotation page

- **Arrow keys:** This option determines how many degrees the view will rotate each time a user clicks the arrow button.

- **Mouse speed:** By default, the SolidWorks mouse settings are the same as the Windows mouse settings for cursor speed.

- **View animation speed:** When changing between named views or using a Shift-arrow (90-degree rotation) key combination, the view change animates to help prevent the user from becoming disoriented by an immediate and significant change of view. Moving the slider completely to the left (past the Fast setting) disables the view animation.

Backup/Recover

The Backup and Recover options have changed significantly for SolidWorks 2007. Figure B.43 shows the new settings.

FIGURE B.43

The System Options ⇨ Backup/Recover page

 ■ **Save auto-recover info every:** This setting has changed for SolidWorks 2007. It now allows you to specify that SolidWorks save auto-recover information according to a number of changes or an amount of time. You can also specify the folder to be used for the auto-recover data. Auto-recover information is only used if SolidWorks crashes. The next time you launch SolidWorks after a crash, it will offer you the chance to open the recovered files. The auto-recovered files are shown in the Task pane. If SolidWorks exits normally, then the auto-recover information is discarded at the end of the session. This setting can degrade performance, especially of large parts or assemblies, because it periodically saves out data while you are working.

 ■ **Number of backup copies per document:** Another change for SolidWorks 2007 is that SolidWorks has separated the Auto-recover settings from the Backup settings so that they are now two clearly different functions. Backup works differently from auto-recover in that backup occurs only during a save. The previously saved version is renamed (and moved to a new location if the Backup folder is specified). Also new for SolidWorks 2007 is the purge of backup files by age.

■ **Save notification:** This is the kind of setting that you will probably use after you have crashed and lost a lot of work. It is a nice reminder that does not have to get in the way of work, but not everyone has enough patience to deal with persistent (if polite) nagging. You need to balance how much work can you afford to lose with how often can you withstand the persistent reminders.

Hole Wizard/Toolbox

The Hole Wizard and Toolbox operate from the same database of hole/hardware size data. The path shown on the page shown in Figure B.44 establishes where the database for these functions is located on your hard drive or network.

FIGURE B.44

The Hole Wizard/Toolbox settings page

System Options	Document Properties

General
Drawings
— Display Style
— Area Hatch/Fill
Colors
Sketch
— Relations/Snaps
Display/Selection
Performance
Assemblies
External References
Default Templates
File Locations
FeatureManager
Spin Box Increments
View Rotation/Zoom
Backup/Recover
Hole Wizard/Toolbox
File Explorer
Search
Collaboration

HoleWizard/ToolBox folder:

`D:\program files\common files\solidworks dat` [...]

[Configure...]

The Configure button shown here displays some of the settings for establishing how Toolbox functions. More details can be found about the Toolbox product in Chapter 17.

File Explorer

The File Explorer is a part of the Task Pane. It can be shown by clicking the icon of the folder with the magnifying glass on it. The options for what you can display in the File Explorer are shown in Figure B.45. The File Explorer can be used as a substitute for Windows Explorer right within SolidWorks, as well as showing data with special significance to SolidWorks such as samples that install by default with SolidWorks, files already open in SolidWorks, and recently opened SolidWorks documents.

FIGURE B.45

The System Options ➪ File Explorer page

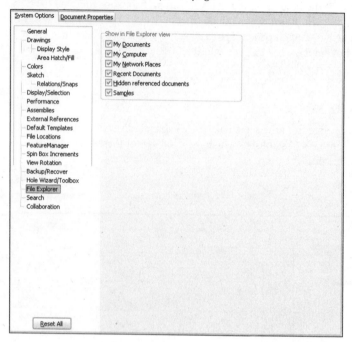

■ **Show in File Explorer view:** File Explorer is the Windows Explorer–like part of the Task Pane, as shown in Figure B.46. Notice that it has a folder for documents that are currently open in SolidWorks, as well as a recent documents list. The panel will disappear after you use it once, although you can click the push-pin icon to keep it displayed. This is a very useful panel.

FIGURE B.46

The File Explorer panel

The Task pane can be detached from its default location on the right side of the screen and either allowed to float or dock on the left side.

Search

The Search options are shown in Figure B.47. Windows Desktop Search is integrated into the new SolidWorks Search function. In order for this function to work properly, Windows Desktop Search must be installed (it is located on the SolidWorks CD-ROM), and then your drive or drives must be indexed, which will take some time.

FIGURE B.47

The System Options ⇨ Search page

   ■ **Search while typing:** With this option enabled, the search takes place immediately as you type the string to be searched instead of waiting for you to press Enter. This enables you to see results on partial strings as well as the complete search name. The SolidWorks Search feature is shown in Figure B.48.

FIGURE B.48

The SolidWorks Search function

- **Results per page:** The search returns results in the Search panel of the Task pane, with easy-to-see previews, filenames, and path information, as shown in Figure B.49. You can also search on custom property information, as well as keywords.

FIGURE B.49

SolidWorks Search results

- **Maximum results per data source:** This setting allows you to specify limits, so that you are not overwhelmed with all of the available data.

- **Index Now:** After guiding you through a wizard to narrow down the hard drive areas where you keep data that you want to be indexed, this option initiates the Windows Desktop Search Indexing function, as shown in Figure B.50. You can also specify search paths through the Search Paths option at System Options ⇨ File Locations.

FIGURE B.50

The Windows Desktop Search Indexing Status dialog box

Collaboration

You should consider using the Collaboration settings when setting up a PDM application or a manual document management system between multiple users. The Collaboration settings are shown in Figure B.51.

- **Enable multi-user environment:** This option enables the rest of the collaboration options.

- **Add shortcut menu items for multi-user environment:** When you select this option, the items Make Read-Only and Get Write Access become available on the RMB (shortcut) menu and the File menu.

> **TIP** There is no indication on the FeatureManager whether individual parts in an assembly are read-only or read-write. The only indication appears at the top of the screen, after the filename, where it is indicated in brackets, for example, as [Read-Only]. Another way to check is to look at the File ⇨ Find References lists; a read-only indicator appears after the filename.

- **Check if files opened read-only have been modified by other users:** This option will check open read-only documents, at the indicated interval, for changes.

The System Options ⇨ Collaboration page

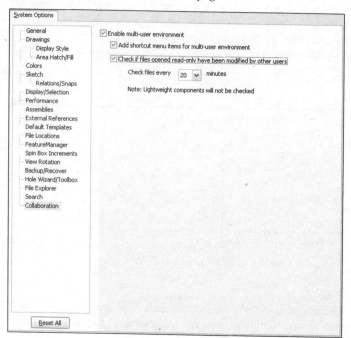

Document Properties

In this case, the term "Document Properties" refers to the settings that are specific to each individual document. This does not have anything to do with File Properties or Custom Properties. Document Properties settings are stored in templates and reused when you use the template to create a new document.

I often hear the question, "Can I change the template used by a document?" The answer is always "No." However, you can change the settings. Some tools exist that can help you take a list of settings and write them to a group of documents. These tools are available on the Internet for download. One that I am familiar with is an Excel spreadsheet with some VBA programming that handles this function.

The following list details each of the Document Properties settings and gives some insight about when and why you should use each setting.

Detailing

The Detailing Document Properties page is shown in Figure B.52.

The Document Properties ⇨ Detailing page

- **Dimensioning Standard:** The options are ANSI, BSI, DIN, GB, GOST, ISO, and JIS.

CAUTION   A very important note for American users is that for some default SolidWorks document templates, ISO is the standard. When the ISO standard is used, First Angle Projection is used for projected views rather than Third Angle Projection, which is the standard for ANSI. This can lead to drawings that are incorrect by the ANSI standard, and will seem more than a little confusing until you understand what is going on.

Another situation where you encounter the First-versus-Third-angle-projection problem is in the System Options tab, on the Display/Selection page. The Viewport tool is set to use First Angle, whether you install with ANSI or not.

There is no comprehensive list of all of the differences in SolidWorks settings between the various standards. If you use documents with different standards, then you will need to create different templates for each standard. Be sure to search through the options to find out the differences between the standards.

- **Dual Dimensions Display:** Users of older versions will cheer when they see the options that are available in Dual dimensions display. Figure B.53 shows the effects of the display options.

FIGURE B.53

The different options for Dual Dimensions Display

[107.31]   4.225
  4.225   [107.31]   4.225[107.31]   [107.31]4.225

- **Fixed Size Weld Symbols:** This option toggles between the control of the size of the weld symbol being taken from the drawing standard (the option is turned on) or the document font size (the option is turned off).

- **Display Datums per 1982:** Figure B.54 shows the difference between the 1982 and 1994 standards for datum display.

FIGURE B.54

The 1982 and 1994 standards for datum display

1994   1982

- **Leading Zeroes:** Generally, *leading zeroes* refers to a single zero to the left side of the decimal if that place is not occupied by a number. The options are Standard, Show, and Remove. Standard means that the leading zero display for that dimension will follow the standard. Show will always show a leading zero, and Remove will always remove the leading zero.

NOTE   Standards for leading zeroes may be different for different units. For example, using the ANSI standard, the dimension .015in. does not get a leading zero, but the dual dimension 0.38mm does.

- **Trailing Zeroes:** The options are Smart, Show, Remove, and Standard. While the last three options are self-explanatory, the Smart option means that even if the standard calls for trailing zeroes, they will be removed if they follow a whole metric number. For example, in the measurements, 4.00mm and 4.50mm, the Smart option only removes the trailing zeroes from the 4.00mm value, to make it 4mm.

■ **Alternate Section Display:** Figure B.55 shows the difference between standard and alternate section displays.

Using standard and alternate section displays

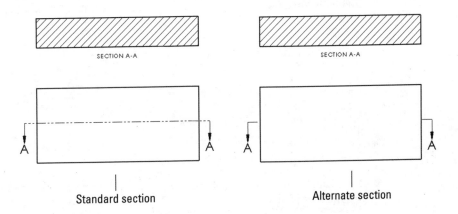

■ **Centerline Extension:** When a centerline lies on top of a section line, the centerline extends past the section line by a value determined by the standard, unless the distance in this text field is changed.

■ **Extension Line Gap:** This is the distance between the part and the extension line, as shown in Figure B.56.

The Extension Line Gap, and the distance beyond the dimension line

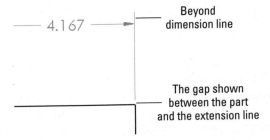

- **Beyond Dimension Line:** This is the distance that the extension line extends beyond the dimension line, as shown in Figure B.56.

- **Datum Feature Display Type:** The options are Per Standard, Square, and Round (GB). Figure B.57 shows the difference between square and round datum feature symbols.

FIGURE B.57

Square and Round Datum Feature Symbols

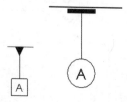

- **Next Label:** This option establishes the next letter to be used in the Datum feature symbol.

- **Surface Finish Symbols, Display Symbols per 2002:** This option alters the display of the surface finish symbols for the following standards to reflect changes to those standards in that year: BSI, DIN, GB, GOST, and ISO.

Up to now, I have discussed options that pertain to all document types. Starting from here, I will discuss settings and options that are available only to drawing documents.

- **Auto Insert on View Creation:** This setting determines which entity types you want to be automatically inserted from the model into drawings when the view is created. New for SolidWorks 2007 is the differentiation between center marks for holes and fillets. You can choose multiple items from the following options:

  - Center Marks-Holes

  - Center Marks-Fillets

  - Centerlines

  - Balloons

  - Dimensions Marked for Drawing

- **Bill Of Materials, Automatic Update of BOM:** For this drawing document, the BOM either will or will not be updated automatically. This usually means that for every rebuild, the BOM will be updated. If you want the BOM to remain static, then you can turn off this option. You can also turn this option off to increase speed. For updated BOMs, turn this option on.

- **Cosmetic Thread Display, High Quality:** Cosmetic threads on the backside of a part will be hidden if this option is on. To increase speed, you can turn this option off. Figure B.58 demonstrates that this setting only makes a difference for shaded model views on the drawing. For any Wireframe mode, the hidden cosmetic thread is not shown unless the hidden lines of the view are visible.

FIGURE B.58

Cosmetic Thread display, using High Quality and Draft Quality

Draft and high quality   Draft quality   High quality

- **Area Hatch Display, Show Halo Around Annotations:** A halo is simply a gap in the hatch pattern, as shown in Figure B.59.

FIGURE B.59

A measurement with the Show Halo Around Annotations option turned on and off

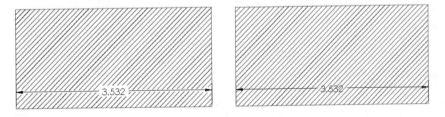

- **Center Marks, Size:** You can specify the diameter of the circle that the crosshairs of the center mark fit into.

- **Extended Lines:** When this option is selected, extended lines go past the circular edge that they were created from, as shown in Figure B.60.

- **Centerline Font:** This option applies a centerline font to the extended lines. If this option is off, then the extended lines will be solid.

FIGURE B.60

Extended lines on a center mark

- **Break Lines, Gap:** This refers to the gap between break lines on a broken view, as shown in Figure B.61.

- **Extension:** This refers to the extension of the broken view break line past the model edge, as shown in Figure B.61.

FIGURE B.61

Break Lines Gap and Extension

DimXpert

 The DimXpert enables you to apply dimensions to a drawing to fully dimension the selected features. The options for the DimXpert are shown in Figure B.62.

FIGURE B.62

The DimXpert options

- **Chamfer Dimension Scheme:** This option allows you to select between angle-by-distance or distance-by-distance dimensions for chamfers.

- **Slot Dimension Scheme:** This option allows you to select between center-to-center or end-to-end dimensioning for slots.

- **Fillet and Chamfer Options:** When several fillets with the same radius are found, you can specify whether SolidWorks uses "Typ," the number of instances (Instant count), or neither (None).

Dimensions

The Dimensions page of the Document Properties controls how dimensions look. The options on this page, shown in Figure B.63, are exactly the same for models and drawings.

- **Add Parentheses By Default:** This option applies parentheses around any reference dimension. Parentheses are not applied to driving dimensions.

- **Snap Text to Grid:** This option causes the dimension text to snap to regular intervals to help alignment, whether or not the grid is displayed.

The Document Properties ⇨ Dimensions page

- **Center Between Extension Lines:** This option causes the dimension text to snap to a location in the center of the extension lines, when originally created or when dragged.
- **Include prefix inside basic tolerance box:** Any prefix added before the dimension will be included in a Basic tolerance box, if used. This is demonstrated in Figure B.64.

A prefix inside a Basic tolerance box

- **Automatically Jog Ordinates:** When ordinate dimensions become too closely spaced, this option jogs the dimension lines to space them out.

 ■ **Show Dimensions As Broken In Broken Views:** Dimensions that go across breaks show a broken dimension line, as shown in Figure B.65.

FIGURE B.65
_____

A broken dimension on a broken view

- **Offset Distances:** These are the spacing distances from the part to the dimension, and between dimensions for Baseline dimensions.

- **Text Alignment:** The Horizontal alignment affects justification of the dimension text as well as any added text. This is also controlled by the justification buttons in the PropertyManager, as shown in Figure B.66. The Vertical alignment specifies the line of text that the leader aligns with. The justification (Horizontal) setting applies to all standards, but the leader position (Vertical) setting applies only to the ANSI standard.

FIGURE B.66
_____

The Text Alignment settings

This row corresponds to the vertical setting

Top row corresponds to the horizontal setting

■ **Arrow Style:** You can select the arrow style for dimensions. The list of options is shown in Figure B.67.

■ **Outside, Inside, Smart:** The Outside and Inside options force all of the arrows to go either outside or inside the extension lines. The Smart option allows the arrows to change sides automatically, depending on how far apart the extension lines are. You can change this setting manually by clicking one of handles on the arrows, as shown in Figure B.67.

FIGURE B.67

The Arrow Style settings

■ **Display 2ⁿᵈ Outside Arrow (Radial):** According to SolidWorks Help, this option works with radial dimensions. However, it is for diameter dimensions, and does nothing for radial dimensions. Enabling the option turns on the second arrow, as shown in Figure B.68.

FIGURE B.68

Diameter dimension outside arrows

Adds this arrow for diameter dimensions
where the dimension is placed to
the outside of the circle

■ **Arrows Follow Position Of Text (Radial):** This option is activated only when the arrows are set to Smart. When this option is off, radial dimension arrows are always to the inside of an arc. When the option is on, the arrow goes to the inside or outside of the arc, depending on whether the text is inside or outside. This option is illustrated in Figure B.69.

FIGURE B.69

Using the Arrows Follow Position of Text option

Option on   Option off

■ **Angled/Linear-Angled Display:** This option is only available for the ANSI standard. This option simply determines whether bent leaders will be used for angle dimensions and linear dimensions that are at an angle.

■ **Break Dimension Extension/Leader Lines:** These settings control breaks in dimension and extension lines. Dimension lines are the ones with the arrows, and extension lines act as extensions of model edges. Both line types can break. The Gap number is simply the width of the gap.

If the Break Around Dimension Arrows Only option is on, then breaks always involve arrows. Figure B.70 shows the dimension line of the 6.374 dimension broken where the extension lines of the other two dimensions cross it. To determine which dimension is broken, select the Break Lines check box in the dimension PropertyManager.

FIGURE B.70

Specifying the Break Dimension and Extension Lines

 ■ **Fractional Display:** For units with fractional displays, this setting determines how the fractions are displayed. The Stack Size setting allows you to use smaller characters for the fractions than for the whole numbers. Examples of the settings are shown in Figure B.71.

FIGURE B.71

Changing the Fractional Display

2 1/2"   2½"   2½"   2½"   2-1/2"

Stack height of 70 percent

■ **Bent Leader Length:** Bent leaders can be controlled individually for dimensions, notes, and balloons. The lengths are not linked, and so to get them all the same, you must manually make them all the same, and ensure that bent leaders are enabled for each type.

 ■ **Radial Leader Snap Angle:** When dragging or placing a radial dimension, the arrow snaps to angles. To disable this snapping behavior, set the angle to zero.

■ **Leaders:** If you want to override the dimensioning standard (such as ANSI or ISO) behavior to dimension leaders, click the Leaders button on the Dimensions page, and select the desired behavior. The available overrides are shown in Figure B.72.

FIGURE B.72

The Leader Override options

■ **Precision:** This is where the number of decimal places is set for the primary, secondary, and angular units, as well as tolerances. The Units page duplicates these settings, but does not allow for setting the number of decimal places for the tolerance. The Dimension Precision dialog box is shown in Figure B.73.

FIGURE B.73

Setting decimal places

■ **Tolerance:** When you click the Tolerance button, the Dimension Tolerance dialog box appears. In this dialog box, you can set default tolerances, and you can change the tolerance font scale, as shown in Figure B.74.

987

FIGURE B.74

The Dimension Tolerance dialog box

Notes

The various settings for notes are found on the Notes page, as shown in Figure B.75.

FIGURE B.75

The Notes settings

- **Text Alignment:** When you use multi-line notes, each line is aligned, or justified, as specified in this selection box.
- **Leader Anchor:** The leader attaches to notes, as selected here.

■ **Leader Style:** Straight and Bent leaders are common and self-explanatory. The Bent and Underlined leaders are shown in Figure B.76. These options are also available in the Notes PropertyManager, as shown to the right in Figure B.76. When you select the Bent leader option, the Leader Length option also becomes available.

FIGURE B.76

Leader Style options

  ■ **Leader Justification Snapping:** This setting is only available for DIN and JIS standards.

■ **Border:** Balloons are just notes with borders. When you use these settings, SolidWorks puts borders on notes, by default. Border styles are shown with the Balloons settings.

Balloons

Although balloons are used for Bill of Materials item numbering, you can also generically use them for other types of items, or for manual part numbering. The options for balloons are shown in Figure B.77. The figure also shows a set of stacked balloons, which you can stack either horizontally or vertically.

FIGURE B.77

The Balloons settings

Although you can use balloons in parts and assemblies, here they are only referred to as being used in assembly drawings. Remember that because the settings being discussed here are Document Properties, you will need to save each document type with the correct template settings so that they will behave the same across document types.

- **Balloon Style Options:** As shown in Figure B.78, the style options for both single and stacked balloons are:
  - Circular
  - Triangle
  - Hexagon
  - Box
  - Diamond
  - Pentagon
  - Flag – Five Sided
  - Flag – Triangle
  - Circular Split Line

FIGURE B.78

Balloon style options

Circular   Triangle   Hexagon   Box   Diamond

Pentagon   Flag-Five Sided   Flag-Triangle   Circular Split Line

- **Balloon Size Options:** Balloon size settings range from one to five characters, as well as a Tight Fit setting, which enables the balloon to resize automatically, depending on its contents. The other settings are fixed sizes, regardless of contents.

- **Balloon Text:** The Upper and Lower settings are only used at the same time if the style is Circular Split Line. Default settings are Item Number for the Upper setting and Quantity for the Lower setting. If you use a style other than split balloon, then the Upper setting represents the only value inside the balloon. The options for balloon text are as follows:
  - **Text:** The Text selection enables the user to enter custom text into the balloon.
  - **Item Number:** This option pulls the Item Number from the BOM. This is typically related to the order of a component in an assembly. When connected to a part in a

drawing, a question mark is displayed in the Item Number area because a single part has no Item Number.

- **Quantity:** This option pulls the quantity of the part that it points to from the assembly. If you use this setting on a part drawing, then the Item Number still defaults to a question mark, but the Quantity value defaults to one.

- **Custom Property:** The blank, grayed-out fields below the Balloon Text options are for custom property names. Custom Properties will pull values from the part custom properties and place these values in the balloon.

- **Auto Balloon Layout:** When auto-ballooning an assembly drawing, this setting determines how the balloons will be laid out.

- **Bent Leaders:** This setting determines whether the current document uses bent leaders, and if so, how long they should be.

Arrows

You can use arrows on dimensions, notes, and balloons, but the arrow sizes are grouped together for these three annotation types. Only Section Line arrows are given a different size. The settings for arrows are shown in Figure B.79.

FIGURE B.79

The Document Properties ⇨ Arrows page

- **Size:** The Scale With Dimension Height option disables the number selection box options and resets any custom numbers that you may have entered. This option is new for SolidWorks 2007. Proportion of the arrows cannot be controlled when you use the scale option.

- **Section View Size:** This setting works just like the numbers in the Size section, but it applies only to arrows on the ends of section lines.
- **Attachments:** The Attachments settings enable you to specify which arrow type is used when the arrow is attached to edges or vertices, and faces or surfaces, or whether the arrow is unattached. Figure B.80 shows the options for arrow display.

FIGURE B.80

Arrow display options

- **Foreshortened Diameter:** You can control the Foreshortened Diameter dimension display by using this setting.

Virtual Sharps

Virtual Sharp display on a drawing (and in sketches) is controlled on this page. A virtual sharp is the corner where two edges would intersect if they were not interrupted by a fillet, chamfer, or other item breaking the edge. The options for Virtual Sharp display are shown in Figure B.81.

FIGURE B.81

The Virtual Sharps display options

Annotations Display

Annotations Display options are also available by RMB clicking the Annotations folder in the FeatureManager and selecting Details. This page also displays differently, depending on whether you are editing the properties of a part, assembly, or drawing. Figure B.82 shows the available options for Annotations Display.

FIGURE B.82

The Annotations Display options

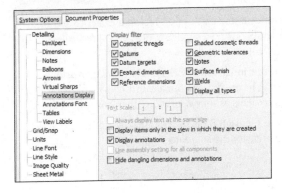

- **Display Filter:** You can select the entity types to be displayed in this particular document or template. The Display All Types option shows everything.

Of special note here is the Shaded Cosmetic Threads option. The difference between normal Cosmetic Threads and Shaded Cosmetic Threads is shown in Figure B.83.

FIGURE B.83

Using the Shaded Cosmetic Threads option

Shaded Cosmetic Thread
display

- **Text Scale:** The Text Scale setting is available only for parts and assemblies, and only when the Always Display Text At The Same Size option is off.

- **Always Display Text At The Same Size:** This option causes annotations and dimensions to appear the same size on the screen, regardless of zoom state. It is not active in drawings because drawings always need to show text at 1:1 size.

- **Display Items Only In The View In Which They Are Created:** This option is sometimes frustrating, because it hides annotations unless the model is in exactly the view in which the annotation was created. It becomes very easy to lose annotations. However, if you are disciplined in how you create annotations (consider using Annotation Views), then this can help to reduce clutter in drawing and model views.

- **Use Assembly's Setting For All Components:** This option makes it easier to see all of the component annotations in the assembly using a single set of settings, regardless of differences between settings in individual component files.

- **Hide Dangling Dimensions And Annotations:** SolidWorks has become increasingly "error-phobic" in recent releases, offering more options to make errors invisible. Best practice is definitely on the side of fixing problems as they rise, rather than covering them up.

- **JIS Surface Finish Size:** Not shown in Figure B.83 is the JIS Surface Finish Size option, which is available only with the JIS dimensioning standard.

Annotations Font

The Annotations Font page is where you can set the default fonts for each annotation type. Figure B.84 shows the types and the Choose Font dialog box that enables you to change fonts.

FIGURE B.84

The Annotations Font page and the Choose Font dialog box

Tables

The Tables options page is available for drawing documents only. Figure B.85 shows the Tables options.

The Tables options page

- **Hole Table:** A Hole Table is a chart that shows the centers and diameters of holes on a face with respect to a selected table Origin. Although these settings are listed in the Document Properties tab, they are probably best suited to being changed from the PropertyManager of the table. Hole Tables use a separate template.

  - **Origin indicator:** The options for displaying the Origin are either to link the display to the dimensioning standard (Per Standard), or to select a standard. The symbol on the options page updates to show how the Origin indicator looks for each standard. The various standards include displays without zeroes (as shown), with zeroes, and with dots.

  - **Tag Angle/Offset From Profile Center:** These settings position the text at an angle and distance from the center of the hole. The "A1" shown in Figure B.85 is closest to where it would be positioned if the angle were zero. It appears to be positioning the lower-left corner of the text.

■ **Alpha/Numerical Control:** This setting controls the hole labels. When letters are chosen, numbers are still shown after the numbers, as shown in Figure B.86. The only time the number after the letter increments is when holes of the same diameter are found; in this situation, they are all labeled with the same letter, and different numbers.

The Hole Table interface and a chart

■ **Scheme:** The Combine Same Size option combines all of the table cells that contain the same diameter hole. Combine Same Tags causes the A1, A2 tags for same-diameter holes to all be labeled "A" in the table.

■ **Location Precision:** This setting determines how many decimal places are used in the hole X, Y position.

The Show Hole Centers option, when used from the Document Properties options page, appears to have no effect, but the same (albeit inverted) function works from the Hole Table PropertyManager under the name of Hide Hole Centers.

■ **Revision Table:** Revision tables help keep track of revisions to drawings. These can be used in conjunction with PDMWorks or other PDM products. The revision level is stored in a custom property in the file. A simple revision table is shown in Figure B.87.

FIGURE B.87

A simple revision table

		REVISIONS		
ZONE	REV.	DESCRIPTION	DATE	APPROVED
	A	Changed Material	10/29/2006	
	b	Changed Surface Finish	10/29/2006	

- **Symbol Shapes:** When a new revision is added to the table, you are prompted to place a symbol containing the new revision letter near the item on the drawing that has changed in the new revision. This setting determines the shape of the symbol.

- **Alpha/Numerical Control:** Revisions driven by revision tables can be either alphabetical or numerical.

 ■ **Multiple Sheet Style:** Different users may want to control revision tables differently on different sheets of a drawing. SolidWorks 2007 now offers three options:

- **See Sheet 1:** This is just a note in the revision table that directs the drawing reader to the first sheet for the revision history.

- **Linked:** The revision tables on each sheet are linked.

- **Independent:** The revision tables on each sheet of the drawing are independent.

■ **Bill of Materials Table:** Bills of Materials (BOMs) also have their own templates, which have settings of their own, but drawing document property settings do contain a couple of relevant options and settings.

- **Zero Quantity:** Before you ask why parts with a zero quantity are shown on a BOM, this is usually for assemblies that are shown with configurations.

  The options for a zero quantity are to show a dash, a zero, or a blank.

- **Missing Component:** Missing components are created by having deleted or suppressed parts or subassemblies in the top-level assembly.

- **Don't Add "QTY" Next To Configuration Name:** This option eliminates the QTY letters from the configuration column in the BOM.

- **Don't copy QTY column name from template:** This option puts the configuration name in the BOM QTY column, instead of a custom name in the template.

- **Restrict Top Level Only BOMs To One Configuration:** This option means that if a BOM is designated "Top Level Only," then the BOM can show only a single configuration.

View Labels

Three types of views — Detail, Auxiliary, and Section — can have special text labels, along with a custom scale label that accompanies the view. The options on this page are shown in Figure B.88. The name for each type can either be blank, VIEW, or the name of the type of view (DETAIL, AUXILIARY, or SECTION). The label can either be the letter assigned to the view or blank.

The Scale label can be SCALE, SCALE:, or blank. Options for the scale delimiter are blank, X:Y, (X:Y), X/Y, (X/Y), or #X, where # is an integer.

FIGURE B.88

The View Labels options page

 Display Label Above View is a new option in SolidWorks 2007. The default setting is to display the label below the view.

Grid/Snap

One of the first questions that new users tend to ask is how to turn off the grid in sketches. This is unfortunate, because the grid is most useful for new users, mainly to help them keep track of when they are in or out of Sketch mode. The Grid/Snap options are shown in Figure B.89.

FIGURE B.89

The Grid/Snap options page

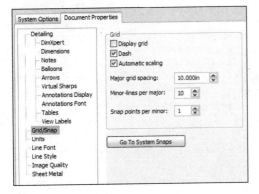

- **Display Grid:** This option turns the display of the grid on or off in the sketch.
- **Dash:** Minor grid lines, specified below, are dashed. If this option is off, then the minor grid lines are solid.
- **Automatic Scaling:** As you zoom in and out, the minor grid goes from ten divisions to five to two, depending on your settings.

Units

The Units options page enables you to either select a predefined unit system or create custom settings, including primary and dual length units, angular units, and special units for mass and section properties. Units of force are included for the strength properties that are associated with COSMOS products. The Units options page is shown in Figure B.90.

After the "How do I turn off the grid" question, the next most popular question regarding settings is, "How do I make SolidWorks remember that I want to use inches instead of millimeters?" Of course, the answer is to use templates. Set the units the way you want them on a blank document (or delete all of the features from an existing document), and save the file as a template. This applies to parts, assemblies, and drawings.

FIGURE B.90

The Units options page

Fractions

SolidWorks can use fractional dimensions, and convert decimals to fractions. To set up fractions, set the Denominator selection box to the smallest division that you will want to use, and select the Round To Nearest Fraction option. Be aware that when you do this, some values will be approximated.

The only units that will accept fractional values are all of the English units except for feet. Interestingly, you can use fractional mils (.001, thousandths of an inch) and micro-inches (.000001, millionths of an inch). Fractions are most appropriate for inches, and feet and inches.

Decimal places or Denominator

Depending on whether Decimal or Fractions has been selected for the units, the precision is set either with a number of decimal places or a denominator for the fraction.

Line Font

Many types of edges, identified in Figure B.91, can have special line fonts assigned to them. You can even create custom line fonts, although the custom line styles are limited to being used in drawings, not in parts or assemblies. New line styles are discussed in the next section on Line Styles.

The Line Font options page

 The one setting that is not self-explanatory on this page is the End Cap Style. This is new to SolidWorks 2007. In the past, thicker line types would have poorly jointed corners, as shown in Figure B.92 in the image to the left. This line is using the Flat end cap style. The square end cap style is shown to the right. If this problem occurs when you use thick lines, you now have a way to fix it.

Using the End Cap Style option to make thicker lines look better

Line Style

The Line Style option page is where you can modify existing styles and even create new line styles. You can follow the instructions on the page, using a simple code to create special line styles, as shown in Figure B.93.

The Line Style options page

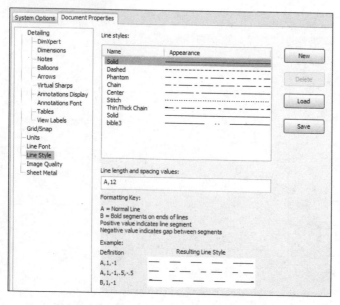

Colors

The Document Properties ➪ Colors page enables you to specify colors for certain feature types. System Options ➪ Colors options specify colors for parts of the interface, rather than part geometry. The Document Properties ➪ Colors page is shown in Figure B.94.

- **Advanced:** This button enables you to specify transparency and other effects.
- **Curvature:** The curvature window is shown to the right in Figure B.93. This enables you to specify the color spread for various curvature values. Remember that curvature is the inverse of radius (c=1/r), and so the smaller the radius, the bigger the curvature.

■ **Apply Same Color To Wireframe, HLR and Shaded:** This setting is only valid in part documents. This is probably one of the least-appreciated options in SolidWorks. Many parts built and provided by SolidWorks Corporation as sample or tutorial parts do not use this setting, and so when you open an assembly where the parts do not have this option applied, and you turn the assembly to Wireframe mode, all of the edges become black. This can make you feel as if you had gone back 15 years to using modeling wireframes in AutoCAD.

Do yourself a favor and save your part templates to use this setting.

BEST PRACTICE Use the Apply Same Color To Wireframe, HLR and Shaded option to be able to differentiate parts in an assembly by color when they are shown in Wireframe mode. The alternative is a black-on-black wireframe display.

FIGURE B.94

The Document Properties ⇨ Colors page

Image Quality

Image quality can have a definite effect on the performance of parts and assemblies. This setting is highly dependent on a couple of things: primarily your graphics card, but also part complexity and the number of parts in an assembly. The Image Quality options page is shown in Figure B.95.

FIGURE B.95

The Image Quality options page

BEST PRACTICE   The best practice recommendation for image quality is to set it as low as you can stand it. This may be at different levels for different parts.

The way SolidWorks (and indeed most 3D graphics applications) displays curved 3D geometry is to create a set of smaller, flat, triangular facets. This is called tessellation. If these triangles become too large, then curved surfaces are not recognizable, and they may look more like hexagons than circles. However, if the triangular facets become too small, then your graphics card may not be able to process them quickly enough. As a result, image quality settings require a compromise.

- **Shaded and draft quality HLR/HLV resolution:** The slider at the top of the window applies to shaded models.

  - **Deviation:** This setting measures how far from the real shape the displayed shape is. By making a curved edge into a series of straight lines, the number shown represents the maximum distance from the line to the curve. As the quality becomes higher, the deviation becomes lower.

  - **Optimize Edge Length (higher quality, but slower):** SolidWorks is not explicit about this, but it is assumed that what is being "optimized" is the quality of the display, and not the speed of the system.

  - **Apply To All Referenced Part Documents:** This setting is valid for assembly documents only. In an assembly, display quality settings from individual part documents are used unless this option is used in the assembly, in which case the assembly setting is propagated to each of the individual parts. However, if you use high part-quality settings for good visualization, and the assembly setting is low for increased speed, then you will need to change the part settings back to high after you have them open in the assembly. This can become frustrating unless you can find a good middle ground or a macro that changes the settings for you quickly and easily.

■ **Save Tessellation With Part Document:** This setting is valid for part documents only. This option toggles the tessellated display data that is being saved in the part file. This can have an impact on save time and file size. However, do not become overly excited about turning this option off; you need to remember that it is faster to read existing data than it is to recalculate it. There may be times when you need the extra data such as when using eDrawings as a viewer.

■ **Wireframe And High Quality HLR/HLV Resolution:** This slider works for wireframe display and drawings. Again, set it as low as you can stand it if you are having performance problems.

Plane Display

Planes in SolidWorks can be displayed either with just a rectangular outline or with a transparent shaded face. Each "side" of the plane can be viewed with different colors. Although this may not seem useful immediately, I find it very useful when working in detail on a larger part. It helps me to keep my bearings. The slider shown in Figure B.96 also enables you to change the transparency of the planes.

FIGURE B.96

The Plane Display options page

Plane intersections can also be shown by a dotted line of a specified color, but because you cannot select them or actually use them for anything other than visualization, I tend to turn them off.

Appendix C

Finding Help

SolidWorks software has been around for over ten years now. In that time, the resources available to users seeking help have increased dramatically. The available help takes many forms, from personal Web sites with information obtained from individual experience, to commercial on-line magazines or forums with advanced Flash interfaces. In this appendix, I have assembled some of the more useful sources of quality information.

It is not the goal of this book to endorse any commercial sites or services, but some of the listed resources are commercial in nature, and may feature advertisements, logins, or both.

SolidWorks Help

The SolidWorks Help file is also called the Online Users Guide. It contains most of the information that you need to find out how a function works. There are topics for which searchability is poor, or when topics do not appear under expected headings, but this is the exception rather than the norm. It is more common to find that some features are poorly documented or not documented at all. For example, when looking up the significance of the Engage Belt option in the Belt/Chain sketch function described in Chapter 4, SolidWorks Help merely states, "Engage belt. Clear to disengage the belt mechanism," which is not at all helpful to the user. It turns out that "Engage belt" means that when one pulley turns, all of the pulleys should turn as if they were all physically joined by a belt.

However, some functions, such as sheet metal bend allowances and the referenced documents search routine, are extraordinarily well documented.

Contents

One problem with SolidWorks is its tendency to not alphabetize lists that users browse through, such as the Help Contents. Although these lists may be full of useful information, many users will never find it because the information is so difficult to locate.

SolidWorks Fundamentals

If you are just getting started with SolidWorks, then this section of the Help feature can be useful. In any case, you should read it as a primer along with the tutorials, before attending a training course.

Glossary

SolidWorks terminology has at times caused difficulty in the writing of this book because terms are either unclear or overlap each other. Still, it is difficult for two people to talk about the software if they are not using the same terminology. The Glossary is one of the most useful and yet most underused sections of the Help files. Often when I am asked a question by a new user, it can be impossible to discern what they are talking about because they are not familiar with the SolidWorks terminology. As dull as it may be, this Glossary should be required reading for all new users. Simply understanding the language being used by the training materials, Help files, and other users can offer a big head start when it comes to learning the software. Look through it; I promise that you will learn something.

Index

This is the section of the Help files that I use the most because I can type something in, and if the terminology is correct, then most of the time I will quickly arrive very close to where I want to be. Sometimes you need to change the order of words, try an alternate term, or check your spelling, but the Index works well when you have a good idea of what you are looking for.

Search

The Search function is for when you are not exactly sure of what you are looking for. For example, you may know that there is a feature that uses stripes to analyze curvature across edges, but you cannot remember its name. In this example, there are two words that you can use for your search: curvature and stripes. If you use curvature, then the Search function returns about sixty possibilities. The term that you are looking for is Zebra Stripes, but you may not quickly find it from scanning such a long list. If you search using the term stripe, then Zebra Stripes appears at the top of the list.

The biggest complaint that you can have about the Search function in Help is that it will sometimes return too many options, and it is not immediately clear what the connection is between the word that you searched on and the topic title that appears in the list. Still, too much information is better than not enough.

Many users overlook three options that are found at the bottom of the Search window: Search Previous Results, Match Similar Words, and Search Titles Only. All of these options are useful in narrowing down the search to find a meaningful result.

SolidWorks Web site

Most of the valuable information on the SolidWorks Web site (www.solidworks.com) is behind the subscription login, but there is also some free information available. It may be worthwhile to look around a little bit on the SolidWorks Web site because there is a large amount of information ranging from graphics card evaluations to training files.

Graphics Cards

The link to this area is located on the SolidWorks Web site main page. SolidWorks has tested the most popular graphics cards and drivers for compatibility with various versions of SolidWorks, and has rated them at various levels, using the following criteria:

- Passed all tests
- Passed with limitations
- Card has significant stability or repaint problems
- Use the graphics card display settings for SolidWorks
- Multi-head hardware accelerated
- Supports RealView
- 64-bit native support
- Supports 3D-Stereo effects

Customer Portal

The Customer Portal is full of useful information, and first appeared in 2006.

Knowledge Base

If you have used the Knowledge Base before and found it less than satisfying, then you owe it to yourself to try it again. Searches actually turn up a lot of information that you can really use. Results may include tech support responses to customer issues, software performance reports (SPRs — also called bug reports), white papers, articles, and so on. In addition, you can look up SPR numbers that you have received from tech support to check the status. I have consulted the knowledge base many times to write this book. It has been built from vast amounts of internal SolidWorks Corporate support documentation, as well as the support database. I give it very high usability marks!

Software downloads

Manually downloading and installing software and upgrades for SolidWorks is becoming a thing of the past, although you can still do it. The SolidWorks Installation Manager works in many respects like Microsoft Automatic Update. It downloads and even installs updates for you automatically. It can also be made to work with administrative image installations. I particularly like the way that it can download service packs before the links on the SolidWorks Web site are active. Of course, if you need or simply want to download manually, then this option is also available.

Release Notes

All of the Release Notes for all of the service packs of the current version are also available from the main Customer Portal window. This is essential information for CAD Administrators. Technical Alerts, changes to the System Requirements (such as SolidWorks 2007 dropping support for Windows 2000), and new installation details are listed here.

Even if you do not think that you need to know any of this information, it still makes for interesting (and at times alarming) reading. The Technical Alerts typically warn of severe bugs or other problems, and how to work around or fix them.

What's New

This is a great document to refer to when learning about a new version of SolidWorks.

Installation and administration guides

Installation and administration guides are available for SolidWorks, eDrawings, and Cosmos. These contain basic information about the topics, and are not as detailed as other sources of information (such as this book).

PDMWorks Workgroup Vault Debug Guide

When the vault gives you an error code, why should you have to call tech support to find out what is going on? It is all listed here. All of the error codes are listed with the name of the error. This is a must-have document for the PDMWorks Administrator.

FLEXlm End Users Guide

The FLEXlm End Users Guide is required reading for a network license Administrator. While the network license is easy to install, set up, and maintain, this guide explains many of the details and options that are available.

Discussion Forum

The SolidWorks Discussion Forum is a very active moderated forum for discussing SolidWorks topics. SolidWorks employees will often respond to questions, although more frequently, questions are answered by other users.

There are many topic areas, such as Sheet Metal, Surfacing, API, Configurations, Assemblies, User Groups, and probably thirty more topics to choose from. The forum moderator does not heavily censor the material. Discussions of real problems, and even passionate rants, have been allowed to remain. Posts that are removed are typically wildly off topic and inappropriate by any measure.

This is another area that to me has immeasurable value. Almost any question you can come up with has either already been asked and answered, or there is someone waiting to answer it. Whether your question is about tips, tools, techniques, or something more generically engineering related, you are bound to get a useful answer.

Tech Tips

The Tech Tips Web site is a listing of Cadalyst and SolidWorks Express (two relevant on-line magazines) articles about specific functionality. I would not classify any of these articles as particularly detailed or advanced, and they do at times appear to be more like sales pitches than informational pieces, but they are useful as articles of general interest to SolidWorks users.

More tips come in the form of PowerPoint presentations, most of which originate from SolidWorks World sessions.

Also valuable in this area are the API examples and the Utilities collection. If you do a bit of macro writing, then you will want to check these out.

User Groups

The main SolidWorks Web site for user groups is `www.swugn.org`. There are too many individual user groups to keep track of or to list here, but you can find a user group in your area on the SolidWorks User Group Network, or SWUGN, Web site. The SWUGN site also has sample presentations in Powerpoint or PDF format that have been given at some of the regional events or SolidWorks World.

Online Forums

There are many types of online forums for SolidWorks. (The forum on the SolidWorks Web site has already been discussed.) Other forums are not directly sponsored by the SolidWorks Corporation, and they may vary in quality.

comp.cad.solidworks

The next most valuable resource is `comp.cad.solidworks`, the notorious SolidWorks newsgroup. This is a Usenet newsgroup, and is best accessed through a news server with a newsreader. Many newsreader applications are free, such as Microplanet Gravity, Xnews, Mozilla Thunderbird, Netscape, and Outlook Express. Generally, your ISP will supply you with a news server, which works similarly in some respects to an e-mail server. If you are unfamiliar with all of this terminology and not inclined to investigate it, then the easiest thing to do is to go to Google Groups, which archives all of the messages. If you choose this method, then you will quickly discover the downside to using Google Groups: it does not filter or sort the messages.

In any event, `comp.cad.solidworks` reminds us all that www also stands for Wild Wild West. This newsgroup is not moderated in any way, and so people can (and do) say whatever they want. Of course, this is not an attraction unless you are having a bad day and need to vent your frustration. The attraction of this newsgroup is that it can be a great way to get an answer to almost any

SolidWorks question that you can think of because there are such a wide range of people accessing it that have a wide range of experience. (In fact, I have done some of the research for this book by asking questions on this forum.) There are people who monitor the group who seem to enjoy fixing programming, or researching obscure functionality. Of course, you are just as likely to get an answer from someone who misunderstands the question, and so you definitely have to be able to sort through different quality levels of information. You will find many highly opinionated responses, but this is also part of the attraction. Many topics in SolidWorks do not have clear cut answers, and different points of view can be valuable to understand various aspects of an issue such as file management or naming conventions. Very frequently, questions are answered in less than 30 minutes, which rivals most reseller tech support organizations.

Other forums

Most of the other forums are commercial, which to me means that they contain advertising. They are listed here with brief introductions and the site URL:

- `www.cadforums.net` uses minimal advertising, and requires no sign-ins, but it has several CAD forums with varying topics. The traffic on this Web site seems to be light.

- `www.mcadforums.com` has more traffic and content, but also uses Flash advertisements.

- `www.eng-tips.com` has plenty of traffic, but has an irritating sign-in popup and is highly censored. My posts were removed for responding to a question about how to go about becoming a consultant.

- `www.3dcadtips.com` is a Web site that you should avoid if you do not like flashing advertisements. Although there appears to be a fair amount of content, it is chaotic and filled with advertising.

Non-Commercial Web Sites

Individuals run all of the Web sites listed here without advertising, and they all contain information that is created by the owner of the Web site. These are my favorite types of places to find information. Even though most of these people are not professional HTML coders, the information is useful and well presented.

- **Rob Rodriguez** (`www.robrodriguez.com`) features the PhotoWorks contest and a PhotoWorks forum.

- **Sean Adams** (`www.sheetmetaldesign.com`) contains a lot of very useful information that Sean has accumulated.

- **Paul Salvador** (`www.zxys.com`) has some nice models and images.

- **Stefan Berlitz** (`http://solidworks.cad.de`) is the unofficial German SolidWorks Web site. If you read German, then this Web site is loaded with great information. Although it does seem to contain some advertisements, I still include it with the non-commercial Web sites.

- **Scott Baugh** (`www.scottjbaugh.com`) has several sample models and a Tips section.

- **Lenny Kikstra** (`www.lennyworks.com/solidworks`) has plenty of tips and tricks as well as macros. Check this Web site out.

- **Mike Wilson** (`www.mikejwilson.com`) has some simply amazing things that Mike has done with SolidWorks. Great models to learn from.

- **Matt Lombard** (`http://mysite.verizon.net/mjlombard/`) has some sections that are getting a bit dated, and it needs a refresh, but it is still a useful site with a lot of good information and a macro library.

Appendix D

What's on the CD-ROM

T he only file you see on this book's companion CD-ROM is a single zip file. Extract the contents of the file to your hard drive in a location that is easy to access.

The CD contains example and tutorial parts, assemblies, and drawings, as well as templates, macros, and tables as appropriate for each chapter. The files are organized within folders for each chapter and are named for the chapter and the function they demonstrate. Some of the files are starting points for tutorials, and some are finished models meant to be examined.

If you make changes to files, I recommend that you perform a Save As command to keep the original file intact. You can retrieve originals from the CD when needed.

CAUTION I do not recommend that you open files directly from the CD because SolidWorks will react with messages about read-only files.

IN THIS APPENDIX

Using the CD

System Requirements

Troubleshooting

System Requirements

Make sure that your computer meets the minimum system requirements listed in this section. If your computer doesn't match up to these requirements, you may have a problem using the contents of the CD.

For Windows XP Professional:

- Intel Pentium, Intel Xeon, Intel Core; AMD Athlon, AMD Opteron, AMD Turion.
- 512MB RAM (1GB recommended).

- Virtual memory twice the amount of RAM (recommended).
- A certified OpenGL workstation graphics card and driver.
- A mouse or other pointing device.
- Microsoft Internet Explorer 6.
- A CD drive.

For Vista:

- 1GB RAM (1.5GB recommended).
- Other minimum requirements are the same as for Windows XP Professional.

For more details about the system requirements for SolidWorks 2007 and a list of certified graphics cards and drivers, visit `solidworks.com`.

Some systems that run Windows XP Professional may not be compatible with Vista. For the latest information on system compatibility with Vista, visit `microsoft.com`.

Troubleshooting

If you have difficulty installing or using any of the material on the companion CD, try the following solutions:

- **Turn off any anti-virus software that you may have running.** Installers sometimes mimic virus activity and can make your computer incorrectly believe that it is being infected by a virus. (Be sure to turn the anti-virus software back on later.)
- **Close all running programs.** The more programs you're running, the less memory is available to other programs. Installers also typically update files and programs; if you keep other programs running, installation may not work properly.
- **See the ReadMe file.** Please refer to the ReadMe file located at the root of the CD for the latest product information at the time of publication.

Customer Care

If you still have trouble with the CD, please call the Wiley Product Technical Support telephone number: (800) 762-2974. Outside the United States, call 1 (317) 572-3994. You can also contact Wiley Product Technical Support at `http://support.wiley.com`. John Wiley & Sons will provide technical support only for installation and other general quality control items. For technical support on the applications themselves, consult the program's vendor or author.

To place additional orders or to request information about other Wiley products, please call (800) 225-5945.

Index

NUMERICS

I

M